ENORMOUSLY FOXTROT

A FOXTROT TREASURY

BY BILL AMEND

Other FoxTrot Books by Bill Amend

FoxTrot

Pass the Loot

Black Bart Says Draw

Eight Yards, Down and Out

Bury My Heart at Fun-Fun Mountain

Say Hello to Cactus Flats

May the Force Be With Us, Please

Take Us to Your Mall

The Return Of The Lone Iguana

At Least This Place Sells T-Shirts

Come Closer, Roger, There's a Mosquito on Your Nose

Anthologies

FoxTrot: The Works

FoxTrot en masse

Wildly FoxTrot

FoxTrot Beyond a Doubt

ENORMOUSLY FOXTROT

A FOXTROT TREASURY

BY BILL AMEND

Andrews and McMeel
A Universal Press Syndicate Company
Kansas City

FOXTROT is distributed internationally by Universal Press Syndicate.

ISBN: 0-8362-1759-4

Library of Congress Catalog Card Number: 94-71741

Printed on recycled paper

Special Paige and Pierre artwork prepared with the assistance of Kallen Godsey and Michael Grove.

98 99 00 01 02 BAM 10 9 8 7 6 5

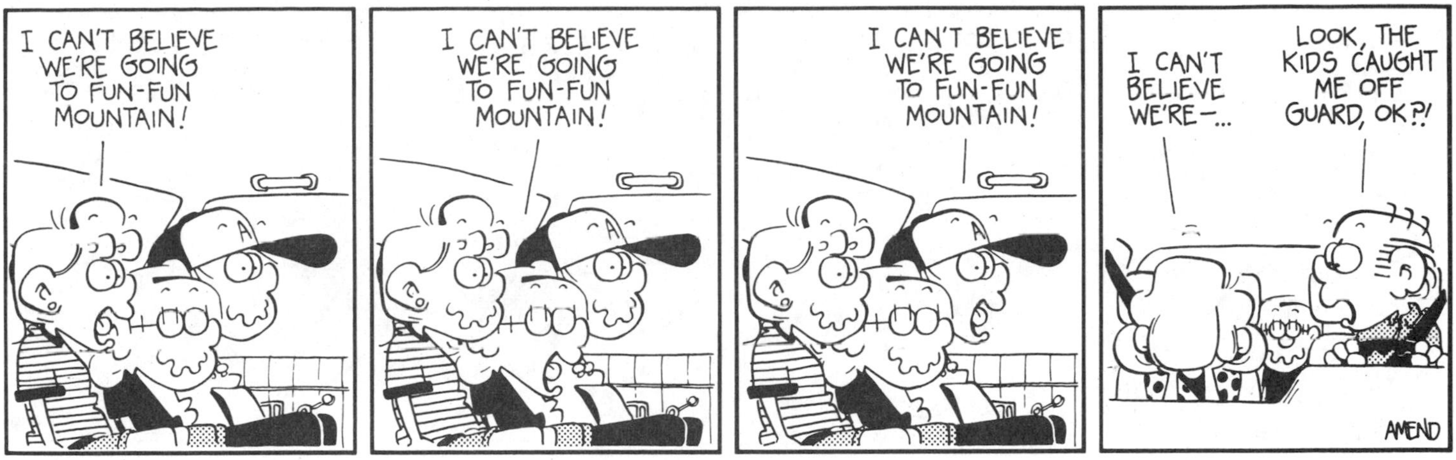
I CAN'T BELIEVE WE'RE GOING TO FUN-FUN MOUNTAIN!
I CAN'T BELIEVE WE'RE GOING TO FUN-FUN MOUNTAIN!
I CAN'T BELIEVE WE'RE GOING TO FUN-FUN MOUNTAIN!
I CAN'T BELIEVE WE'RE—...
LOOK, THE KIDS CAUGHT ME OFF GUARD, OK?!
AMEND

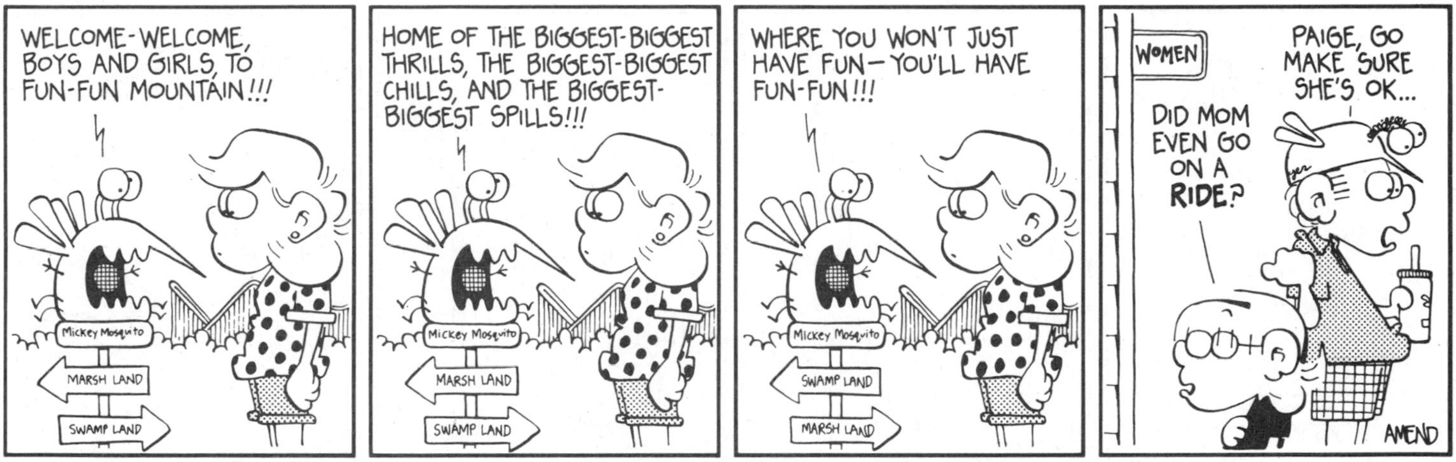
WELCOME-WELCOME, BOYS AND GIRLS, TO FUN-FUN MOUNTAIN!!!
Mickey Mosquito
MARSH LAND
SWAMP LAND
HOME OF THE BIGGEST-BIGGEST THRILLS, THE BIGGEST-BIGGEST CHILLS, AND THE BIGGEST-BIGGEST SPILLS!!!
Mickey Mosquito
MARSH LAND
SWAMP LAND
WHERE YOU WON'T JUST HAVE FUN—YOU'LL HAVE FUN-FUN!!!
Mickey Mosquito
SWAMP LAND
MARSH LAND
WOMEN
PAIGE, GO MAKE SURE SHE'S OK...
DID MOM EVEN GO ON A RIDE?
AMEND

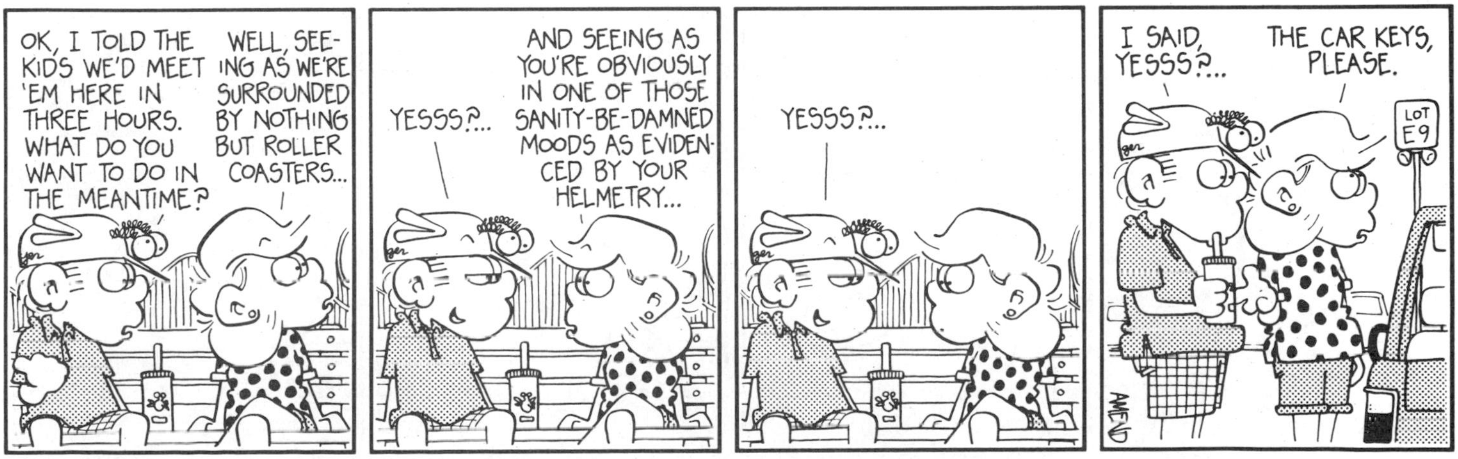
OK, I TOLD THE KIDS WE'D MEET 'EM HERE IN THREE HOURS. WHAT DO YOU WANT TO DO IN THE MEANTIME?
WELL, SEEING AS WE'RE SURROUNDED BY NOTHING BUT ROLLER COASTERS...
YESSS?...
AND SEEING AS YOU'RE OBVIOUSLY IN ONE OF THOSE SANITY-BE-DAMNED MOODS AS EVIDENCED BY YOUR HELMETRY...
YESSS?...
I SAID, YESSS?...
THE CAR KEYS, PLEASE.
LOT E9
AMEND

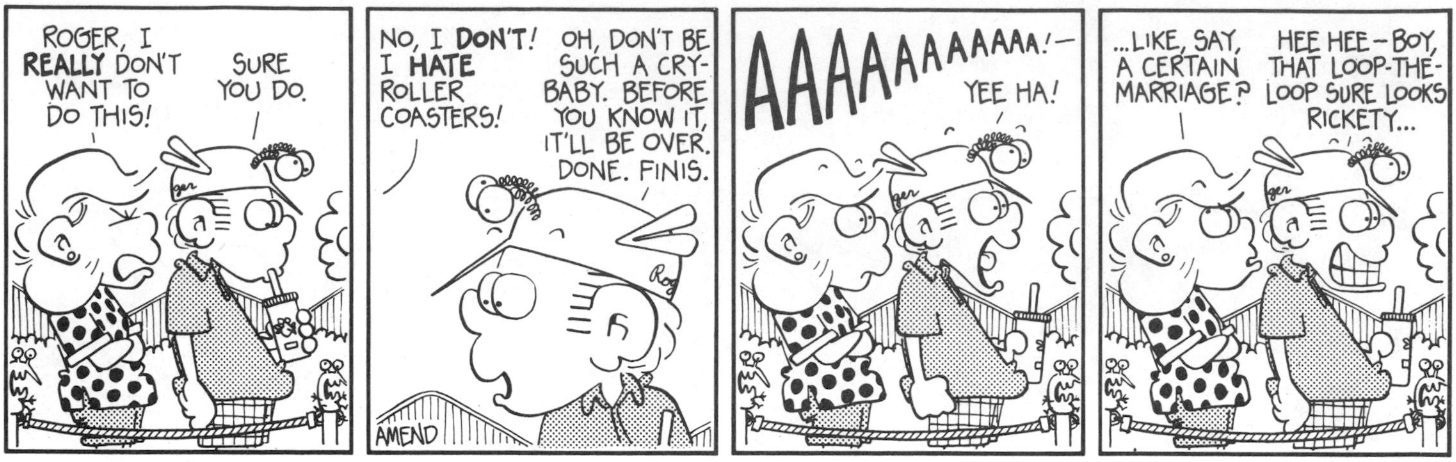
ROGER, I **REALLY** DON'T WANT TO DO THIS!
SURE YOU DO.
NO, I **DON'T**! I **HATE** ROLLER COASTERS!
OH, DON'T BE SUCH A CRY-BABY. BEFORE YOU KNOW IT, IT'LL BE OVER. DONE. FINIS.
AMEND
AAAAAAAAAAA!—
YEE HA!
...LIKE, SAY, A CERTAIN MARRIAGE?
HEE HEE—BOY, THAT LOOP-THE-LOOP SURE LOOKS RICKETY...

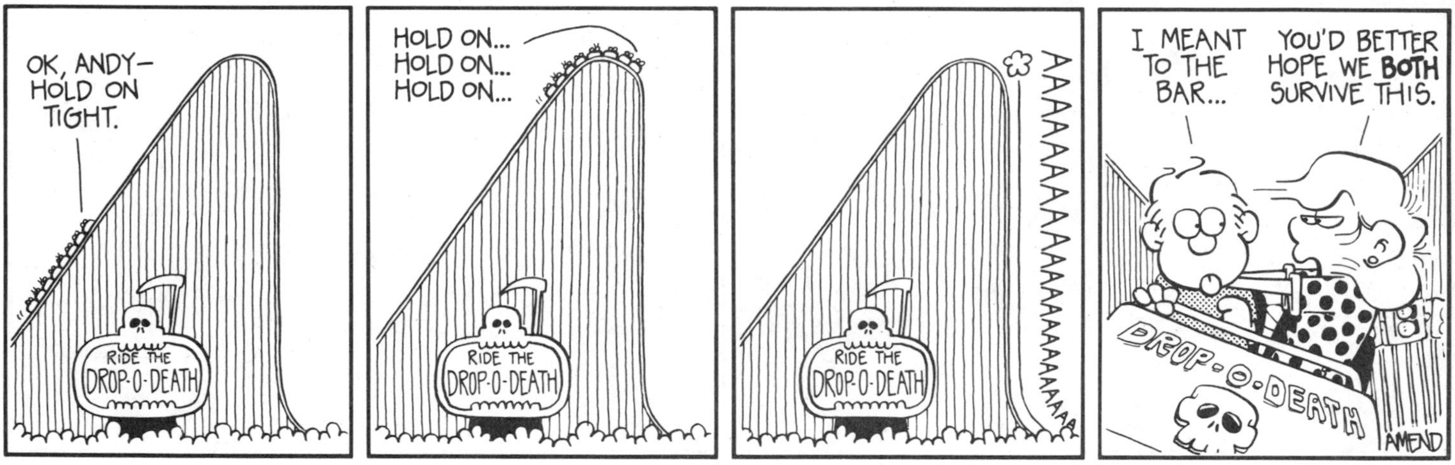
OK, ANDY—HOLD ON TIGHT.
RIDE THE DROP-O-DEATH
HOLD ON... HOLD ON... HOLD ON...
RIDE THE DROP-O-DEATH
AAAAAAAAAAAAAAAAAAAAAAA
RIDE THE DROP-O-DEATH
I MEANT TO THE BAR...
YOU'D BETTER HOPE WE **BOTH** SURVIVE THIS.
DROP-O-DEATH
AMEND

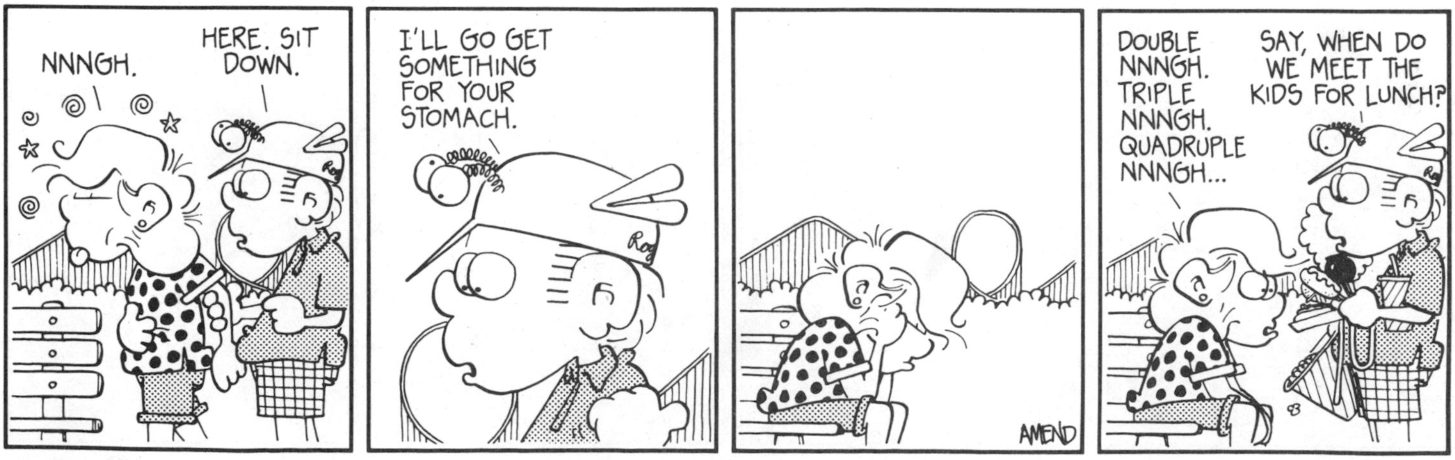
NNNGH.
HERE. SIT DOWN.
I'LL GO GET SOMETHING FOR YOUR STOMACH.
AMEND
DOUBLE NNNGH. TRIPLE NNNGH. QUADRUPLE NNNGH...
SAY, WHEN DO WE MEET THE KIDS FOR LUNCH?

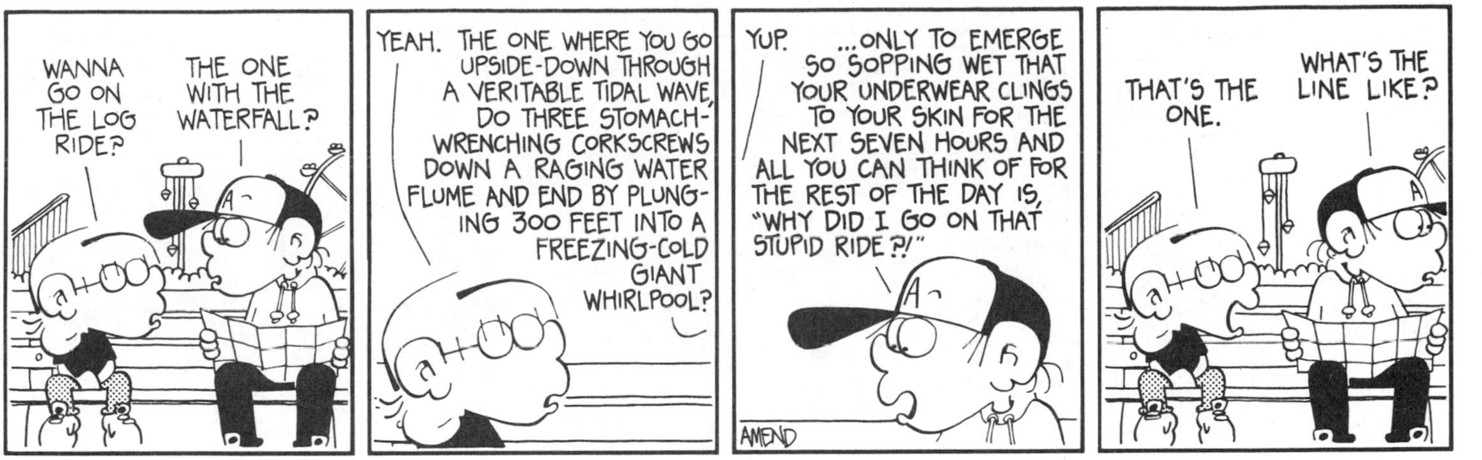
WANNA GO ON THE LOG RIDE?
THE ONE WITH THE WATERFALL?
YEAH. THE ONE WHERE YOU GO UPSIDE-DOWN THROUGH A VERITABLE TIDAL WAVE, DO THREE STOMACH-WRENCHING CORKSCREWS DOWN A RAGING WATER FLUME AND END BY PLUNGING 300 FEET INTO A FREEZING-COLD GIANT WHIRLPOOL?
YUP.
...ONLY TO EMERGE SO SOPPING WET THAT YOUR UNDERWEAR CLINGS TO YOUR SKIN FOR THE NEXT SEVEN HOURS AND ALL YOU CAN THINK OF FOR THE REST OF THE DAY IS, "WHY DID I GO ON THAT STUPID RIDE?!"
AMEND
THAT'S THE ONE.
WHAT'S THE LINE LIKE?

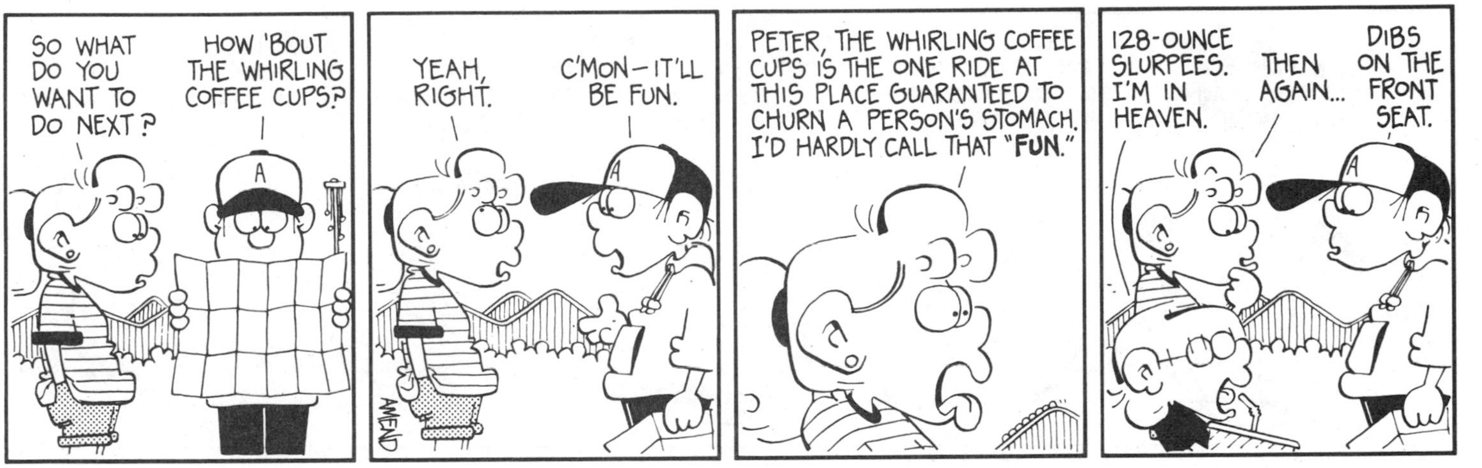
SO WHAT DO YOU WANT TO DO NEXT?
HOW 'BOUT THE WHIRLING COFFEE CUPS?
YEAH, RIGHT.
C'MON – IT'LL BE FUN.
AMEND
PETER, THE WHIRLING COFFEE CUPS IS THE ONE RIDE AT THIS PLACE GUARANTEED TO CHURN A PERSON'S STOMACH. I'D HARDLY CALL THAT "**FUN**."
128-OUNCE SLURPEES. I'M IN HEAVEN.
THEN AGAIN...
DIBS ON THE FRONT SEAT.

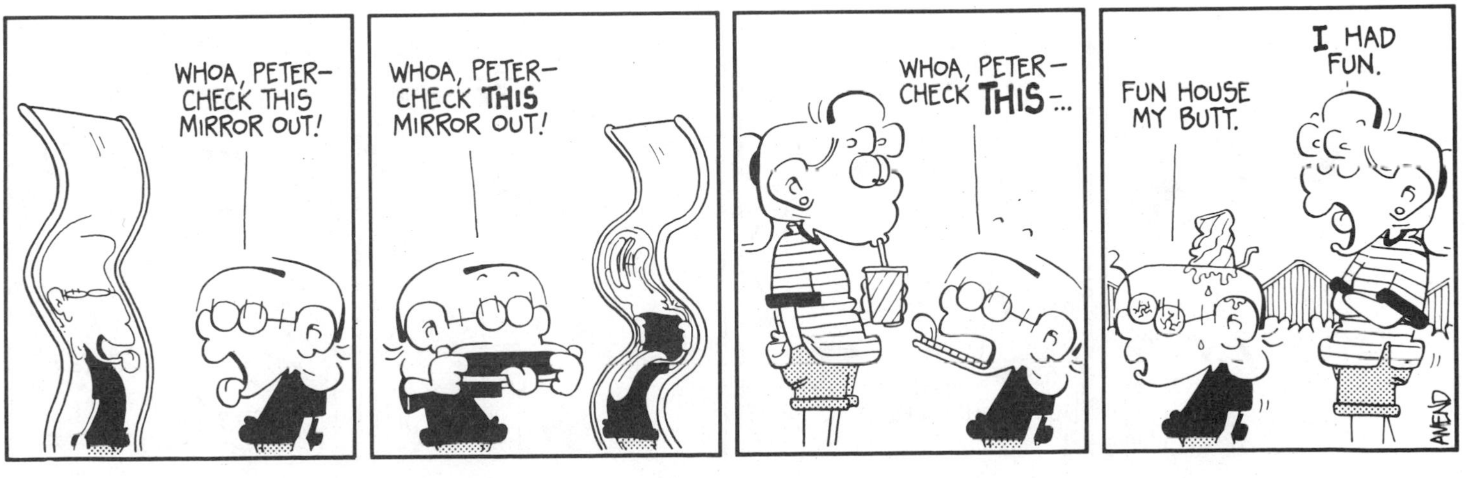
WHOA, PETER– CHECK THIS MIRROR OUT!
WHOA, PETER– CHECK **THIS** MIRROR OUT!
WHOA, PETER– CHECK **THIS**–...
FUN HOUSE MY BUTT.
I HAD FUN.
AMEND

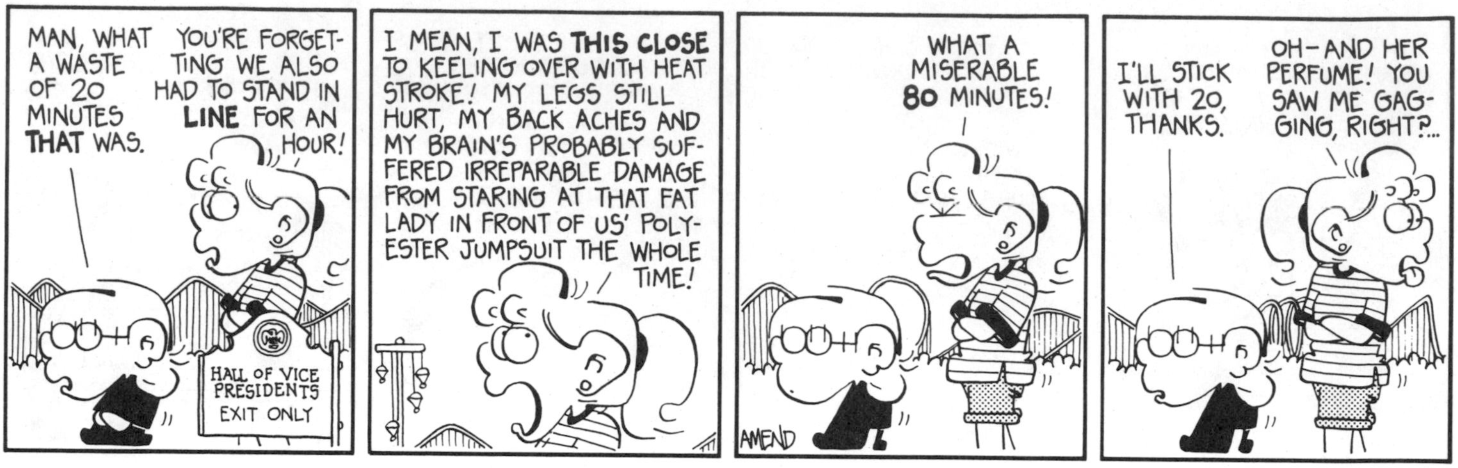
MAN, WHAT A WASTE OF 20 MINUTES THAT WAS.
YOU'RE FORGETTING WE ALSO HAD TO STAND IN LINE FOR AN HOUR!
HALL OF VICE PRESIDENTS
EXIT ONLY
I MEAN, I WAS THIS CLOSE TO KEELING OVER WITH HEAT STROKE! MY LEGS STILL HURT, MY BACK ACHES AND MY BRAIN'S PROBABLY SUFFERED IRREPARABLE DAMAGE FROM STARING AT THAT FAT LADY IN FRONT OF US' POLYESTER JUMPSUIT THE WHOLE TIME!
WHAT A MISERABLE 80 MINUTES!
AMEND
I'LL STICK WITH 20, THANKS.
OH—AND HER PERFUME! YOU SAW ME GAGGING, RIGHT?...

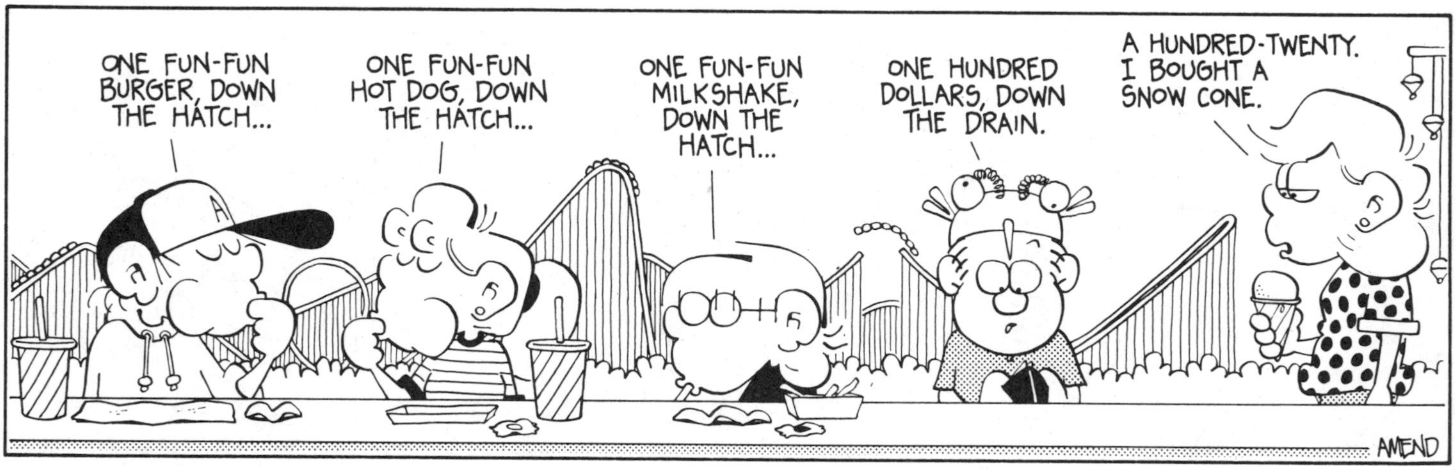
ONE FUN-FUN BURGER, DOWN THE HATCH...
ONE FUN-FUN HOT DOG, DOWN THE HATCH...
ONE FUN-FUN MILKSHAKE, DOWN THE HATCH...
ONE HUNDRED DOLLARS, DOWN THE DRAIN.
A HUNDRED-TWENTY. I BOUGHT A SNOW CONE.
AMEND

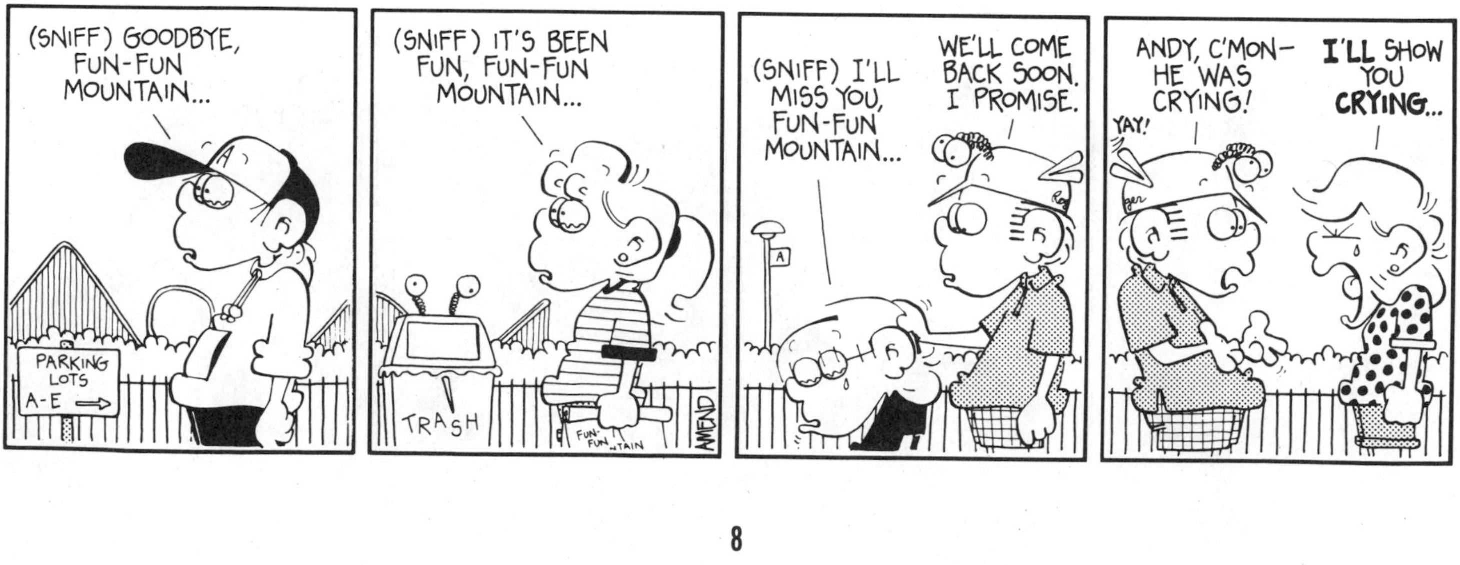
(SNIFF) GOODBYE, FUN-FUN MOUNTAIN...
PARKING LOTS A-E
(SNIFF) IT'S BEEN FUN, FUN-FUN MOUNTAIN...
TRASH
AMEND
(SNIFF) I'LL MISS YOU, FUN-FUN MOUNTAIN...
WE'LL COME BACK SOON. I PROMISE.
YAY!
ANDY, C'MON—HE WAS CRYING!
I'LL SHOW YOU CRYING...

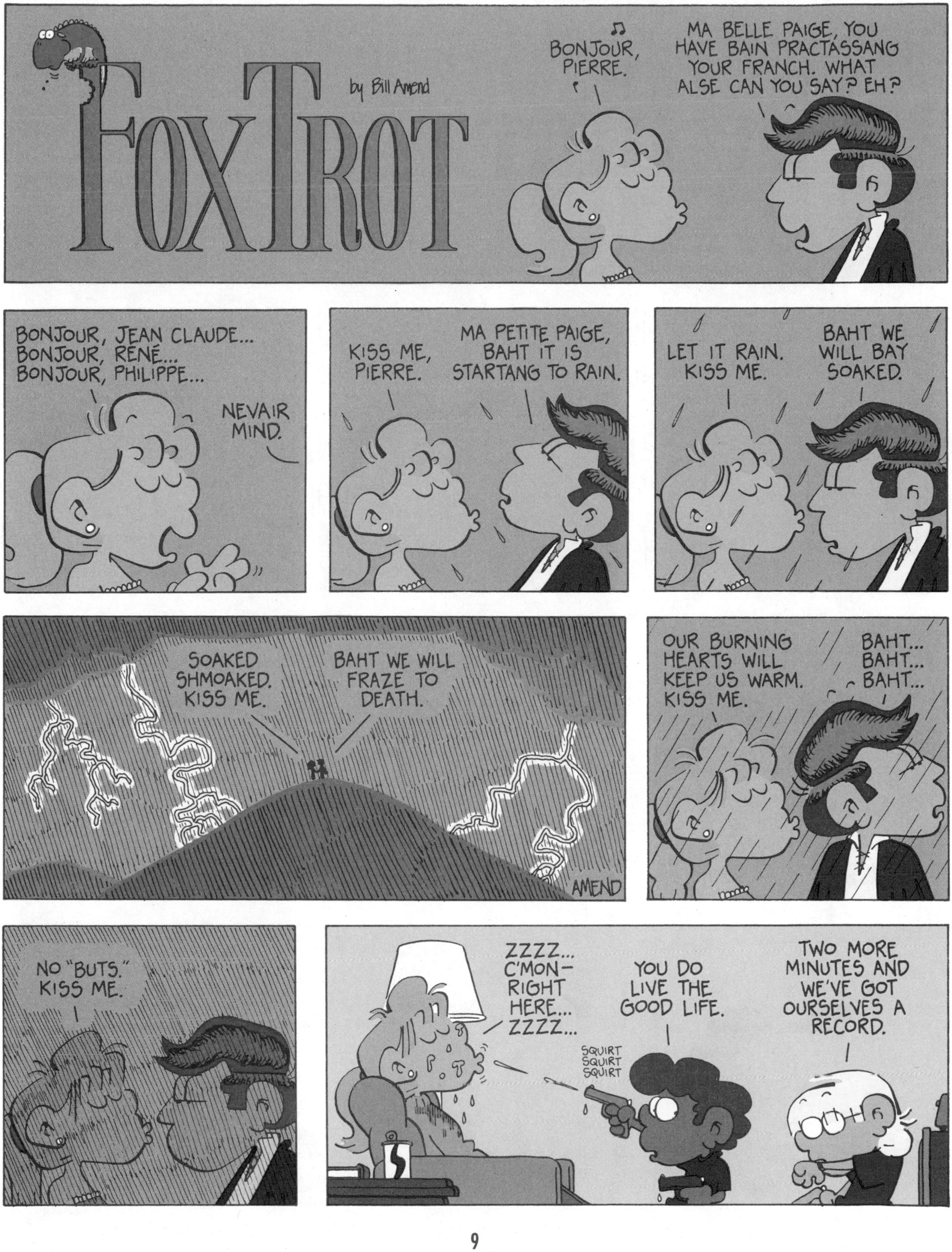
FoxTrot
by Bill Amend
BONJOUR, PIERRE.
MA BELLE PAIGE, YOU HAVE BAIN PRACTASSANG YOUR FRANCH. WHAT ALSE CAN YOU SAY? EH?
BONJOUR, JEAN CLAUDE... BONJOUR, RENÉ... BONJOUR, PHILIPPE...
NEVAIR MIND.
KISS ME, PIERRE.
MA PETITE PAIGE, BAHT IT IS STARTANG TO RAIN.
LET IT RAIN. KISS ME.
BAHT WE WILL BAY SOAKED.
SOAKED SHMOAKED. KISS ME.
BAHT WE WILL FRAZE TO DEATH.
AMEND
OUR BURNING HEARTS WILL KEEP US WARM. KISS ME.
BAHT... BAHT... BAHT...
NO "BUTS." KISS ME.
ZZZZ... C'MON— RIGHT HERE... ZZZZ...
SQUIRT SQUIRT SQUIRT
YOU DO LIVE THE GOOD LIFE.
TWO MORE MINUTES AND WE'VE GOT OURSELVES A RECORD.

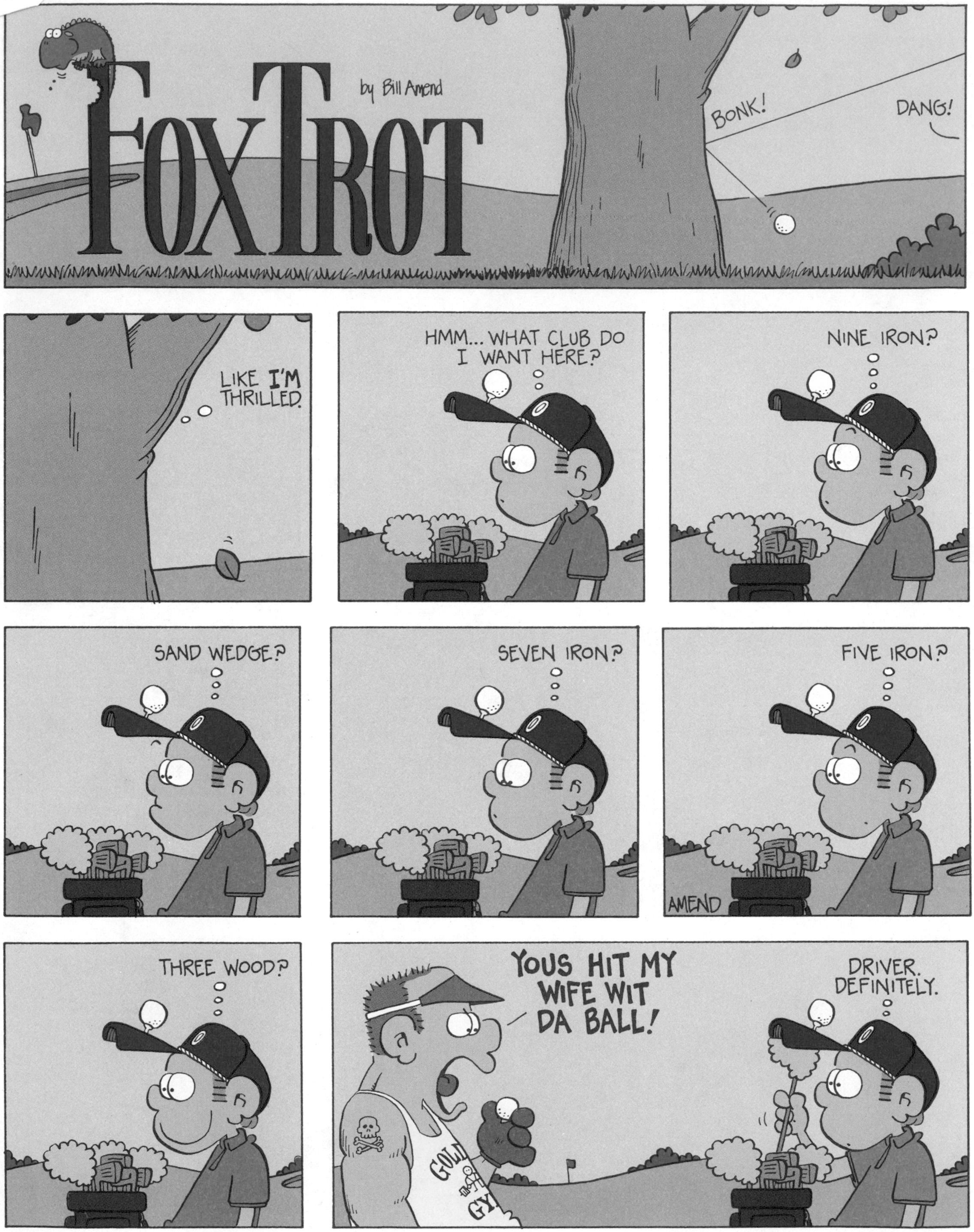
FoxTrot
by Bill Amend
BONK!
DANG!
LIKE I'M THRILLED.
HMM... WHAT CLUB DO I WANT HERE?
NINE IRON?
SAND WEDGE?
SEVEN IRON?
FIVE IRON?
AMEND
THREE WOOD?
YOUS HIT MY WIFE WIT DA BALL!
DRIVER. DEFINITELY.

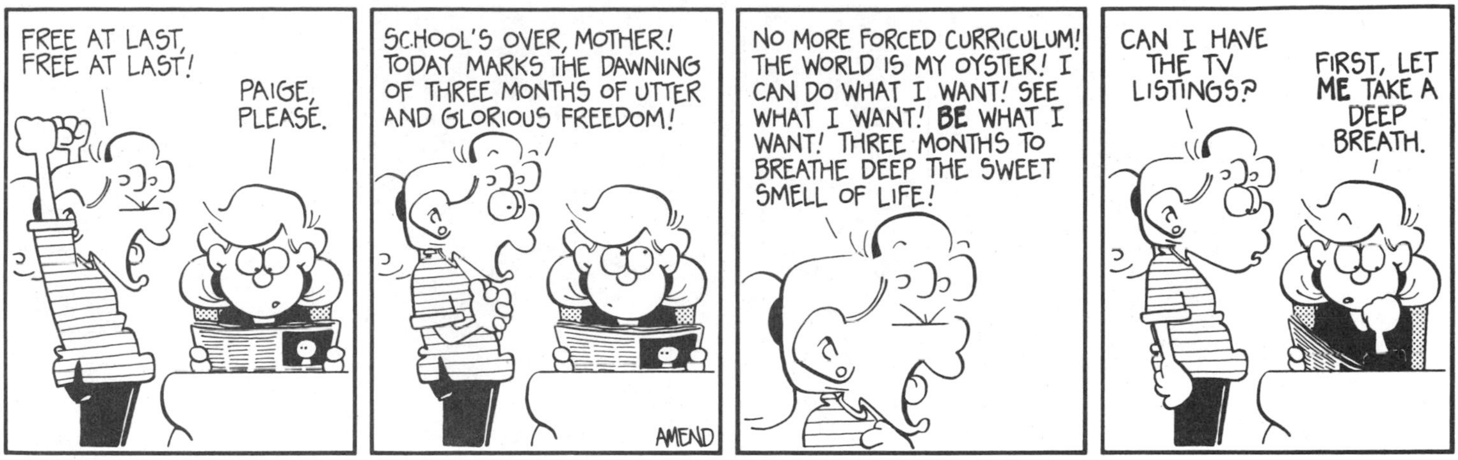
FREE AT LAST, FREE AT LAST!
PAIGE, PLEASE.
SCHOOL'S OVER, MOTHER! TODAY MARKS THE DAWNING OF THREE MONTHS OF UTTER AND GLORIOUS FREEDOM!
AMEND
NO MORE FORCED CURRICULUM! THE WORLD IS MY OYSTER! I CAN DO WHAT I WANT! SEE WHAT I WANT! **BE** WHAT I WANT! THREE MONTHS TO BREATHE DEEP THE SWEET SMELL OF LIFE!
CAN I HAVE THE TV LISTINGS?
FIRST, LET **ME** TAKE A DEEP BREATH.

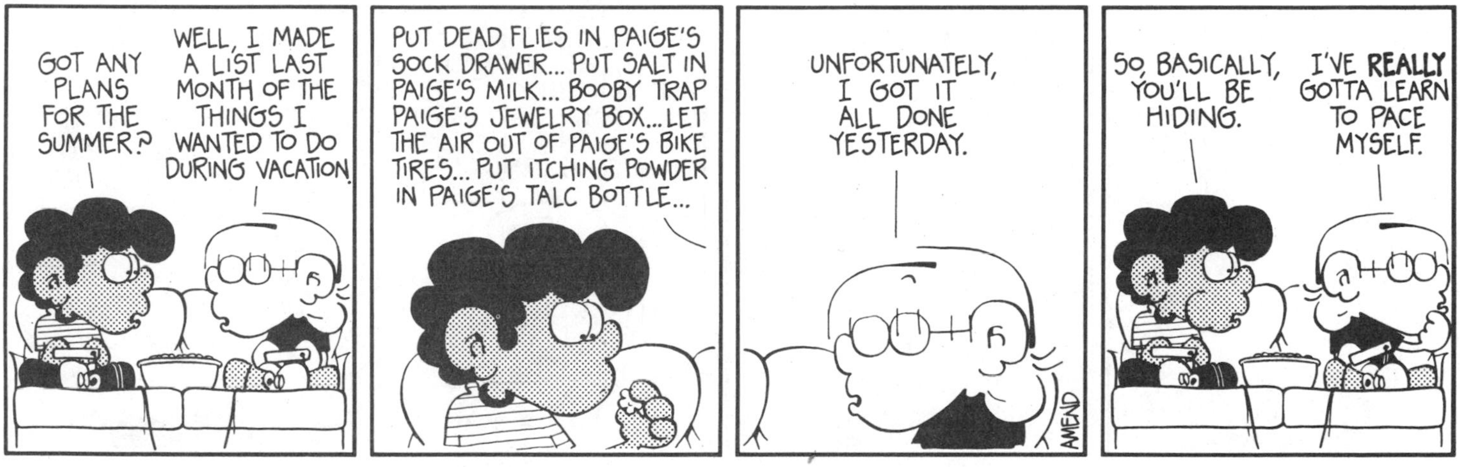
GOT ANY PLANS FOR THE SUMMER?
WELL, I MADE A LIST LAST MONTH OF THE THINGS I WANTED TO DO DURING VACATION.
PUT DEAD FLIES IN PAIGE'S SOCK DRAWER... PUT SALT IN PAIGE'S MILK... BOOBY TRAP PAIGE'S JEWELRY BOX... LET THE AIR OUT OF PAIGE'S BIKE TIRES... PUT ITCHING POWDER IN PAIGE'S TALC BOTTLE...
UNFORTUNATELY, I GOT IT ALL DONE YESTERDAY.
AMEND
SO, BASICALLY, YOU'LL BE HIDING.
I'VE **REALLY** GOTTA LEARN TO PACE MYSELF.

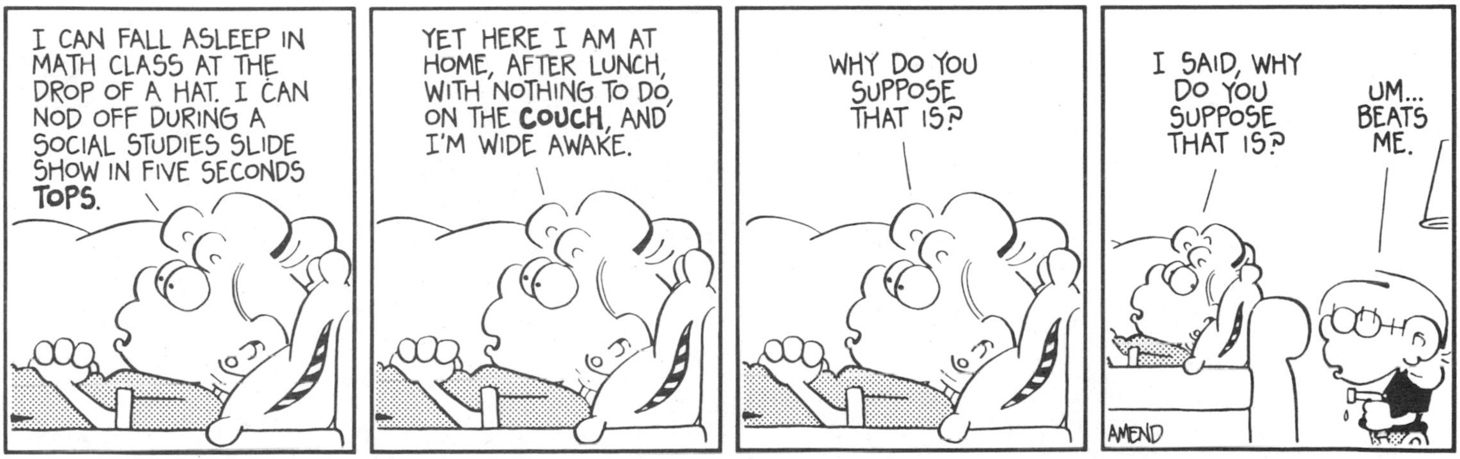
I CAN FALL ASLEEP IN MATH CLASS AT THE DROP OF A HAT. I CAN NOD OFF DURING A SOCIAL STUDIES SLIDE SHOW IN FIVE SECONDS **TOPS**.
YET HERE I AM AT HOME, AFTER LUNCH, WITH NOTHING TO DO, ON THE **COUCH**, AND I'M WIDE AWAKE.
WHY DO YOU SUPPOSE THAT IS?
I SAID, WHY DO YOU SUPPOSE THAT IS?
UM... BEATS ME.
AMEND

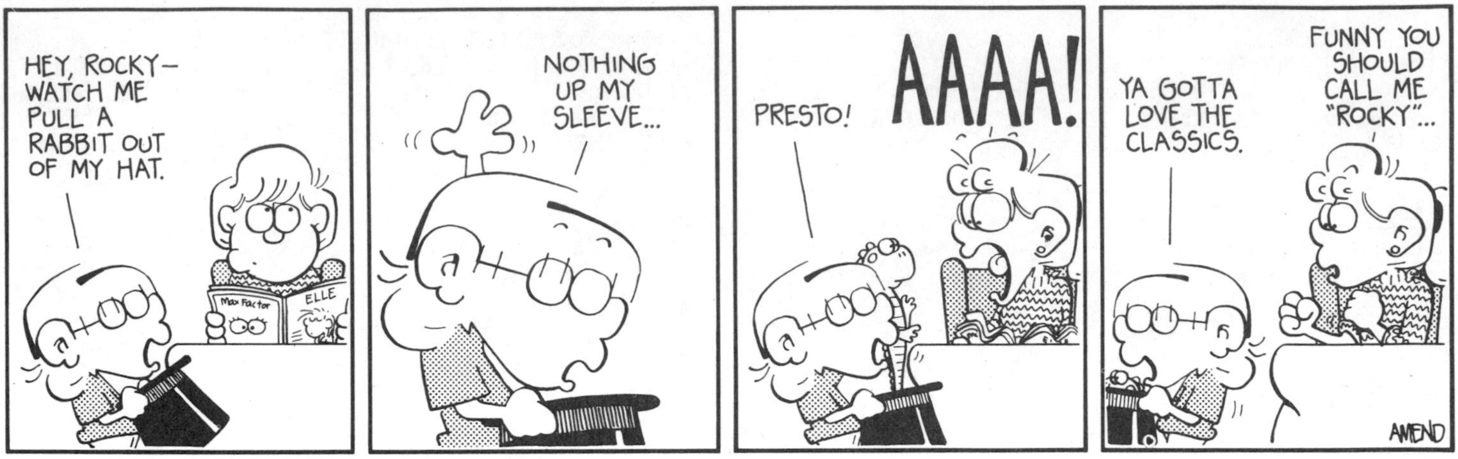
HEY, ROCKY— WATCH ME PULL A RABBIT OUT OF MY HAT.
Max Factor
ELLE
NOTHING UP MY SLEEVE...
PRESTO!
AAAA!
YA GOTTA LOVE THE CLASSICS.
FUNNY YOU SHOULD CALL ME "ROCKY"...
AMEND

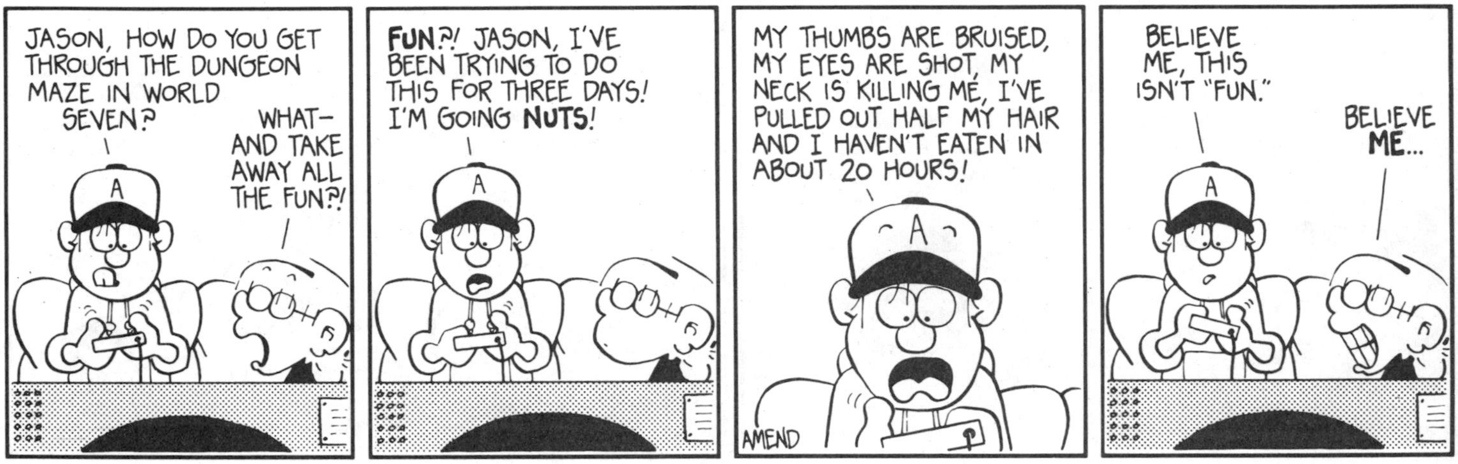
JASON, HOW DO YOU GET THROUGH THE DUNGEON MAZE IN WORLD SEVEN?
WHAT— AND TAKE AWAY ALL THE FUN?!
FUN?! JASON, I'VE BEEN TRYING TO DO THIS FOR THREE DAYS! I'M GOING NUTS!
MY THUMBS ARE BRUISED, MY EYES ARE SHOT, MY NECK IS KILLING ME, I'VE PULLED OUT HALF MY HAIR AND I HAVEN'T EATEN IN ABOUT 20 HOURS!
AMEND
BELIEVE ME, THIS ISN'T "FUN."
BELIEVE ME...

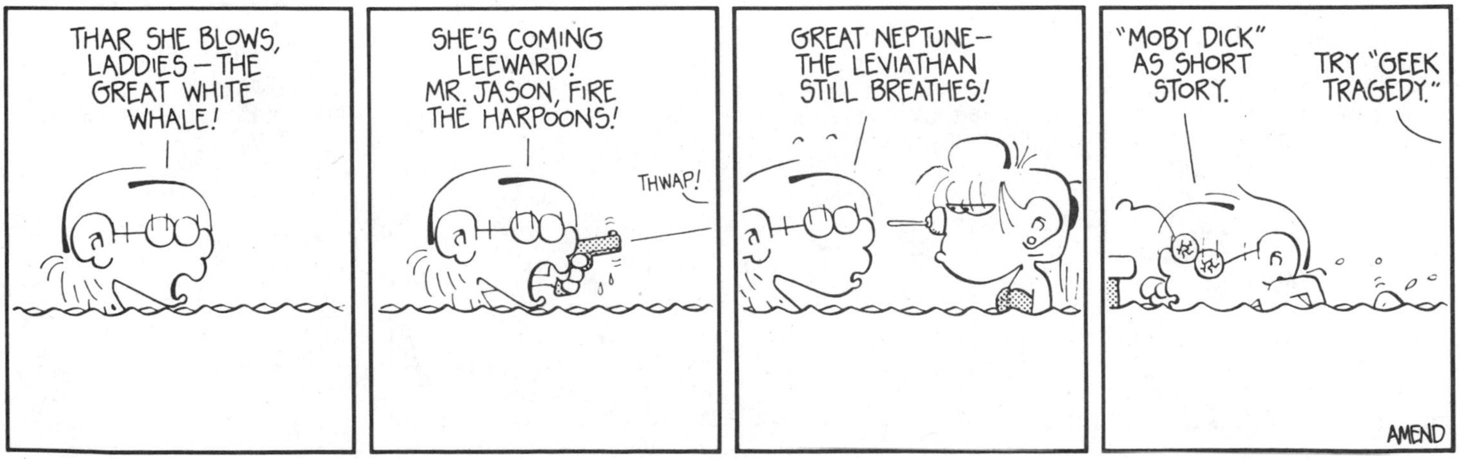
THAR SHE BLOWS, LADDIES — THE GREAT WHITE WHALE!
SHE'S COMING LEEWARD! MR. JASON, FIRE THE HARPOONS!
THWAP!
GREAT NEPTUNE— THE LEVIATHAN STILL BREATHES!
"MOBY DICK" AS SHORT STORY.
TRY "GEEK TRAGEDY."
AMEND

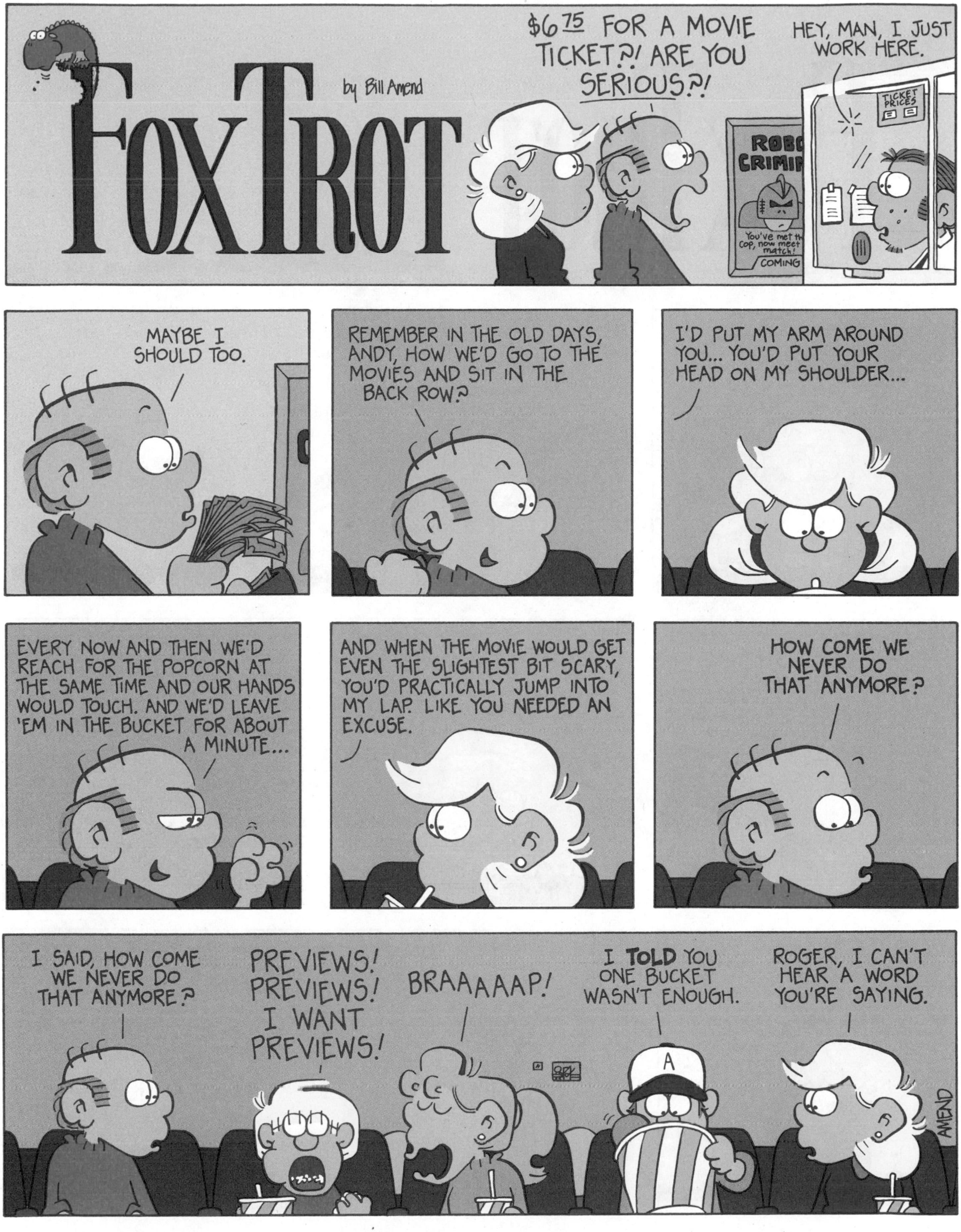
FoxTrot
by Bill Amend
$6.75 FOR A MOVIE TICKET?! ARE YOU SERIOUS?!
HEY, MAN, I JUST WORK HERE.
TICKET PRICES
ROBO CRIMI
You've met the cop, now meet match!
COMING
MAYBE I SHOULD TOO.
REMEMBER IN THE OLD DAYS, ANDY, HOW WE'D GO TO THE MOVIES AND SIT IN THE BACK ROW?
I'D PUT MY ARM AROUND YOU... YOU'D PUT YOUR HEAD ON MY SHOULDER...
EVERY NOW AND THEN WE'D REACH FOR THE POPCORN AT THE SAME TIME AND OUR HANDS WOULD TOUCH. AND WE'D LEAVE 'EM IN THE BUCKET FOR ABOUT A MINUTE...
AND WHEN THE MOVIE WOULD GET EVEN THE SLIGHTEST BIT SCARY, YOU'D PRACTICALLY JUMP INTO MY LAP. LIKE YOU NEEDED AN EXCUSE.
HOW COME WE NEVER DO THAT ANYMORE?
I SAID, HOW COME WE NEVER DO THAT ANYMORE?
PREVIEWS! PREVIEWS! I WANT PREVIEWS!
BRAAAAAP!
I **TOLD** YOU ONE BUCKET WASN'T ENOUGH.
ROGER, I CAN'T HEAR A WORD YOU'RE SAYING.
A
AMEND

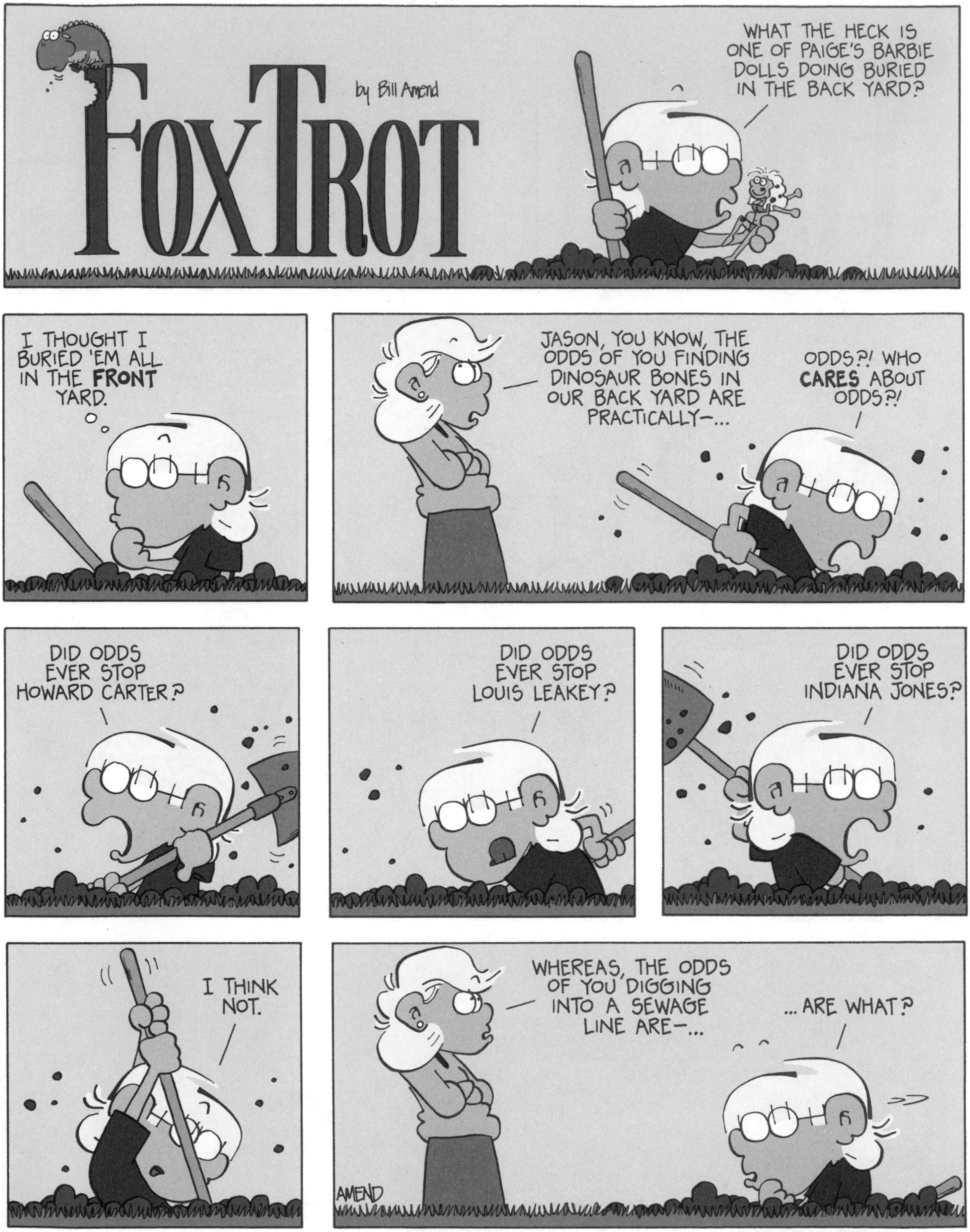
FoxTrot
by Bill Amend
WHAT THE HECK IS ONE OF PAIGE'S BARBIE DOLLS DOING BURIED IN THE BACK YARD?
I THOUGHT I BURIED 'EM ALL IN THE **FRONT** YARD.
JASON, YOU KNOW, THE ODDS OF YOU FINDING DINOSAUR BONES IN OUR BACK YARD ARE PRACTICALLY–...
ODDS?! WHO **CARES** ABOUT ODDS?!
DID ODDS EVER STOP HOWARD CARTER?
DID ODDS EVER STOP LOUIS LEAKEY?
DID ODDS EVER STOP INDIANA JONES?
I THINK NOT.
WHEREAS, THE ODDS OF YOU DIGGING INTO A SEWAGE LINE ARE–...
... ARE WHAT?
AMEND

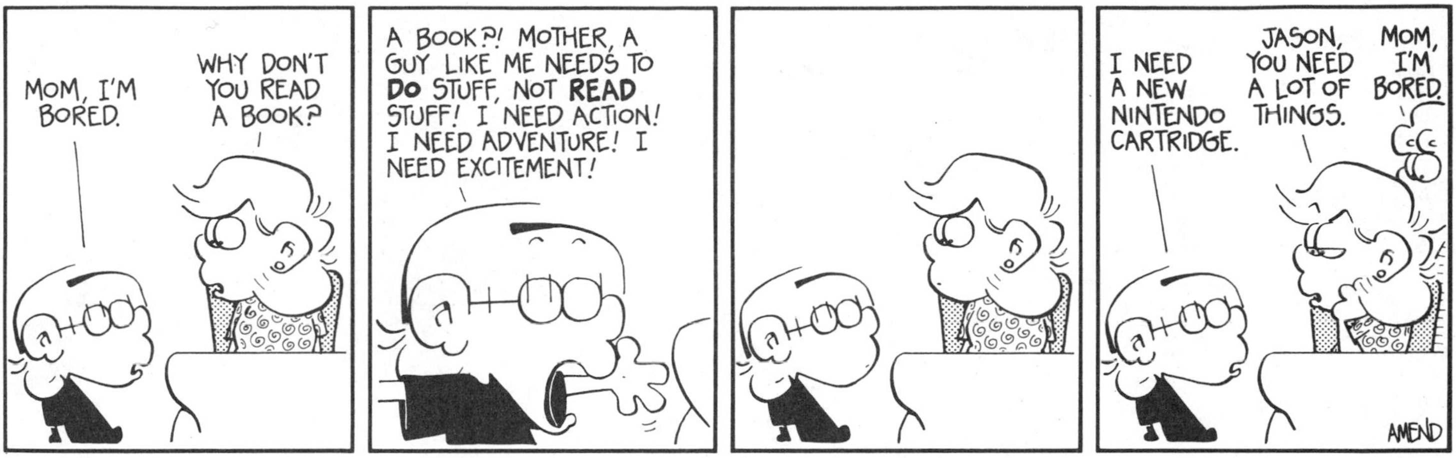
MOM, I'M BORED.
WHY DON'T YOU READ A BOOK?
A BOOK?! MOTHER, A GUY LIKE ME NEEDS TO **DO** STUFF, NOT **READ** STUFF! I NEED ACTION! I NEED ADVENTURE! I NEED EXCITEMENT!
I NEED A NEW NINTENDO CARTRIDGE.
JASON, YOU NEED A LOT OF THINGS.
MOM, I'M BORED.

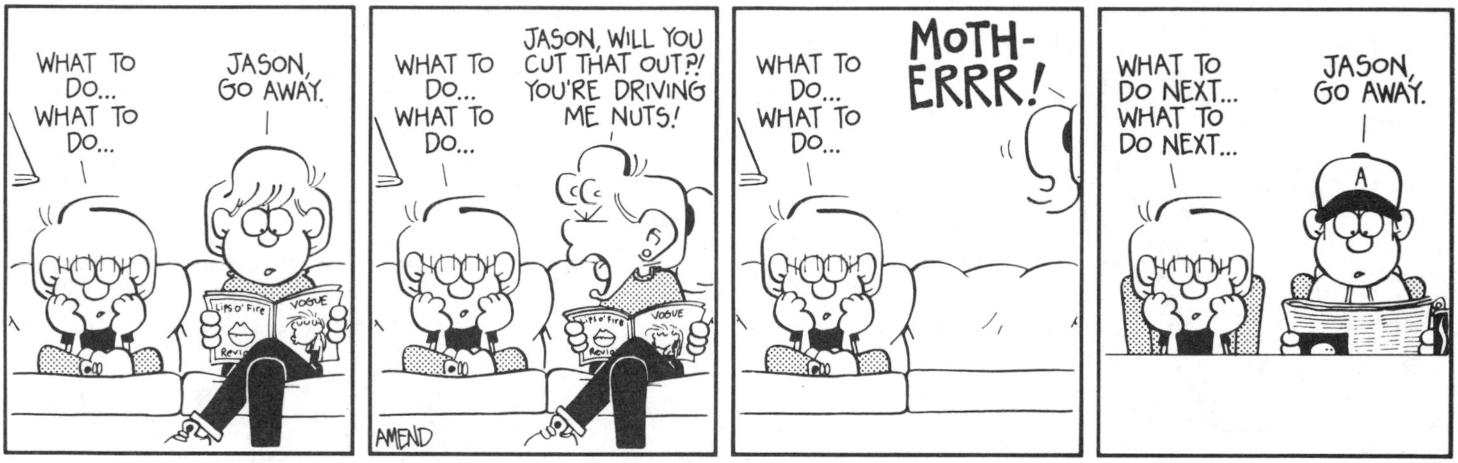
WHAT TO DO... WHAT TO DO...
JASON, GO AWAY.
WHAT TO DO... WHAT TO DO...
JASON, WILL YOU CUT THAT OUT?! YOU'RE DRIVING ME NUTS!
WHAT TO DO... WHAT TO DO...
MOTH-ERRR!
WHAT TO DO NEXT... WHAT TO DO NEXT...
JASON, GO AWAY.

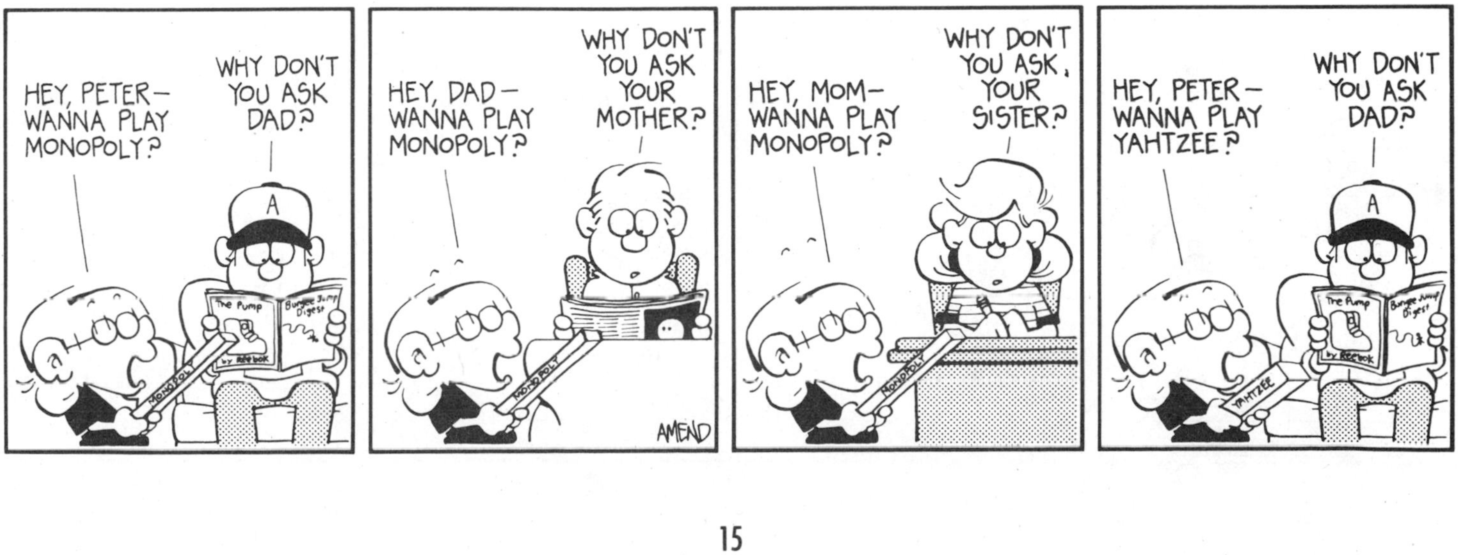
HEY, PETER— WANNA PLAY MONOPOLY?
WHY DON'T YOU ASK DAD?
HEY, DAD— WANNA PLAY MONOPOLY?
WHY DON'T YOU ASK YOUR MOTHER?
HEY, MOM— WANNA PLAY MONOPOLY?
WHY DON'T YOU ASK YOUR SISTER?
HEY, PETER— WANNA PLAY YAHTZEE?
WHY DON'T YOU ASK DAD?

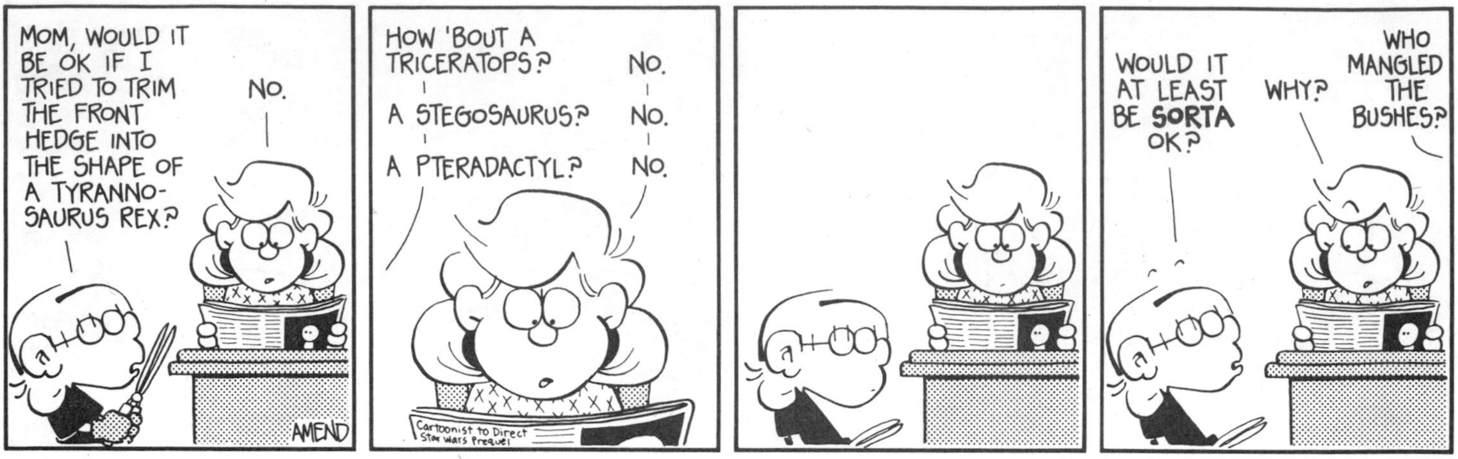
MOM, WOULD IT BE OK IF I TRIED TO TRIM THE FRONT HEDGE INTO THE SHAPE OF A TYRANNOSAURUS REX?
NO.
AMEND
HOW 'BOUT A TRICERATOPS?
NO.
A STEGOSAURUS?
NO.
A PTERADACTYL?
NO.
Cartoonist to Direct Star Wars Prequel
WOULD IT AT LEAST BE **SORTA** OK?
WHY?
WHO MANGLED THE BUSHES?

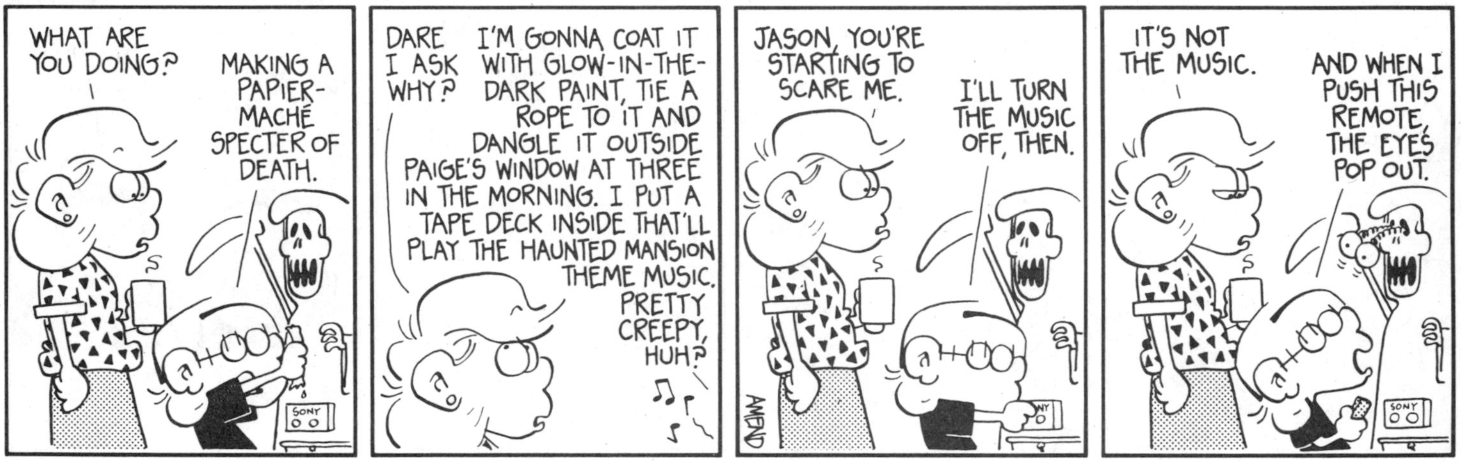
WHAT ARE YOU DOING?
MAKING A PAPIER-MACHÉ SPECTER OF DEATH.
SONY
DARE I ASK WHY?
I'M GONNA COAT IT WITH GLOW-IN-THE-DARK PAINT, TIE A ROPE TO IT AND DANGLE IT OUTSIDE PAIGE'S WINDOW AT THREE IN THE MORNING. I PUT A TAPE DECK INSIDE THAT'LL PLAY THE HAUNTED MANSION THEME MUSIC. PRETTY CREEPY, HUH?
JASON, YOU'RE STARTING TO SCARE ME.
I'LL TURN THE MUSIC OFF, THEN.
AMEND
IT'S NOT THE MUSIC.
AND WHEN I PUSH THIS REMOTE, THE EYES POP OUT.
SONY

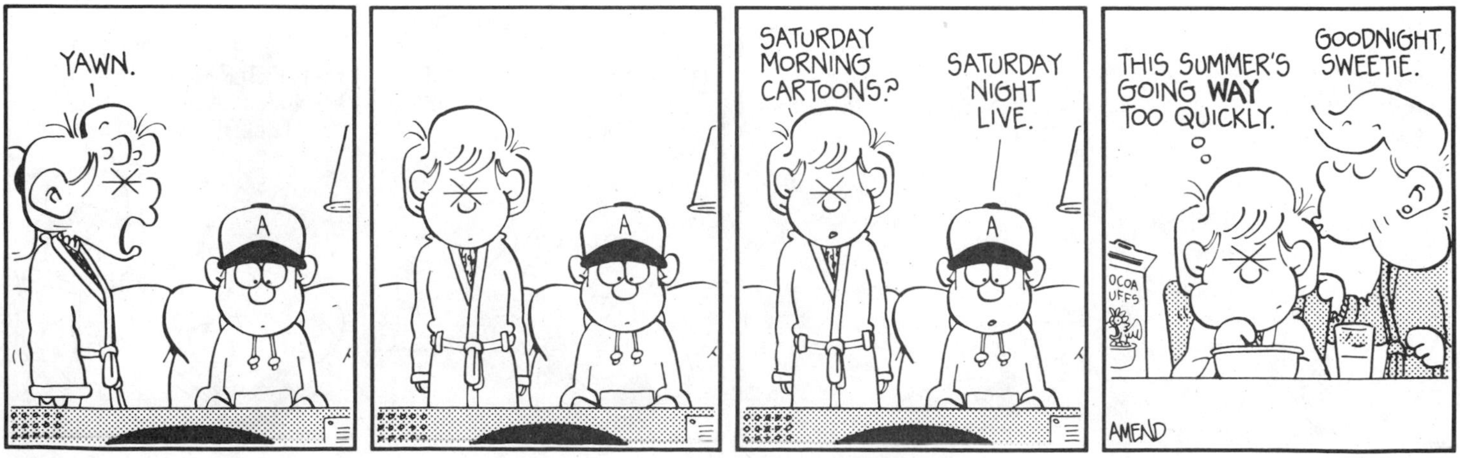
YAWN.
SATURDAY MORNING CARTOONS?
SATURDAY NIGHT LIVE.
THIS SUMMER'S GOING **WAY** TOO QUICKLY.
GOODNIGHT, SWEETIE.
AMEND

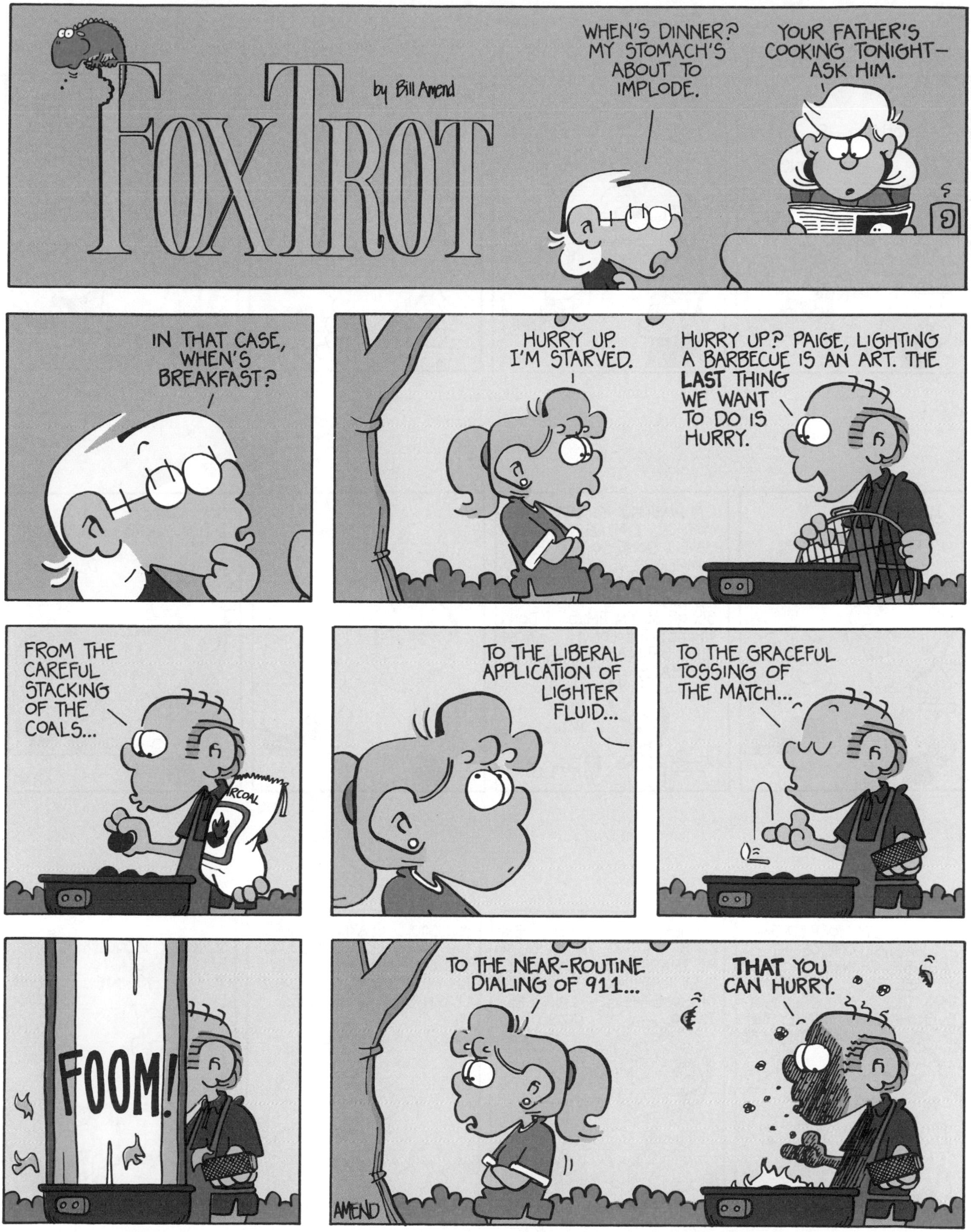
FoxTrot
by Bill Amend
WHEN'S DINNER? MY STOMACH'S ABOUT TO IMPLODE.
YOUR FATHER'S COOKING TONIGHT— ASK HIM.
IN THAT CASE, WHEN'S BREAKFAST?
HURRY UP. I'M STARVED.
HURRY UP? PAIGE, LIGHTING A BARBECUE IS AN ART. THE **LAST** THING WE WANT TO DO IS HURRY.
FROM THE CAREFUL STACKING OF THE COALS...
TO THE LIBERAL APPLICATION OF LIGHTER FLUID...
TO THE GRACEFUL TOSSING OF THE MATCH...
FOOM!
TO THE NEAR-ROUTINE DIALING OF 911...
THAT YOU CAN HURRY.
AMEND

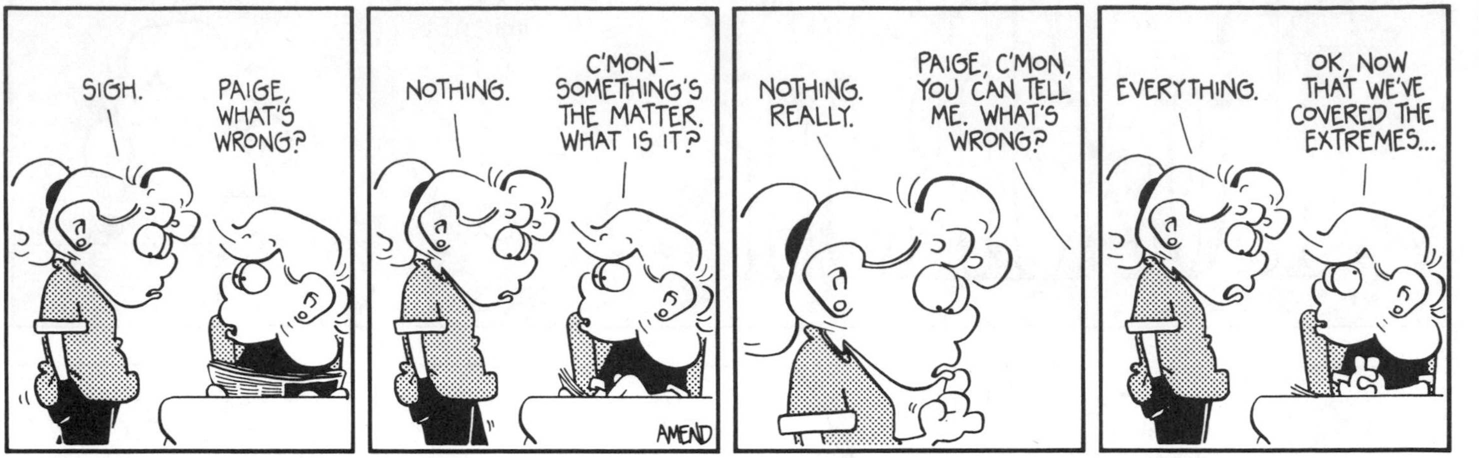
SIGH.
PAIGE, WHAT'S WRONG?
NOTHING.
C'MON— SOMETHING'S THE MATTER. WHAT IS IT?
AMEND
NOTHING. REALLY.
PAIGE, C'MON, YOU CAN TELL ME. WHAT'S WRONG?
EVERYTHING.
OK, NOW THAT WE'VE COVERED THE EXTREMES...

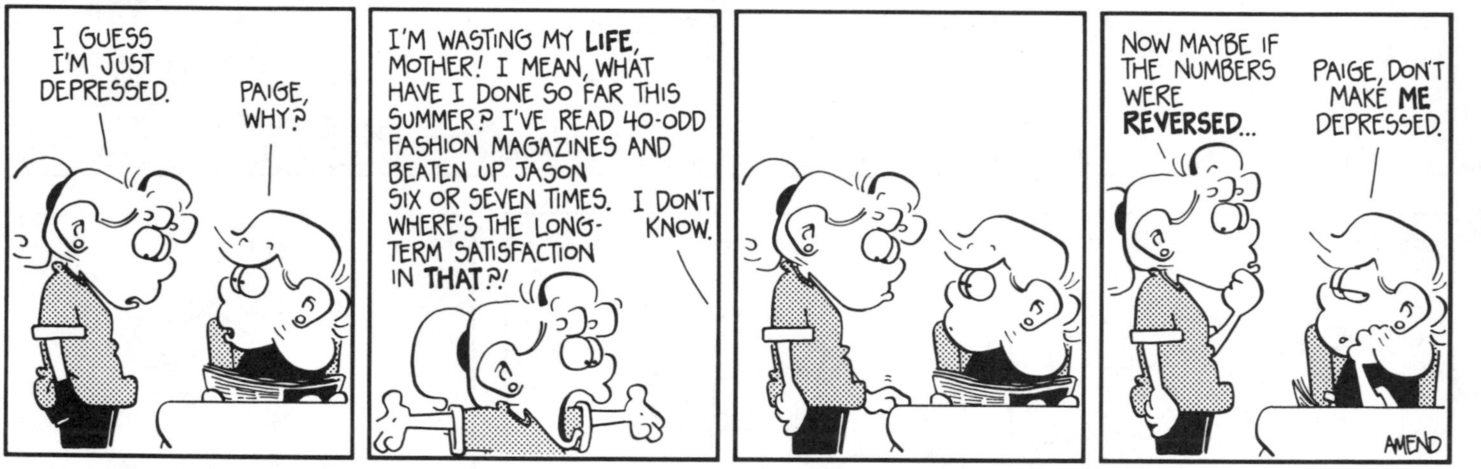
I GUESS I'M JUST DEPRESSED.
PAIGE, WHY?
I'M WASTING MY LIFE, MOTHER! I MEAN, WHAT HAVE I DONE SO FAR THIS SUMMER? I'VE READ 40-ODD FASHION MAGAZINES AND BEATEN UP JASON SIX OR SEVEN TIMES. WHERE'S THE LONG-TERM SATISFACTION IN THAT?!
I DON'T KNOW.
NOW MAYBE IF THE NUMBERS WERE REVERSED...
PAIGE, DON'T MAKE ME DEPRESSED.
AMEND

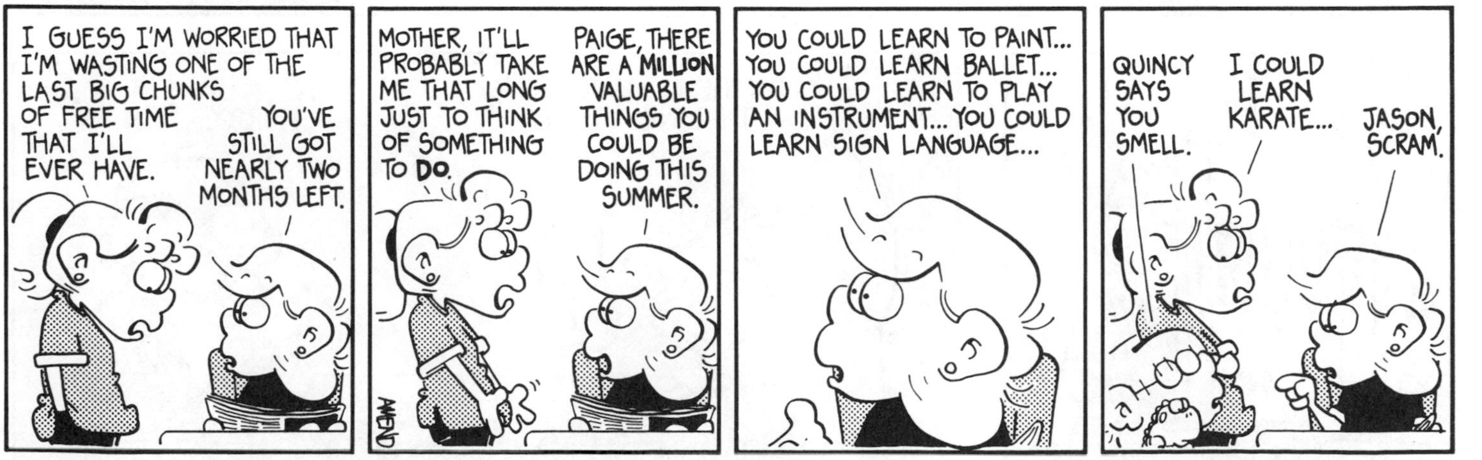
I GUESS I'M WORRIED THAT I'M WASTING ONE OF THE LAST BIG CHUNKS OF FREE TIME THAT I'LL EVER HAVE.
YOU'VE STILL GOT NEARLY TWO MONTHS LEFT.
MOTHER, IT'LL PROBABLY TAKE ME THAT LONG JUST TO THINK OF SOMETHING TO DO.
PAIGE, THERE ARE A MILLION VALUABLE THINGS YOU COULD BE DOING THIS SUMMER.
AMEND
YOU COULD LEARN TO PAINT... YOU COULD LEARN BALLET... YOU COULD LEARN TO PLAY AN INSTRUMENT... YOU COULD LEARN SIGN LANGUAGE...
QUINCY SAYS YOU SMELL.
I COULD LEARN KARATE...
JASON, SCRAM.

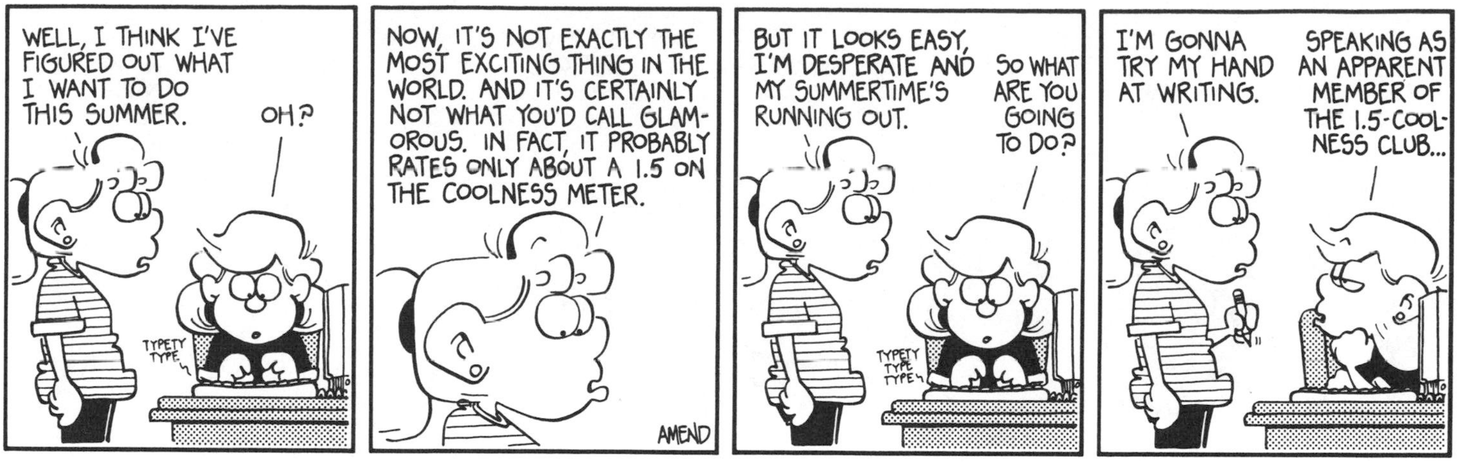
WELL, I THINK I'VE FIGURED OUT WHAT I WANT TO DO THIS SUMMER.
OH?
TYPETY TYPE
NOW, IT'S NOT EXACTLY THE MOST EXCITING THING IN THE WORLD. AND IT'S CERTAINLY NOT WHAT YOU'D CALL GLAMOROUS. IN FACT, IT PROBABLY RATES ONLY ABOUT A 1.5 ON THE COOLNESS METER.
AMEND
BUT IT LOOKS EASY, I'M DESPERATE AND MY SUMMERTIME'S RUNNING OUT.
SO WHAT ARE YOU GOING TO DO?
TYPETY TYPE TYPE
I'M GONNA TRY MY HAND AT WRITING.
SPEAKING AS AN APPARENT MEMBER OF THE 1.5-COOLNESS CLUB...

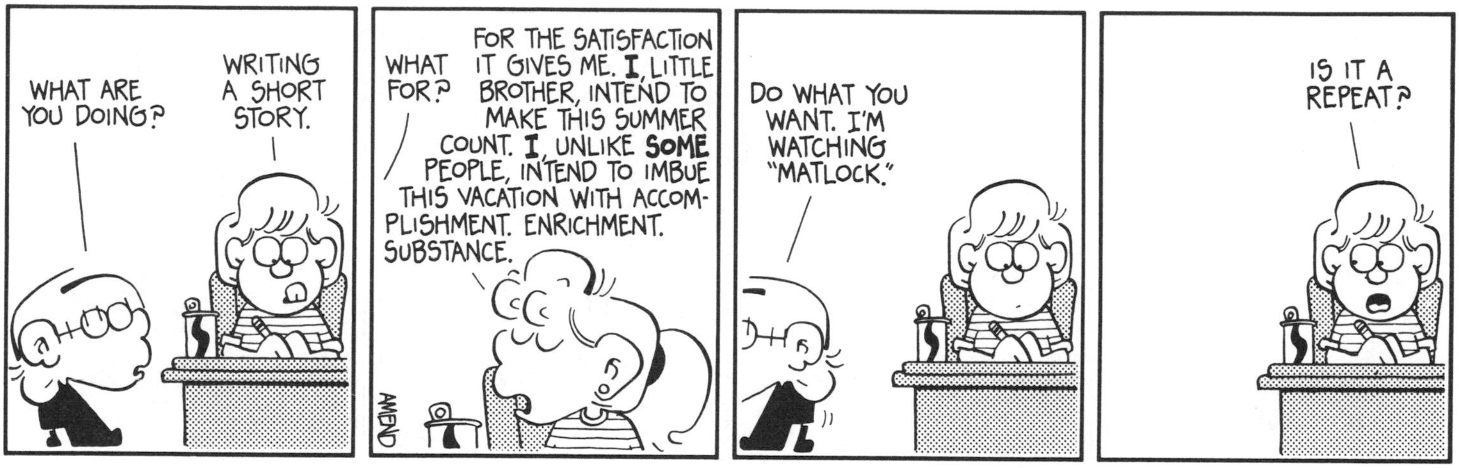
WHAT ARE YOU DOING?
WRITING A SHORT STORY.
WHAT FOR?
FOR THE SATISFACTION IT GIVES ME. **I**, LITTLE BROTHER, INTEND TO MAKE THIS SUMMER COUNT. **I**, UNLIKE **SOME** PEOPLE, INTEND TO IMBUE THIS VACATION WITH ACCOMPLISHMENT. ENRICHMENT. SUBSTANCE.
AMEND
DO WHAT YOU WANT. I'M WATCHING "MATLOCK."
IS IT A REPEAT?

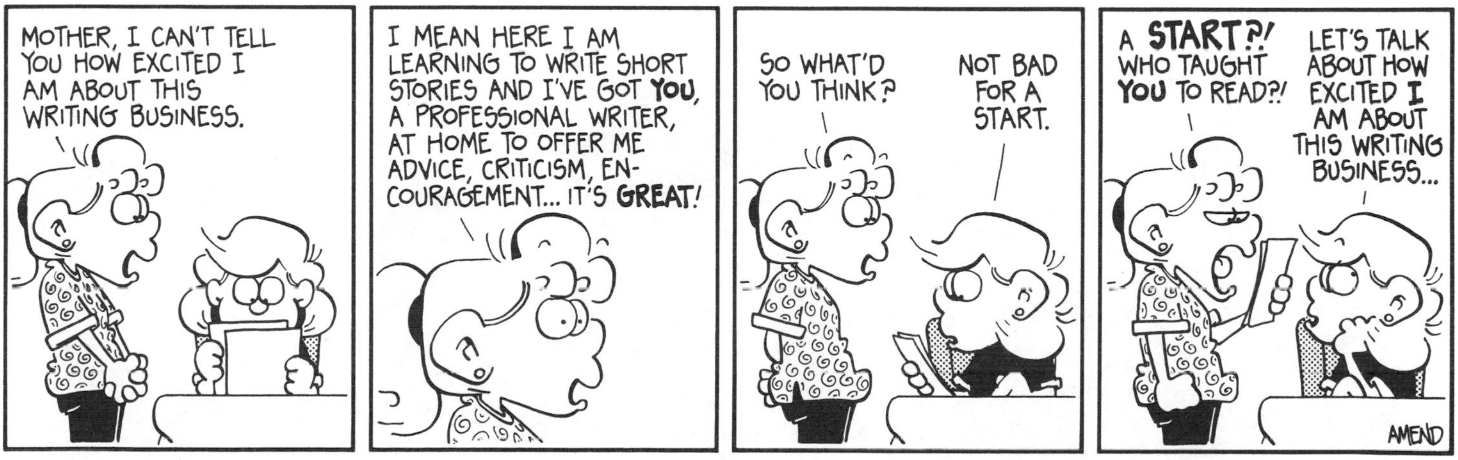
MOTHER, I CAN'T TELL YOU HOW EXCITED I AM ABOUT THIS WRITING BUSINESS.
I MEAN HERE I AM LEARNING TO WRITE SHORT STORIES AND I'VE GOT **YOU**, A PROFESSIONAL WRITER, AT HOME TO OFFER ME ADVICE, CRITICISM, ENCOURAGEMENT... IT'S **GREAT**!
SO WHAT'D YOU THINK?
NOT BAD FOR A START.
A **START**?! WHO TAUGHT **YOU** TO READ?!
LET'S TALK ABOUT HOW EXCITED **I** AM ABOUT THIS WRITING BUSINESS...
AMEND

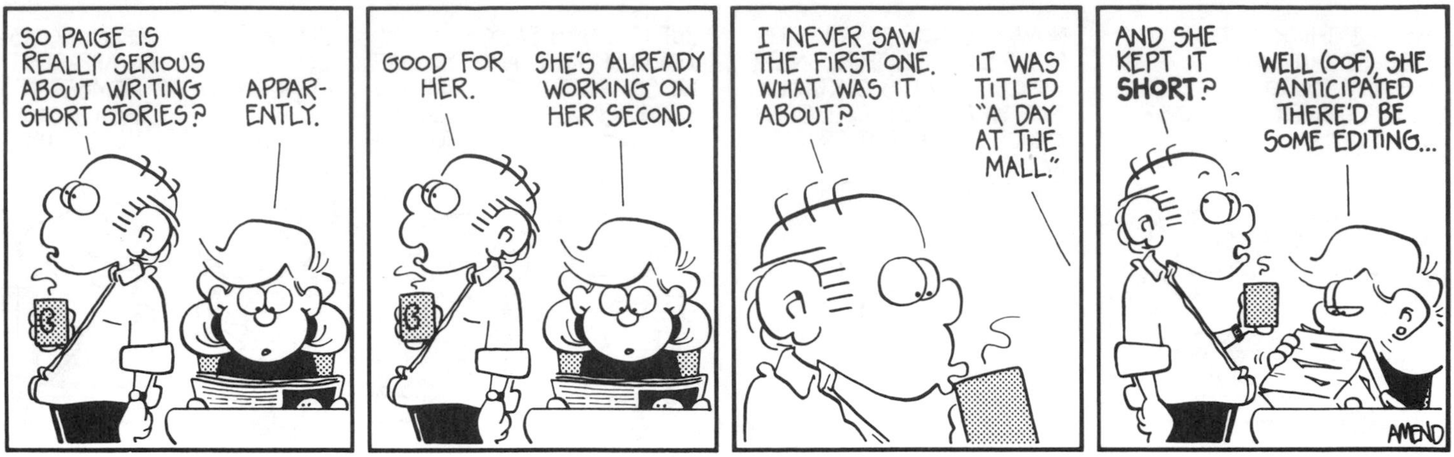
SO PAIGE IS REALLY SERIOUS ABOUT WRITING SHORT STORIES?
APPAR-ENTLY.
GOOD FOR HER.
SHE'S ALREADY WORKING ON HER SECOND.
I NEVER SAW THE FIRST ONE. WHAT WAS IT ABOUT?
IT WAS TITLED "A DAY AT THE MALL."
AND SHE KEPT IT **SHORT**?
WELL (OOF), SHE ANTICIPATED THERE'D BE SOME EDITING...
AMEND

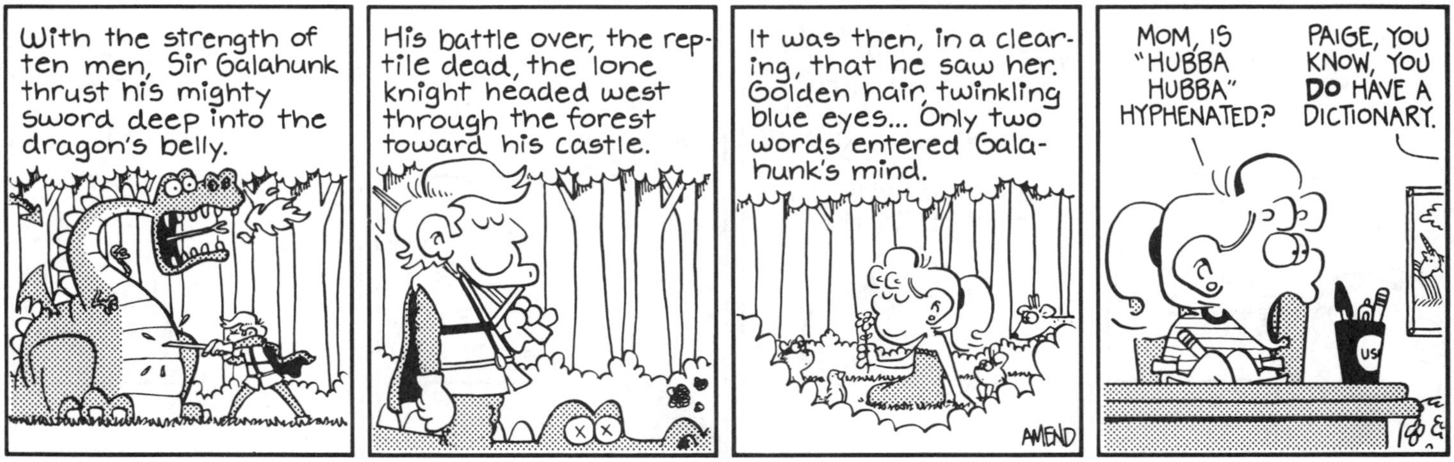
With the strength of ten men, Sir Galahunk thrust his mighty sword deep into the dragon's belly.
His battle over, the rep-tile dead, the lone knight headed west through the forest toward his castle.
It was then, in a clear-ing, that he saw her. Golden hair, twinkling blue eyes... Only two words entered Gala-hunk's mind.
AMEND
MOM, IS "HUBBA HUBBA" HYPHENATED?
PAIGE, YOU KNOW, YOU **DO** HAVE A DICTIONARY.

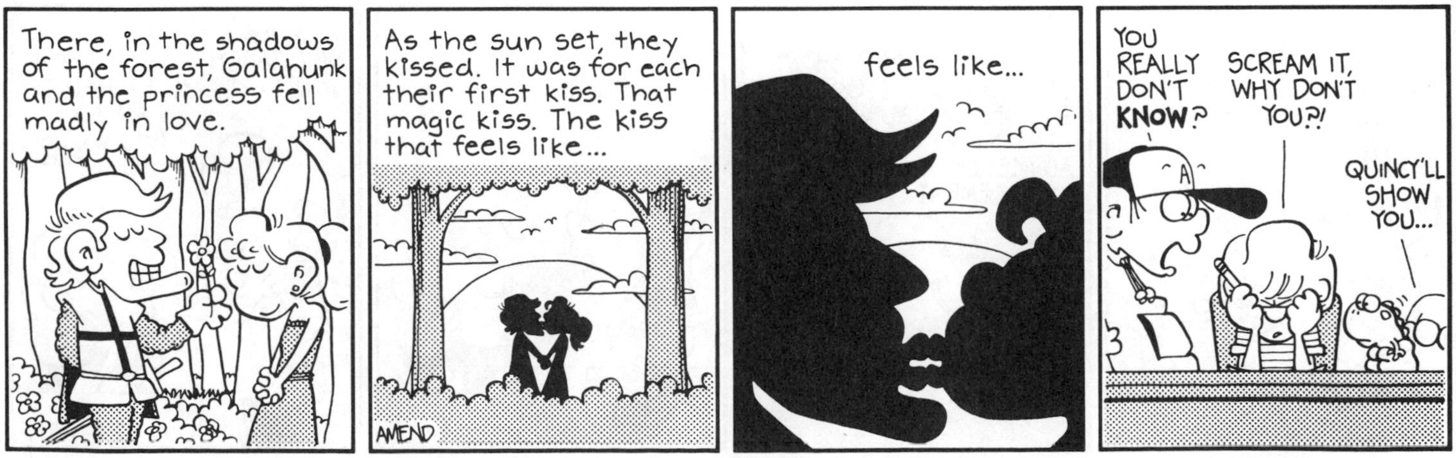
There, in the shadows of the forest, Galahunk and the princess fell madly in love.
As the sun set, they kissed. It was for each their first kiss. That magic kiss. The kiss that feels like...
AMEND
feels like...
YOU REALLY DON'T **KNOW**?
SCREAM IT, WHY DON'T YOU?!
QUINCY'LL SHOW YOU...

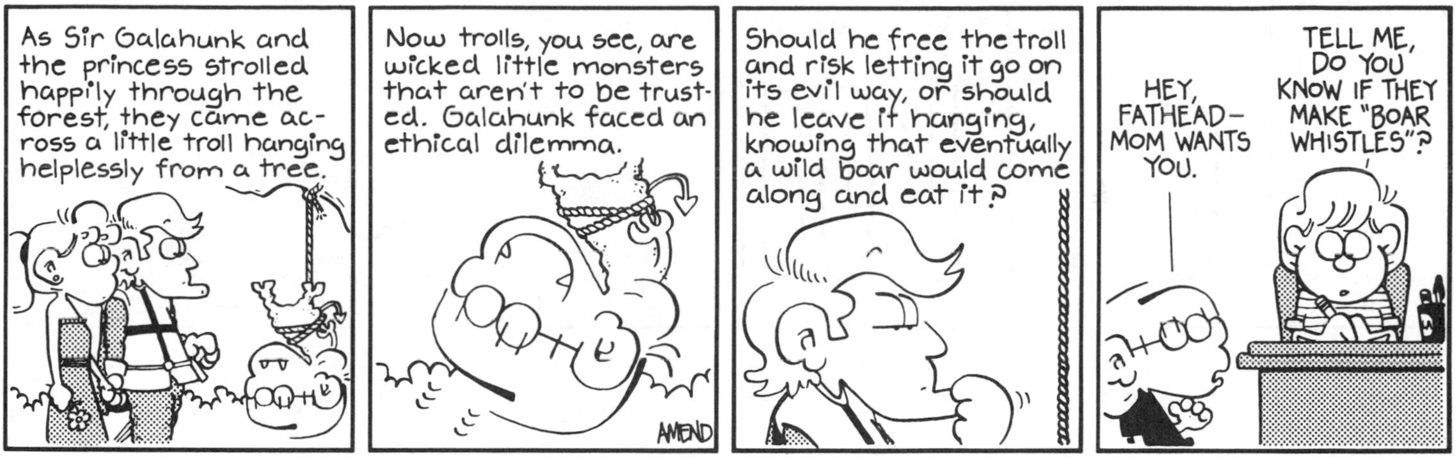
As Sir Galahunk and the princess strolled happily through the forest, they came across a little troll hanging helplessly from a tree.
Now trolls, you see, are wicked little monsters that aren't to be trusted. Galahunk faced an ethical dilemma.
AMEND
Should he free the troll and risk letting it go on its evil way, or should he leave it hanging, knowing that eventually a wild boar would come along and eat it?
HEY, FATHEAD– MOM WANTS YOU.
TELL ME, DO YOU KNOW IF THEY MAKE "BOAR WHISTLES"?

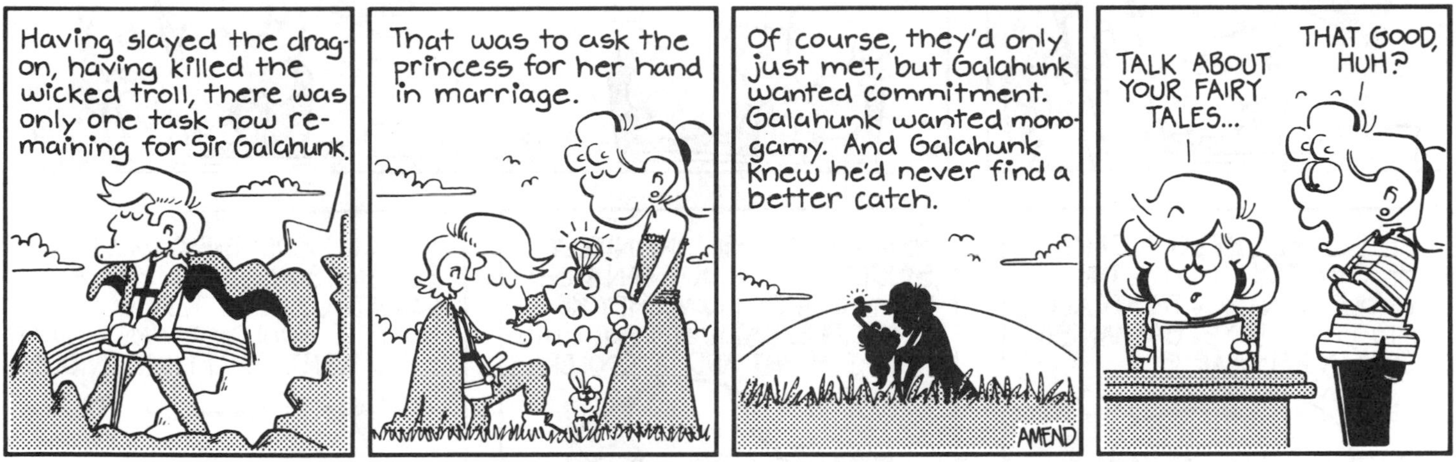
Having slayed the dragon, having killed the wicked troll, there was only one task now remaining for Sir Galahunk.
That was to ask the princess for her hand in marriage.
Of course, they'd only just met, but Galahunk wanted commitment. Galahunk wanted monogamy. And Galahunk knew he'd never find a better catch.
AMEND
TALK ABOUT YOUR FAIRY TALES...
THAT GOOD, HUH?

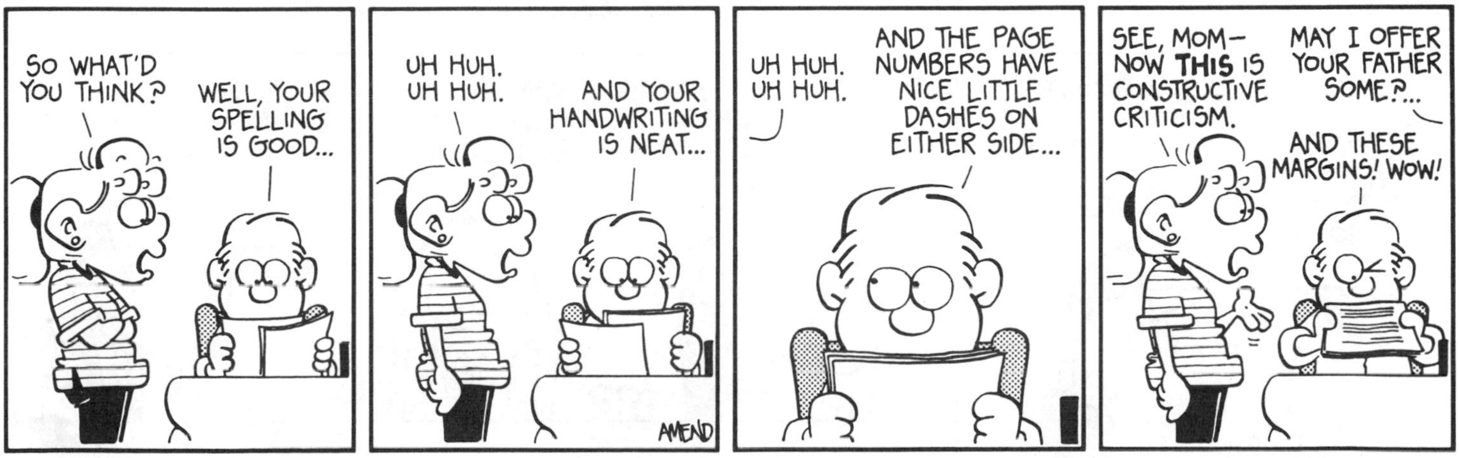
SO WHAT'D YOU THINK?
WELL, YOUR SPELLING IS GOOD...
UH HUH. UH HUH.
AND YOUR HANDWRITING IS NEAT...
AMEND
UH HUH. UH HUH.
AND THE PAGE NUMBERS HAVE NICE LITTLE DASHES ON EITHER SIDE...
SEE, MOM– NOW **THIS** IS CONSTRUCTIVE CRITICISM.
MAY I OFFER YOUR FATHER SOME?...
AND THESE MARGINS! WOW!

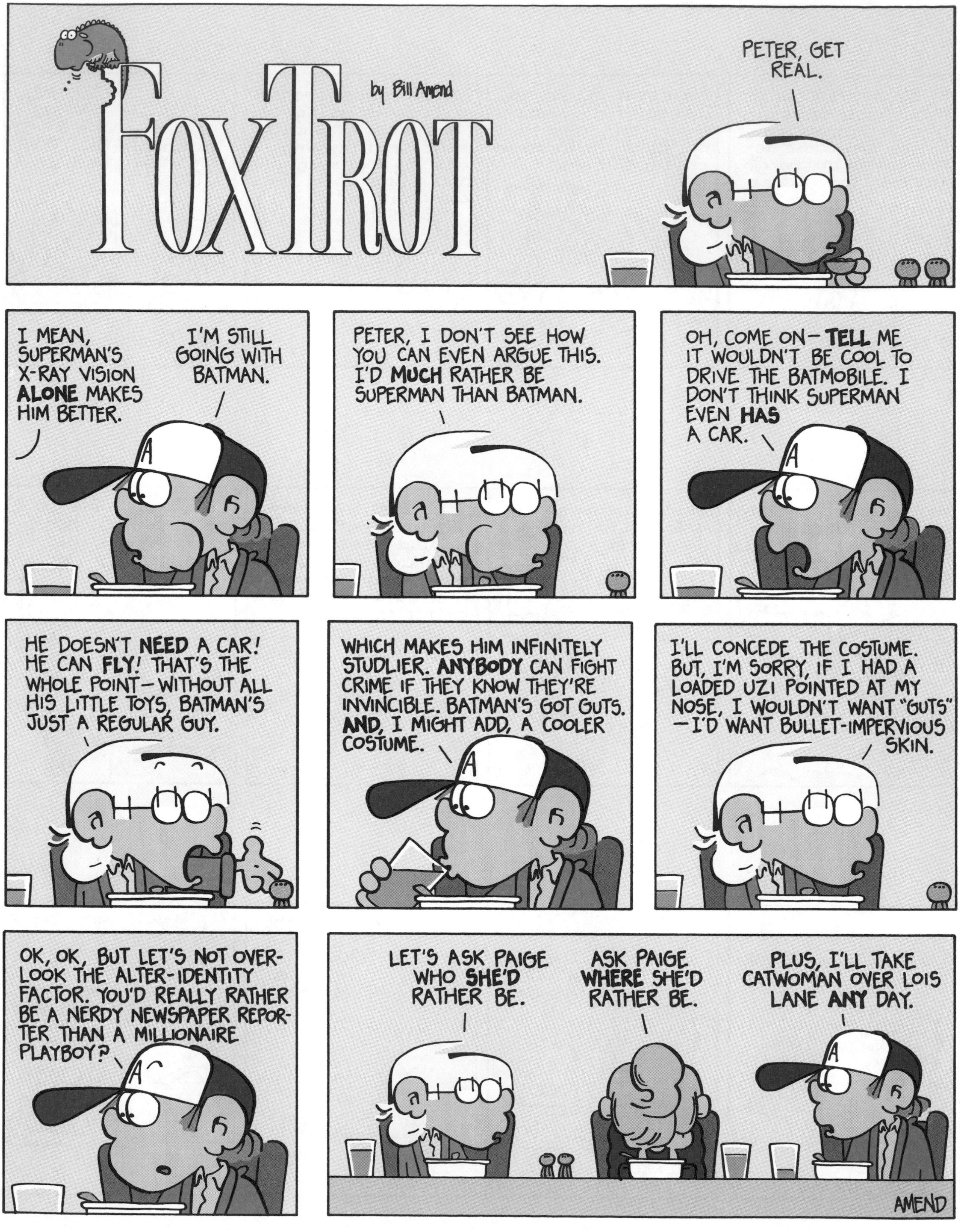
FoxTrot
by Bill Amend
PETER, GET REAL.
I MEAN, SUPERMAN'S X-RAY VISION **ALONE** MAKES HIM BETTER.
I'M STILL GOING WITH BATMAN.
PETER, I DON'T SEE HOW YOU CAN EVEN ARGUE THIS. I'D **MUCH** RATHER BE SUPERMAN THAN BATMAN.
OH, COME ON— **TELL** ME IT WOULDN'T BE COOL TO DRIVE THE BATMOBILE. I DON'T THINK SUPERMAN EVEN **HAS** A CAR.
HE DOESN'T **NEED** A CAR! HE CAN **FLY**! THAT'S THE WHOLE POINT— WITHOUT ALL HIS LITTLE TOYS, BATMAN'S JUST A REGULAR GUY.
WHICH MAKES HIM INFINITELY STUDLIER. **ANYBODY** CAN FIGHT CRIME IF THEY KNOW THEY'RE INVINCIBLE. BATMAN'S GOT GUTS. **AND**, I MIGHT ADD, A COOLER COSTUME.
I'LL CONCEDE THE COSTUME. BUT, I'M SORRY, IF I HAD A LOADED UZI POINTED AT MY NOSE, I WOULDN'T WANT "GUTS" —I'D WANT BULLET-IMPERVIOUS SKIN.
OK, OK, BUT LET'S NOT OVERLOOK THE ALTER-IDENTITY FACTOR. YOU'D REALLY RATHER BE A NERDY NEWSPAPER REPORTER THAN A MILLIONAIRE PLAYBOY?
LET'S ASK PAIGE WHO **SHE'D** RATHER BE.
ASK PAIGE **WHERE** SHE'D RATHER BE.
PLUS, I'LL TAKE CATWOMAN OVER LOIS LANE **ANY** DAY.
AMEND

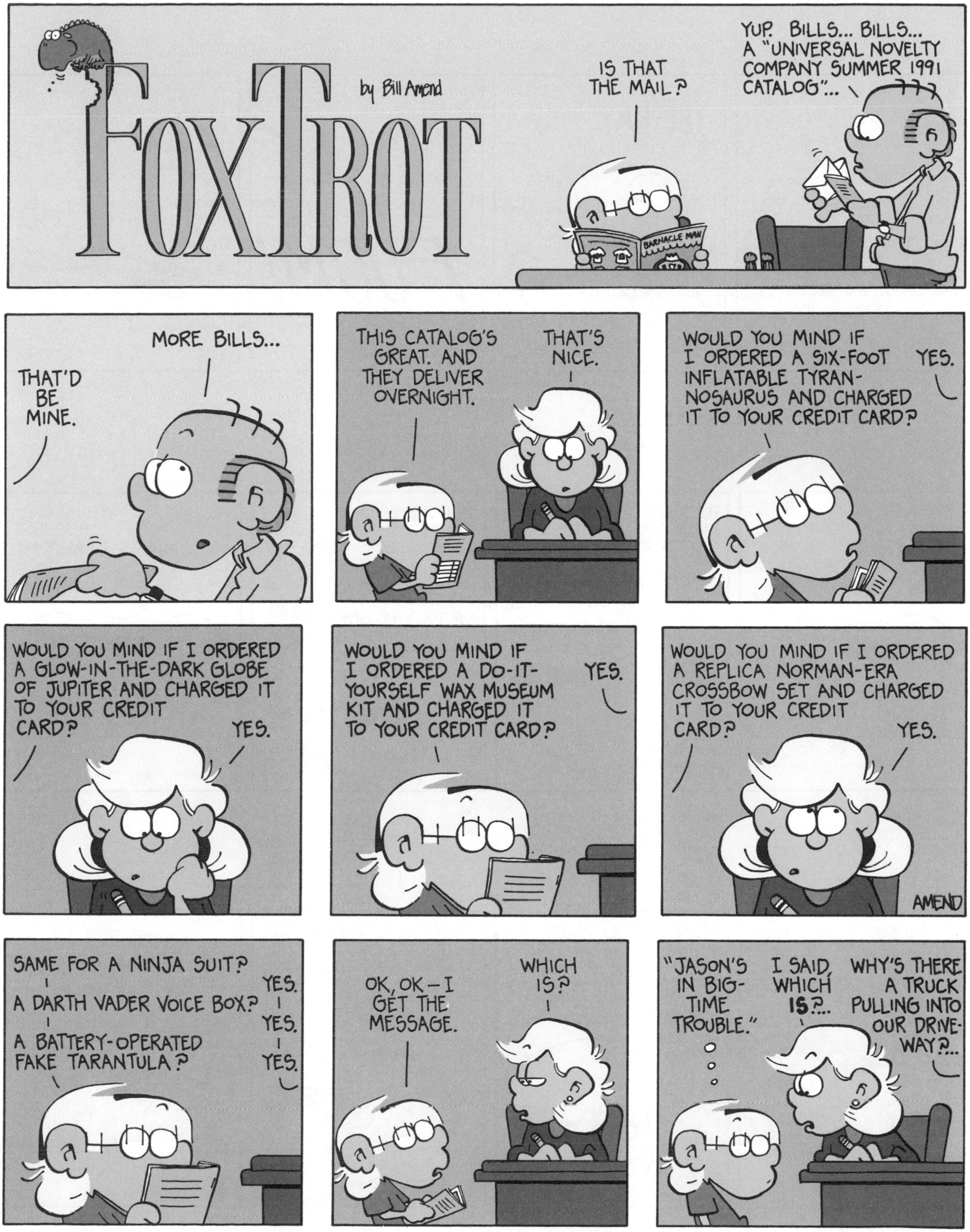
FoxTrot
by Bill Amend
IS THAT THE MAIL?
YUP. BILLS... BILLS... A "UNIVERSAL NOVELTY COMPANY SUMMER 1991 CATALOG"...
BARNACLE MAN
MORE BILLS...
THAT'D BE MINE.
THIS CATALOG'S GREAT. AND THEY DELIVER OVERNIGHT.
THAT'S NICE.
WOULD YOU MIND IF I ORDERED A SIX-FOOT INFLATABLE TYRAN-NOSAURUS AND CHARGED IT TO YOUR CREDIT CARD?
YES.
WOULD YOU MIND IF I ORDERED A GLOW-IN-THE-DARK GLOBE OF JUPITER AND CHARGED IT TO YOUR CREDIT CARD?
YES.
WOULD YOU MIND IF I ORDERED A DO-IT-YOURSELF WAX MUSEUM KIT AND CHARGED IT TO YOUR CREDIT CARD?
YES.
WOULD YOU MIND IF I ORDERED A REPLICA NORMAN-ERA CROSSBOW SET AND CHARGED IT TO YOUR CREDIT CARD?
YES.
AMEND
SAME FOR A NINJA SUIT?
YES.
A DARTH VADER VOICE BOX?
YES.
A BATTERY-OPERATED FAKE TARANTULA?
YES.
OK, OK – I GET THE MESSAGE.
WHICH IS?
"JASON'S IN BIG-TIME TROUBLE."
I SAID, WHICH IS?...
WHY'S THERE A TRUCK PULLING INTO OUR DRIVE-WAY?...

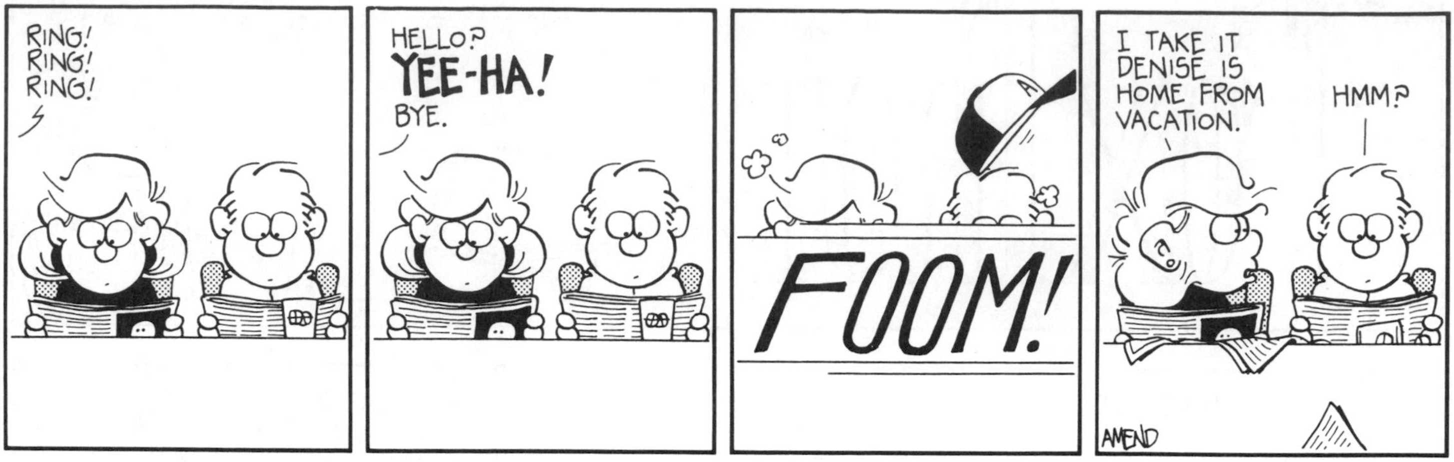
RING! RING! RING!
HELLO?
YEE-HA!
BYE.
FOOM!
I TAKE IT DENISE IS HOME FROM VACATION.
HMM?
AMEND

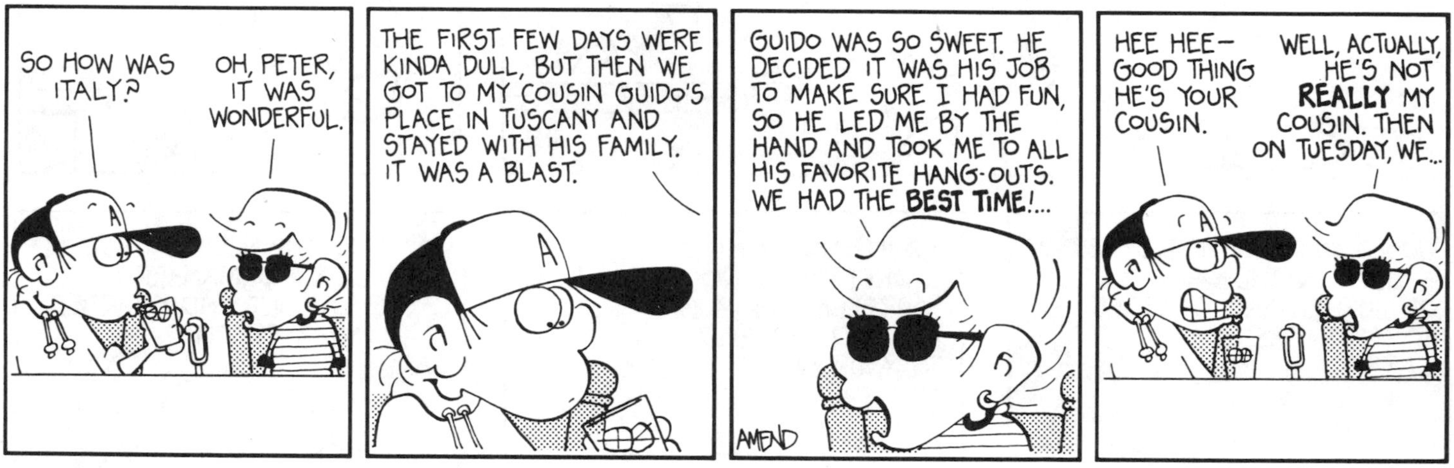
SO HOW WAS ITALY?
OH, PETER, IT WAS WONDERFUL.
THE FIRST FEW DAYS WERE KINDA DULL, BUT THEN WE GOT TO MY COUSIN GUIDO'S PLACE IN TUSCANY AND STAYED WITH HIS FAMILY. IT WAS A BLAST.
GUIDO WAS SO SWEET. HE DECIDED IT WAS HIS JOB TO MAKE SURE I HAD FUN, SO HE LED ME BY THE HAND AND TOOK ME TO ALL HIS FAVORITE HANG-OUTS. WE HAD THE BEST TIME!...
AMEND
HEE HEE– GOOD THING HE'S YOUR COUSIN.
WELL, ACTUALLY, HE'S NOT REALLY MY COUSIN. THEN ON TUESDAY, WE...

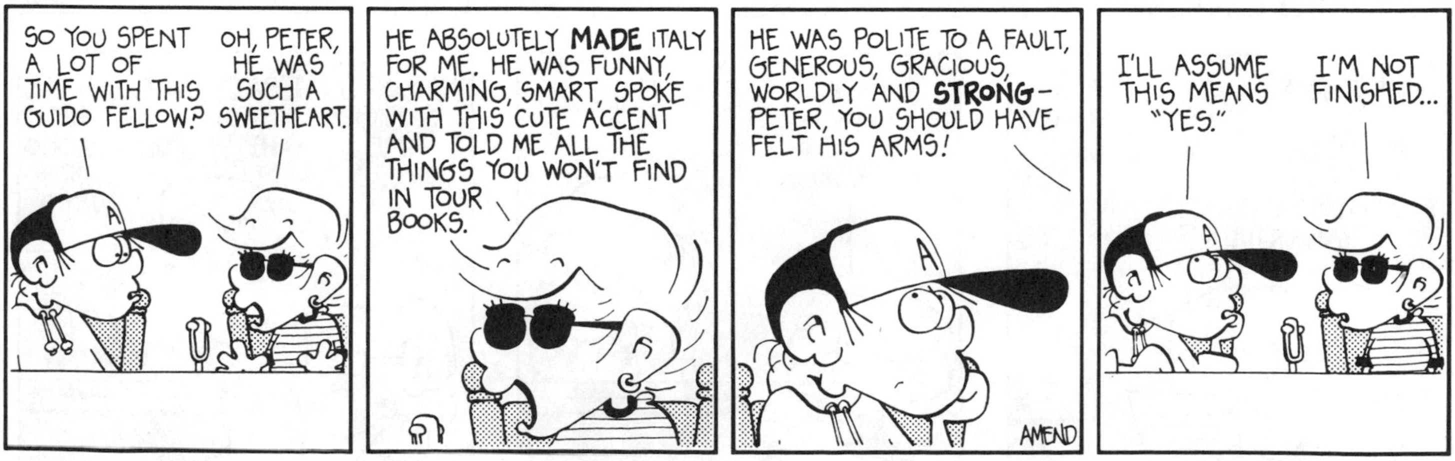
SO YOU SPENT A LOT OF TIME WITH THIS GUIDO FELLOW?
OH, PETER, HE WAS SUCH A SWEETHEART.
HE ABSOLUTELY MADE ITALY FOR ME. HE WAS FUNNY, CHARMING, SMART, SPOKE WITH THIS CUTE ACCENT AND TOLD ME ALL THE THINGS YOU WON'T FIND IN TOUR BOOKS.
HE WAS POLITE TO A FAULT, GENEROUS, GRACIOUS, WORLDLY AND STRONG– PETER, YOU SHOULD HAVE FELT HIS ARMS!
AMEND
I'LL ASSUME THIS MEANS "YES."
I'M NOT FINISHED...

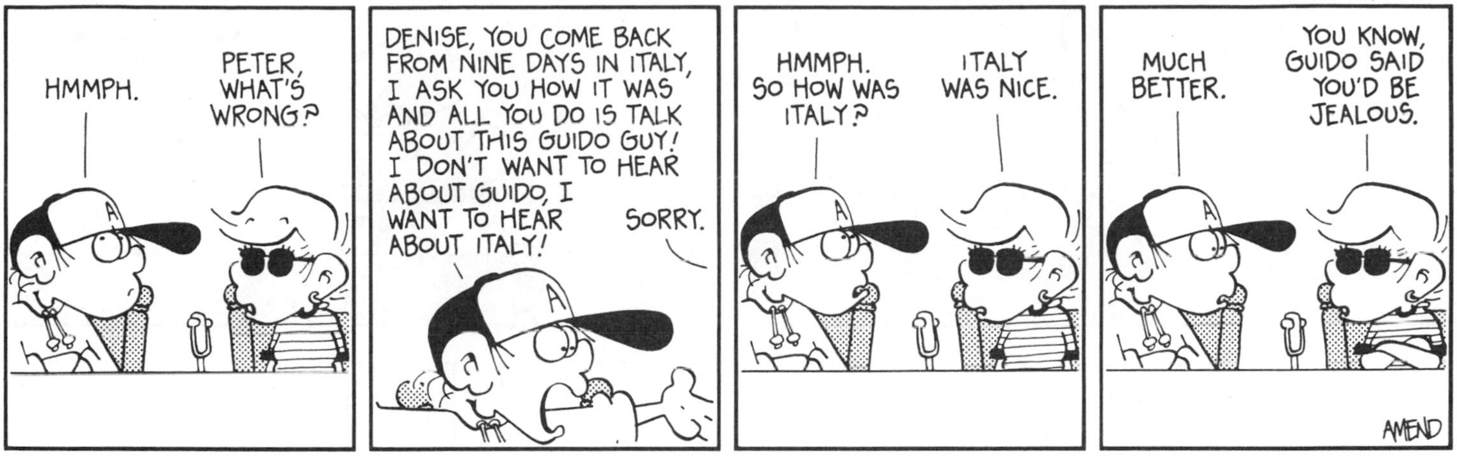
HMMPH.
PETER, WHAT'S WRONG?
DENISE, YOU COME BACK FROM NINE DAYS IN ITALY, I ASK YOU HOW IT WAS AND ALL YOU DO IS TALK ABOUT THIS GUIDO GUY! I DON'T WANT TO HEAR ABOUT GUIDO, I WANT TO HEAR ABOUT ITALY!
SORRY.
HMMPH. SO HOW WAS ITALY?
ITALY WAS NICE.
MUCH BETTER.
YOU KNOW, GUIDO SAID YOU'D BE JEALOUS.
AMEND

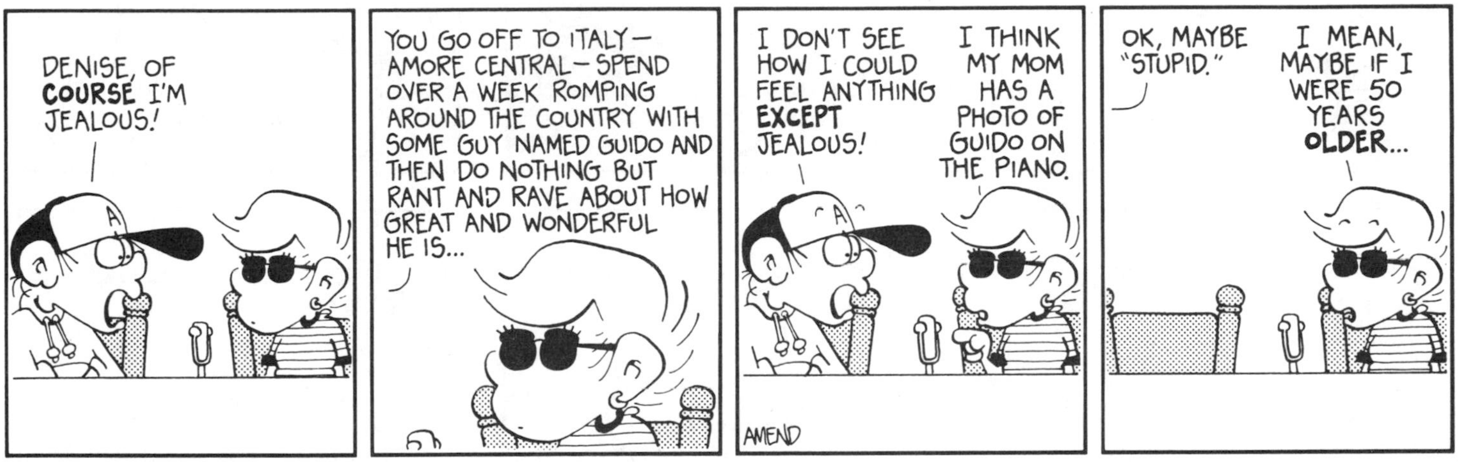
DENISE, OF COURSE I'M JEALOUS!
YOU GO OFF TO ITALY — AMORE CENTRAL — SPEND OVER A WEEK ROMPING AROUND THE COUNTRY WITH SOME GUY NAMED GUIDO AND THEN DO NOTHING BUT RANT AND RAVE ABOUT HOW GREAT AND WONDERFUL HE IS...
I DON'T SEE HOW I COULD FEEL ANYTHING EXCEPT JEALOUS!
I THINK MY MOM HAS A PHOTO OF GUIDO ON THE PIANO.
AMEND
OK, MAYBE "STUPID."
I MEAN, MAYBE IF I WERE 50 YEARS OLDER...

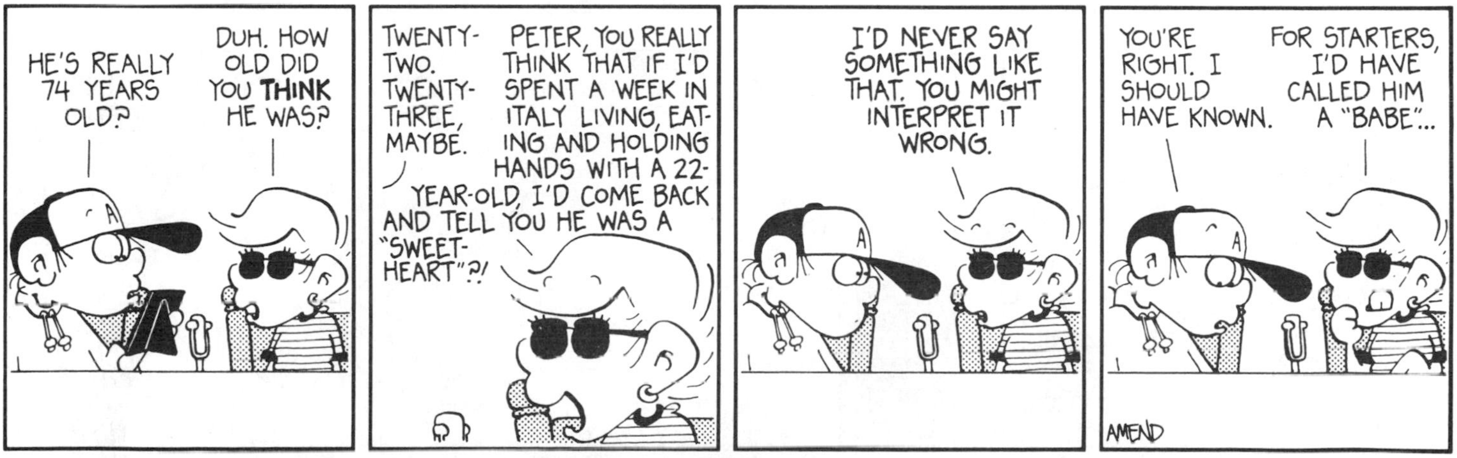
HE'S REALLY 74 YEARS OLD?
DUH. HOW OLD DID YOU THINK HE WAS?
TWENTY-TWO. TWENTY-THREE, MAYBE.
PETER, YOU REALLY THINK THAT IF I'D SPENT A WEEK IN ITALY LIVING, EATING AND HOLDING HANDS WITH A 22-YEAR-OLD, I'D COME BACK AND TELL YOU HE WAS A "SWEET-HEART"?!
I'D NEVER SAY SOMETHING LIKE THAT. YOU MIGHT INTERPRET IT WRONG.
YOU'RE RIGHT. I SHOULD HAVE KNOWN.
FOR STARTERS, I'D HAVE CALLED HIM A "BABE"...
AMEND

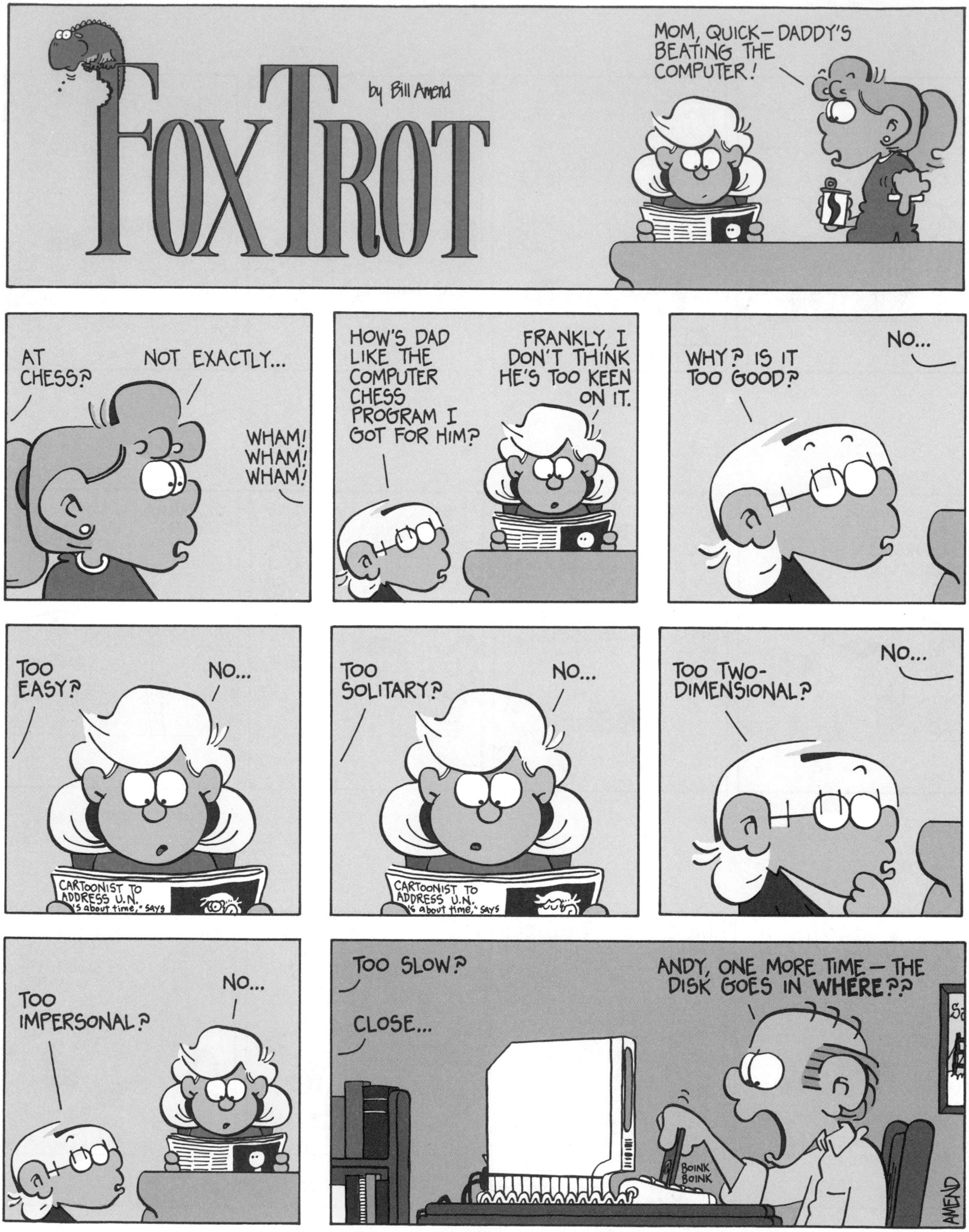
FOXTROT
by Bill Amend
MOM, QUICK— DADDY'S BEATING THE COMPUTER!
AT CHESS?
NOT EXACTLY...
WHAM! WHAM! WHAM!
HOW'S DAD LIKE THE COMPUTER CHESS PROGRAM I GOT FOR HIM?
FRANKLY, I DON'T THINK HE'S TOO KEEN ON IT.
WHY? IS IT TOO GOOD?
NO...
TOO EASY?
NO...
CARTOONIST TO ADDRESS U.N.
TOO SOLITARY?
NO...
CARTOONIST TO ADDRESS U.N.
TOO TWO-DIMENSIONAL?
NO...
TOO IMPERSONAL?
NO...
TOO SLOW?
CLOSE...
ANDY, ONE MORE TIME— THE DISK GOES IN **WHERE**??
BOINK BOINK
AMEND

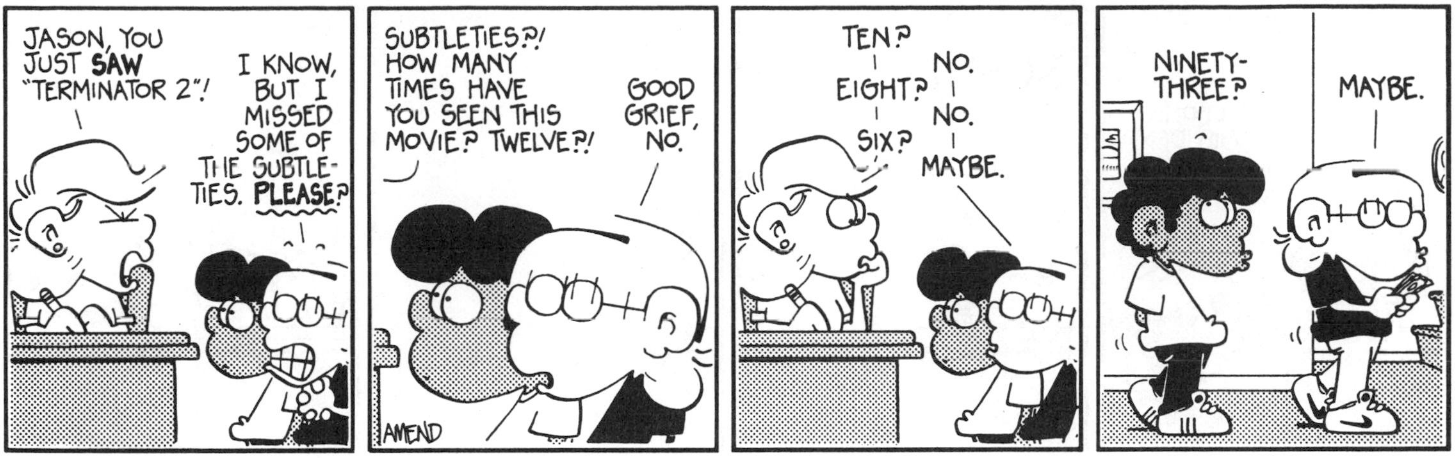
JASON, YOU JUST **SAW** "TERMINATOR 2"!
I KNOW, BUT I MISSED SOME OF THE SUBTLE-TIES. **PLEASE?**
SUBTLETIES?! HOW MANY TIMES HAVE YOU SEEN THIS MOVIE? TWELVE?!
GOOD GRIEF, NO.
AMEND
TEN?
NO.
EIGHT?
NO.
SIX?
MAYBE.
NINETY-THREE?
MAYBE.

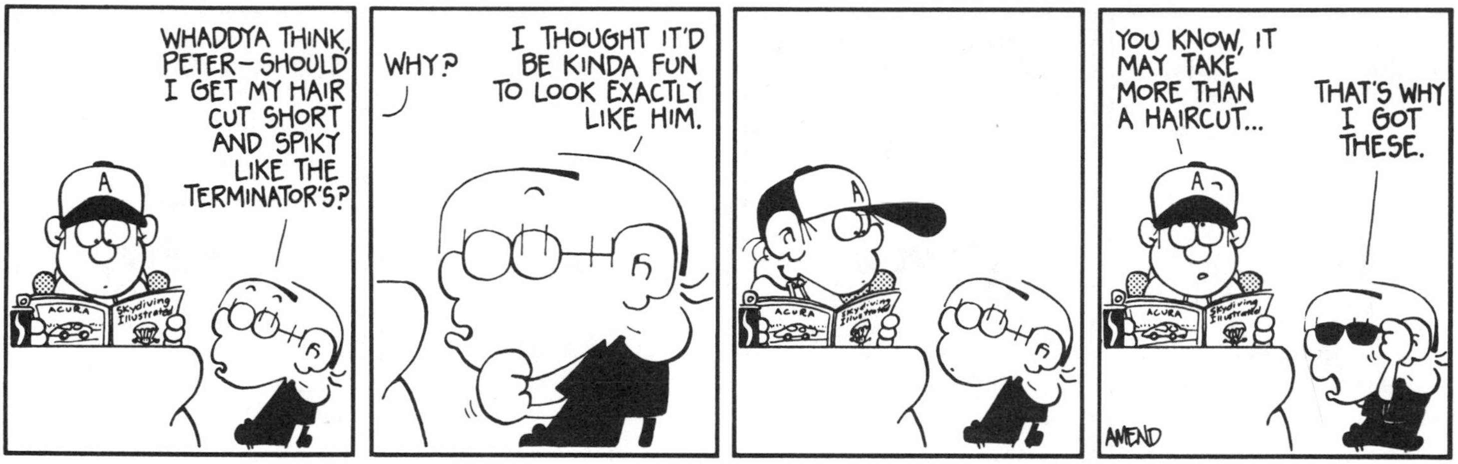
WHADDYA THINK, PETER– SHOULD I GET MY HAIR CUT SHORT AND SPIKY LIKE THE TERMINATOR'S?
WHY?
I THOUGHT IT'D BE KINDA FUN TO LOOK EXACTLY LIKE HIM.
YOU KNOW, IT MAY TAKE MORE THAN A HAIRCUT...
THAT'S WHY I GOT THESE.
AMEND

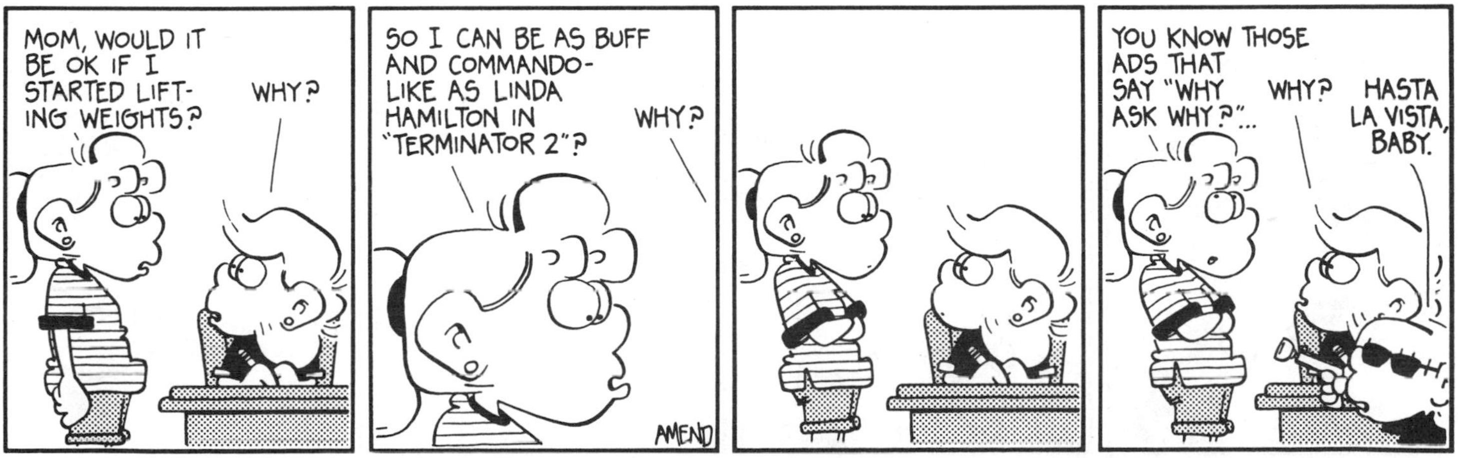
MOM, WOULD IT BE OK IF I STARTED LIFT-ING WEIGHTS?
WHY?
SO I CAN BE AS BUFF AND COMMANDO-LIKE AS LINDA HAMILTON IN "TERMINATOR 2"?
WHY?
AMEND
YOU KNOW THOSE ADS THAT SAY "WHY ASK WHY?"...
WHY?
HASTA LA VISTA, BABY.

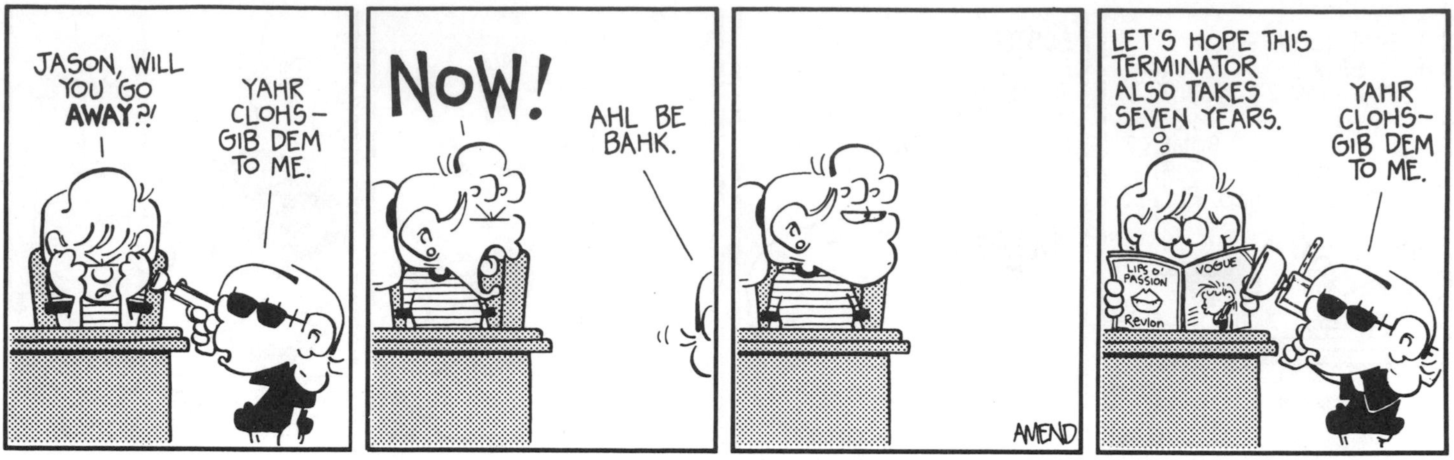
JASON, WILL YOU GO AWAY?!
YAHR CLOHS-GIB DEM TO ME.
NOW!
AHL BE BAHK.
AMEND
LET'S HOPE THIS TERMINATOR ALSO TAKES SEVEN YEARS.
YAHR CLOHS-GIB DEM TO ME.
LIPS O' PASSION
Revlon
VOGUE

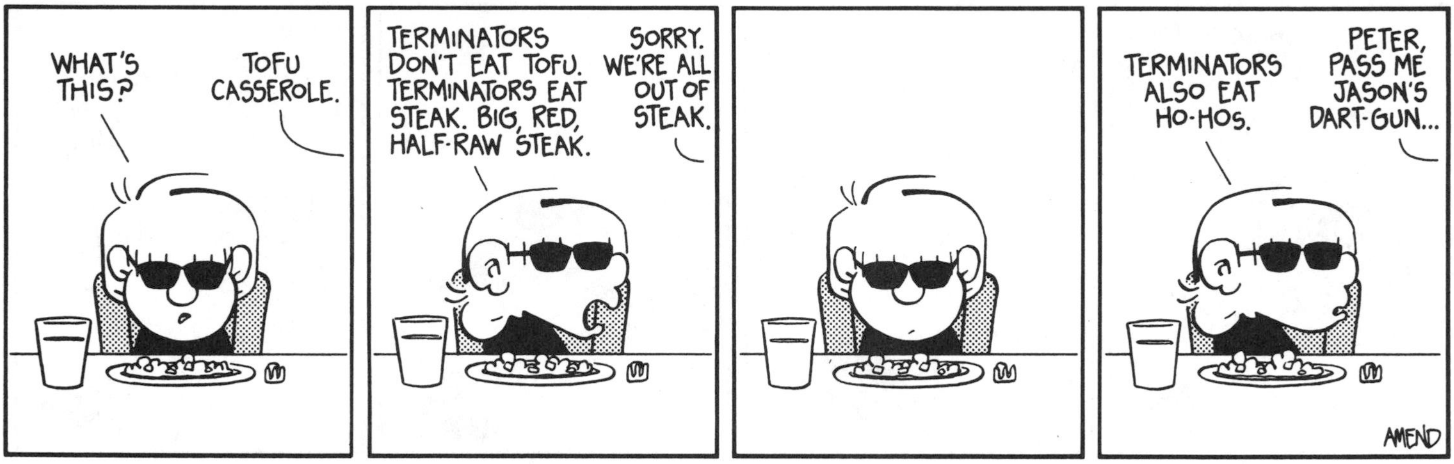
WHAT'S THIS?
TOFU CASSEROLE.
TERMINATORS DON'T EAT TOFU. TERMINATORS EAT STEAK. BIG, RED, HALF-RAW STEAK.
SORRY. WE'RE ALL OUT OF STEAK.
TERMINATORS ALSO EAT HO-HOS.
PETER, PASS ME JASON'S DART-GUN...
AMEND

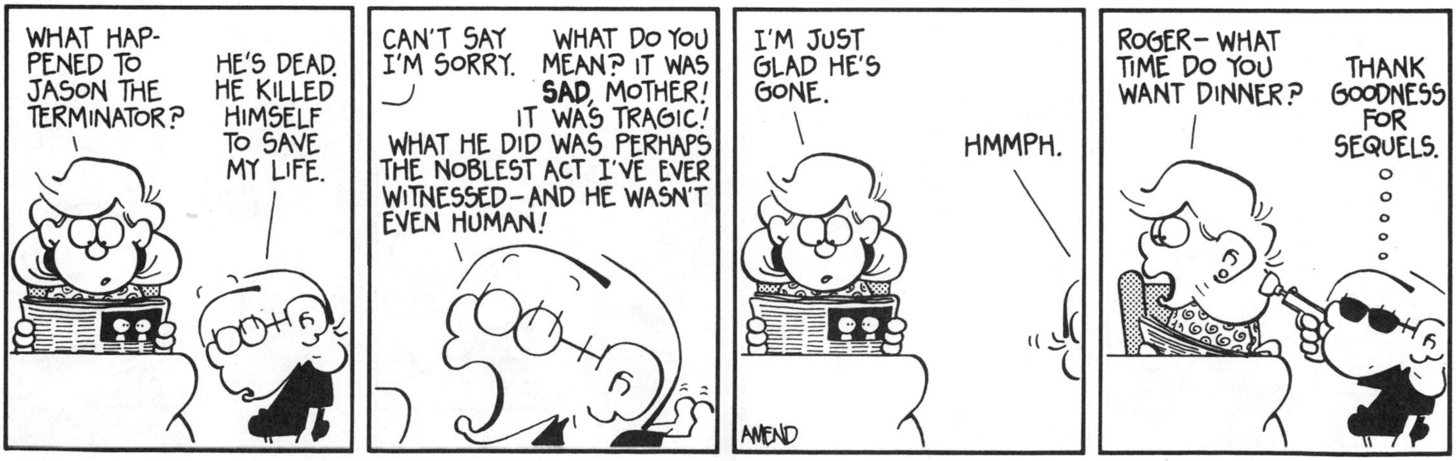
WHAT HAPPENED TO JASON THE TERMINATOR?
HE'S DEAD. HE KILLED HIMSELF TO SAVE MY LIFE.
CAN'T SAY I'M SORRY.
WHAT DO YOU MEAN? IT WAS SAD, MOTHER! IT WAS TRAGIC! WHAT HE DID WAS PERHAPS THE NOBLEST ACT I'VE EVER WITNESSED–AND HE WASN'T EVEN HUMAN!
I'M JUST GLAD HE'S GONE.
HMMPH.
AMEND
ROGER–WHAT TIME DO YOU WANT DINNER?
THANK GOODNESS FOR SEQUELS.

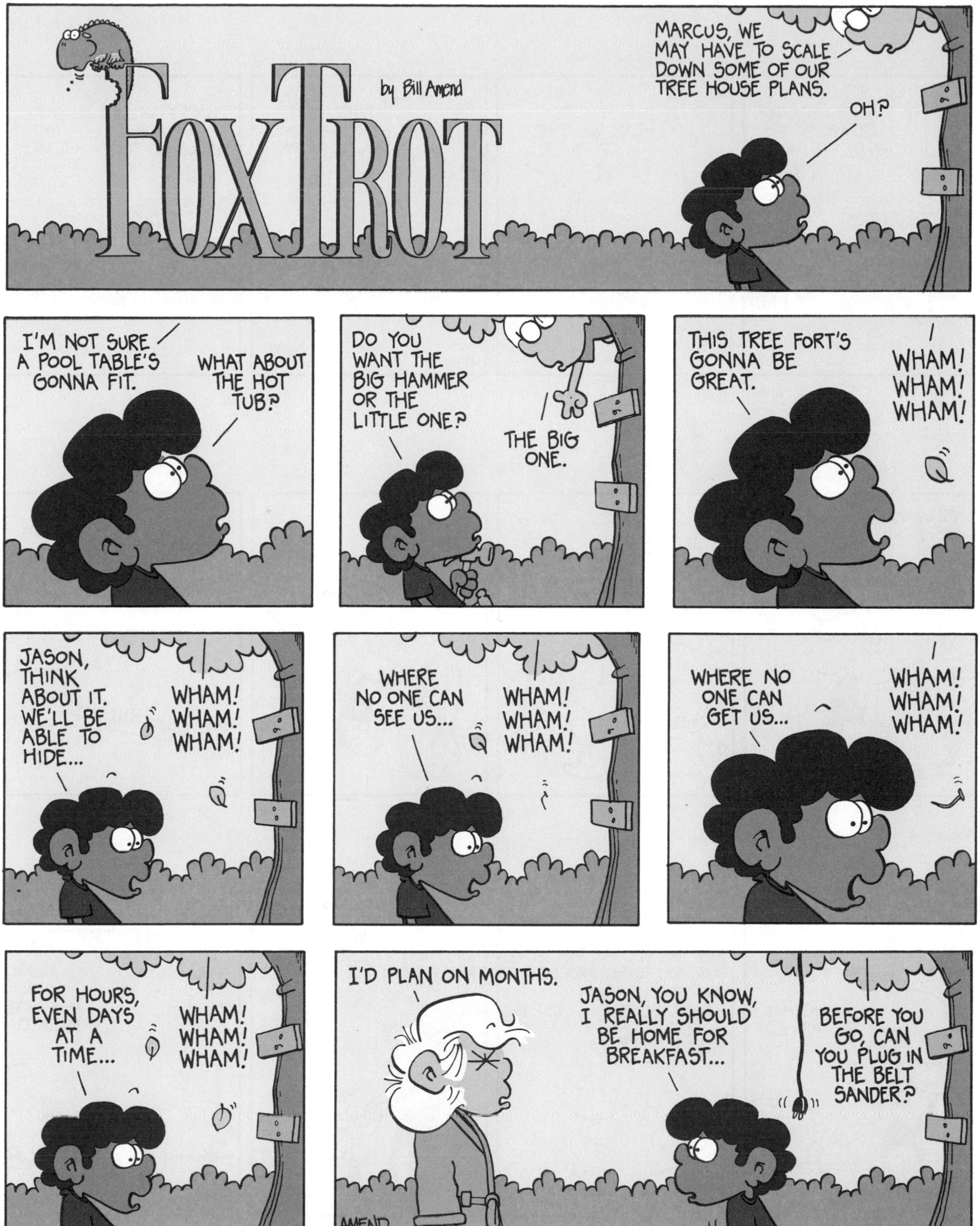
FoxTrot
by Bill Amend
MARCUS, WE MAY HAVE TO SCALE DOWN SOME OF OUR TREE HOUSE PLANS.
OH?
I'M NOT SURE A POOL TABLE'S GONNA FIT.
WHAT ABOUT THE HOT TUB?
DO YOU WANT THE BIG HAMMER OR THE LITTLE ONE?
THE BIG ONE.
THIS TREE FORT'S GONNA BE GREAT.
WHAM! WHAM! WHAM!
JASON, THINK ABOUT IT. WE'LL BE ABLE TO HIDE...
WHAM! WHAM! WHAM!
WHERE NO ONE CAN SEE US...
WHAM! WHAM! WHAM!
WHERE NO ONE CAN GET US...
WHAM! WHAM! WHAM!
FOR HOURS, EVEN DAYS AT A TIME...
WHAM! WHAM! WHAM!
I'D PLAN ON MONTHS.
JASON, YOU KNOW, I REALLY SHOULD BE HOME FOR BREAKFAST...
BEFORE YOU GO, CAN YOU PLUG IN THE BELT SANDER?
AMEND

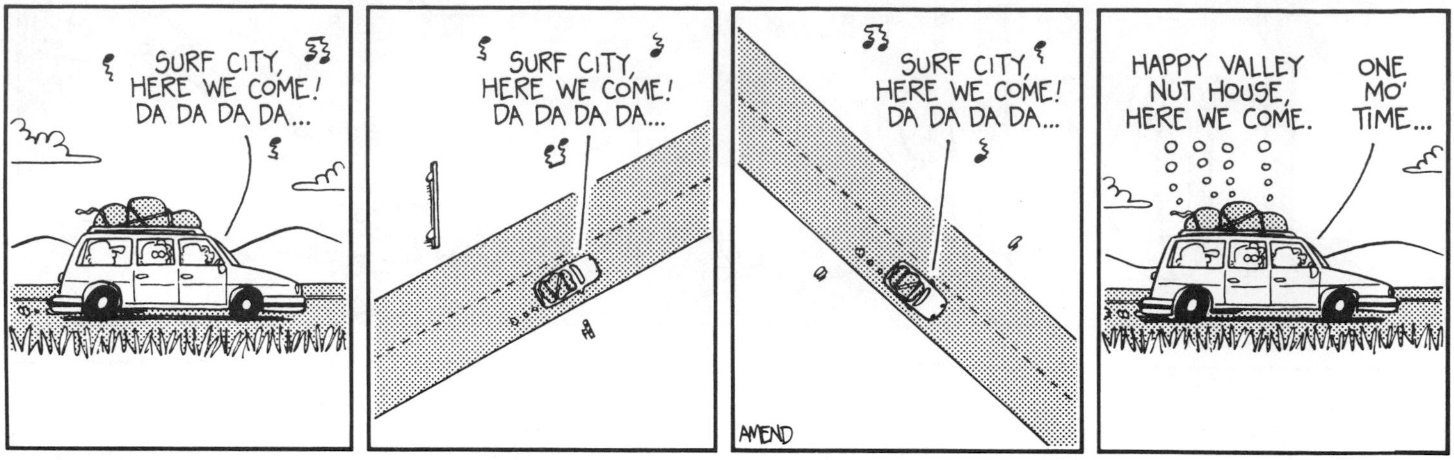
SURF CITY, HERE WE COME! DA DA DA DA...
SURF CITY, HERE WE COME! DA DA DA DA...
SURF CITY, HERE WE COME! DA DA DA DA...
AMEND
HAPPY VALLEY NUT HOUSE, HERE WE COME.
ONE MO' TIME...

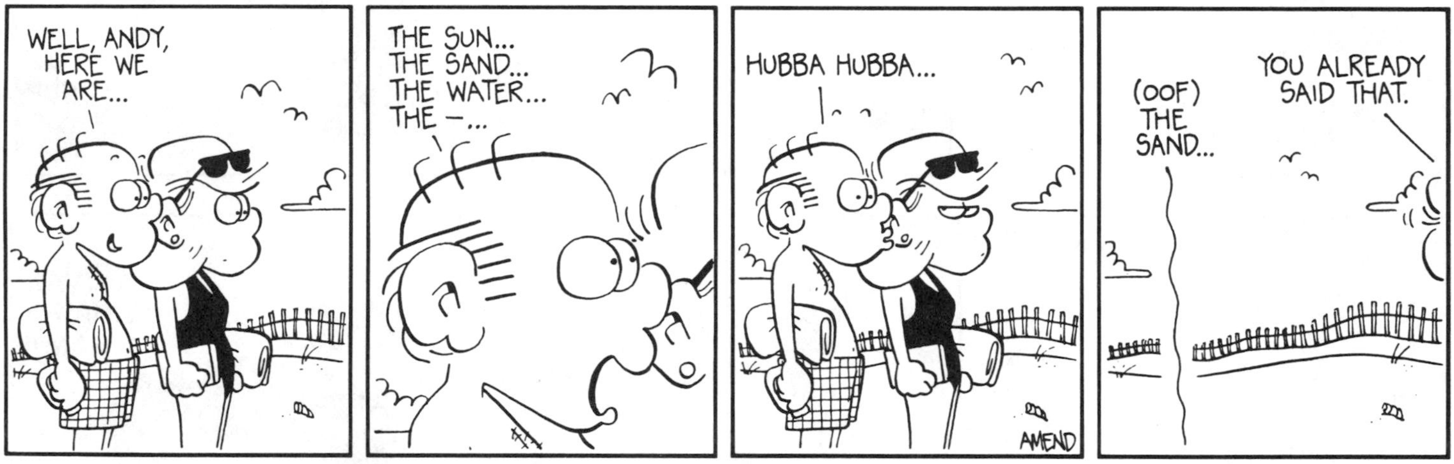
WELL, ANDY, HERE WE ARE...
THE SUN... THE SAND... THE WATER... THE —...
HUBBA HUBBA...
AMEND
(OOF) THE SAND...
YOU ALREADY SAID THAT.

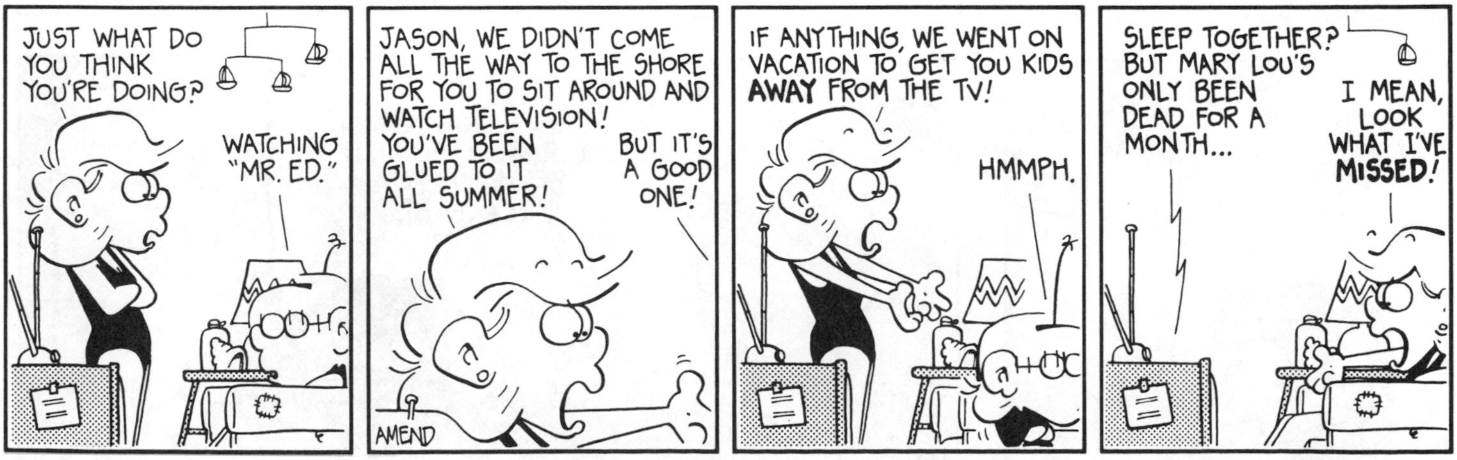
JUST WHAT DO YOU THINK YOU'RE DOING?
WATCHING "MR. ED."
JASON, WE DIDN'T COME ALL THE WAY TO THE SHORE FOR YOU TO SIT AROUND AND WATCH TELEVISION! YOU'VE BEEN GLUED TO IT ALL SUMMER!
BUT IT'S A GOOD ONE!
AMEND
IF ANYTHING, WE WENT ON VACATION TO GET YOU KIDS AWAY FROM THE TV!
HMMPH.
SLEEP TOGETHER? BUT MARY LOU'S ONLY BEEN DEAD FOR A MONTH...
I MEAN, LOOK WHAT I'VE MISSED!

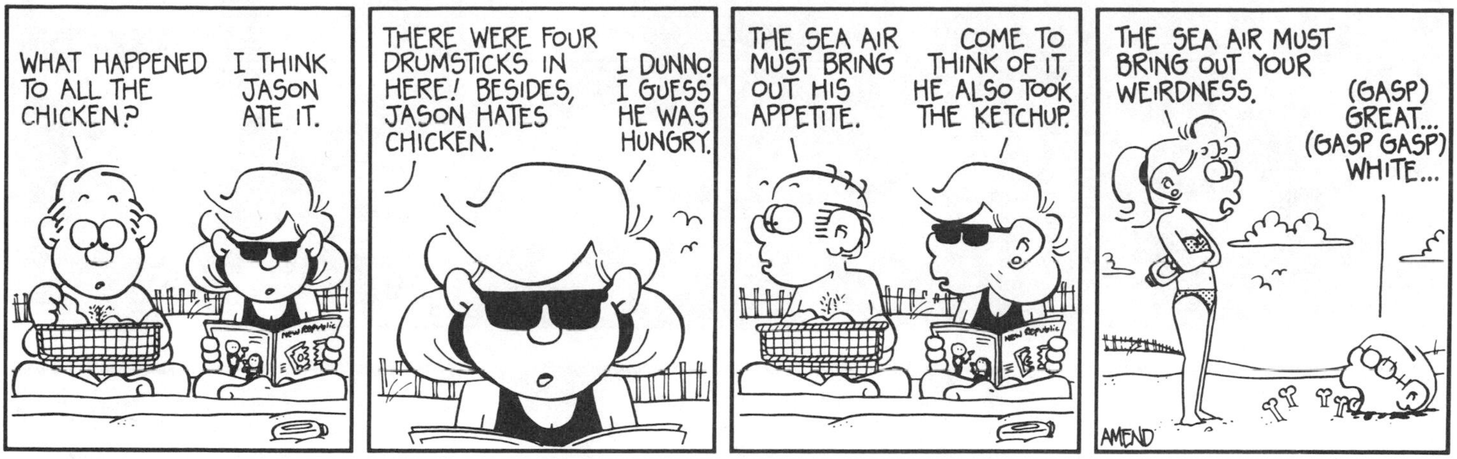
WHAT HAPPENED TO ALL THE CHICKEN?
I THINK JASON ATE IT.
THERE WERE FOUR DRUMSTICKS IN HERE! BESIDES, JASON HATES CHICKEN.
I DUNNO. I GUESS HE WAS HUNGRY.
THE SEA AIR MUST BRING OUT HIS APPETITE.
COME TO THINK OF IT, HE ALSO TOOK THE KETCHUP.
THE SEA AIR MUST BRING OUT YOUR WEIRDNESS.
(GASP) GREAT... (GASP GASP) WHITE...
AMEND

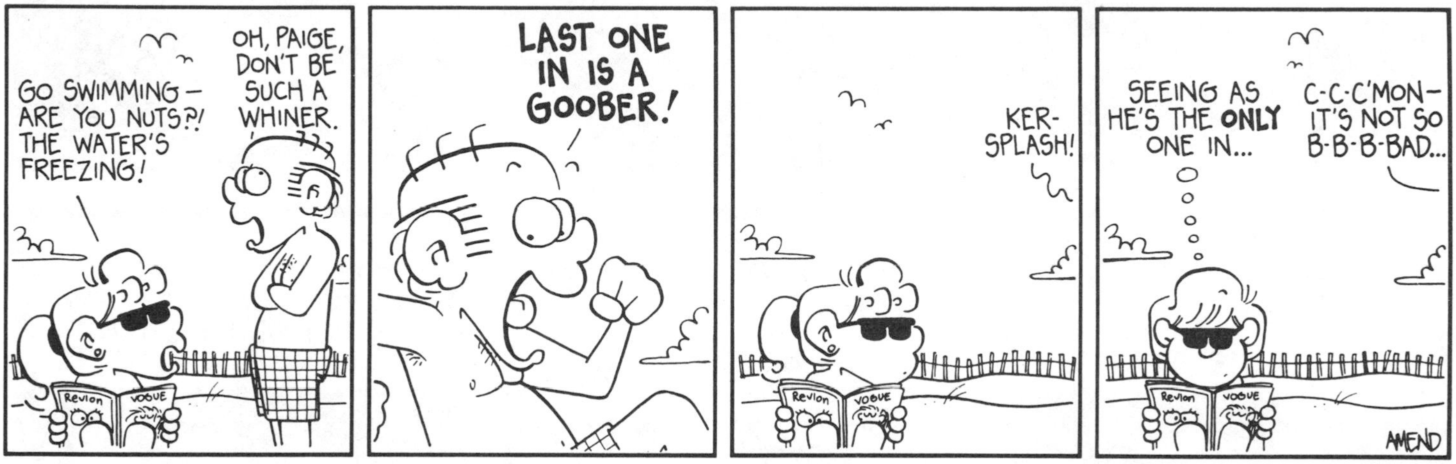
GO SWIMMING – ARE YOU NUTS?! THE WATER'S FREEZING!
OH, PAIGE, DON'T BE SUCH A WHINER.
LAST ONE IN IS A GOOBER!
KER-SPLASH!
SEEING AS HE'S THE **ONLY** ONE IN...
C-C-C'MON– IT'S NOT SO B-B-B-BAD...
Revlon
VOGUE
AMEND

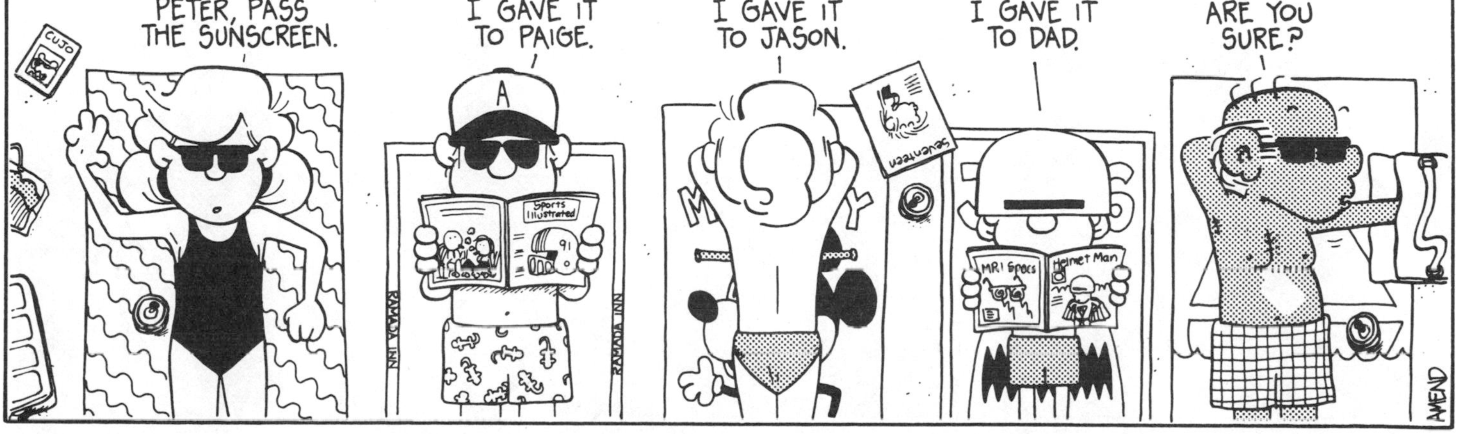
PETER, PASS THE SUNSCREEN.
I GAVE IT TO PAIGE.
I GAVE IT TO JASON.
I GAVE IT TO DAD.
ARE YOU SURE?
CUJO
Sports Illustrated
RAMADA INN
seventeen
MR. Specs
Helmet Man
AMEND

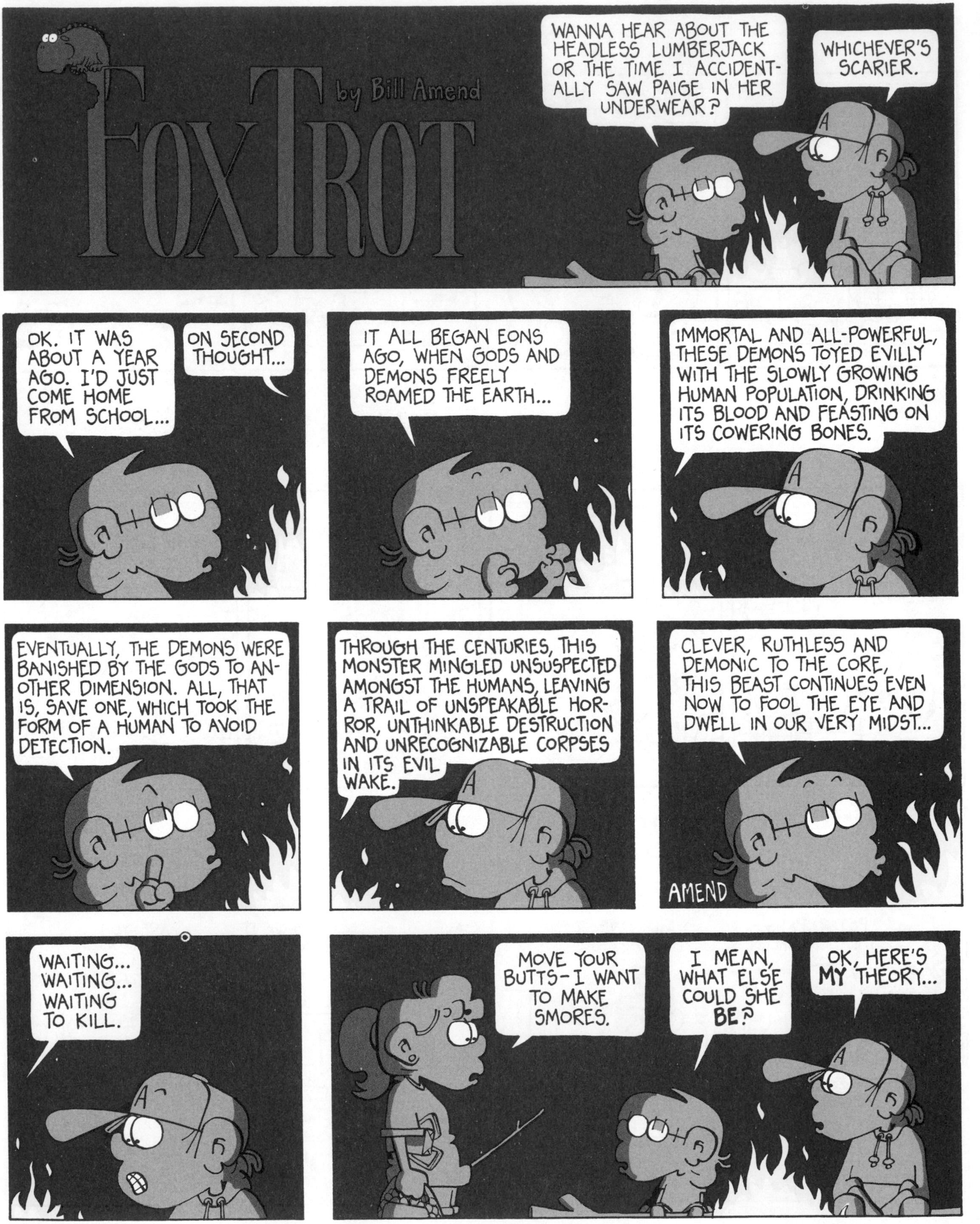
FoxTrot
by Bill Amend
WANNA HEAR ABOUT THE HEADLESS LUMBERJACK OR THE TIME I ACCIDENTALLY SAW PAIGE IN HER UNDERWEAR?
WHICHEVER'S SCARIER.
OK. IT WAS ABOUT A YEAR AGO. I'D JUST COME HOME FROM SCHOOL...
ON SECOND THOUGHT...
IT ALL BEGAN EONS AGO, WHEN GODS AND DEMONS FREELY ROAMED THE EARTH...
IMMORTAL AND ALL-POWERFUL, THESE DEMONS TOYED EVILLY WITH THE SLOWLY GROWING HUMAN POPULATION, DRINKING ITS BLOOD AND FEASTING ON ITS COWERING BONES.
EVENTUALLY, THE DEMONS WERE BANISHED BY THE GODS TO ANOTHER DIMENSION. ALL, THAT IS, SAVE ONE, WHICH TOOK THE FORM OF A HUMAN TO AVOID DETECTION.
THROUGH THE CENTURIES, THIS MONSTER MINGLED UNSUSPECTED AMONGST THE HUMANS, LEAVING A TRAIL OF UNSPEAKABLE HORROR, UNTHINKABLE DESTRUCTION AND UNRECOGNIZABLE CORPSES IN ITS EVIL WAKE.
CLEVER, RUTHLESS AND DEMONIC TO THE CORE, THIS BEAST CONTINUES EVEN NOW TO FOOL THE EYE AND DWELL IN OUR VERY MIDST...
AMEND
WAITING... WAITING... WAITING TO KILL.
MOVE YOUR BUTTS- I WANT TO MAKE SMORES.
I MEAN, WHAT ELSE COULD SHE **BE**?
OK, HERE'S **MY** THEORY...

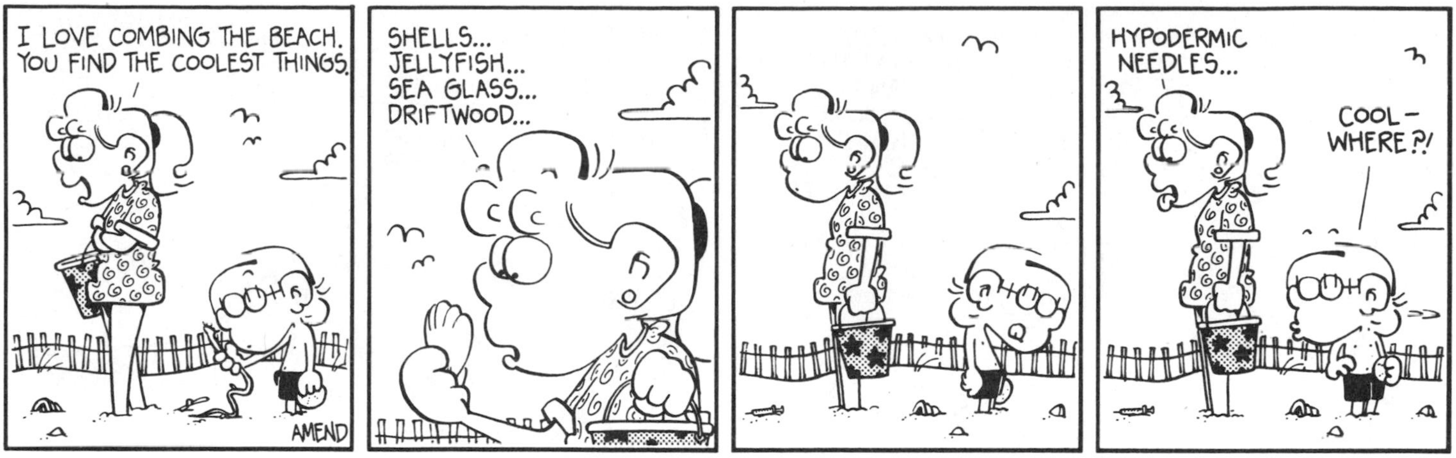
I LOVE COMBING THE BEACH. YOU FIND THE COOLEST THINGS.
AMEND
SHELLS... JELLYFISH... SEA GLASS... DRIFTWOOD...
HYPODERMIC NEEDLES...
COOL- WHERE?!

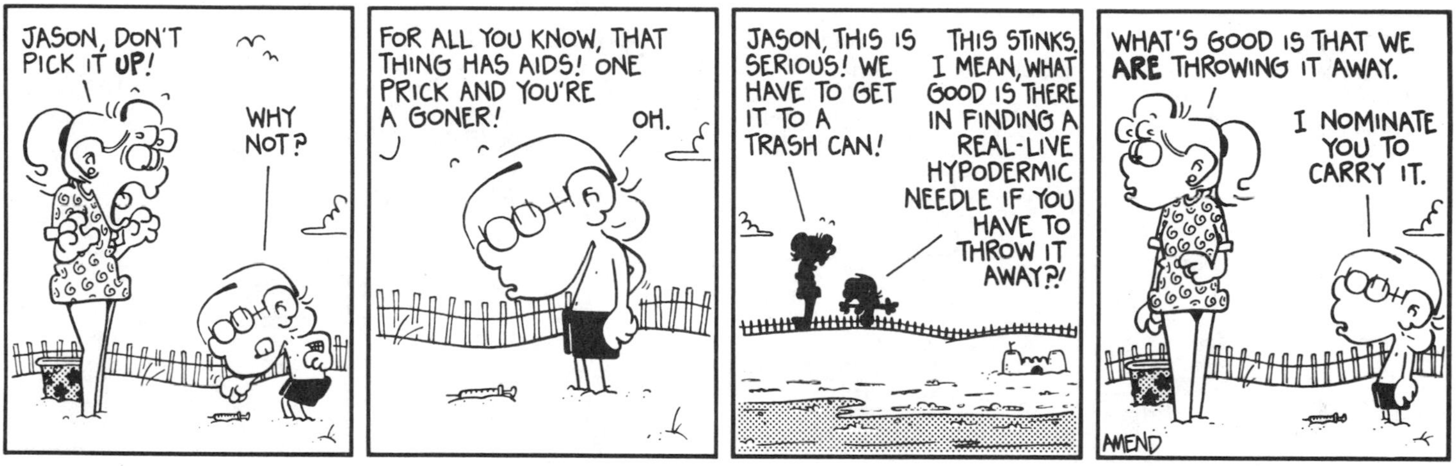
JASON, DON'T PICK IT **UP**!
WHY NOT?
FOR ALL YOU KNOW, THAT THING HAS AIDS! ONE PRICK AND YOU'RE A GONER!
OH.
JASON, THIS IS SERIOUS! WE HAVE TO GET IT TO A TRASH CAN!
THIS STINKS. I MEAN, WHAT GOOD IS THERE IN FINDING A REAL-LIVE HYPODERMIC NEEDLE IF YOU HAVE TO THROW IT AWAY?!
WHAT'S GOOD IS THAT WE **ARE** THROWING IT AWAY.
I NOMINATE YOU TO CARRY IT.
AMEND

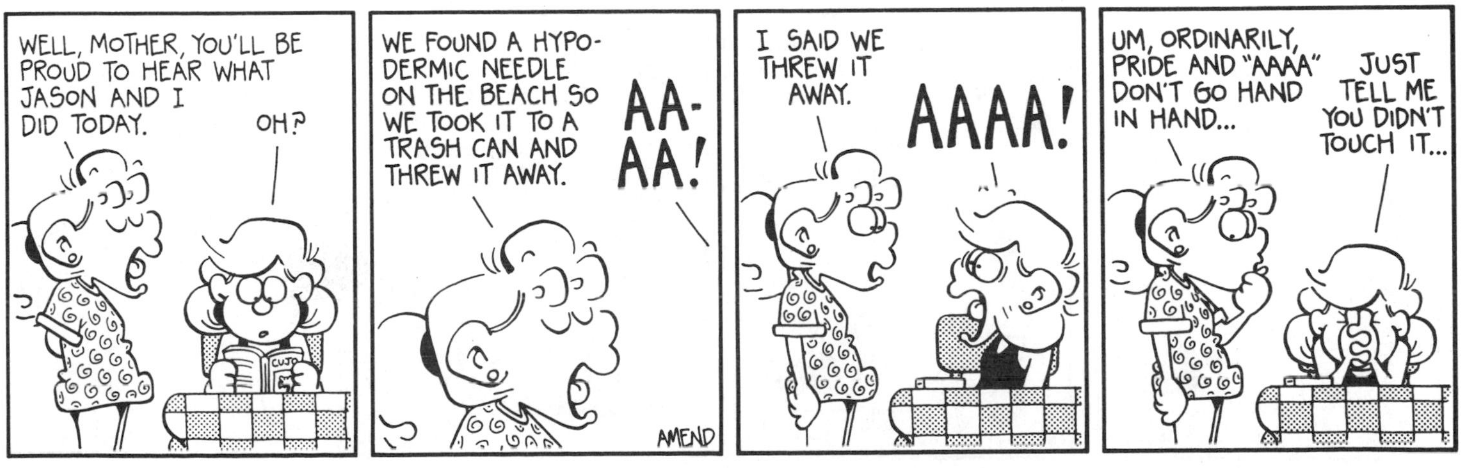
WELL, MOTHER, YOU'LL BE PROUD TO HEAR WHAT JASON AND I DID TODAY.
OH?
CUJO
WE FOUND A HYPO-DERMIC NEEDLE ON THE BEACH SO WE TOOK IT TO A TRASH CAN AND THREW IT AWAY.
AA-AA!
AMEND
I SAID WE THREW IT AWAY.
AAAA!
UM, ORDINARILY, PRIDE AND "AAAA" DON'T GO HAND IN HAND...
JUST TELL ME YOU DIDN'T TOUCH IT...

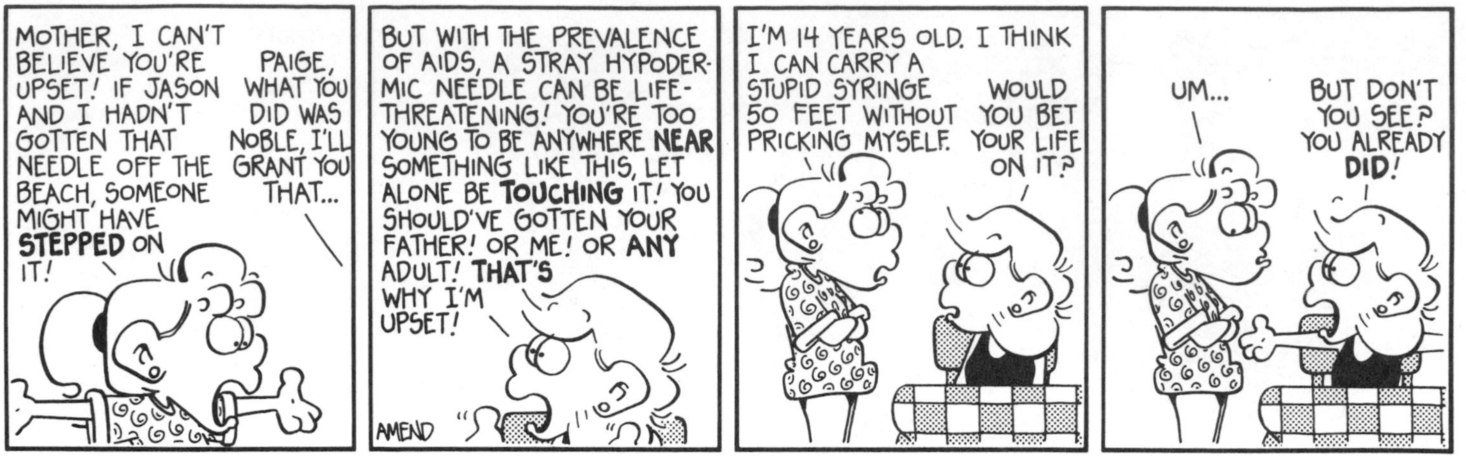
MOTHER, I CAN'T BELIEVE YOU'RE UPSET! IF JASON AND I HADN'T GOTTEN THAT NEEDLE OFF THE BEACH, SOMEONE MIGHT HAVE **STEPPED** ON IT!
PAIGE, WHAT YOU DID WAS NOBLE, I'LL GRANT YOU THAT...
BUT WITH THE PREVALENCE OF AIDS, A STRAY HYPODERMIC NEEDLE CAN BE LIFE-THREATENING! YOU'RE TOO YOUNG TO BE ANYWHERE **NEAR** SOMETHING LIKE THIS, LET ALONE BE **TOUCHING** IT! YOU SHOULD'VE GOTTEN YOUR FATHER! OR ME! OR **ANY** ADULT! **THAT'S** WHY I'M UPSET!
AMEND
I'M 14 YEARS OLD. I THINK I CAN CARRY A STUPID SYRINGE 50 FEET WITHOUT PRICKING MYSELF.
WOULD YOU BET YOUR LIFE ON IT?
UM...
BUT DON'T YOU SEE? YOU ALREADY **DID**!

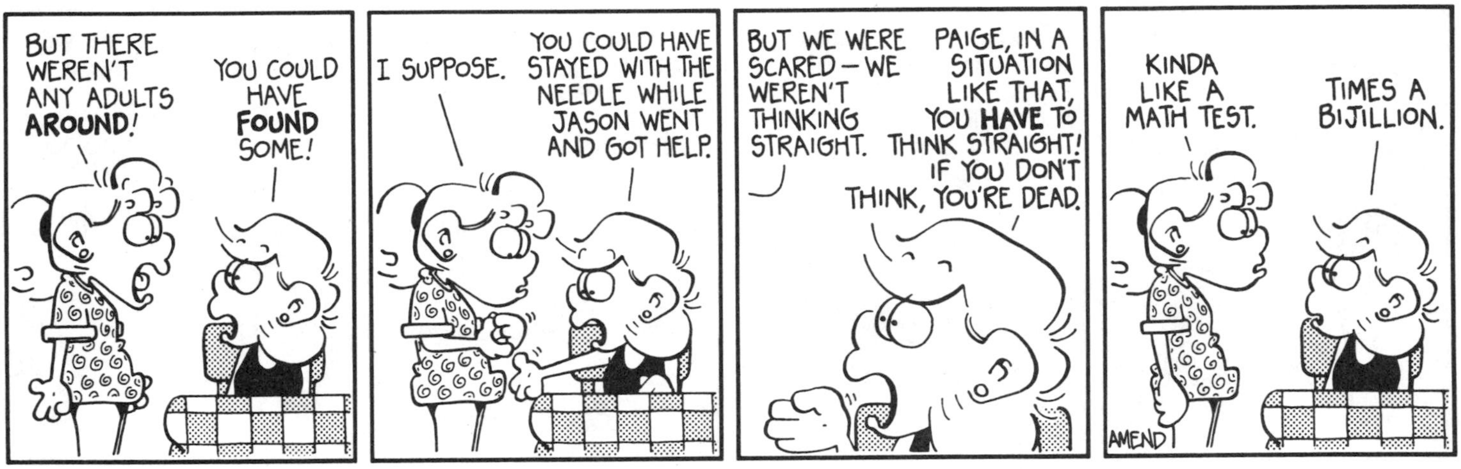
BUT THERE WEREN'T ANY ADULTS **AROUND**!
YOU COULD HAVE **FOUND** SOME!
I SUPPOSE.
YOU COULD HAVE STAYED WITH THE NEEDLE WHILE JASON WENT AND GOT HELP.
BUT WE WERE SCARED — WE WEREN'T THINKING STRAIGHT.
PAIGE, IN A SITUATION LIKE THAT, YOU **HAVE** TO THINK STRAIGHT! IF YOU DON'T THINK, YOU'RE DEAD.
KINDA LIKE A MATH TEST.
TIMES A BIJILLION.
AMEND

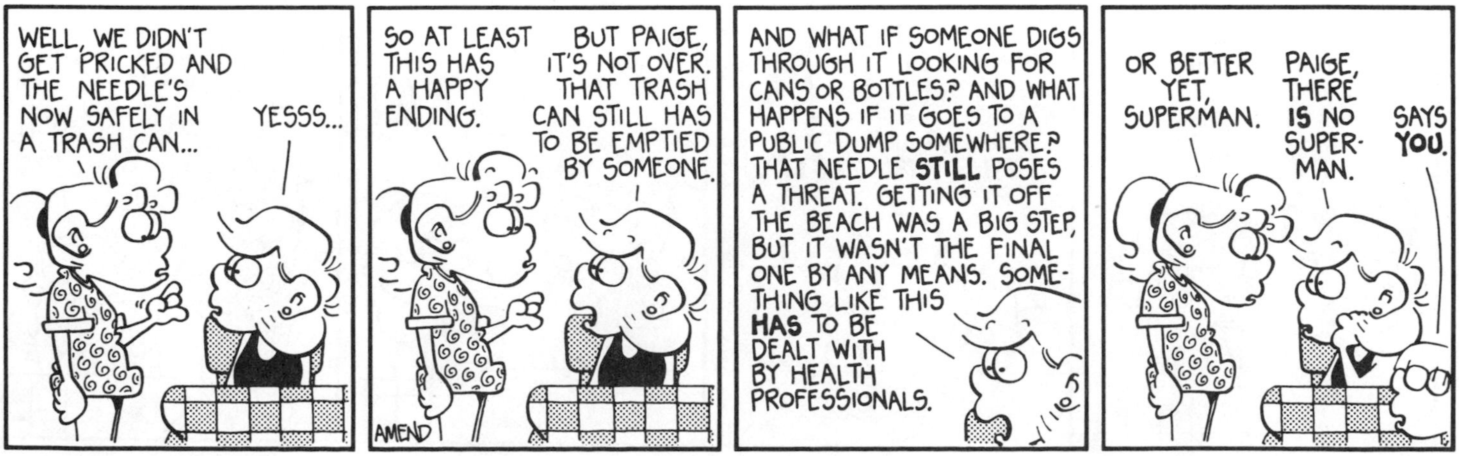
WELL, WE DIDN'T GET PRICKED AND THE NEEDLE'S NOW SAFELY IN A TRASH CAN...
YESSS...
SO AT LEAST THIS HAS A HAPPY ENDING.
BUT PAIGE, IT'S NOT OVER. THAT TRASH CAN STILL HAS TO BE EMPTIED BY SOMEONE.
AMEND
AND WHAT IF SOMEONE DIGS THROUGH IT LOOKING FOR CANS OR BOTTLES? AND WHAT HAPPENS IF IT GOES TO A PUBLIC DUMP SOMEWHERE? THAT NEEDLE **STILL** POSES A THREAT. GETTING IT OFF THE BEACH WAS A BIG STEP, BUT IT WASN'T THE FINAL ONE BY ANY MEANS. SOMETHING LIKE THIS **HAS** TO BE DEALT WITH BY HEALTH PROFESSIONALS.
OR BETTER YET, SUPERMAN.
PAIGE, THERE **IS** NO SUPERMAN.
SAYS **YOU**.

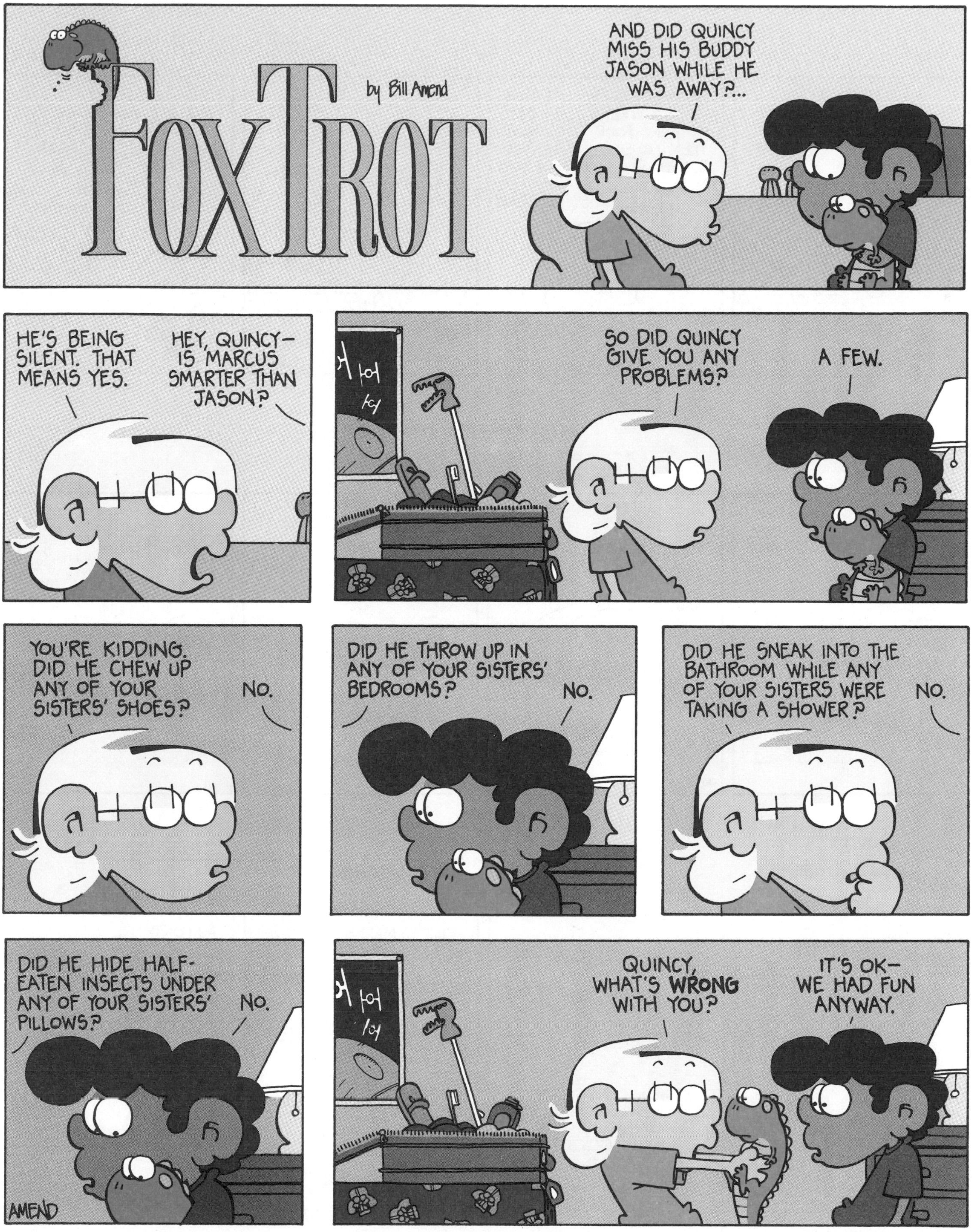
FoxTrot
by Bill Amend
AND DID QUINCY MISS HIS BUDDY JASON WHILE HE WAS AWAY?...
HE'S BEING SILENT. THAT MEANS YES.
HEY, QUINCY- IS MARCUS SMARTER THAN JASON?
SO DID QUINCY GIVE YOU ANY PROBLEMS?
A FEW.
YOU'RE KIDDING. DID HE CHEW UP ANY OF YOUR SISTERS' SHOES?
NO.
DID HE THROW UP IN ANY OF YOUR SISTERS' BEDROOMS?
NO.
DID HE SNEAK INTO THE BATHROOM WHILE ANY OF YOUR SISTERS WERE TAKING A SHOWER?
NO.
DID HE HIDE HALF-EATEN INSECTS UNDER ANY OF YOUR SISTERS' PILLOWS?
NO.
AMEND
QUINCY, WHAT'S **WRONG** WITH YOU?
IT'S OK- WE HAD FUN ANYWAY.

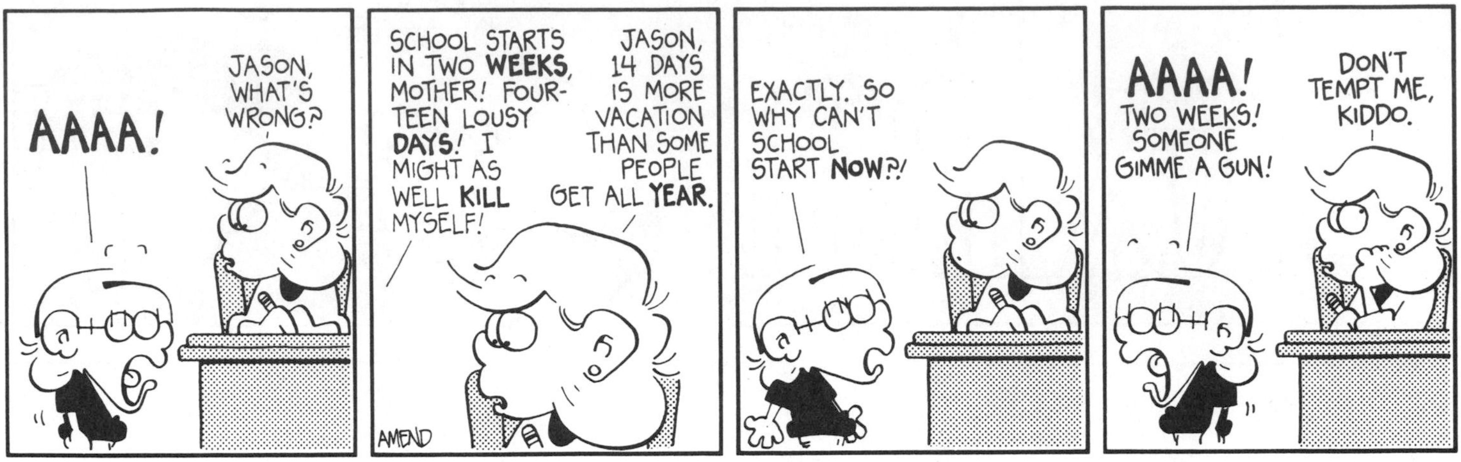
AAAA!
JASON, WHAT'S WRONG?
SCHOOL STARTS IN TWO **WEEKS**, MOTHER! FOURTEEN LOUSY **DAYS**! I MIGHT AS WELL **KILL** MYSELF!
JASON, 14 DAYS IS MORE VACATION THAN SOME PEOPLE GET ALL **YEAR**.
EXACTLY. SO WHY CAN'T SCHOOL START **NOW**?!
AAAA! TWO WEEKS! SOMEONE GIMME A GUN!
DON'T TEMPT ME, KIDDO.
AMEND

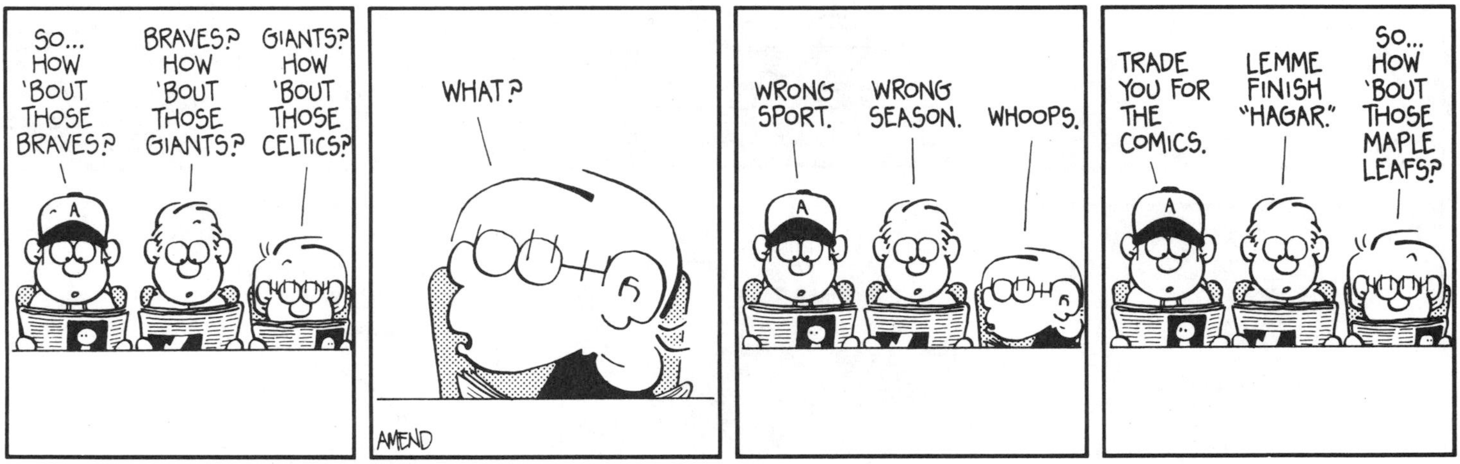
SO... HOW 'BOUT THOSE BRAVES?
BRAVES? HOW 'BOUT THOSE GIANTS?
GIANTS? HOW 'BOUT THOSE CELTICS?
WHAT?
WRONG SPORT.
WRONG SEASON.
WHOOPS.
TRADE YOU FOR THE COMICS.
LEMME FINISH "HAGAR."
SO... HOW 'BOUT THOSE MAPLE LEAFS?
AMEND

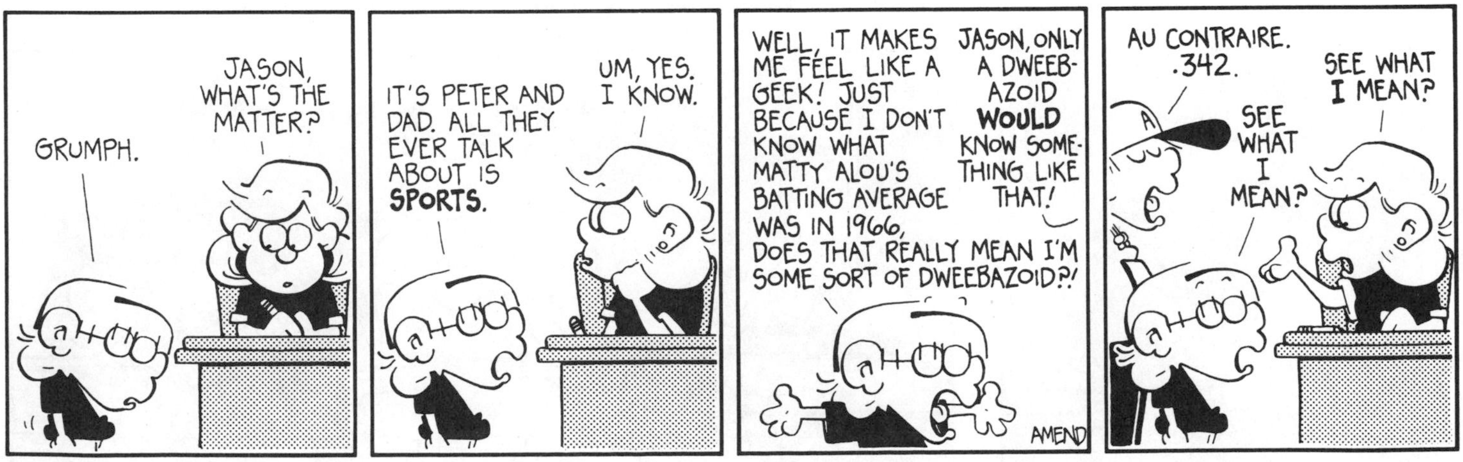
GRUMPH.
JASON, WHAT'S THE MATTER?
IT'S PETER AND DAD. ALL THEY EVER TALK ABOUT IS **SPORTS**.
UM, YES. I KNOW.
WELL, IT MAKES ME FEEL LIKE A GEEK! JUST BECAUSE I DON'T KNOW WHAT MATTY ALOU'S BATTING AVERAGE WAS IN 1966, DOES THAT REALLY MEAN I'M SOME SORT OF DWEEBAZOID?!
JASON, ONLY A DWEEB-AZOID **WOULD** KNOW SOMETHING LIKE THAT!
AU CONTRAIRE. .342.
SEE WHAT I MEAN?
SEE WHAT **I** MEAN?
AMEND

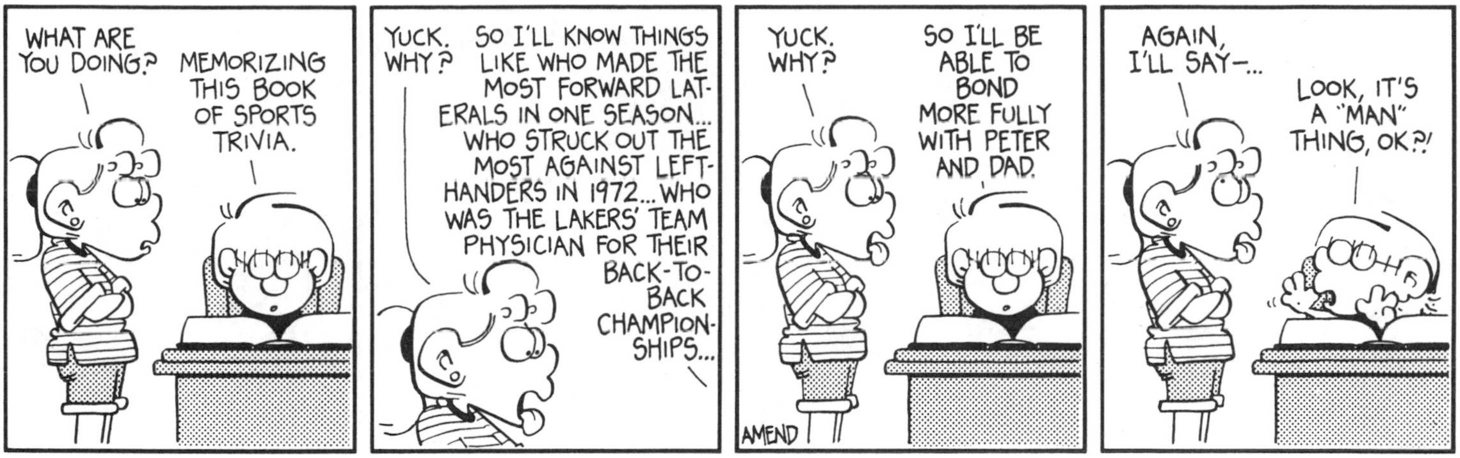
WHAT ARE YOU DOING?
MEMORIZING THIS BOOK OF SPORTS TRIVIA.
YUCK. WHY?
SO I'LL KNOW THINGS LIKE WHO MADE THE MOST FORWARD LATERALS IN ONE SEASON... WHO STRUCK OUT THE MOST AGAINST LEFT-HANDERS IN 1972... WHO WAS THE LAKERS' TEAM PHYSICIAN FOR THEIR BACK-TO-BACK CHAMPIONSHIPS...
YUCK. WHY?
SO I'LL BE ABLE TO BOND MORE FULLY WITH PETER AND DAD.
AMEND
AGAIN, I'LL SAY—...
LOOK, IT'S A "MAN" THING, OK?!

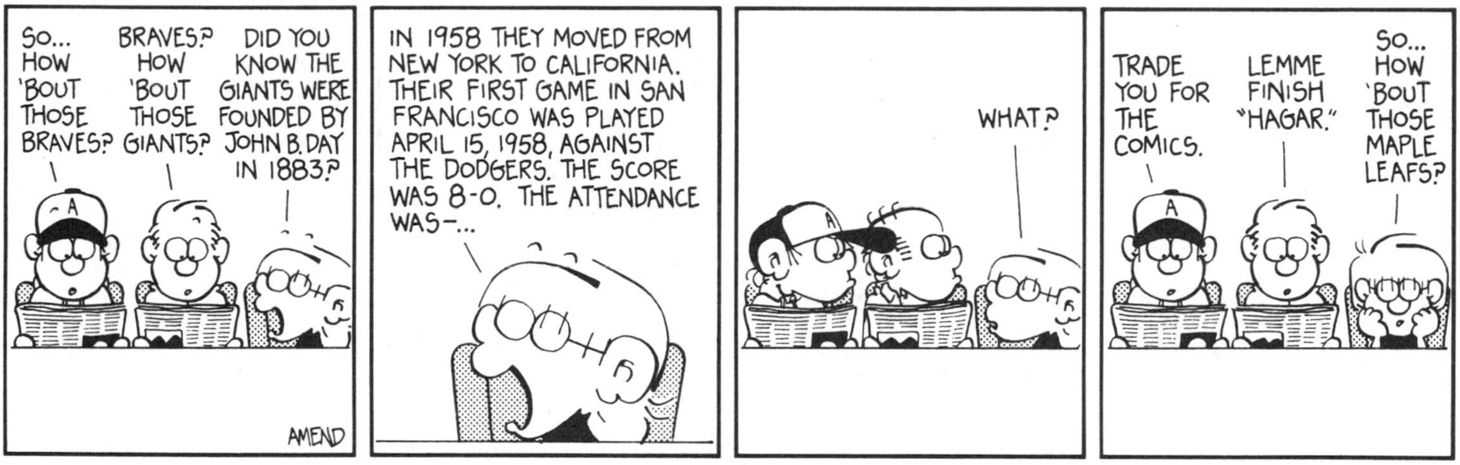
SO... HOW 'BOUT THOSE BRAVES?
BRAVES? HOW 'BOUT THOSE GIANTS?
DID YOU KNOW THE GIANTS WERE FOUNDED BY JOHN B. DAY IN 1883?
AMEND
IN 1958 THEY MOVED FROM NEW YORK TO CALIFORNIA. THEIR FIRST GAME IN SAN FRANCISCO WAS PLAYED APRIL 15, 1958, AGAINST THE DODGERS. THE SCORE WAS 8-0. THE ATTENDANCE WAS—...
WHAT?
TRADE YOU FOR THE COMICS.
LEMME FINISH "HAGAR."
SO... HOW 'BOUT THOSE MAPLE LEAFS?

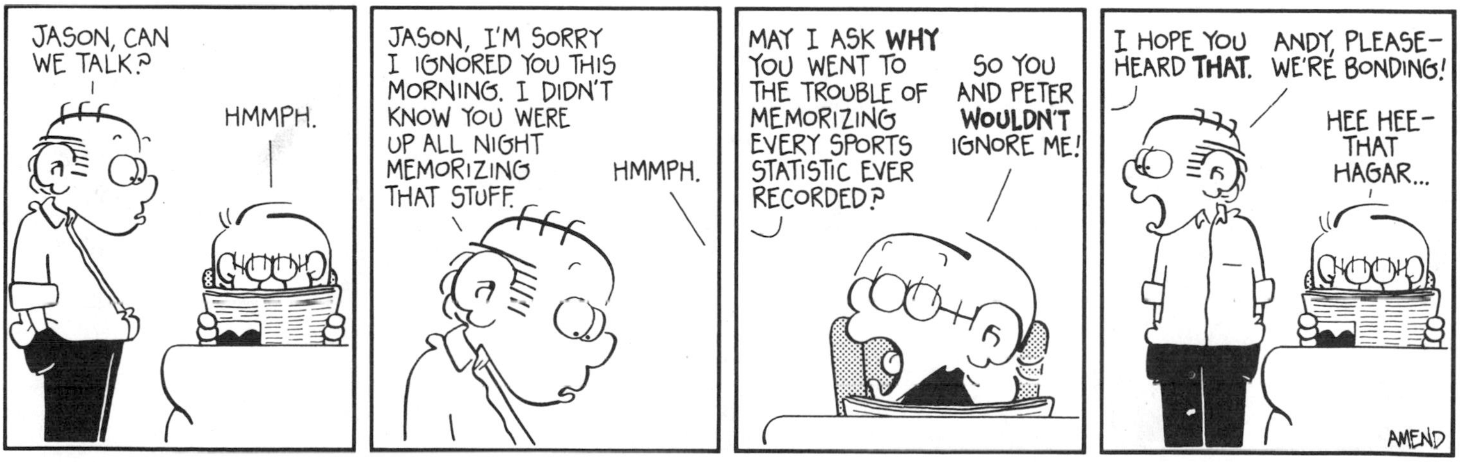
JASON, CAN WE TALK?
HMMPH.
JASON, I'M SORRY I IGNORED YOU THIS MORNING. I DIDN'T KNOW YOU WERE UP ALL NIGHT MEMORIZING THAT STUFF.
HMMPH.
MAY I ASK WHY YOU WENT TO THE TROUBLE OF MEMORIZING EVERY SPORTS STATISTIC EVER RECORDED?
SO YOU AND PETER WOULDN'T IGNORE ME!
I HOPE YOU HEARD THAT.
ANDY, PLEASE—WE'RE BONDING!
HEE HEE—THAT HAGAR...
AMEND

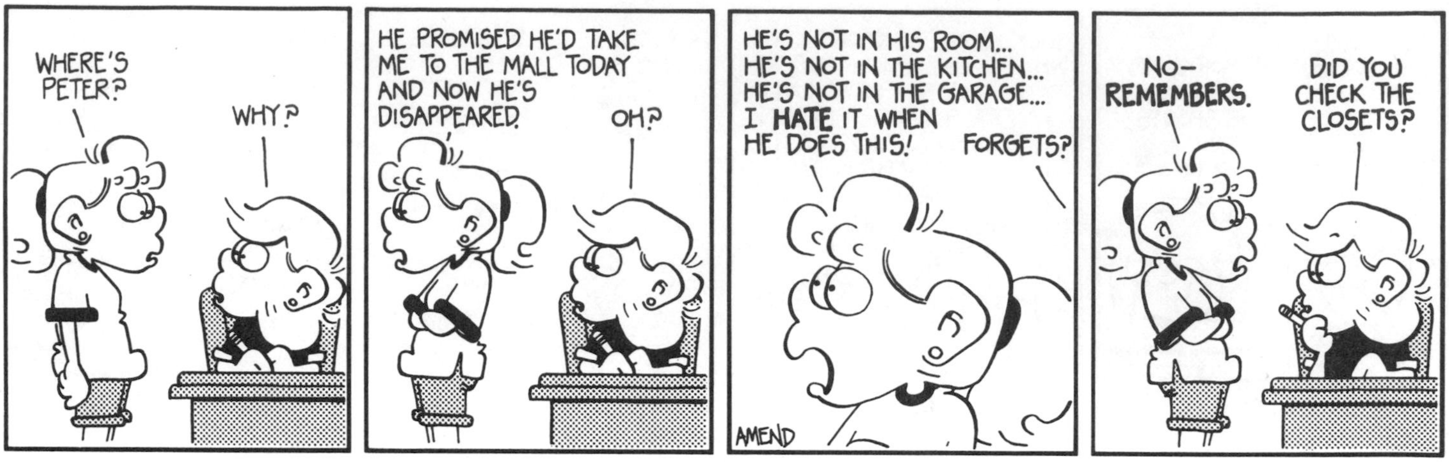
WHERE'S PETER?
WHY?
HE PROMISED HE'D TAKE ME TO THE MALL TODAY AND NOW HE'S DISAPPEARED.
OH?
HE'S NOT IN HIS ROOM... HE'S NOT IN THE KITCHEN... HE'S NOT IN THE GARAGE... I HATE IT WHEN HE DOES THIS!
FORGETS?
AMEND
NO— REMEMBERS.
DID YOU CHECK THE CLOSETS?

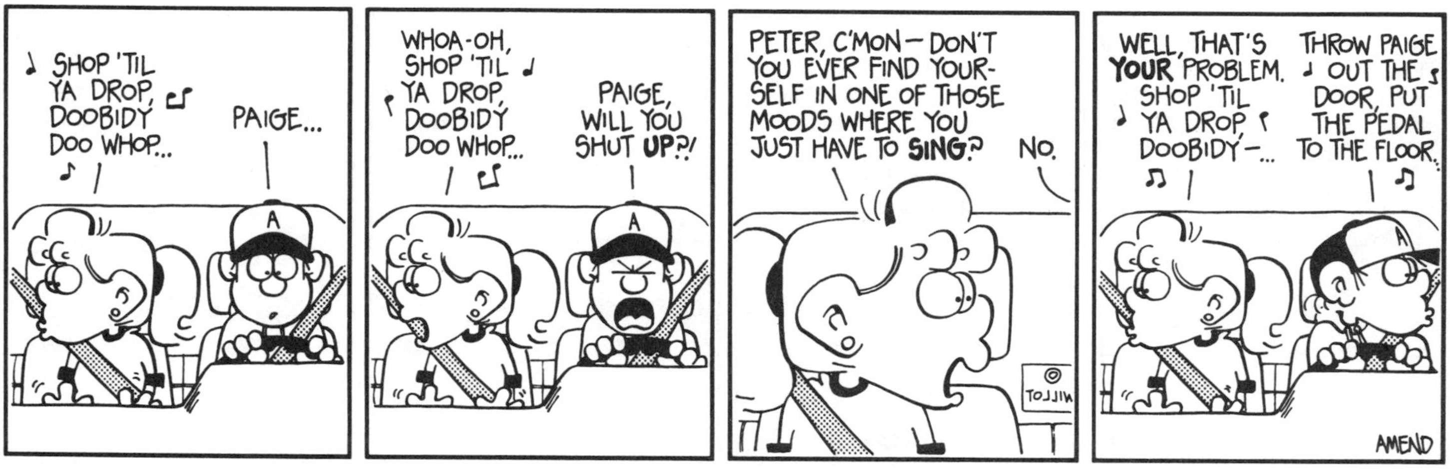
SHOP 'TIL YA DROP, DOOBIDY DOO WHOP...
PAIGE...
WHOA-OH, SHOP 'TIL YA DROP, DOOBIDY DOO WHOP...
PAIGE, WILL YOU SHUT UP?!
PETER, C'MON — DON'T YOU EVER FIND YOURSELF IN ONE OF THOSE MOODS WHERE YOU JUST HAVE TO SING?
NO.
WELL, THAT'S YOUR PROBLEM. SHOP 'TIL YA DROP, DOOBIDY—...
THROW PAIGE OUT THE DOOR, PUT THE PEDAL TO THE FLOOR...
AMEND

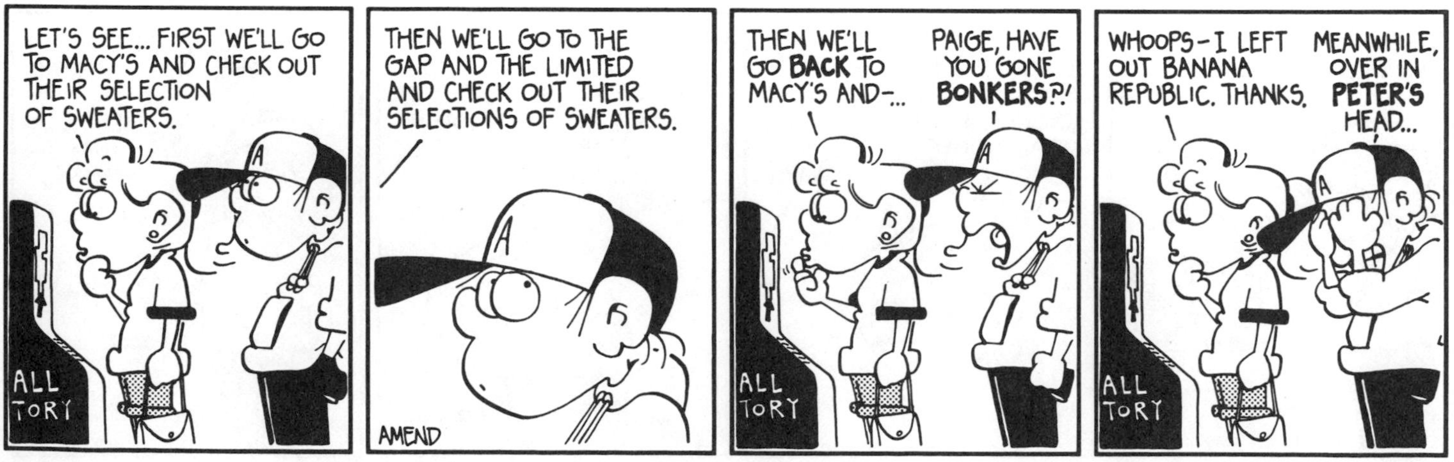
LET'S SEE... FIRST WE'LL GO TO MACY'S AND CHECK OUT THEIR SELECTION OF SWEATERS.
ALL TORY
THEN WE'LL GO TO THE GAP AND THE LIMITED AND CHECK OUT THEIR SELECTIONS OF SWEATERS.
AMEND
THEN WE'LL GO BACK TO MACY'S AND—...
PAIGE, HAVE YOU GONE BONKERS?!
WHOOPS - I LEFT OUT BANANA REPUBLIC. THANKS.
MEANWHILE, OVER IN PETER'S HEAD...

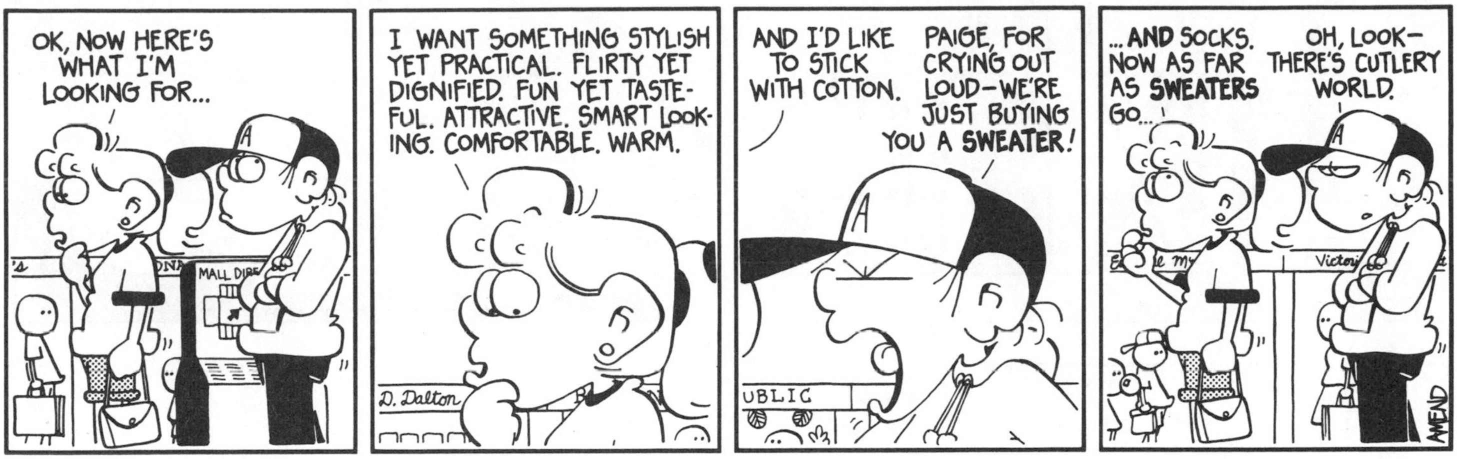
OK, NOW HERE'S WHAT I'M LOOKING FOR...
I WANT SOMETHING STYLISH YET PRACTICAL. FLIRTY YET DIGNIFIED. FUN YET TASTEFUL. ATTRACTIVE. SMART LOOKING. COMFORTABLE. WARM.
D. Dalton
AND I'D LIKE TO STICK WITH COTTON.
PAIGE, FOR CRYING OUT LOUD—WE'RE JUST BUYING YOU A **SWEATER**!
...**AND** SOCKS. NOW AS FAR AS **SWEATERS** GO...
OH, LOOK—THERE'S CUTLERY WORLD.
AMEND

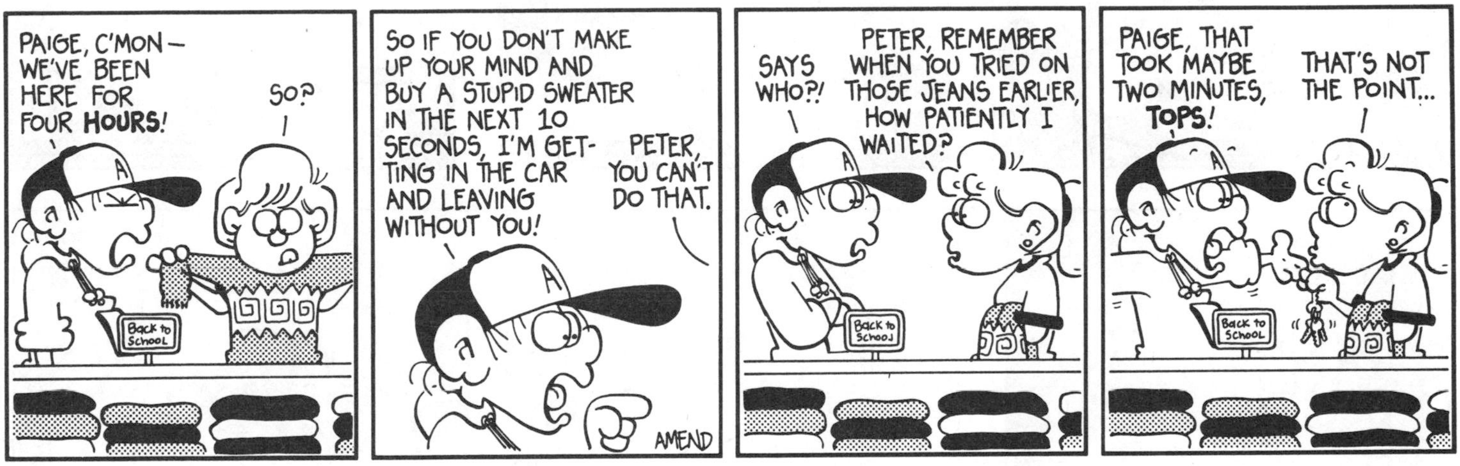
PAIGE, C'MON—WE'VE BEEN HERE FOR FOUR **HOURS**!
SO?
Back to School
SO IF YOU DON'T MAKE UP YOUR MIND AND BUY A STUPID SWEATER IN THE NEXT 10 SECONDS, I'M GETTING IN THE CAR AND LEAVING WITHOUT YOU!
PETER, YOU CAN'T DO THAT.
AMEND
SAYS WHO?!
PETER, REMEMBER WHEN YOU TRIED ON THOSE JEANS EARLIER, HOW PATIENTLY I WAITED?
Back to School
PAIGE, THAT TOOK MAYBE TWO MINUTES, **TOPS**!
THAT'S NOT THE POINT...
Back to School

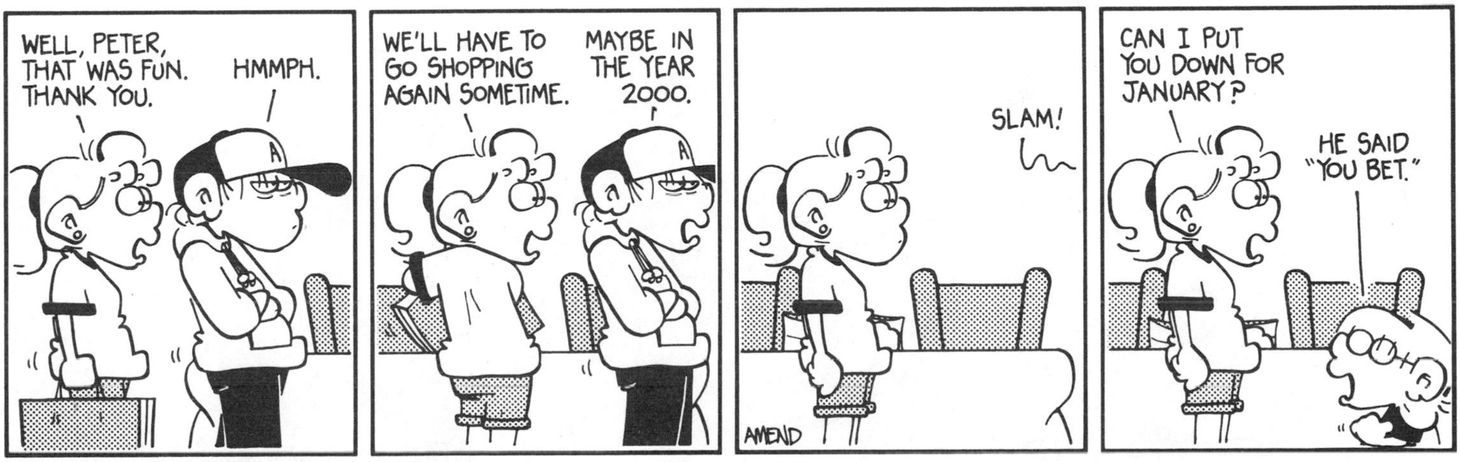
WELL, PETER, THAT WAS FUN. THANK YOU.
HMMPH.
WE'LL HAVE TO GO SHOPPING AGAIN SOMETIME.
MAYBE IN THE YEAR 2000.
SLAM!
AMEND
CAN I PUT YOU DOWN FOR JANUARY?
HE SAID "YOU BET."

... $256 \times 253 = 64{,}768$
$256 \times 254 = 65{,}024$
$256 \times 255 = 65{,}280$
$256 \times 256 = 65{,}536$

SIX MINUTES?! MAN, I AM OUT OF SHAPE!

WHAT ARE YOU DOING?

BRUSHING UP ON MY TIMES TABLES.

YUCK. WHY?

SO I'LL BE IN PEAK FORM WHEN SCHOOL STARTS.

FOOL. THAT'S WHAT CALCULATORS ARE FOR.

MAYBE. BUT WATCH HOW QUICKLY I CAN RATTLE 'EM OFF...

$6 \times 5 = 30$
$6 \times 6 = 36$
$6 \times 7 = 42$
$6 \times 8 = 48$
$6 \times 9 = 54$

$7 \times 5 = 8$
$7 \times 6 = 99$
$7 \times 7 = -4$
$7 \times 8 = \sqrt{255}$
$7 \times 9 = 0$

$8 \times 5 = 1$
$8 \times 6 = \pi r^2$
$8 \times 7 = 87$
$8 \times 8 = 1{,}026{,}305$
$8 \times 9 = \sqrt[3]{e}$

AMEND

$9 \times 5 = 0.01$
$9 \times 6 = 5555$
$9 \times 7 = \ln\beta$
$9 \times 8 = 1/3$
$9 \times 9 = mc^2$

STILL, I'LL BET MY CALCULATOR'S FASTER.

WANNA BET, OH, 8×8 CENTS?

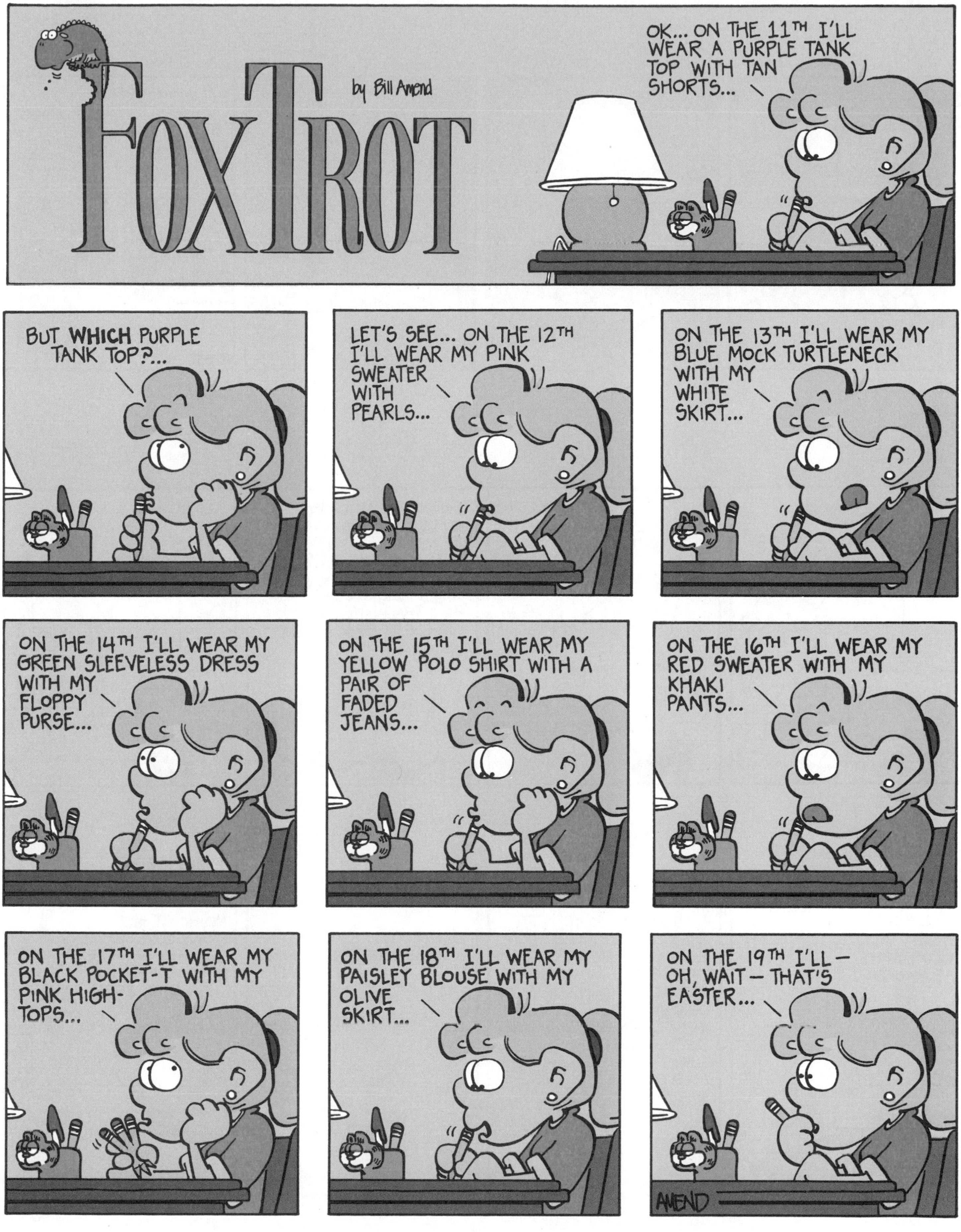
FOXTROT
by Bill Amend
OK... ON THE 11TH I'LL WEAR A PURPLE TANK TOP WITH TAN SHORTS...
BUT WHICH PURPLE TANK TOP?...
LET'S SEE... ON THE 12TH I'LL WEAR MY PINK SWEATER WITH PEARLS...
ON THE 13TH I'LL WEAR MY BLUE MOCK TURTLENECK WITH MY WHITE SKIRT...
ON THE 14TH I'LL WEAR MY GREEN SLEEVELESS DRESS WITH MY FLOPPY PURSE...
ON THE 15TH I'LL WEAR MY YELLOW POLO SHIRT WITH A PAIR OF FADED JEANS...
ON THE 16TH I'LL WEAR MY RED SWEATER WITH MY KHAKI PANTS...
ON THE 17TH I'LL WEAR MY BLACK POCKET-T WITH MY PINK HIGH-TOPS...
ON THE 18TH I'LL WEAR MY PAISLEY BLOUSE WITH MY OLIVE SKIRT...
ON THE 19TH I'LL— OH, WAIT— THAT'S EASTER...
AMEND

SCHOOL STARTS TOMORROW.

SCHOOL STARTS TOMORROW.

SCHOOL STARTS TOMORROW.

CORRECTION...

MAN, WHO'DA THOUGHT...

WHAT?

BATTY OL' MISS GRINCHLEY RETIRED OVER THE SUMMER.

YOU'RE KIDDING. SO WHO'S YOUR TEACHER?

THIS NEW LADY, MISS O'MALLEY. SHE'S YOUNG, IDEALISTIC, ENTHUSIASTIC, ENERGETIC, ORGANIZED AND ABOUT A HUNDRED TIMES MORE ON THE BALL THAN MISS GRINCHLEY EVER WAS.

REALLY...

THIS IS NOT GOOD.

HOW'S "GREAT" SOUND?

JASON, ABOUT YOUR GEOGRAPHY ASSIGNMENT...

YES, MISS O'MALLEY?

I ASKED YOU TO IDENTIFY THE SEVEN CONTINENTS ON THIS MAP. I DIDN'T SAY ANYTHING ABOUT INDICATING THE KNOWN LOCATIONS OF MAJOR DINOSAUR FOSSIL DEPOSITS IN NORTH AMERICA. DID YOU DO THIS SORT OF THING WHEN MISS GRINCHLEY WAS YOUR TEACHER?

MAYBE.

AND WHAT DID SHE DO?

USUALLY SHE'D KINDA GET ALL FLUSTERED AND BUG-EYED.

NO, NO — I MEAN GRADE-WISE. YOU'VE GOT THE '67 PTERANADON FIND IN THE WRONG STATE.

HUH?!

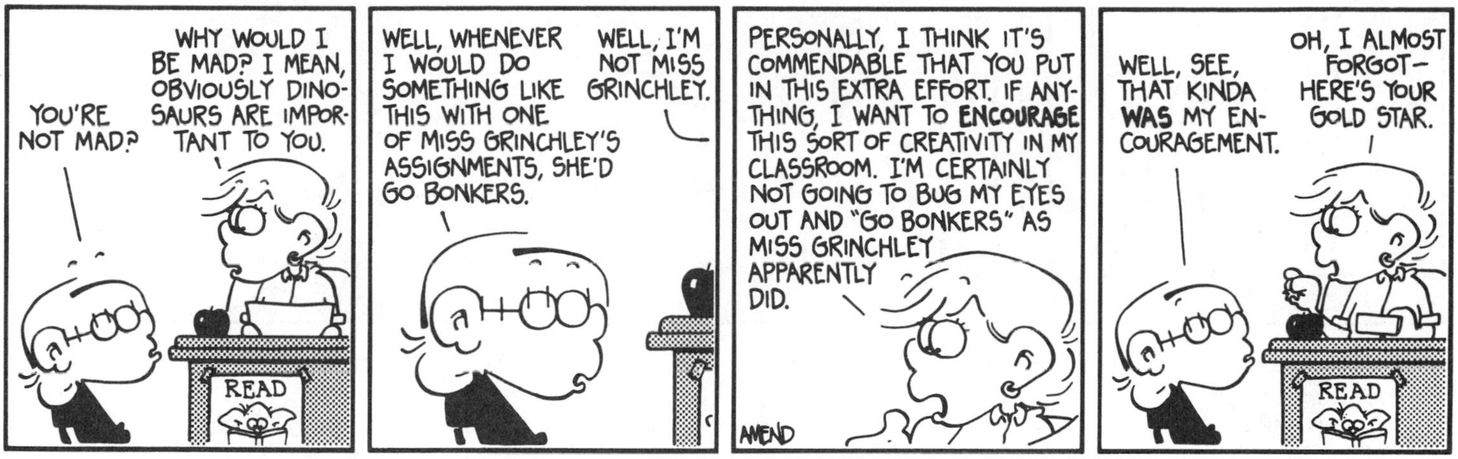
YOU'RE NOT MAD?
WHY WOULD I BE MAD? I MEAN, OBVIOUSLY DINOSAURS ARE IMPORTANT TO YOU.
WELL, WHENEVER I WOULD DO SOMETHING LIKE THIS WITH ONE OF MISS GRINCHLEY'S ASSIGNMENTS, SHE'D GO BONKERS.
WELL, I'M NOT MISS GRINCHLEY.
PERSONALLY, I THINK IT'S COMMENDABLE THAT YOU PUT IN THIS EXTRA EFFORT. IF ANYTHING, I WANT TO **ENCOURAGE** THIS SORT OF CREATIVITY IN MY CLASSROOM. I'M CERTAINLY NOT GOING TO BUG MY EYES OUT AND "GO BONKERS" AS MISS GRINCHLEY APPARENTLY DID.
AMEND
WELL, SEE, THAT KINDA **WAS** MY ENCOURAGEMENT.
OH, I ALMOST FORGOT— HERE'S YOUR GOLD STAR.
READ

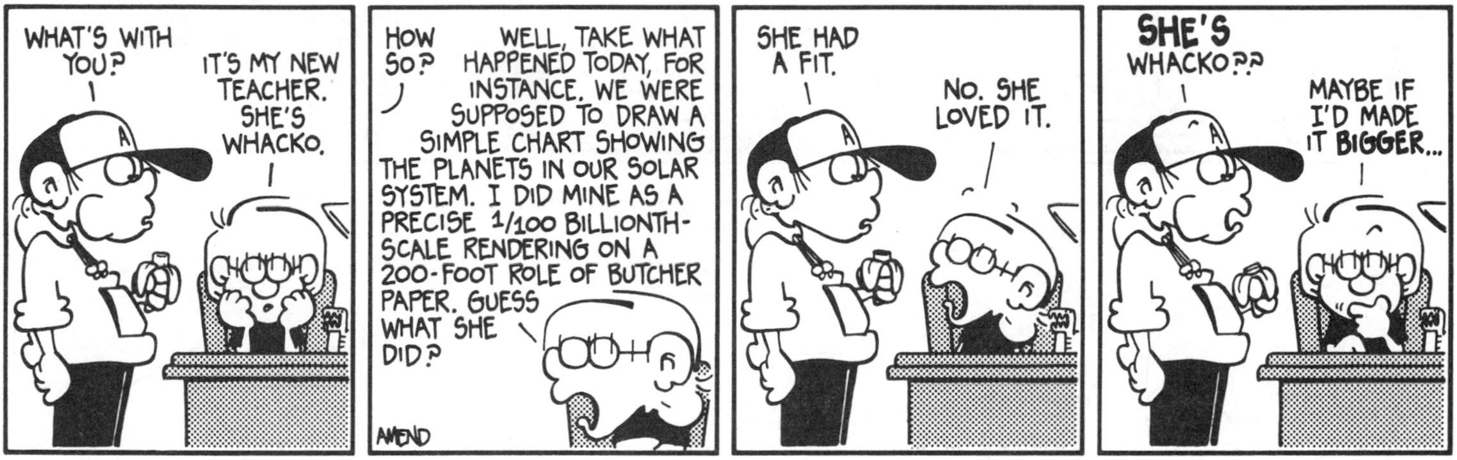
WHAT'S WITH YOU?
IT'S MY NEW TEACHER. SHE'S WHACKO.
HOW SO?
WELL, TAKE WHAT HAPPENED TODAY, FOR INSTANCE. WE WERE SUPPOSED TO DRAW A SIMPLE CHART SHOWING THE PLANETS IN OUR SOLAR SYSTEM. I DID MINE AS A PRECISE 1/100 BILLIONTH-SCALE RENDERING ON A 200-FOOT ROLE OF BUTCHER PAPER. GUESS WHAT SHE DID?
AMEND
SHE HAD A FIT.
NO. SHE LOVED IT.
SHE'S WHACKO??
MAYBE IF I'D MADE IT **BIGGER**...

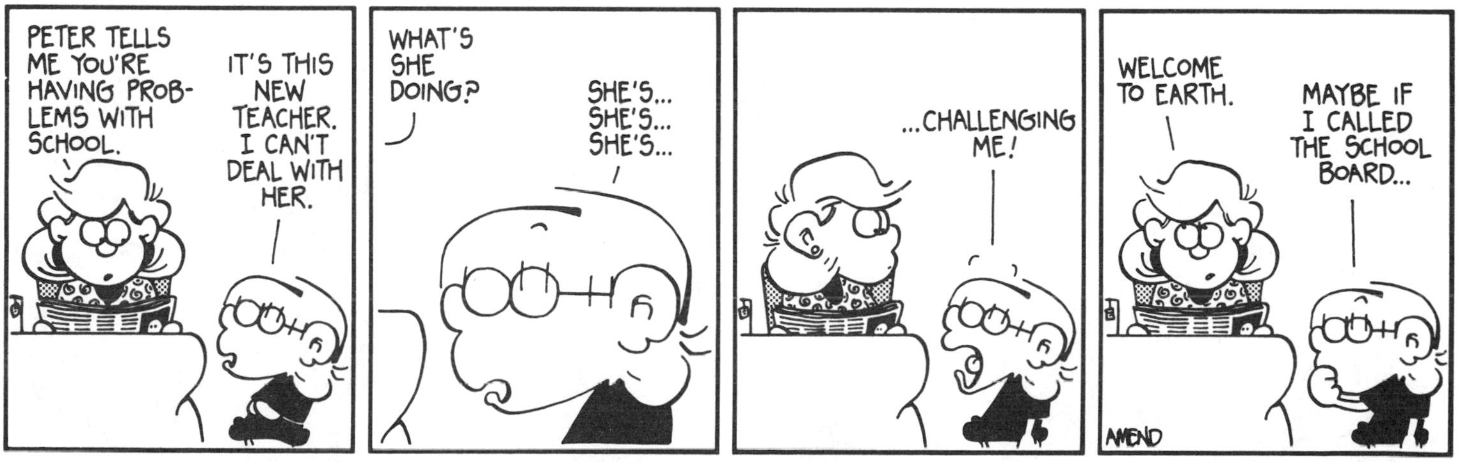
PETER TELLS ME YOU'RE HAVING PROBLEMS WITH SCHOOL.
IT'S THIS NEW TEACHER. I CAN'T DEAL WITH HER.
WHAT'S SHE DOING?
SHE'S... SHE'S... SHE'S...
...CHALLENGING ME!
WELCOME TO EARTH.
MAYBE IF I CALLED THE SCHOOL BOARD...
AMEND

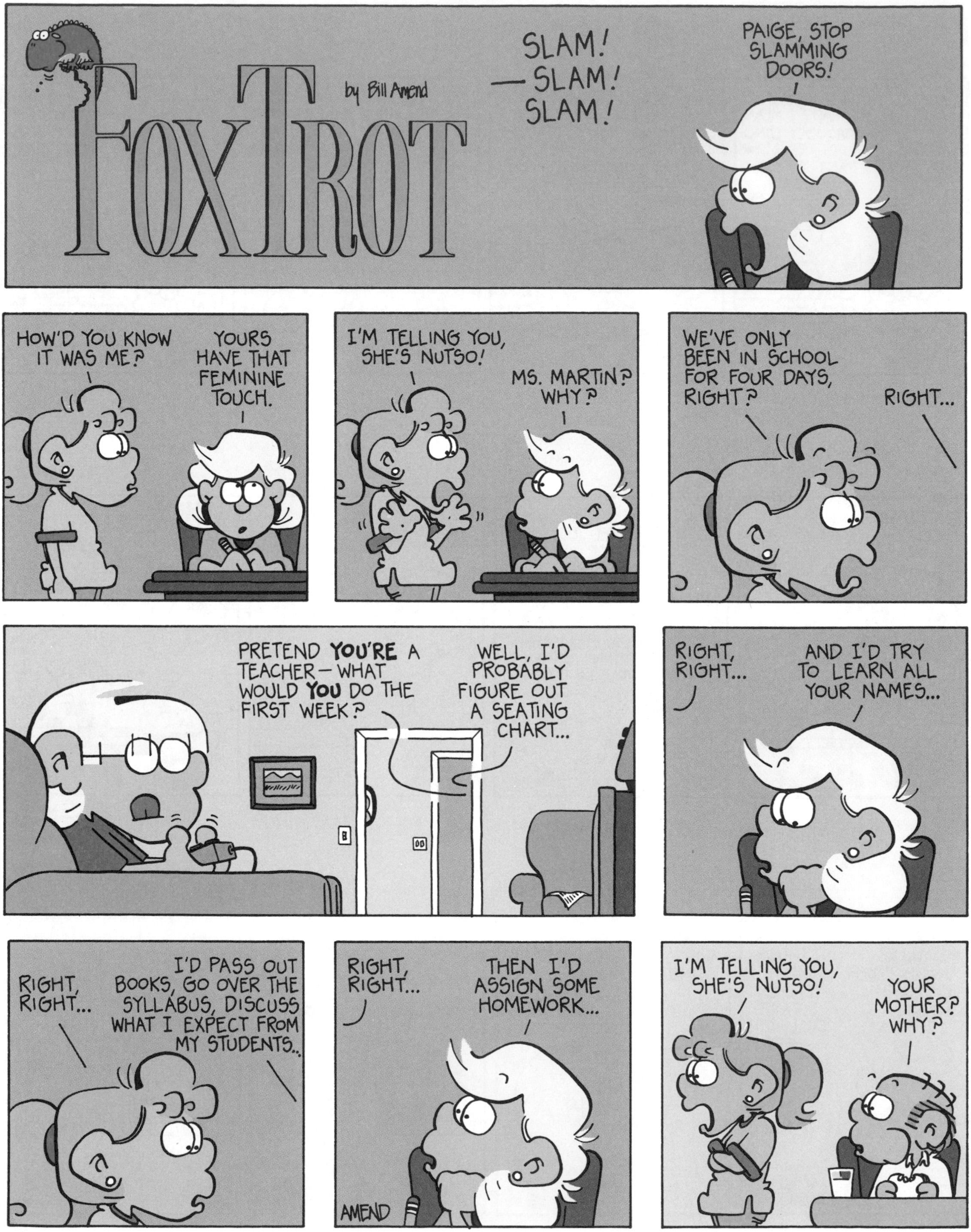
FoxTrot
by Bill Amend
SLAM! —SLAM! SLAM!
PAIGE, STOP SLAMMING DOORS!
HOW'D YOU KNOW IT WAS ME?
YOURS HAVE THAT FEMININE TOUCH.
I'M TELLING YOU, SHE'S NUTSO!
MS. MARTIN? WHY?
WE'VE ONLY BEEN IN SCHOOL FOR FOUR DAYS, RIGHT?
RIGHT...
PRETEND YOU'RE A TEACHER— WHAT WOULD YOU DO THE FIRST WEEK?
WELL, I'D PROBABLY FIGURE OUT A SEATING CHART...
RIGHT, RIGHT...
AND I'D TRY TO LEARN ALL YOUR NAMES...
RIGHT, RIGHT...
I'D PASS OUT BOOKS, GO OVER THE SYLLABUS, DISCUSS WHAT I EXPECT FROM MY STUDENTS...
RIGHT, RIGHT...
THEN I'D ASSIGN SOME HOMEWORK...
AMEND
I'M TELLING YOU, SHE'S NUTSO!
YOUR MOTHER? WHY?

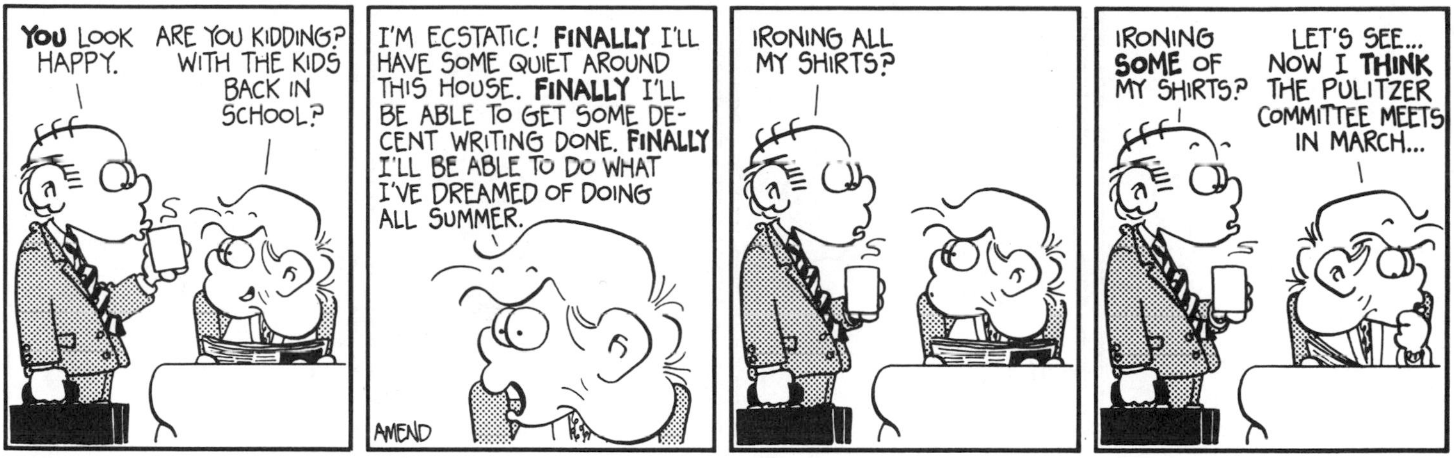
YOU LOOK HAPPY.
ARE YOU KIDDING? WITH THE KIDS BACK IN SCHOOL?
I'M ECSTATIC! FINALLY I'LL HAVE SOME QUIET AROUND THIS HOUSE. FINALLY I'LL BE ABLE TO GET SOME DECENT WRITING DONE. FINALLY I'LL BE ABLE TO DO WHAT I'VE DREAMED OF DOING ALL SUMMER.
AMEND
IRONING ALL MY SHIRTS?
IRONING SOME OF MY SHIRTS?
LET'S SEE... NOW I THINK THE PULITZER COMMITTEE MEETS IN MARCH...

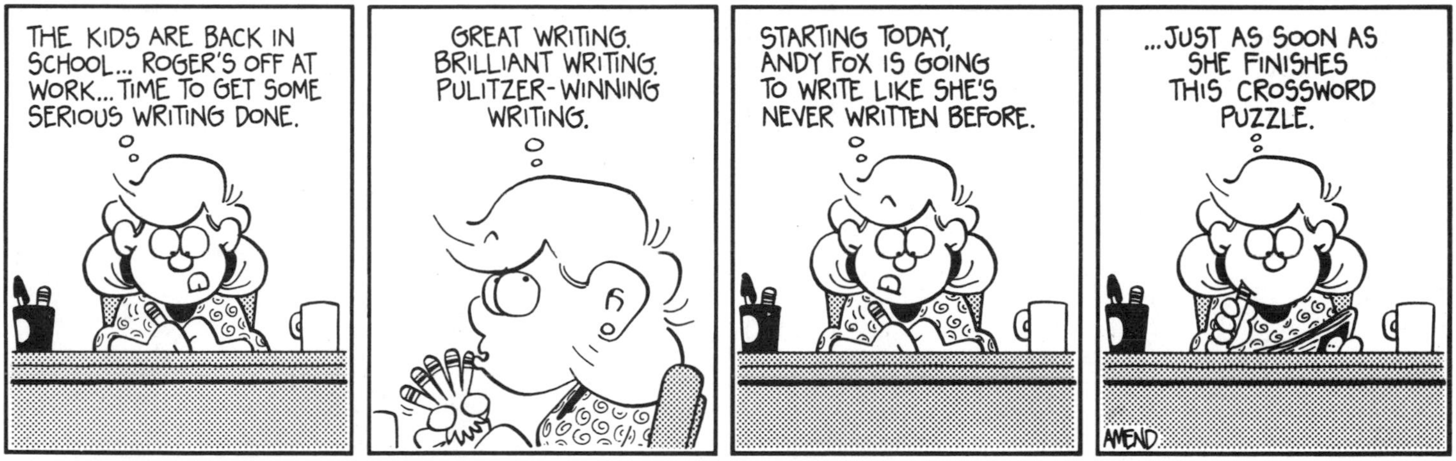
THE KIDS ARE BACK IN SCHOOL... ROGER'S OFF AT WORK... TIME TO GET SOME SERIOUS WRITING DONE.
GREAT WRITING. BRILLIANT WRITING. PULITZER-WINNING WRITING.
STARTING TODAY, ANDY FOX IS GOING TO WRITE LIKE SHE'S NEVER WRITTEN BEFORE.
...JUST AS SOON AS SHE FINISHES THIS CROSSWORD PUZZLE.
AMEND

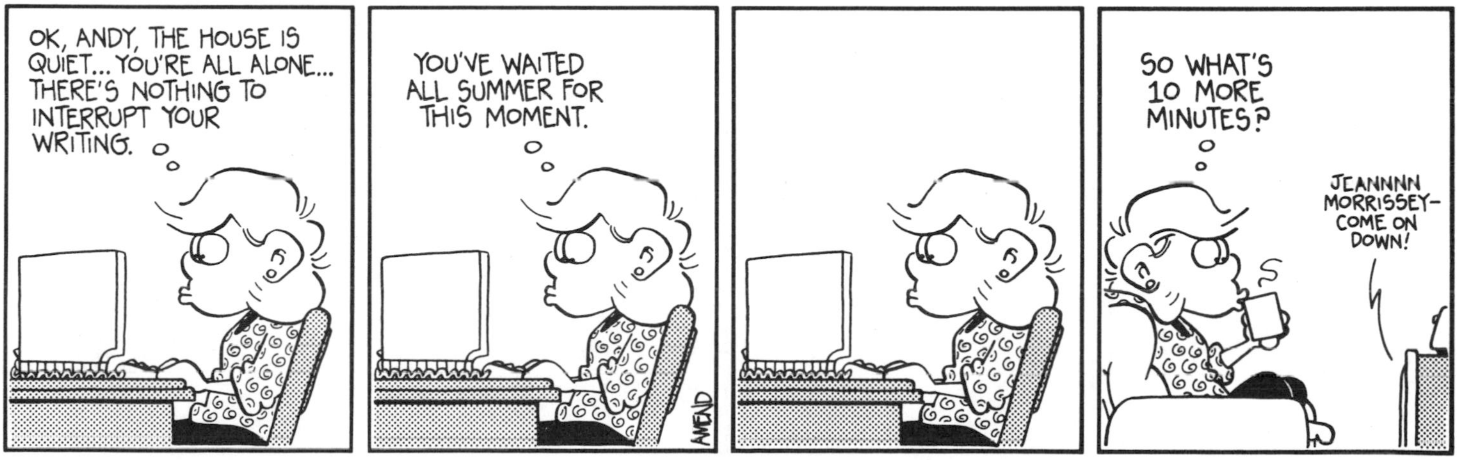
OK, ANDY, THE HOUSE IS QUIET... YOU'RE ALL ALONE... THERE'S NOTHING TO INTERRUPT YOUR WRITING.
YOU'VE WAITED ALL SUMMER FOR THIS MOMENT.
AMEND
SO WHAT'S 10 MORE MINUTES?
JEANNNN MORRISSEY-COME ON DOWN!

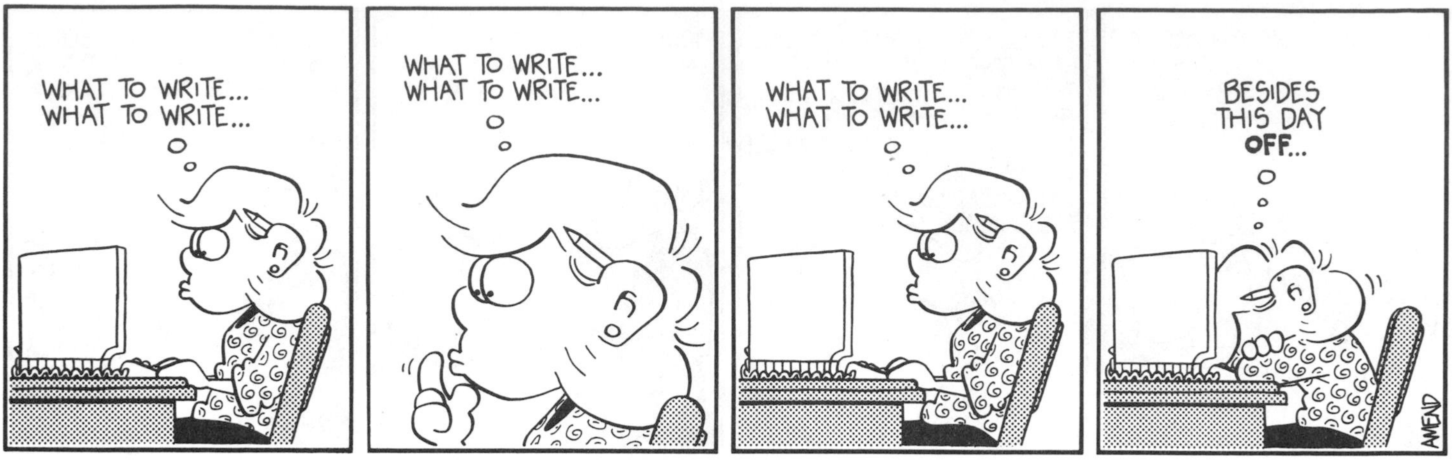
WHAT TO WRITE...
WHAT TO WRITE...
WHAT TO WRITE...
WHAT TO WRITE...
WHAT TO WRITE...
WHAT TO WRITE...
BESIDES THIS DAY **OFF**...
AMEND

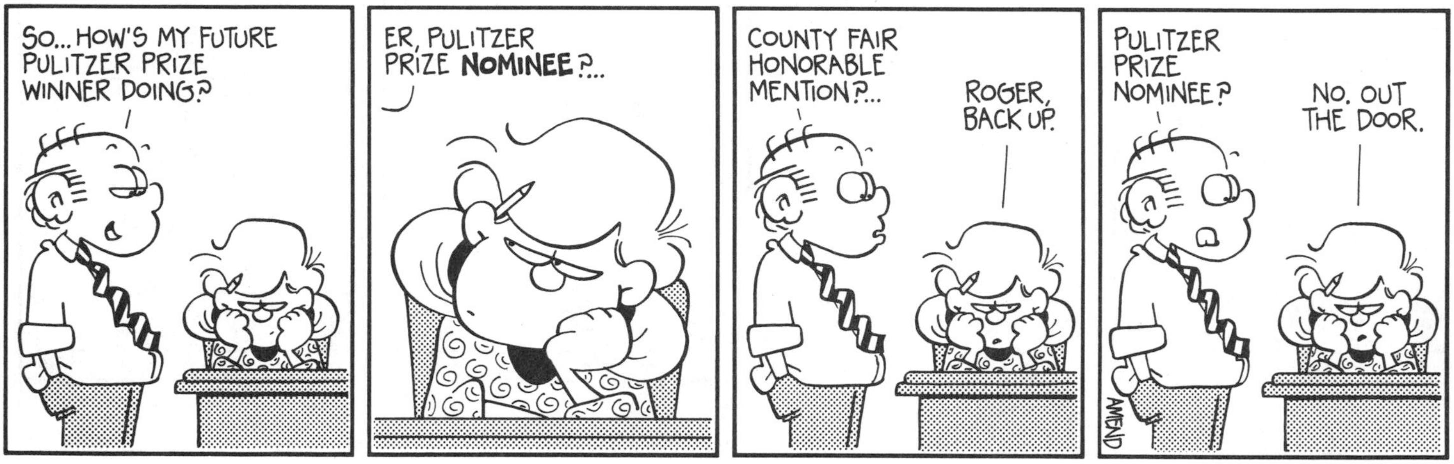
SO... HOW'S MY FUTURE PULITZER PRIZE WINNER DOING?
ER, PULITZER PRIZE **NOMINEE**?...
COUNTY FAIR HONORABLE MENTION?...
ROGER, BACK UP.
PULITZER PRIZE NOMINEE?
NO. OUT THE DOOR.
AMEND

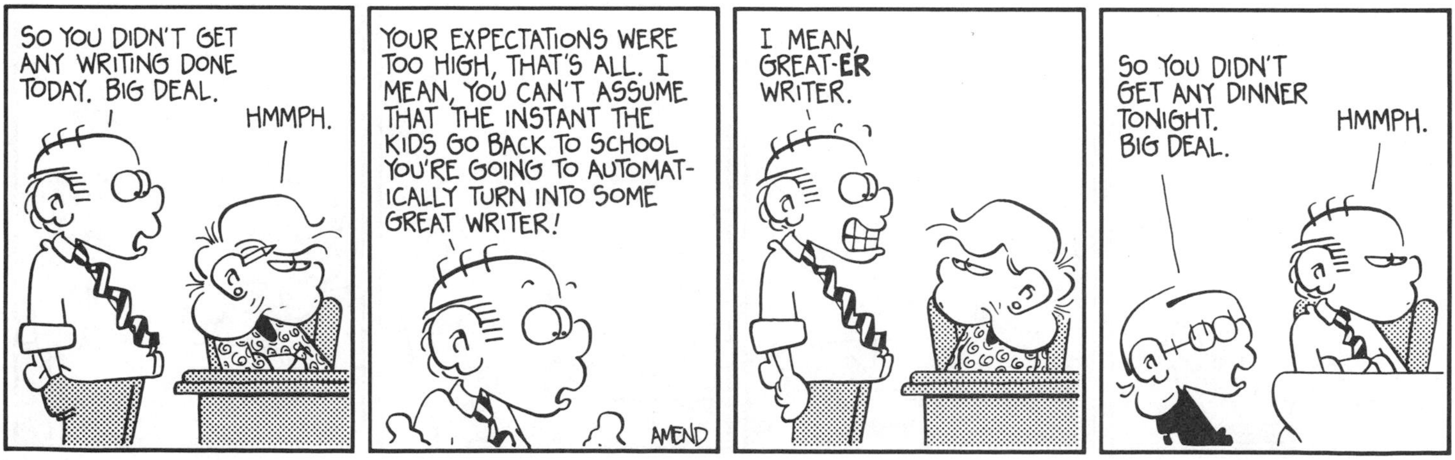
SO YOU DIDN'T GET ANY WRITING DONE TODAY. BIG DEAL.
HMMPH.
YOUR EXPECTATIONS WERE TOO HIGH, THAT'S ALL. I MEAN, YOU CAN'T ASSUME THAT THE INSTANT THE KIDS GO BACK TO SCHOOL YOU'RE GOING TO AUTOMATICALLY TURN INTO SOME GREAT WRITER!
AMEND
I MEAN, GREAT-**ER** WRITER.
SO YOU DIDN'T GET ANY DINNER TONIGHT. BIG DEAL.
HMMPH.

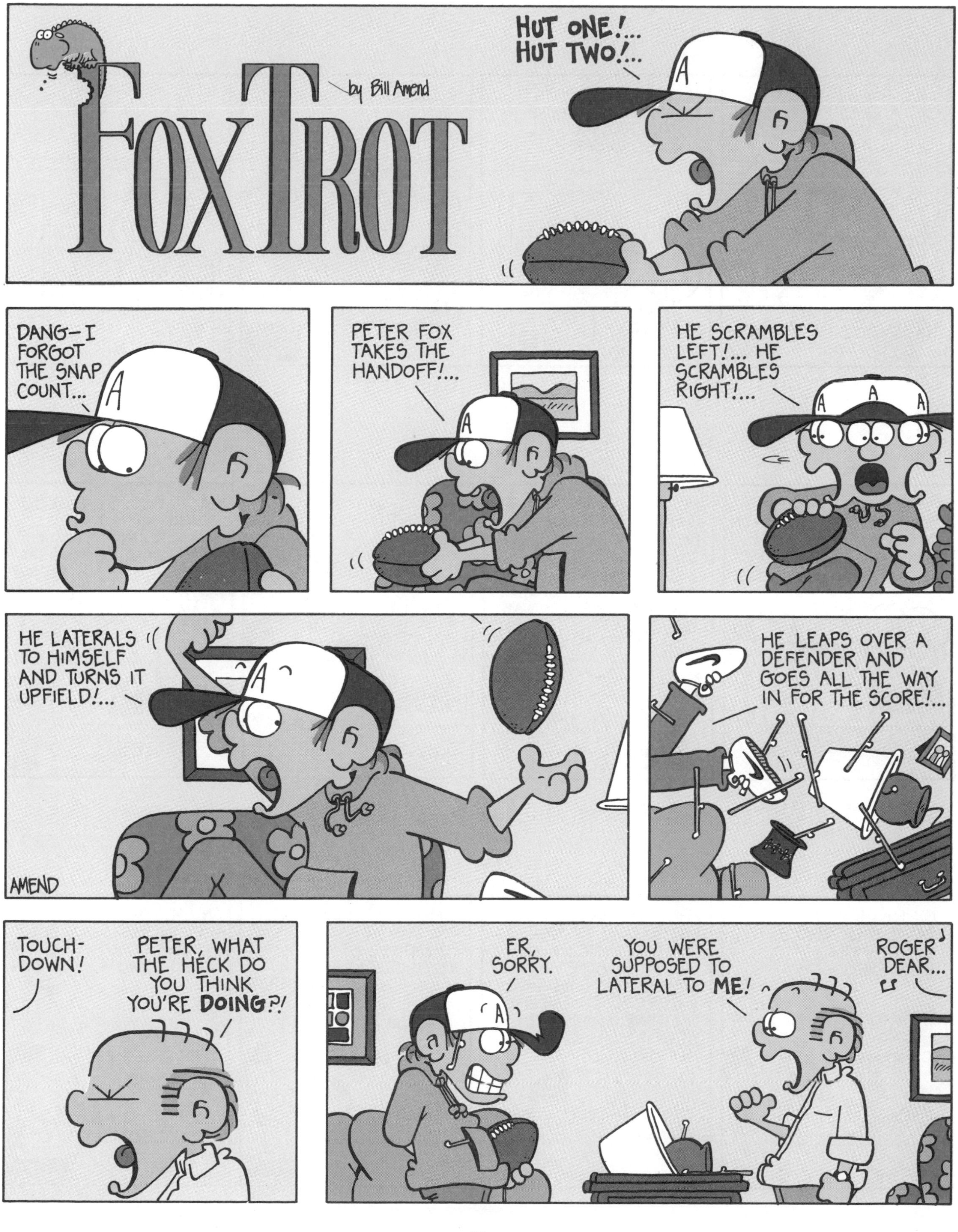
FoxTrot
by Bill Amend
HUT ONE!... HUT TWO!...
DANG— I FORGOT THE SNAP COUNT...
PETER FOX TAKES THE HANDOFF!...
HE SCRAMBLES LEFT!... HE SCRAMBLES RIGHT!...
HE LATERALS TO HIMSELF AND TURNS IT UPFIELD!...
AMEND
HE LEAPS OVER A DEFENDER AND GOES ALL THE WAY IN FOR THE SCORE!...
TOUCH-DOWN!
PETER, WHAT THE HECK DO YOU THINK YOU'RE DOING?!
ER, SORRY.
YOU WERE SUPPOSED TO LATERAL TO ME!
ROGER DEAR...

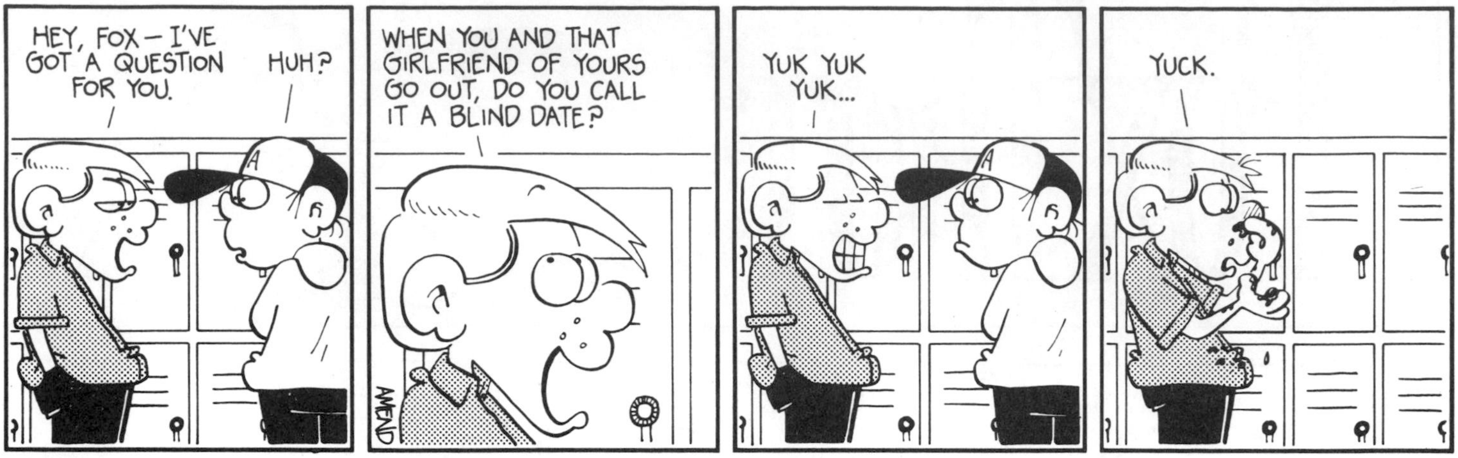
HEY, FOX — I'VE GOT A QUESTION FOR YOU.
HUH?
WHEN YOU AND THAT GIRLFRIEND OF YOURS GO OUT, DO YOU CALL IT A BLIND DATE?
AMEND
YUK YUK YUK...
YUCK.

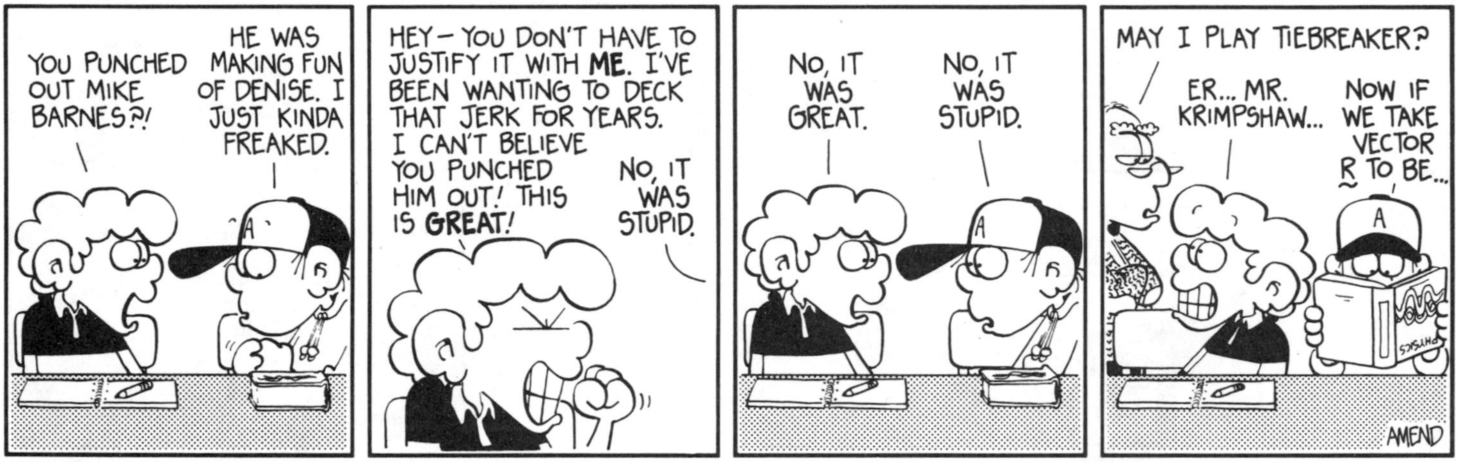
YOU PUNCHED OUT MIKE BARNES?!
HE WAS MAKING FUN OF DENISE. I JUST KINDA FREAKED.
HEY — YOU DON'T HAVE TO JUSTIFY IT WITH **ME**. I'VE BEEN WANTING TO DECK THAT JERK FOR YEARS. I CAN'T BELIEVE YOU PUNCHED HIM OUT! THIS IS **GREAT**!
NO, IT WAS STUPID.
NO, IT WAS GREAT.
NO, IT WAS STUPID.
MAY I PLAY TIEBREAKER?
ER... MR. KRIMPSHAW...
NOW IF WE TAKE VECTOR R TO BE...
AMEND

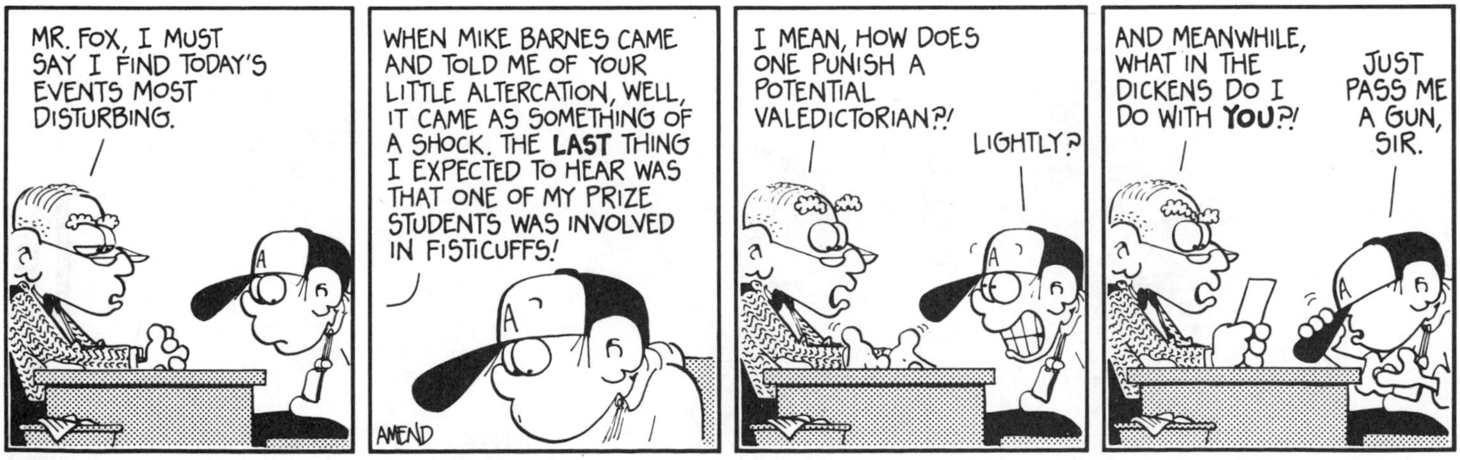
MR. FOX, I MUST SAY I FIND TODAY'S EVENTS MOST DISTURBING.
WHEN MIKE BARNES CAME AND TOLD ME OF YOUR LITTLE ALTERCATION, WELL, IT CAME AS SOMETHING OF A SHOCK. THE **LAST** THING I EXPECTED TO HEAR WAS THAT ONE OF MY PRIZE STUDENTS WAS INVOLVED IN FISTICUFFS!
AMEND
I MEAN, HOW DOES ONE PUNISH A POTENTIAL VALEDICTORIAN?!
LIGHTLY?
AND MEANWHILE, WHAT IN THE DICKENS DO I DO WITH **YOU**?!
JUST PASS ME A GUN, SIR.

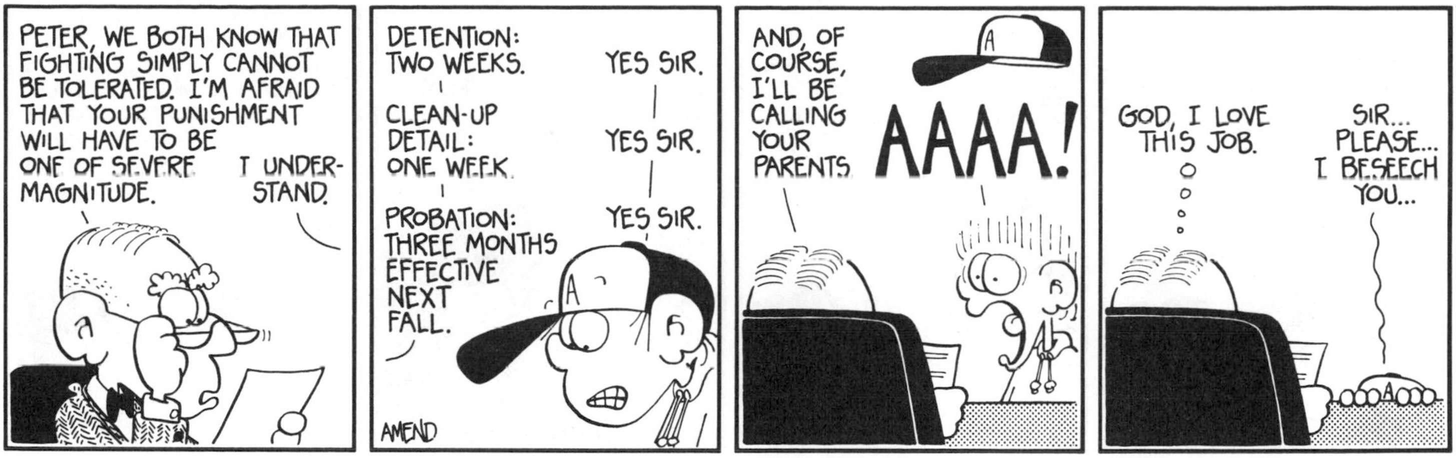
PETER, WE BOTH KNOW THAT FIGHTING SIMPLY CANNOT BE TOLERATED. I'M AFRAID THAT YOUR PUNISHMENT WILL HAVE TO BE ONE OF SEVERE MAGNITUDE.
I UNDERSTAND.
DETENTION: TWO WEEKS.
YES SIR.
CLEAN-UP DETAIL: ONE WEEK.
YES SIR.
PROBATION: THREE MONTHS EFFECTIVE NEXT FALL.
YES SIR.
AMEND
AND, OF COURSE, I'LL BE CALLING YOUR PARENTS.
AAAA!
GOD, I LOVE THIS JOB.
SIR... PLEASE... I BESEECH YOU...

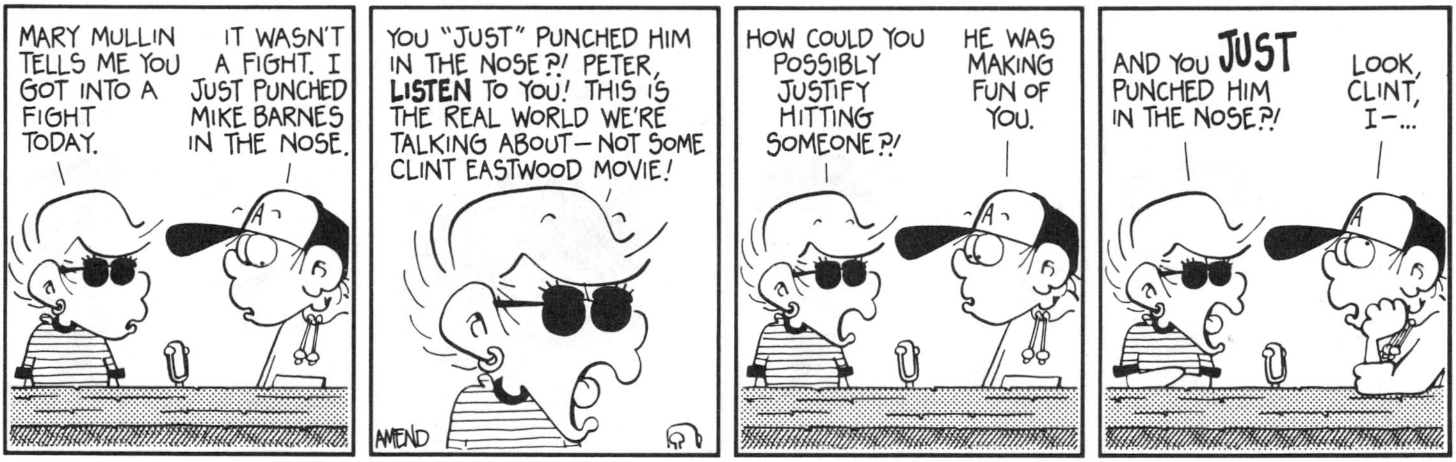
MARY MULLIN TELLS ME YOU GOT INTO A FIGHT TODAY.
IT WASN'T A FIGHT. I JUST PUNCHED MIKE BARNES IN THE NOSE.
YOU "JUST" PUNCHED HIM IN THE NOSE?! PETER, LISTEN TO YOU! THIS IS THE REAL WORLD WE'RE TALKING ABOUT— NOT SOME CLINT EASTWOOD MOVIE!
AMEND
HOW COULD YOU POSSIBLY JUSTIFY HITTING SOMEONE?!
HE WAS MAKING FUN OF YOU.
AND YOU JUST PUNCHED HIM IN THE NOSE?!
LOOK, CLINT, I—...

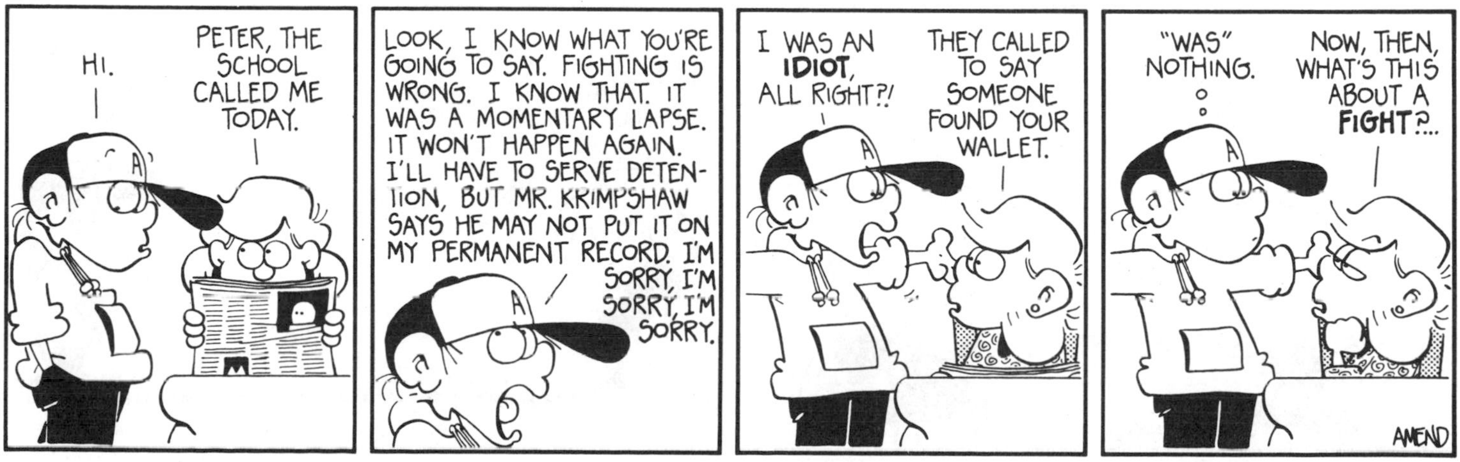
HI.
PETER, THE SCHOOL CALLED ME TODAY.
LOOK, I KNOW WHAT YOU'RE GOING TO SAY. FIGHTING IS WRONG. I KNOW THAT. IT WAS A MOMENTARY LAPSE. IT WON'T HAPPEN AGAIN. I'LL HAVE TO SERVE DETENTION, BUT MR. KRIMPSHAW SAYS HE MAY NOT PUT IT ON MY PERMANENT RECORD. I'M SORRY, I'M SORRY, I'M SORRY.
I WAS AN IDIOT, ALL RIGHT?!
THEY CALLED TO SAY SOMEONE FOUND YOUR WALLET.
"WAS" NOTHING.
NOW, THEN, WHAT'S THIS ABOUT A FIGHT?...
AMEND

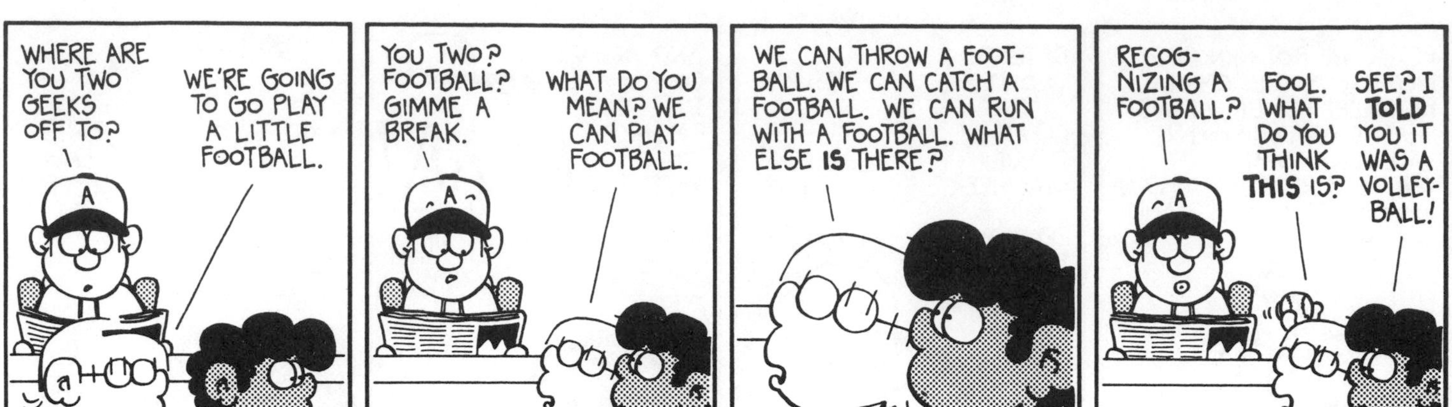
WHERE ARE YOU TWO GEEKS OFF TO?
WE'RE GOING TO GO PLAY A LITTLE FOOTBALL.
YOU TWO? FOOTBALL? GIMME A BREAK.
WHAT DO YOU MEAN? WE CAN PLAY FOOTBALL.
WE CAN THROW A FOOTBALL. WE CAN CATCH A FOOTBALL. WE CAN RUN WITH A FOOTBALL. WHAT ELSE IS THERE?
AMEND
RECOGNIZING A FOOTBALL?
FOOL. WHAT DO YOU THINK THIS IS?
SEE? I TOLD YOU IT WAS A VOLLEYBALL!

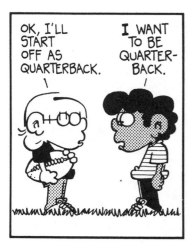

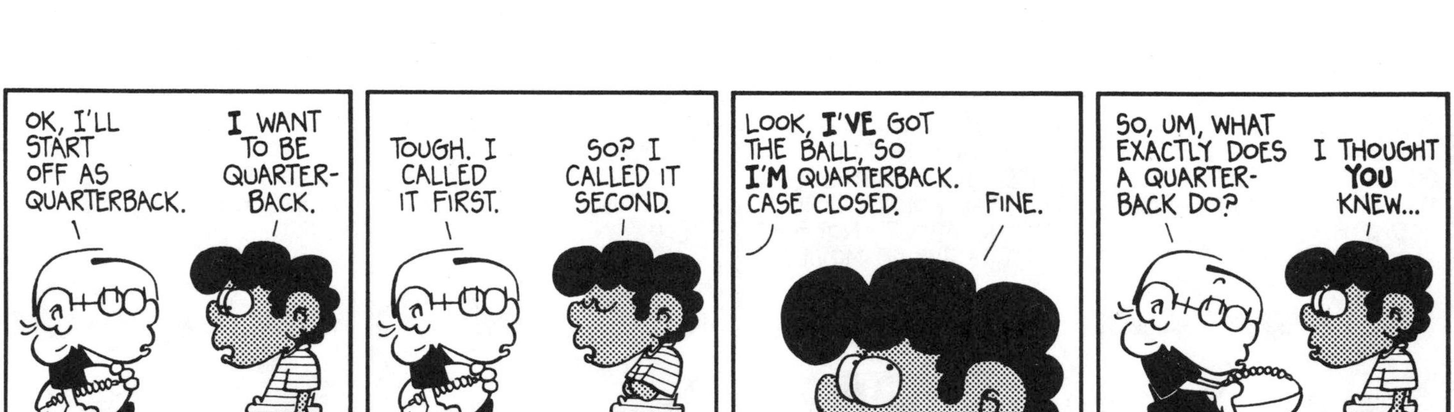
OK, I'LL START OFF AS QUARTERBACK.
I WANT TO BE QUARTERBACK.
TOUGH. I CALLED IT FIRST.
SO? I CALLED IT SECOND.
AMEND
LOOK, I'VE GOT THE BALL, SO I'M QUARTERBACK. CASE CLOSED.
FINE.
SO, UM, WHAT EXACTLY DOES A QUARTERBACK DO?
I THOUGHT YOU KNEW...

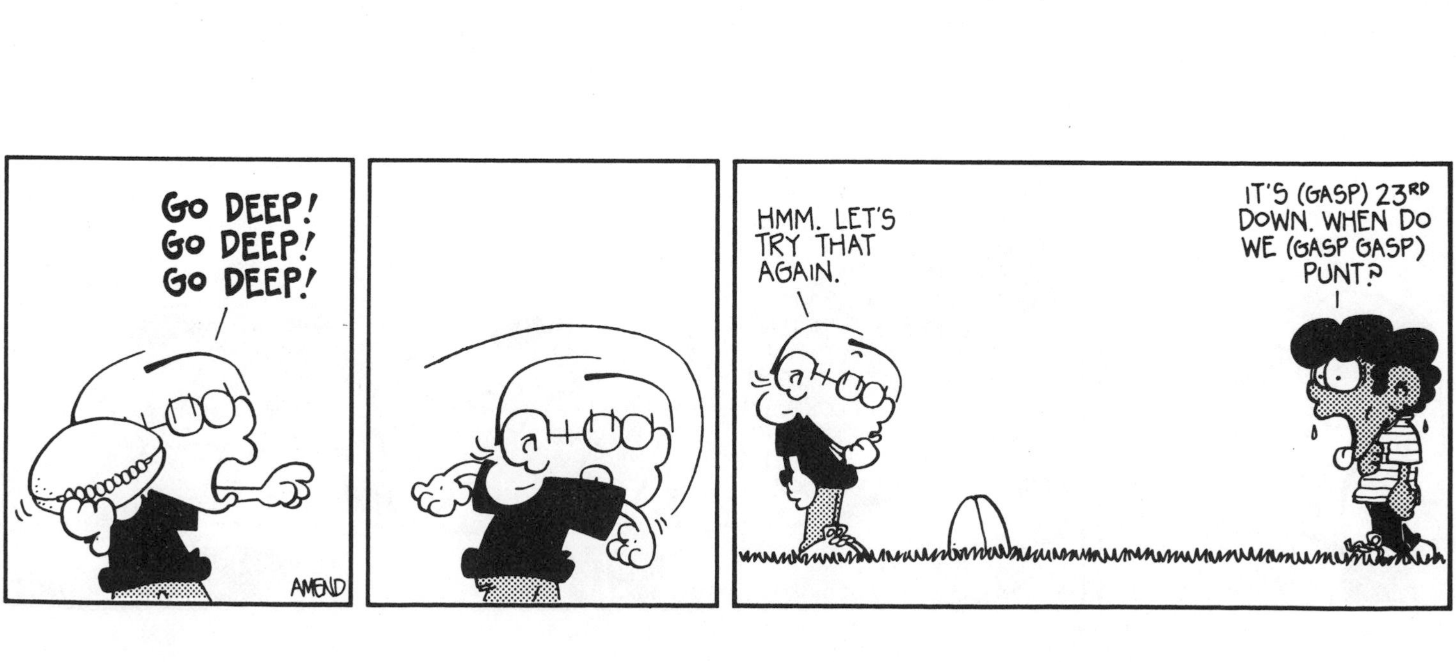
GO DEEP! GO DEEP! GO DEEP!
AMEND
HMM. LET'S TRY THAT AGAIN.
IT'S (GASP) 23RD DOWN. WHEN DO WE (GASP GASP) PUNT?

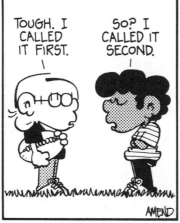

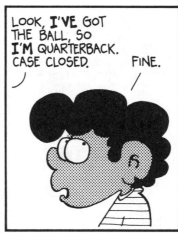

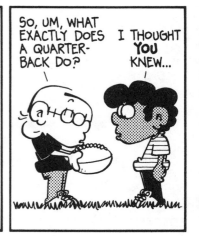

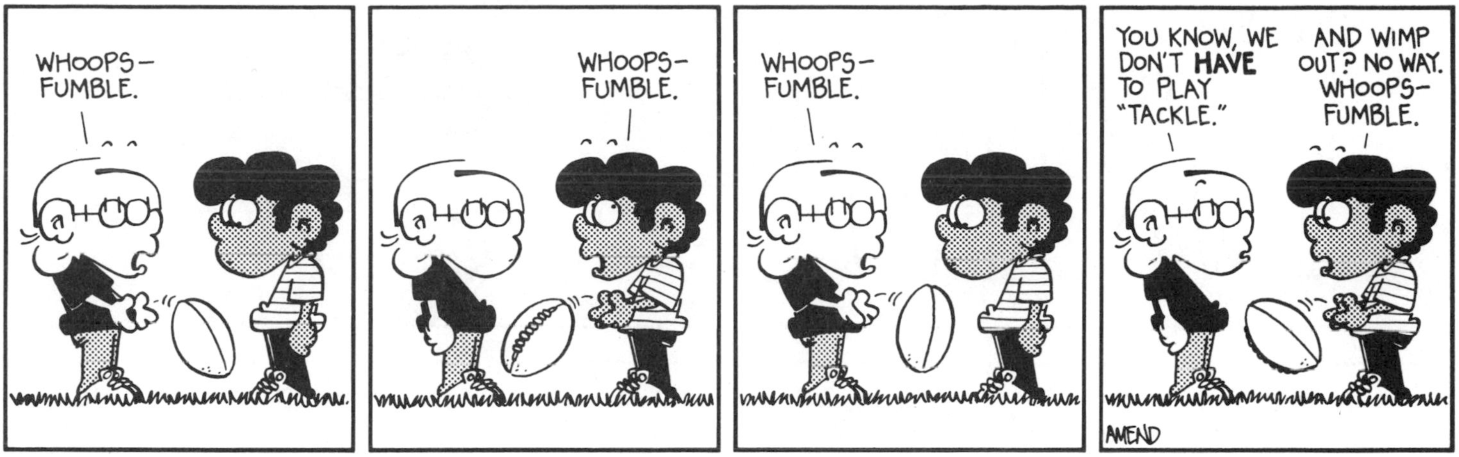
WHOOPS–
FUMBLE.
WHOOPS–
FUMBLE.
WHOOPS–
FUMBLE.
YOU KNOW, WE DON'T **HAVE** TO PLAY "TACKLE."
AND WIMP OUT? NO WAY. WHOOPS– FUMBLE.
AMEND

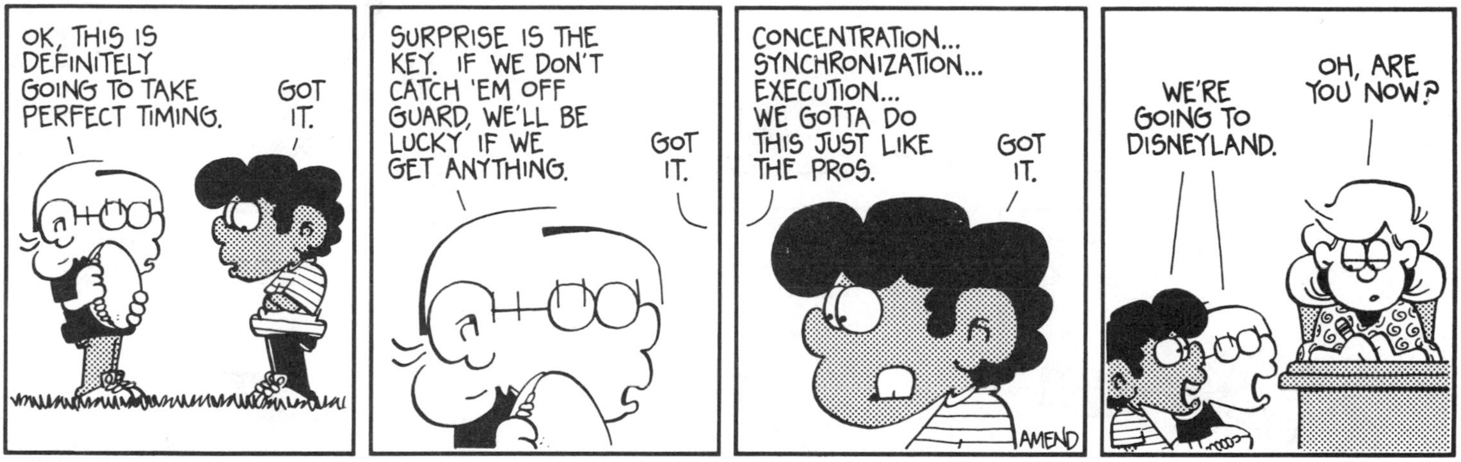
OK, THIS IS DEFINITELY GOING TO TAKE PERFECT TIMING.
GOT IT.
SURPRISE IS THE KEY. IF WE DON'T CATCH 'EM OFF GUARD, WE'LL BE LUCKY IF WE GET ANYTHING.
GOT IT.
CONCENTRATION... SYNCHRONIZATION... EXECUTION... WE GOTTA DO THIS JUST LIKE THE PROS.
GOT IT.
AMEND
WE'RE GOING TO DISNEYLAND.
OH, ARE YOU NOW?

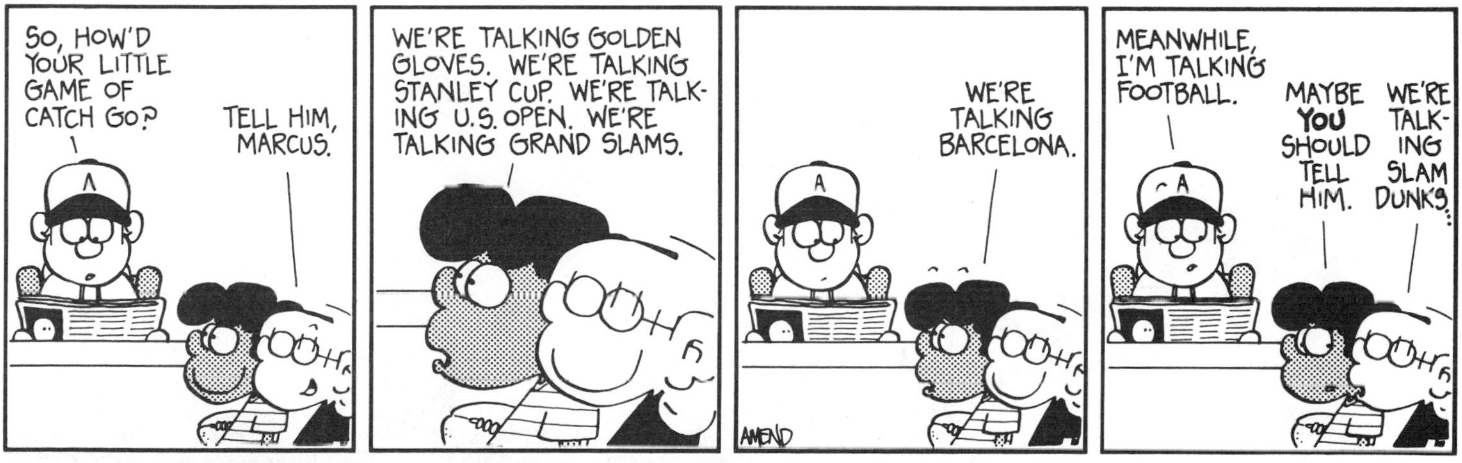
SO, HOW'D YOUR LITTLE GAME OF CATCH GO?
TELL HIM, MARCUS.
WE'RE TALKING GOLDEN GLOVES. WE'RE TALKING STANLEY CUP. WE'RE TALKING U.S. OPEN. WE'RE TALKING GRAND SLAMS.
WE'RE TALKING BARCELONA.
AMEND
MEANWHILE, I'M TALKING FOOTBALL.
MAYBE **YOU** SHOULD TELL HIM.
WE'RE TALKING SLAM DUNKS...

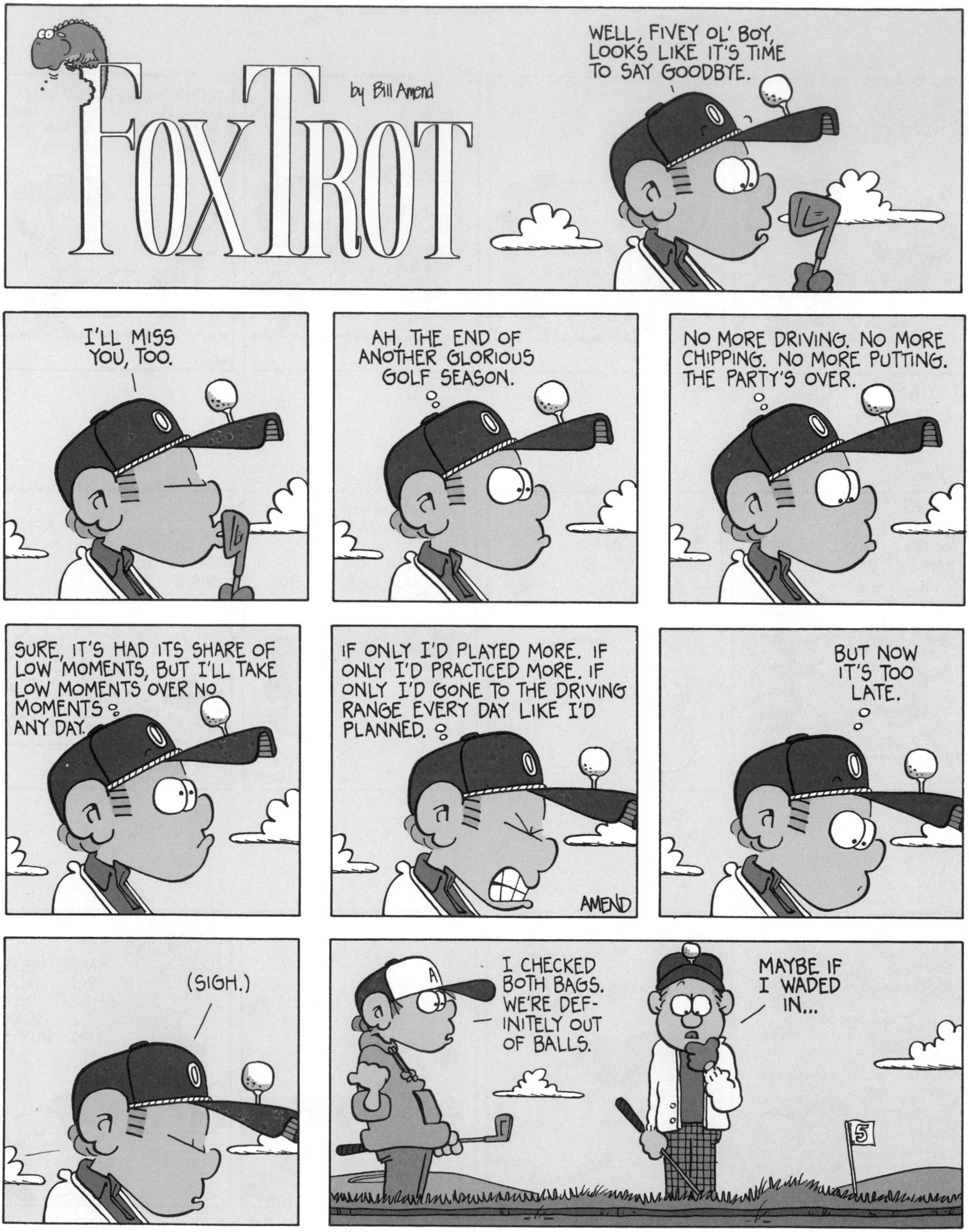
FoxTrot
by Bill Amend
WELL, FIVEY OL' BOY, LOOKS LIKE IT'S TIME TO SAY GOODBYE.
I'LL MISS YOU, TOO.
AH, THE END OF ANOTHER GLORIOUS GOLF SEASON.
NO MORE DRIVING. NO MORE CHIPPING. NO MORE PUTTING. THE PARTY'S OVER.
SURE, IT'S HAD ITS SHARE OF LOW MOMENTS, BUT I'LL TAKE LOW MOMENTS OVER NO MOMENTS ANY DAY.
IF ONLY I'D PLAYED MORE. IF ONLY I'D PRACTICED MORE. IF ONLY I'D GONE TO THE DRIVING RANGE EVERY DAY LIKE I'D PLANNED.
AMEND
BUT NOW IT'S TOO LATE.
(SIGH.)
I CHECKED BOTH BAGS. WE'RE DEFINITELY OUT OF BALLS.
MAYBE IF I WADED IN...
5

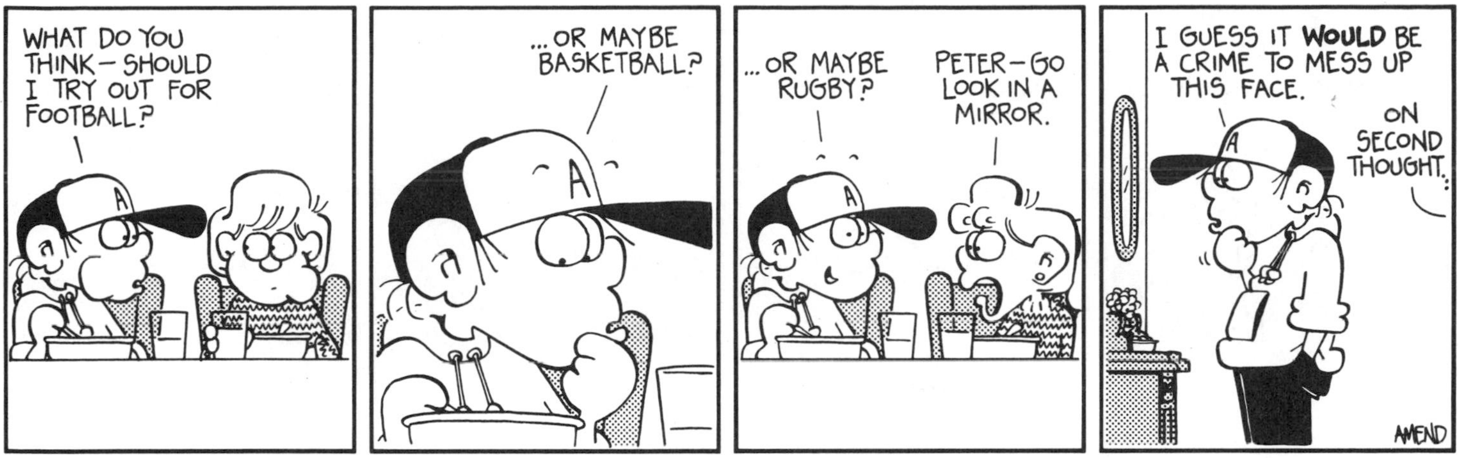
WHAT DO YOU THINK—SHOULD I TRY OUT FOR FOOTBALL?
...OR MAYBE BASKETBALL?
...OR MAYBE RUGBY?
PETER—GO LOOK IN A MIRROR.
I GUESS IT **WOULD** BE A CRIME TO MESS UP THIS FACE.
ON SECOND THOUGHT...
AMEND

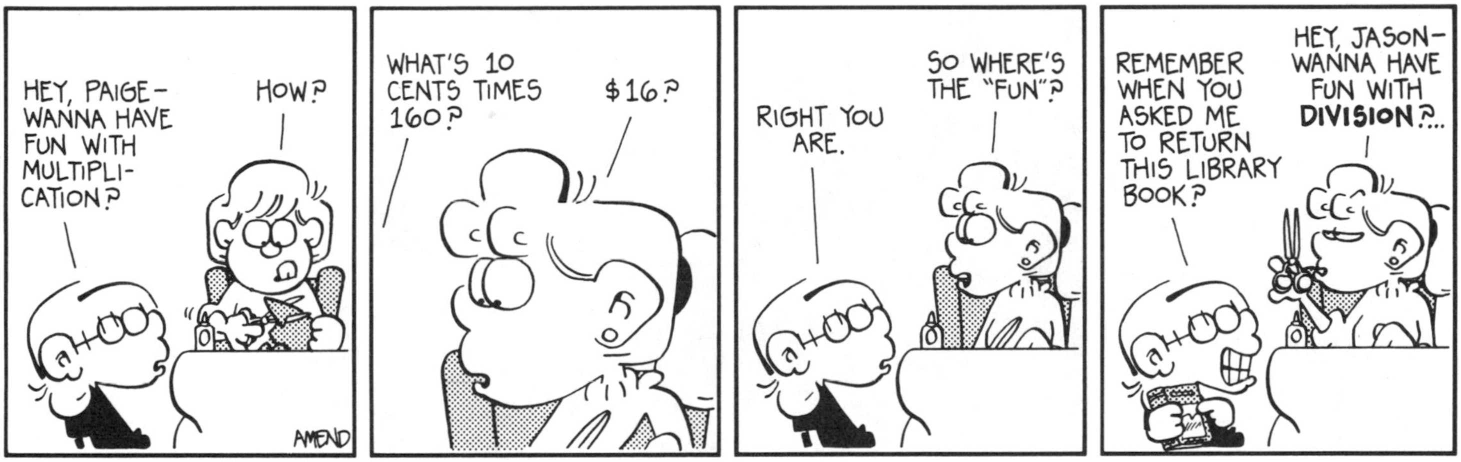
HEY, PAIGE—WANNA HAVE FUN WITH MULTIPLI-CATION?
HOW?
AMEND
WHAT'S 10 CENTS TIMES 160?
$16?
RIGHT YOU ARE.
SO WHERE'S THE "FUN"?
REMEMBER WHEN YOU ASKED ME TO RETURN THIS LIBRARY BOOK?
HEY, JASON—WANNA HAVE FUN WITH **DIVISION**?...

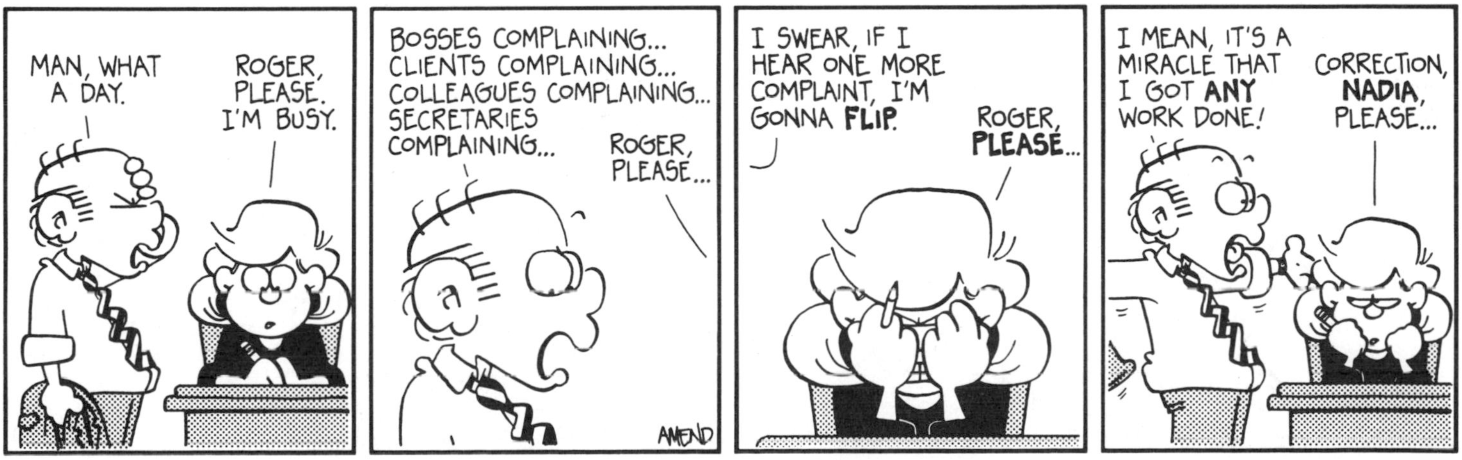
MAN, WHAT A DAY.
ROGER, PLEASE. I'M BUSY.
BOSSES COMPLAINING... CLIENTS COMPLAINING... COLLEAGUES COMPLAINING... SECRETARIES COMPLAINING...
ROGER, PLEASE...
AMEND
I SWEAR, IF I HEAR ONE MORE COMPLAINT, I'M GONNA **FLIP**.
ROGER, **PLEASE**...
I MEAN, IT'S A MIRACLE THAT I GOT **ANY** WORK DONE!
CORRECTION, **NADIA**, PLEASE...

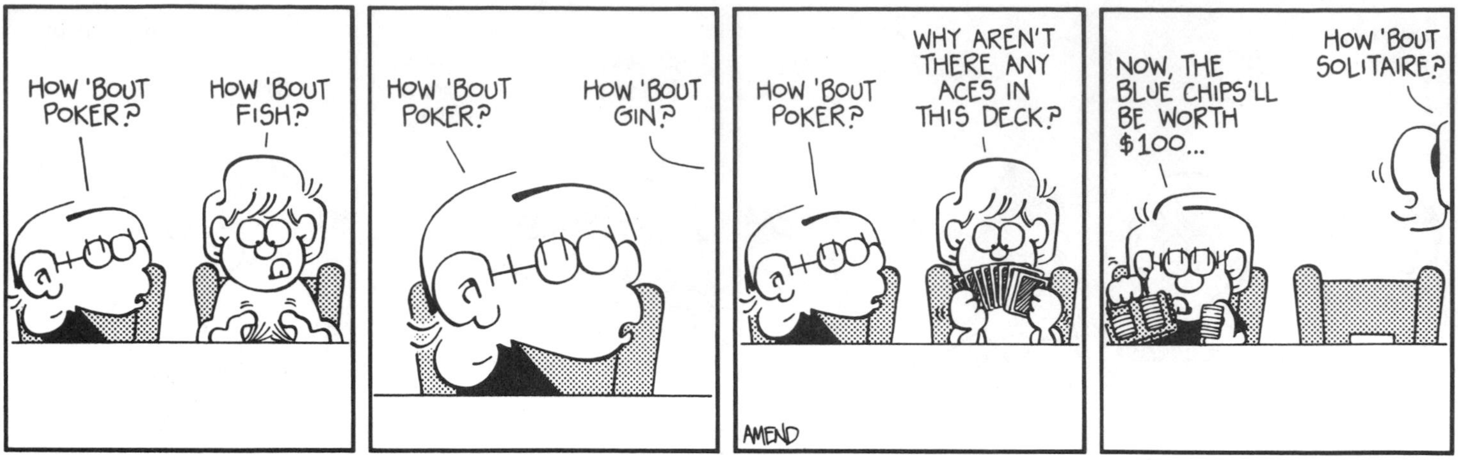
HOW 'BOUT POKER?
HOW 'BOUT FISH?
HOW 'BOUT POKER?
HOW 'BOUT GIN?
HOW 'BOUT POKER?
WHY AREN'T THERE ANY ACES IN THIS DECK?
AMEND
NOW, THE BLUE CHIPS'LL BE WORTH $100...
HOW 'BOUT SOLITAIRE?

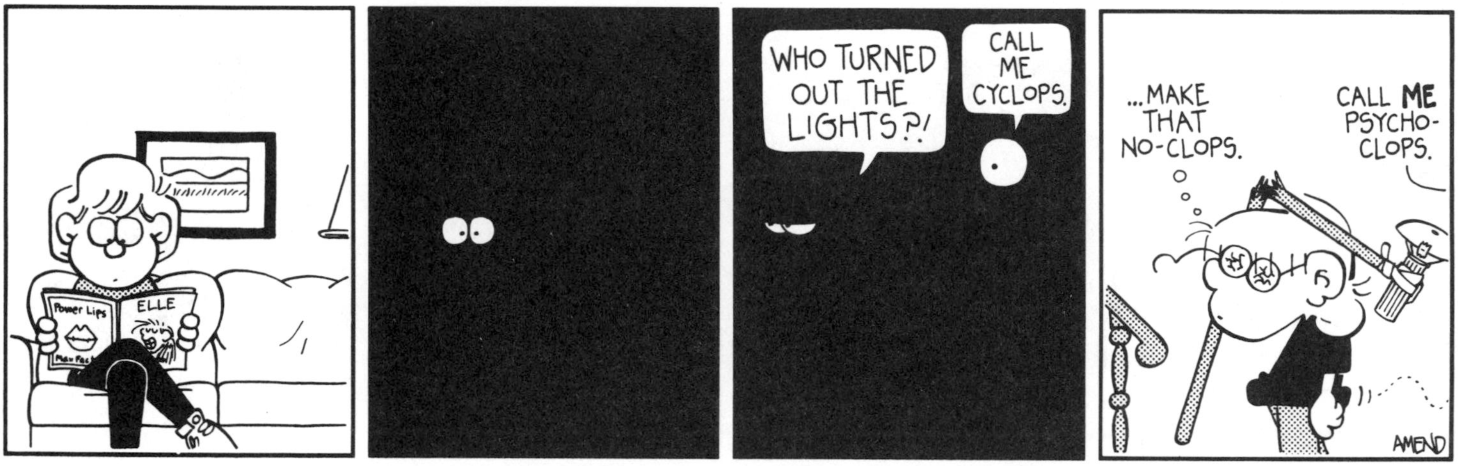
Power Lips
ELLE
WHO TURNED OUT THE LIGHTS?!
CALL ME CYCLOPS.
...MAKE THAT NO-CLOPS.
CALL **ME** PSYCHO-CLOPS.
AMEND

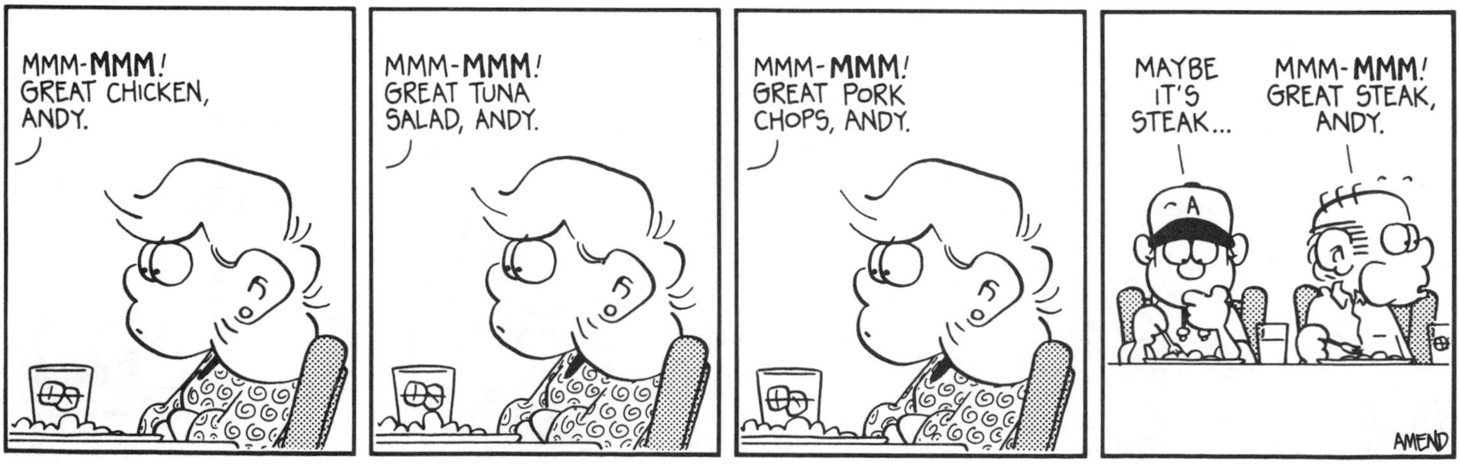
MMM-**MMM**! GREAT CHICKEN, ANDY.
MMM-**MMM**! GREAT TUNA SALAD, ANDY.
MMM-**MMM**! GREAT PORK CHOPS, ANDY.
MAYBE IT'S STEAK...
MMM-**MMM**! GREAT STEAK, ANDY.
A
AMEND

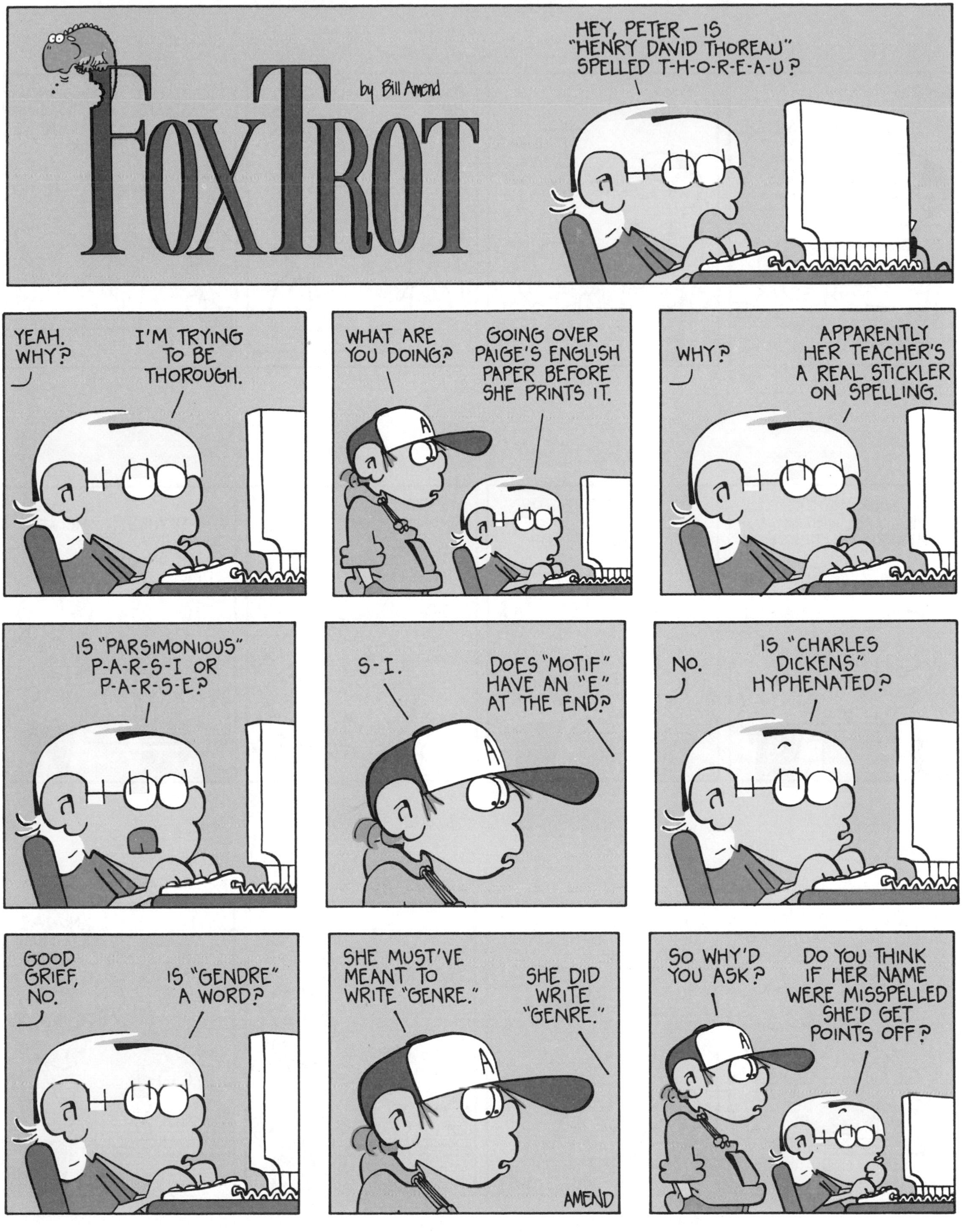
FoxTrot
by Bill Amend
HEY, PETER — IS "HENRY DAVID THOREAU" SPELLED T-H-O-R-E-A-U?
YEAH. WHY?
I'M TRYING TO BE THOROUGH.
WHAT ARE YOU DOING?
GOING OVER PAIGE'S ENGLISH PAPER BEFORE SHE PRINTS IT.
WHY?
APPARENTLY HER TEACHER'S A REAL STICKLER ON SPELLING.
IS "PARSIMONIOUS" P-A-R-S-I OR P-A-R-S-E?
S-I.
DOES "MOTIF" HAVE AN "E" AT THE END?
NO.
IS "CHARLES DICKENS" HYPHENATED?
GOOD GRIEF, NO.
IS "GENDRE" A WORD?
SHE MUST'VE MEANT TO WRITE "GENRE."
SHE DID WRITE "GENRE."
AMEND
SO WHY'D YOU ASK?
DO YOU THINK IF HER NAME WERE MISSPELLED SHE'D GET POINTS OFF?

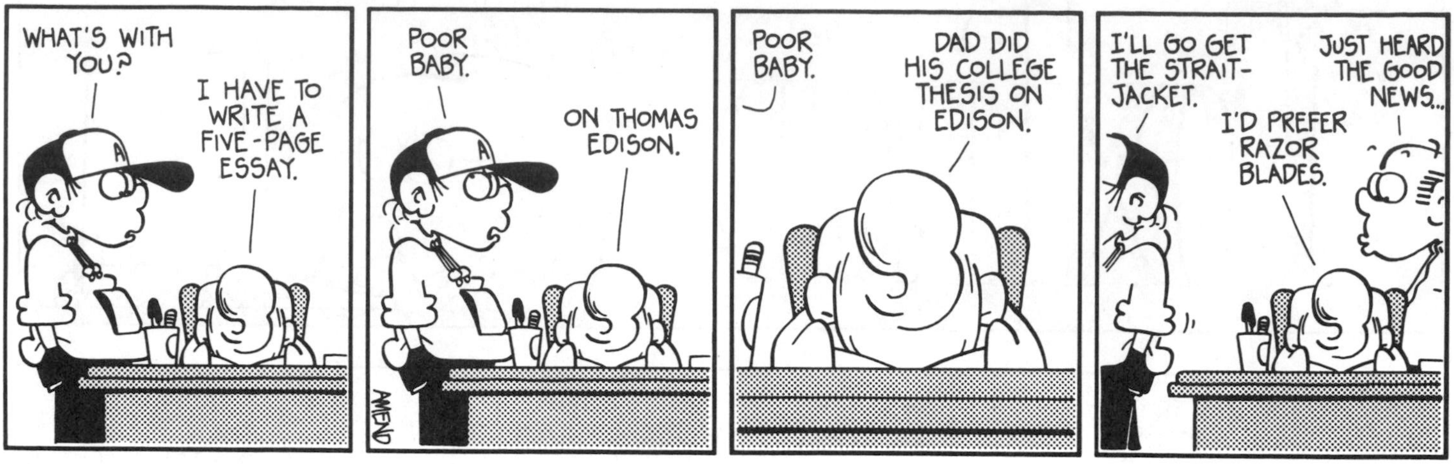
WHAT'S WITH YOU?
I HAVE TO WRITE A FIVE-PAGE ESSAY.
POOR BABY.
ON THOMAS EDISON.
POOR BABY.
DAD DID HIS COLLEGE THESIS ON EDISON.
I'LL GO GET THE STRAIT-JACKET.
JUST HEARD THE GOOD NEWS...
I'D PREFER RAZOR BLADES.
AMEND

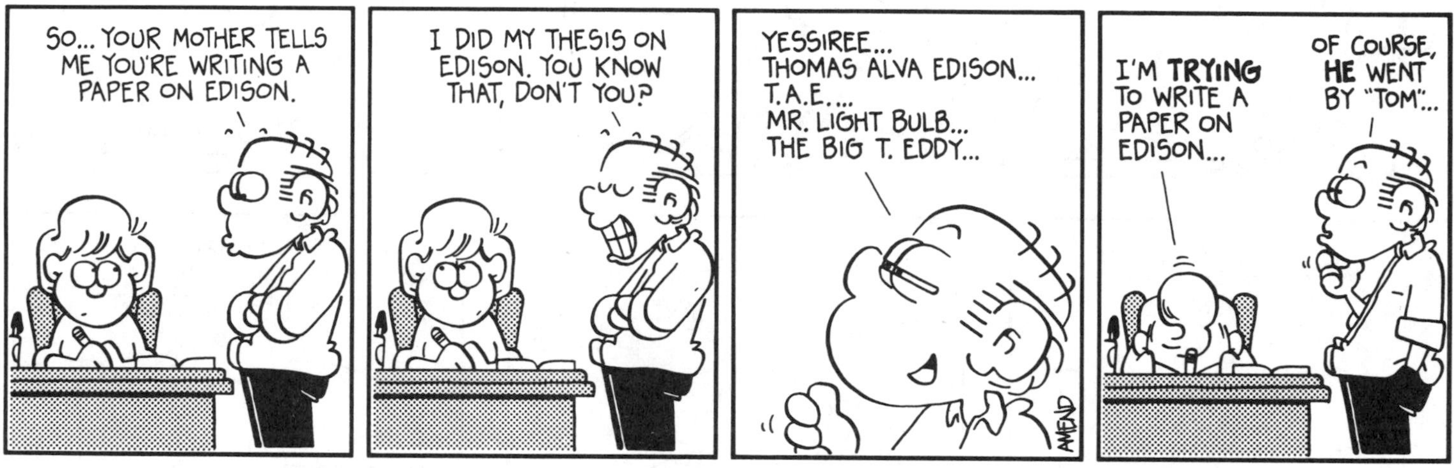
SO... YOUR MOTHER TELLS ME YOU'RE WRITING A PAPER ON EDISON.
I DID MY THESIS ON EDISON. YOU KNOW THAT, DON'T YOU?
YESSIREE... THOMAS ALVA EDISON... T.A.E.... MR. LIGHT BULB... THE BIG T. EDDY...
I'M **TRYING** TO WRITE A PAPER ON EDISON...
OF COURSE, **HE** WENT BY "TOM"...
AMEND

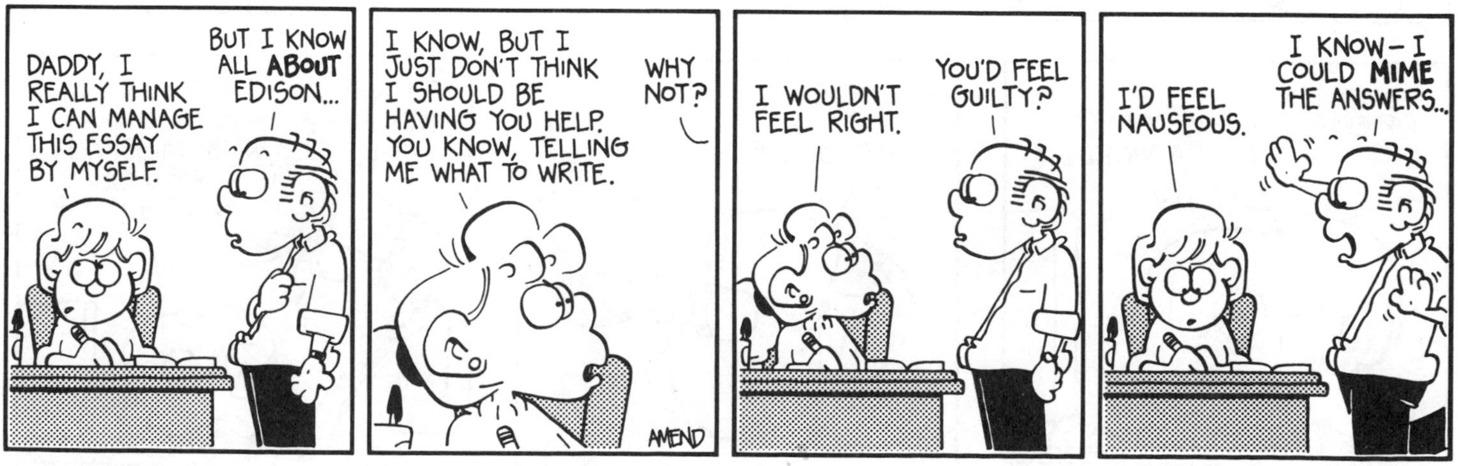
DADDY, I REALLY THINK I CAN MANAGE THIS ESSAY BY MYSELF.
BUT I KNOW ALL **ABOUT** EDISON...
I KNOW, BUT I JUST DON'T THINK I SHOULD BE HAVING YOU HELP. YOU KNOW, TELLING ME WHAT TO WRITE.
WHY NOT?
I WOULDN'T FEEL RIGHT.
YOU'D FEEL GUILTY?
I'D FEEL NAUSEOUS.
I KNOW – I COULD **MIME** THE ANSWERS...
AMEND

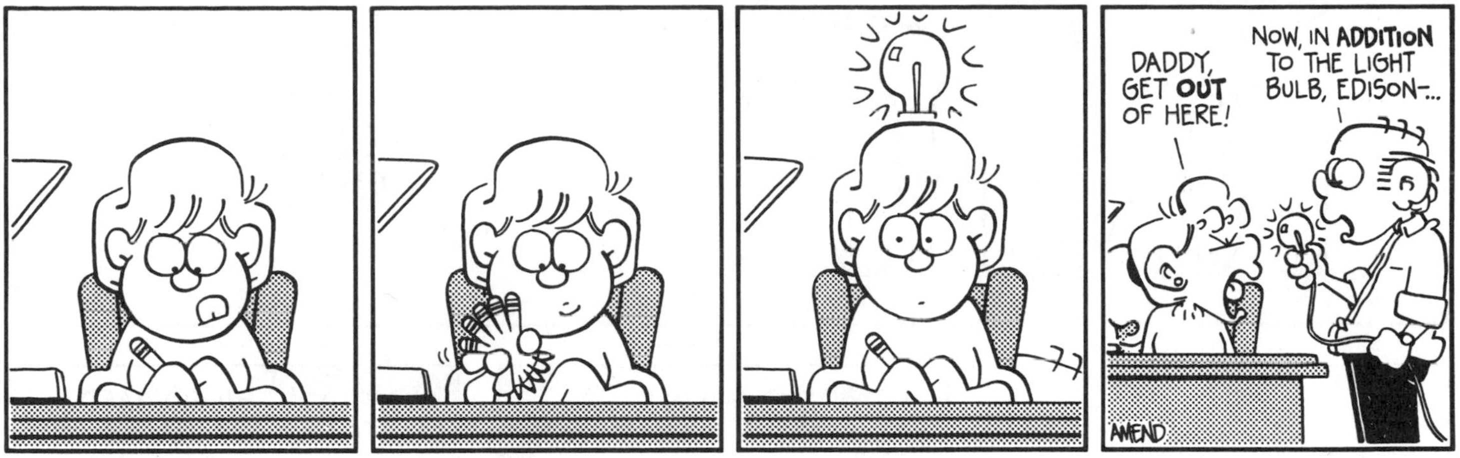
DADDY, GET OUT OF HERE!
NOW, IN ADDITION TO THE LIGHT BULB, EDISON-...
AMEND

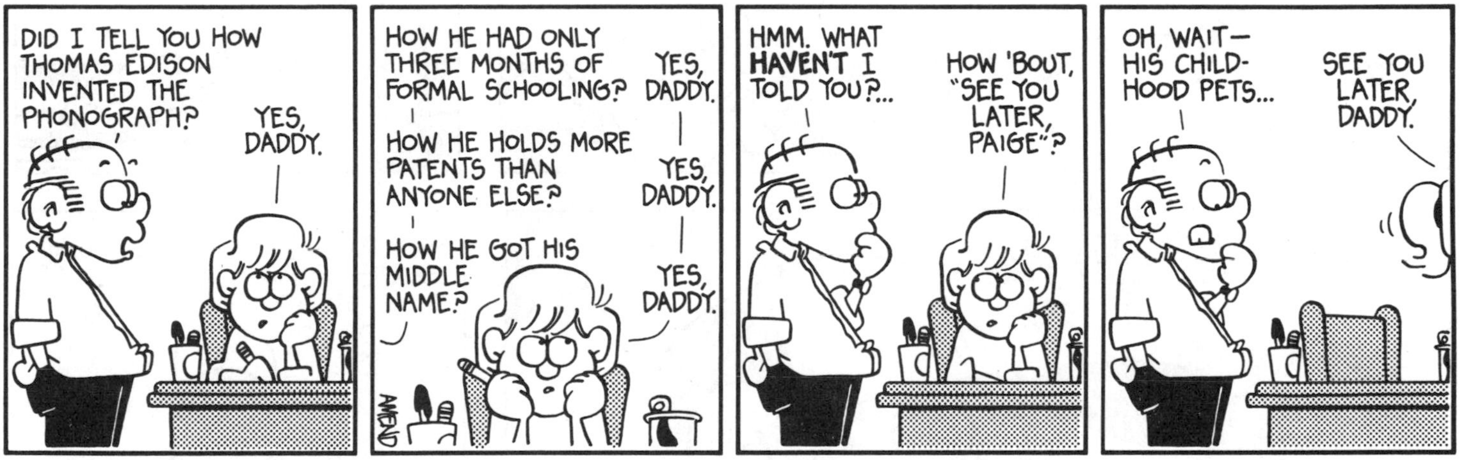
DID I TELL YOU HOW THOMAS EDISON INVENTED THE PHONOGRAPH?
YES, DADDY.
HOW HE HAD ONLY THREE MONTHS OF FORMAL SCHOOLING?
YES, DADDY.
HOW HE HOLDS MORE PATENTS THAN ANYONE ELSE?
YES, DADDY.
HOW HE GOT HIS MIDDLE NAME?
YES, DADDY.
AMEND
HMM. WHAT HAVEN'T I TOLD YOU?...
HOW 'BOUT, "SEE YOU LATER, PAIGE"?
OH, WAIT— HIS CHILDHOOD PETS...
SEE YOU LATER, DADDY.

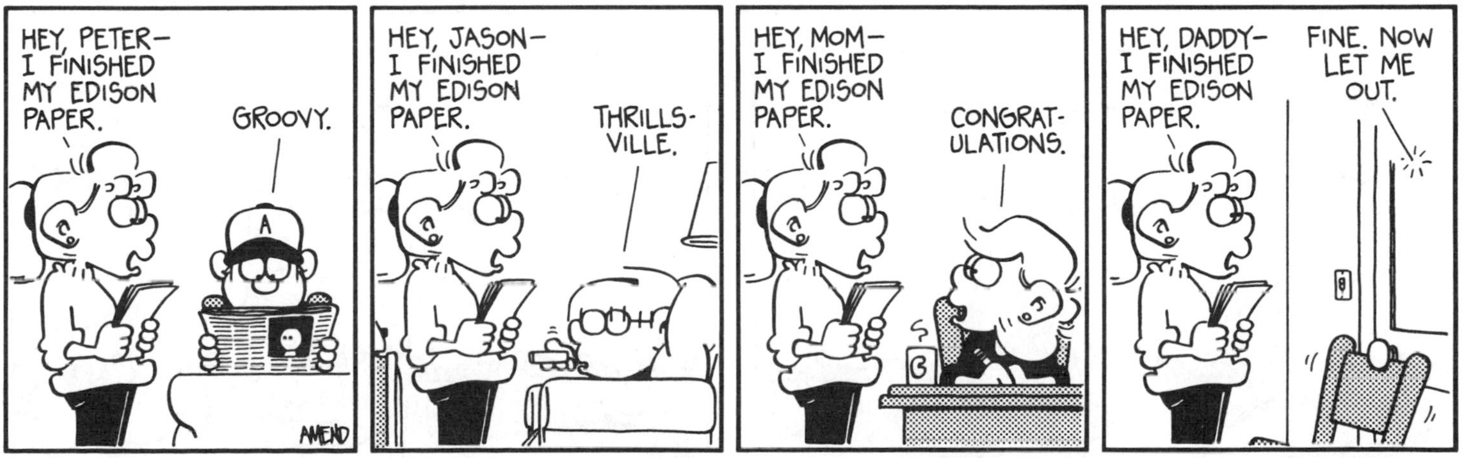
HEY, PETER— I FINISHED MY EDISON PAPER.
GROOVY.
AMEND
HEY, JASON— I FINISHED MY EDISON PAPER.
THRILLSVILLE.
HEY, MOM— I FINISHED MY EDISON PAPER.
CONGRATULATIONS.
HEY, DADDY— I FINISHED MY EDISON PAPER.
FINE. NOW LET ME OUT.

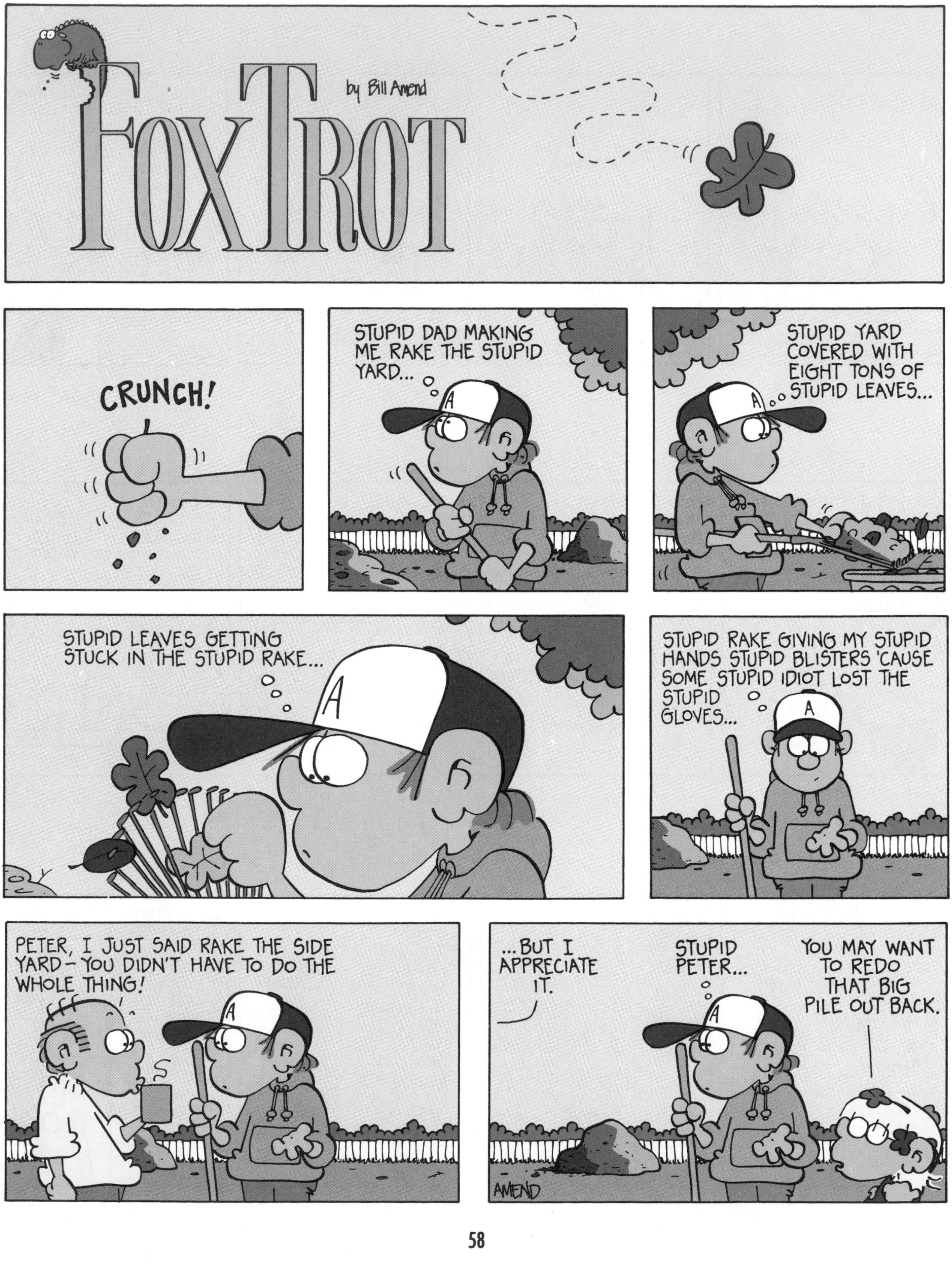
FoxTrot
by Bill Amend
CRUNCH!
STUPID DAD MAKING ME RAKE THE STUPID YARD...
STUPID YARD COVERED WITH EIGHT TONS OF STUPID LEAVES...
STUPID LEAVES GETTING STUCK IN THE STUPID RAKE...
STUPID RAKE GIVING MY STUPID HANDS STUPID BLISTERS 'CAUSE SOME STUPID IDIOT LOST THE STUPID GLOVES...
PETER, I JUST SAID RAKE THE SIDE YARD – YOU DIDN'T HAVE TO DO THE WHOLE THING!
...BUT I APPRECIATE IT.
STUPID PETER...
YOU MAY WANT TO REDO THAT BIG PILE OUT BACK.
AMEND

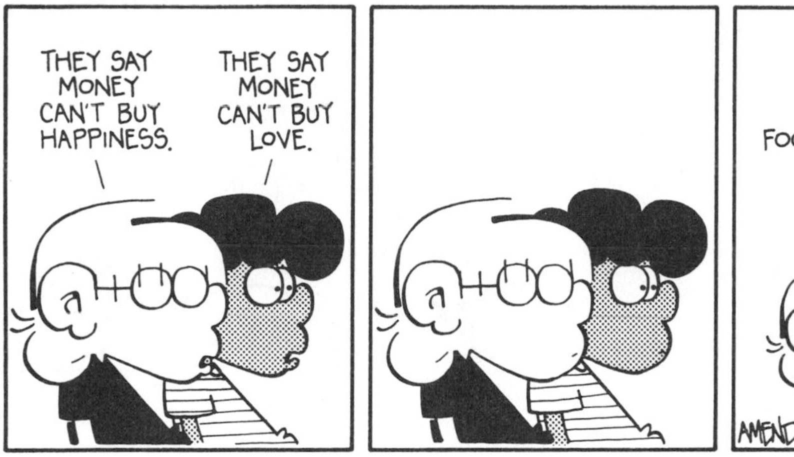
THEY SAY MONEY CAN'T BUY HAPPINESS.
THEY SAY MONEY CAN'T BUY LOVE.
FOOLS.
MAYBE WE COULD JUST GO IN AND **TOUCH** IT...
Televis
SUPER NINTENDO NOW IN STOCK! ONLY $198⁰⁰
VISA
AMEND

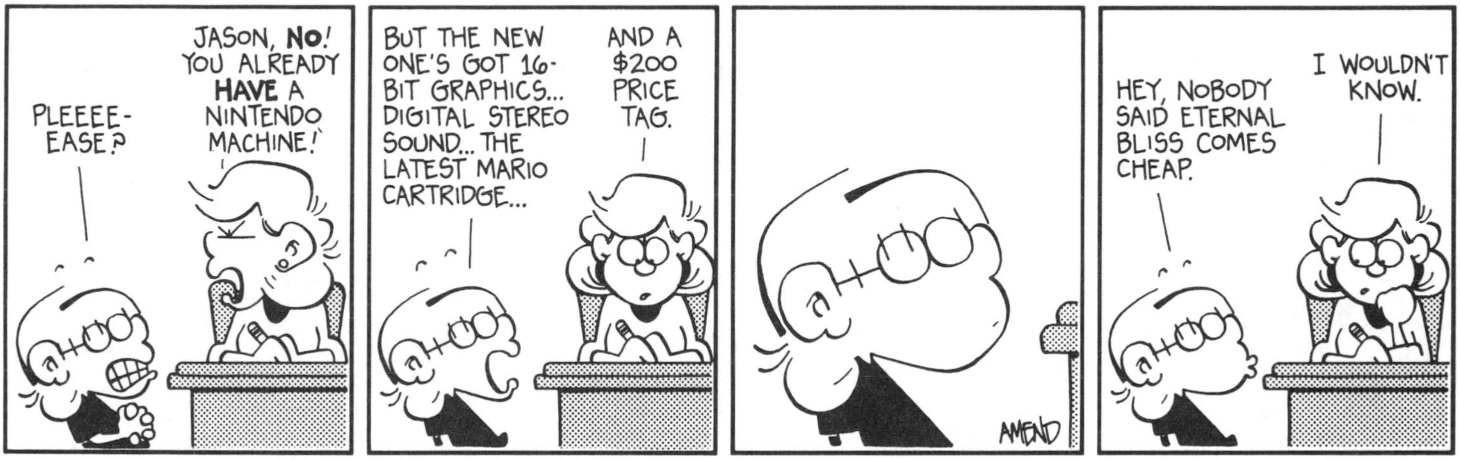
PLEEEE-EASE?
JASON, **NO**! YOU ALREADY **HAVE** A NINTENDO MACHINE!
BUT THE NEW ONE'S GOT 16-BIT GRAPHICS... DIGITAL STEREO SOUND... THE LATEST MARIO CARTRIDGE...
AND A $200 PRICE TAG.
AMEND
HEY, NOBODY SAID ETERNAL BLISS COMES CHEAP.
I WOULDN'T KNOW.

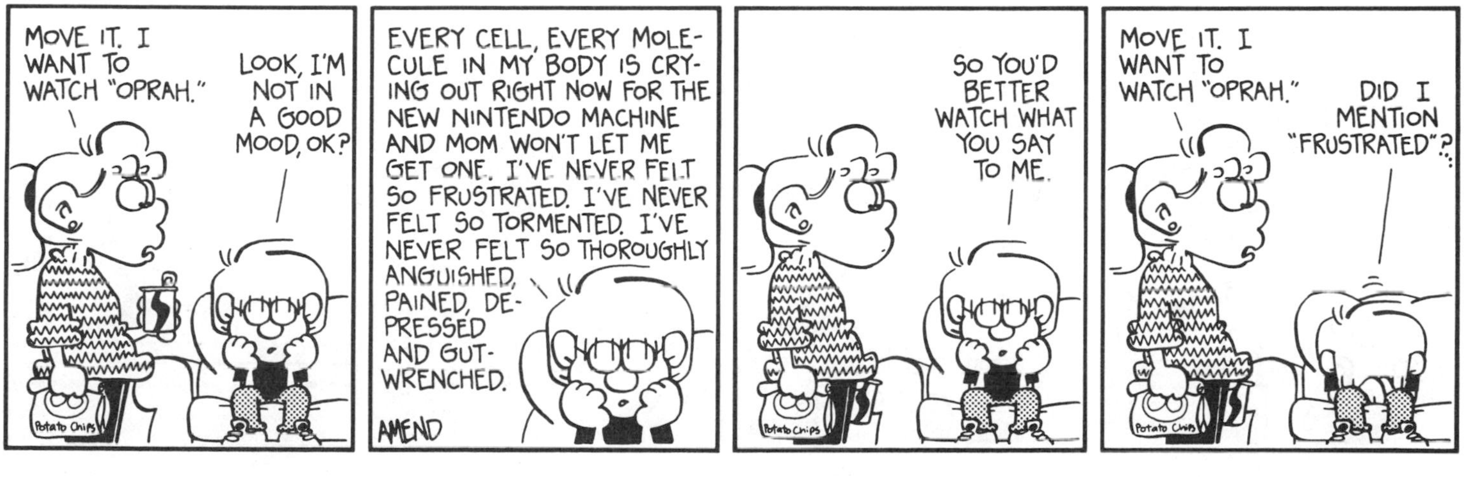
MOVE IT. I WANT TO WATCH "OPRAH."
LOOK, I'M NOT IN A GOOD MOOD, OK?
Potato Chips
EVERY CELL, EVERY MOLECULE IN MY BODY IS CRYING OUT RIGHT NOW FOR THE NEW NINTENDO MACHINE AND MOM WON'T LET ME GET ONE. I'VE NEVER FELT SO FRUSTRATED. I'VE NEVER FELT SO TORMENTED. I'VE NEVER FELT SO THOROUGHLY ANGUISHED, PAINED, DEPRESSED AND GUT-WRENCHED.
AMEND
SO YOU'D BETTER WATCH WHAT YOU SAY TO ME.
Potato Chips
MOVE IT. I WANT TO WATCH "OPRAH."
DID I MENTION "FRUSTRATED"?
Potato Chips

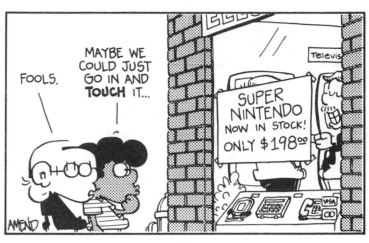

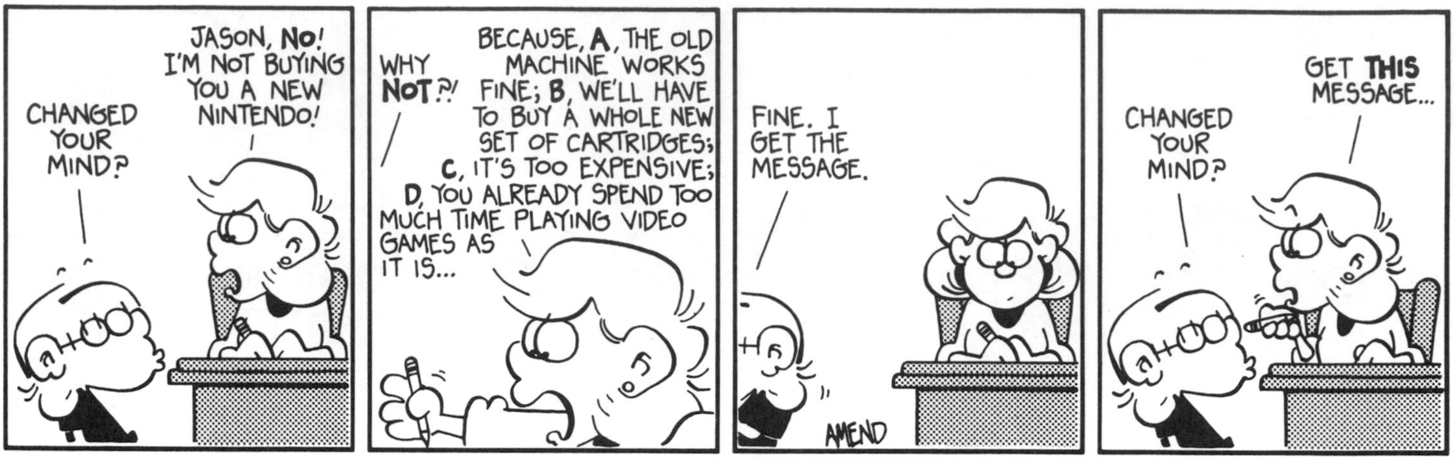
CHANGED YOUR MIND?
JASON, NO! I'M NOT BUYING YOU A NEW NINTENDO!
WHY NOT?!
BECAUSE, A, THE OLD MACHINE WORKS FINE; B, WE'LL HAVE TO BUY A WHOLE NEW SET OF CARTRIDGES; C, IT'S TOO EXPENSIVE; D, YOU ALREADY SPEND TOO MUCH TIME PLAYING VIDEO GAMES AS IT IS...
FINE. I GET THE MESSAGE.
AMEND
CHANGED YOUR MIND?
GET THIS MESSAGE...

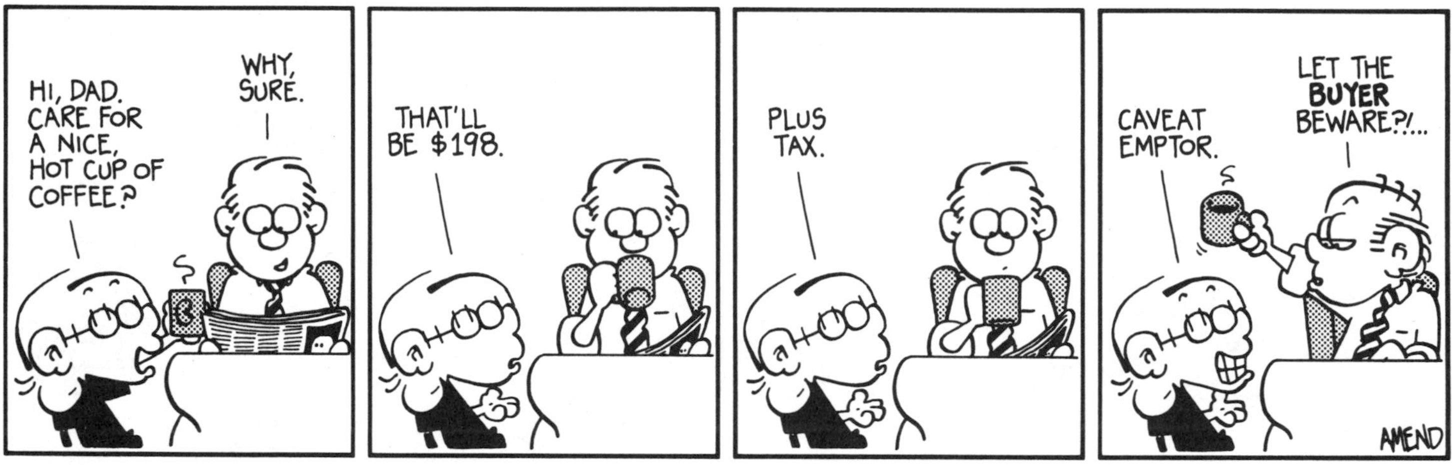
HI, DAD. CARE FOR A NICE, HOT CUP OF COFFEE?
WHY, SURE.
THAT'LL BE $198.
PLUS TAX.
CAVEAT EMPTOR.
LET THE BUYER BEWARE?!...
AMEND

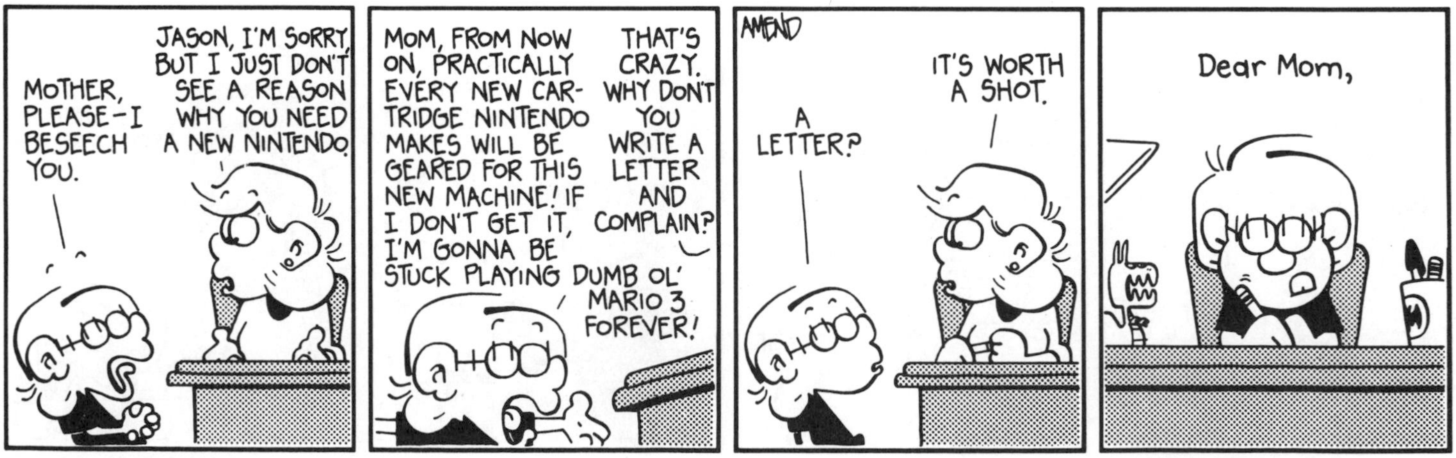
MOTHER, PLEASE-I BESEECH YOU.
JASON, I'M SORRY, BUT I JUST DON'T SEE A REASON WHY YOU NEED A NEW NINTENDO.
MOM, FROM NOW ON, PRACTICALLY EVERY NEW CARTRIDGE NINTENDO MAKES WILL BE GEARED FOR THIS NEW MACHINE! IF I DON'T GET IT, I'M GONNA BE STUCK PLAYING DUMB OL' MARIO 3 FOREVER!
THAT'S CRAZY. WHY DON'T YOU WRITE A LETTER AND COMPLAIN?
AMEND
A LETTER?
IT'S WORTH A SHOT.
Dear Mom,

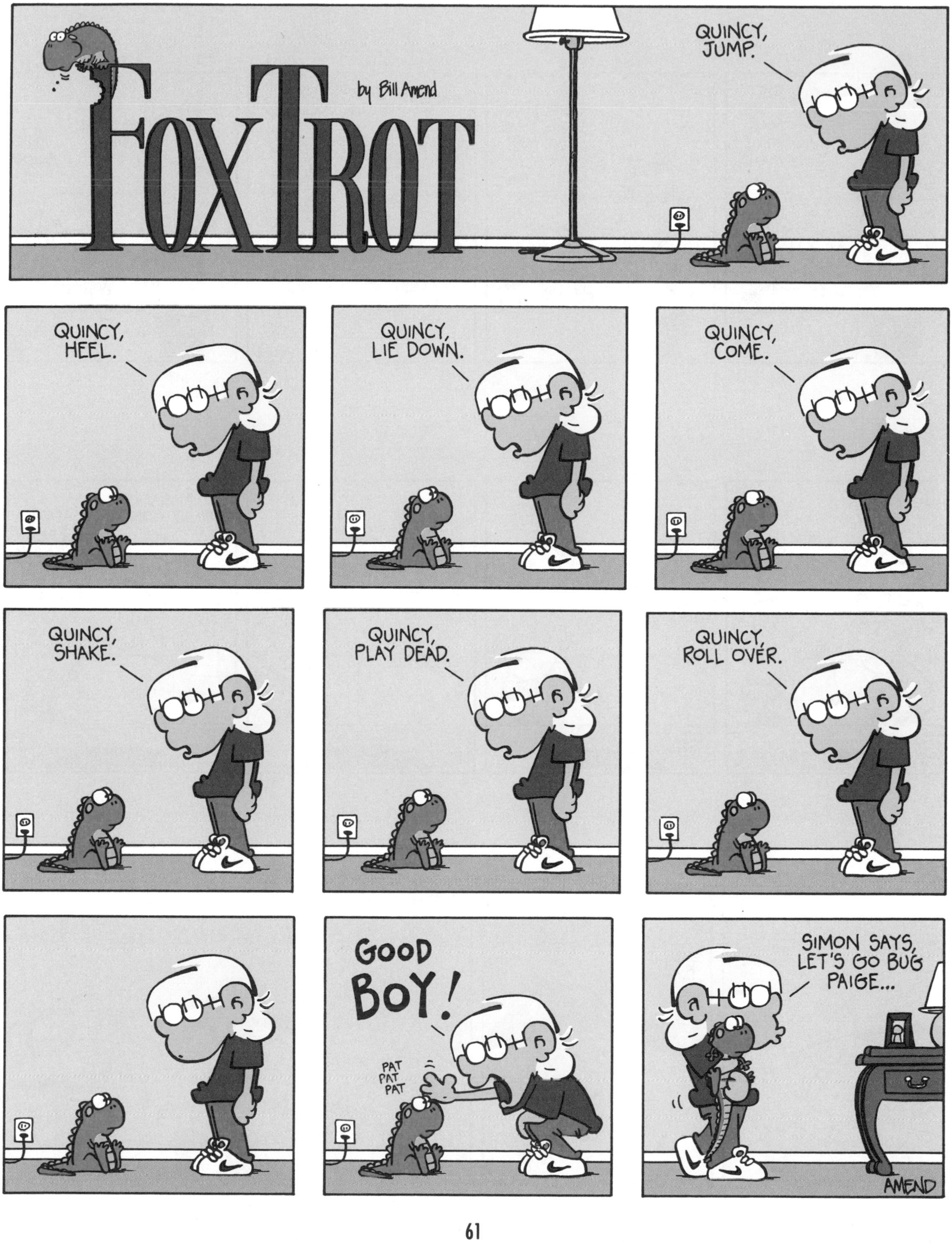
FoxTrot
by Bill Amend
QUINCY, JUMP.
QUINCY, HEEL.
QUINCY, LIE DOWN.
QUINCY, COME.
QUINCY, SHAKE.
QUINCY, PLAY DEAD.
QUINCY, ROLL OVER.
GOOD BOY!
PAT PAT PAT
SIMON SAYS, LET'S GO BUG PAIGE...
AMEND

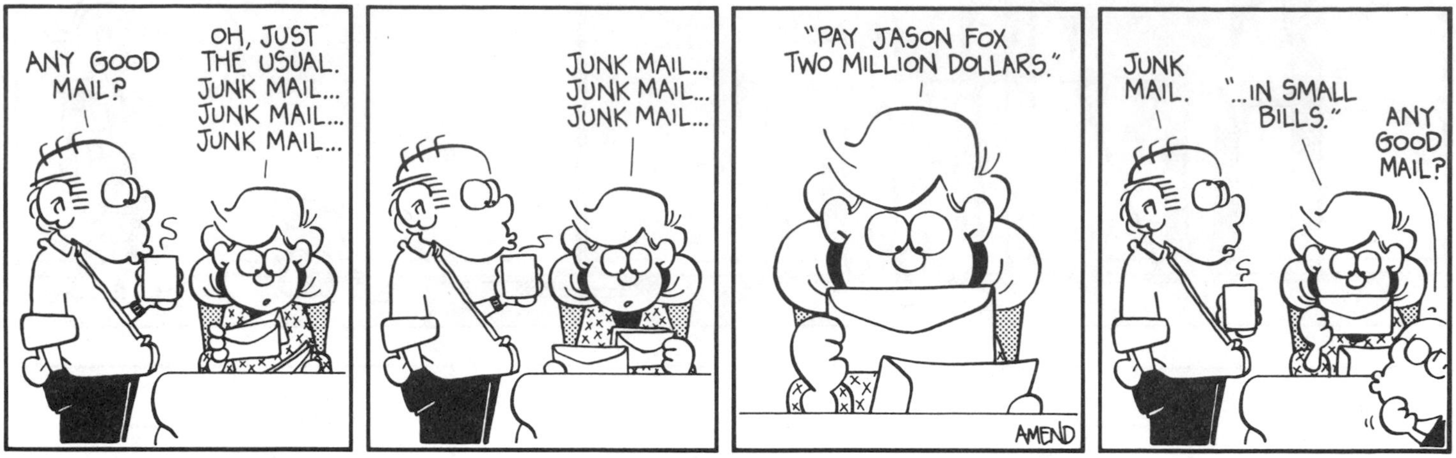
ANY GOOD MAIL?
OH, JUST THE USUAL. JUNK MAIL... JUNK MAIL... JUNK MAIL...
JUNK MAIL... JUNK MAIL... JUNK MAIL...
"PAY JASON FOX TWO MILLION DOLLARS."
AMEND
JUNK MAIL.
"...IN SMALL BILLS."
ANY GOOD MAIL?

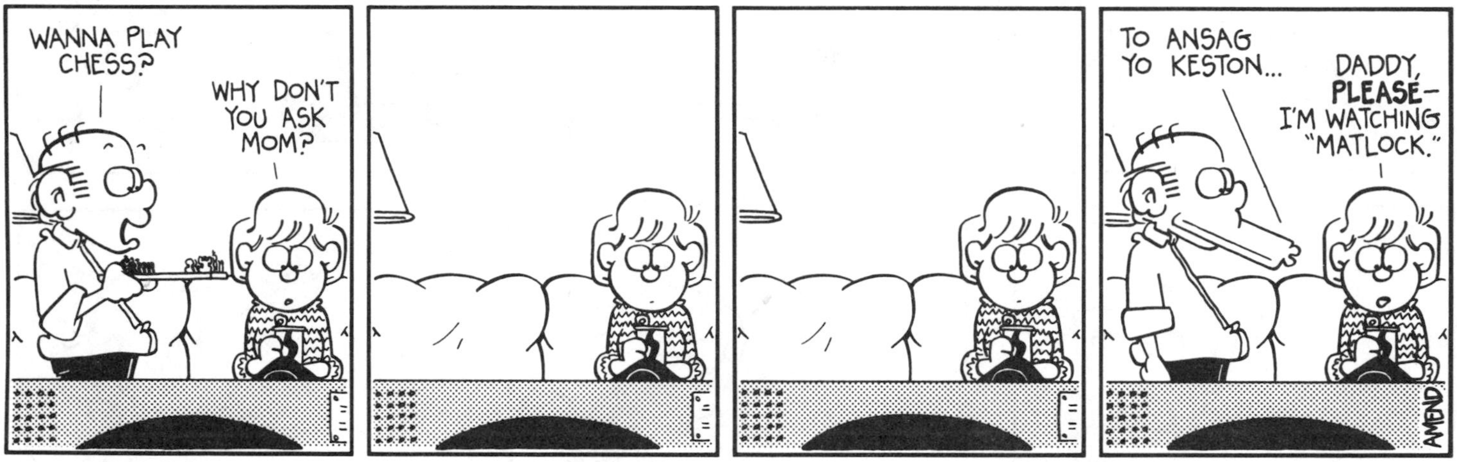
WANNA PLAY CHESS?
WHY DON'T YOU ASK MOM?
TO ANSAG YO KESTON...
DADDY, **PLEASE**– I'M WATCHING "MATLOCK."
AMEND

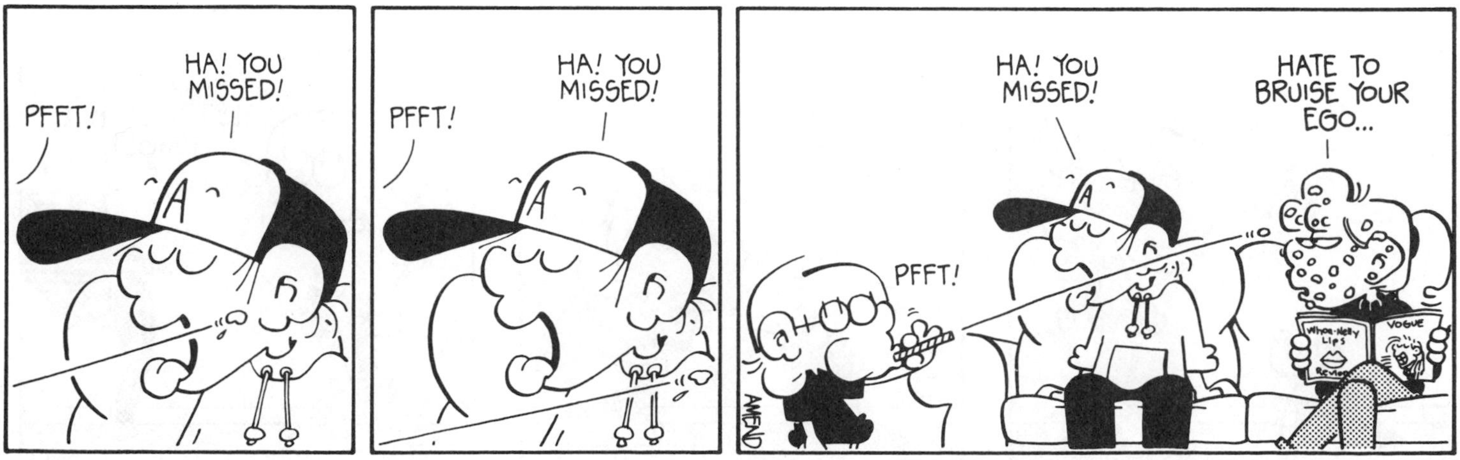
PFFT!
HA! YOU MISSED!
PFFT!
HA! YOU MISSED!
AMEND
PFFT!
HA! YOU MISSED!
HATE TO BRUISE YOUR EGO...
VOGUE

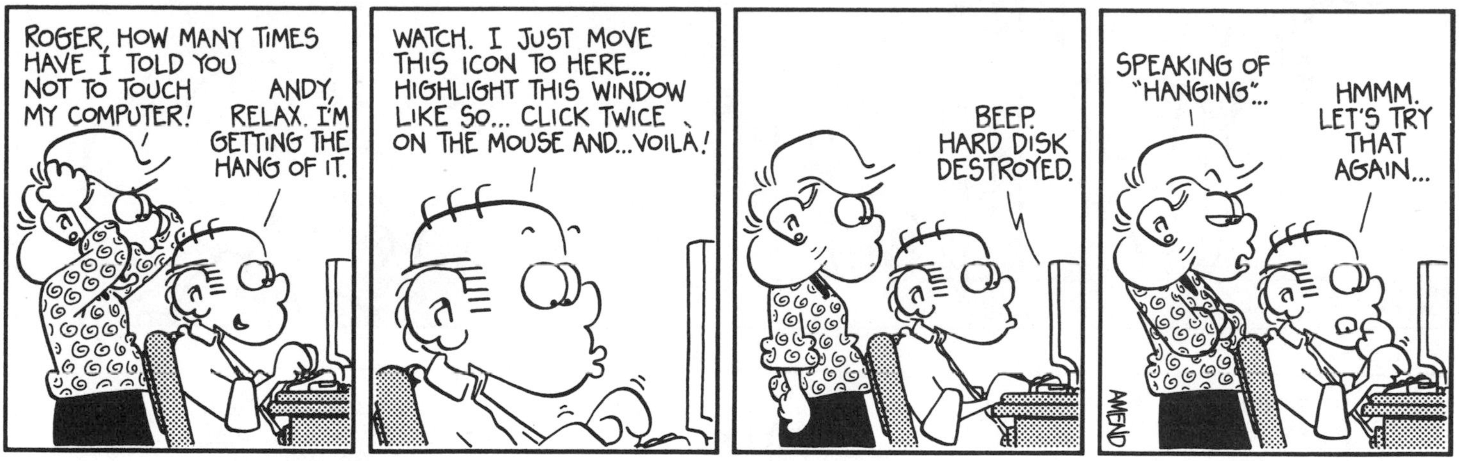
ROGER, HOW MANY TIMES HAVE I TOLD YOU NOT TO TOUCH MY COMPUTER!
ANDY, RELAX. I'M GETTING THE HANG OF IT.
WATCH. I JUST MOVE THIS ICON TO HERE... HIGHLIGHT THIS WINDOW LIKE SO... CLICK TWICE ON THE MOUSE AND...VOILÀ!
BEEP. HARD DISK DESTROYED.
SPEAKING OF "HANGING"...
HMMM. LET'S TRY THAT AGAIN...
AMEND

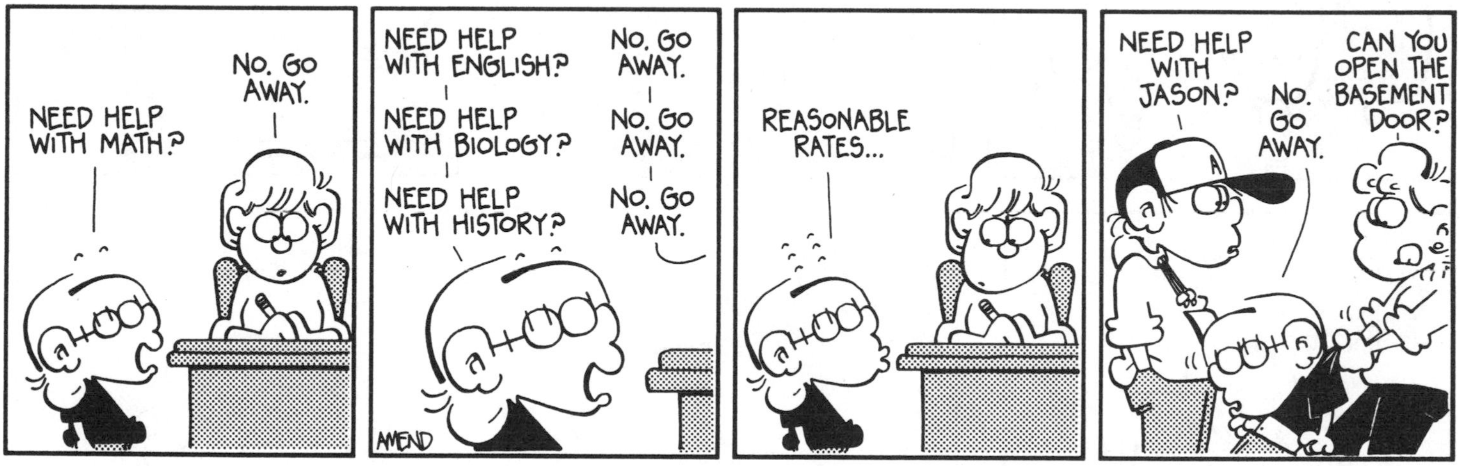
NEED HELP WITH MATH?
NO. GO AWAY.
NEED HELP WITH ENGLISH?
NO. GO AWAY.
NEED HELP WITH BIOLOGY?
NO. GO AWAY.
NEED HELP WITH HISTORY?
NO. GO AWAY.
AMEND
REASONABLE RATES...
NEED HELP WITH JASON?
NO. GO AWAY.
CAN YOU OPEN THE BASEMENT DOOR?

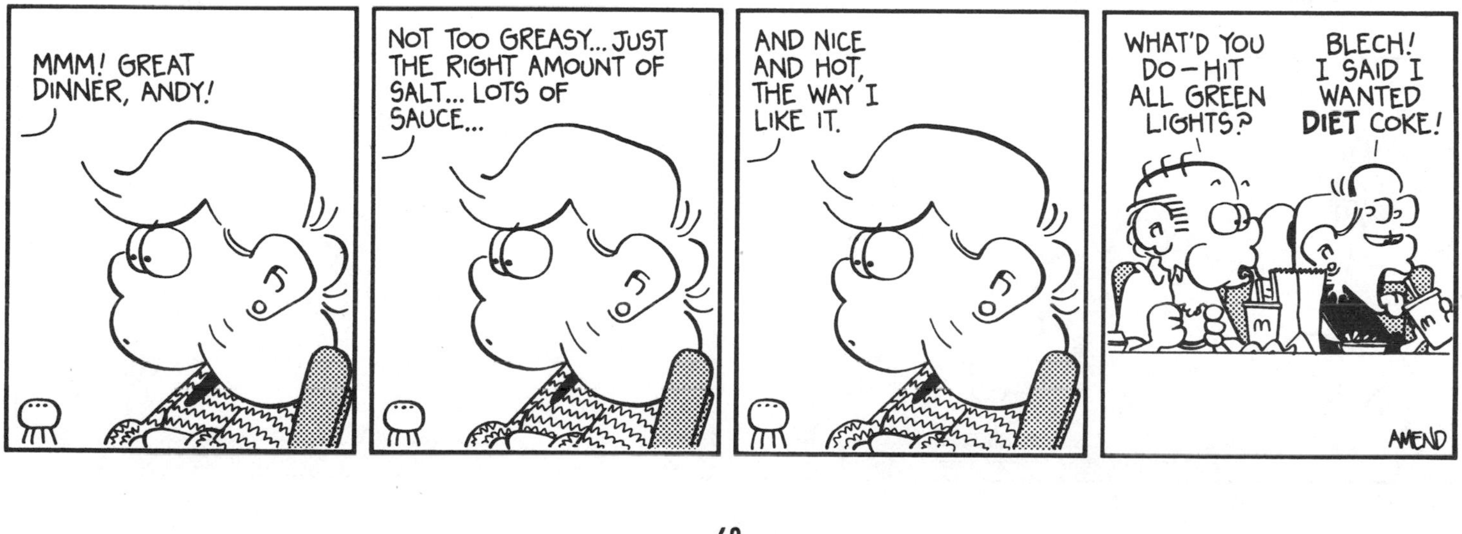
MMM! GREAT DINNER, ANDY!
NOT TOO GREASY... JUST THE RIGHT AMOUNT OF SALT... LOTS OF SAUCE...
AND NICE AND HOT, THE WAY I LIKE IT.
WHAT'D YOU DO–HIT ALL GREEN LIGHTS?
BLECH! I SAID I WANTED **DIET** COKE!
AMEND

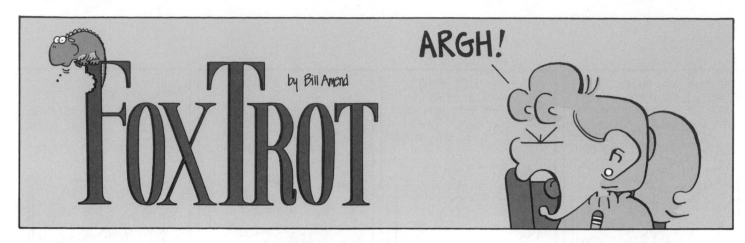

ARGH!

AARGH!

AAARGH!

WHAT'S WRONG?

THIS STUPID MATH IS WHAT'S WRONG! IT'S **POINTLESS**, MOTHER!

PAIGE...

I MEAN, WHO **CARES** IF I DON'T KNOW THE AREA OF A CIRCLE WITH A RADIUS OF THREE?!

WHO **CARES** IF I DON'T KNOW HOW TO FIND THE DOT PRODUCT OF TWO VECTORS?!

WHO **CARES** IF I CAN'T SIMPLIFY THE CUBE ROOT OF 256?!

9π.
$AB\cos\theta$.
$4\sqrt[3]{4}$.

BONEHEAD.

BESIDES HIM.

YOU KNOW, IF YOU WERE TO **LEARN** THESE THINGS...

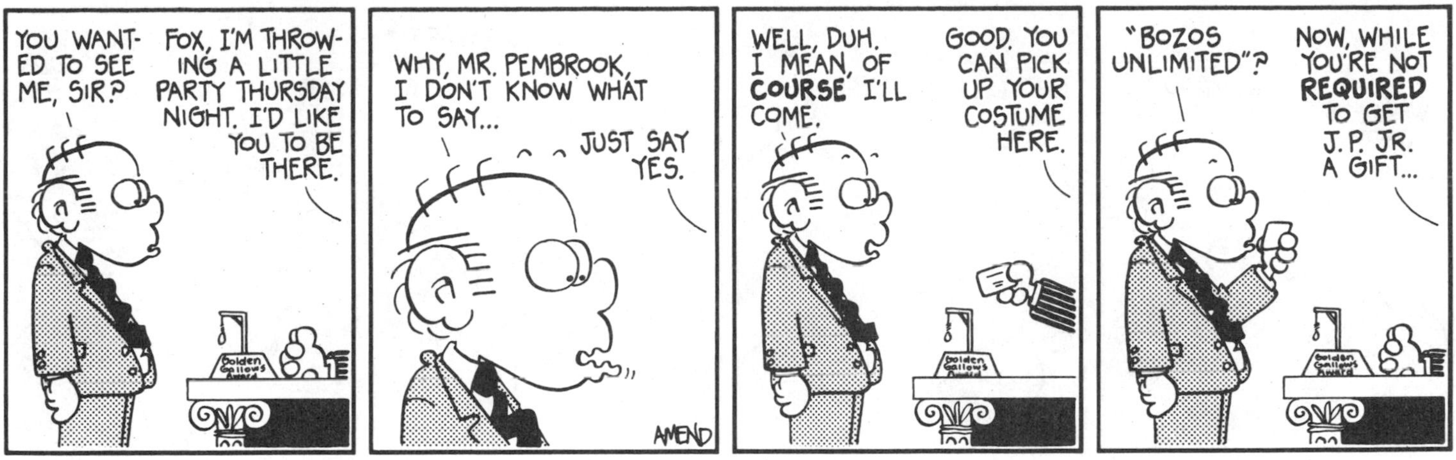
YOU WANTED TO SEE ME, SIR?
FOX, I'M THROWING A LITTLE PARTY THURSDAY NIGHT. I'D LIKE YOU TO BE THERE.
WHY, MR. PEMBROOK, I DON'T KNOW WHAT TO SAY...
JUST SAY YES.
WELL, DUH. I MEAN, OF **COURSE** I'LL COME.
GOOD. YOU CAN PICK UP YOUR COSTUME HERE.
"BOZOS UNLIMITED"?
NOW, WHILE YOU'RE NOT **REQUIRED** TO GET J.P. JR. A GIFT...
AMEND

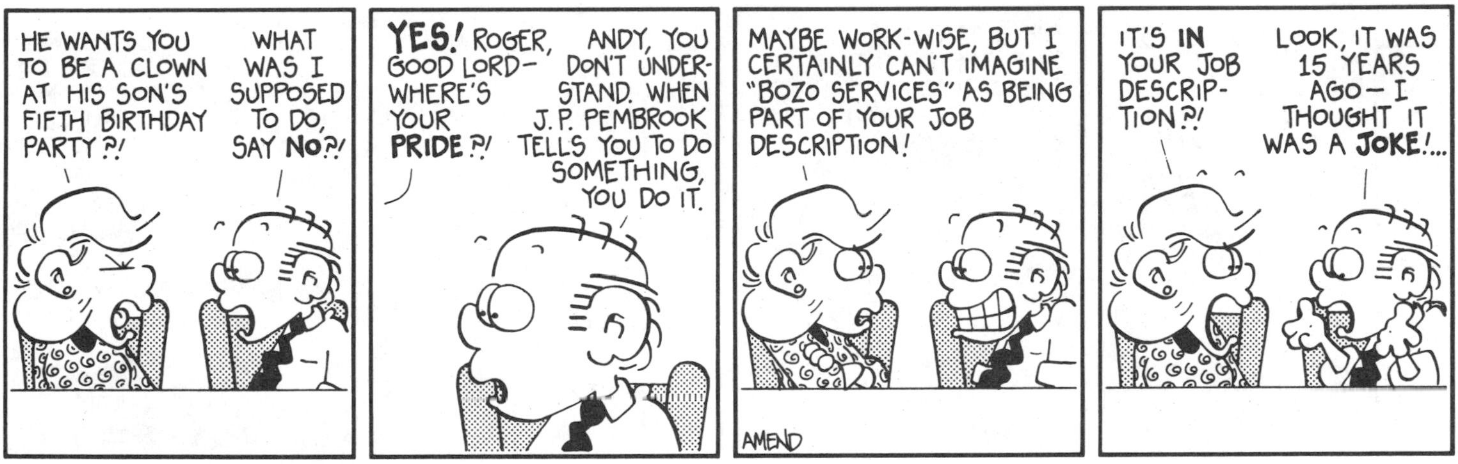
HE WANTS YOU TO BE A CLOWN AT HIS SON'S FIFTH BIRTHDAY PARTY?!
WHAT WAS I SUPPOSED TO DO, SAY **NO**?!
YES! ROGER, GOOD LORD— WHERE'S YOUR **PRIDE**?!
ANDY, YOU DON'T UNDERSTAND. WHEN J.P. PEMBROOK TELLS YOU TO DO SOMETHING, YOU DO IT.
MAYBE WORK-WISE, BUT I CERTAINLY CAN'T IMAGINE "BOZO SERVICES" AS BEING PART OF YOUR JOB DESCRIPTION!
AMEND
IT'S **IN** YOUR JOB DESCRIPTION?!
LOOK, IT WAS 15 YEARS AGO— I THOUGHT IT WAS A **JOKE**!...

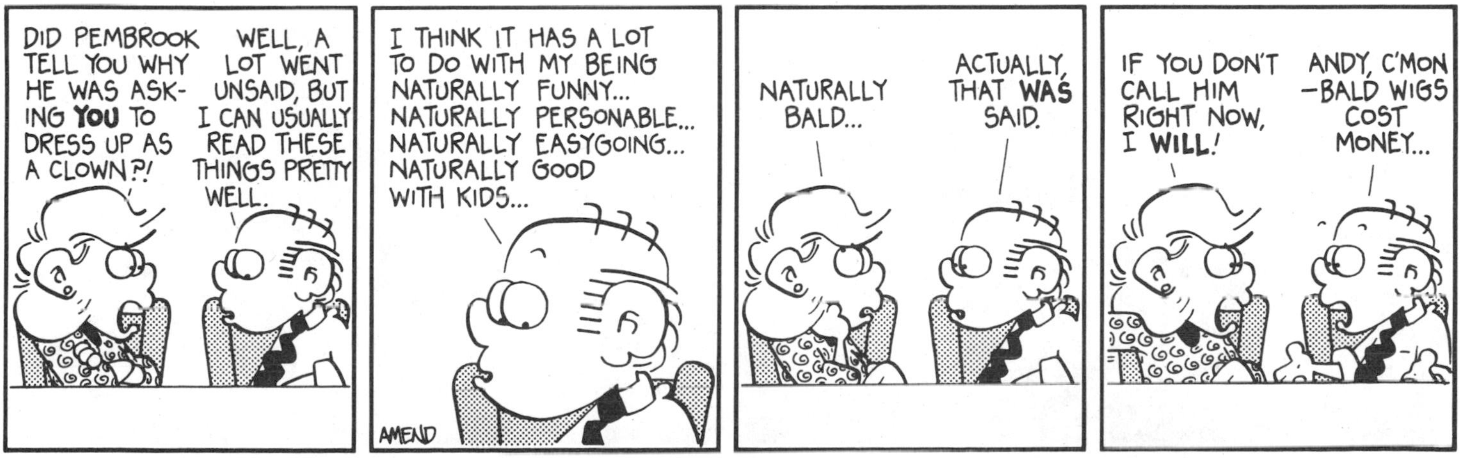
DID PEMBROOK TELL YOU WHY HE WAS ASKING **YOU** TO DRESS UP AS A CLOWN?!
WELL, A LOT WENT UNSAID, BUT I CAN USUALLY READ THESE THINGS PRETTY WELL.
I THINK IT HAS A LOT TO DO WITH MY BEING NATURALLY FUNNY... NATURALLY PERSONABLE... NATURALLY EASYGOING... NATURALLY GOOD WITH KIDS...
AMEND
NATURALLY BALD...
ACTUALLY, THAT **WAS** SAID.
IF YOU DON'T CALL HIM RIGHT NOW, I **WILL**!
ANDY, C'MON —BALD WIGS COST MONEY...

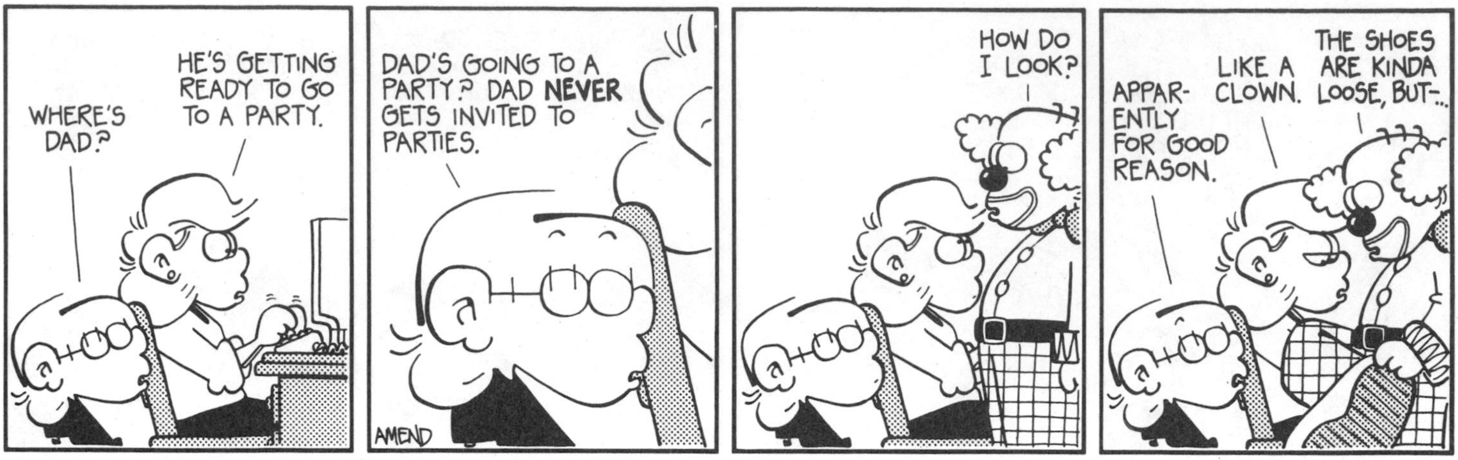
WHERE'S DAD?
HE'S GETTING READY TO GO TO A PARTY.
DAD'S GOING TO A PARTY? DAD **NEVER** GETS INVITED TO PARTIES.
AMEND
HOW DO I LOOK?
APPAR-ENTLY FOR GOOD REASON.
LIKE A CLOWN.
THE SHOES ARE KINDA LOOSE, BUT-...

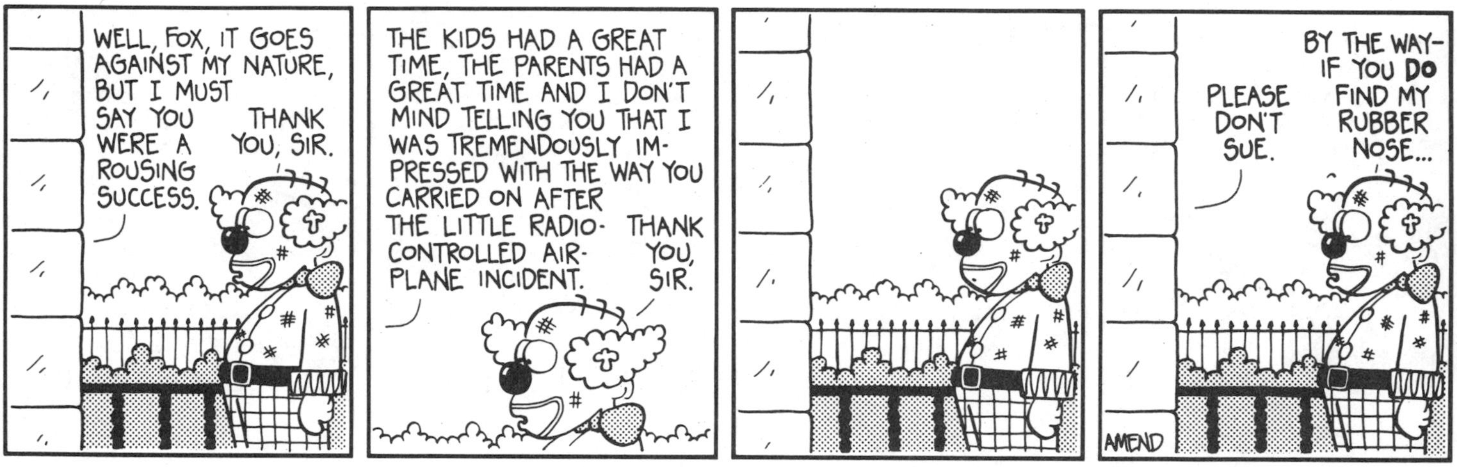
WELL, FOX, IT GOES AGAINST MY NATURE, BUT I MUST SAY YOU WERE A ROUSING SUCCESS.
THANK YOU, SIR.
THE KIDS HAD A GREAT TIME, THE PARENTS HAD A GREAT TIME AND I DON'T MIND TELLING YOU THAT I WAS TREMENDOUSLY IM-PRESSED WITH THE WAY YOU CARRIED ON AFTER THE LITTLE RADIO-CONTROLLED AIR-PLANE INCIDENT.
THANK YOU, SIR.
PLEASE DON'T SUE.
BY THE WAY- IF YOU **DO** FIND MY RUBBER NOSE...
AMEND

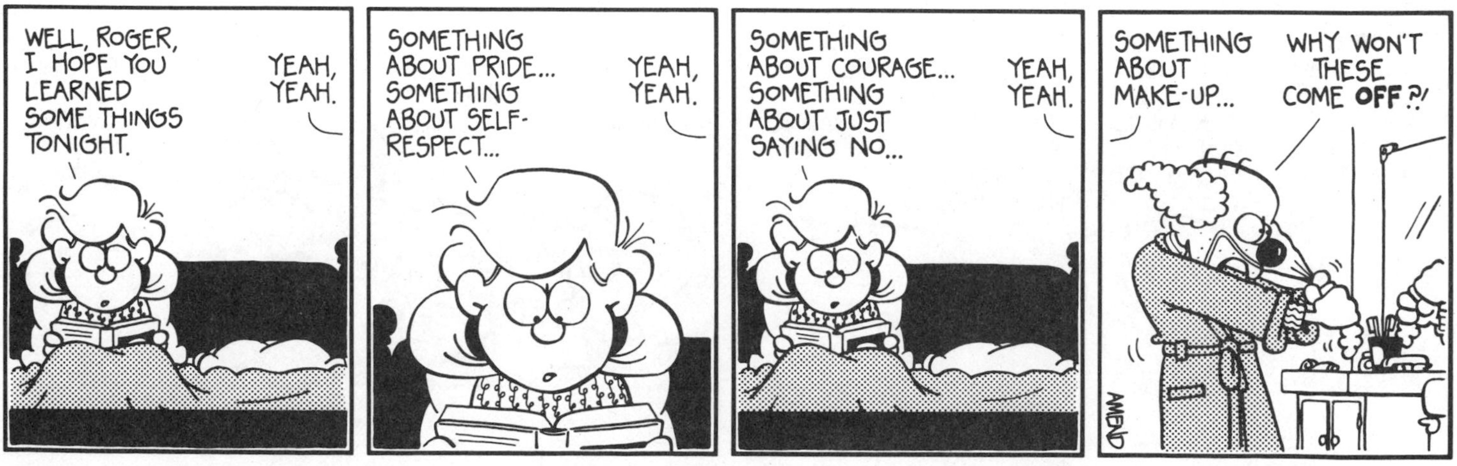
WELL, ROGER, I HOPE YOU LEARNED SOME THINGS TONIGHT.
YEAH, YEAH.
SOMETHING ABOUT PRIDE... SOMETHING ABOUT SELF-RESPECT...
YEAH, YEAH.
SOMETHING ABOUT COURAGE... SOMETHING ABOUT JUST SAYING NO...
YEAH, YEAH.
SOMETHING ABOUT MAKE-UP...
WHY WON'T THESE COME **OFF**?!
AMEND

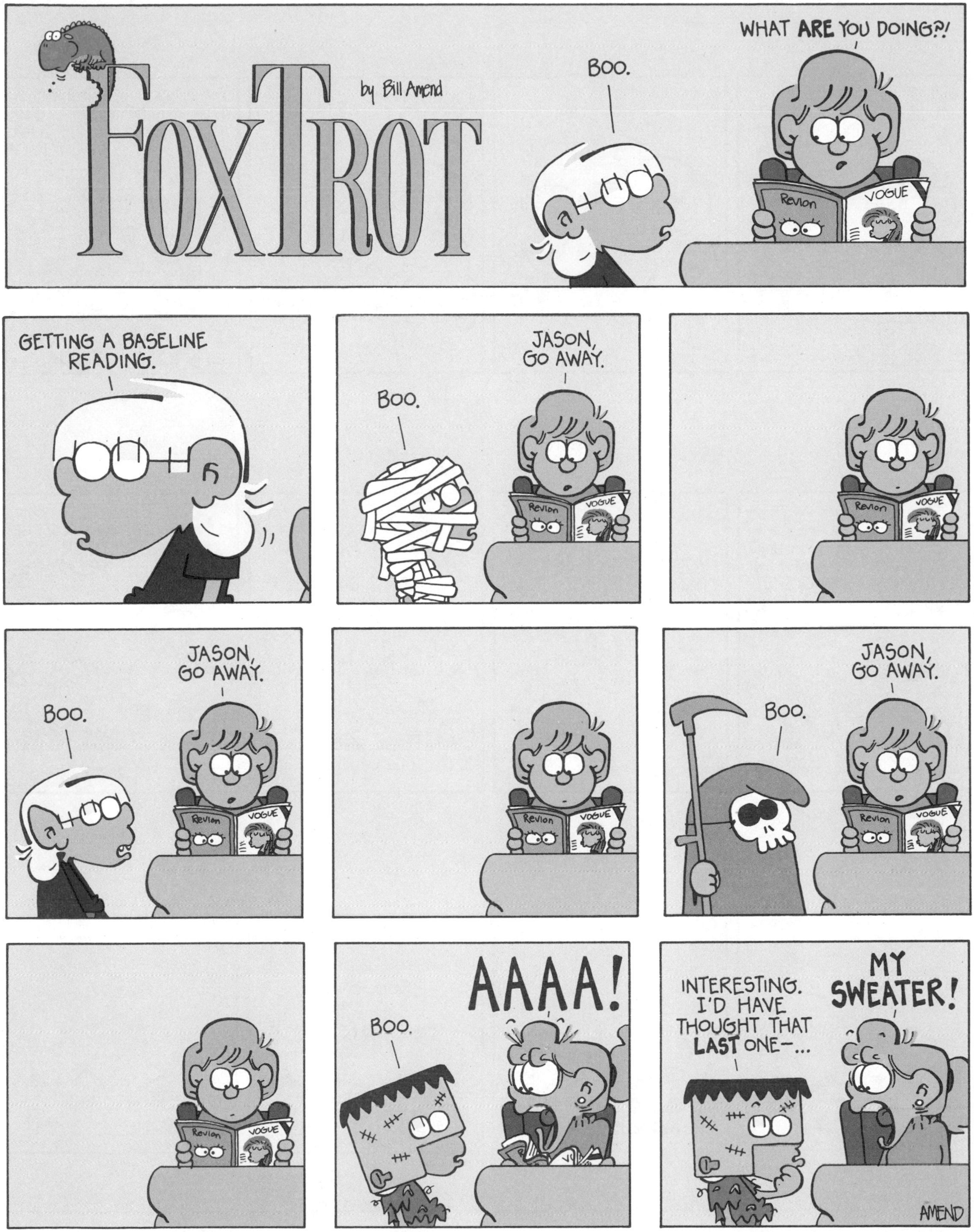
FoxTrot
by Bill Amend
BOO.
WHAT ARE YOU DOING?!
GETTING A BASELINE READING.
BOO.
JASON, GO AWAY.
BOO.
JASON, GO AWAY.
BOO.
JASON, GO AWAY.
BOO.
AAAA!
INTERESTING. I'D HAVE THOUGHT THAT LAST ONE—...
MY SWEATER!
AMEND

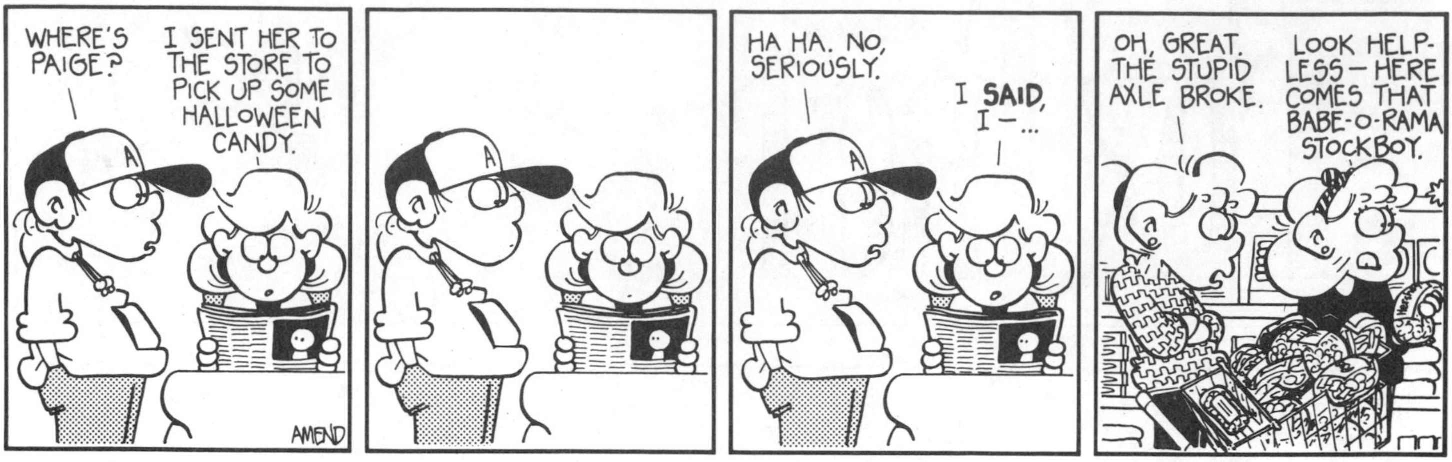
WHERE'S PAIGE?
I SENT HER TO THE STORE TO PICK UP SOME HALLOWEEN CANDY.
AMEND
HA HA. NO, SERIOUSLY.
I **SAID**, I—...
OH, GREAT. THE STUPID AXLE BROKE.
LOOK HELPLESS—HERE COMES THAT BABE-O-RAMA STOCKBOY.

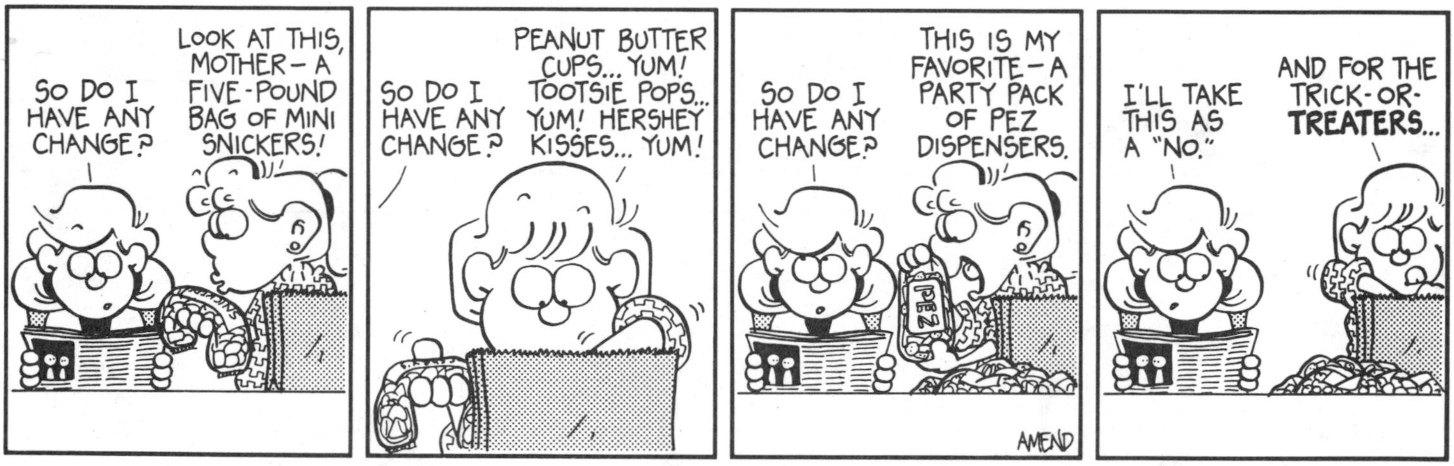
SO DO I HAVE ANY CHANGE?
LOOK AT THIS, MOTHER—A FIVE-POUND BAG OF MINI SNICKERS!
SO DO I HAVE ANY CHANGE?
PEANUT BUTTER CUPS... YUM! TOOTSIE POPS... YUM! HERSHEY KISSES... YUM!
SO DO I HAVE ANY CHANGE?
THIS IS MY FAVORITE—A PARTY PACK OF PEZ DISPENSERS.
PEZ
AMEND
I'LL TAKE THIS AS A "NO."
AND FOR THE TRICK-OR-**TREATERS**...

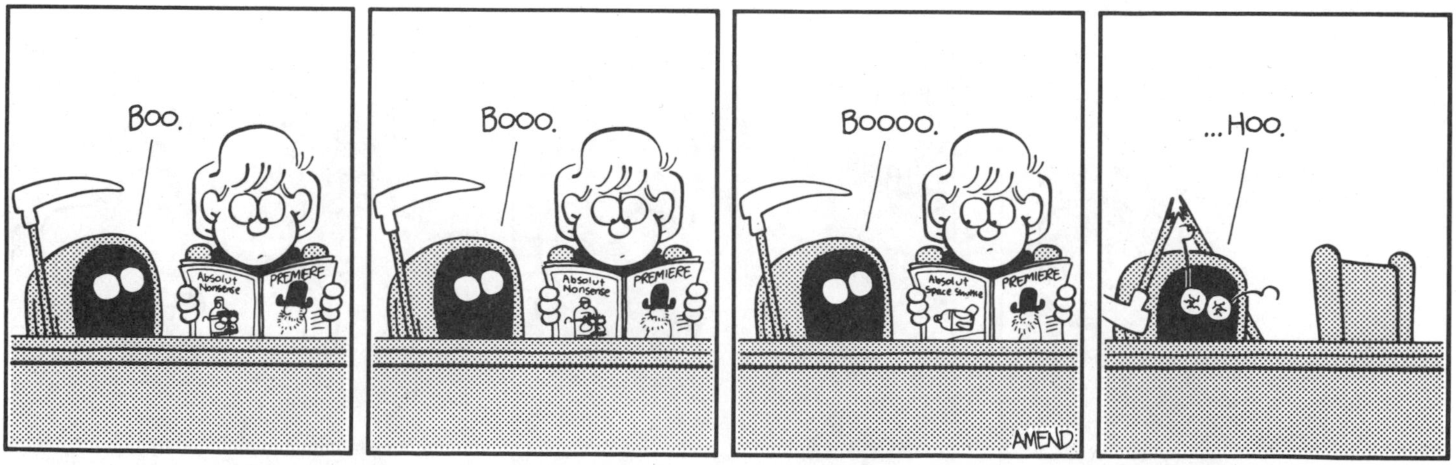
BOO.
PREMIERE
BOOO.
PREMIERE
BOOOO.
PREMIERE
AMEND
...HOO.

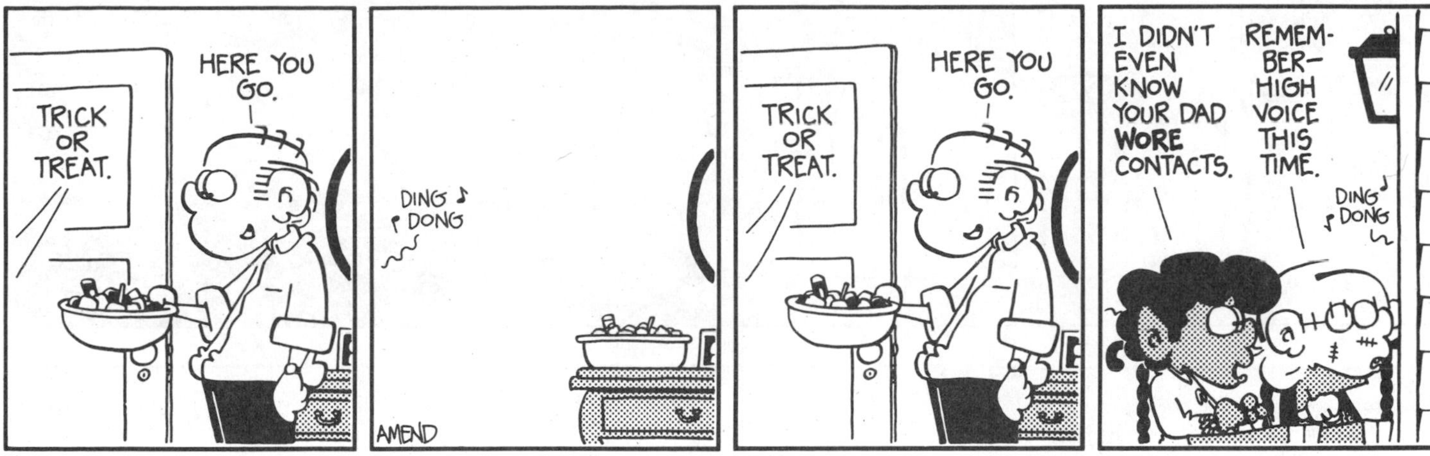
TRICK OR TREAT.
HERE YOU GO.
DING DONG
AMEND
TRICK OR TREAT.
HERE YOU GO.
I DIDN'T EVEN KNOW YOUR DAD **WORE** CONTACTS.
REMEMBER- HIGH VOICE THIS TIME.
DING DONG

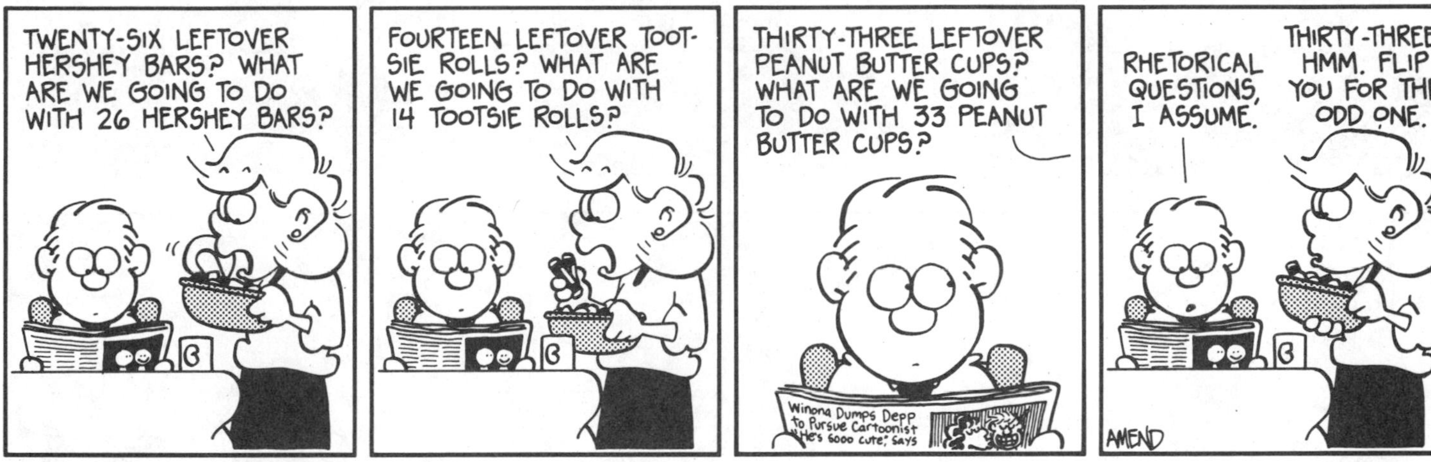
TWENTY-SIX LEFTOVER HERSHEY BARS? WHAT ARE WE GOING TO DO WITH 26 HERSHEY BARS?
FOURTEEN LEFTOVER TOOTSIE ROLLS? WHAT ARE WE GOING TO DO WITH 14 TOOTSIE ROLLS?
THIRTY-THREE LEFTOVER PEANUT BUTTER CUPS? WHAT ARE WE GOING TO DO WITH 33 PEANUT BUTTER CUPS?
Winona Dumps Depp to Pursue Cartoonist
"He's Sooo cute," Says
RHETORICAL QUESTIONS, I ASSUME.
THIRTY-THREE. HMM. FLIP YOU FOR THE ODD ONE.
AMEND

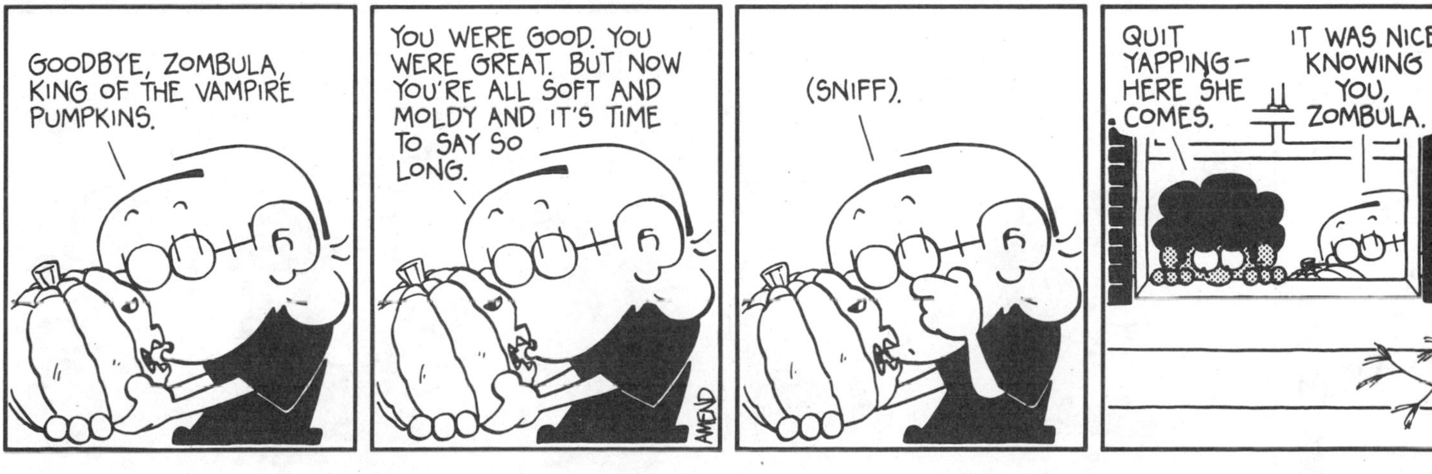
GOODBYE, ZOMBULA, KING OF THE VAMPIRE PUMPKINS.
YOU WERE GOOD. YOU WERE GREAT. BUT NOW YOU'RE ALL SOFT AND MOLDY AND IT'S TIME TO SAY SO LONG.
AMEND
(SNIFF).
QUIT YAPPING- HERE SHE COMES.
IT WAS NICE KNOWING YOU, ZOMBULA.

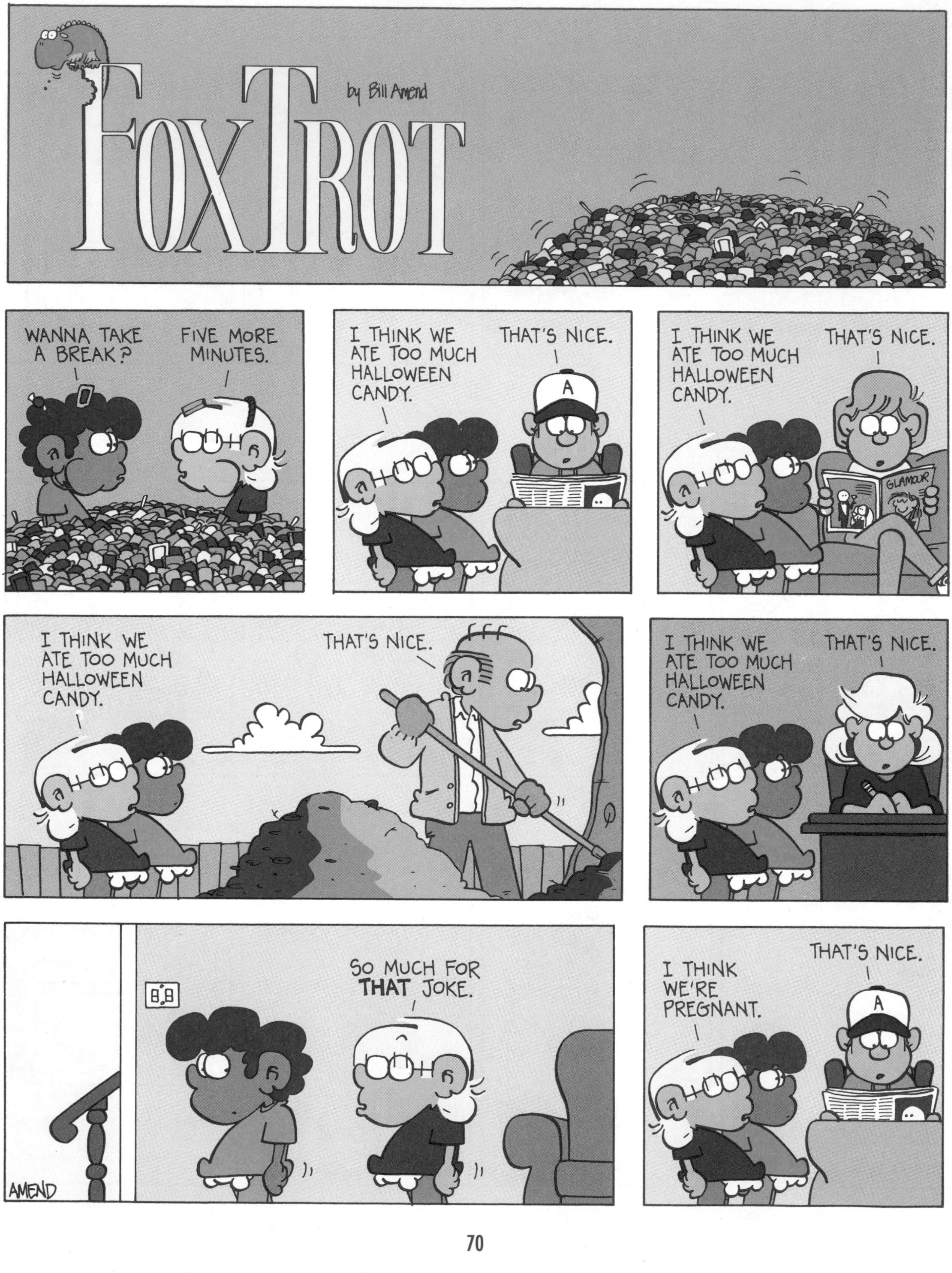
FoxTrot
by Bill Amend
WANNA TAKE A BREAK?
FIVE MORE MINUTES.
I THINK WE ATE TOO MUCH HALLOWEEN CANDY.
THAT'S NICE.
I THINK WE ATE TOO MUCH HALLOWEEN CANDY.
THAT'S NICE.
GLAMOUR
I THINK WE ATE TOO MUCH HALLOWEEN CANDY.
THAT'S NICE.
I THINK WE ATE TOO MUCH HALLOWEEN CANDY.
THAT'S NICE.
SO MUCH FOR **THAT** JOKE.
AMEND
I THINK WE'RE PREGNANT.
THAT'S NICE.

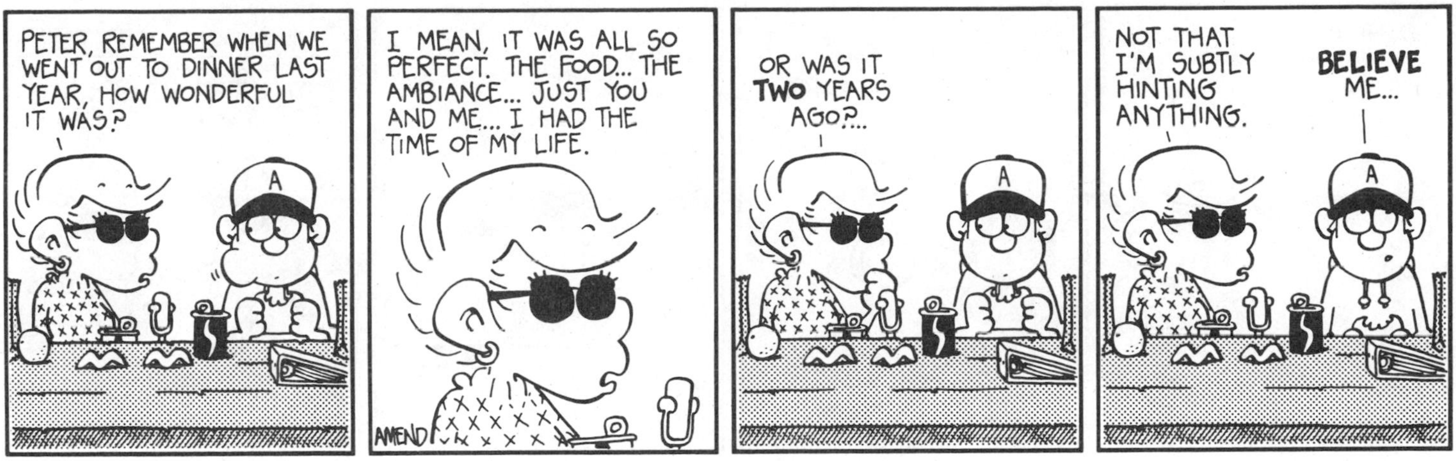
PETER, REMEMBER WHEN WE WENT OUT TO DINNER LAST YEAR, HOW WONDERFUL IT WAS?
I MEAN, IT WAS ALL SO PERFECT. THE FOOD... THE AMBIANCE... JUST YOU AND ME... I HAD THE TIME OF MY LIFE.
AMEND
OR WAS IT **TWO** YEARS AGO?...
NOT THAT I'M SUBTLY HINTING ANYTHING.
BELIEVE ME...

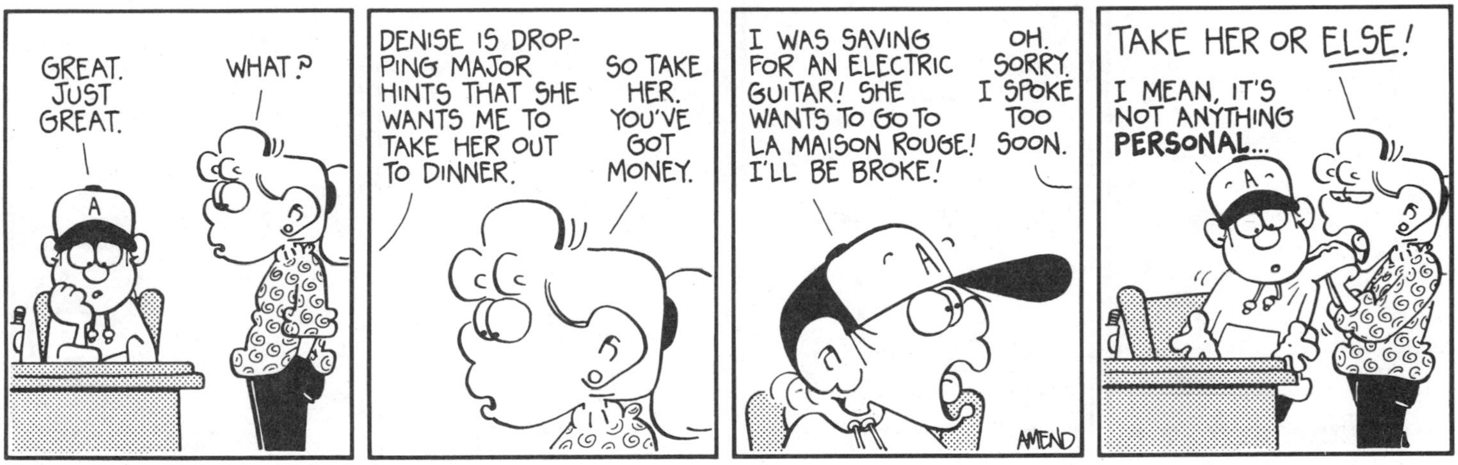
GREAT. JUST GREAT.
WHAT?
DENISE IS DROPPING MAJOR HINTS THAT SHE WANTS ME TO TAKE HER OUT TO DINNER.
SO TAKE HER. YOU'VE GOT MONEY.
I WAS SAVING FOR AN ELECTRIC GUITAR! SHE WANTS TO GO TO LA MAISON ROUGE! I'LL BE BROKE!
OH. SORRY. I SPOKE TOO SOON.
AMEND
TAKE HER OR ELSE!
I MEAN, IT'S NOT ANYTHING **PERSONAL**...

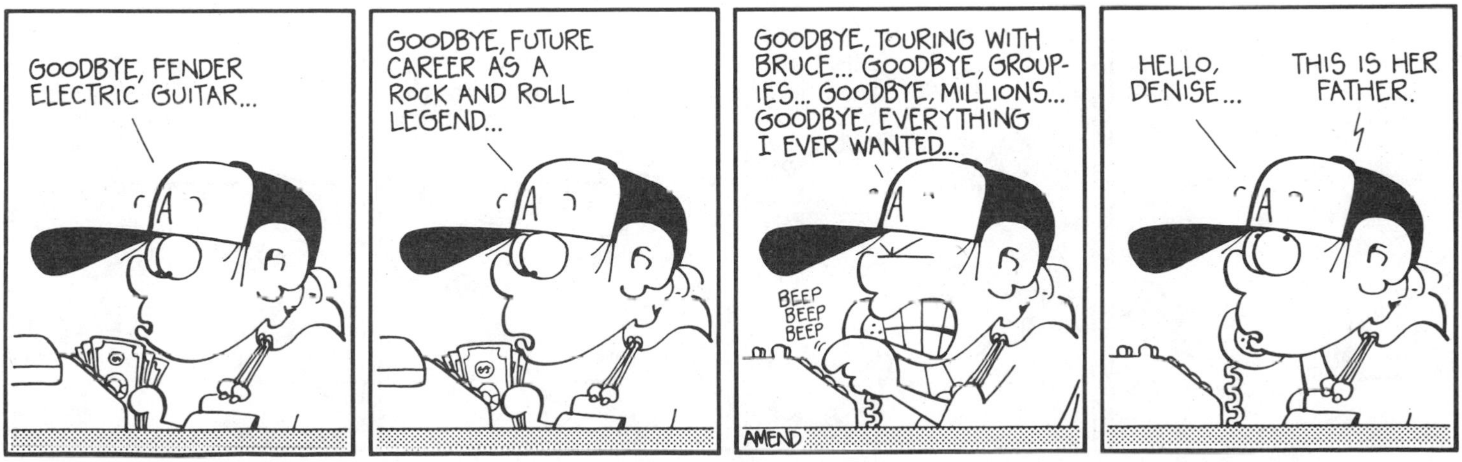
GOODBYE, FENDER ELECTRIC GUITAR...
GOODBYE, FUTURE CAREER AS A ROCK AND ROLL LEGEND...
GOODBYE, TOURING WITH BRUCE... GOODBYE, GROUPIES... GOODBYE, MILLIONS... GOODBYE, EVERYTHING I EVER WANTED...
BEEP BEEP BEEP
AMEND
HELLO, DENISE...
THIS IS HER FATHER.

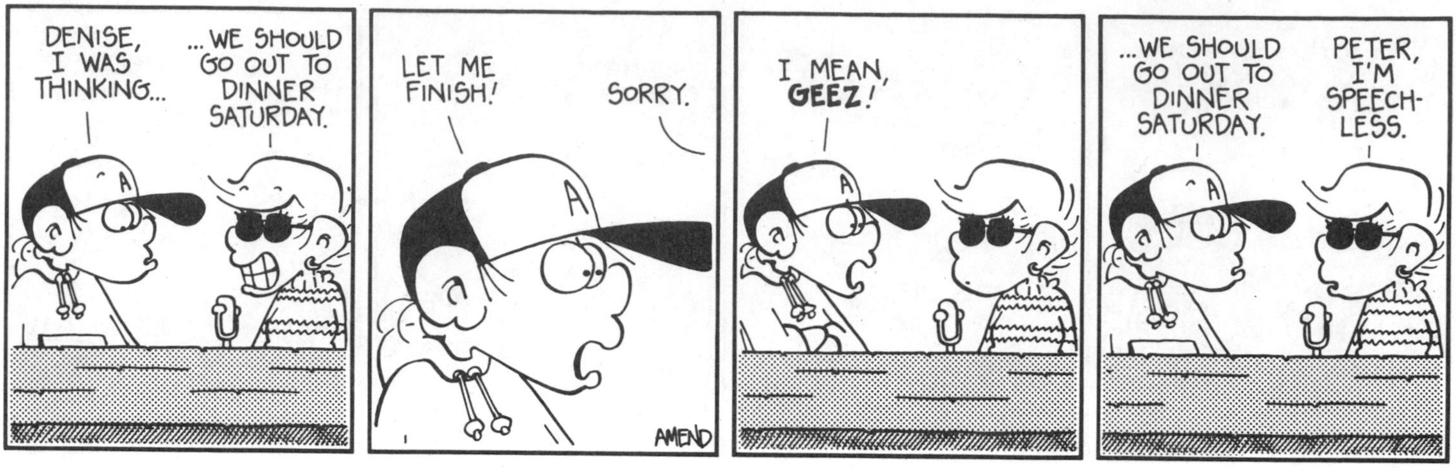
DENISE, I WAS THINKING...
...WE SHOULD GO OUT TO DINNER SATURDAY.
LET ME FINISH!
SORRY.
I MEAN, GEEZ!
...WE SHOULD GO OUT TO DINNER SATURDAY.
PETER, I'M SPEECH-LESS.
AMEND

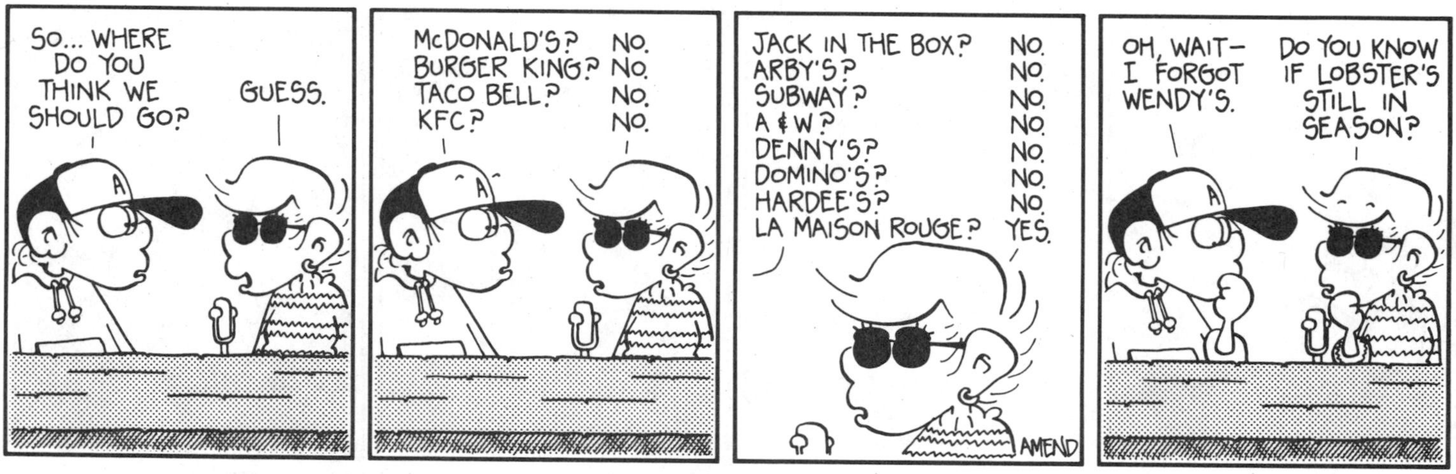
SO... WHERE DO YOU THINK WE SHOULD GO?
GUESS.
McDONALD'S? NO.
BURGER KING? NO.
TACO BELL? NO.
KFC? NO.
JACK IN THE BOX? NO.
ARBY'S? NO.
SUBWAY? NO.
A & W? NO.
DENNY'S? NO.
DOMINO'S? NO.
HARDEE'S? NO.
LA MAISON ROUGE? YES.
AMEND
OH, WAIT– I FORGOT WENDY'S.
DO YOU KNOW IF LOBSTER'S STILL IN SEASON?

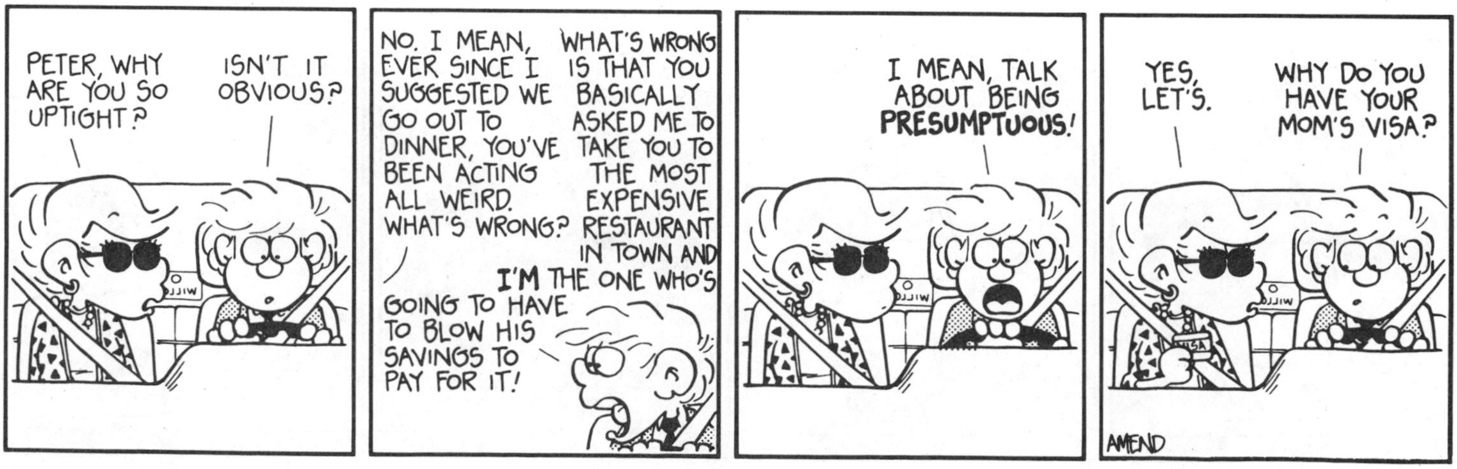
PETER, WHY ARE YOU SO UPTIGHT?
ISN'T IT OBVIOUS?
NO. I MEAN, EVER SINCE I SUGGESTED WE GO OUT TO DINNER, YOU'VE BEEN ACTING ALL WEIRD. WHAT'S WRONG?
WHAT'S WRONG IS THAT YOU BASICALLY ASKED ME TO TAKE YOU TO THE MOST EXPENSIVE RESTAURANT IN TOWN AND I'M THE ONE WHO'S GOING TO HAVE TO BLOW HIS SAVINGS TO PAY FOR IT!
I MEAN, TALK ABOUT BEING PRESUMPTUOUS!
YES, LET'S.
WHY DO YOU HAVE YOUR MOM'S VISA?
AMEND

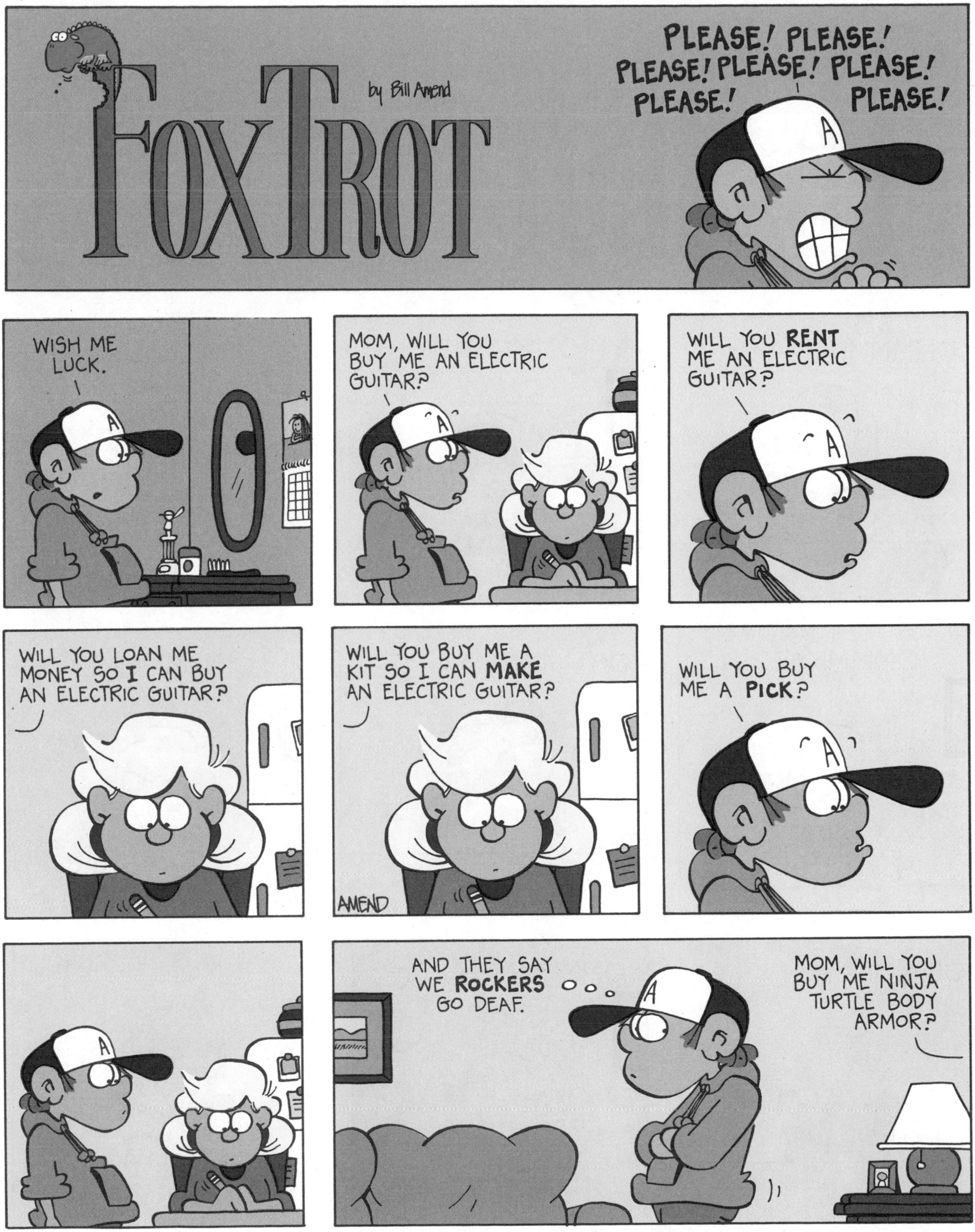
FoxTrot
by Bill Amend
PLEASE! PLEASE! PLEASE! PLEASE! PLEASE! PLEASE! PLEASE!
WISH ME LUCK.
MOM, WILL YOU BUY ME AN ELECTRIC GUITAR?
WILL YOU **RENT** ME AN ELECTRIC GUITAR?
WILL YOU LOAN ME MONEY SO **I** CAN BUY AN ELECTRIC GUITAR?
WILL YOU BUY ME A KIT SO I CAN **MAKE** AN ELECTRIC GUITAR?
AMEND
WILL YOU BUY ME A **PICK**?
AND THEY SAY WE **ROCKERS** GO DEAF.
MOM, WILL YOU BUY ME NINJA TURTLE BODY ARMOR?

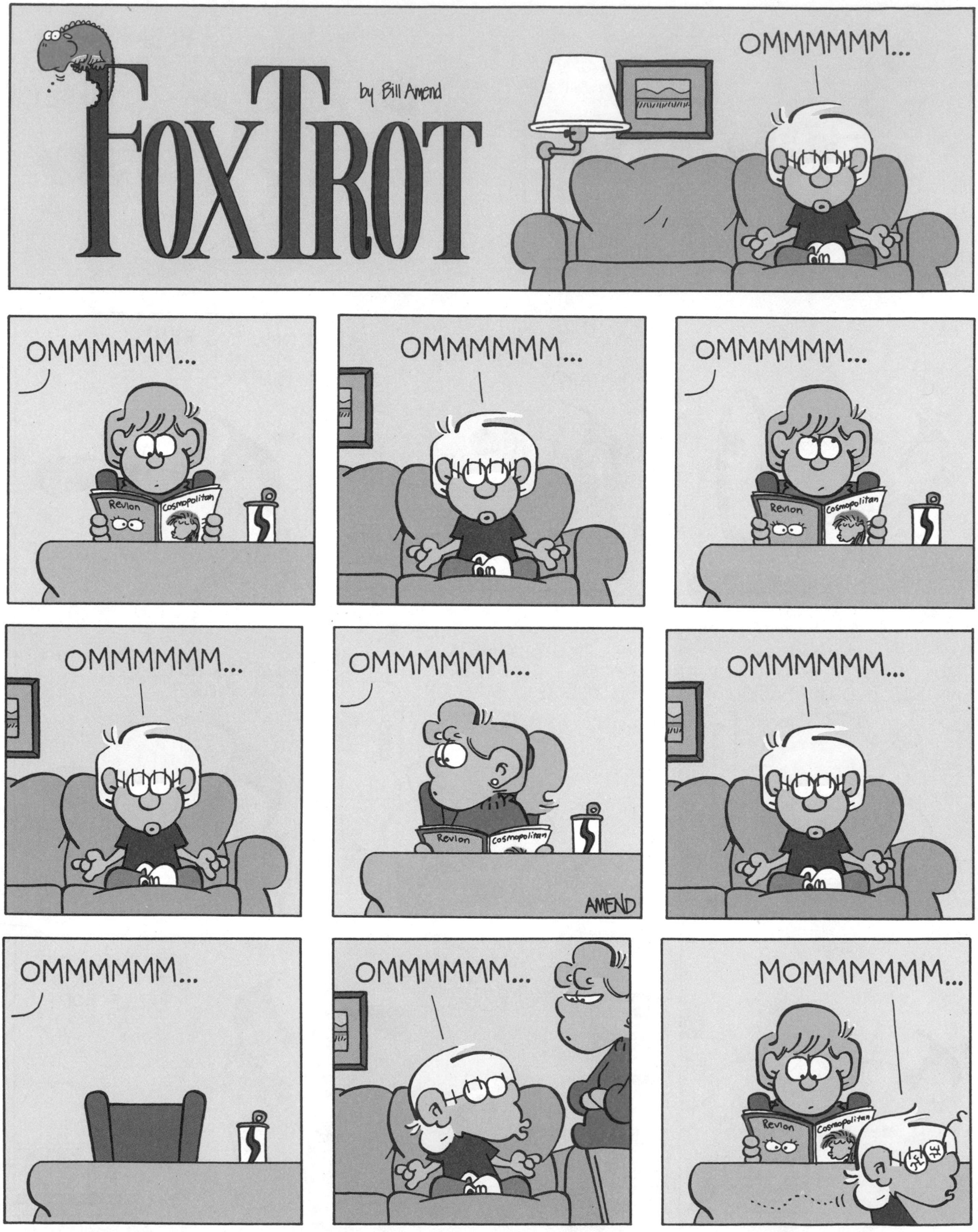
FoxTrot
by Bill Amend
OMMMMMM...
OMMMMMM...
OMMMMMM...
OMMMMMM...
OMMMMMM...
OMMMMMM...
OMMMMMM...
OMMMMMM...
OMMMMMM...
MOMMMMMM...
Revlon
Cosmopolitan
AMEND

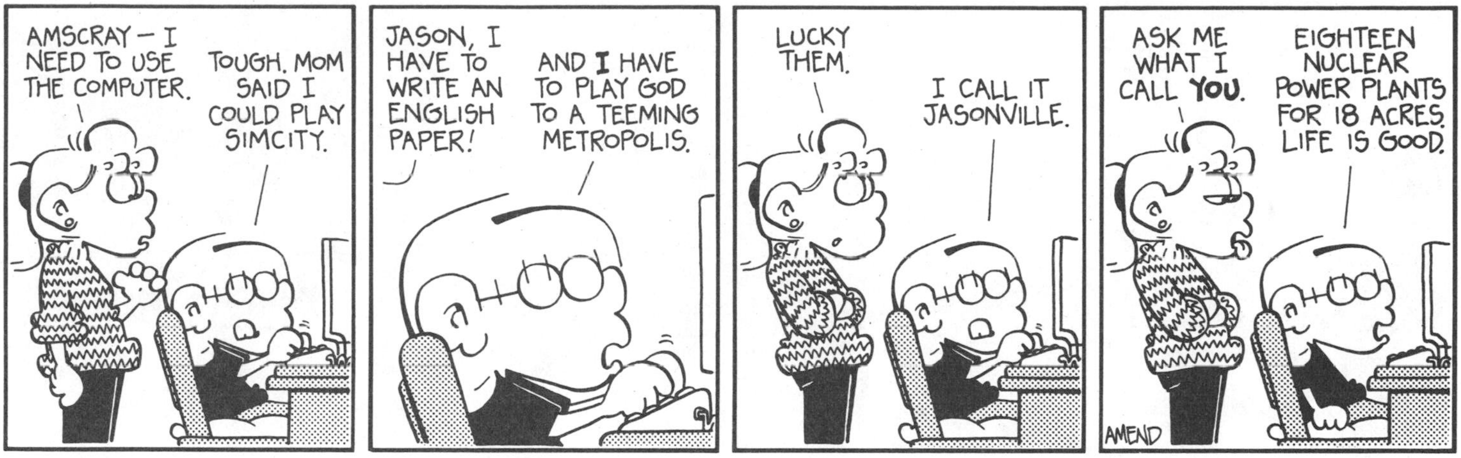
AMSCRAY – I NEED TO USE THE COMPUTER.
TOUGH. MOM SAID I COULD PLAY SIMCITY.
JASON, I HAVE TO WRITE AN ENGLISH PAPER!
AND **I** HAVE TO PLAY GOD TO A TEEMING METROPOLIS.
LUCKY THEM.
I CALL IT JASONVILLE.
ASK ME WHAT I CALL **YOU**.
EIGHTEEN NUCLEAR POWER PLANTS FOR 18 ACRES. LIFE IS GOOD.
AMEND

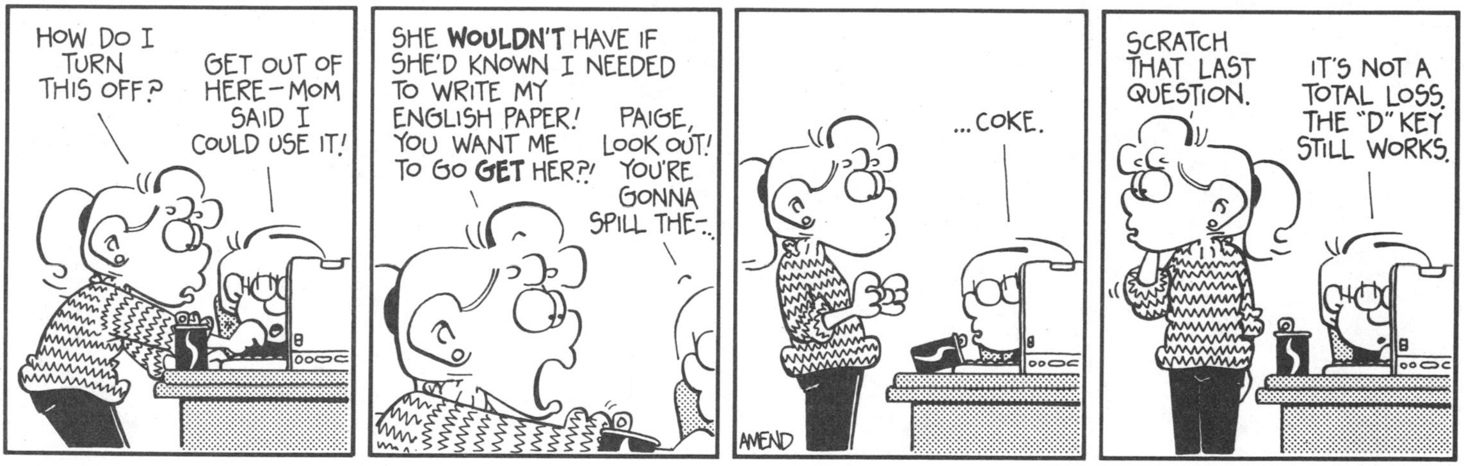
HOW DO I TURN THIS OFF?
GET OUT OF HERE – MOM SAID I COULD USE IT!
SHE **WOULDN'T** HAVE IF SHE'D KNOWN I NEEDED TO WRITE MY ENGLISH PAPER! YOU WANT ME TO GO **GET** HER?!
PAIGE, LOOK OUT! YOU'RE GONNA SPILL THE–...
...COKE.
AMEND
SCRATCH THAT LAST QUESTION.
IT'S NOT A TOTAL LOSS. THE "D" KEY STILL WORKS.

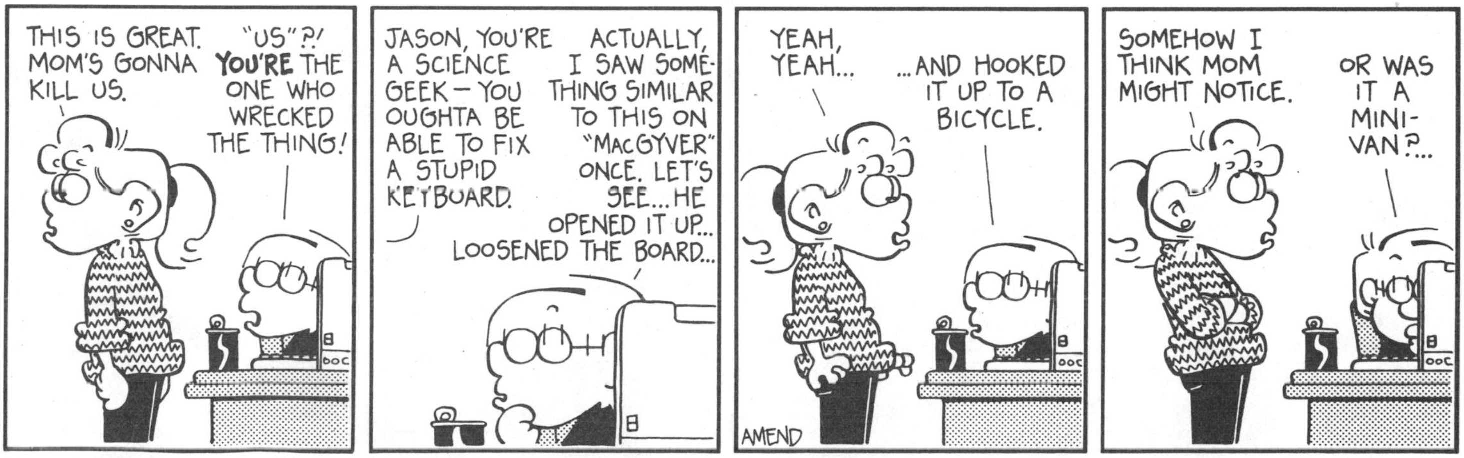
THIS IS GREAT. MOM'S GONNA KILL US.
"US"?! **YOU'RE** THE ONE WHO WRECKED THE THING!
JASON, YOU'RE A SCIENCE GEEK – YOU OUGHTA BE ABLE TO FIX A STUPID KEYBOARD.
ACTUALLY, I SAW SOMETHING SIMILAR TO THIS ON "MACGYVER" ONCE. LET'S SEE... HE OPENED IT UP... LOOSENED THE BOARD...
YEAH, YEAH...
...AND HOOKED IT UP TO A BICYCLE.
AMEND
SOMEHOW I THINK MOM MIGHT NOTICE.
OR WAS IT A MINI-VAN?...

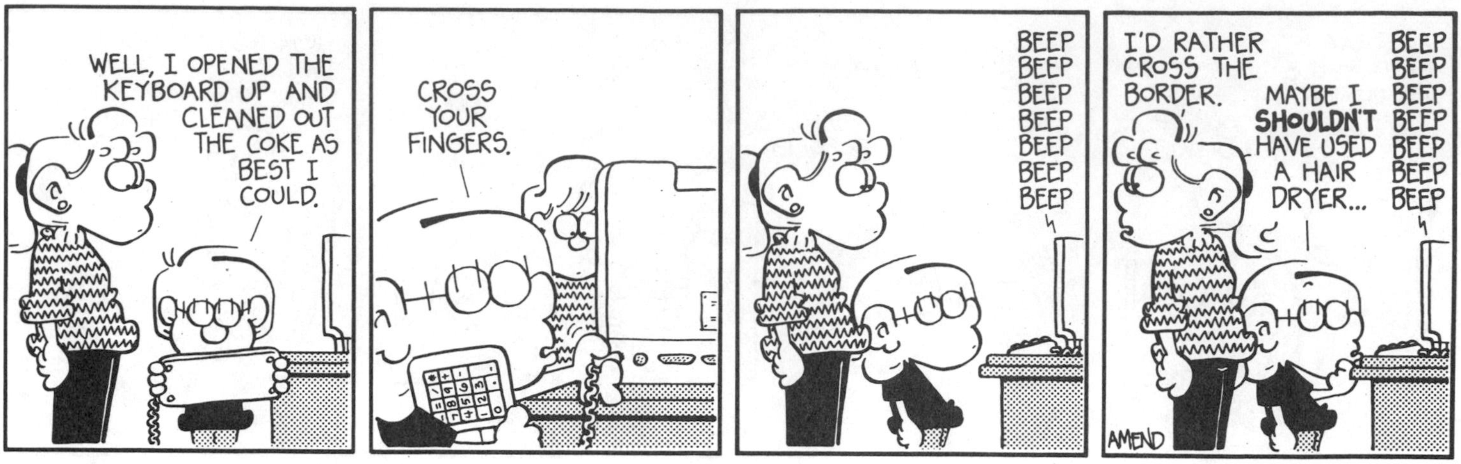
WELL, I OPENED THE KEYBOARD UP AND CLEANED OUT THE COKE AS BEST I COULD.
CROSS YOUR FINGERS.
BEEP BEEP BEEP BEEP BEEP BEEP BEEP
I'D RATHER CROSS THE BORDER.
MAYBE I SHOULDN'T HAVE USED A HAIR DRYER...
BEEP BEEP BEEP BEEP BEEP BEEP BEEP
AMEND

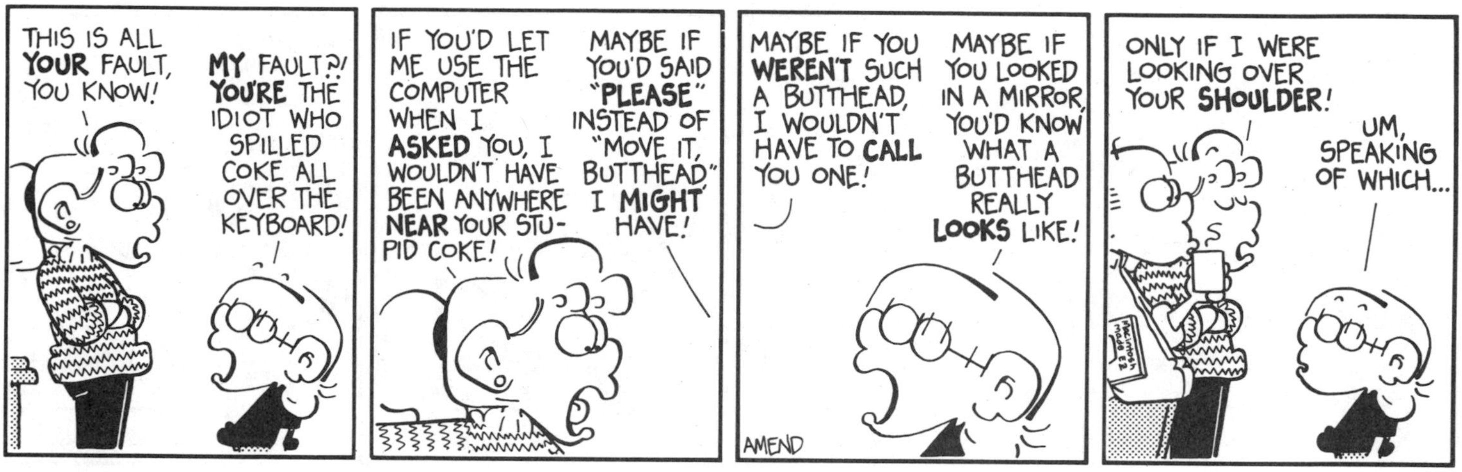
THIS IS ALL YOUR FAULT, YOU KNOW!
MY FAULT?! YOU'RE THE IDIOT WHO SPILLED COKE ALL OVER THE KEYBOARD!
IF YOU'D LET ME USE THE COMPUTER WHEN I ASKED YOU, I WOULDN'T HAVE BEEN ANYWHERE NEAR YOUR STUPID COKE!
MAYBE IF YOU'D SAID "PLEASE" INSTEAD OF "MOVE IT, BUTTHEAD" I MIGHT HAVE!
MAYBE IF YOU WEREN'T SUCH A BUTTHEAD, I WOULDN'T HAVE TO CALL YOU ONE!
MAYBE IF YOU LOOKED IN A MIRROR, YOU'D KNOW WHAT A BUTTHEAD REALLY LOOKS LIKE!
AMEND
ONLY IF I WERE LOOKING OVER YOUR SHOULDER!
UM, SPEAKING OF WHICH...

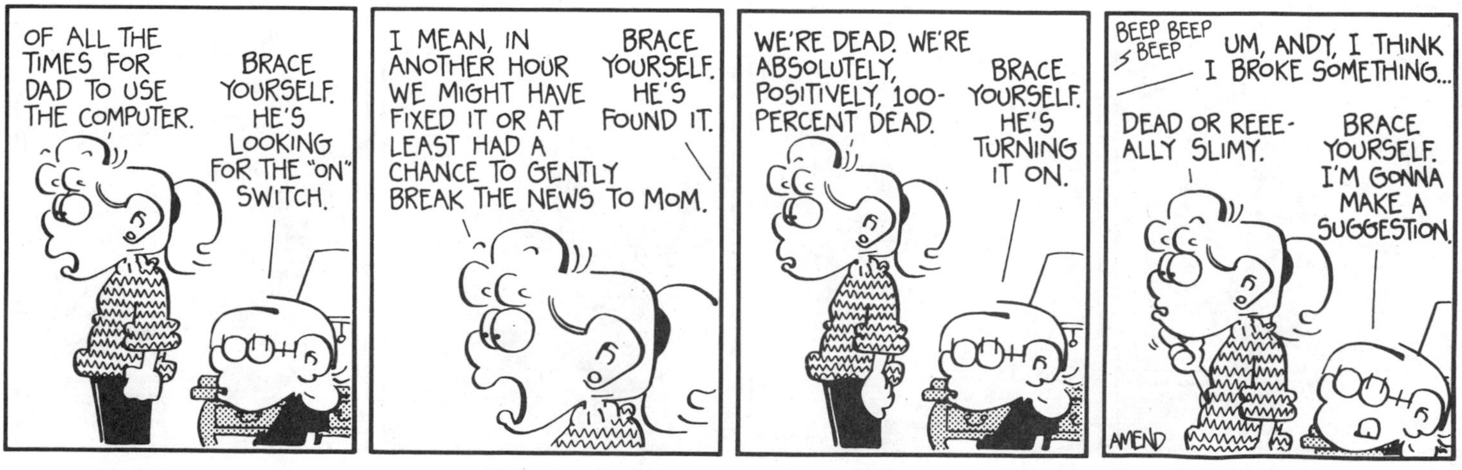
OF ALL THE TIMES FOR DAD TO USE THE COMPUTER.
BRACE YOURSELF. HE'S LOOKING FOR THE "ON" SWITCH.
I MEAN, IN ANOTHER HOUR WE MIGHT HAVE FIXED IT OR AT LEAST HAD A CHANCE TO GENTLY BREAK THE NEWS TO MOM.
BRACE YOURSELF. HE'S FOUND IT.
WE'RE DEAD. WE'RE ABSOLUTELY, POSITIVELY, 100-PERCENT DEAD.
BRACE YOURSELF. HE'S TURNING IT ON.
BEEP BEEP BEEP
UM, ANDY, I THINK I BROKE SOMETHING...
DEAD OR REEE-ALLY SLIMY.
BRACE YOURSELF. I'M GONNA MAKE A SUGGESTION.
AMEND

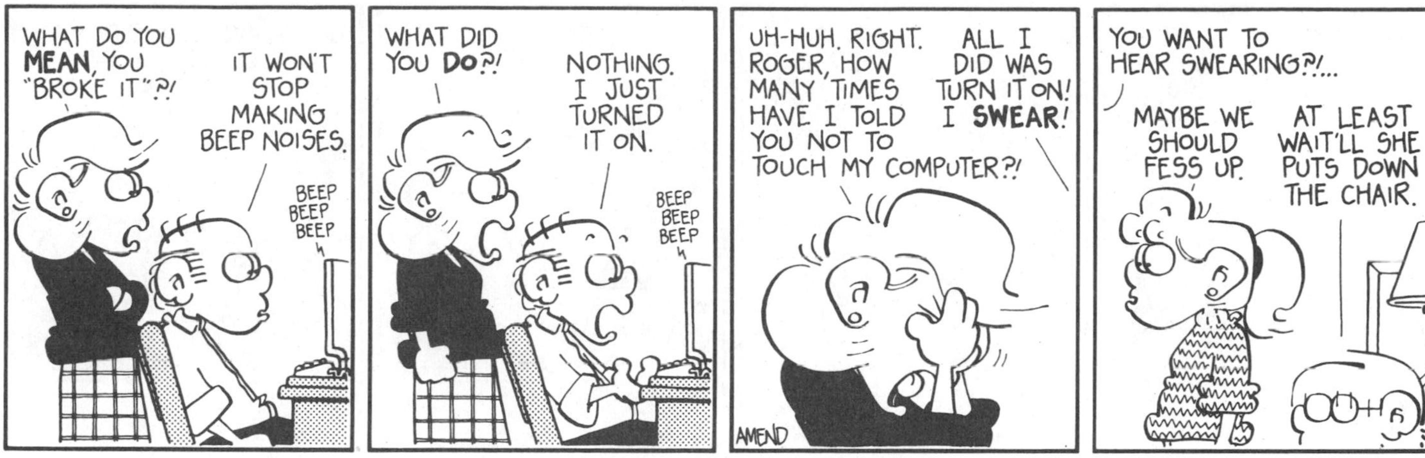
WHAT DO YOU MEAN, YOU "BROKE IT"?!
IT WON'T STOP MAKING BEEP NOISES.
BEEP BEEP BEEP
WHAT DID YOU DO?!
NOTHING. I JUST TURNED IT ON.
BEEP BEEP BEEP
UH-HUH. RIGHT. ROGER, HOW MANY TIMES HAVE I TOLD YOU NOT TO TOUCH MY COMPUTER?!
ALL I DID WAS TURN IT ON! I SWEAR!
AMEND
YOU WANT TO HEAR SWEARING?!...
MAYBE WE SHOULD FESS UP.
AT LEAST WAIT'LL SHE PUTS DOWN THE CHAIR.

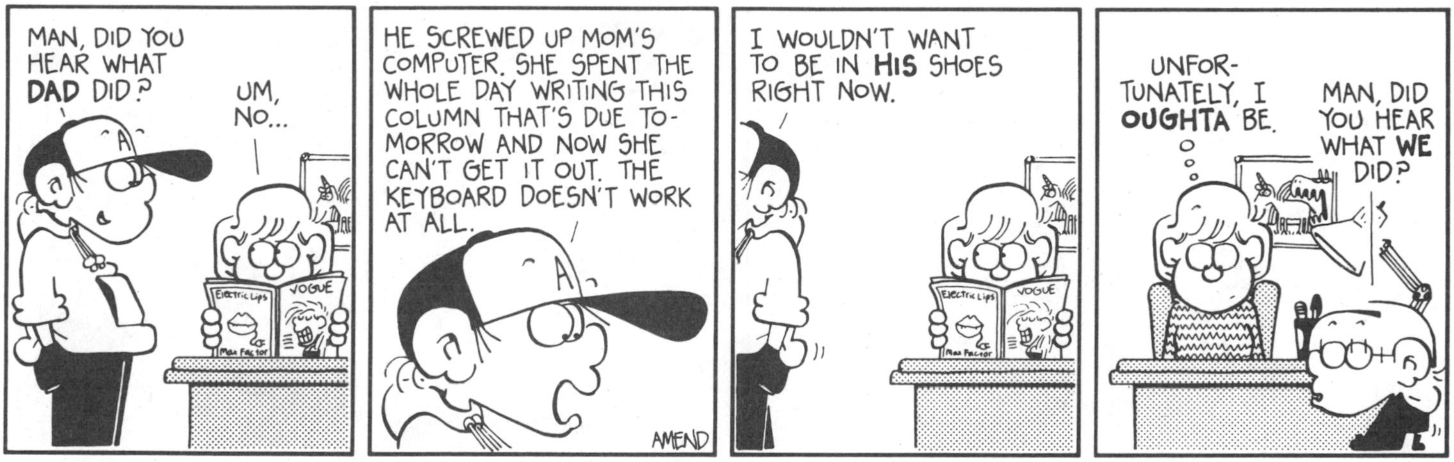
MAN, DID YOU HEAR WHAT DAD DID?
UM, NO...
HE SCREWED UP MOM'S COMPUTER. SHE SPENT THE WHOLE DAY WRITING THIS COLUMN THAT'S DUE TO-MORROW AND NOW SHE CAN'T GET IT OUT. THE KEYBOARD DOESN'T WORK AT ALL.
AMEND
I WOULDN'T WANT TO BE IN HIS SHOES RIGHT NOW.
UNFOR-TUNATELY, I OUGHTA BE.
MAN, DID YOU HEAR WHAT WE DID?

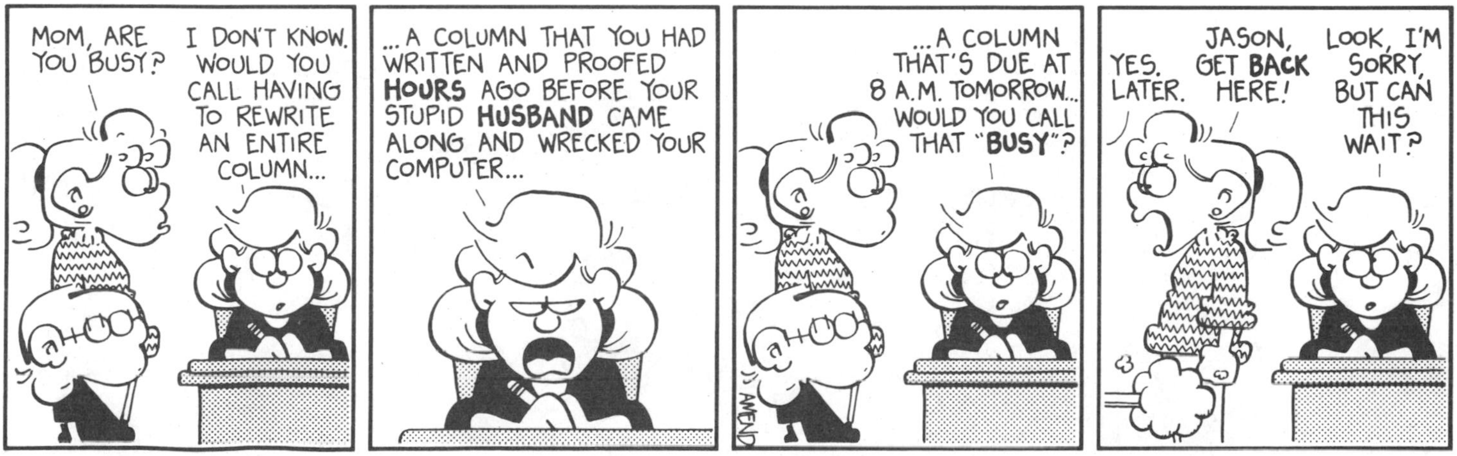
MOM, ARE YOU BUSY?
I DON'T KNOW. WOULD YOU CALL HAVING TO REWRITE AN ENTIRE COLUMN...
...A COLUMN THAT YOU HAD WRITTEN AND PROOFED HOURS AGO BEFORE YOUR STUPID HUSBAND CAME ALONG AND WRECKED YOUR COMPUTER...
...A COLUMN THAT'S DUE AT 8 A.M. TOMORROW... WOULD YOU CALL THAT "BUSY"?
AMEND
YES. LATER.
JASON, GET BACK HERE!
LOOK, I'M SORRY, BUT CAN THIS WAIT?

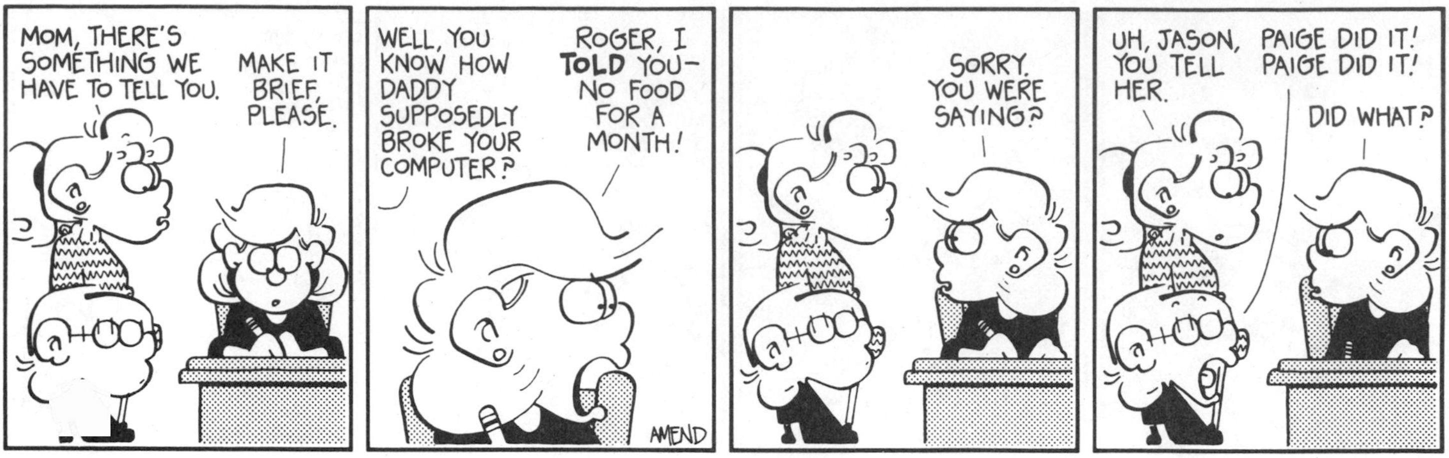
MOM, THERE'S SOMETHING WE HAVE TO TELL YOU.
MAKE IT BRIEF, PLEASE.
WELL, YOU KNOW HOW DADDY SUPPOSEDLY BROKE YOUR COMPUTER?
ROGER, I **TOLD** YOU– NO FOOD FOR A MONTH!
AMEND
SORRY. YOU WERE SAYING?
UH, JASON, YOU TELL HER.
PAIGE DID IT! PAIGE DID IT!
DID WHAT?

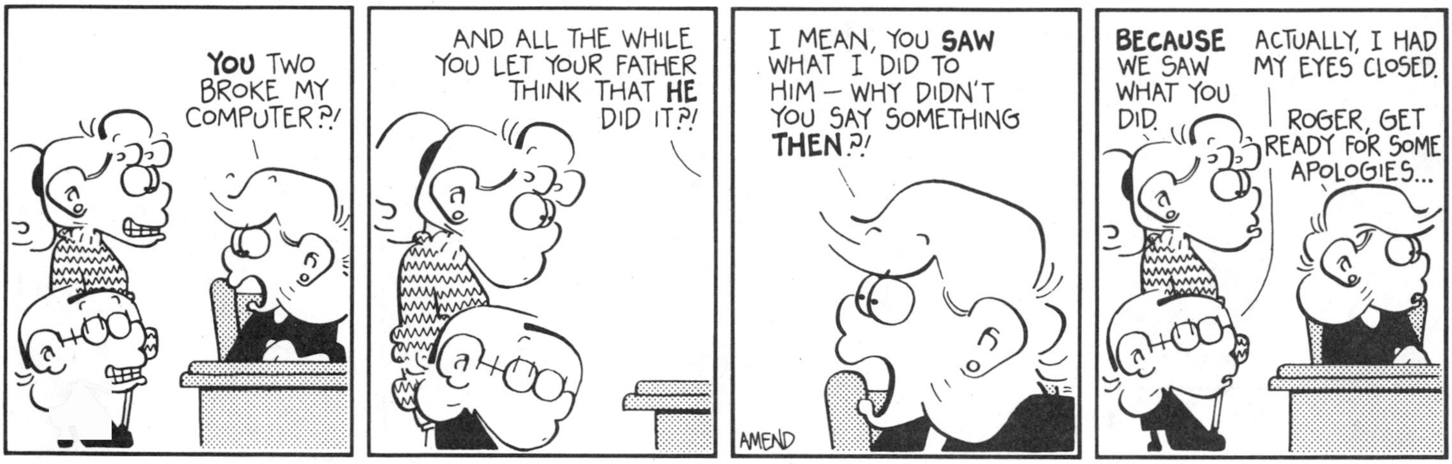
YOU TWO BROKE MY COMPUTER?!
AND ALL THE WHILE YOU LET YOUR FATHER THINK THAT **HE** DID IT?!
I MEAN, YOU **SAW** WHAT I DID TO HIM – WHY DIDN'T YOU SAY SOMETHING **THEN**?!
AMEND
BECAUSE WE SAW WHAT YOU DID.
ACTUALLY, I HAD MY EYES CLOSED.
ROGER, GET READY FOR SOME APOLOGIES...

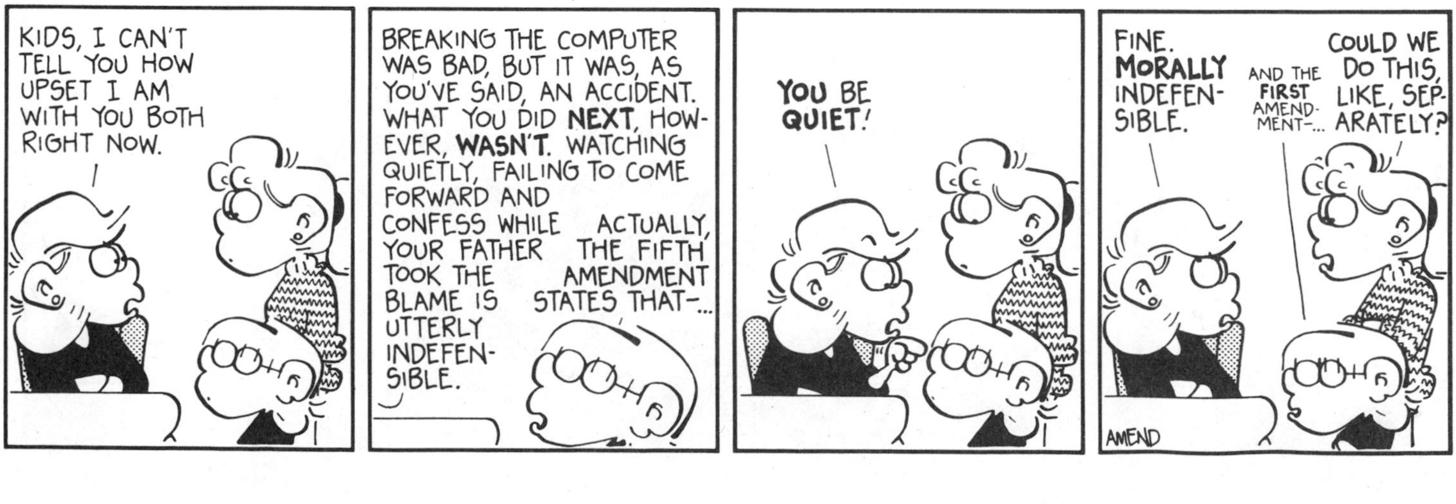
KIDS, I CAN'T TELL YOU HOW UPSET I AM WITH YOU BOTH RIGHT NOW.
BREAKING THE COMPUTER WAS BAD, BUT IT WAS, AS YOU'VE SAID, AN ACCIDENT. WHAT YOU DID **NEXT**, HOWEVER, **WASN'T**. WATCHING QUIETLY, FAILING TO COME FORWARD AND CONFESS WHILE YOUR FATHER TOOK THE BLAME IS UTTERLY INDEFENSIBLE.
ACTUALLY, THE FIFTH AMENDMENT STATES THAT–...
YOU BE **QUIET**!
FINE. **MORALLY** INDEFENSIBLE.
AND THE **FIRST** AMENDMENT–...
COULD WE DO THIS, LIKE, SEPARATELY?
AMEND

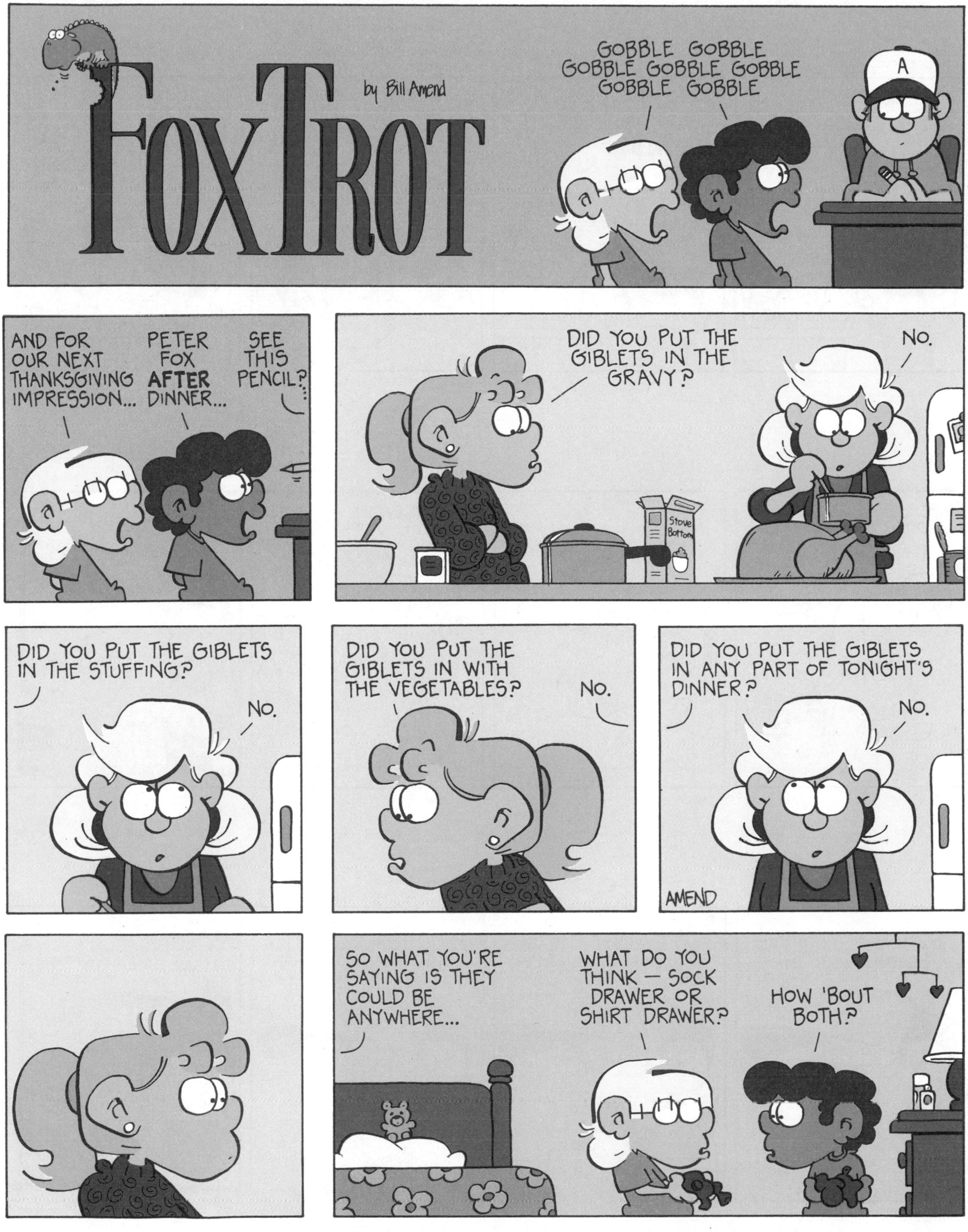
FoxTrot
by Bill Amend
GOBBLE GOBBLE GOBBLE GOBBLE GOBBLE GOBBLE GOBBLE
AND FOR OUR NEXT THANKSGIVING IMPRESSION...
PETER FOX AFTER DINNER...
SEE THIS PENCIL?
DID YOU PUT THE GIBLETS IN THE GRAVY?
NO.
Stove Bottom
DID YOU PUT THE GIBLETS IN THE STUFFING?
NO.
DID YOU PUT THE GIBLETS IN WITH THE VEGETABLES?
NO.
DID YOU PUT THE GIBLETS IN ANY PART OF TONIGHT'S DINNER?
NO.
AMEND
SO WHAT YOU'RE SAYING IS THEY COULD BE ANYWHERE...
WHAT DO YOU THINK — SOCK DRAWER OR SHIRT DRAWER?
HOW 'BOUT BOTH?

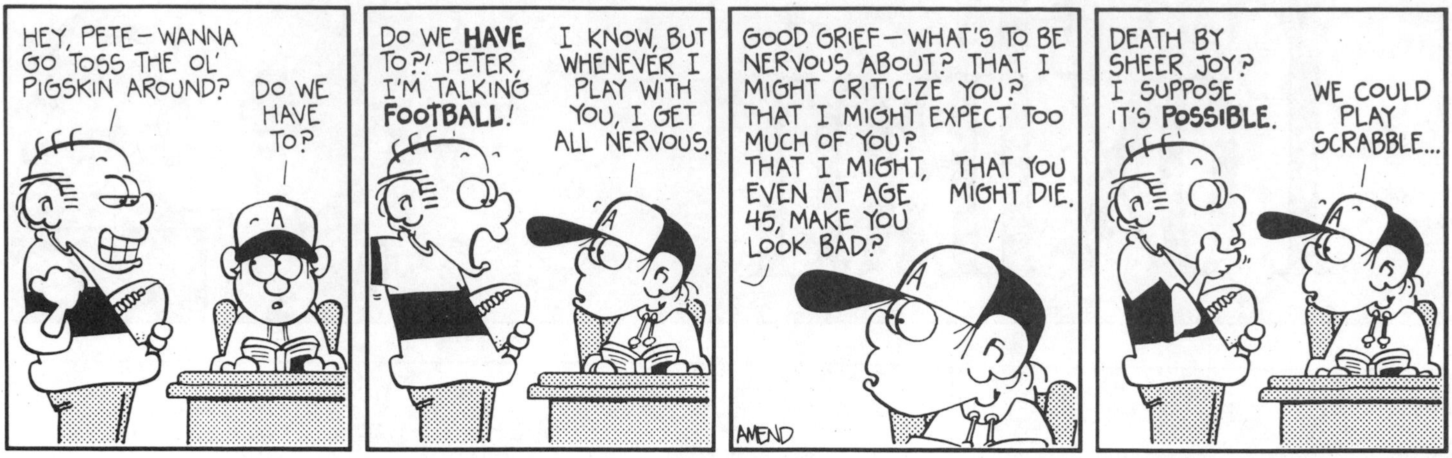
HEY, PETE—WANNA GO TOSS THE OL' PIGSKIN AROUND?
DO WE HAVE TO?
DO WE **HAVE** TO?! PETER, I'M TALKING **FOOTBALL**!
I KNOW, BUT WHENEVER I PLAY WITH YOU, I GET ALL NERVOUS.
GOOD GRIEF—WHAT'S TO BE NERVOUS ABOUT? THAT I MIGHT CRITICIZE YOU? THAT I MIGHT EXPECT TOO MUCH OF YOU? THAT I MIGHT, EVEN AT AGE 45, MAKE YOU LOOK BAD?
THAT YOU MIGHT DIE.
AMEND
DEATH BY SHEER JOY? I SUPPOSE IT'S **POSSIBLE**.
WE COULD PLAY SCRABBLE...

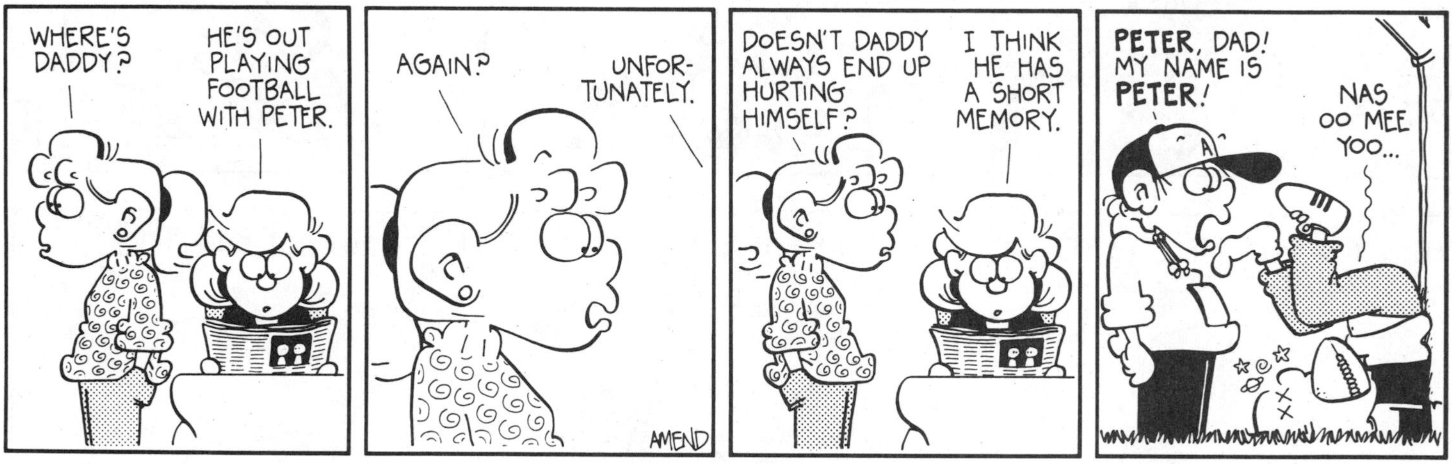
WHERE'S DADDY?
HE'S OUT PLAYING FOOTBALL WITH PETER.
AGAIN?
UNFORTUNATELY.
AMEND
DOESN'T DADDY ALWAYS END UP HURTING HIMSELF?
I THINK HE HAS A SHORT MEMORY.
PETER, DAD! MY NAME IS **PETER**!
NAS OO MEE YOO...

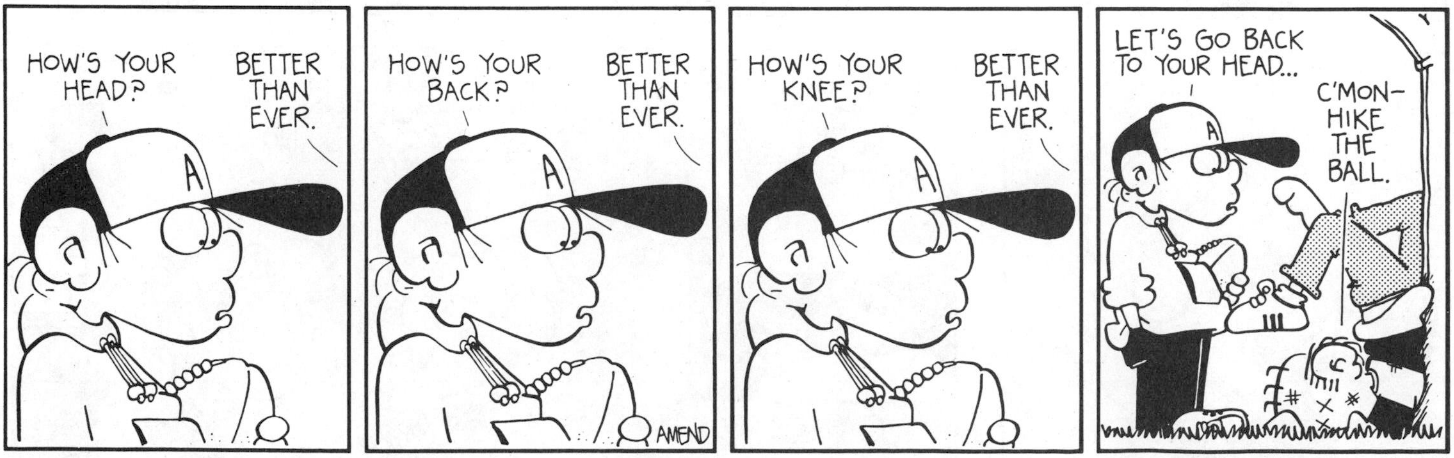
HOW'S YOUR HEAD?
BETTER THAN EVER.
HOW'S YOUR BACK?
BETTER THAN EVER.
AMEND
HOW'S YOUR KNEE?
BETTER THAN EVER.
LET'S GO BACK TO YOUR HEAD...
C'MON—HIKE THE BALL.

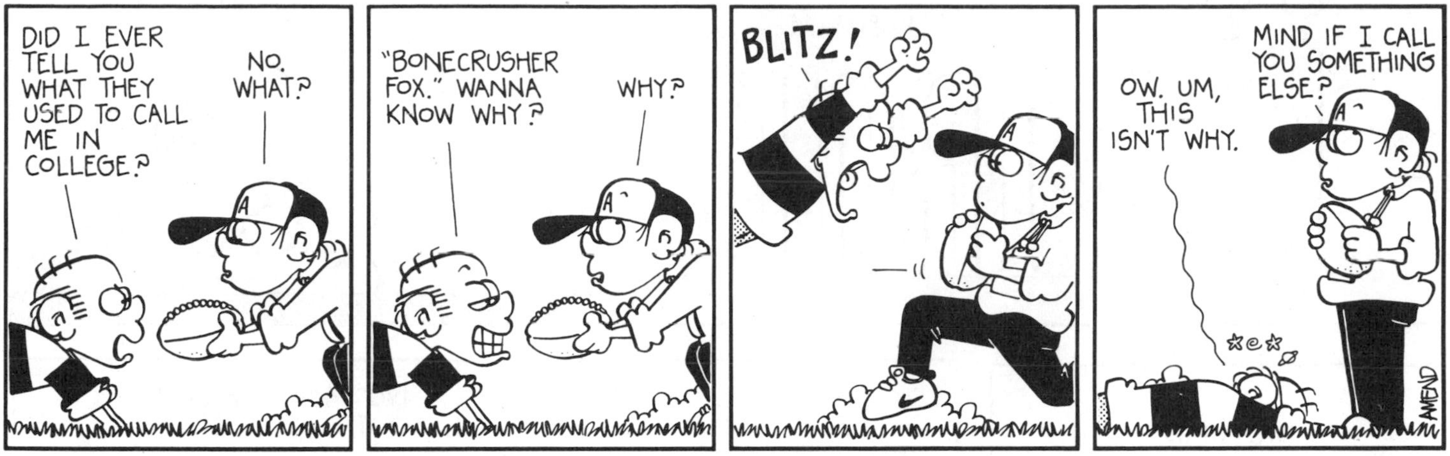
DID I EVER TELL YOU WHAT THEY USED TO CALL ME IN COLLEGE?
NO. WHAT?
"BONECRUSHER FOX." WANNA KNOW WHY?
WHY?
BLITZ!
OW. UM, THIS ISN'T WHY.
MIND IF I CALL YOU SOMETHING ELSE?
AMEND

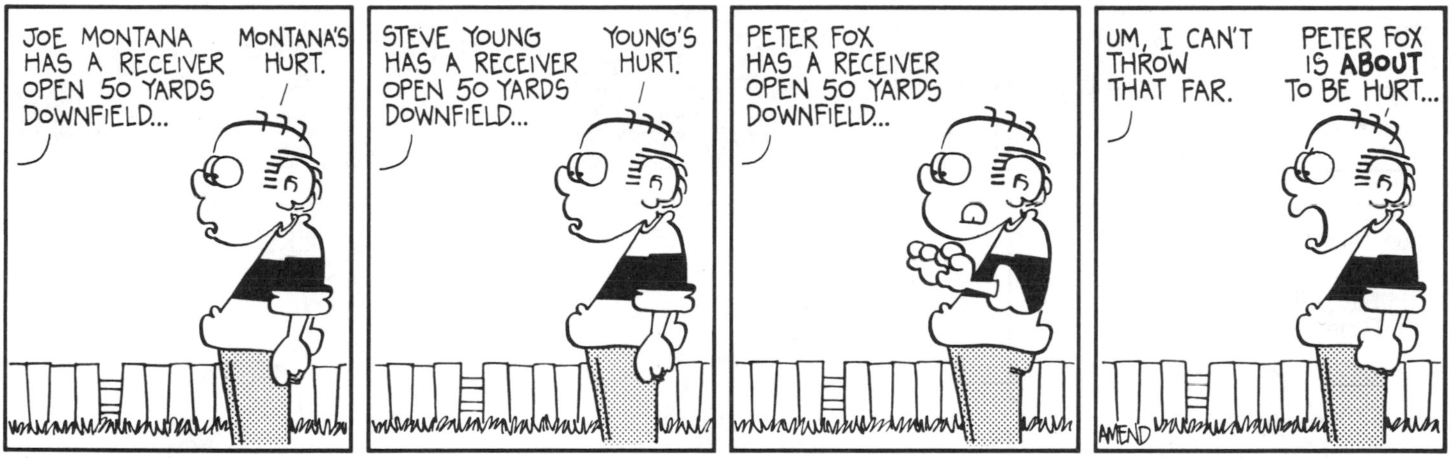
JOE MONTANA HAS A RECEIVER OPEN 50 YARDS DOWNFIELD...
MONTANA'S HURT.
STEVE YOUNG HAS A RECEIVER OPEN 50 YARDS DOWNFIELD...
YOUNG'S HURT.
PETER FOX HAS A RECEIVER OPEN 50 YARDS DOWNFIELD...
UM, I CAN'T THROW THAT FAR.
PETER FOX IS **ABOUT** TO BE HURT...
AMEND

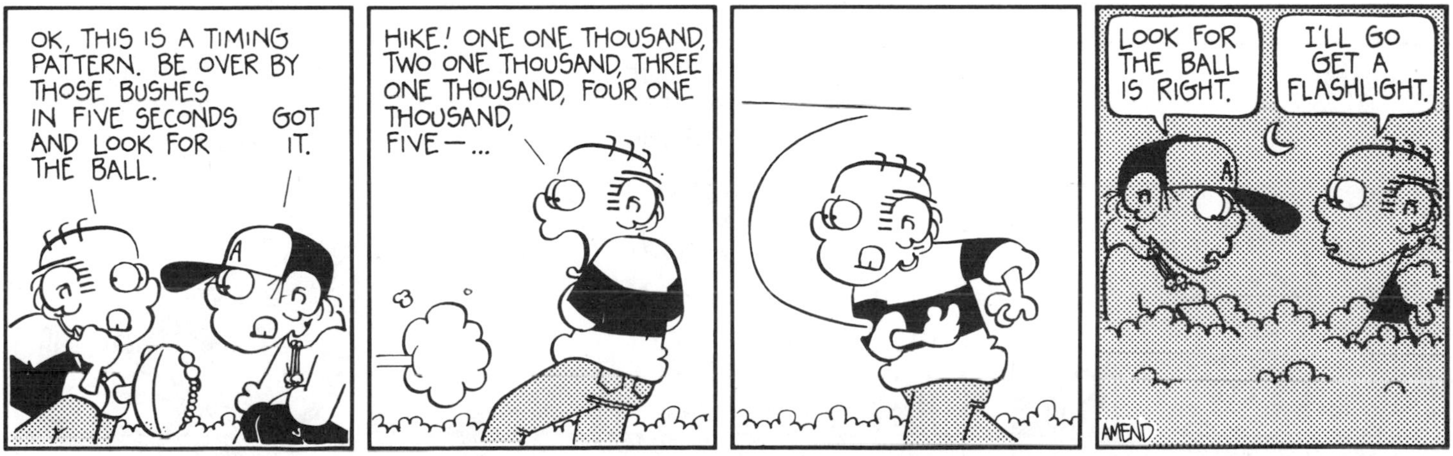
OK, THIS IS A TIMING PATTERN. BE OVER BY THOSE BUSHES IN FIVE SECONDS AND LOOK FOR THE BALL.
GOT IT.
HIKE! ONE ONE THOUSAND, TWO ONE THOUSAND, THREE ONE THOUSAND, FOUR ONE THOUSAND, FIVE—...
LOOK FOR THE BALL IS RIGHT.
I'LL GO GET A FLASHLIGHT.
AMEND

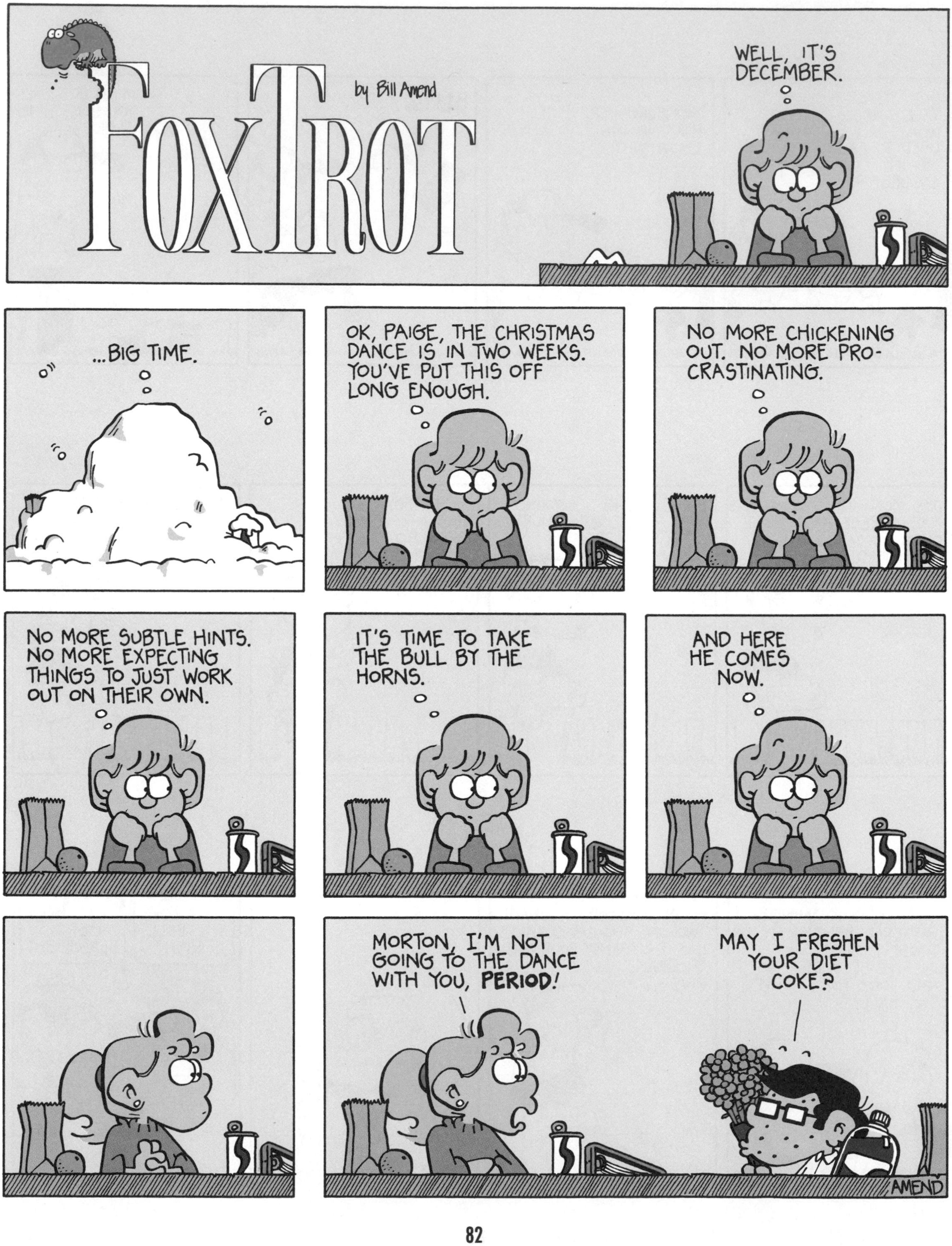
FoxTrot
by Bill Amend
WELL, IT'S DECEMBER.
...BIG TIME.
OK, PAIGE, THE CHRISTMAS DANCE IS IN TWO WEEKS. YOU'VE PUT THIS OFF LONG ENOUGH.
NO MORE CHICKENING OUT. NO MORE PRO-CRASTINATING.
NO MORE SUBTLE HINTS. NO MORE EXPECTING THINGS TO JUST WORK OUT ON THEIR OWN.
IT'S TIME TO TAKE THE BULL BY THE HORNS.
AND HERE HE COMES NOW.
MORTON, I'M NOT GOING TO THE DANCE WITH YOU, **PERIOD**!
MAY I FRESHEN YOUR DIET COKE?
AMEND

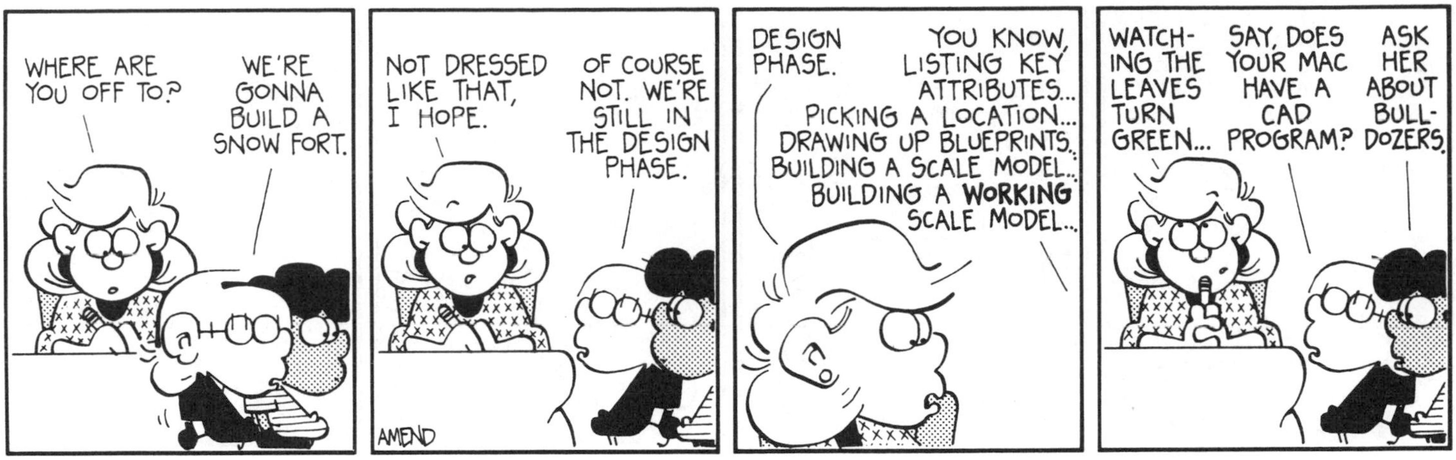
WHERE ARE YOU OFF TO?
WE'RE GONNA BUILD A SNOW FORT.
NOT DRESSED LIKE THAT, I HOPE.
OF COURSE NOT. WE'RE STILL IN THE DESIGN PHASE.
AMEND
DESIGN PHASE.
YOU KNOW, LISTING KEY ATTRIBUTES... PICKING A LOCATION... DRAWING UP BLUEPRINTS... BUILDING A SCALE MODEL... BUILDING A **WORKING** SCALE MODEL...
WATCHING THE LEAVES TURN GREEN...
SAY, DOES YOUR MAC HAVE A CAD PROGRAM?
ASK HER ABOUT BULLDOZERS.

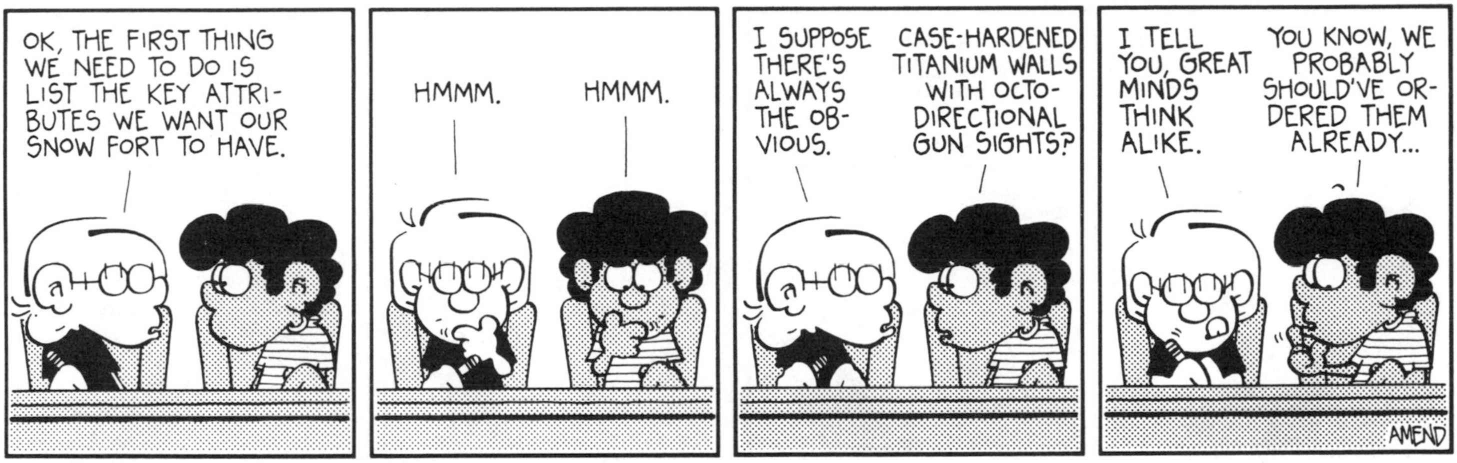
OK, THE FIRST THING WE NEED TO DO IS LIST THE KEY ATTRIBUTES WE WANT OUR SNOW FORT TO HAVE.
HMMM.
HMMM.
I SUPPOSE THERE'S ALWAYS THE OBVIOUS.
CASE-HARDENED TITANIUM WALLS WITH OCTO-DIRECTIONAL GUN SIGHTS?
I TELL YOU, GREAT MINDS THINK ALIKE.
YOU KNOW, WE PROBABLY SHOULD'VE ORDERED THEM ALREADY...
AMEND

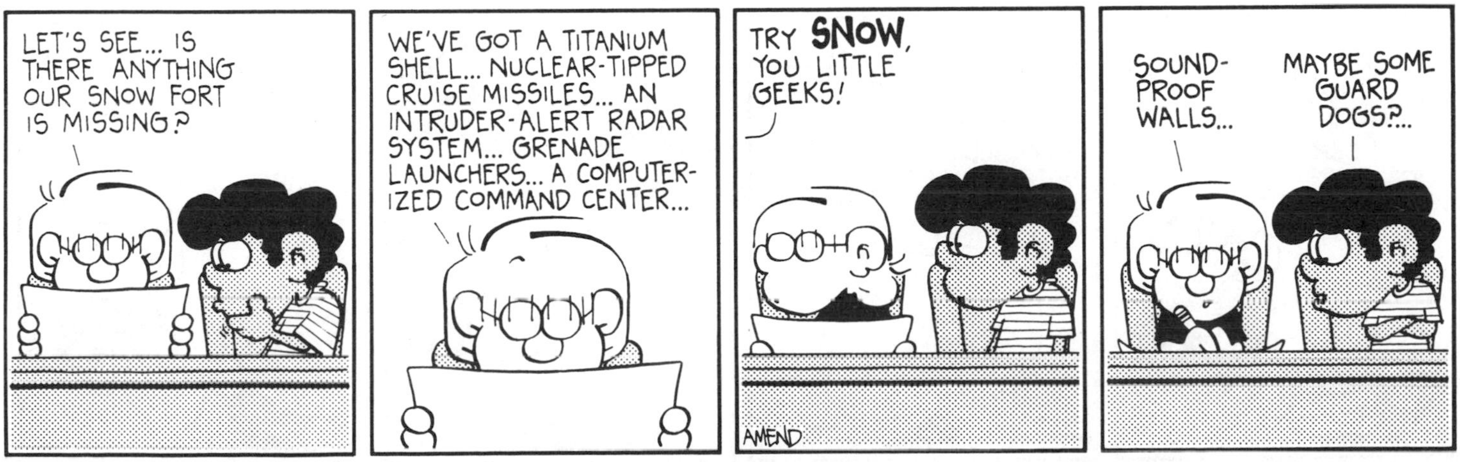
LET'S SEE... IS THERE ANYTHING OUR SNOW FORT IS MISSING?
WE'VE GOT A TITANIUM SHELL... NUCLEAR-TIPPED CRUISE MISSILES... AN INTRUDER-ALERT RADAR SYSTEM... GRENADE LAUNCHERS... A COMPUTERIZED COMMAND CENTER...
TRY **SNOW**, YOU LITTLE GEEKS!
AMEND
SOUND-PROOF WALLS...
MAYBE SOME GUARD DOGS?...

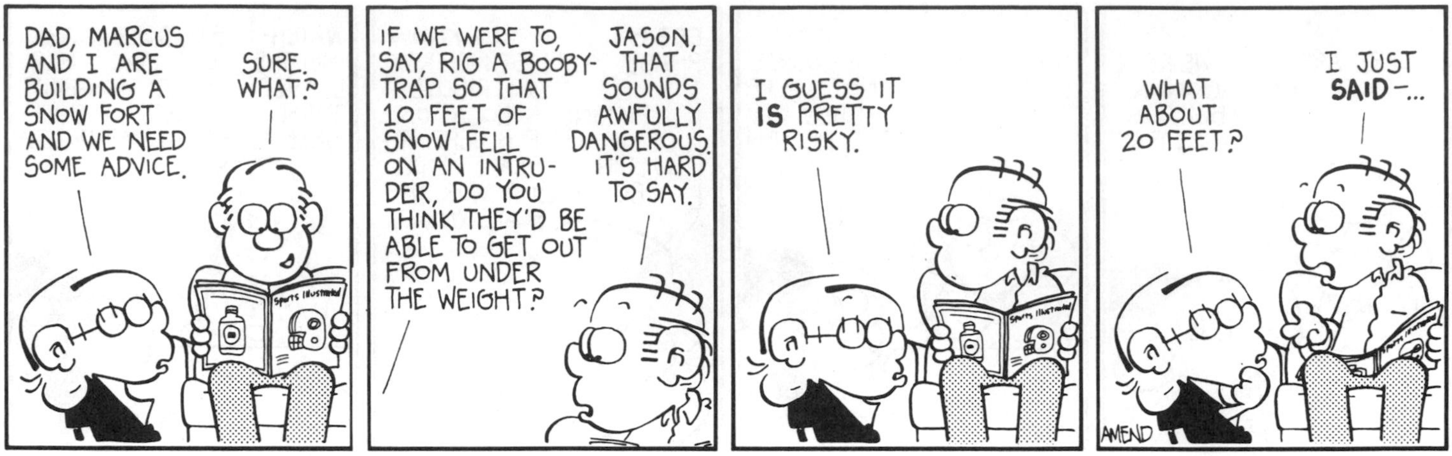
DAD, MARCUS AND I ARE BUILDING A SNOW FORT AND WE NEED SOME ADVICE.
SURE. WHAT?
IF WE WERE TO, SAY, RIG A BOOBY-TRAP SO THAT 10 FEET OF SNOW FELL ON AN INTRUDER, DO YOU THINK THEY'D BE ABLE TO GET OUT FROM UNDER THE WEIGHT?
JASON, THAT SOUNDS AWFULLY DANGEROUS. IT'S HARD TO SAY.
I GUESS IT **IS** PRETTY RISKY.
WHAT ABOUT 20 FEET?
I JUST **SAID**—...
AMEND

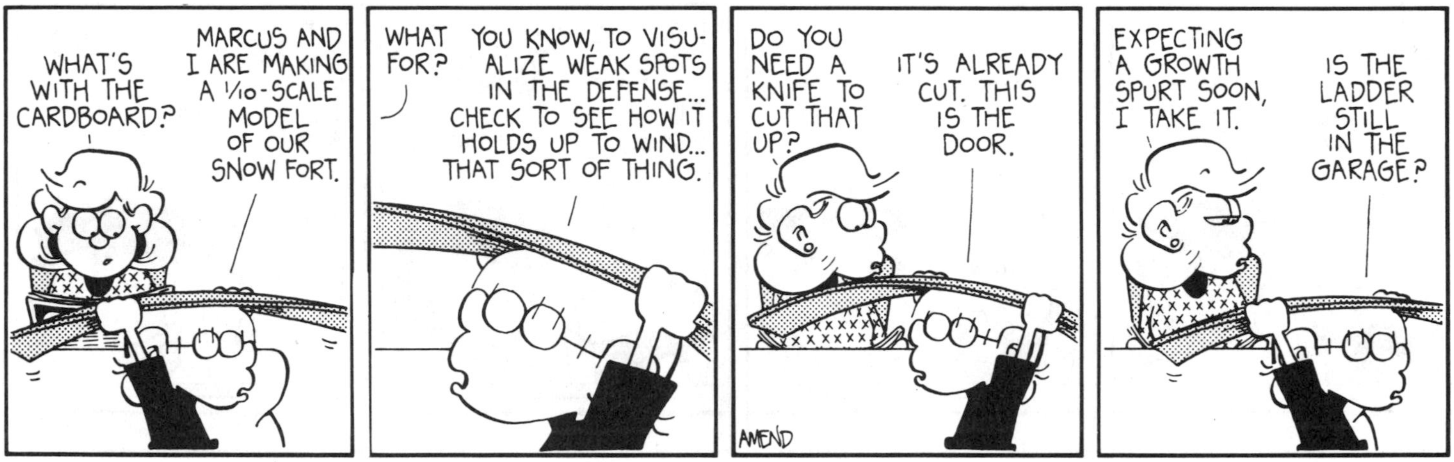
WHAT'S WITH THE CARDBOARD?
MARCUS AND I ARE MAKING A 1/10-SCALE MODEL OF OUR SNOW FORT.
WHAT FOR?
YOU KNOW, TO VISUALIZE WEAK SPOTS IN THE DEFENSE... CHECK TO SEE HOW IT HOLDS UP TO WIND... THAT SORT OF THING.
DO YOU NEED A KNIFE TO CUT THAT UP?
IT'S ALREADY CUT. THIS IS THE DOOR.
EXPECTING A GROWTH SPURT SOON, I TAKE IT.
IS THE LADDER STILL IN THE GARAGE?
AMEND

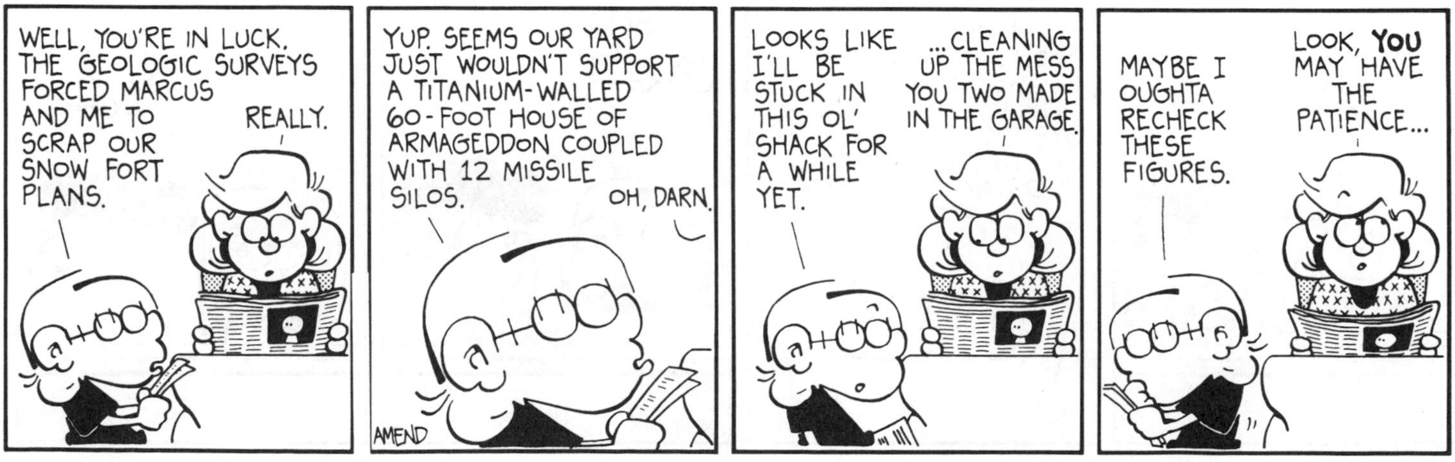
WELL, YOU'RE IN LUCK. THE GEOLOGIC SURVEYS FORCED MARCUS AND ME TO SCRAP OUR SNOW FORT PLANS.
REALLY.
YUP. SEEMS OUR YARD JUST WOULDN'T SUPPORT A TITANIUM-WALLED 60-FOOT HOUSE OF ARMAGEDDON COUPLED WITH 12 MISSILE SILOS.
OH, DARN.
AMEND
LOOKS LIKE I'LL BE STUCK IN THIS OL' SHACK FOR A WHILE YET.
...CLEANING UP THE MESS YOU TWO MADE IN THE GARAGE.
MAYBE I OUGHTA RECHECK THESE FIGURES.
LOOK, **YOU** MAY HAVE THE PATIENCE...

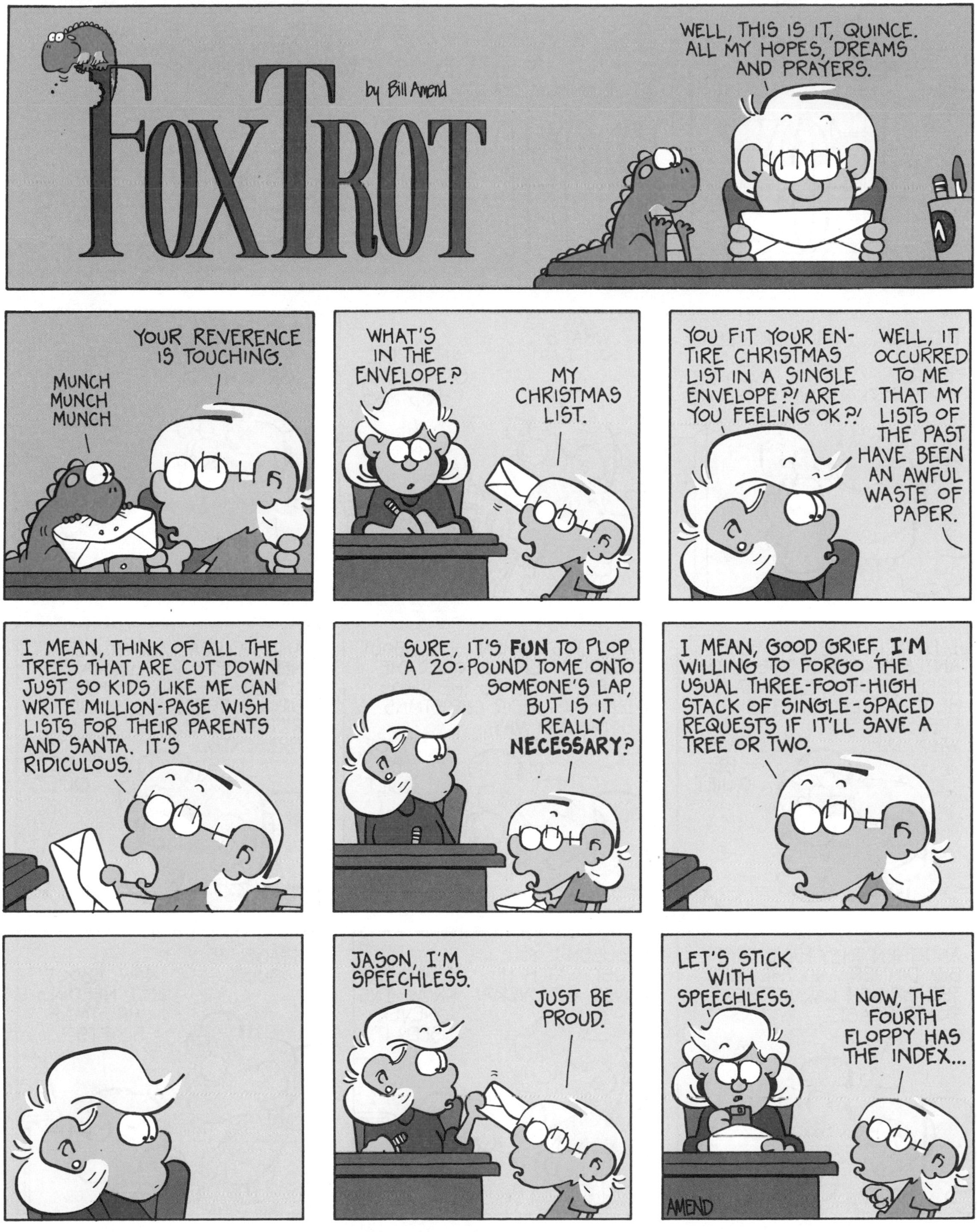
FoxTrot
by Bill Amend
WELL, THIS IS IT, QUINCE. ALL MY HOPES, DREAMS AND PRAYERS.
MUNCH MUNCH MUNCH
YOUR REVERENCE IS TOUCHING.
WHAT'S IN THE ENVELOPE?
MY CHRISTMAS LIST.
YOU FIT YOUR ENTIRE CHRISTMAS LIST IN A SINGLE ENVELOPE?! ARE YOU FEELING OK?!
WELL, IT OCCURRED TO ME THAT MY LISTS OF THE PAST HAVE BEEN AN AWFUL WASTE OF PAPER.
I MEAN, THINK OF ALL THE TREES THAT ARE CUT DOWN JUST SO KIDS LIKE ME CAN WRITE MILLION-PAGE WISH LISTS FOR THEIR PARENTS AND SANTA. IT'S RIDICULOUS.
SURE, IT'S **FUN** TO PLOP A 20-POUND TOME ONTO SOMEONE'S LAP, BUT IS IT REALLY **NECESSARY**?
I MEAN, GOOD GRIEF, **I'M** WILLING TO FORGO THE USUAL THREE-FOOT-HIGH STACK OF SINGLE-SPACED REQUESTS IF IT'LL SAVE A TREE OR TWO.
JASON, I'M SPEECHLESS.
JUST BE PROUD.
LET'S STICK WITH SPEECHLESS.
NOW, THE FOURTH FLOPPY HAS THE INDEX...
AMEND

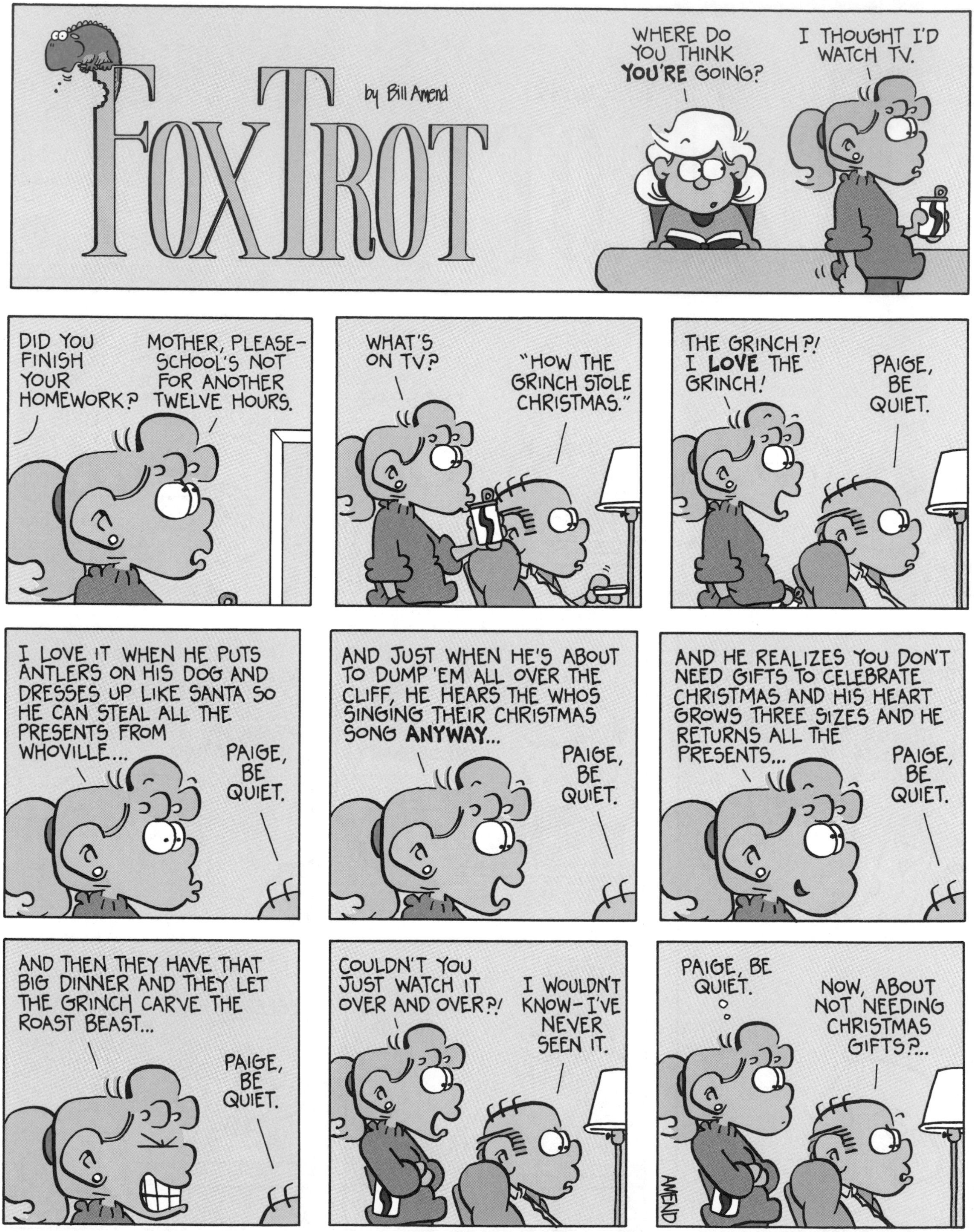
FoxTrot
by Bill Amend
WHERE DO YOU THINK **YOU'RE** GOING?
I THOUGHT I'D WATCH TV.
DID YOU FINISH YOUR HOMEWORK?
MOTHER, PLEASE- SCHOOL'S NOT FOR ANOTHER TWELVE HOURS.
WHAT'S ON TV?
"HOW THE GRINCH STOLE CHRISTMAS."
THE GRINCH?! I **LOVE** THE GRINCH!
PAIGE, BE QUIET.
I LOVE IT WHEN HE PUTS ANTLERS ON HIS DOG AND DRESSES UP LIKE SANTA SO HE CAN STEAL ALL THE PRESENTS FROM WHOVILLE...
PAIGE, BE QUIET.
AND JUST WHEN HE'S ABOUT TO DUMP 'EM ALL OVER THE CLIFF, HE HEARS THE WHOS SINGING THEIR CHRISTMAS SONG **ANYWAY**...
PAIGE, BE QUIET.
AND HE REALIZES YOU DON'T NEED GIFTS TO CELEBRATE CHRISTMAS AND HIS HEART GROWS THREE SIZES AND HE RETURNS ALL THE PRESENTS...
PAIGE, BE QUIET.
AND THEN THEY HAVE THAT BIG DINNER AND THEY LET THE GRINCH CARVE THE ROAST BEAST...
PAIGE, BE QUIET.
COULDN'T YOU JUST WATCH IT OVER AND OVER?!
I WOULDN'T KNOW- I'VE NEVER SEEN IT.
PAIGE, BE QUIET.
NOW, ABOUT NOT NEEDING CHRISTMAS GIFTS?...
AMEND

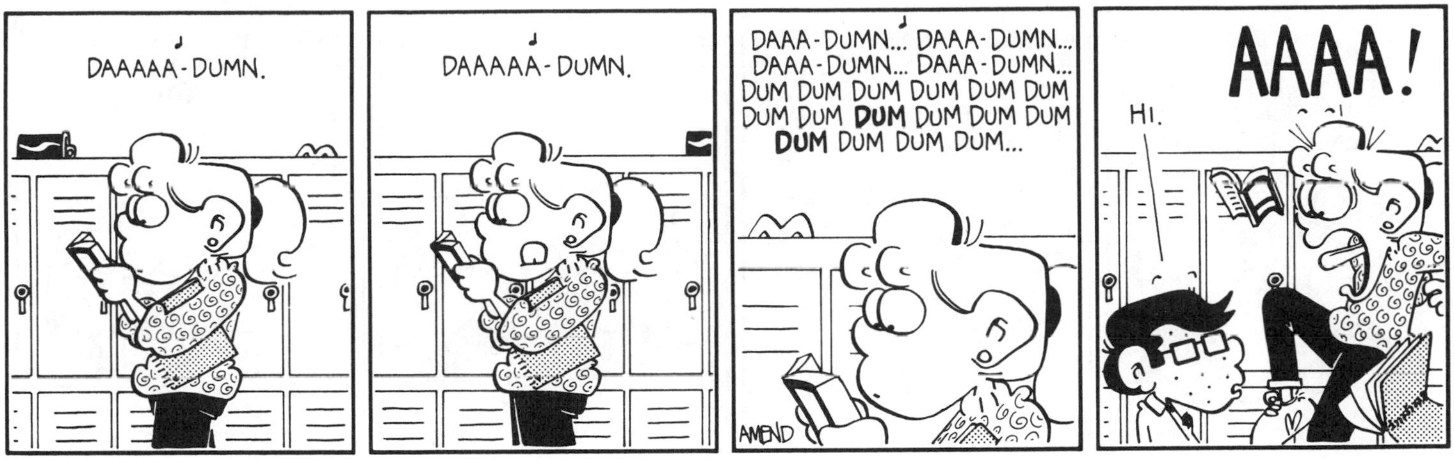
DAAAAA-DUMN.
DAAAAA-DUMN.
DAAA-DUMN... DAAA-DUMN... DAAA-DUMN... DAAA-DUMN... DUM DUM DUM DUM DUM DUM DUM DUM **DUM** DUM DUM DUM **DUM** DUM DUM DUM...
AMEND
HI.
AAAA!

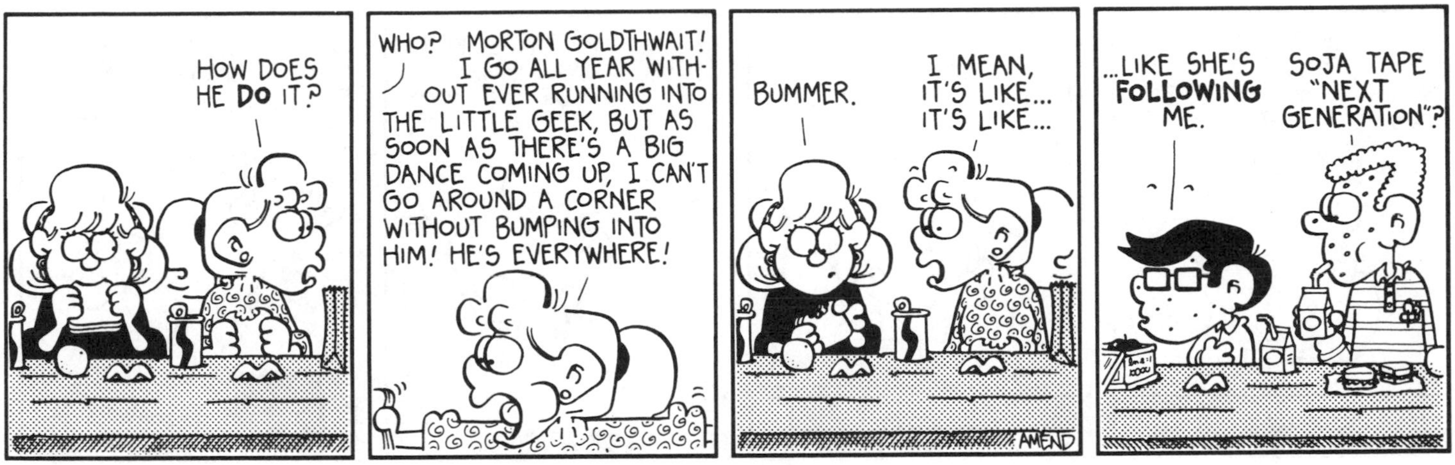
HOW DOES HE **DO** IT?
WHO?
MORTON GOLDTHWAIT! I GO ALL YEAR WITHOUT EVER RUNNING INTO THE LITTLE GEEK, BUT AS SOON AS THERE'S A BIG DANCE COMING UP, I CAN'T GO AROUND A CORNER WITHOUT BUMPING INTO HIM! HE'S EVERYWHERE!
BUMMER.
I MEAN, IT'S LIKE... IT'S LIKE...
AMEND
...LIKE SHE'S **FOLLOWING** ME.
SOJA TAPE "NEXT GENERATION"?

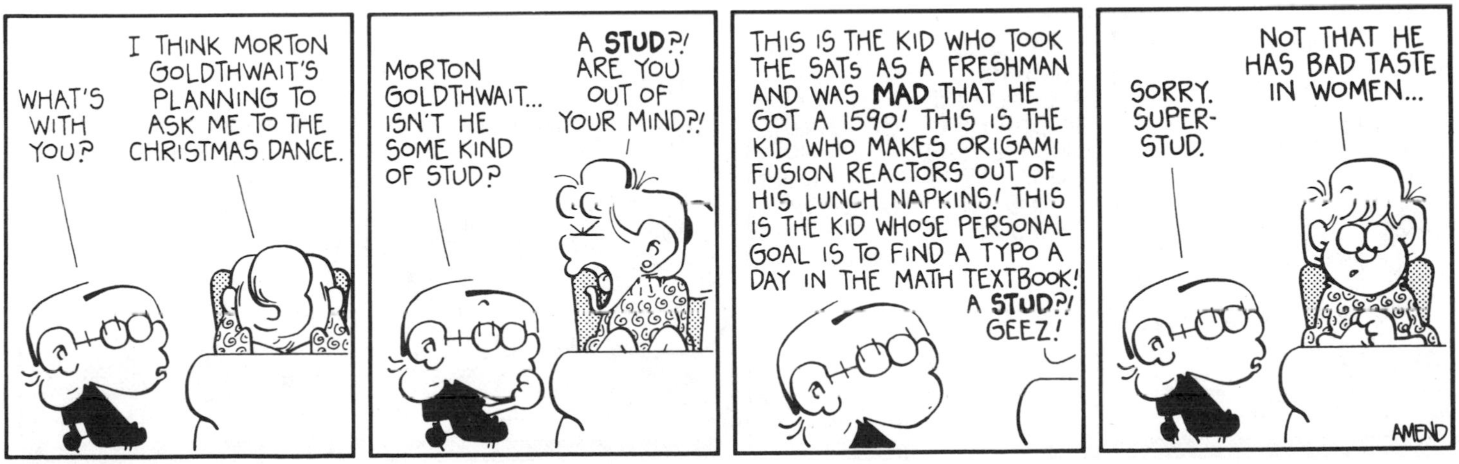
WHAT'S WITH YOU?
I THINK MORTON GOLDTHWAIT'S PLANNING TO ASK ME TO THE CHRISTMAS DANCE.
MORTON GOLDTHWAIT... ISN'T HE SOME KIND OF STUD?
A **STUD**?! ARE YOU OUT OF YOUR MIND?!
THIS IS THE KID WHO TOOK THE SATS AS A FRESHMAN AND WAS **MAD** THAT HE GOT A 1590! THIS IS THE KID WHO MAKES ORIGAMI FUSION REACTORS OUT OF HIS LUNCH NAPKINS! THIS IS THE KID WHOSE PERSONAL GOAL IS TO FIND A TYPO A DAY IN THE MATH TEXTBOOK! A **STUD**?! GEEZ!
SORRY. SUPER-STUD.
NOT THAT HE HAS BAD TASTE IN WOMEN...
AMEND

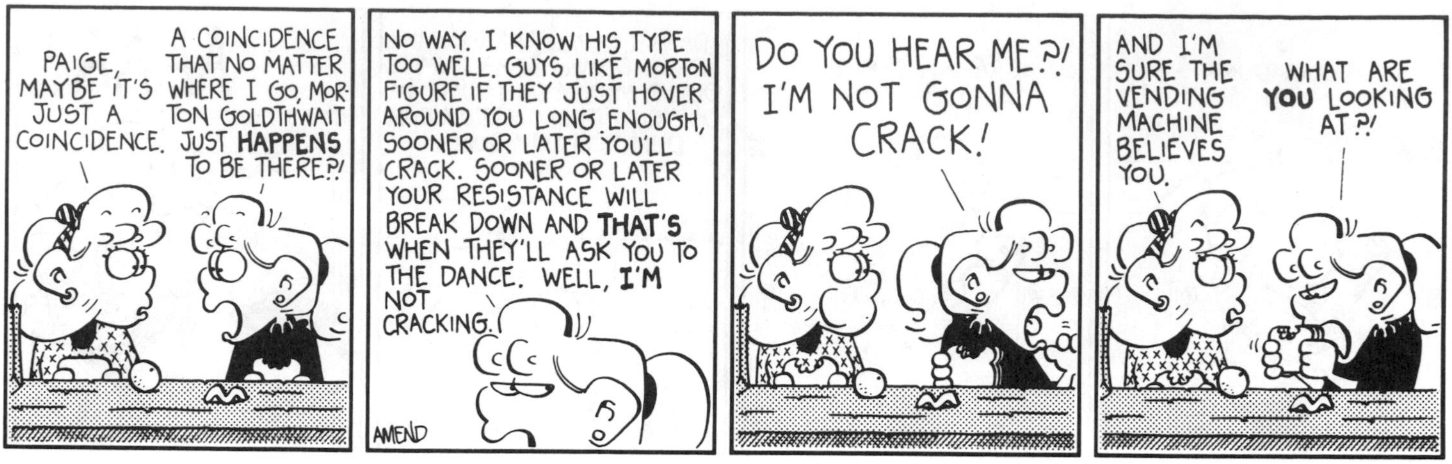
PAIGE, MAYBE IT'S JUST A COINCIDENCE.
A COINCIDENCE THAT NO MATTER WHERE I GO, MORTON GOLDTHWAIT JUST **HAPPENS** TO BE THERE?!
NO WAY. I KNOW HIS TYPE TOO WELL. GUYS LIKE MORTON FIGURE IF THEY JUST HOVER AROUND YOU LONG ENOUGH, SOONER OR LATER YOU'LL CRACK. SOONER OR LATER YOUR RESISTANCE WILL BREAK DOWN AND **THAT'S** WHEN THEY'LL ASK YOU TO THE DANCE. WELL, **I'M** NOT CRACKING.
AMEND
DO YOU HEAR ME?! I'M NOT GONNA CRACK!
AND I'M SURE THE VENDING MACHINE BELIEVES YOU.
WHAT ARE **YOU** LOOKING AT?!

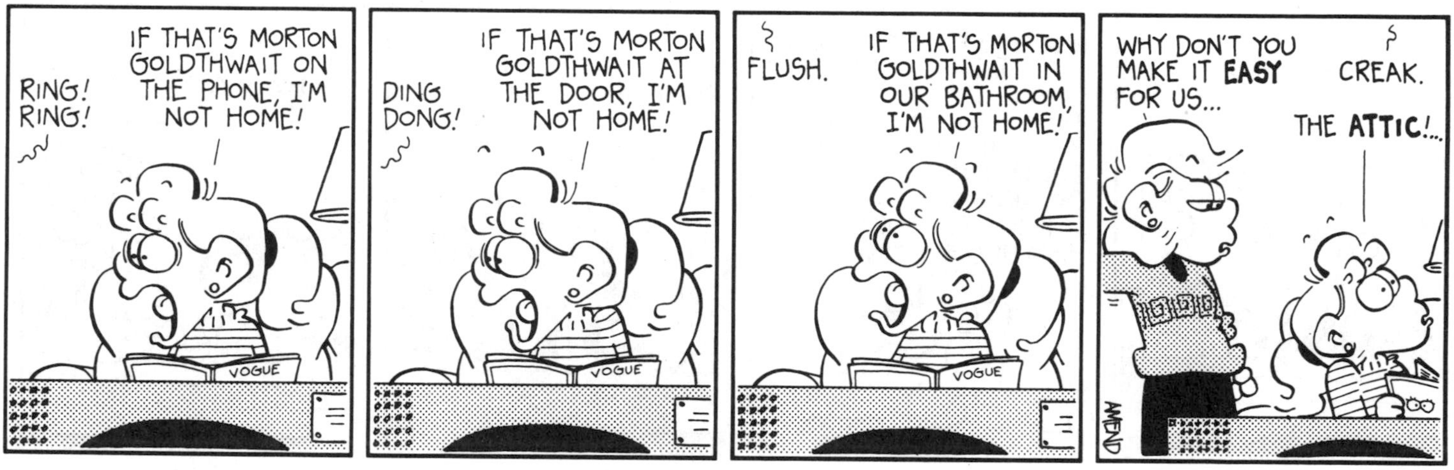
RING! RING!
IF THAT'S MORTON GOLDTHWAIT ON THE PHONE, I'M NOT HOME!
VOGUE
DING DONG!
IF THAT'S MORTON GOLDTHWAIT AT THE DOOR, I'M NOT HOME!
VOGUE
FLUSH.
IF THAT'S MORTON GOLDTHWAIT IN OUR BATHROOM, I'M NOT HOME!
VOGUE
WHY DON'T YOU MAKE IT **EASY** FOR US...
CREAK.
THE **ATTIC**!...
AMEND

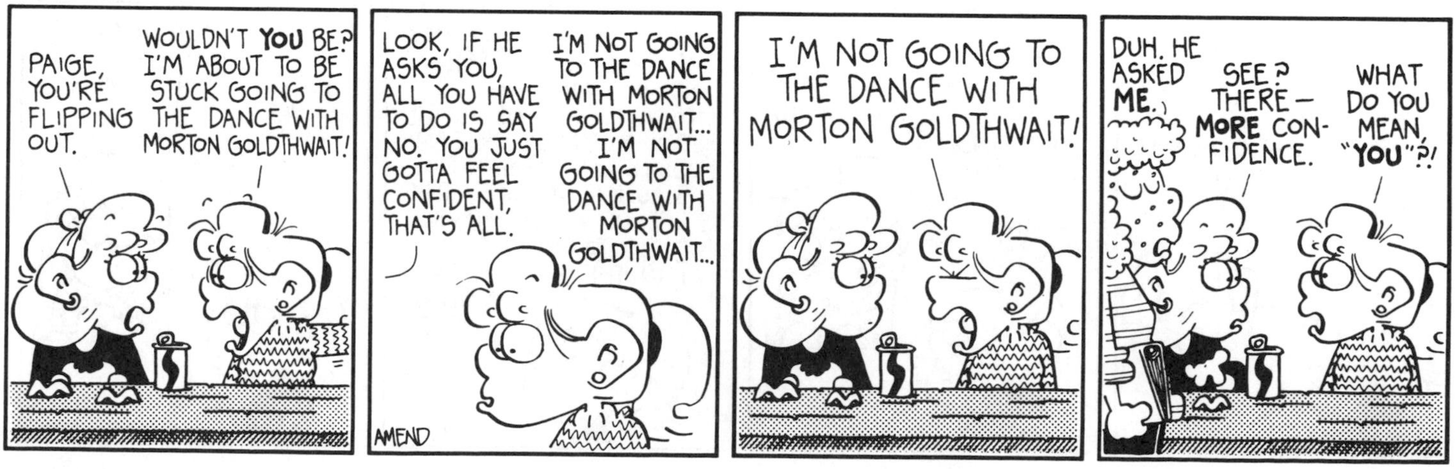
PAIGE, YOU'RE FLIPPING OUT.
WOULDN'T **YOU** BE?! I'M ABOUT TO BE STUCK GOING TO THE DANCE WITH MORTON GOLDTHWAIT!
LOOK, IF HE ASKS YOU, ALL YOU HAVE TO DO IS SAY NO. YOU JUST GOTTA FEEL CONFIDENT, THAT'S ALL.
I'M NOT GOING TO THE DANCE WITH MORTON GOLDTHWAIT... I'M NOT GOING TO THE DANCE WITH MORTON GOLDTHWAIT...
AMEND
I'M NOT GOING TO THE DANCE WITH MORTON GOLDTHWAIT!
DUH. HE ASKED **ME**.
SEE? THERE— **MORE** CONFIDENCE.
WHAT DO YOU MEAN, "**YOU**"?!

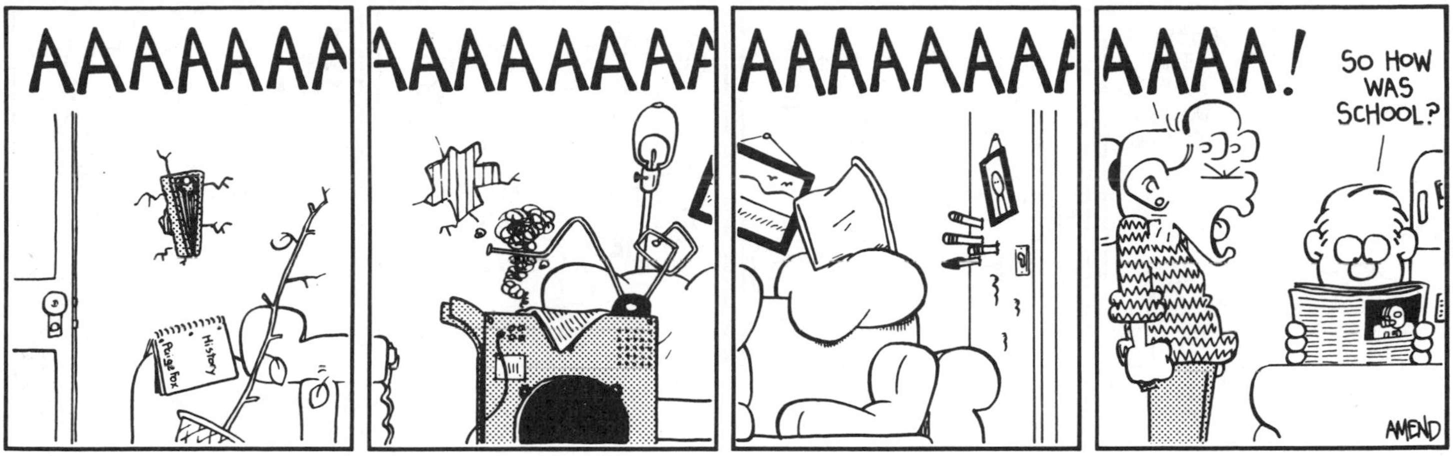
AAAAAAAAAAAAAAAAAAAAAAAAA!
SO HOW WAS SCHOOL?
AMEND

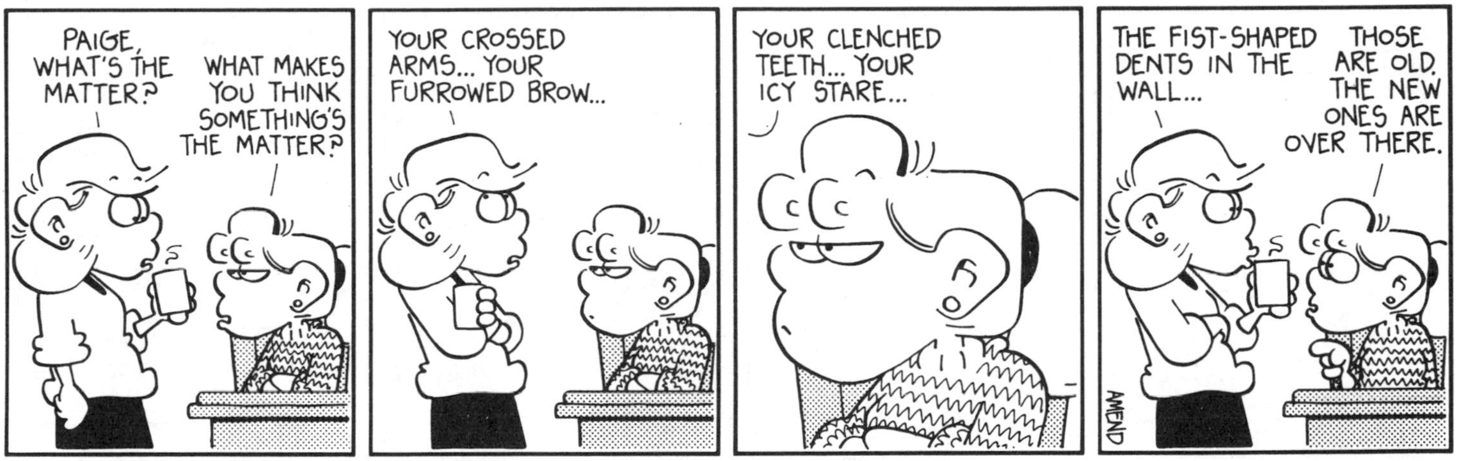
PAIGE, WHAT'S THE MATTER?
WHAT MAKES YOU THINK SOMETHING'S THE MATTER?
YOUR CROSSED ARMS... YOUR FURROWED BROW...
YOUR CLENCHED TEETH... YOUR ICY STARE...
THE FIST-SHAPED DENTS IN THE WALL...
THOSE ARE OLD. THE NEW ONES ARE OVER THERE.
AMEND

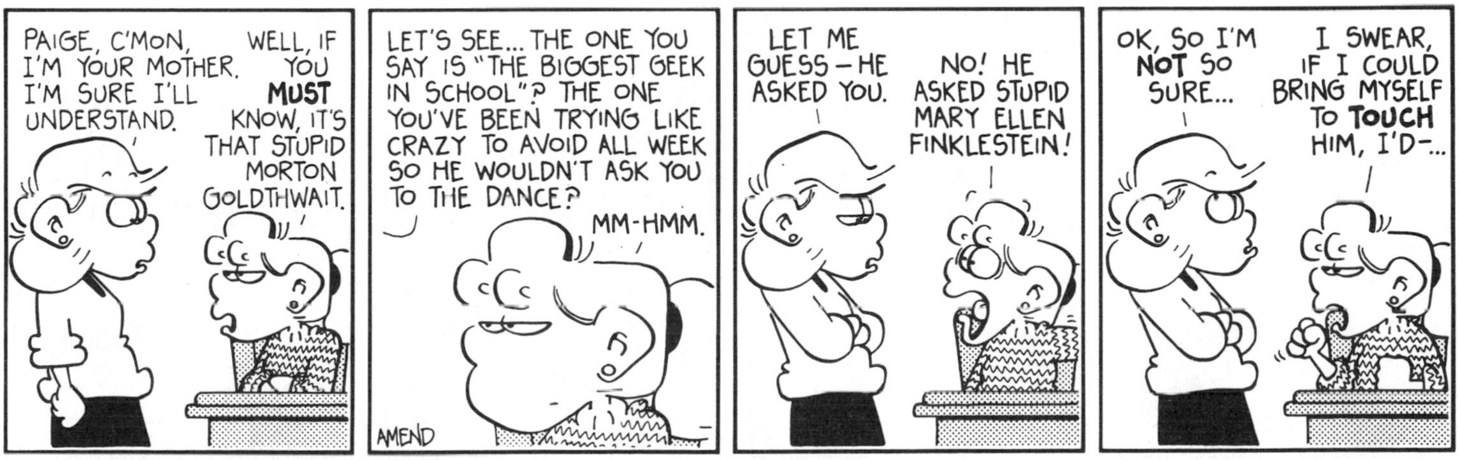
PAIGE, C'MON, I'M YOUR MOTHER. I'M SURE I'LL UNDERSTAND.
WELL, IF YOU **MUST** KNOW, IT'S THAT STUPID MORTON GOLDTHWAIT.
LET'S SEE... THE ONE YOU SAY IS "THE BIGGEST GEEK IN SCHOOL"? THE ONE YOU'VE BEEN TRYING LIKE CRAZY TO AVOID ALL WEEK SO HE WOULDN'T ASK YOU TO THE DANCE?
MM-HMM.
AMEND
LET ME GUESS – HE ASKED YOU.
NO! HE ASKED STUPID MARY ELLEN FINKLESTEIN!
OK, SO I'M **NOT** SO SURE...
I SWEAR, IF I COULD BRING MYSELF TO **TOUCH** HIM, I'D–...

Panel 1: BUT PAIGE, YOU DIDN'T **WANT** TO GO TO THE DANCE WITH MORTON.

SO? WHAT'S THAT HAVE TO DO WITH ANYTHING?

Panel 2: HUH?

THE POINT IS THAT HE DIDN'T EVEN **ASK** ME!

Panel 3: ME! PAIGE FOX! GIRL OF HIS DREAMS! THE WOMAN HE'S HAD SOME WEIRDO CRUSH ON FOR TWO YEARS! I MEAN, WHY ON **EARTH** WOULD HE ASK SOMEONE LIKE MARY ELLEN FINKLESTEIN TO THE DANCE AND NOT **ME**?!

Panel 4: I DUNNO. WHY DON'T YOU ASK HIM?

EEEW! AND **TALK** TO THAT GEEK?! NO WAY!

Panel 5: PAIGE, PUT YOURSELF IN MORTON'S SHOES.

WHY?

Panel 6: JUST BECAUSE. NOW PRETEND THERE'S THIS GIRL YOU REALLY LIKE, BUT EVERY TIME YOU GET NEAR HER SHE RUNS AND EVERY TIME YOU ASK HER TO A DANCE SHE SCREAMS IN HORROR.

Panel 7: NOW, WOULDN'T EVEN **YOU** BE INCLINED TO JUST GIVE UP AFTER A WHILE?

NOT IF SHE WERE **ME**.

Panel 8: OK, WHY DON'T **I** PRETEND I'M MORTON...

WHOA— DO YOU SUPPOSE HE WENT INSANE?

Panel 9: GOLDTHWAIT— WE NEED TO TALK.

ABOUT WHAT?

Panel 10: ABOUT WHAT?! ABOUT WHY YOU DIDN'T ASK ME TO THE CHRISTMAS DANCE! YOU **ALWAYS** ASK ME TO THE STUPID DANCES! YOU'D ASK ME, I'D SAY NO, THEN WE'D START ALL OVER AGAIN THE NEXT MONTH! IT WAS LIKE TRADITION!

Panel 11: I CAN'T BELIEVE YOU'D FORGET ABOUT ME!

THE TRUTH IS, I REMEMBERED.

Panel 12: MORTON, YOU'RE KILLING MY EGO.

EGOS HEAL.

THERE YOU ARE, POOKIE...

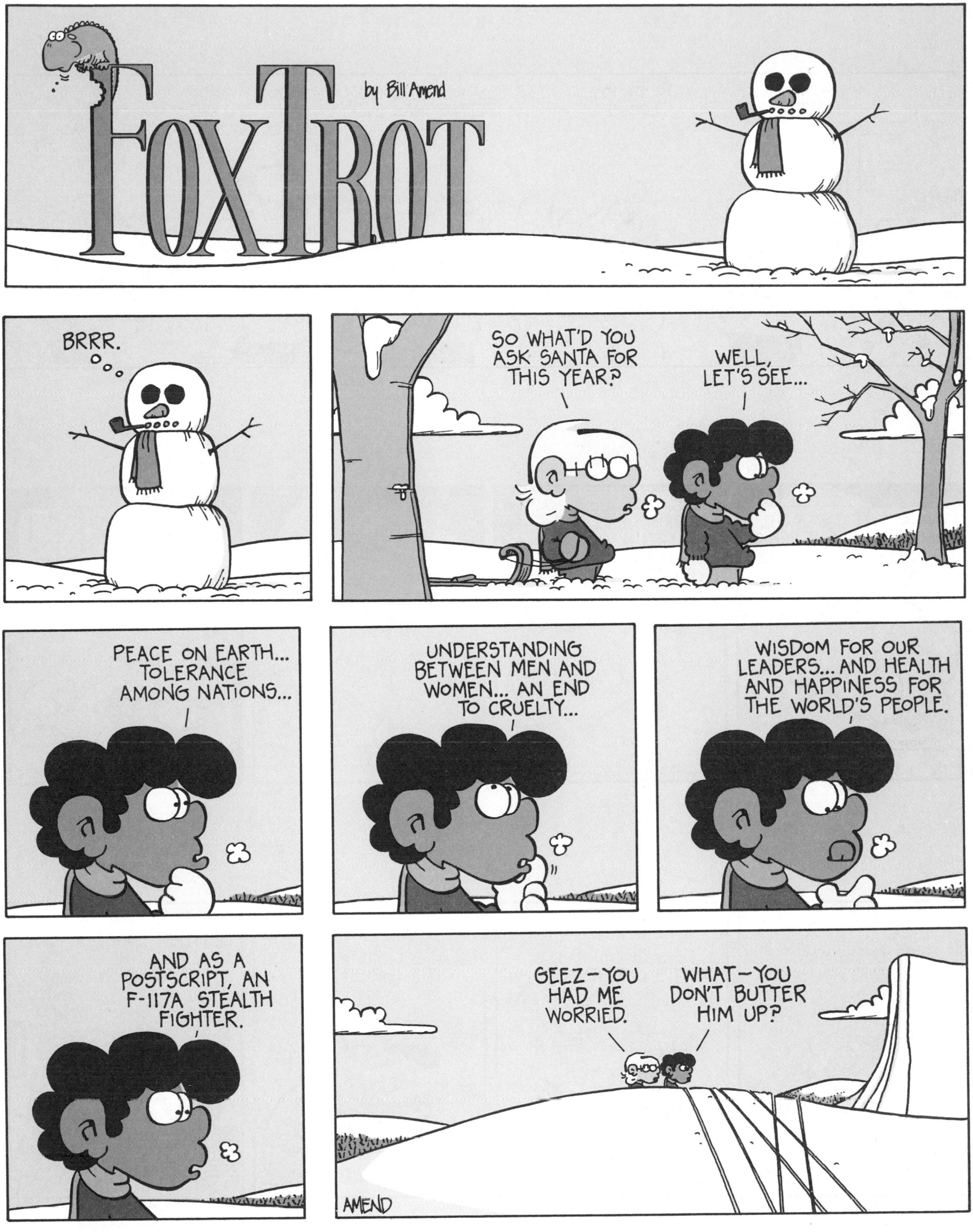
FoxTrot
by Bill Amend
BRRR.
SO WHAT'D YOU ASK SANTA FOR THIS YEAR?
WELL, LET'S SEE...
PEACE ON EARTH... TOLERANCE AMONG NATIONS...
UNDERSTANDING BETWEEN MEN AND WOMEN... AN END TO CRUELTY...
WISDOM FOR OUR LEADERS... AND HEALTH AND HAPPINESS FOR THE WORLD'S PEOPLE.
AND AS A POSTSCRIPT, AN F-117A STEALTH FIGHTER.
GEEZ—YOU HAD ME WORRIED.
WHAT—YOU DON'T BUTTER HIM UP?
AMEND

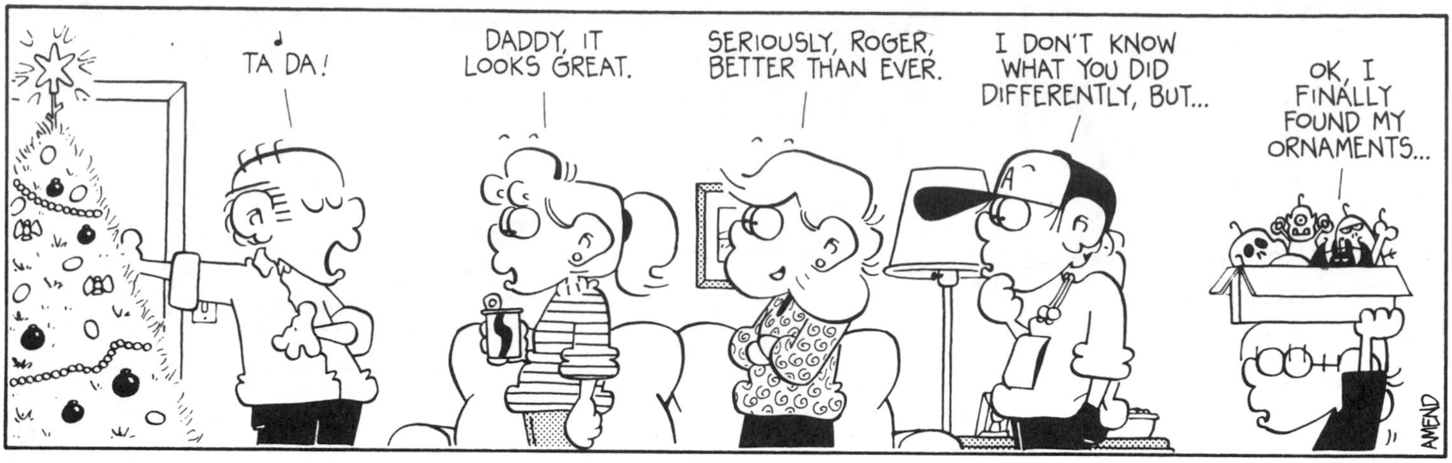
TA DA!
DADDY, IT LOOKS GREAT.
SERIOUSLY, ROGER, BETTER THAN EVER.
I DON'T KNOW WHAT YOU DID DIFFERENTLY, BUT...
OK, I FINALLY FOUND MY ORNAMENTS...
AMEND

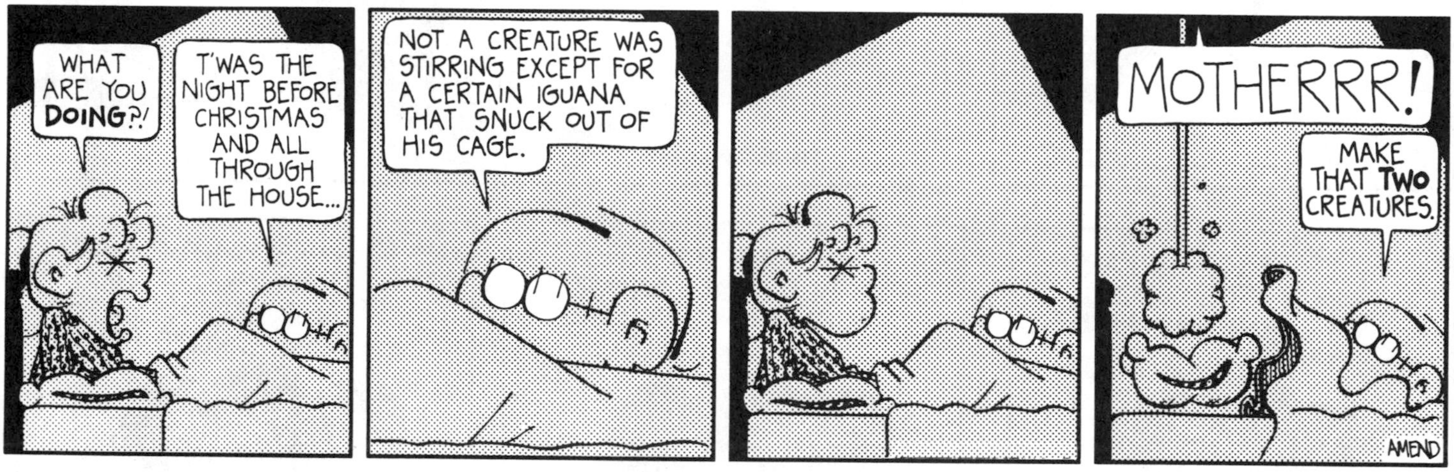
WHAT ARE YOU **DOING**?!
T'WAS THE NIGHT BEFORE CHRISTMAS AND ALL THROUGH THE HOUSE...
NOT A CREATURE WAS STIRRING EXCEPT FOR A CERTAIN IGUANA THAT SNUCK OUT OF HIS CAGE.
MOTHERRR!
MAKE THAT **TWO** CREATURES.
AMEND

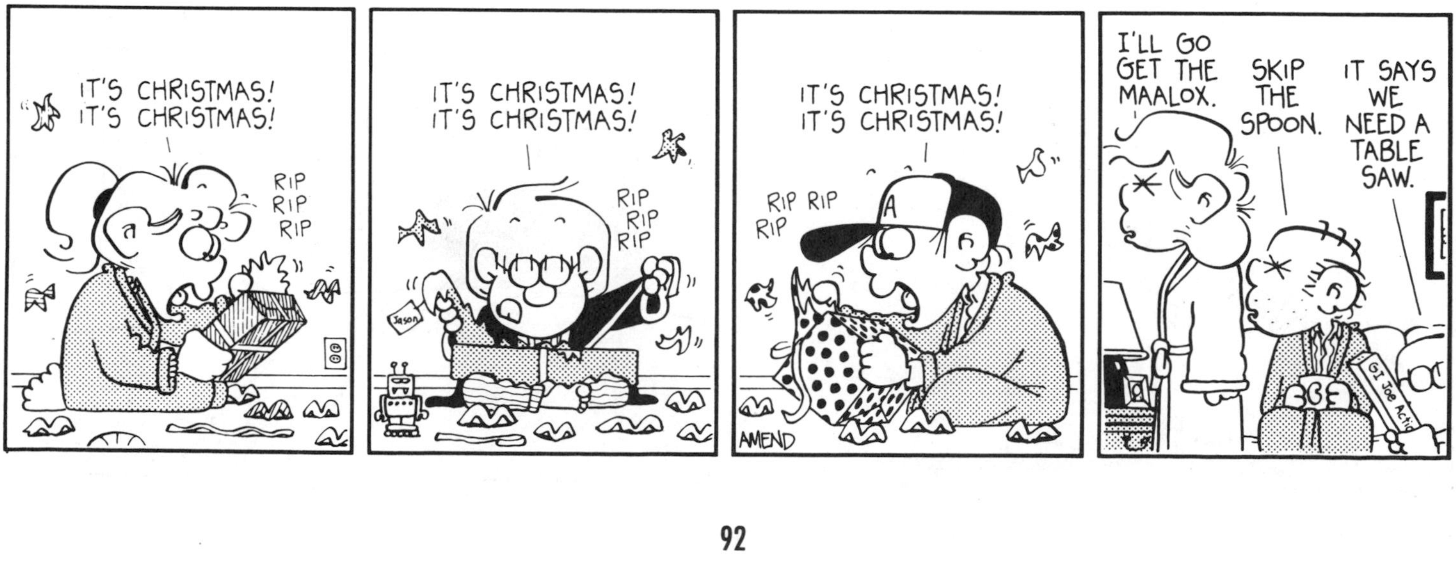
IT'S CHRISTMAS! IT'S CHRISTMAS!
RIP RIP RIP
IT'S CHRISTMAS! IT'S CHRISTMAS!
RIP RIP RIP
IT'S CHRISTMAS! IT'S CHRISTMAS!
RIP RIP RIP
AMEND
I'LL GO GET THE MAALOX.
SKIP THE SPOON.
IT SAYS WE NEED A TABLE SAW.

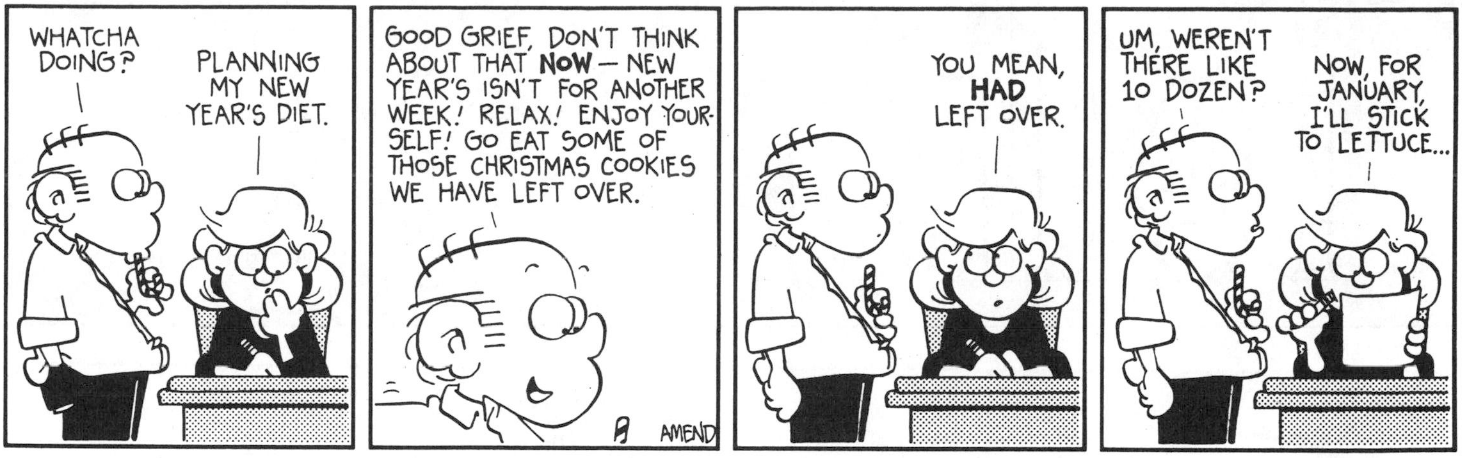
WHATCHA DOING?
PLANNING MY NEW YEAR'S DIET.
GOOD GRIEF, DON'T THINK ABOUT THAT NOW — NEW YEAR'S ISN'T FOR ANOTHER WEEK! RELAX! ENJOY YOURSELF! GO EAT SOME OF THOSE CHRISTMAS COOKIES WE HAVE LEFT OVER.
AMEND
YOU MEAN, HAD LEFT OVER.
UM, WEREN'T THERE LIKE 10 DOZEN?
NOW, FOR JANUARY, I'LL STICK TO LETTUCE...

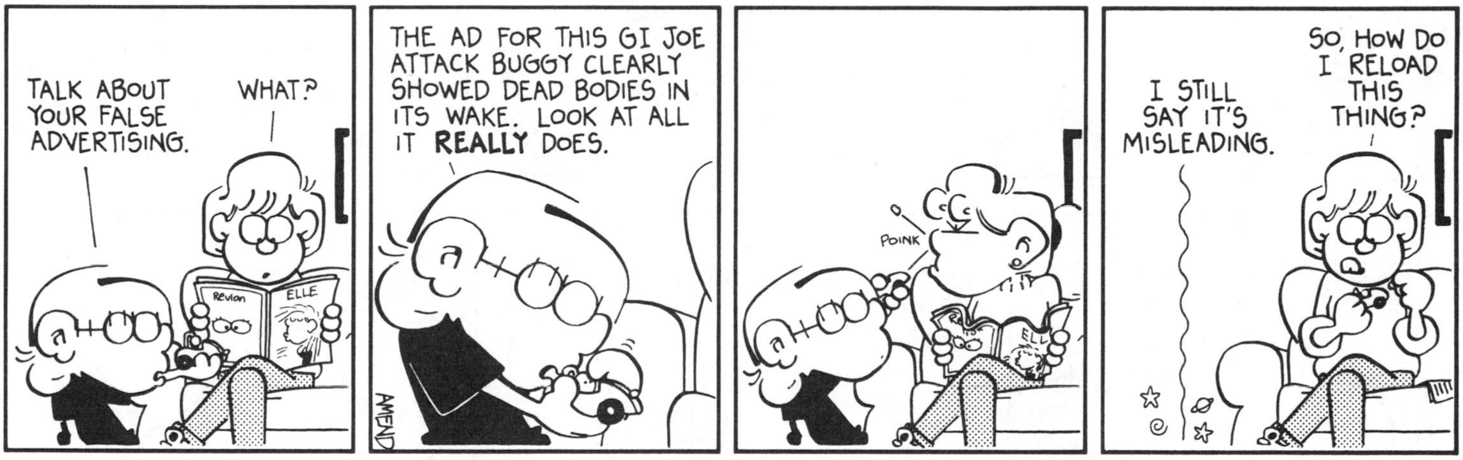
TALK ABOUT YOUR FALSE ADVERTISING.
WHAT?
Revlon
ELLE
THE AD FOR THIS GI JOE ATTACK BUGGY CLEARLY SHOWED DEAD BODIES IN ITS WAKE. LOOK AT ALL IT REALLY DOES.
AMEND
POINK
I STILL SAY IT'S MISLEADING.
SO, HOW DO I RELOAD THIS THING?

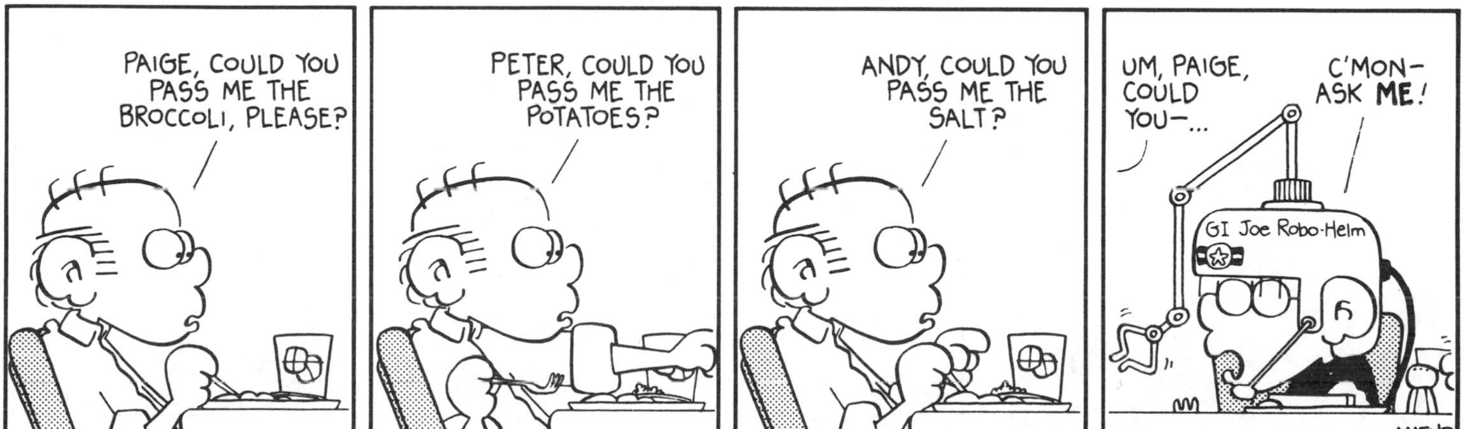
PAIGE, COULD YOU PASS ME THE BROCCOLI, PLEASE?
PETER, COULD YOU PASS ME THE POTATOES?
ANDY, COULD YOU PASS ME THE SALT?
UM, PAIGE, COULD YOU—...
C'MON— ASK ME!
GI Joe Robo-Helm
AMEND

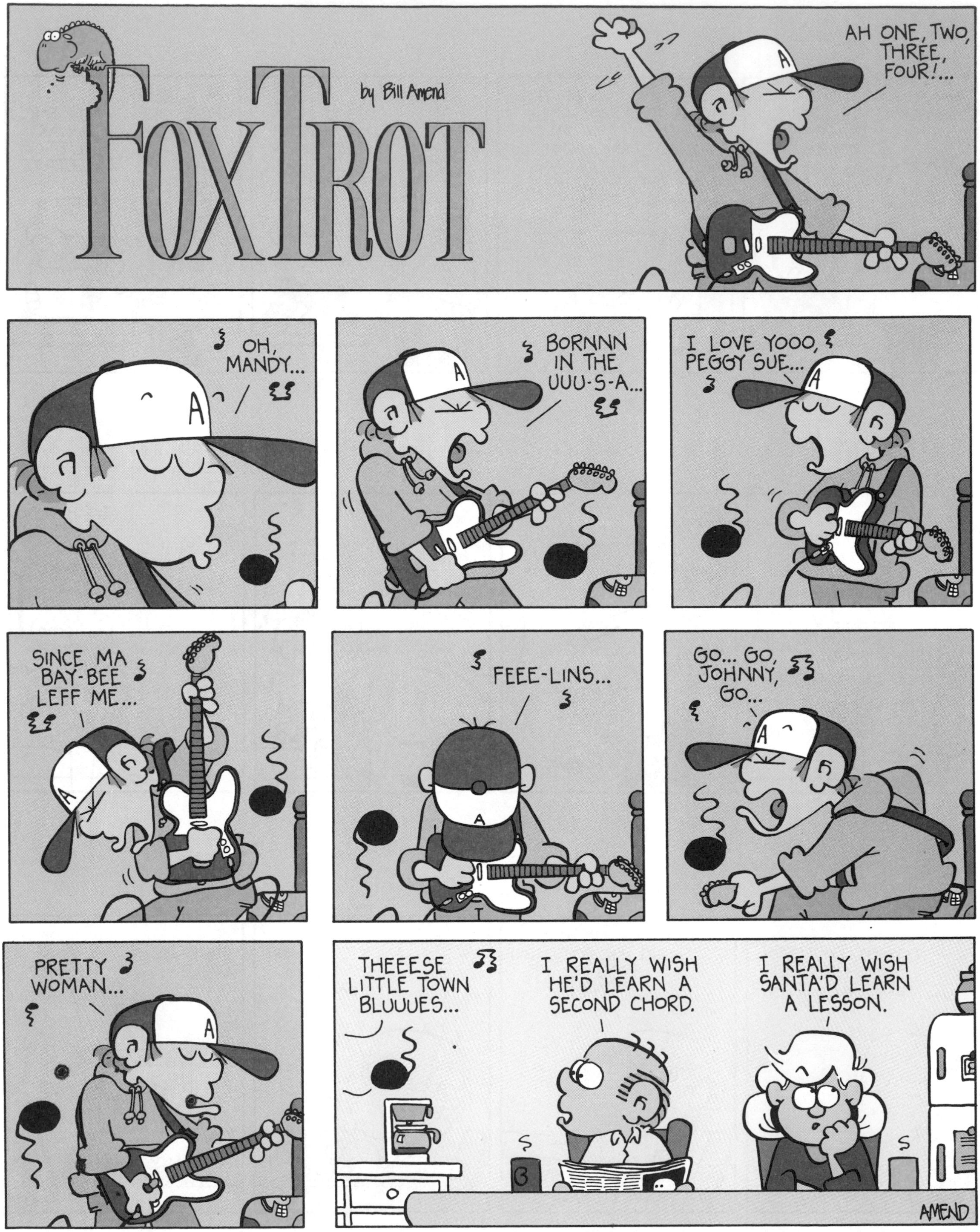
FoxTrot
by Bill Amend
AH ONE, TWO, THREE, FOUR!...
OH, MANDY...
BORNNN IN THE UUU-S-A...
I LOVE YOOO, PEGGY SUE...
SINCE MA BAY-BEE LEFF ME...
FEEE-LINS...
GO... GO, JOHNNY, GO...
PRETTY WOMAN...
THEEESE LITTLE TOWN BLUUUES...
I REALLY WISH HE'D LEARN A SECOND CHORD.
I REALLY WISH SANTA'D LEARN A LESSON.
AMEND

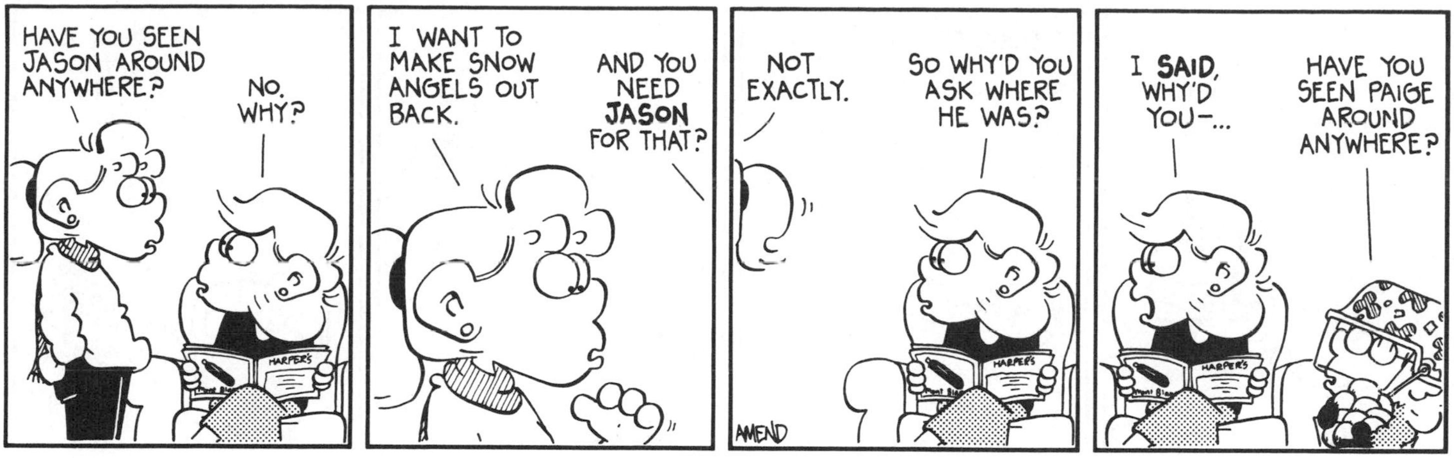
HAVE YOU SEEN JASON AROUND ANYWHERE?
NO. WHY?
I WANT TO MAKE SNOW ANGELS OUT BACK.
AND YOU NEED **JASON** FOR THAT?
NOT EXACTLY.
SO WHY'D YOU ASK WHERE HE WAS?
I **SAID**, WHY'D YOU–...
HAVE YOU SEEN PAIGE AROUND ANYWHERE?
AMEND

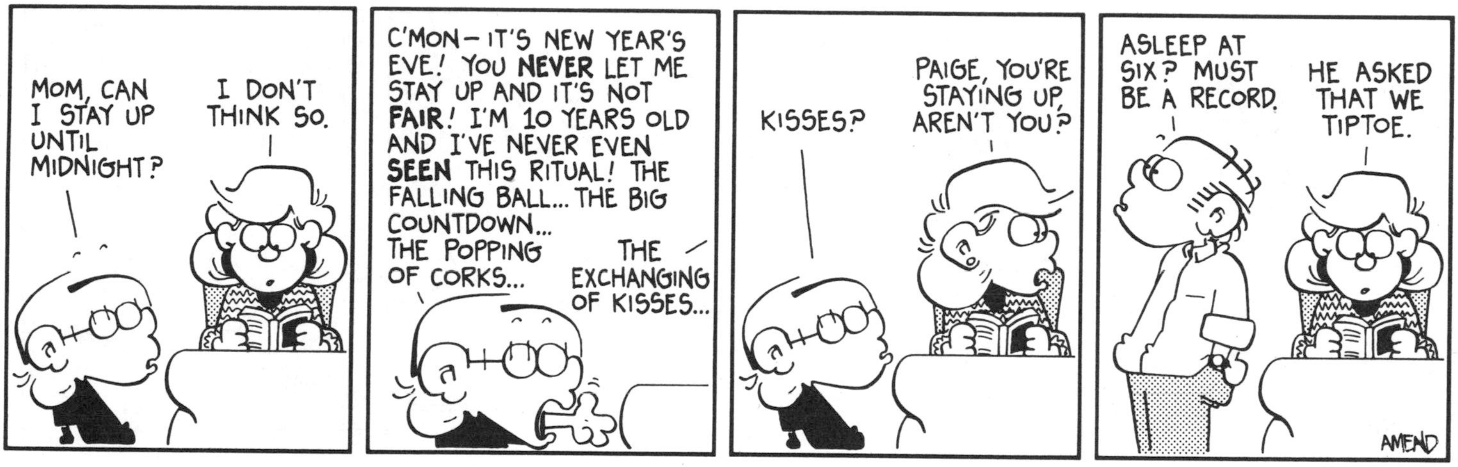
MOM, CAN I STAY UP UNTIL MIDNIGHT?
I DON'T THINK SO.
C'MON– IT'S NEW YEAR'S EVE! YOU **NEVER** LET ME STAY UP AND IT'S NOT **FAIR**! I'M 10 YEARS OLD AND I'VE NEVER EVEN **SEEN** THIS RITUAL! THE FALLING BALL... THE BIG COUNTDOWN...
THE POPPING OF CORKS...
THE EXCHANGING OF KISSES...
KISSES?
PAIGE, YOU'RE STAYING UP, AREN'T YOU?
ASLEEP AT SIX? MUST BE A RECORD.
HE ASKED THAT WE TIPTOE.
AMEND

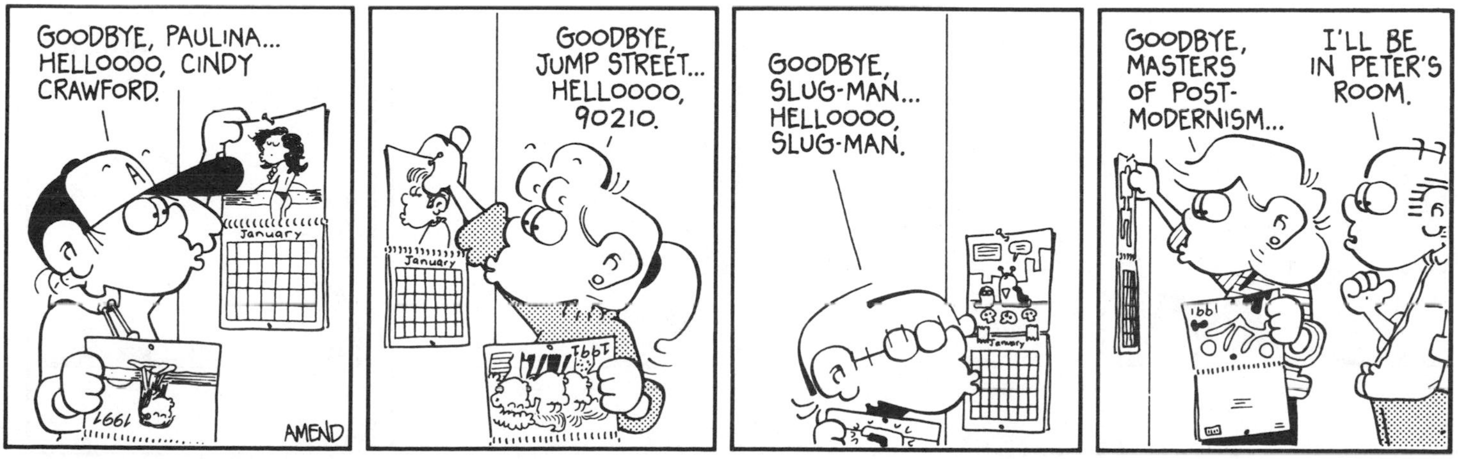
GOODBYE, PAULINA... HELLOOOO, CINDY CRAWFORD.
GOODBYE, JUMP STREET... HELLOOOO, 90210.
GOODBYE, SLUG-MAN... HELLOOOO, SLUG-MAN.
GOODBYE, MASTERS OF POST-MODERNISM...
I'LL BE IN PETER'S ROOM.
AMEND

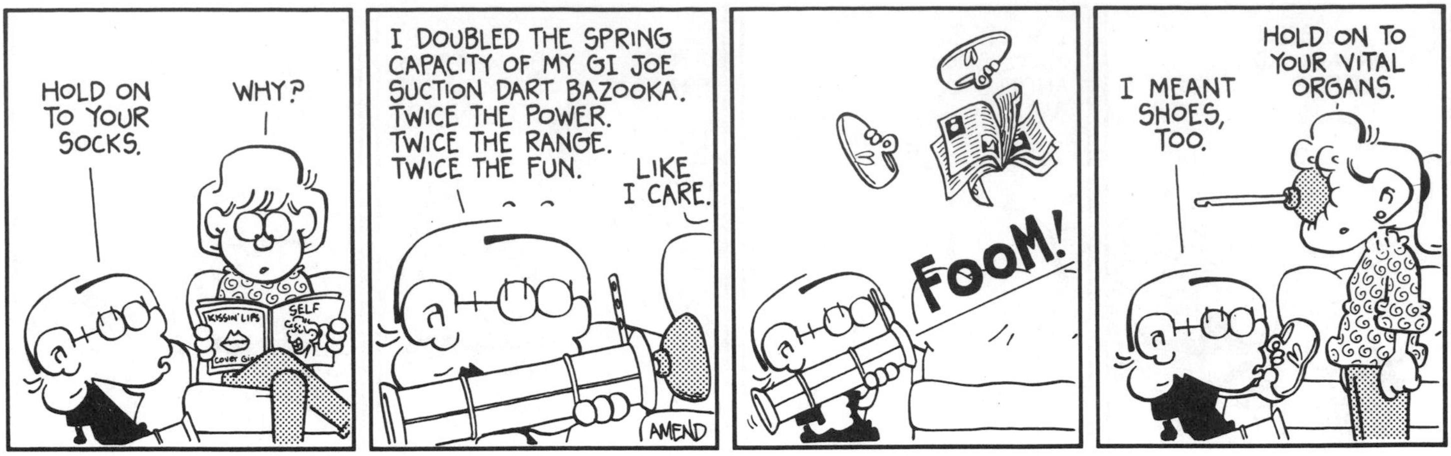
HOLD ON TO YOUR SOCKS.
WHY?
I DOUBLED THE SPRING CAPACITY OF MY GI JOE SUCTION DART BAZOOKA. TWICE THE POWER. TWICE THE RANGE. TWICE THE FUN.
LIKE I CARE.
AMEND
FOOM!
I MEANT SHOES, TOO.
HOLD ON TO YOUR VITAL ORGANS.

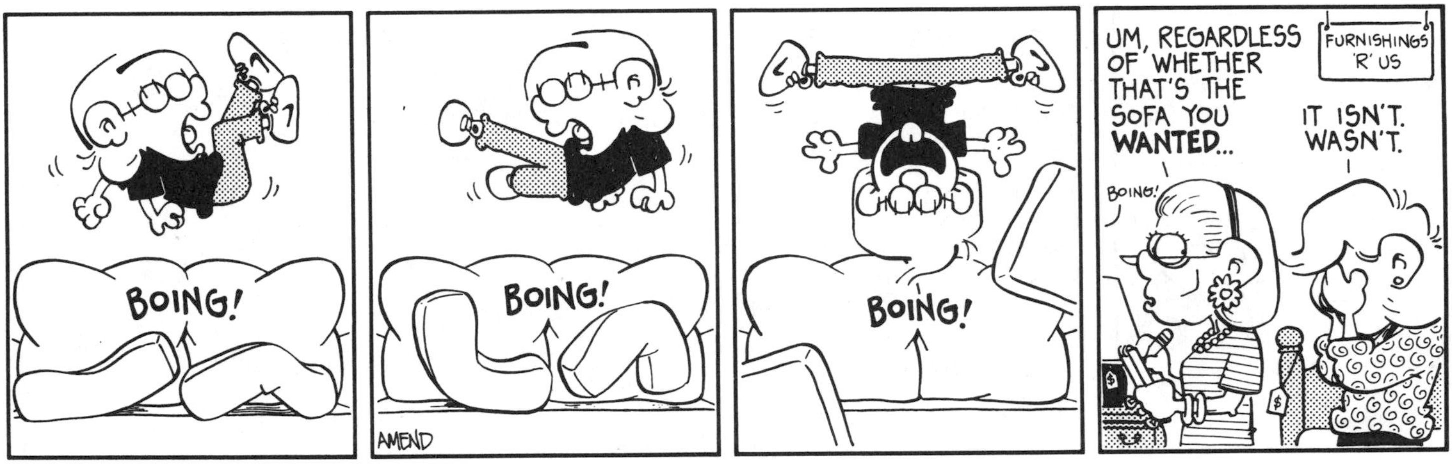
BOING!
BOING!
AMEND
BOING!
FURNISHINGS 'R' US
UM, REGARDLESS OF WHETHER THAT'S THE SOFA YOU **WANTED**...
BOING!
IT ISN'T. WASN'T.

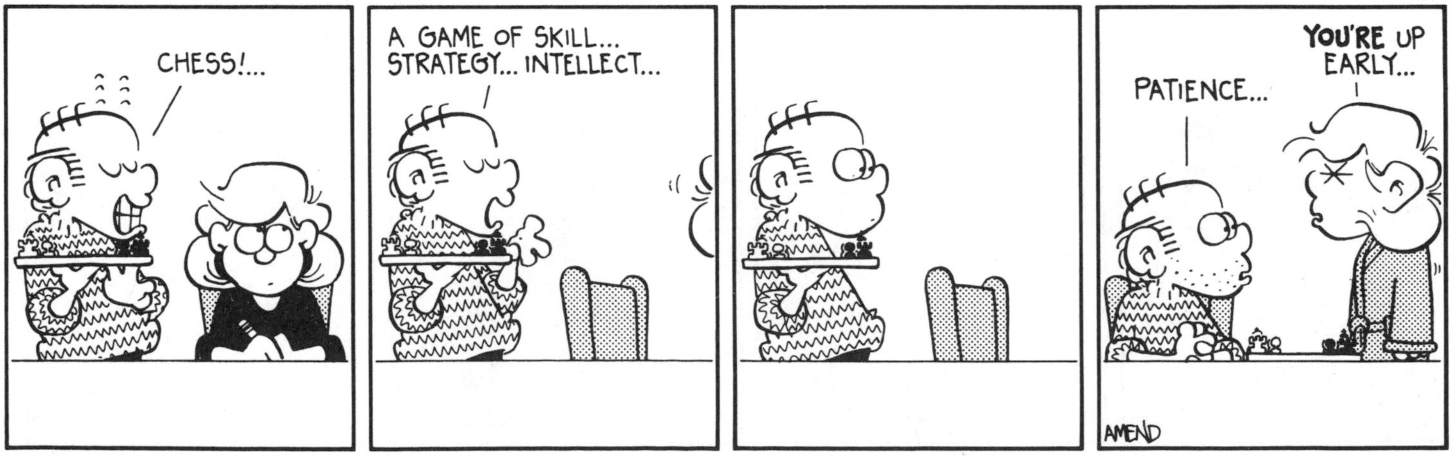
CHESS!...
A GAME OF SKILL... STRATEGY... INTELLECT...
PATIENCE...
YOU'RE UP EARLY...
AMEND

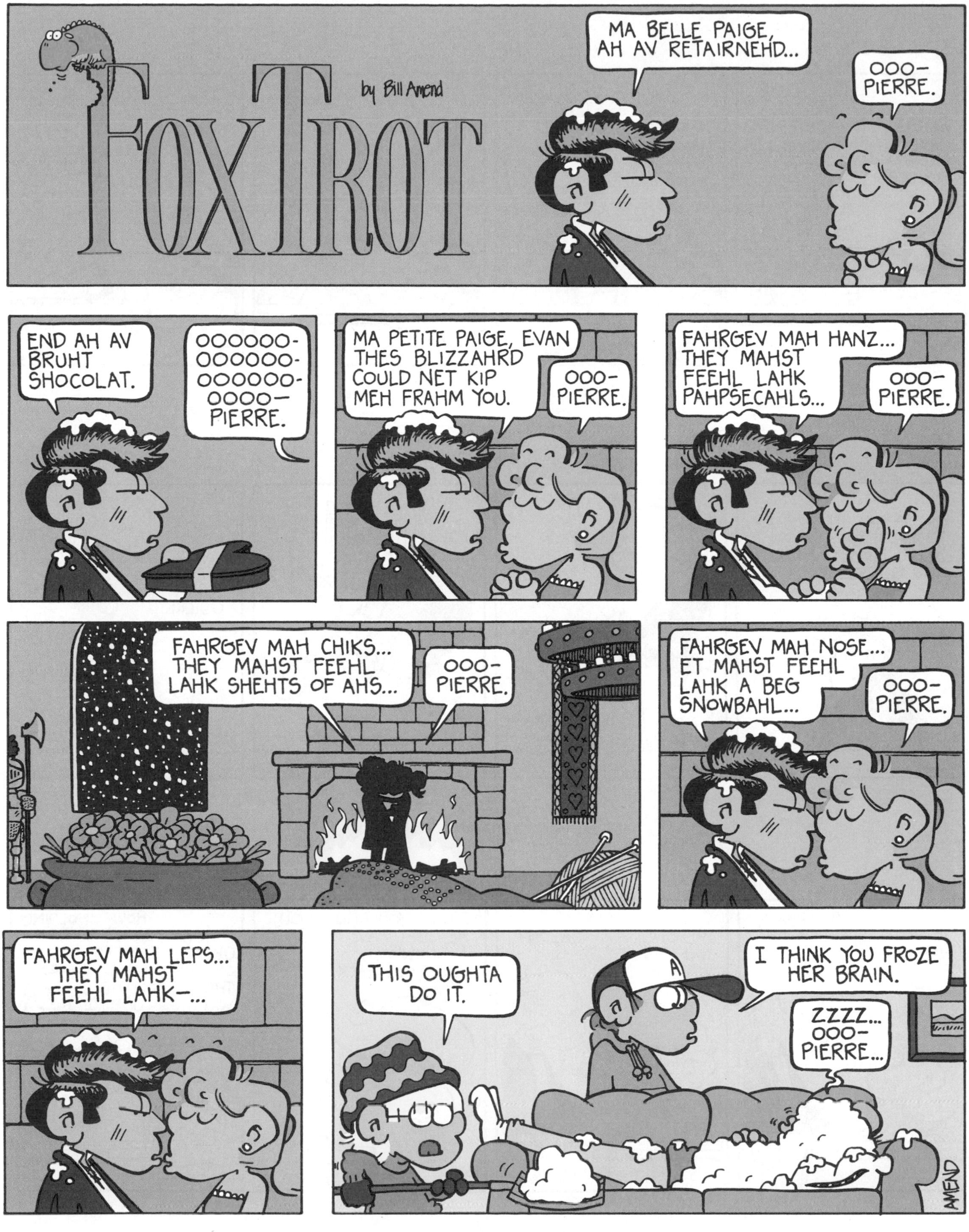
FoxTrot
by Bill Amend
MA BELLE PAIGE, AH AV RETAIRNEHD...
OOO-PIERRE.
END AH AV BRUHT SHOCOLAT.
OOOOOO-OOOOOO-OOOOOO-OOOO—PIERRE.
MA PETITE PAIGE, EVAN THES BLIZZAHRD COULD NET KIP MEH FRAHM YOU.
OOO-PIERRE.
FAHRGEV MAH HANZ... THEY MAHST FEEHL LAHK PAHPSECAHLS...
OOO-PIERRE.
FAHRGEV MAH CHIKS... THEY MAHST FEEHL LAHK SHEHTS OF AHS...
OOO-PIERRE.
FAHRGEV MAH NOSE... ET MAHST FEEHL LAHK A BEG SNOWBAHL...
OOO-PIERRE.
FAHRGEV MAH LEPS... THEY MAHST FEEHL LAHK—...
THIS OUGHTA DO IT.
I THINK YOU FROZE HER BRAIN.
ZZZZ... OOO-PIERRE...
AMEND

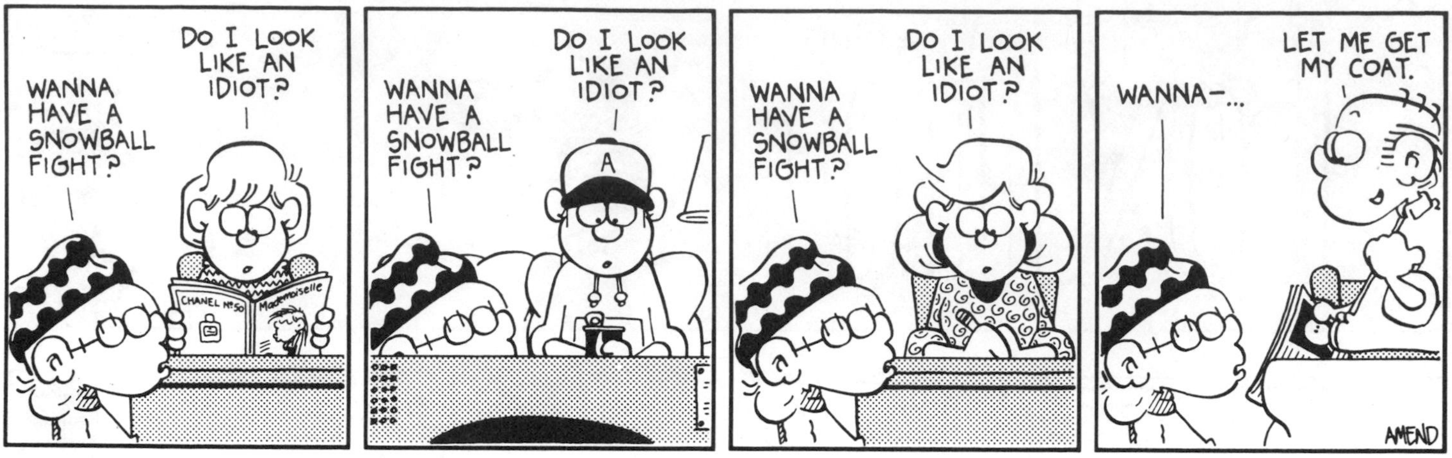
WANNA HAVE A SNOWBALL FIGHT?
DO I LOOK LIKE AN IDIOT?
CHANEL Nº50
Mademoiselle
WANNA HAVE A SNOWBALL FIGHT?
DO I LOOK LIKE AN IDIOT?
A
WANNA HAVE A SNOWBALL FIGHT?
DO I LOOK LIKE AN IDIOT?
WANNA–...
LET ME GET MY COAT.
AMEND

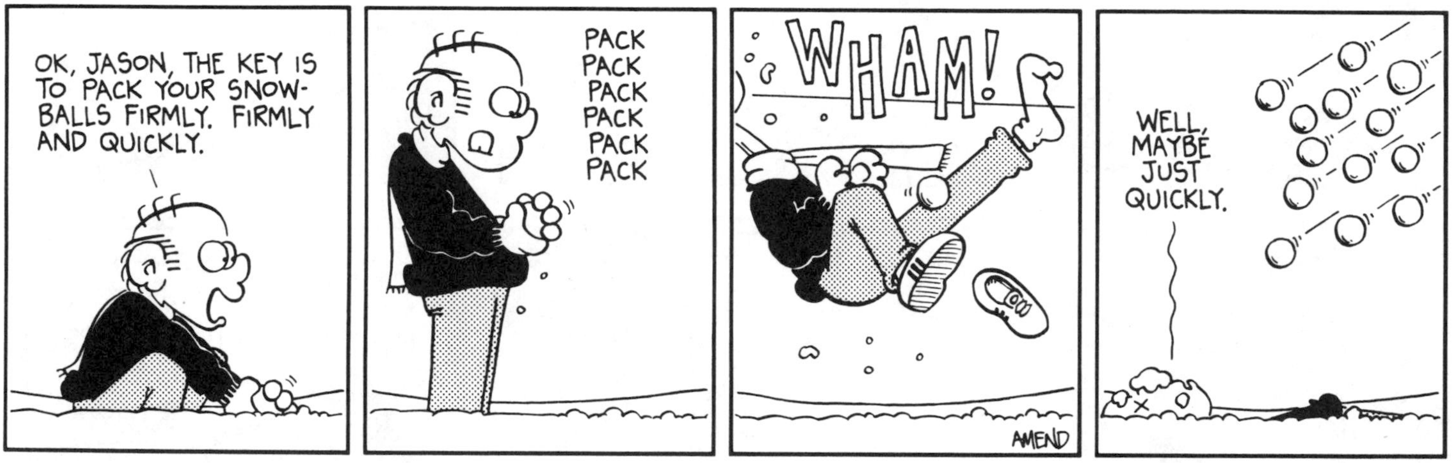
OK, JASON, THE KEY IS TO PACK YOUR SNOWBALLS FIRMLY. FIRMLY AND QUICKLY.
PACK PACK PACK PACK PACK PACK
WHAM!
WELL, MAYBE JUST QUICKLY.
AMEND

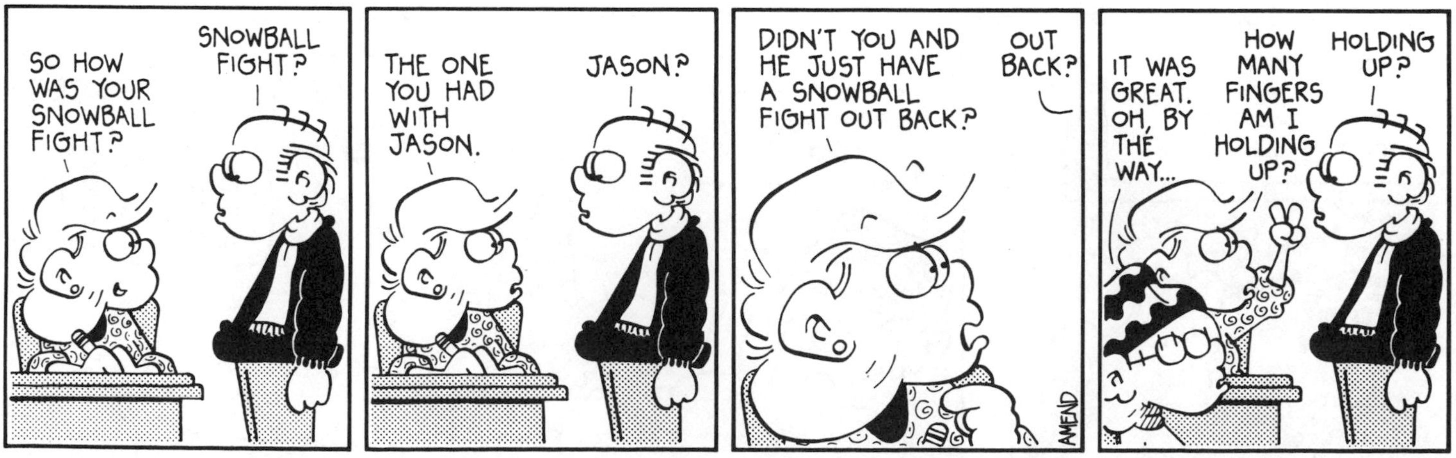
SO HOW WAS YOUR SNOWBALL FIGHT?
SNOWBALL FIGHT?
THE ONE YOU HAD WITH JASON.
JASON?
DIDN'T YOU AND HE JUST HAVE A SNOWBALL FIGHT OUT BACK?
OUT BACK?
AMEND
IT WAS GREAT. OH, BY THE WAY...
HOW MANY FINGERS AM I HOLDING UP?
HOLDING UP?

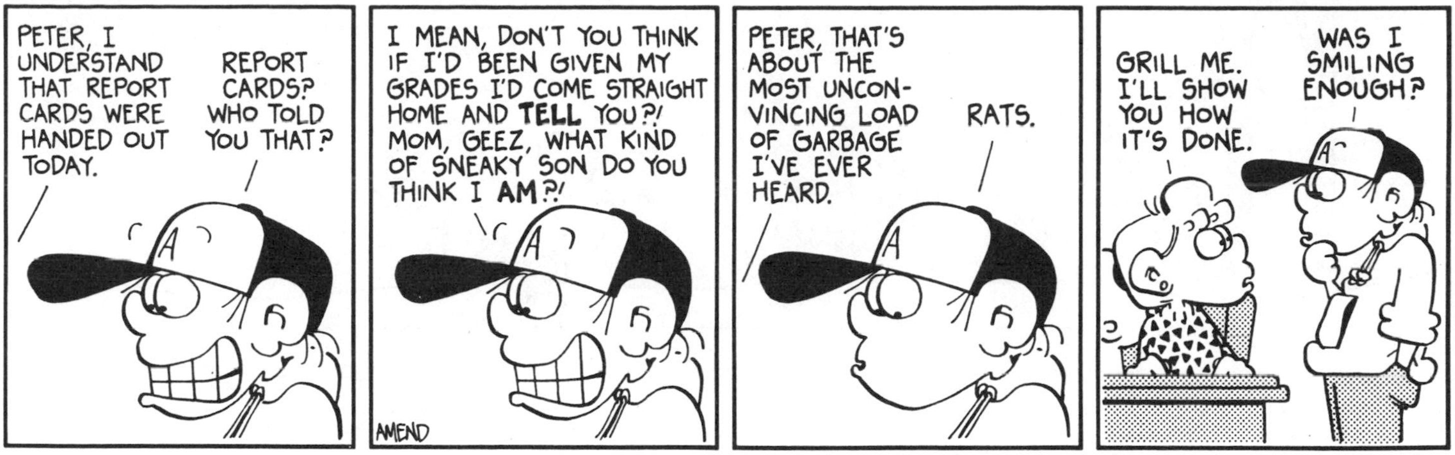
PETER, I UNDERSTAND THAT REPORT CARDS WERE HANDED OUT TODAY.
REPORT CARDS? WHO TOLD YOU THAT?
I MEAN, DON'T YOU THINK IF I'D BEEN GIVEN MY GRADES I'D COME STRAIGHT HOME AND **TELL** YOU?! MOM, GEEZ, WHAT KIND OF SNEAKY SON DO YOU THINK I **AM**?!
AMEND
PETER, THAT'S ABOUT THE MOST UNCONVINCING LOAD OF GARBAGE I'VE EVER HEARD.
RATS.
GRILL ME. I'LL SHOW YOU HOW IT'S DONE.
WAS I SMILING ENOUGH?

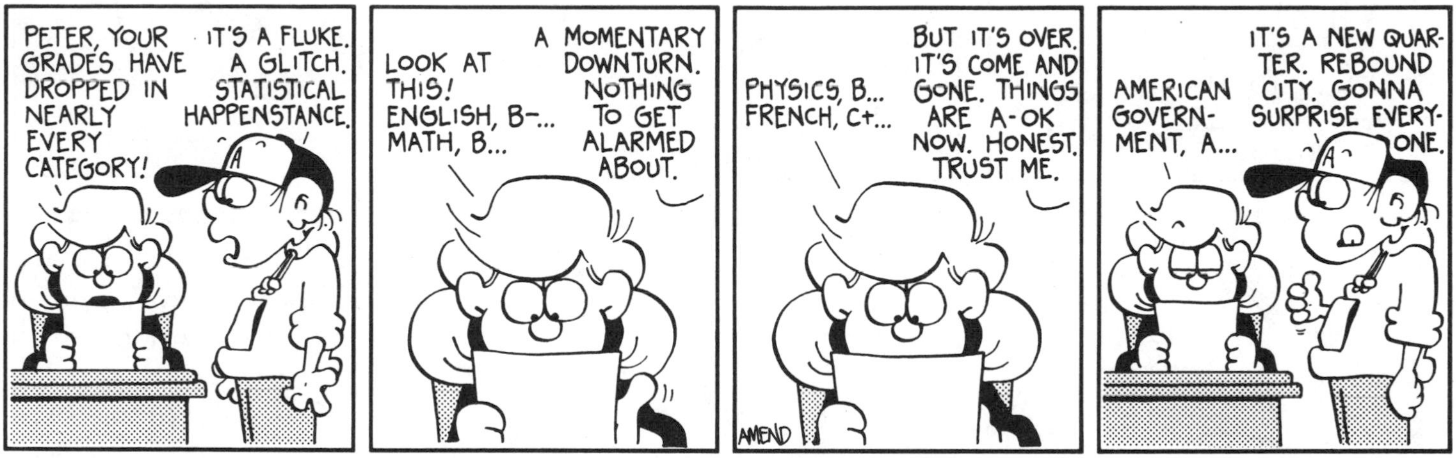
PETER, YOUR GRADES HAVE DROPPED IN NEARLY EVERY CATEGORY!
IT'S A FLUKE. A GLITCH. STATISTICAL HAPPENSTANCE.
LOOK AT THIS! ENGLISH, B–... MATH, B...
A MOMENTARY DOWNTURN. NOTHING TO GET ALARMED ABOUT.
PHYSICS, B... FRENCH, C+...
BUT IT'S OVER. IT'S COME AND GONE. THINGS ARE A-OK NOW. HONEST. TRUST ME.
AMEND
AMERICAN GOVERNMENT, A...
IT'S A NEW QUARTER. REBOUND CITY. GONNA SURPRISE EVERYONE.

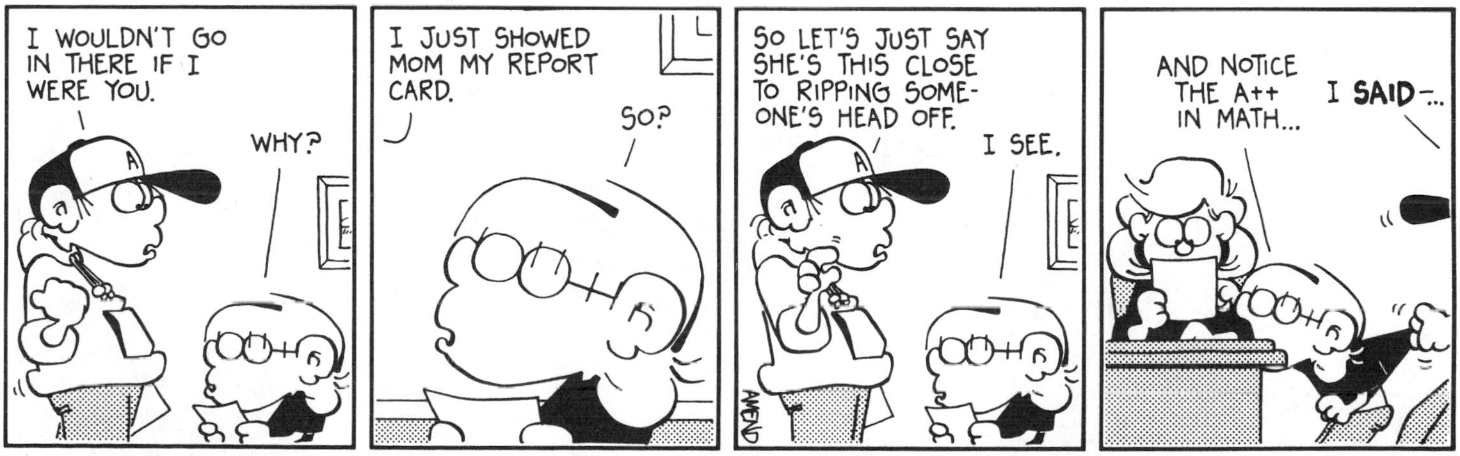
I WOULDN'T GO IN THERE IF I WERE YOU.
WHY?
I JUST SHOWED MOM MY REPORT CARD.
SO?
SO LET'S JUST SAY SHE'S THIS CLOSE TO RIPPING SOMEONE'S HEAD OFF.
I SEE.
AMEND
AND NOTICE THE A++ IN MATH...
I **SAID**–...

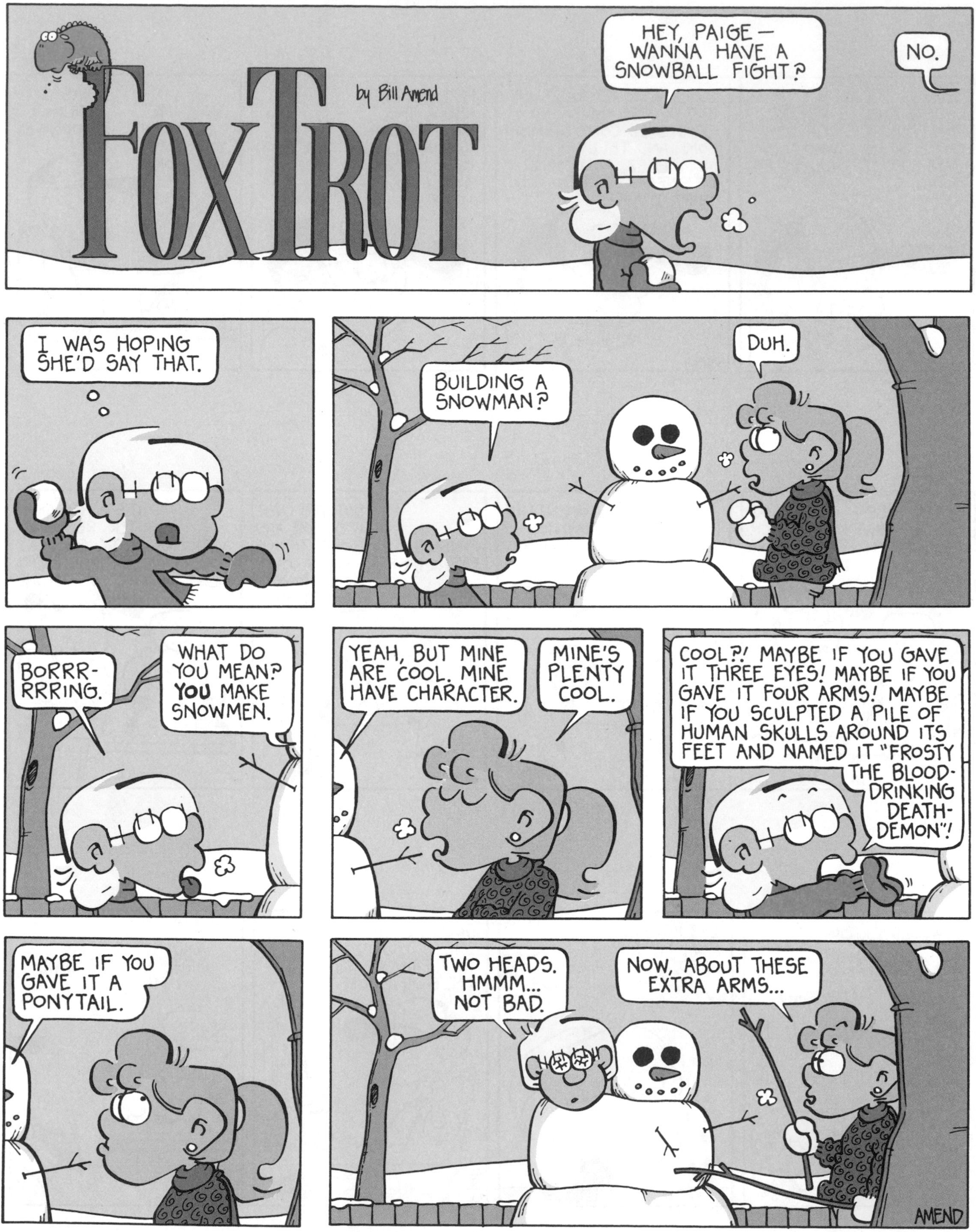
FoxTrot
by Bill Amend
HEY, PAIGE — WANNA HAVE A SNOWBALL FIGHT?
NO.
I WAS HOPING SHE'D SAY THAT.
BUILDING A SNOWMAN?
DUH.
BORRR-RRRING.
WHAT DO YOU MEAN? YOU MAKE SNOWMEN.
YEAH, BUT MINE ARE COOL. MINE HAVE CHARACTER.
MINE'S PLENTY COOL.
COOL?! MAYBE IF YOU GAVE IT THREE EYES! MAYBE IF YOU GAVE IT FOUR ARMS! MAYBE IF YOU SCULPTED A PILE OF HUMAN SKULLS AROUND ITS FEET AND NAMED IT "FROSTY THE BLOOD-DRINKING DEATH-DEMON"!
MAYBE IF YOU GAVE IT A PONYTAIL.
TWO HEADS. HMMM... NOT BAD.
NOW, ABOUT THESE EXTRA ARMS...
AMEND

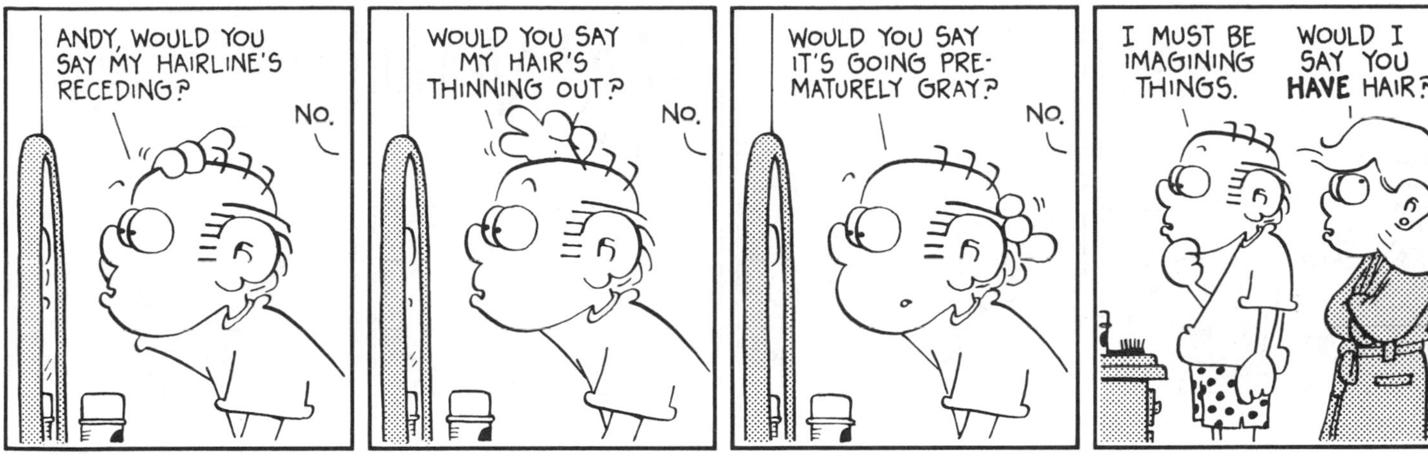
ANDY, WOULD YOU SAY MY HAIRLINE'S RECEDING?
NO.
WOULD YOU SAY MY HAIR'S THINNING OUT?
NO.
WOULD YOU SAY IT'S GOING PRE-MATURELY GRAY?
NO.
I MUST BE IMAGINING THINGS.
WOULD I SAY YOU **HAVE** HAIR?
AMEND

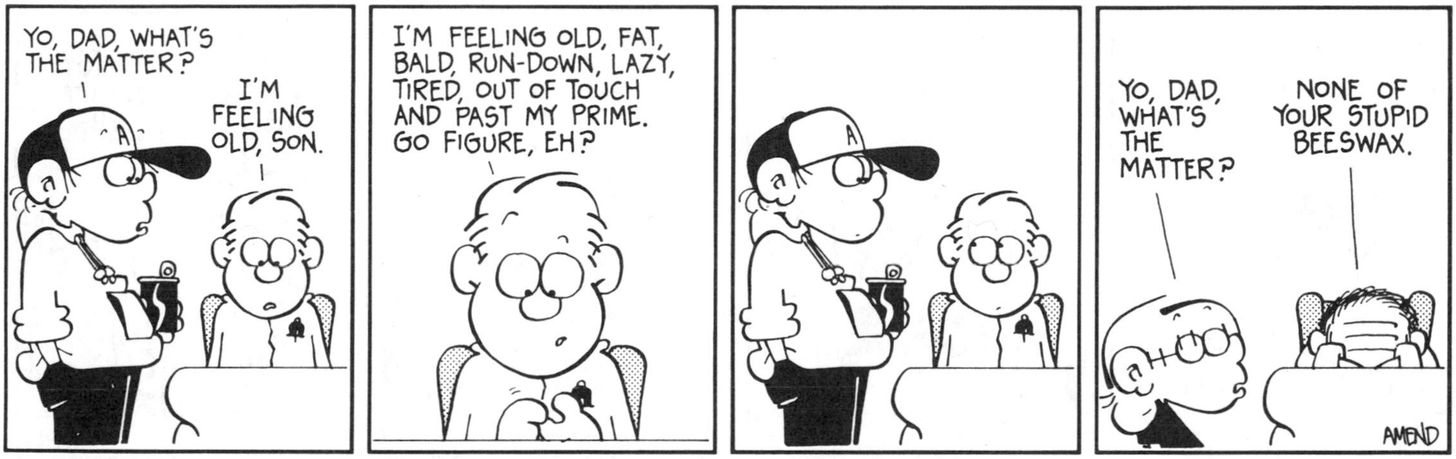
YO, DAD, WHAT'S THE MATTER?
I'M FEELING OLD, SON.
I'M FEELING OLD, FAT, BALD, RUN-DOWN, LAZY, TIRED, OUT OF TOUCH AND PAST MY PRIME. GO FIGURE, EH?
YO, DAD, WHAT'S THE MATTER?
NONE OF YOUR STUPID BEESWAX.
AMEND

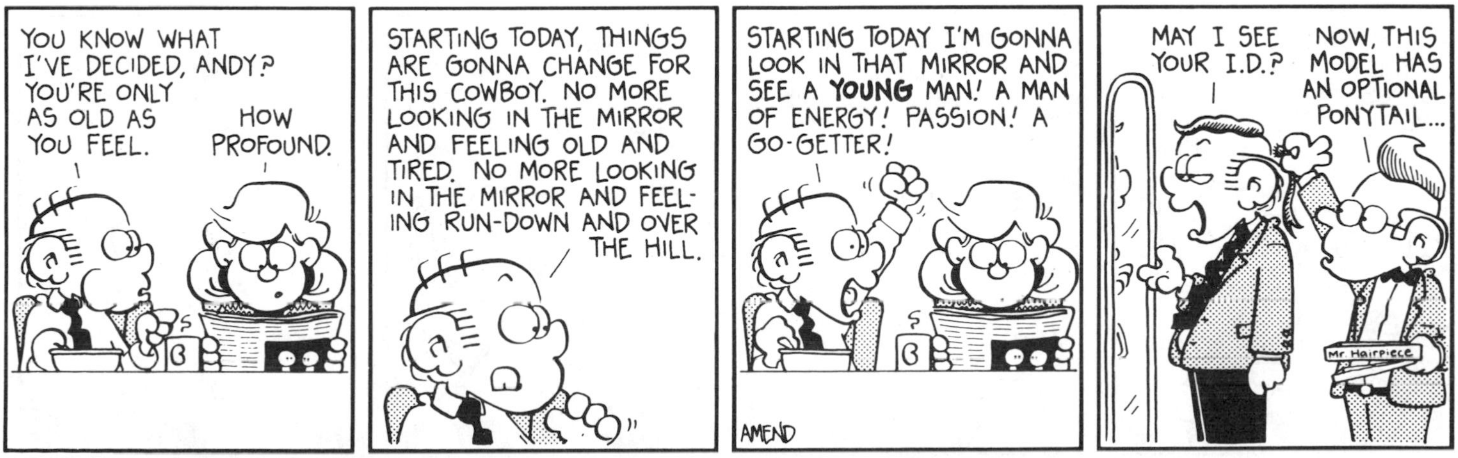
YOU KNOW WHAT I'VE DECIDED, ANDY? YOU'RE ONLY AS OLD AS YOU FEEL.
HOW PROFOUND.
STARTING TODAY, THINGS ARE GONNA CHANGE FOR THIS COWBOY. NO MORE LOOKING IN THE MIRROR AND FEELING OLD AND TIRED. NO MORE LOOKING IN THE MIRROR AND FEEL-ING RUN-DOWN AND OVER THE HILL.
STARTING TODAY I'M GONNA LOOK IN THAT MIRROR AND SEE A **YOUNG** MAN! A MAN OF ENERGY! PASSION! A GO-GETTER!
AMEND
MAY I SEE YOUR I.D.?
NOW, THIS MODEL HAS AN OPTIONAL PONYTAIL...
Mr Hairpiece

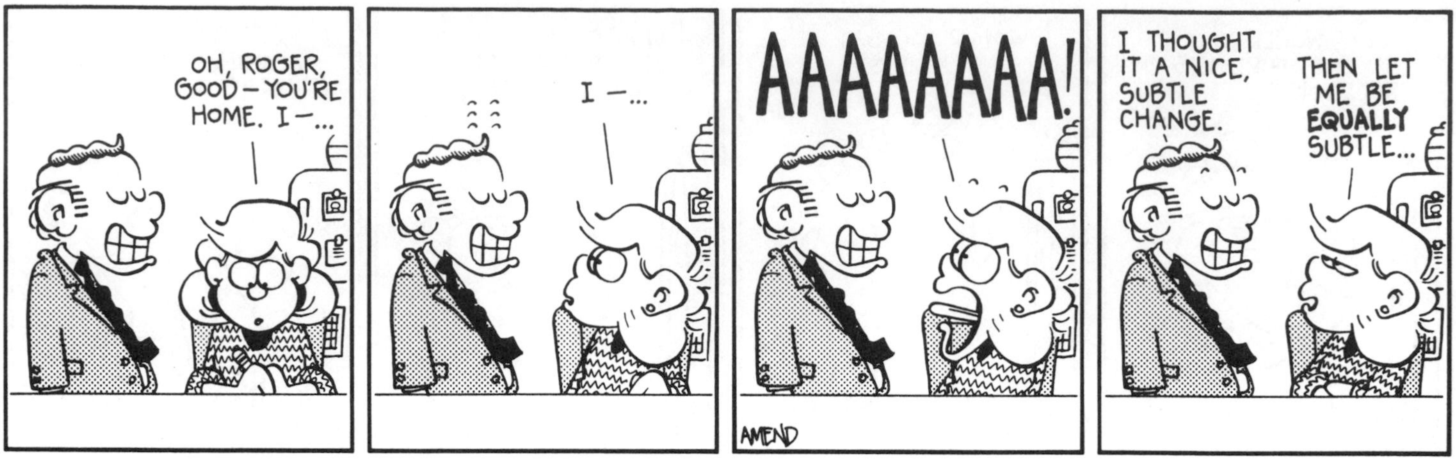
OH, ROGER, GOOD — YOU'RE HOME. I —...
I —...
AAAAAAAA!
I THOUGHT IT A NICE, SUBTLE CHANGE.
THEN LET ME BE **EQUALLY** SUBTLE...
AMEND

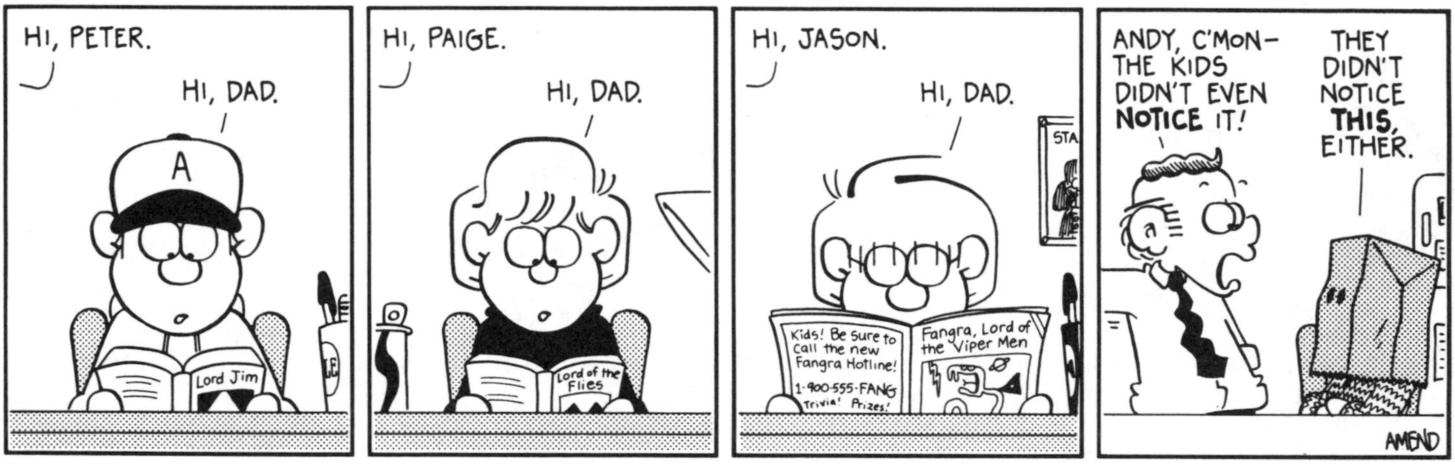
HI, PETER.
HI, DAD.
A
Lord Jim
HI, PAIGE.
HI, DAD.
Lord of the Flies
HI, JASON.
HI, DAD.
Kids! Be sure to call the new Fangra Hotline!
1-900-555-FANG
Trivia! Prizes!
Fangra, Lord of the Viper Men
ANDY, C'MON— THE KIDS DIDN'T EVEN **NOTICE** IT!
THEY DIDN'T NOTICE **THIS,** EITHER.
AMEND

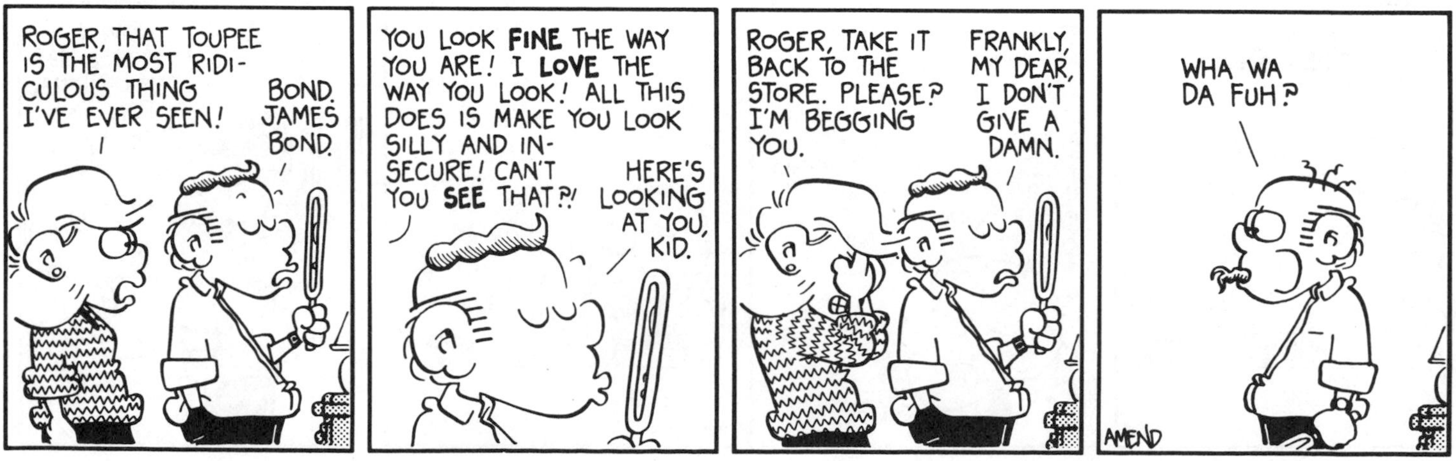
ROGER, THAT TOUPEE IS THE MOST RIDI-CULOUS THING I'VE EVER SEEN!
BOND. JAMES BOND.
YOU LOOK **FINE** THE WAY YOU ARE! I **LOVE** THE WAY YOU LOOK! ALL THIS DOES IS MAKE YOU LOOK SILLY AND IN-SECURE! CAN'T YOU **SEE** THAT?!
HERE'S LOOKING AT YOU, KID.
ROGER, TAKE IT BACK TO THE STORE. PLEASE? I'M BEGGING YOU.
FRANKLY, MY DEAR, I DON'T GIVE A DAMN.
WHA WA DA FUH?
AMEND

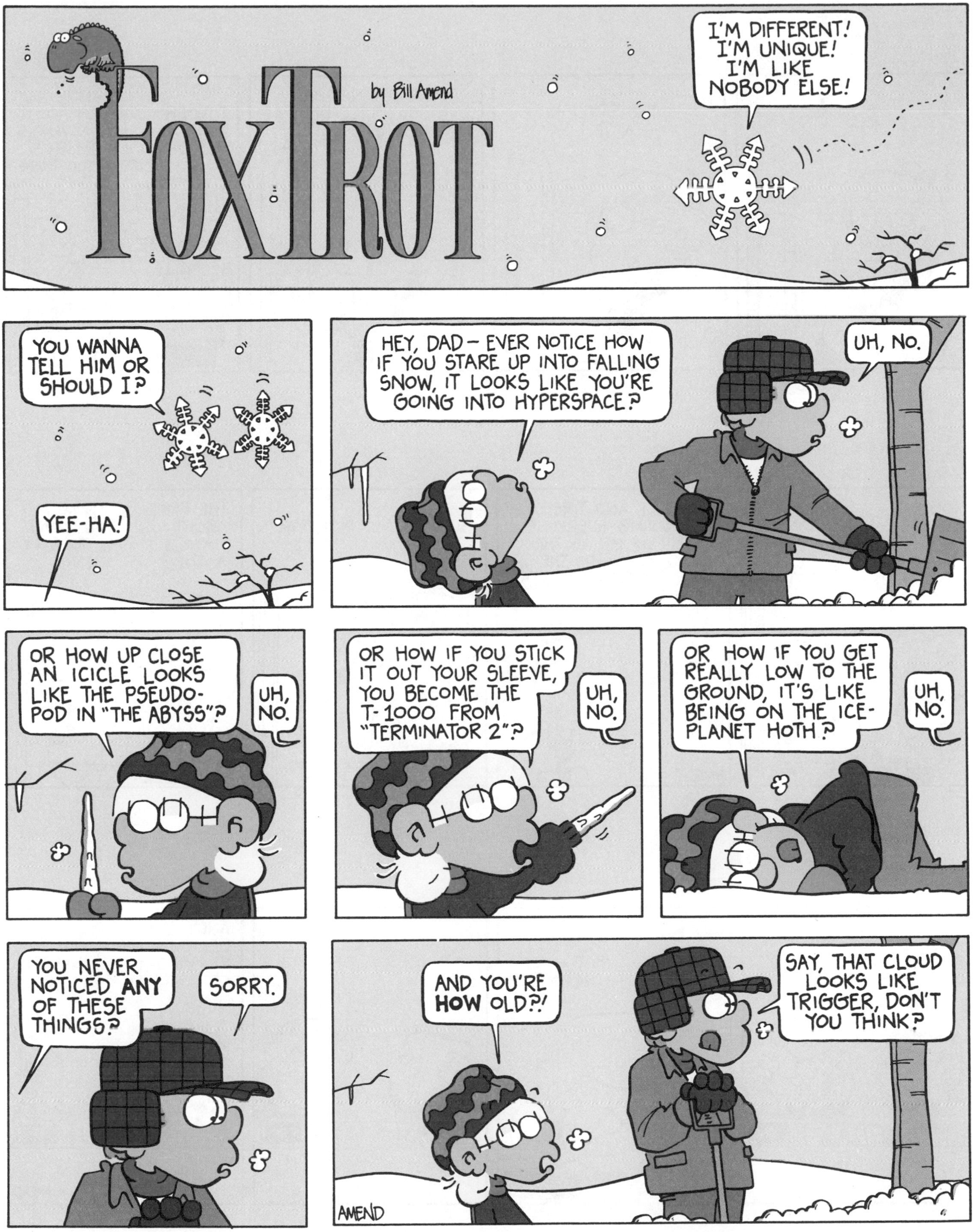
FoxTrot
by Bill Amend
I'M DIFFERENT! I'M UNIQUE! I'M LIKE NOBODY ELSE!
YOU WANNA TELL HIM OR SHOULD I?
YEE-HA!
HEY, DAD – EVER NOTICE HOW IF YOU STARE UP INTO FALLING SNOW, IT LOOKS LIKE YOU'RE GOING INTO HYPERSPACE?
UH, NO.
OR HOW UP CLOSE AN ICICLE LOOKS LIKE THE PSEUDO-POD IN "THE ABYSS"?
UH, NO.
OR HOW IF YOU STICK IT OUT YOUR SLEEVE, YOU BECOME THE T-1000 FROM "TERMINATOR 2"?
UH, NO.
OR HOW IF YOU GET REALLY LOW TO THE GROUND, IT'S LIKE BEING ON THE ICE-PLANET HOTH?
UH, NO.
YOU NEVER NOTICED ANY OF THESE THINGS?
SORRY.
AND YOU'RE HOW OLD?!
SAY, THAT CLOUD LOOKS LIKE TRIGGER, DON'T YOU THINK?
AMEND

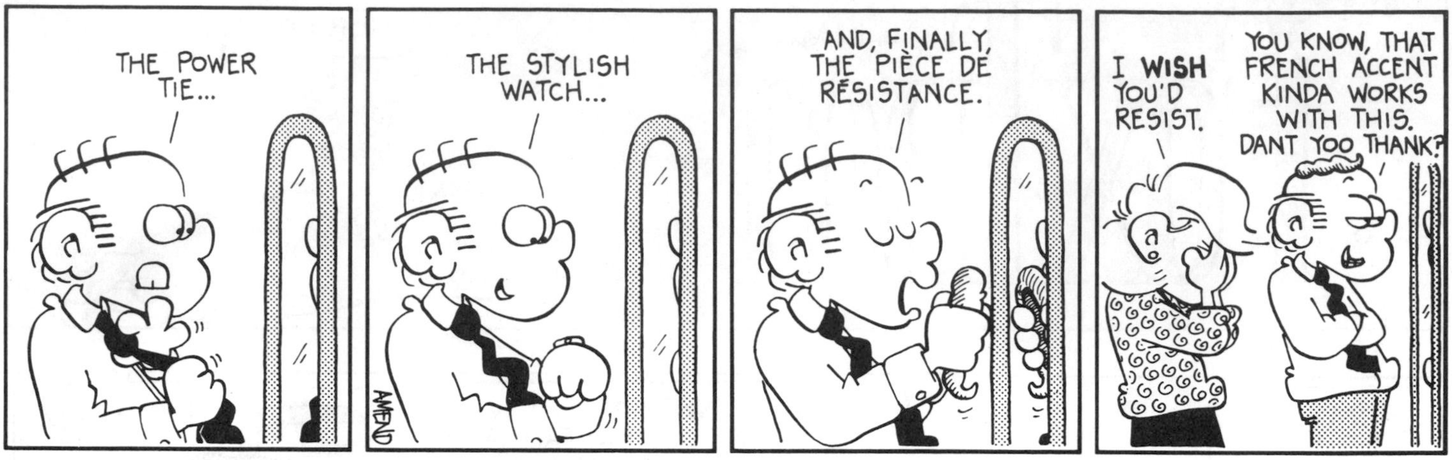
THE POWER TIE...
THE STYLISH WATCH...
AND, FINALLY, THE PIÈCE DE RÉSISTANCE.
I **WISH** YOU'D RESIST.
YOU KNOW, THAT FRENCH ACCENT KINDA WORKS WITH THIS. DANT YOO THANK?
AMEND

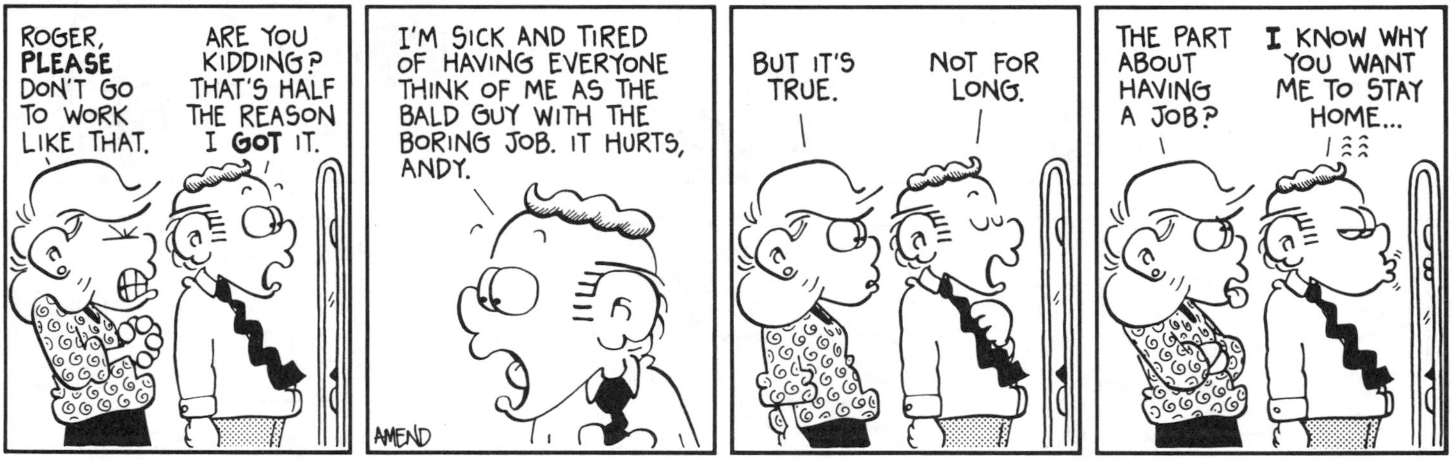
ROGER, **PLEASE** DON'T GO TO WORK LIKE THAT.
ARE YOU KIDDING? THAT'S HALF THE REASON I **GOT** IT.
I'M SICK AND TIRED OF HAVING EVERYONE THINK OF ME AS THE BALD GUY WITH THE BORING JOB. IT HURTS, ANDY.
AMEND
BUT IT'S TRUE.
NOT FOR LONG.
THE PART ABOUT HAVING A JOB?
I KNOW WHY YOU WANT ME TO STAY HOME...

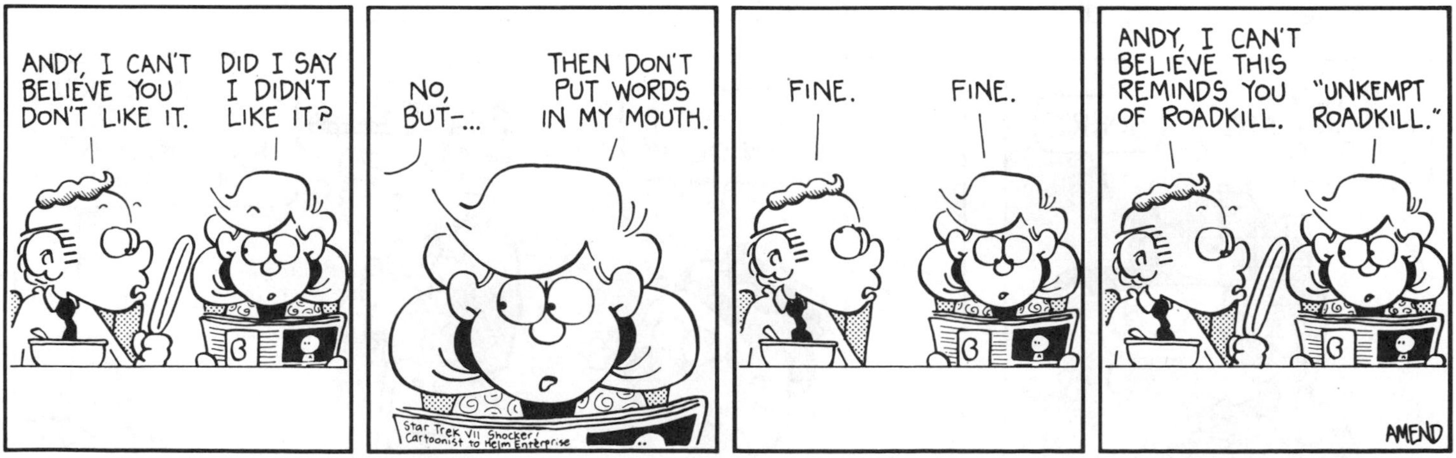
ANDY, I CAN'T BELIEVE YOU DON'T LIKE IT.
DID I SAY I DIDN'T LIKE IT?
NO, BUT-...
THEN DON'T PUT WORDS IN MY MOUTH.
Star Trek VII Shocker! Cartoonist to Helm Enterprise
FINE.
FINE.
ANDY, I CAN'T BELIEVE THIS REMINDS YOU OF ROADKILL.
"UNKEMPT ROADKILL."
AMEND

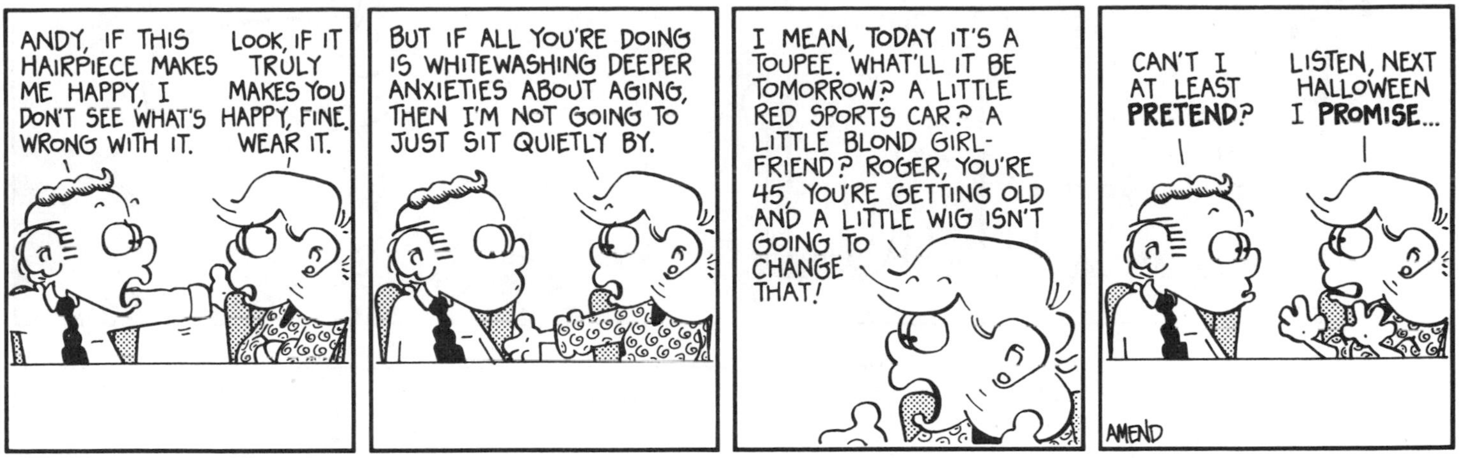
ANDY, IF THIS HAIRPIECE MAKES ME HAPPY, I DON'T SEE WHAT'S WRONG WITH IT.
LOOK, IF IT TRULY MAKES YOU HAPPY, FINE. WEAR IT.
BUT IF ALL YOU'RE DOING IS WHITEWASHING DEEPER ANXIETIES ABOUT AGING, THEN I'M NOT GOING TO JUST SIT QUIETLY BY.
I MEAN, TODAY IT'S A TOUPEE. WHAT'LL IT BE TOMORROW? A LITTLE RED SPORTS CAR? A LITTLE BLOND GIRLFRIEND? ROGER, YOU'RE 45, YOU'RE GETTING OLD AND A LITTLE WIG ISN'T GOING TO CHANGE THAT!
CAN'T I AT LEAST **PRETEND**?
LISTEN, NEXT HALLOWEEN I **PROMISE**...
AMEND

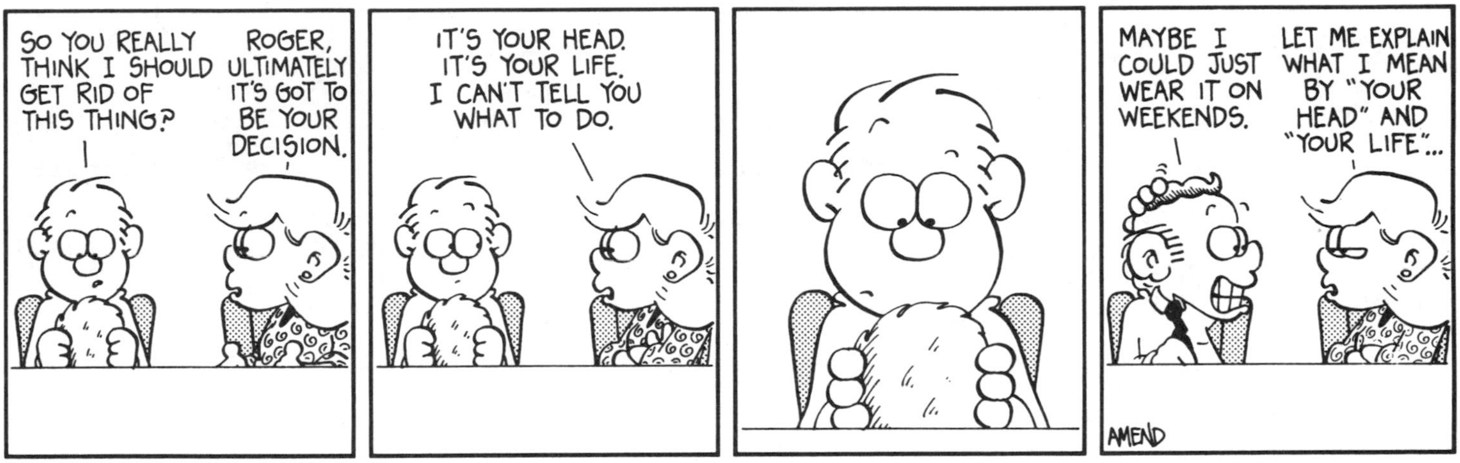
SO YOU REALLY THINK I SHOULD GET RID OF THIS THING?
ROGER, ULTIMATELY IT'S GOT TO BE YOUR DECISION.
IT'S YOUR HEAD. IT'S YOUR LIFE. I CAN'T TELL YOU WHAT TO DO.
MAYBE I COULD JUST WEAR IT ON WEEKENDS.
LET ME EXPLAIN WHAT I MEAN BY "YOUR HEAD" AND "YOUR LIFE"...
AMEND

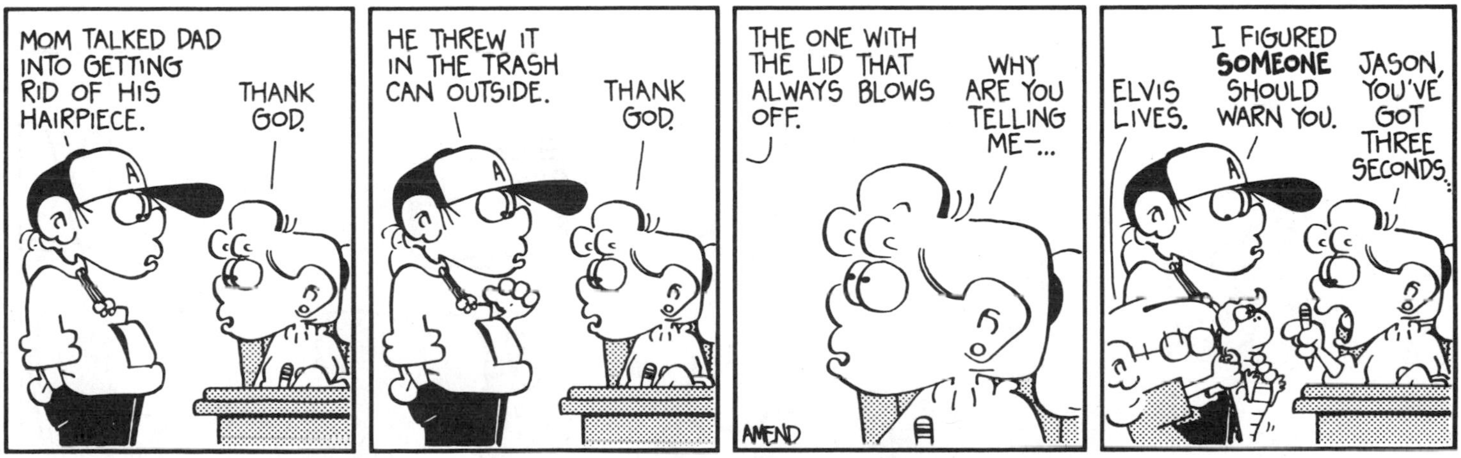
MOM TALKED DAD INTO GETTING RID OF HIS HAIRPIECE.
THANK GOD.
HE THREW IT IN THE TRASH CAN OUTSIDE.
THANK GOD.
THE ONE WITH THE LID THAT ALWAYS BLOWS OFF.
WHY ARE YOU TELLING ME-...
AMEND
ELVIS LIVES.
I FIGURED **SOMEONE** SHOULD WARN YOU.
JASON, YOU'VE GOT THREE SECONDS.

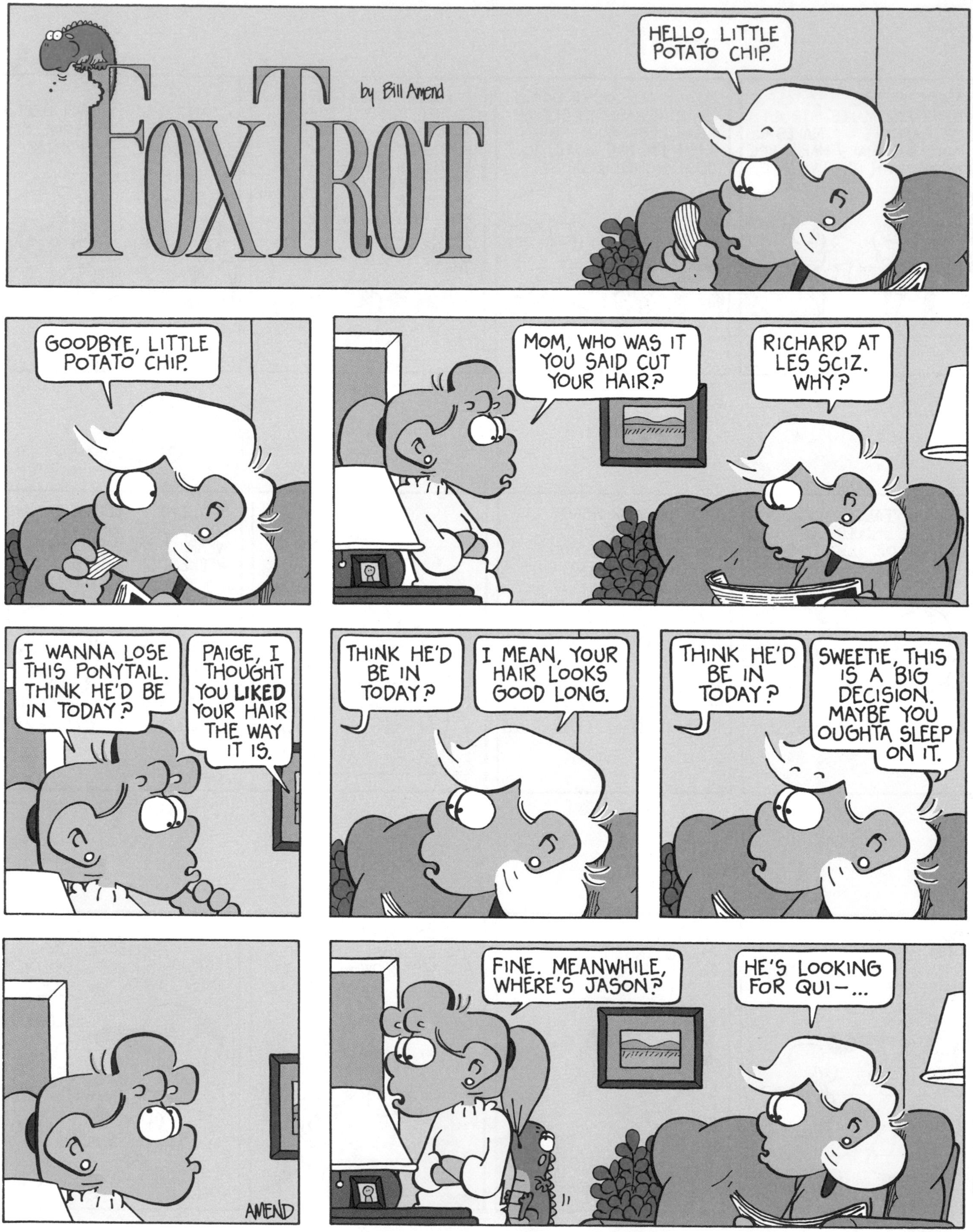
FoxTrot
by Bill Amend
HELLO, LITTLE POTATO CHIP.
GOODBYE, LITTLE POTATO CHIP.
MOM, WHO WAS IT YOU SAID CUT YOUR HAIR?
RICHARD AT LES SCIZ. WHY?
I WANNA LOSE THIS PONYTAIL. THINK HE'D BE IN TODAY?
PAIGE, I THOUGHT YOU **LIKED** YOUR HAIR THE WAY IT IS.
THINK HE'D BE IN TODAY?
I MEAN, YOUR HAIR LOOKS GOOD LONG.
THINK HE'D BE IN TODAY?
SWEETIE, THIS IS A BIG DECISION. MAYBE YOU OUGHTA SLEEP ON IT.
AMEND
FINE. MEANWHILE, WHERE'S JASON?
HE'S LOOKING FOR QUI–...

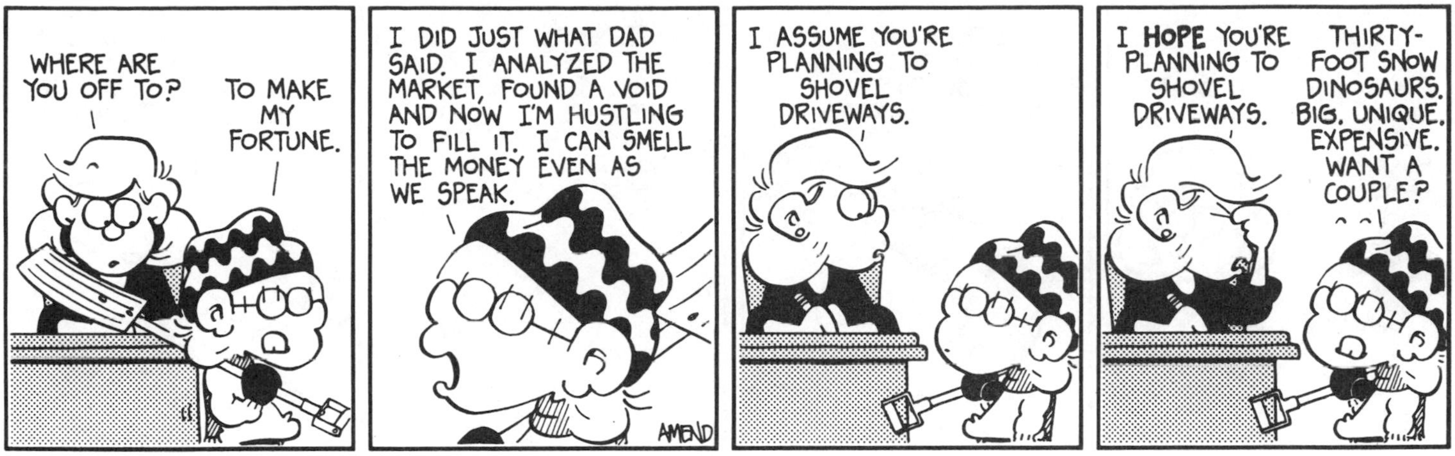
WHERE ARE YOU OFF TO?
TO MAKE MY FORTUNE.
I DID JUST WHAT DAD SAID. I ANALYZED THE MARKET, FOUND A VOID AND NOW I'M HUSTLING TO FILL IT. I CAN SMELL THE MONEY EVEN AS WE SPEAK.
AMEND
I ASSUME YOU'RE PLANNING TO SHOVEL DRIVEWAYS.
I **HOPE** YOU'RE PLANNING TO SHOVEL DRIVEWAYS.
THIRTY-FOOT SNOW DINOSAURS. BIG. UNIQUE. EXPENSIVE. WANT A COUPLE?

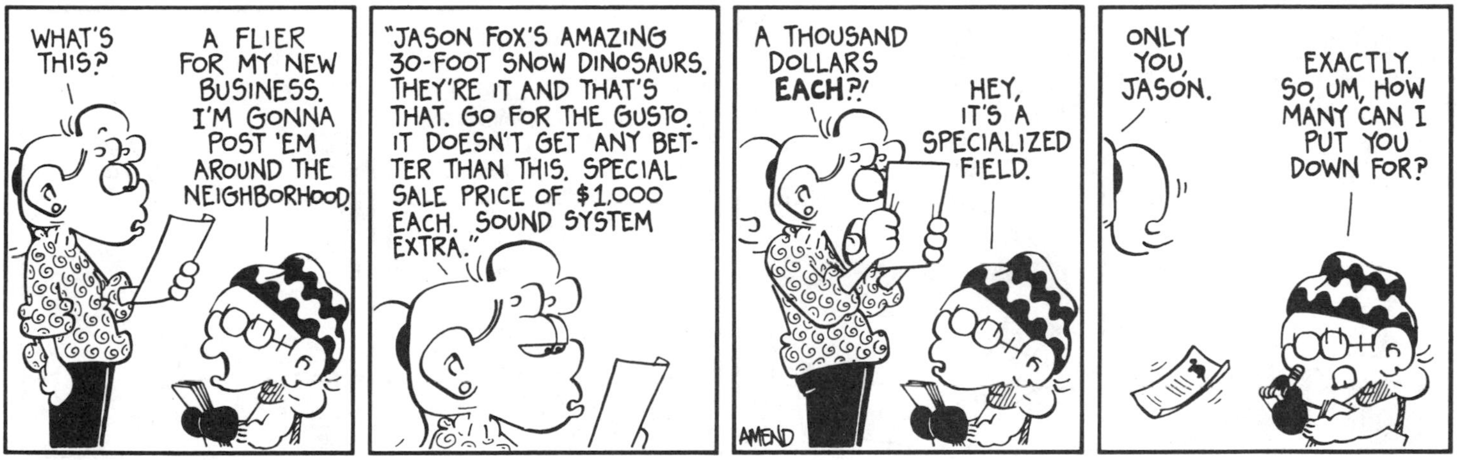
WHAT'S THIS?
A FLIER FOR MY NEW BUSINESS. I'M GONNA POST 'EM AROUND THE NEIGHBORHOOD.
"JASON FOX'S AMAZING 30-FOOT SNOW DINOSAURS. THEY'RE IT AND THAT'S THAT. GO FOR THE GUSTO. IT DOESN'T GET ANY BETTER THAN THIS. SPECIAL SALE PRICE OF $1,000 EACH. SOUND SYSTEM EXTRA."
A THOUSAND DOLLARS **EACH**?!
HEY, IT'S A SPECIALIZED FIELD.
AMEND
ONLY YOU, JASON.
EXACTLY. SO, UM, HOW MANY CAN I PUT YOU DOWN FOR?

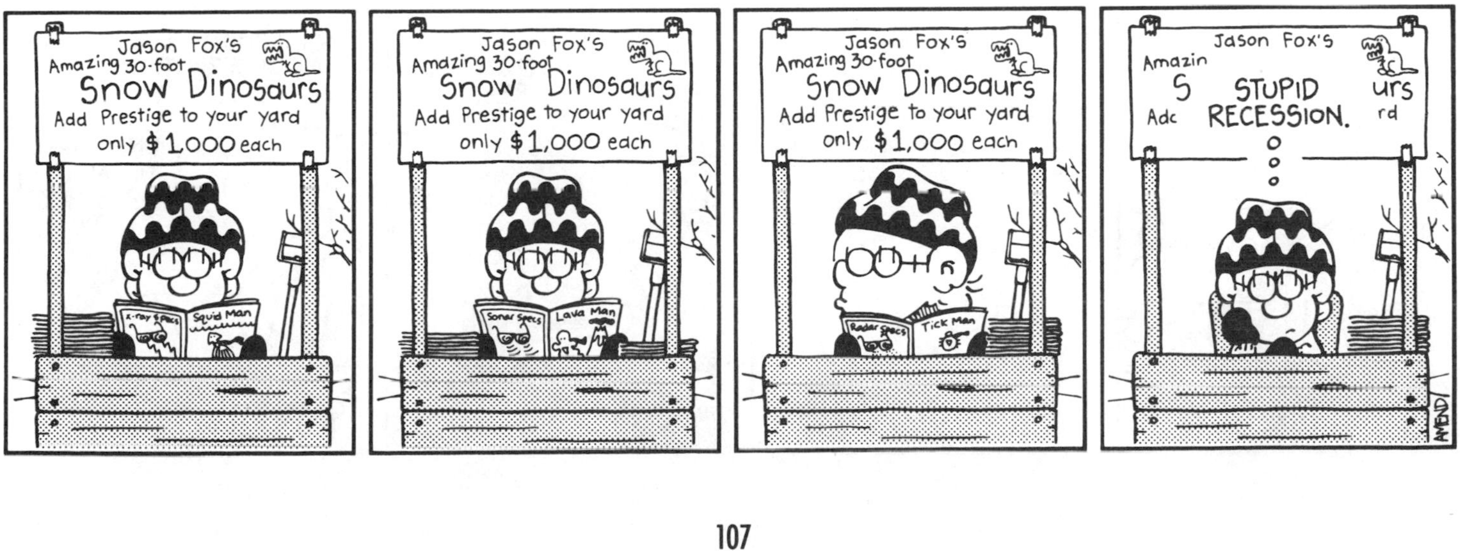
Jason Fox's Amazing 30-foot Snow Dinosaurs Add Prestige to your yard only $1,000 each
X-ray Specs
Squid Man
Jason Fox's Amazing 30-foot Snow Dinosaurs Add Prestige to your yard only $1,000 each
Sonar Specs
Lava Man
Jason Fox's Amazing 30-foot Snow Dinosaurs Add Prestige to your yard only $1,000 each
Radar Specs
Tick Man
Jason Fox's
Amazin
S
urs
Adc
rd
STUPID RECESSION.
AMEND

I KNOW WHAT YOU'RE THINKING.

OH?

YOU'RE THINKING HOW MUCH YOU'D LIKE A 30-FOOT SNOW LEPTOCERATOPS IN THE FRONT YARD BUT THE $1,000 PRICE TAG IS SCARING YOU OFF.

A LEPTO-WHAT?!

SO, SEEING AS YOU'RE MY MOM AND ALL, I FIGURED WE COULD DISCUSS ALTERNATE FORMS OF PAYMENT.

LIKE, SAY, A FRESH BATCH OF YOUR FAVORITE COOKIES?

LIKE, SAY, 24 INSTALLMENTS OF $41.67. NO INTEREST.

THE PUZZLE'S REALLY WHAT **YOU'RE** THINKING...

AMEND

JASON, YOU'VE HAD SOME PRETTY LAME IDEAS IN THE PAST, BUT THIS IS THE LAMEST.

WHAT — ARE YOU KIDDING?

Snow Dinosaur $1000

JASON, SOMEONE **MIGHT** PAY $5 FOR A STUPID SNOW DINOSAUR, BUT A **THOUSAND**?! I BEG YOU'RE **NUTS**!

I BEG TO DIFFER.

WE'RE NOT TALKING MASS PRODUCTION HERE, WE'RE TALKING HAND-CRAFTED, INDIVIDUALLY COMMISSIONED PIECES OF ART. CARVED WITH PRECISION, ANATOMICALLY CORRECT AND CUSTOM POSITIONED FOR EACH SITE, THESE WORKS STAND AS A MONUMENT TO A BYGONE ERA (AN ERA, IRONICALLY, THAT NEVER **SAW** THE ICE AGE), IMBUING ON THEIR OWNER A STATUS AND PRESTIGE THAT'S **EASILY** WORTH A COOL GRAND.

HAVE FUN FREEZING.

SO, UM, YOU'D PAY $5 FOR ONE?...

AMEND

Snow Dinosaur $1000

POOR JASON.

WHAT?

THE KID SET UP A LITTLE STAND TO MAKE SNOW DINOSAURS AND NOBODY WANTED ONE.

AT $1,000 EACH, DO YOU BLAME THEM?

A THOUSAND DOLLARS. EACH.

DIDN'T YOU READ THE SIGN?

SON, ABOUT THAT ORDER I PLACED...

I WAS GOING TO ASK YOU — WOULD IT BE OK IF I DIDN'T START THE APATOSAURUS HERD UNTIL TOMORROW?

AMEND

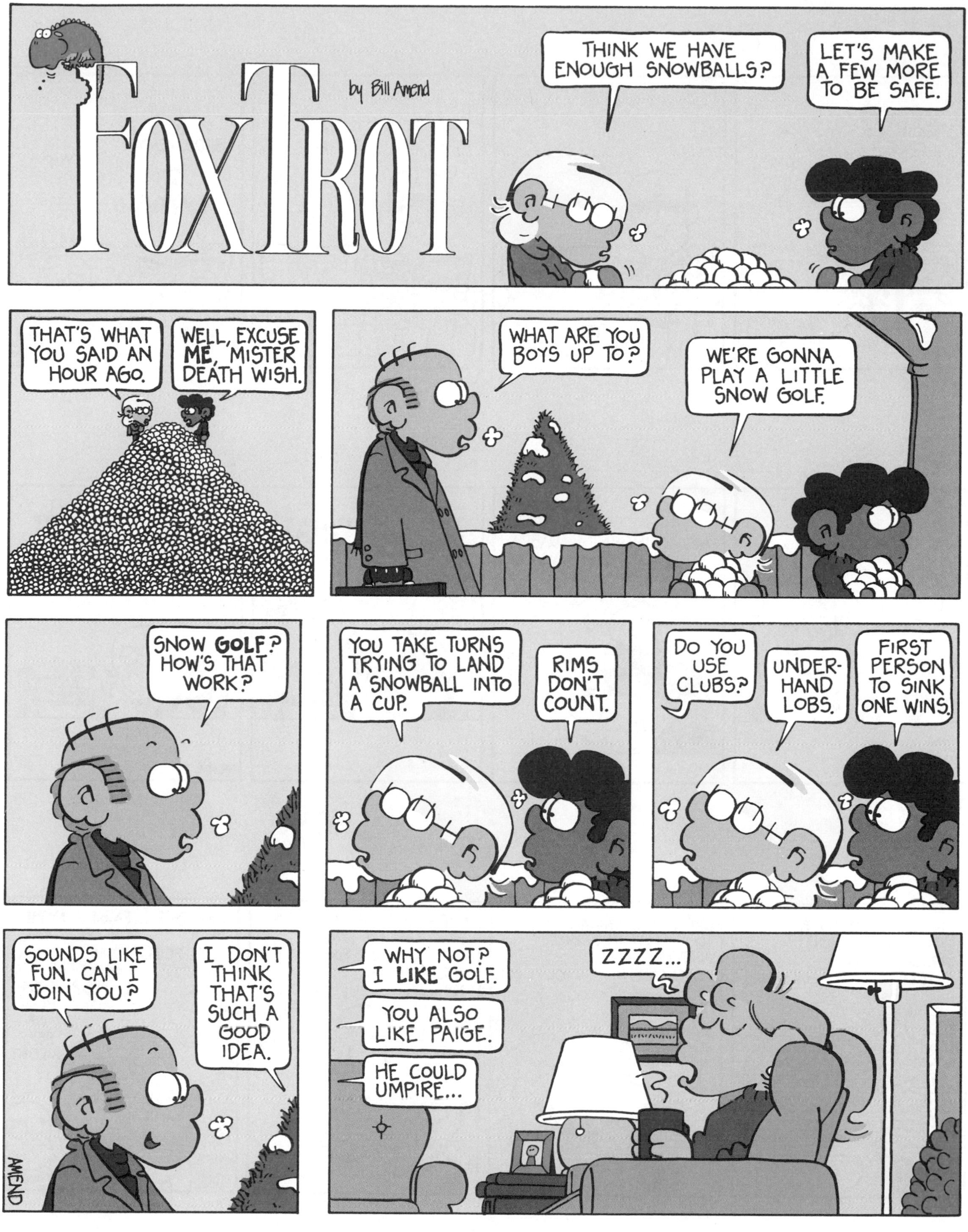
FoxTrot
by Bill Amend
THINK WE HAVE ENOUGH SNOWBALLS?
LET'S MAKE A FEW MORE TO BE SAFE.
THAT'S WHAT YOU SAID AN HOUR AGO.
WELL, EXCUSE **ME**, MISTER DEATH WISH.
WHAT ARE YOU BOYS UP TO?
WE'RE GONNA PLAY A LITTLE SNOW GOLF.
SNOW **GOLF**? HOW'S THAT WORK?
YOU TAKE TURNS TRYING TO LAND A SNOWBALL INTO A CUP.
RIMS DON'T COUNT.
DO YOU USE CLUBS?
UNDER-HAND LOBS.
FIRST PERSON TO SINK ONE WINS.
SOUNDS LIKE FUN. CAN I JOIN YOU?
I DON'T THINK THAT'S SUCH A GOOD IDEA.
WHY NOT? I **LIKE** GOLF.
ZZZZ...
YOU ALSO LIKE PAIGE.
HE COULD UMPIRE...
AMEND

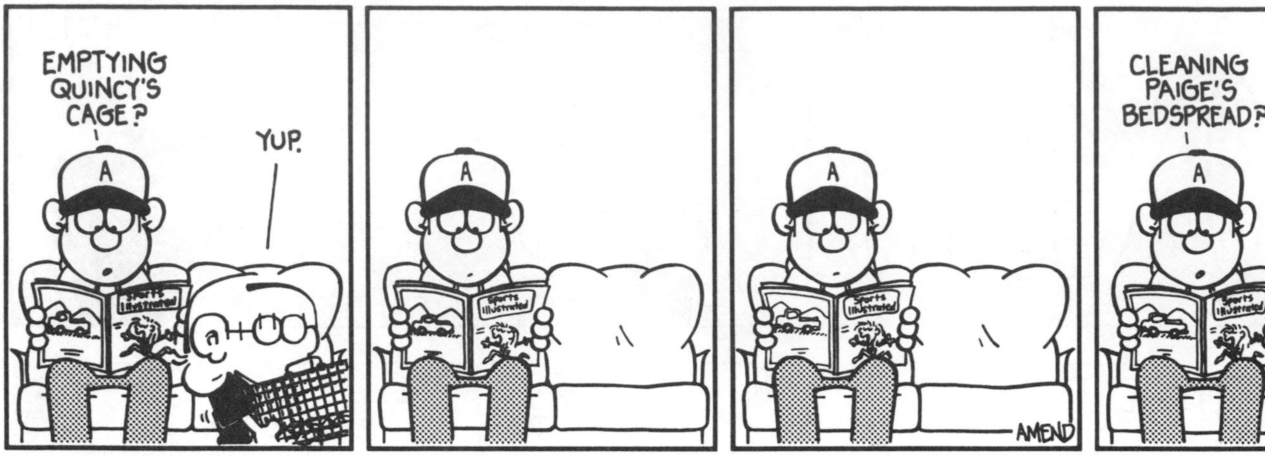
EMPTYING QUINCY'S CAGE?
YUP.
CLEANING PAIGE'S BEDSPREAD?
YUP.
AMEND

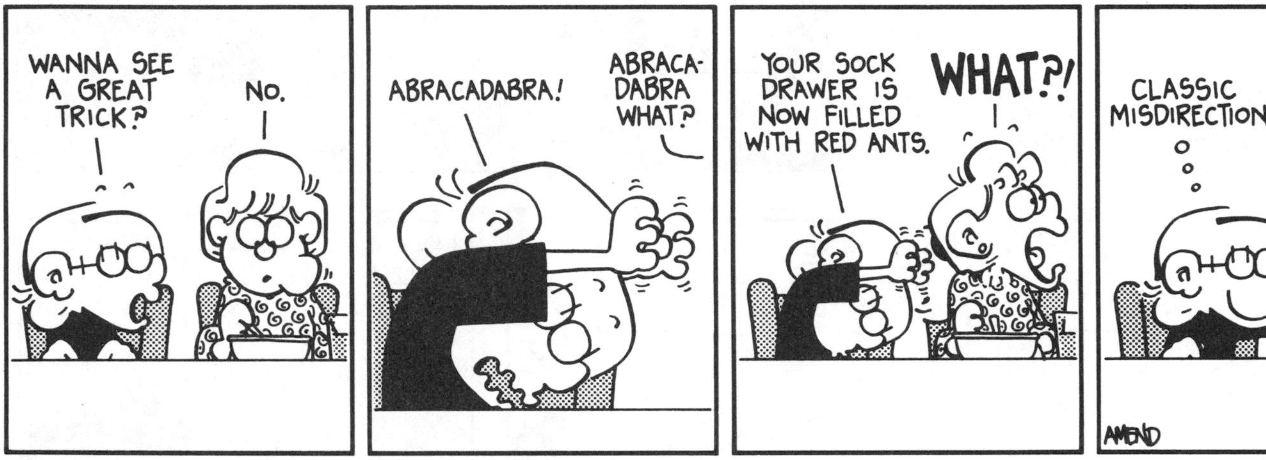
WANNA SEE A GREAT TRICK?
NO.
ABRACADABRA!
ABRACA-DABRA WHAT?
YOUR SOCK DRAWER IS NOW FILLED WITH RED ANTS.
WHAT?!
CLASSIC MISDIRECTION.
LIAR—I DON'T SEE ANY...
AMEND

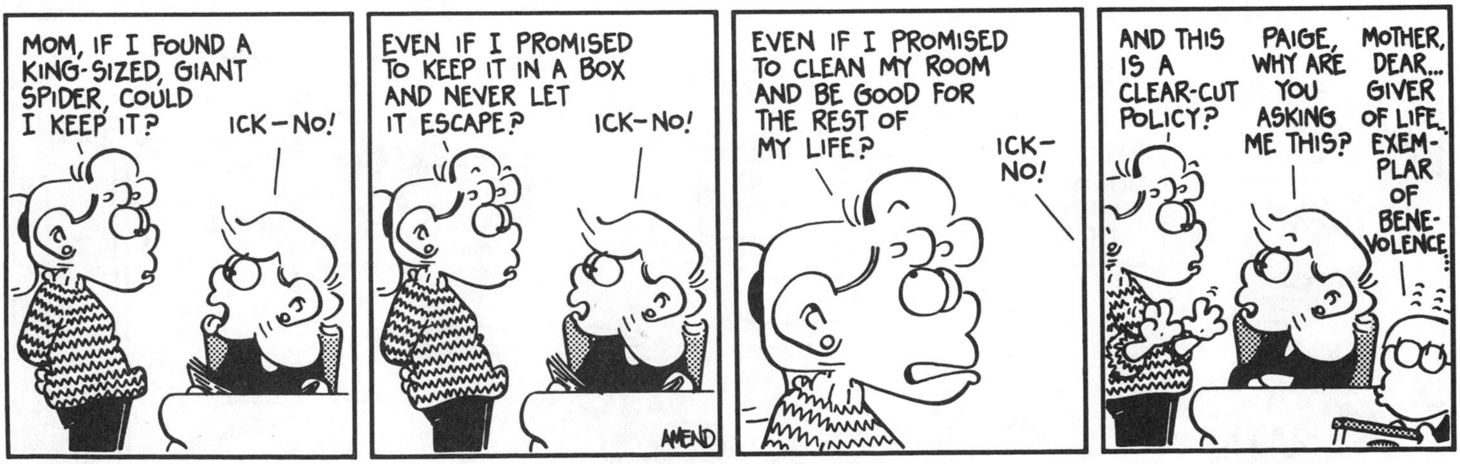
MOM, IF I FOUND A KING-SIZED, GIANT SPIDER, COULD I KEEP IT?
ICK—NO!
EVEN IF I PROMISED TO KEEP IT IN A BOX AND NEVER LET IT ESCAPE?
ICK—NO!
AMEND
EVEN IF I PROMISED TO CLEAN MY ROOM AND BE GOOD FOR THE REST OF MY LIFE?
ICK—NO!
AND THIS IS A CLEAR-CUT POLICY?
PAIGE, WHY ARE YOU ASKING ME THIS?
MOTHER, DEAR... GIVER OF LIFE... EXEMPLAR OF BENEVOLENCE...

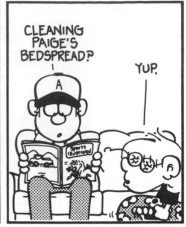

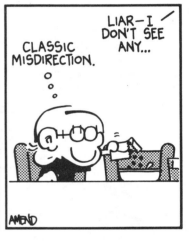

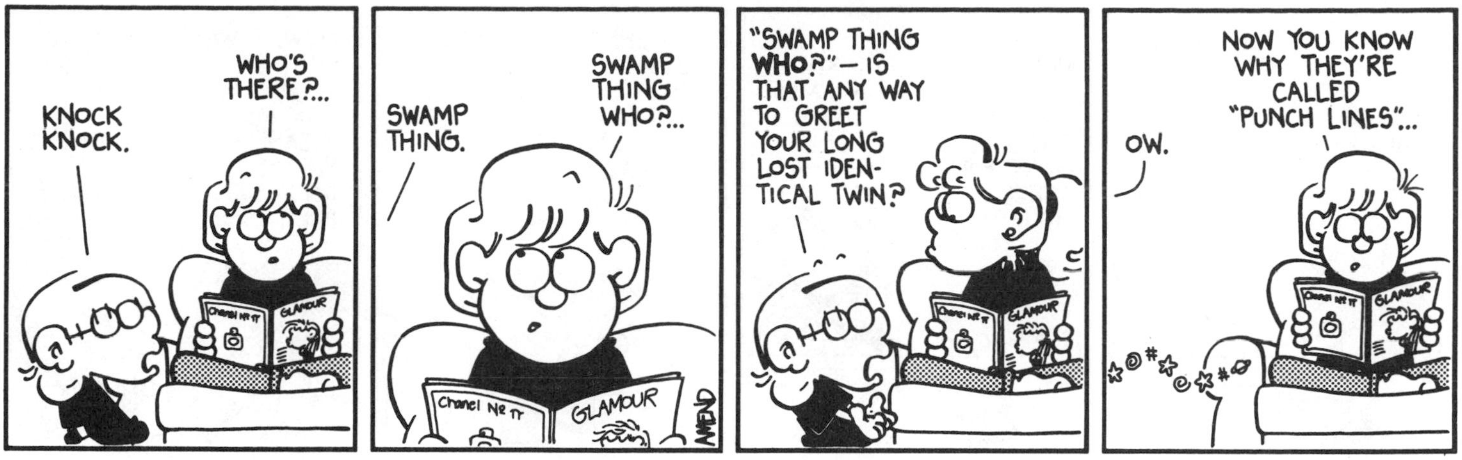
KNOCK KNOCK.
WHO'S THERE?...
SWAMP THING.
SWAMP THING WHO?...
GLAMOUR
AMEND
"SWAMP THING **WHO?**" — IS THAT ANY WAY TO GREET YOUR LONG LOST IDENTICAL TWIN?
OW.
NOW YOU KNOW WHY THEY'RE CALLED "PUNCH LINES"...

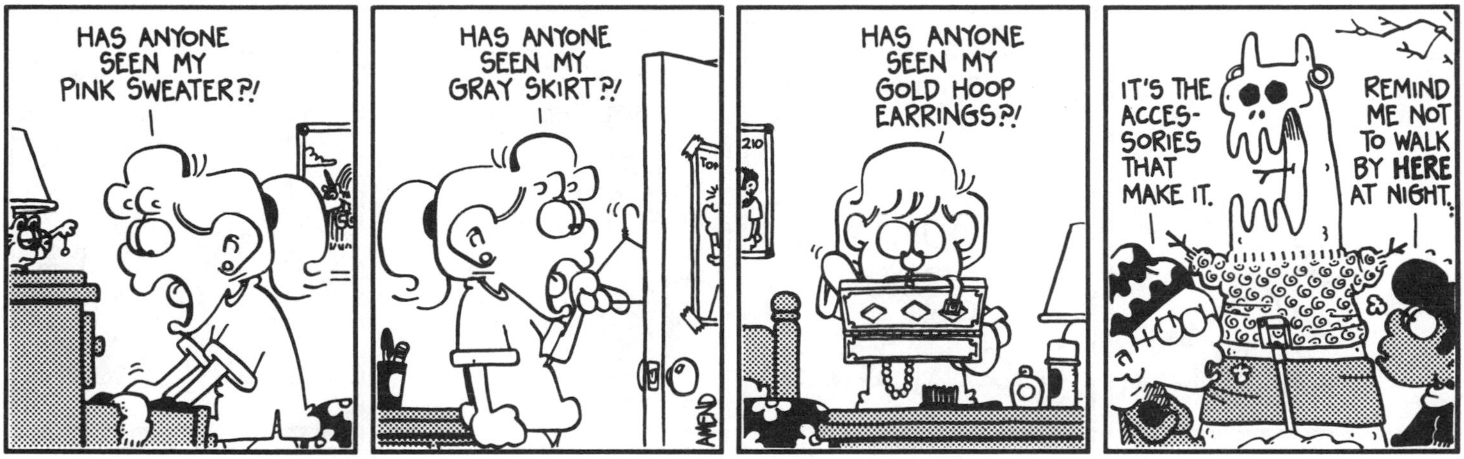
HAS ANYONE SEEN MY PINK SWEATER?!
HAS ANYONE SEEN MY GRAY SKIRT?!
AMEND
HAS ANYONE SEEN MY GOLD HOOP EARRINGS?!
IT'S THE ACCESSORIES THAT MAKE IT.
REMIND ME NOT TO WALK BY **HERE** AT NIGHT.

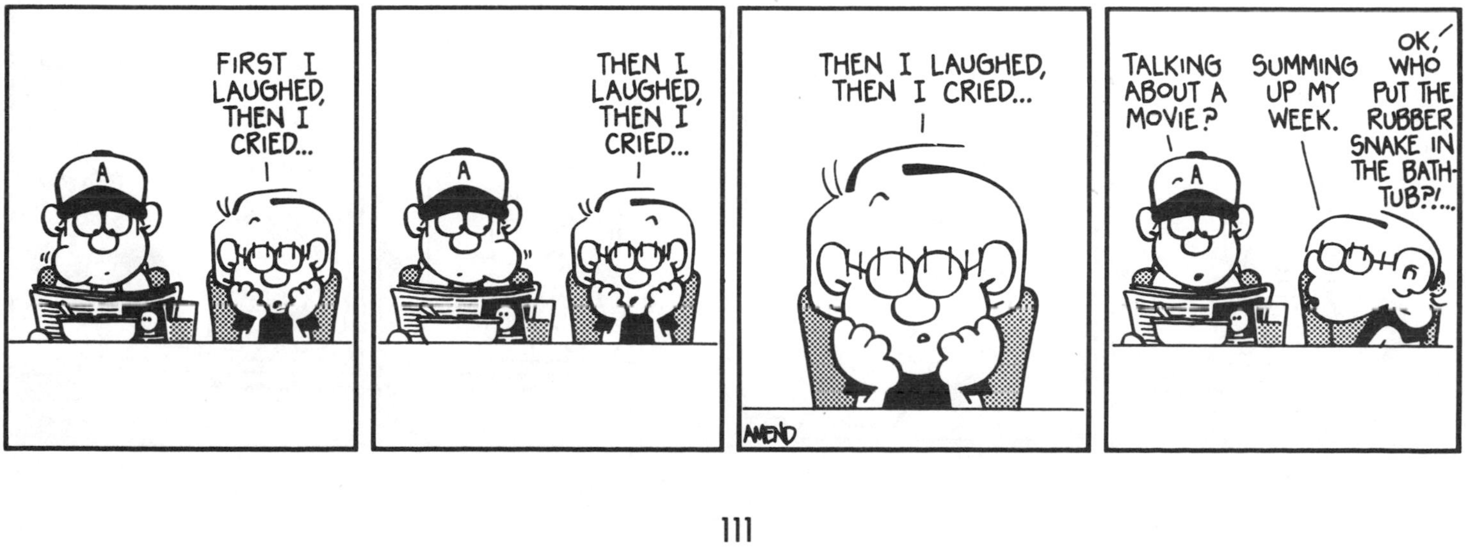
FIRST I LAUGHED, THEN I CRIED...
THEN I LAUGHED, THEN I CRIED...
THEN I LAUGHED, THEN I CRIED...
AMEND
TALKING ABOUT A MOVIE?
SUMMING UP MY WEEK.
OK, WHO PUT THE RUBBER SNAKE IN THE BATHTUB?!...

WHERE'S PAIGE?

SHE WENT OUT TO BUY VALENTINE'S DAY CARDS.

WHERE'D SHE GO?! ITALY?! SHE'S BEEN GONE FOR THREE HOURS!

YOU KNOW HOW PAIGE SHOPS.

ALL SHE'S BUYING IS A LOUSY BOX OF **CARDS**! HOW LONG CAN IT **TAKE**?!

YOUR GUESS IS AS GOOD AS MINE.

AMEND

NOW, I WANT SOMETHING THAT SAYS, "I WANT YOU, I LOVE YOU, I NEED YOU, ASK ME OUT, PLEASE, PLEASE, PLEASE," BUT ONLY SUBLIMINALLY.

IN GARFIELD OR PEANUTS?

THERE HE IS.

OOO—HE'S **CUTE**!

HE JUST SWITCHED INTO MY MATH CLASS. I THINK HIS NAME'S JOHN.

JOHN. OOO—I LIKE IT.

I BOUGHT THE PERFECT VALENTINE'S DAY CARD FOR HIM. THE ONLY PROBLEM IS I DON'T KNOW WHAT TO WRITE.

HMMM. YOU DEFINITELY DON'T WANT TO BLOW IT BY OVERSTATING ANYTHING.

AMEND

HOW'S "DEAR TOTAL HUNK O' HOTNESS" SOUND?

YOU DON'T WANT TO UNDERSTATE THINGS EITHER. OOO—LOOK! HE'S SCRATCHING HIS NOSE!

Dear John,
   I think you're nice. I'm glad you're in my math class.

LOVE,
Paige Fox
xoxoxoxoxoxoxoxoxo
xoxoxoxo xoxoxoxoxo

Hal

Dear John,
   I think you're—...

I JUST **EMPTIED** THIS THING!

AMEND

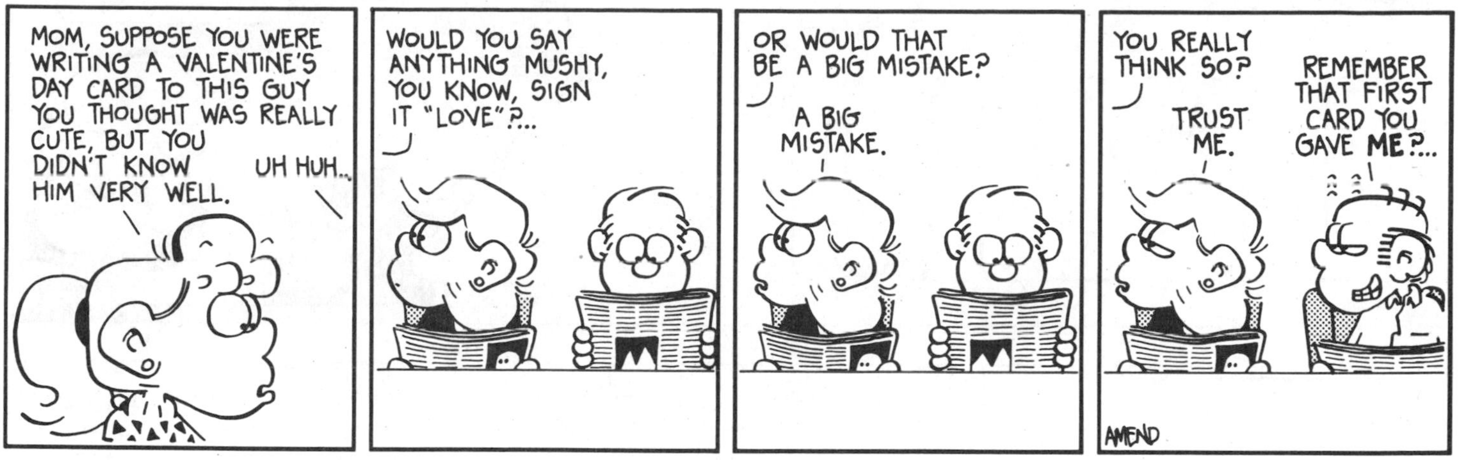
MOM, SUPPOSE YOU WERE WRITING A VALENTINE'S DAY CARD TO THIS GUY YOU THOUGHT WAS REALLY CUTE, BUT YOU DIDN'T KNOW HIM VERY WELL.
UH HUH...
WOULD YOU SAY ANYTHING MUSHY, YOU KNOW, SIGN IT "LOVE"?...
OR WOULD THAT BE A BIG MISTAKE?
A BIG MISTAKE.
YOU REALLY THINK SO?
TRUST ME.
REMEMBER THAT FIRST CARD YOU GAVE **ME**?...
AMEND

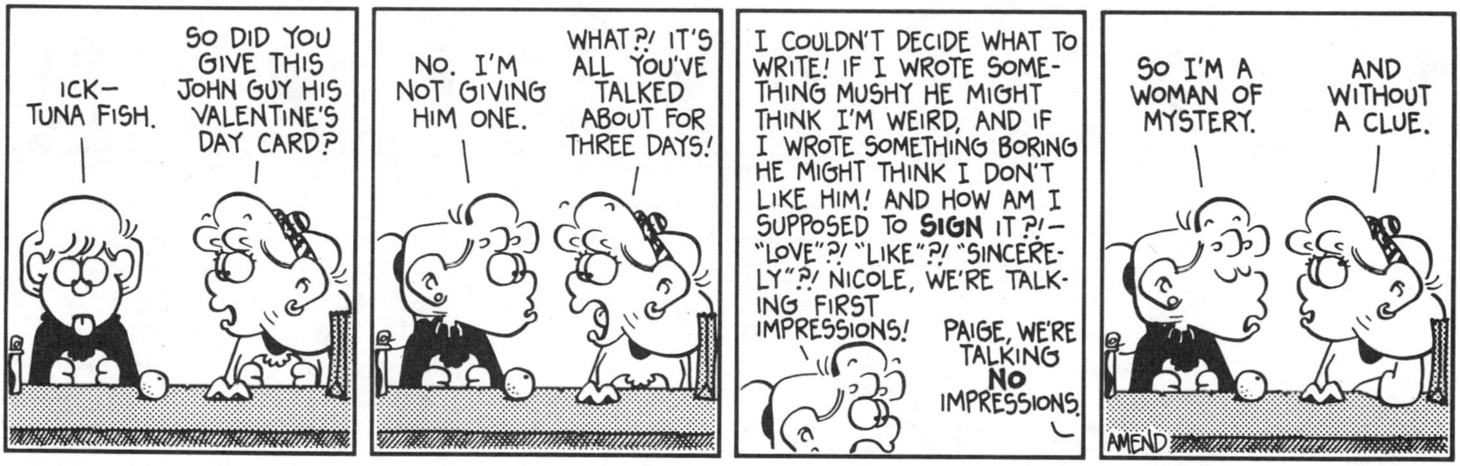
ICK— TUNA FISH.
SO DID YOU GIVE THIS JOHN GUY HIS VALENTINE'S DAY CARD?
NO. I'M NOT GIVING HIM ONE.
WHAT?! IT'S ALL YOU'VE TALKED ABOUT FOR THREE DAYS!
I COULDN'T DECIDE WHAT TO WRITE! IF I WROTE SOMETHING MUSHY HE MIGHT THINK I'M WEIRD, AND IF I WROTE SOMETHING BORING HE MIGHT THINK I DON'T LIKE HIM! AND HOW AM I SUPPOSED TO **SIGN** IT?!—"LOVE"?! "LIKE"?! "SINCERELY"?! NICOLE, WE'RE TALKING FIRST IMPRESSIONS!
PAIGE, WE'RE TALKING **NO** IMPRESSIONS.
SO I'M A WOMAN OF MYSTERY.
AND WITHOUT A CLUE.
AMEND

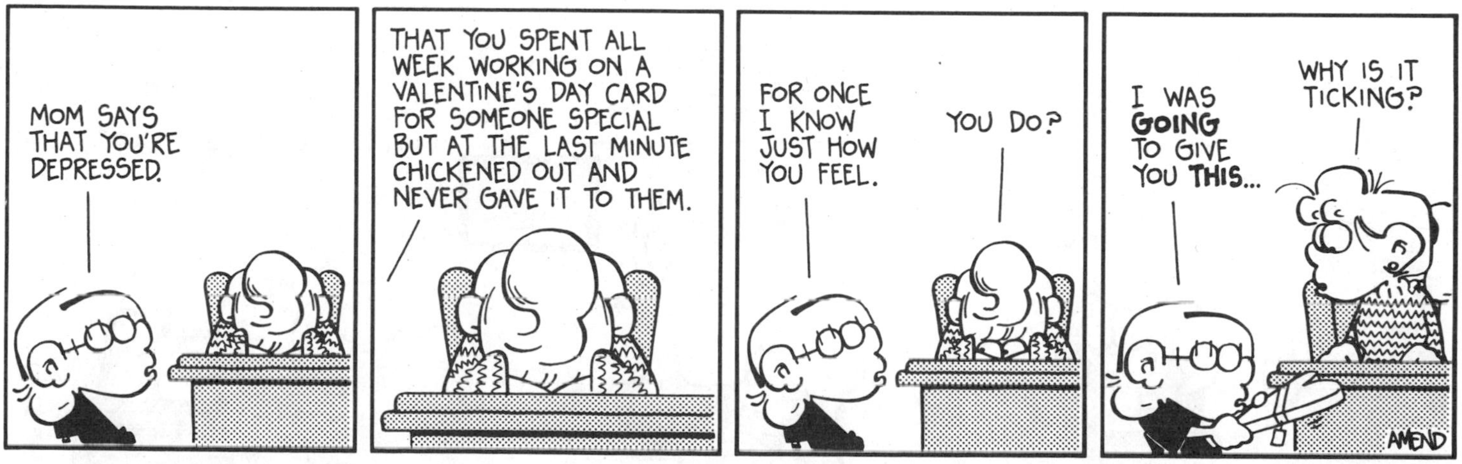
MOM SAYS THAT YOU'RE DEPRESSED.
THAT YOU SPENT ALL WEEK WORKING ON A VALENTINE'S DAY CARD FOR SOMEONE SPECIAL BUT AT THE LAST MINUTE CHICKENED OUT AND NEVER GAVE IT TO THEM.
FOR ONCE I KNOW JUST HOW YOU FEEL.
YOU DO?
I WAS **GOING** TO GIVE YOU **THIS**...
WHY IS IT TICKING?
AMEND

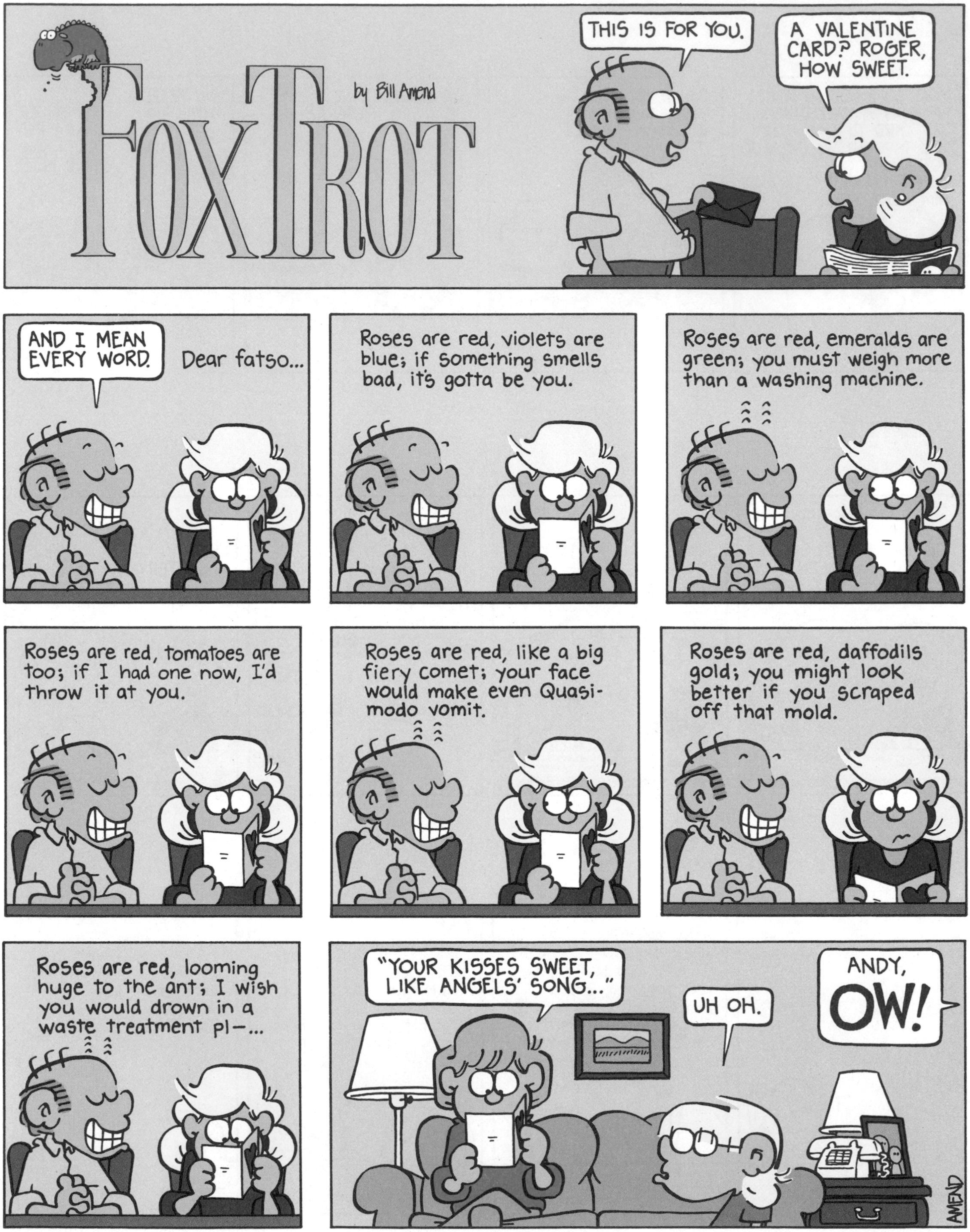
FoxTrot
by Bill Amend
THIS IS FOR YOU.
A VALENTINE CARD? ROGER, HOW SWEET.
AND I MEAN EVERY WORD.
Dear fatso...
Roses are red, violets are blue; if something smells bad, it's gotta be you.
Roses are red, emeralds are green; you must weigh more than a washing machine.
Roses are red, tomatoes are too; if I had one now, I'd throw it at you.
Roses are red, like a big fiery comet; your face would make even Quasi-modo vomit.
Roses are red, daffodils gold; you might look better if you scraped off that mold.
Roses are red, looming huge to the ant; I wish you would drown in a waste treatment pl—...
"YOUR KISSES SWEET, LIKE ANGELS' SONG..."
UH OH.
ANDY, OW!
AMEND

WOOF
WOOF
WOOF

by Bill Amend
FoxTrot

AHEM.

SORRY. CAN WE START OVER?

MY NAME ISN'T IMPORTANT. BUT WHAT I HAVE TO SAY **IS**.

I'M 14 YEARS OLD AND I'VE LIVED A LIFE OF LIES.

PEOPLE THINK I'M HAPPY. PEOPLE THINK I'M NORMAL. BUT THEY DON'T KNOW THE REAL ME.

MY LITTLE BROTHER CALLS ME A MONSTER. IF ONLY HE KNEW HOW RIGHT HE WAS.

I GUESS IT ALL STARTED BACK WHEN I WAS THREE.

THE MASS MURDERS, ANYWAY.

THE TRICK, OF COURSE, WILL BE GETTING GERALDO TO PLAY IT.

OK, OK, MY NAME IS PAIGE FOX. I LIVE AT—...

YOU KNOW, IF WE WERE TO MAKE **COPIES** OF THIS...

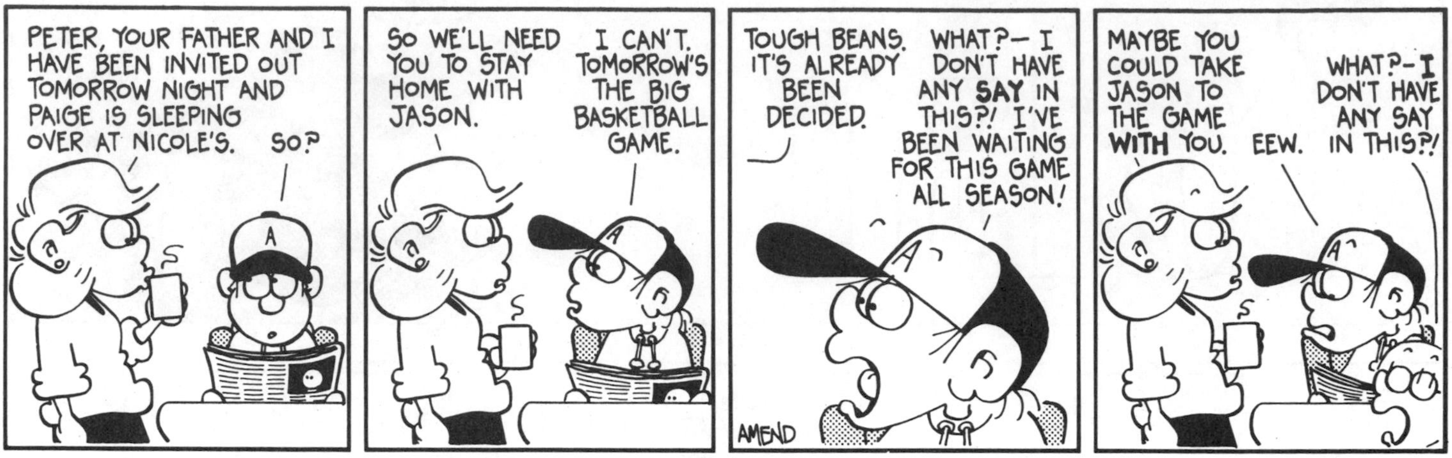
PETER, YOUR FATHER AND I HAVE BEEN INVITED OUT TOMORROW NIGHT AND PAIGE IS SLEEPING OVER AT NICOLE'S.
SO?
SO WE'LL NEED YOU TO STAY HOME WITH JASON.
I CAN'T. TOMORROW'S THE BIG BASKETBALL GAME.
TOUGH BEANS. IT'S ALREADY BEEN DECIDED.
WHAT?— I DON'T HAVE ANY **SAY** IN THIS?! I'VE BEEN WAITING FOR THIS GAME ALL SEASON!
AMEND
MAYBE YOU COULD TAKE JASON TO THE GAME **WITH** YOU.
EEW.
WHAT?– **I** DON'T HAVE ANY SAY IN THIS?!

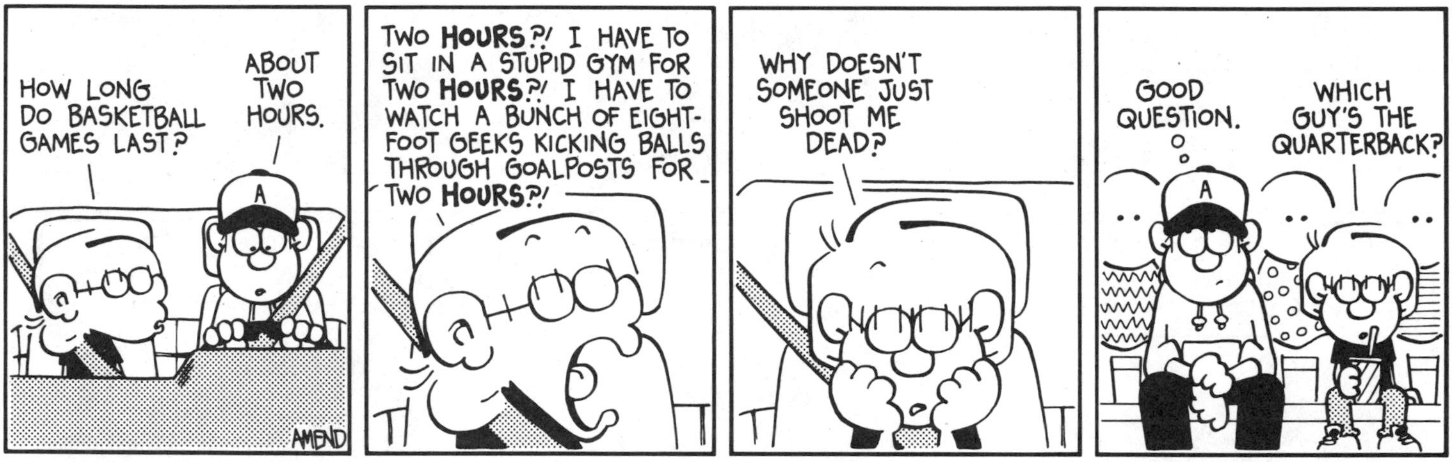
HOW LONG DO BASKETBALL GAMES LAST?
ABOUT TWO HOURS.
AMEND
TWO **HOURS**?! I HAVE TO SIT IN A STUPID GYM FOR TWO **HOURS**?! I HAVE TO WATCH A BUNCH OF EIGHT-FOOT GEEKS KICKING BALLS THROUGH GOALPOSTS FOR TWO **HOURS**?!
WHY DOESN'T SOMEONE JUST SHOOT ME DEAD?
GOOD QUESTION.
WHICH GUY'S THE QUARTERBACK?

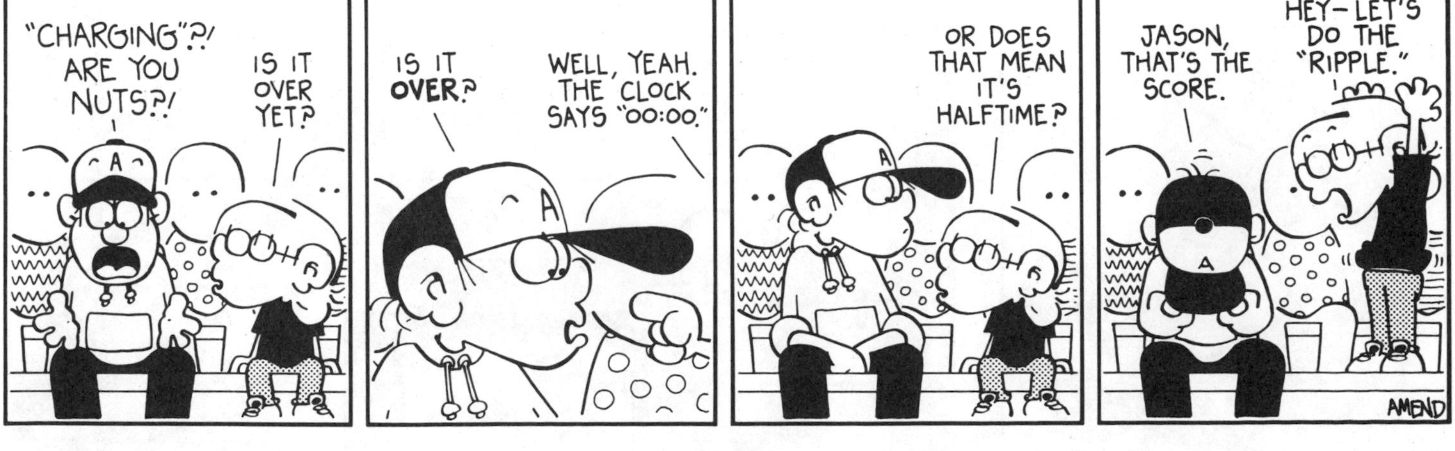
"CHARGING"?! ARE YOU NUTS?!
IS IT OVER YET?
IS IT **OVER**?
WELL, YEAH. THE CLOCK SAYS "00:00."
OR DOES THAT MEAN IT'S HALFTIME?
JASON, THAT'S THE SCORE.
HEY– LET'S DO THE "RIPPLE."
AMEND

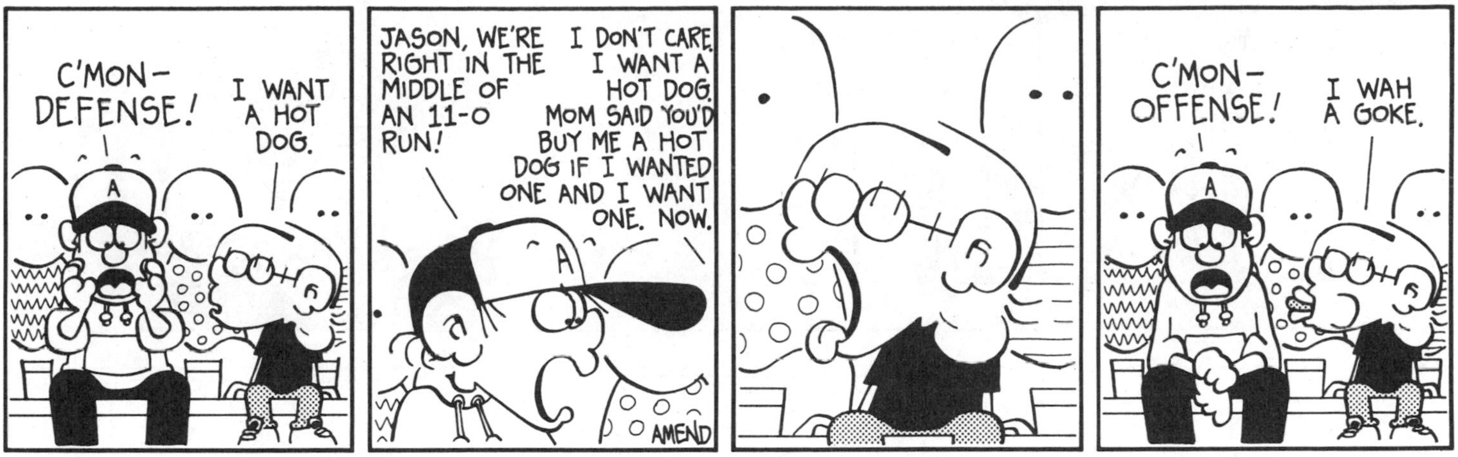
C'MON– DEFENSE!
I WANT A HOT DOG.
JASON, WE'RE RIGHT IN THE MIDDLE OF AN 11-0 RUN!
I DON'T CARE. I WANT A HOT DOG. MOM SAID YOU'D BUY ME A HOT DOG IF I WANTED ONE AND I WANT ONE. NOW.
AMEND
C'MON– OFFENSE!
I WAH A GOKE.

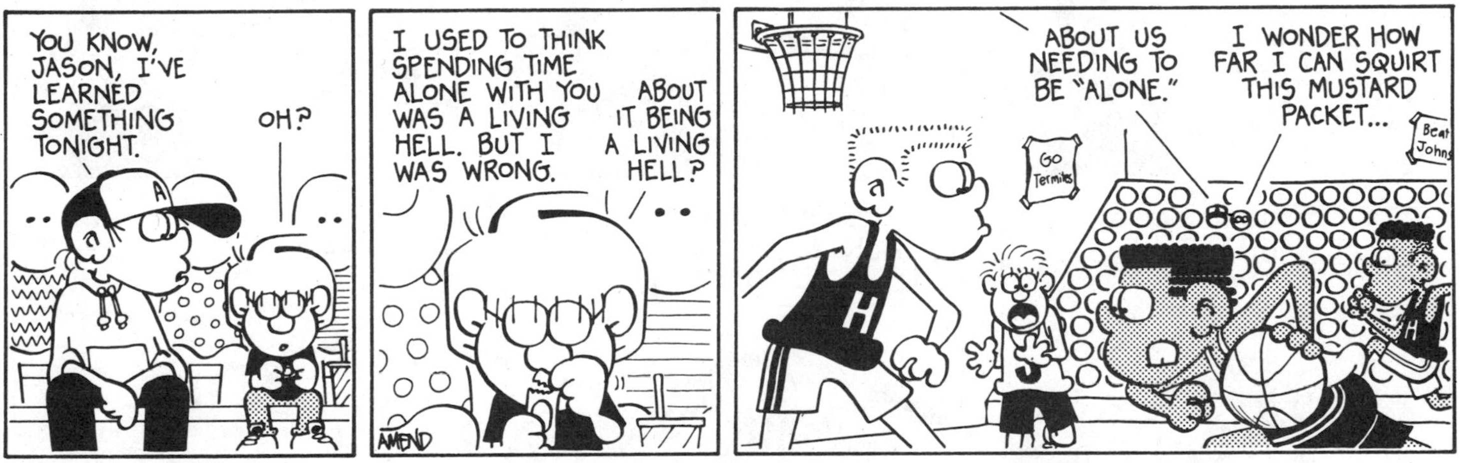
YOU KNOW, JASON, I'VE LEARNED SOMETHING TONIGHT.
OH?
I USED TO THINK SPENDING TIME ALONE WITH YOU WAS A LIVING HELL. BUT I WAS WRONG.
ABOUT IT BEING A LIVING HELL?
AMEND
ABOUT US NEEDING TO BE "ALONE."
I WONDER HOW FAR I CAN SQUIRT THIS MUSTARD PACKET...
Go Termites
Beat

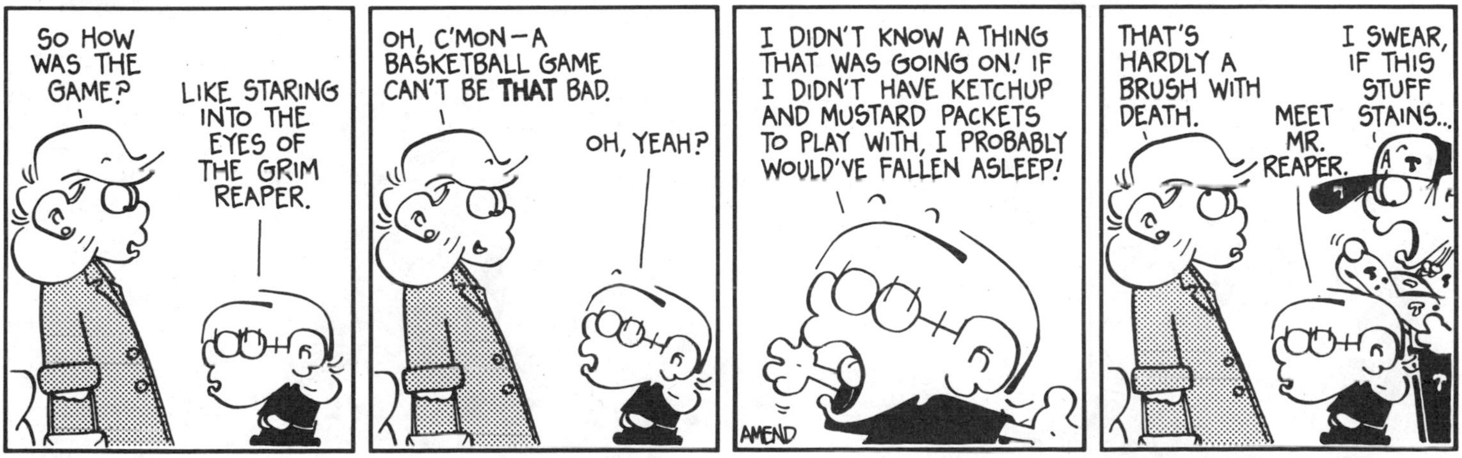
SO HOW WAS THE GAME?
LIKE STARING INTO THE EYES OF THE GRIM REAPER.
OH, C'MON–A BASKETBALL GAME CAN'T BE **THAT** BAD.
OH, YEAH?
I DIDN'T KNOW A THING THAT WAS GOING ON! IF I DIDN'T HAVE KETCHUP AND MUSTARD PACKETS TO PLAY WITH, I PROBABLY WOULD'VE FALLEN ASLEEP!
AMEND
THAT'S HARDLY A BRUSH WITH DEATH.
MEET MR. REAPER.
I SWEAR, IF THIS STUFF STAINS...

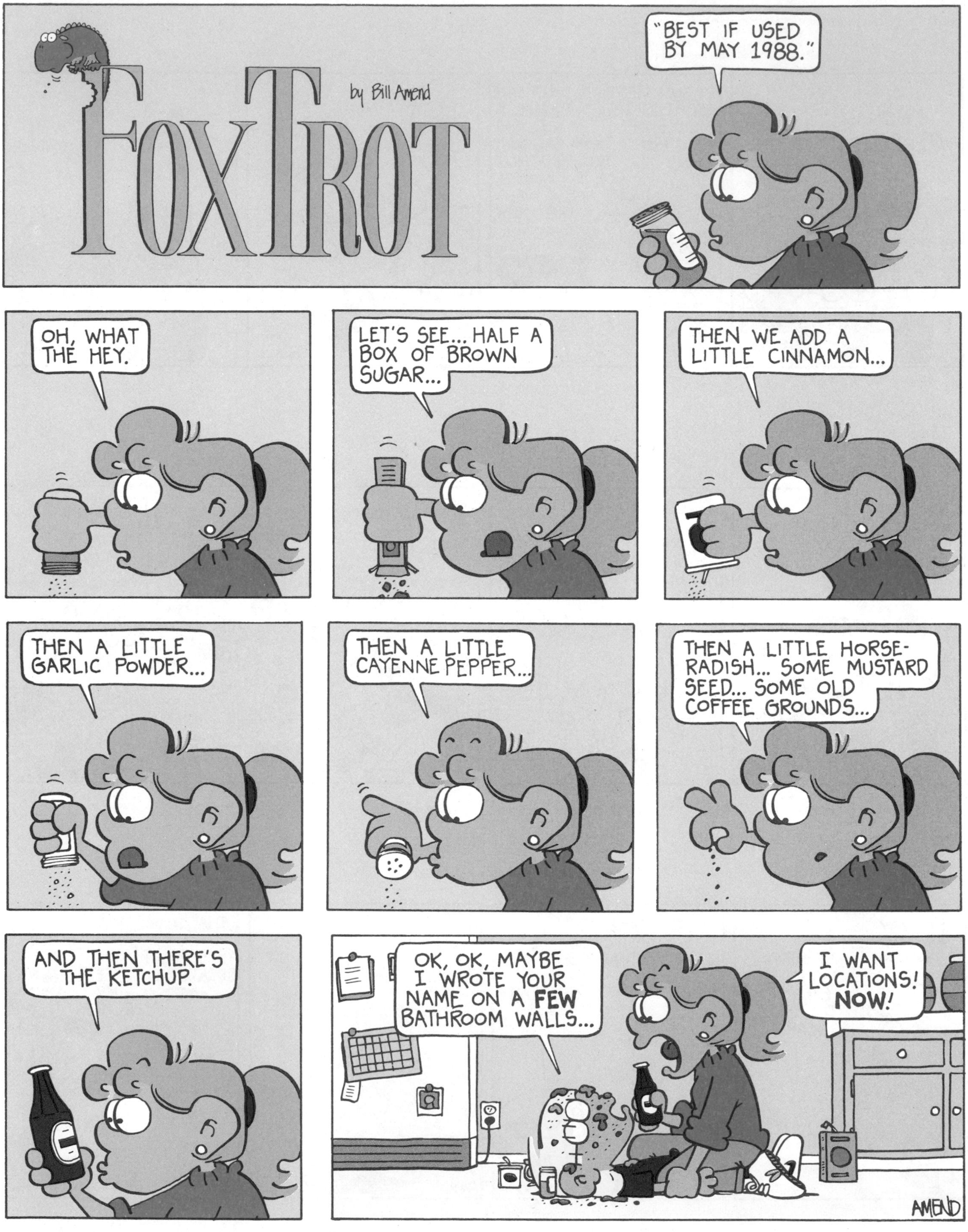
FoxTrot
by Bill Amend
"BEST IF USED BY MAY 1988."
OH, WHAT THE HEY.
LET'S SEE... HALF A BOX OF BROWN SUGAR...
THEN WE ADD A LITTLE CINNAMON...
THEN A LITTLE GARLIC POWDER...
THEN A LITTLE CAYENNE PEPPER...
THEN A LITTLE HORSE-RADISH... SOME MUSTARD SEED... SOME OLD COFFEE GROUNDS...
AND THEN THERE'S THE KETCHUP.
OK, OK, MAYBE I WROTE YOUR NAME ON A **FEW** BATHROOM WALLS...
I WANT LOCATIONS! **NOW**!
AMEND

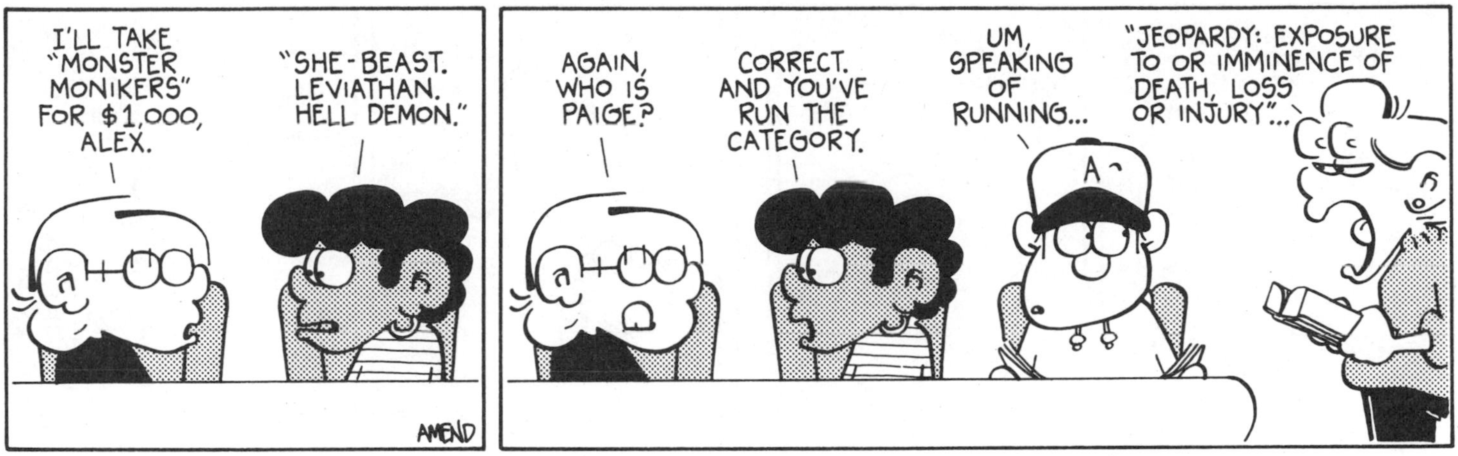
I'LL TAKE "MONSTER MONIKERS" FOR $1,000, ALEX.
"SHE-BEAST. LEVIATHAN. HELL DEMON."
AGAIN, WHO IS PAIGE?
CORRECT. AND YOU'VE RUN THE CATEGORY.
UM, SPEAKING OF RUNNING...
"JEOPARDY: EXPOSURE TO OR IMMINENCE OF DEATH, LOSS OR INJURY"...
AMEND

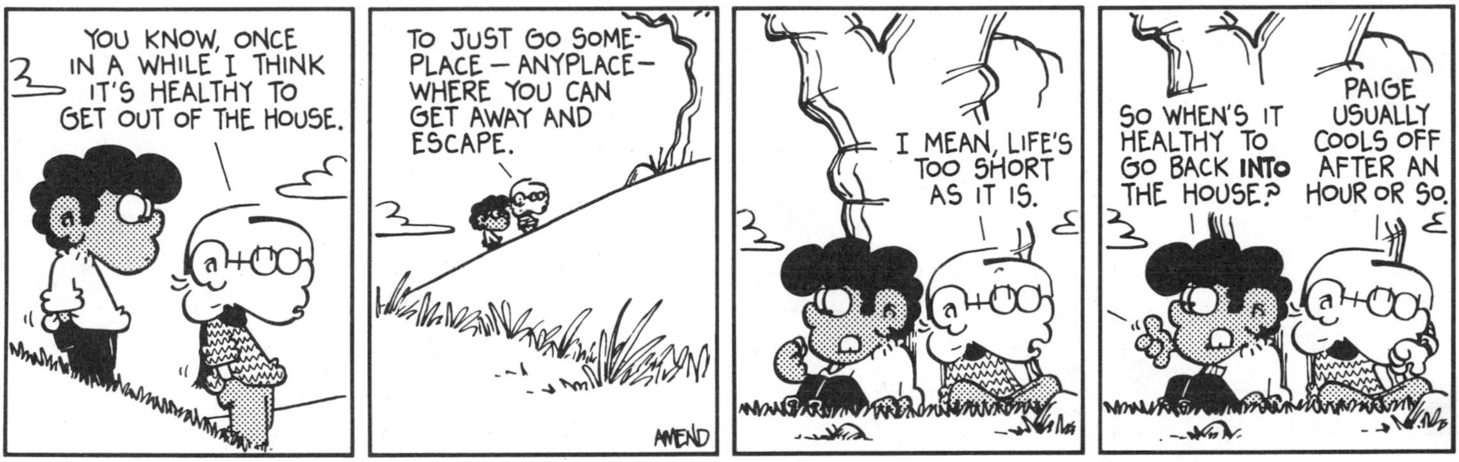
YOU KNOW, ONCE IN A WHILE I THINK IT'S HEALTHY TO GET OUT OF THE HOUSE.
TO JUST GO SOME-PLACE — ANYPLACE — WHERE YOU CAN GET AWAY AND ESCAPE.
AMEND
I MEAN, LIFE'S TOO SHORT AS IT IS.
SO WHEN'S IT HEALTHY TO GO BACK **INTO** THE HOUSE?
PAIGE USUALLY COOLS OFF AFTER AN HOUR OR SO.

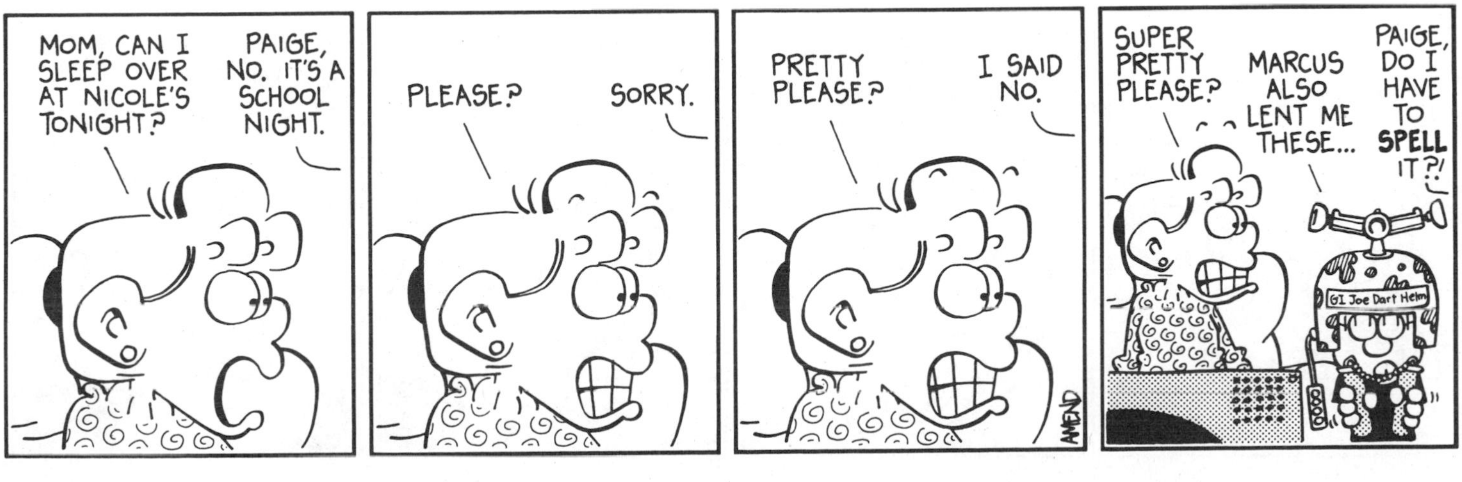
MOM, CAN I SLEEP OVER AT NICOLE'S TONIGHT?
PAIGE, NO. IT'S A SCHOOL NIGHT.
PLEASE?
SORRY.
PRETTY PLEASE?
I SAID NO.
AMEND
SUPER PRETTY PLEASE?
MARCUS ALSO LENT ME THESE...
PAIGE, DO I HAVE TO **SPELL** IT?!
GI Joe Dart Helm

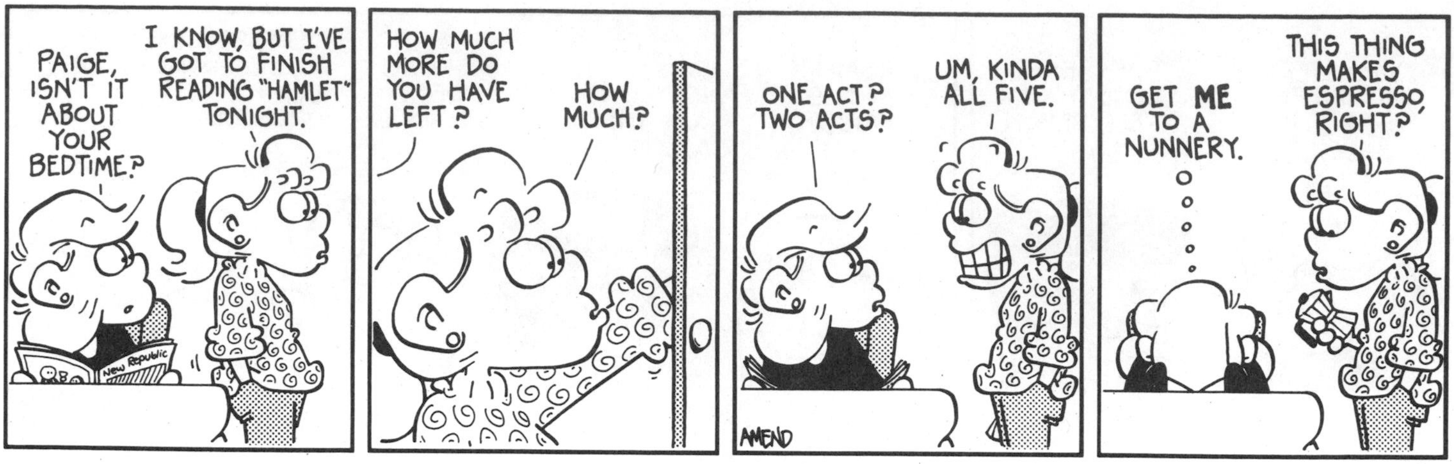
PAIGE, ISN'T IT ABOUT YOUR BEDTIME?
I KNOW, BUT I'VE GOT TO FINISH READING "HAMLET" TONIGHT.
New Republic
HOW MUCH MORE DO YOU HAVE LEFT?
HOW MUCH?
ONE ACT? TWO ACTS?
UM, KINDA ALL FIVE.
AMEND
GET **ME** TO A NUNNERY.
THIS THING MAKES ESPRESSO, RIGHT?

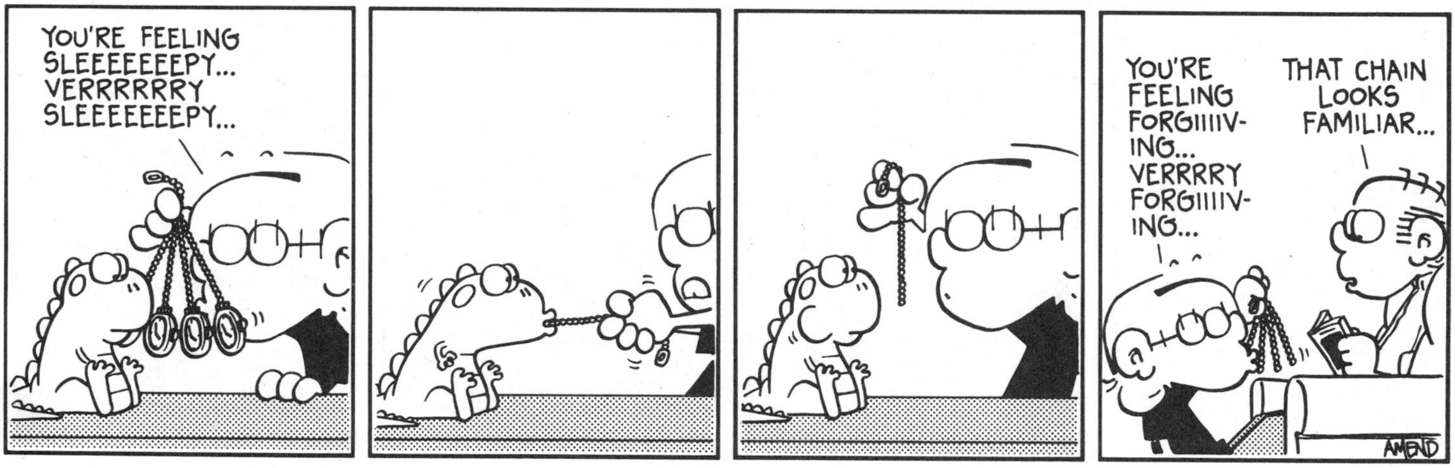
YOU'RE FEELING SLEEEEEEEPY... VERRRRRRY SLEEEEEEEPY...
YOU'RE FEELING FORGIIIIV-ING... VERRRRY FORGIIIIV-ING...
THAT CHAIN LOOKS FAMILIAR...
AMEND

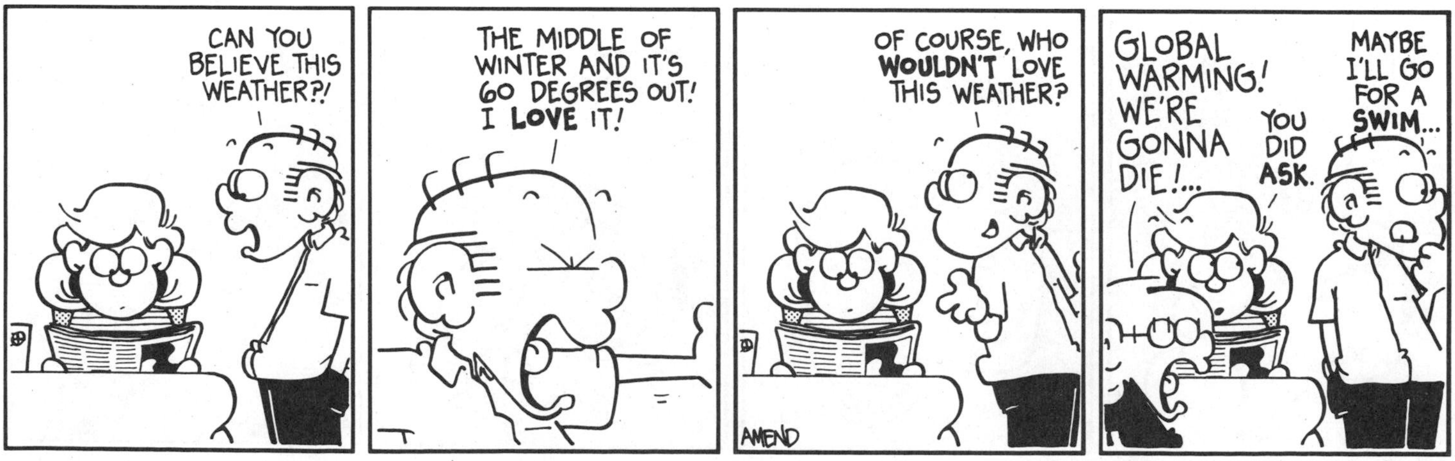
CAN YOU BELIEVE THIS WEATHER?!
THE MIDDLE OF WINTER AND IT'S 60 DEGREES OUT! I **LOVE** IT!
OF COURSE, WHO **WOULDN'T** LOVE THIS WEATHER?
AMEND
GLOBAL WARMING! WE'RE GONNA DIE!...
YOU DID **ASK**.
MAYBE I'LL GO FOR A **SWIM**...

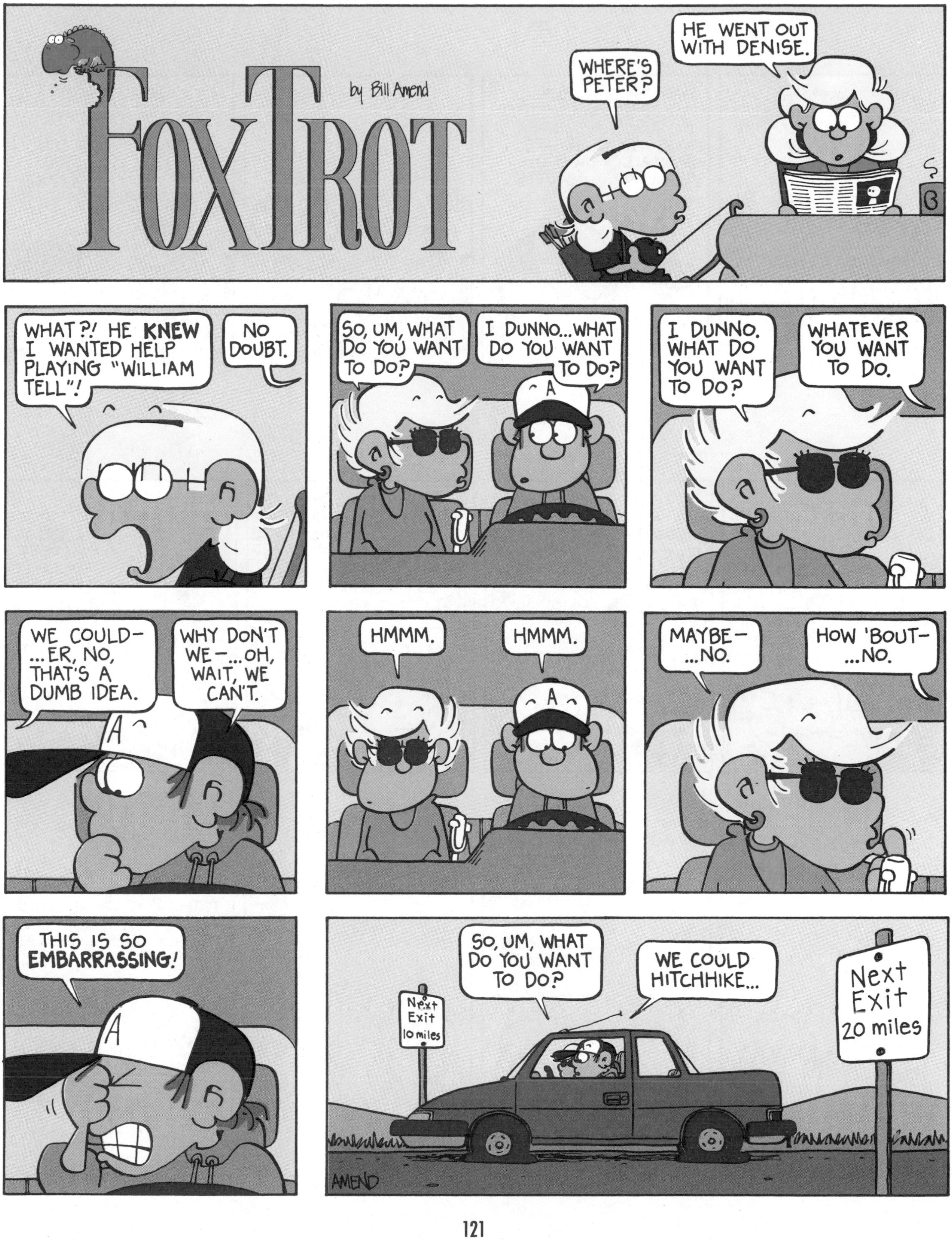
FoxTrot
by Bill Amend
WHERE'S PETER?
HE WENT OUT WITH DENISE.
WHAT?! HE KNEW I WANTED HELP PLAYING "WILLIAM TELL"!
NO DOUBT.
SO, UM, WHAT DO YOU WANT TO DO?
I DUNNO...WHAT DO YOU WANT TO DO?
I DUNNO. WHAT DO YOU WANT TO DO?
WHATEVER YOU WANT TO DO.
WE COULD- ...ER, NO, THAT'S A DUMB IDEA.
WHY DON'T WE-...OH, WAIT, WE CAN'T.
HMMM.
HMMM.
MAYBE- ...NO.
HOW 'BOUT- ...NO.
THIS IS SO EMBARRASSING!
Next Exit 10 miles
SO, UM, WHAT DO YOU WANT TO DO?
WE COULD HITCHHIKE...
Next Exit 20 miles
AMEND

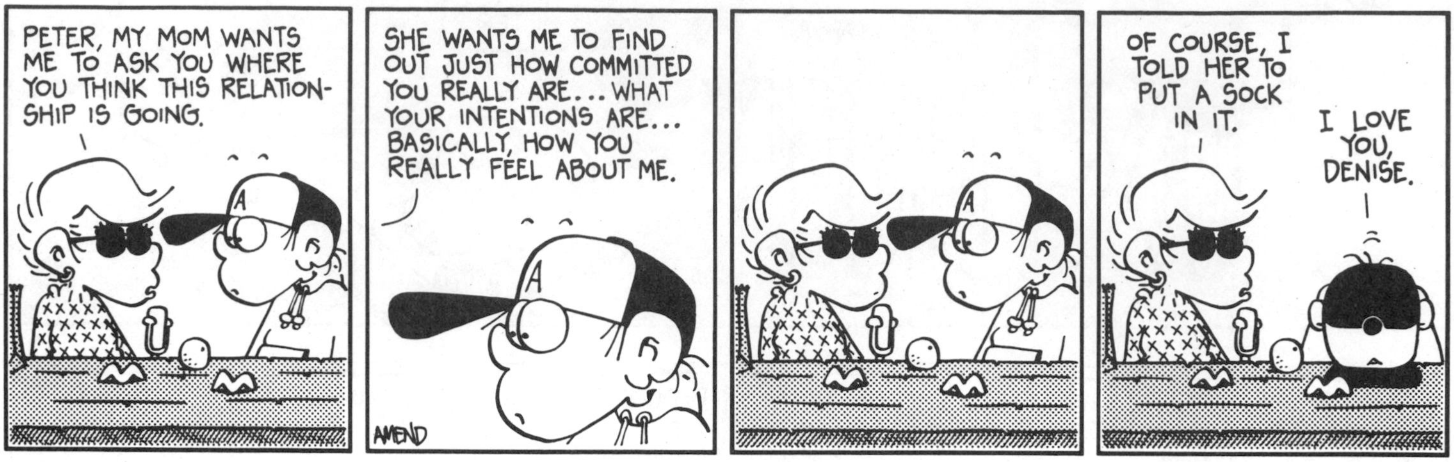
PETER, MY MOM WANTS ME TO ASK YOU WHERE YOU THINK THIS RELATIONSHIP IS GOING.
SHE WANTS ME TO FIND OUT JUST HOW COMMITTED YOU REALLY ARE... WHAT YOUR INTENTIONS ARE... BASICALLY, HOW YOU REALLY FEEL ABOUT ME.
AMEND
OF COURSE, I TOLD HER TO PUT A SOCK IN IT.
I LOVE YOU, DENISE.

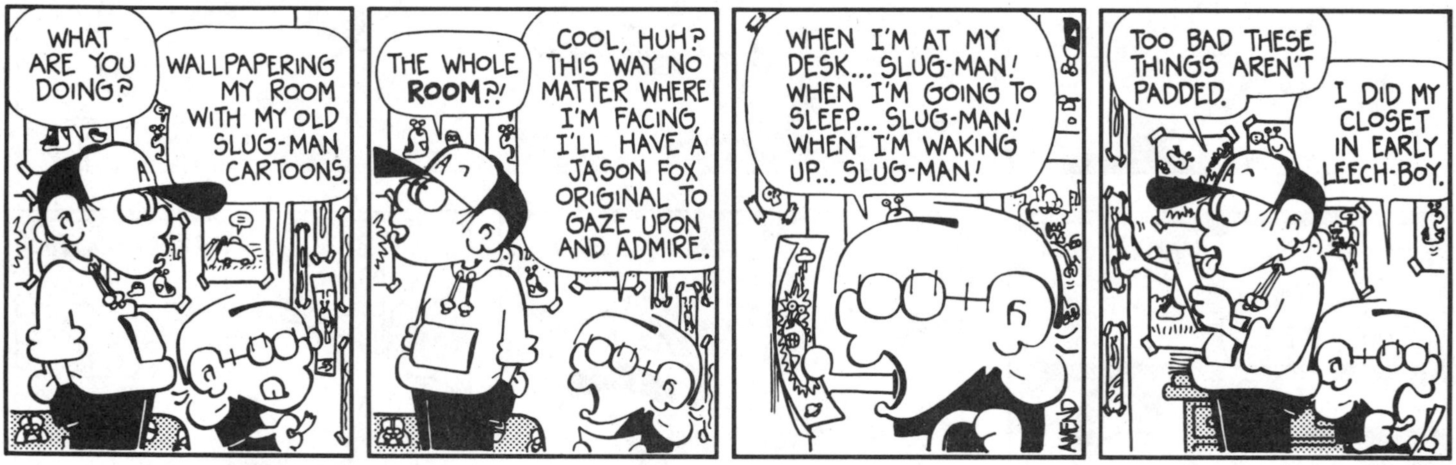
WHAT ARE YOU DOING?
WALLPAPERING MY ROOM WITH MY OLD SLUG-MAN CARTOONS.
THE WHOLE **ROOM**?!
COOL, HUH? THIS WAY NO MATTER WHERE I'M FACING, I'LL HAVE A JASON FOX ORIGINAL TO GAZE UPON AND ADMIRE.
WHEN I'M AT MY DESK... SLUG-MAN! WHEN I'M GOING TO SLEEP... SLUG-MAN! WHEN I'M WAKING UP... SLUG-MAN!
AMEND
TOO BAD THESE THINGS AREN'T PADDED.
I DID MY CLOSET IN EARLY LEECH-BOY.

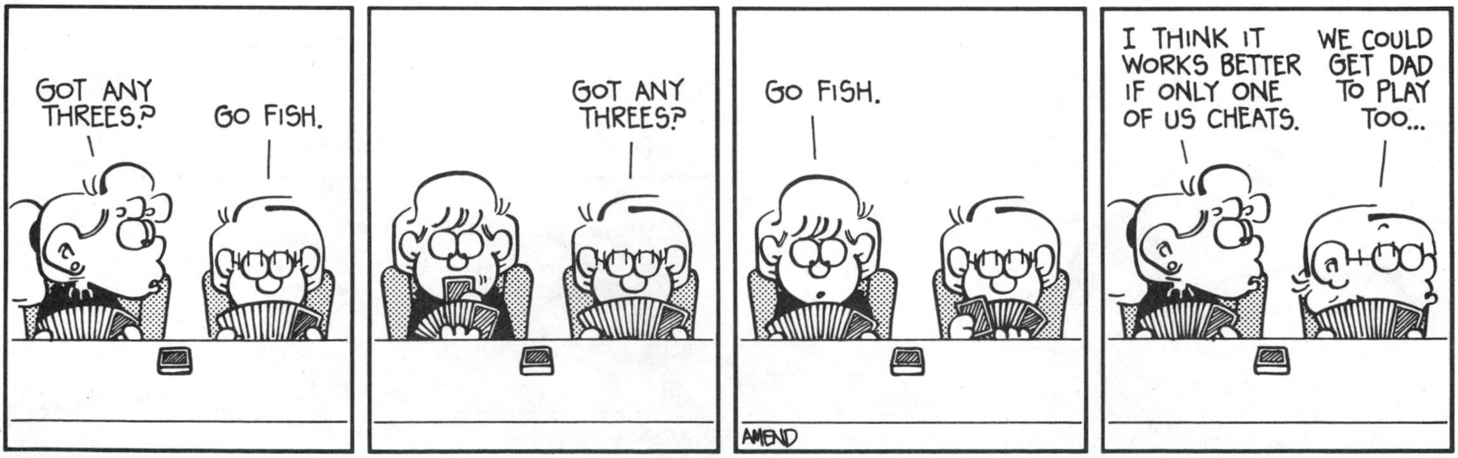
GOT ANY THREES?
GO FISH.
GOT ANY THREES?
GO FISH.
AMEND
I THINK IT WORKS BETTER IF ONLY ONE OF US CHEATS.
WE COULD GET DAD TO PLAY TOO...

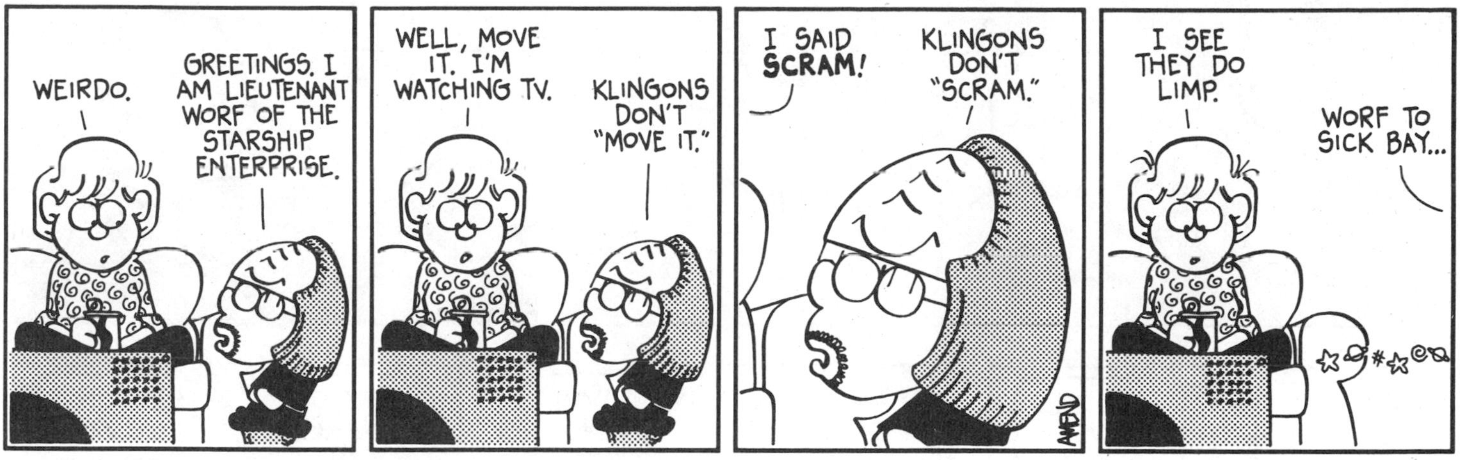
WEIRDO.
GREETINGS. I AM LIEUTENANT WORF OF THE STARSHIP ENTERPRISE.
WELL, MOVE IT. I'M WATCHING TV.
KLINGONS DON'T "MOVE IT."
I SAID **SCRAM**!
KLINGONS DON'T "SCRAM."
I SEE THEY DO LIMP.
WORF TO SICK BAY...
AMEND

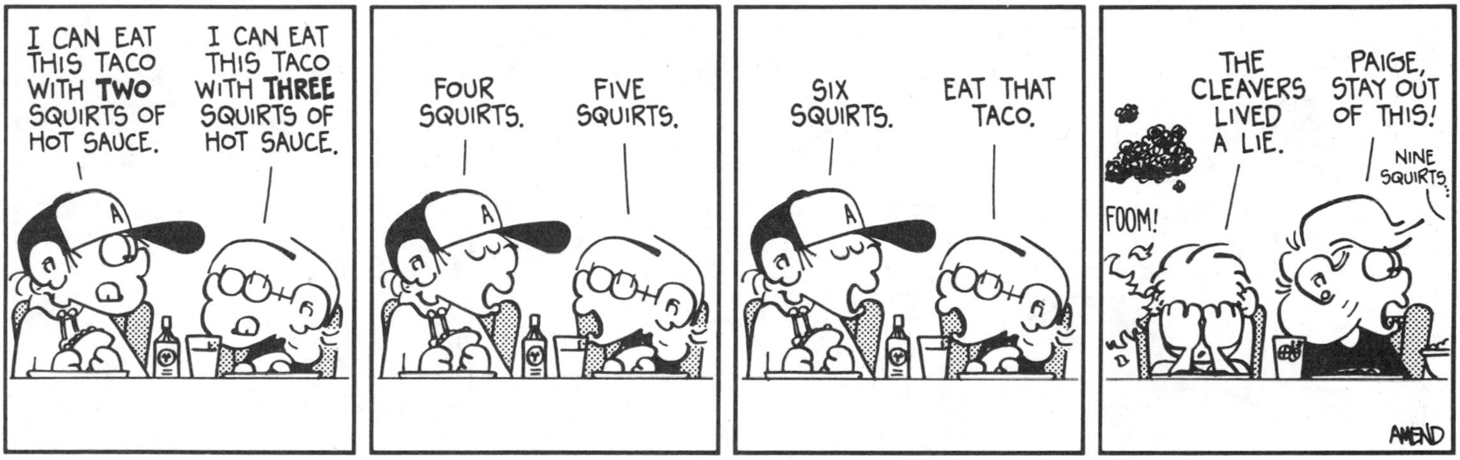
I CAN EAT THIS TACO WITH **TWO** SQUIRTS OF HOT SAUCE.
I CAN EAT THIS TACO WITH **THREE** SQUIRTS OF HOT SAUCE.
FOUR SQUIRTS.
FIVE SQUIRTS.
SIX SQUIRTS.
EAT THAT TACO.
THE CLEAVERS LIVED A LIE.
PAIGE, STAY OUT OF THIS!
NINE SQUIRTS
FOOM!
AMEND

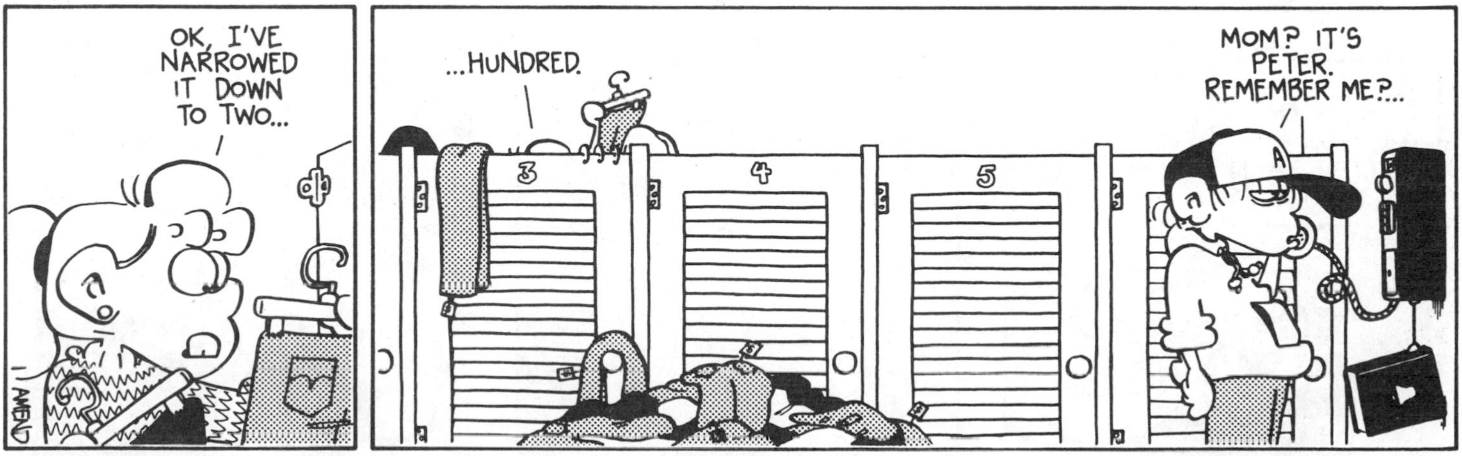
OK, I'VE NARROWED IT DOWN TO TWO...
AMEND
...HUNDRED.
3
4
5
MOM? IT'S PETER. REMEMBER ME?...

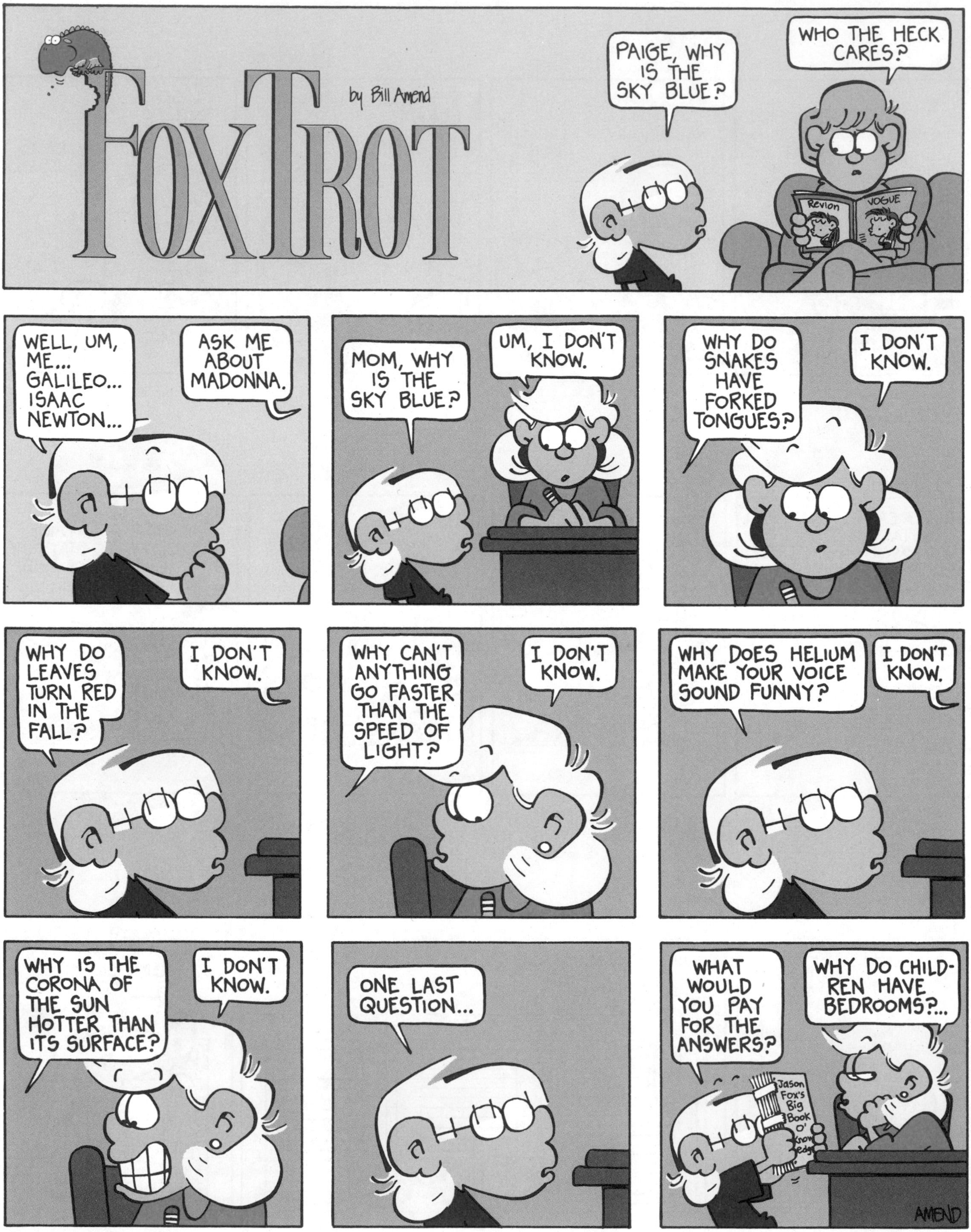
FoxTrot
by Bill Amend
PAIGE, WHY IS THE SKY BLUE?
WHO THE HECK CARES?
Revlon
VOGUE
WELL, UM, ME... GALILEO... ISAAC NEWTON...
ASK ME ABOUT MADONNA.
MOM, WHY IS THE SKY BLUE?
UM, I DON'T KNOW.
WHY DO SNAKES HAVE FORKED TONGUES?
I DON'T KNOW.
WHY DO LEAVES TURN RED IN THE FALL?
I DON'T KNOW.
WHY CAN'T ANYTHING GO FASTER THAN THE SPEED OF LIGHT?
I DON'T KNOW.
WHY DOES HELIUM MAKE YOUR VOICE SOUND FUNNY?
I DON'T KNOW.
WHY IS THE CORONA OF THE SUN HOTTER THAN ITS SURFACE?
I DON'T KNOW.
ONE LAST QUESTION...
WHAT WOULD YOU PAY FOR THE ANSWERS?
WHY DO CHILDREN HAVE BEDROOMS?...
AMEND

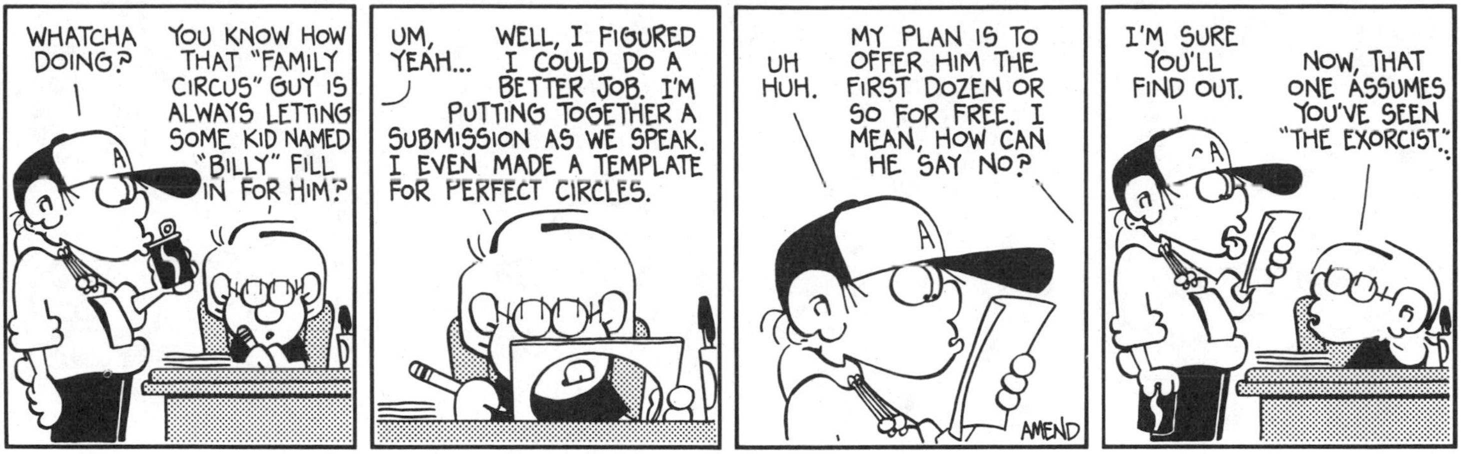
WHATCHA DOING?
YOU KNOW HOW THAT "FAMILY CIRCUS" GUY IS ALWAYS LETTING SOME KID NAMED "BILLY" FILL IN FOR HIM?
UM, YEAH...
WELL, I FIGURED I COULD DO A BETTER JOB. I'M PUTTING TOGETHER A SUBMISSION AS WE SPEAK. I EVEN MADE A TEMPLATE FOR PERFECT CIRCLES.
UH HUH.
MY PLAN IS TO OFFER HIM THE FIRST DOZEN OR SO FOR FREE. I MEAN, HOW CAN HE SAY NO?
AMEND
I'M SURE YOU'LL FIND OUT.
NOW, THAT ONE ASSUMES YOU'VE SEEN "THE EXORCIST."

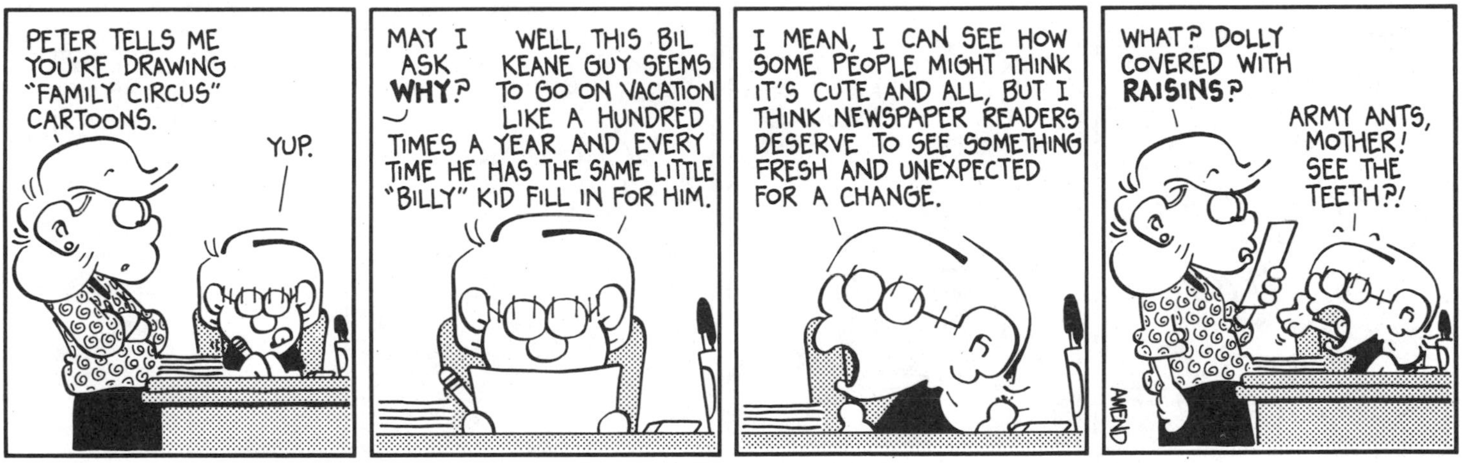
PETER TELLS ME YOU'RE DRAWING "FAMILY CIRCUS" CARTOONS.
YUP.
MAY I ASK **WHY**?
WELL, THIS BIL KEANE GUY SEEMS TO GO ON VACATION LIKE A HUNDRED TIMES A YEAR AND EVERY TIME HE HAS THE SAME LITTLE "BILLY" KID FILL IN FOR HIM.
I MEAN, I CAN SEE HOW SOME PEOPLE MIGHT THINK IT'S CUTE AND ALL, BUT I THINK NEWSPAPER READERS DESERVE TO SEE SOMETHING FRESH AND UNEXPECTED FOR A CHANGE.
WHAT? DOLLY COVERED WITH **RAISINS**?
ARMY ANTS, MOTHER! SEE THE TEETH?!
AMEND

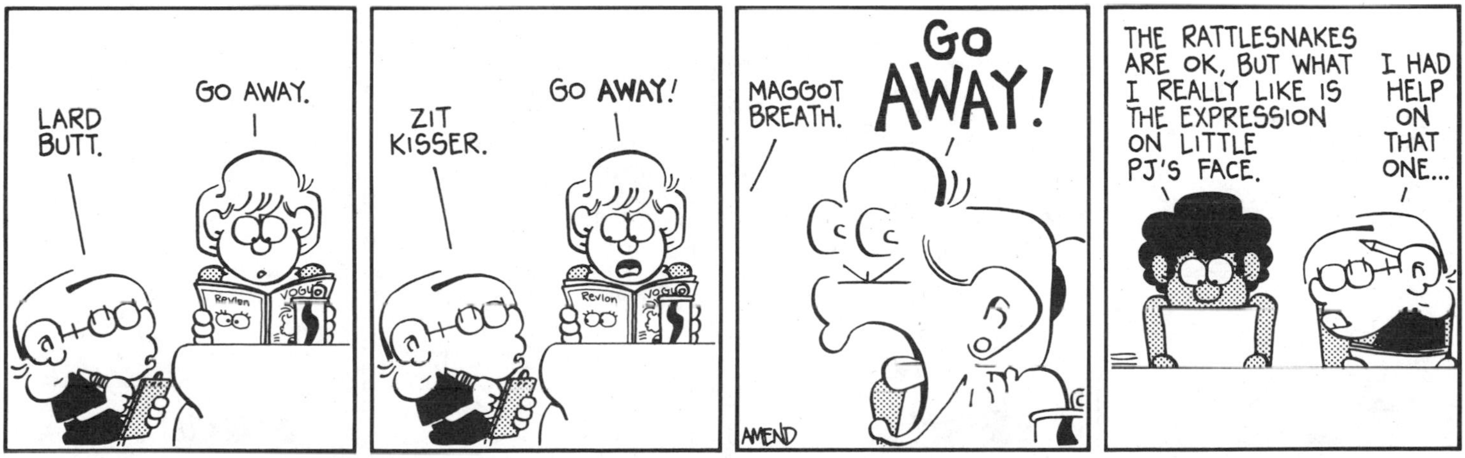
LARD BUTT.
GO AWAY.
Revlon
VOGUE
ZIT KISSER.
GO **AWAY**!
MAGGOT BREATH.
GO AWAY!
AMEND
THE RATTLESNAKES ARE OK, BUT WHAT I REALLY LIKE IS THE EXPRESSION ON LITTLE PJ'S FACE.
I HAD HELP ON THAT ONE...

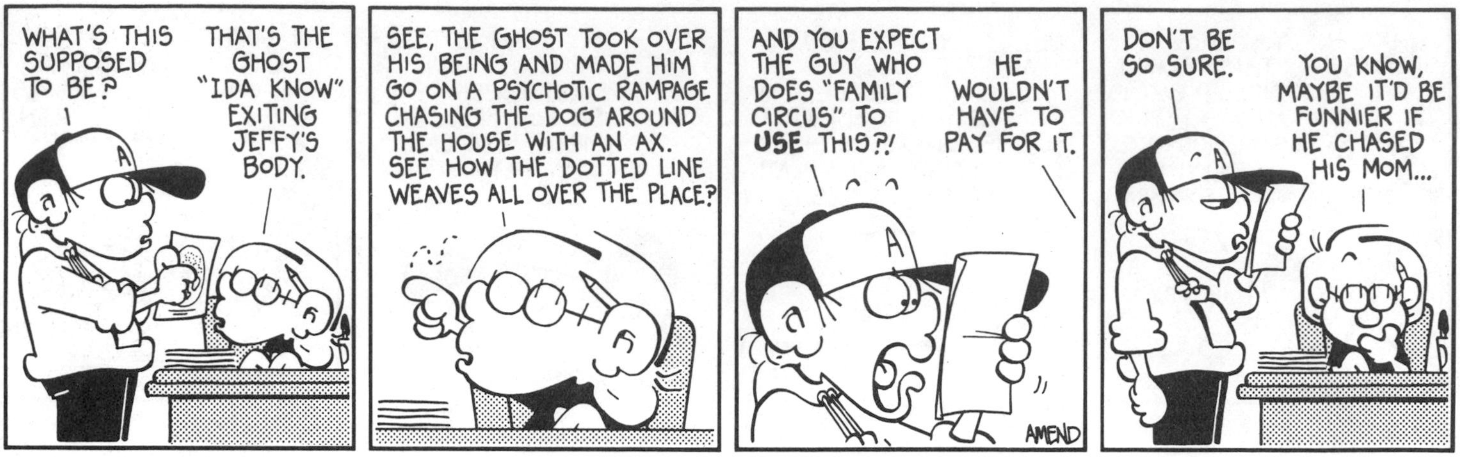
WHAT'S THIS SUPPOSED TO BE?
THAT'S THE GHOST "IDA KNOW" EXITING JEFFY'S BODY.
SEE, THE GHOST TOOK OVER HIS BEING AND MADE HIM GO ON A PSYCHOTIC RAMPAGE CHASING THE DOG AROUND THE HOUSE WITH AN AX. SEE HOW THE DOTTED LINE WEAVES ALL OVER THE PLACE?
AND YOU EXPECT THE GUY WHO DOES "FAMILY CIRCUS" TO **USE** THIS?!
HE WOULDN'T HAVE TO PAY FOR IT.
AMEND
DON'T BE SO SURE.
YOU KNOW, MAYBE IT'D BE FUNNIER IF HE CHASED HIS MOM...

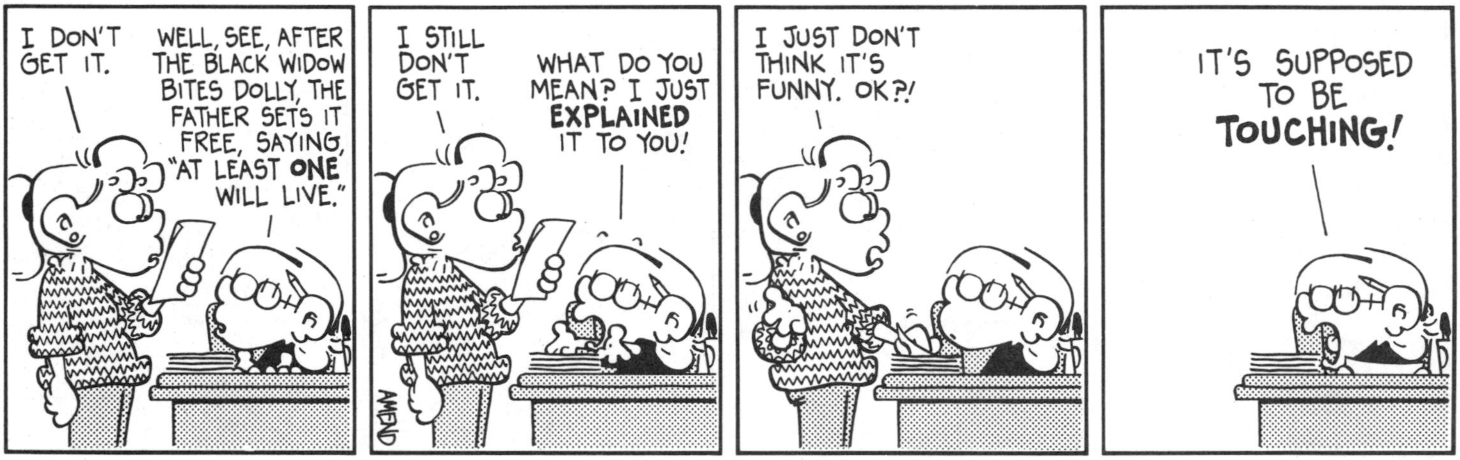
I DON'T GET IT.
WELL, SEE, AFTER THE BLACK WIDOW BITES DOLLY, THE FATHER SETS IT FREE, SAYING, "AT LEAST **ONE** WILL LIVE."
I STILL DON'T GET IT.
WHAT DO YOU MEAN? I JUST **EXPLAINED** IT TO YOU!
AMEND
I JUST DON'T THINK IT'S FUNNY. OK?!
IT'S SUPPOSED TO BE **TOUCHING!**

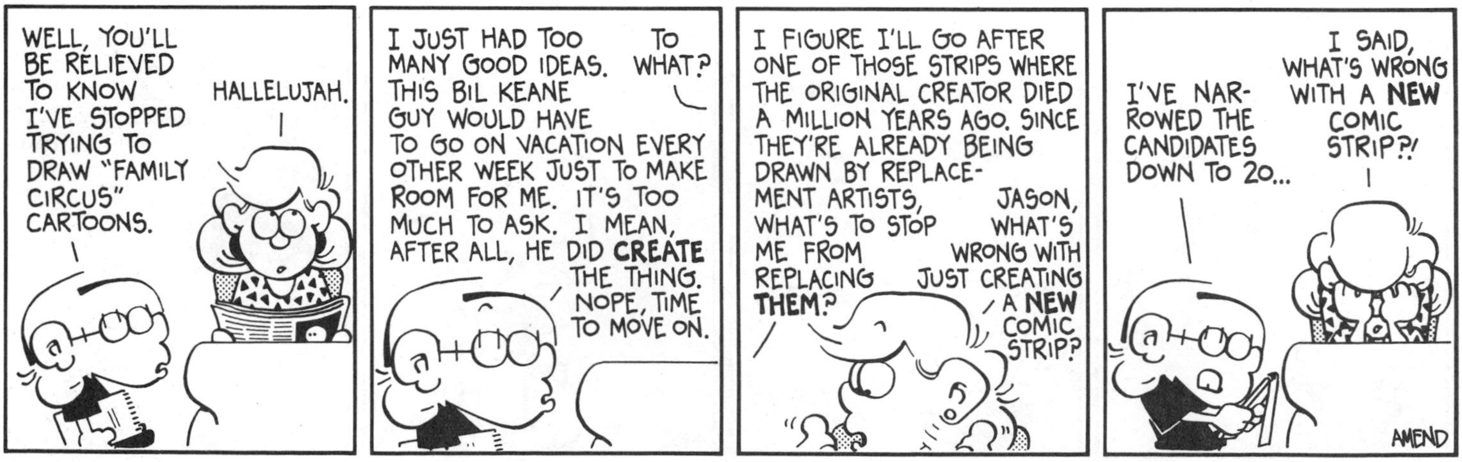
WELL, YOU'LL BE RELIEVED TO KNOW I'VE STOPPED TRYING TO DRAW "FAMILY CIRCUS" CARTOONS.
HALLELUJAH.
I JUST HAD TOO MANY GOOD IDEAS.
TO WHAT?
THIS BIL KEANE GUY WOULD HAVE TO GO ON VACATION EVERY OTHER WEEK JUST TO MAKE ROOM FOR ME. IT'S TOO MUCH TO ASK. I MEAN, AFTER ALL, HE DID **CREATE** THE THING. NOPE, TIME TO MOVE ON.
I FIGURE I'LL GO AFTER ONE OF THOSE STRIPS WHERE THE ORIGINAL CREATOR DIED A MILLION YEARS AGO. SINCE THEY'RE ALREADY BEING DRAWN BY REPLACEMENT ARTISTS, WHAT'S TO STOP ME FROM REPLACING **THEM**?
JASON, WHAT'S WRONG WITH JUST CREATING A **NEW** COMIC STRIP?
I'VE NARROWED THE CANDIDATES DOWN TO 20...
I SAID, WHAT'S WRONG WITH A **NEW** COMIC STRIP?!
AMEND

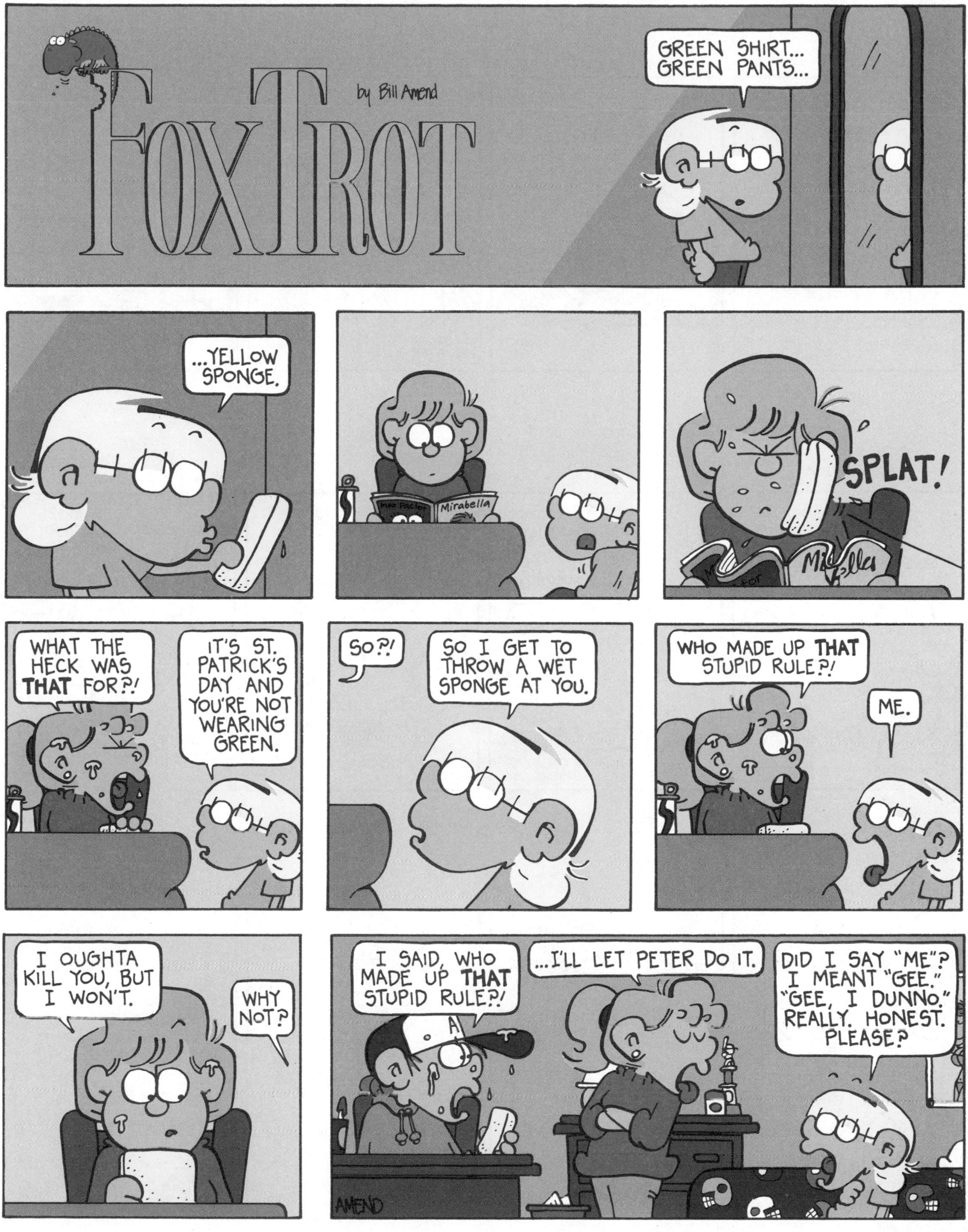

FoxTrot
by Bill Amend
GREEN SHIRT... GREEN PANTS...
...YELLOW SPONGE.
Max Factor
Mirabella
SPLAT!
WHAT THE HECK WAS **THAT** FOR?!
IT'S ST. PATRICK'S DAY AND YOU'RE NOT WEARING GREEN.
SO?!
SO I GET TO THROW A WET SPONGE AT YOU.
WHO MADE UP **THAT** STUPID RULE?!
ME.
I OUGHTA KILL YOU, BUT I WON'T.
WHY NOT?
I SAID, WHO MADE UP **THAT** STUPID RULE?!
...I'LL LET PETER DO IT.
DID I SAY "ME"? I MEANT "GEE." "GEE, I DUNNO." REALLY. HONEST. PLEASE?
AMEND

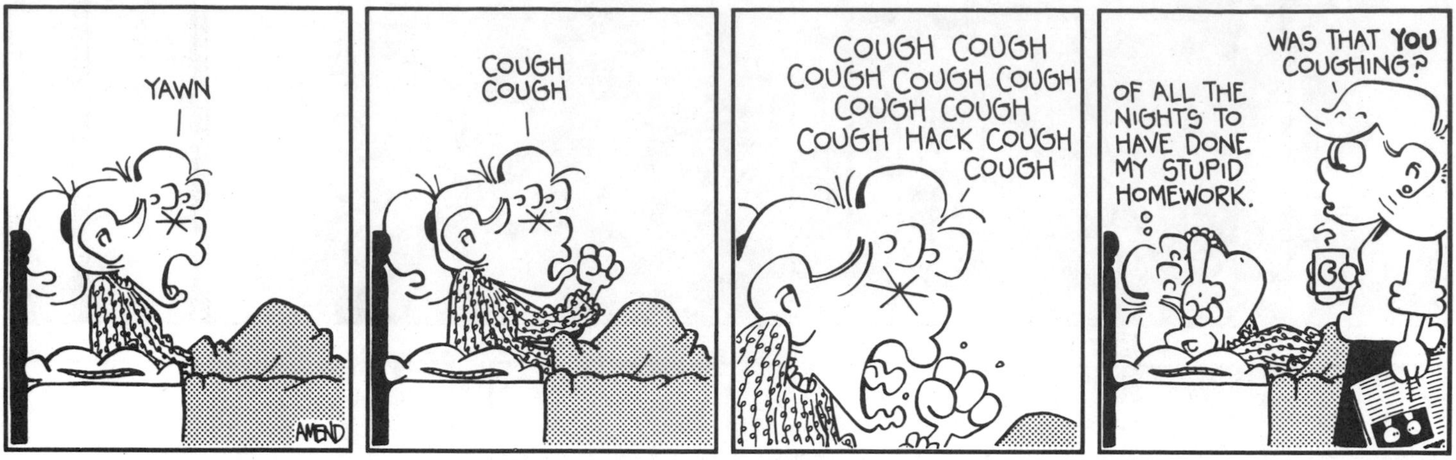
YAWN
COUGH COUGH
COUGH COUGH COUGH COUGH COUGH COUGH COUGH COUGH HACK COUGH COUGH
WAS THAT **YOU** COUGHING?
OF ALL THE NIGHTS TO HAVE DONE MY STUPID HOMEWORK.
AMEND

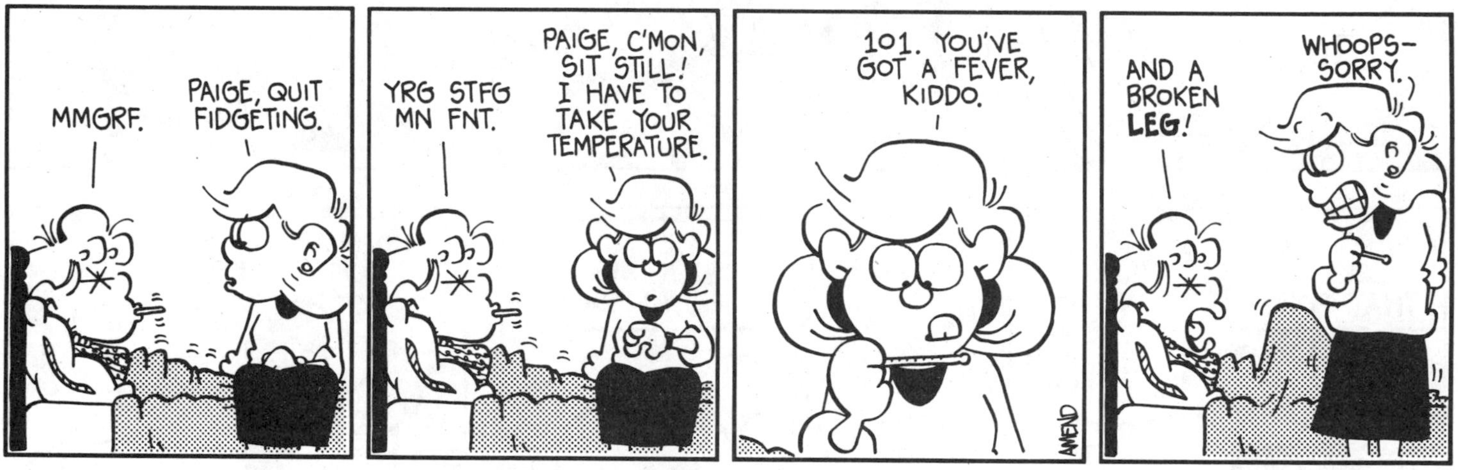
MMGRF.
PAIGE, QUIT FIDGETING.
YRG STFG MN FNT.
PAIGE, C'MON, SIT STILL! I HAVE TO TAKE YOUR TEMPERATURE.
101. YOU'VE GOT A FEVER, KIDDO.
AMEND
AND A BROKEN **LEG**!
WHOOPS- SORRY.

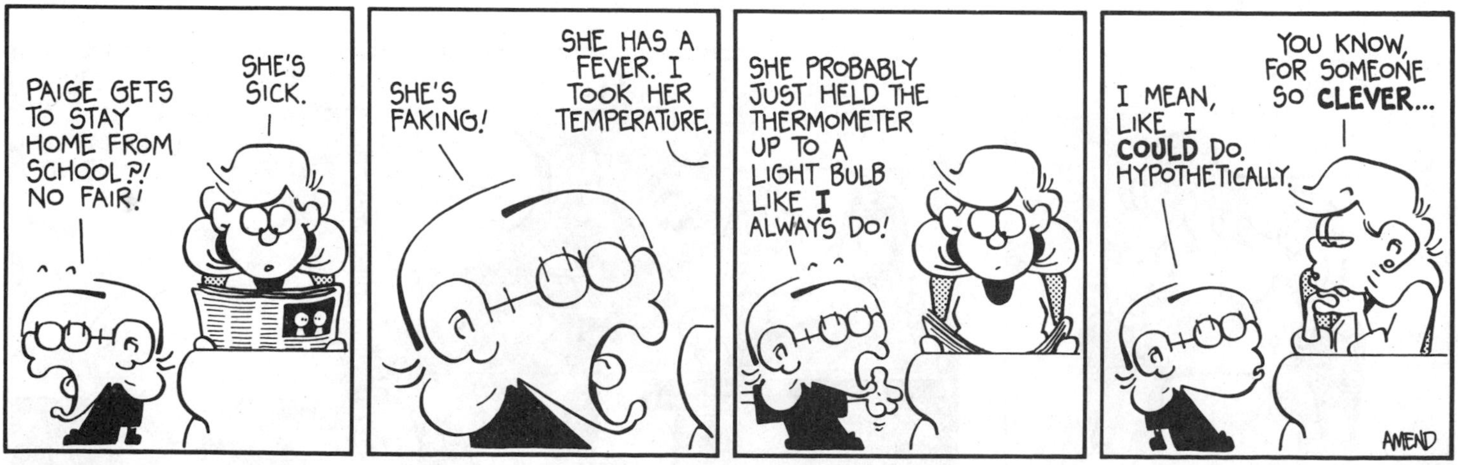
PAIGE GETS TO STAY HOME FROM SCHOOL?! NO FAIR!
SHE'S SICK.
SHE'S FAKING!
SHE HAS A FEVER. I TOOK HER TEMPERATURE.
SHE PROBABLY JUST HELD THE THERMOMETER UP TO A LIGHT BULB LIKE **I** ALWAYS DO!
I MEAN, LIKE I **COULD** DO. HYPOTHETICALLY.
YOU KNOW, FOR SOMEONE SO **CLEVER**...
AMEND

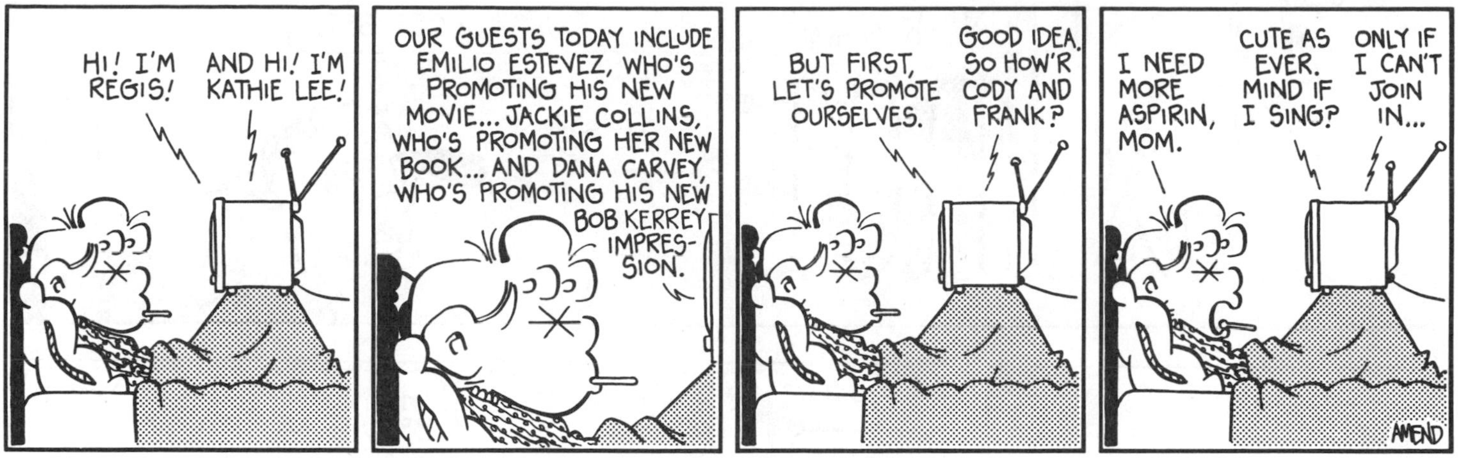
HI! I'M REGIS!
AND HI! I'M KATHIE LEE!
OUR GUESTS TODAY INCLUDE EMILIO ESTEVEZ, WHO'S PROMOTING HIS NEW MOVIE... JACKIE COLLINS, WHO'S PROMOTING HER NEW BOOK... AND DANA CARVEY, WHO'S PROMOTING HIS NEW BOB KERREY IMPRESSION.
BUT FIRST, LET'S PROMOTE OURSELVES.
GOOD IDEA. SO HOW'R CODY AND FRANK?
I NEED MORE ASPIRIN, MOM.
CUTE AS EVER. MIND IF I SING?
ONLY IF I CAN'T JOIN IN...
AMEND

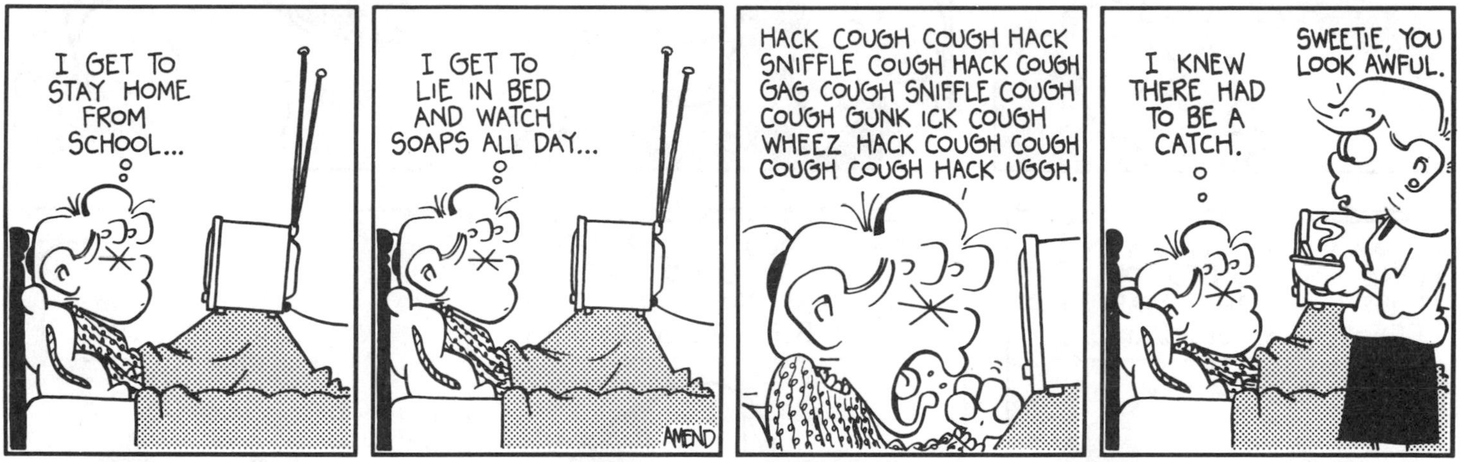
I GET TO STAY HOME FROM SCHOOL...
I GET TO LIE IN BED AND WATCH SOAPS ALL DAY...
AMEND
HACK COUGH COUGH HACK SNIFFLE COUGH HACK COUGH GAG COUGH SNIFFLE COUGH COUGH GUNK ICK COUGH WHEEZ HACK COUGH COUGH COUGH COUGH HACK UGGH.
I KNEW THERE HAD TO BE A CATCH.
SWEETIE, YOU LOOK AWFUL.

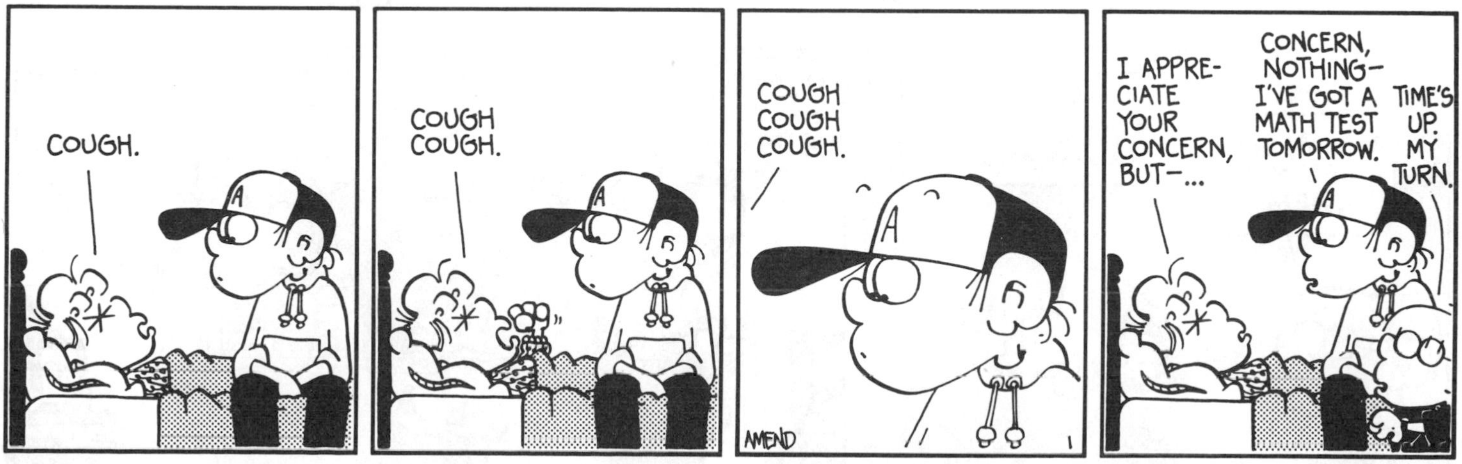
COUGH.
COUGH COUGH.
COUGH COUGH COUGH.
AMEND
I APPRECIATE YOUR CONCERN, BUT—...
CONCERN, NOTHING— I'VE GOT A MATH TEST TOMORROW.
TIME'S UP. MY TURN.

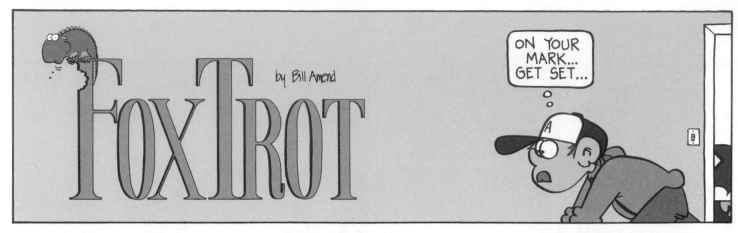

by Bill Amend

FoxTrot

ON YOUR MARK... GET SET...

GET SET... GET SET... GET SET...

WHAT ARE YOU DOING?

GETTING READY FOR THE NEW SPRINGSTEEN ALBUMS.

THE NEWSPAPER SAID THEY'D BE OUT ANY DAY NOW, SO I NEED TO BE PREPARED TO DASH OFF TO THE STORE ON A MOMENT'S NOTICE.

I WAS SEVENTEENTH IN LINE FOR "TUNNEL OF LOVE," BUT THAT WAS BEFORE I COULD DRIVE.

MAN, I MUST'VE BLASTED THAT ALBUM 3,000 TIMES THE FIRST DAY ALONE. I NEARLY BLEW MY SPEAKERS.

AMEND

ANYWAY, THAT'S WHAT I'M DOING.

I, UM, WAS ASKING THEM...

MY STEREO!

YOU'LL GET IT BACK, SOMEDAY.

PAIGE, WATCH THE WIRES.

SO THERE'S WHERE MY MADONNA TAPE WENT!

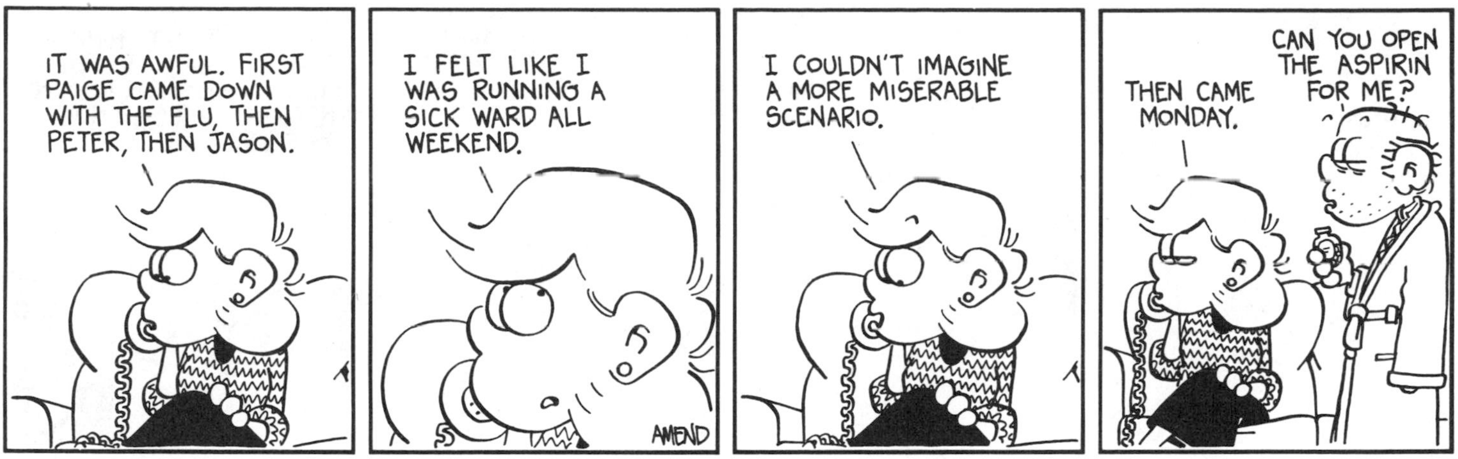
IT WAS AWFUL. FIRST PAIGE CAME DOWN WITH THE FLU, THEN PETER, THEN JASON.
I FELT LIKE I WAS RUNNING A SICK WARD ALL WEEKEND.
AMEND
I COULDN'T IMAGINE A MORE MISERABLE SCENARIO.
THEN CAME MONDAY.
CAN YOU OPEN THE ASPIRIN FOR ME?

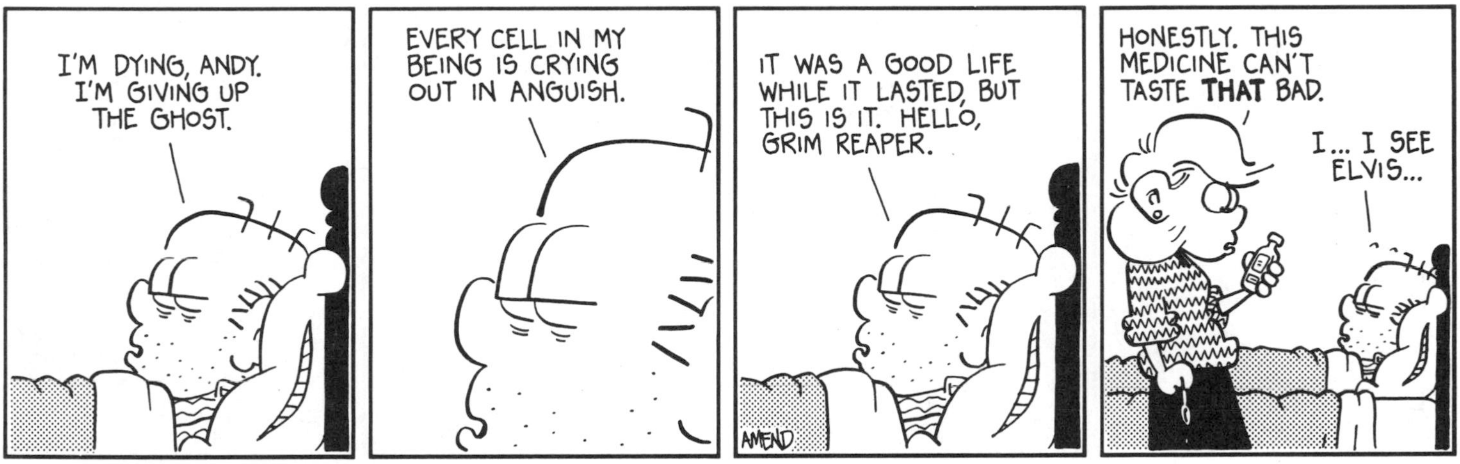
I'M DYING, ANDY. I'M GIVING UP THE GHOST.
EVERY CELL IN MY BEING IS CRYING OUT IN ANGUISH.
IT WAS A GOOD LIFE WHILE IT LASTED, BUT THIS IS IT. HELLO, GRIM REAPER.
AMEND
HONESTLY. THIS MEDICINE CAN'T TASTE **THAT** BAD.
I... I SEE ELVIS...

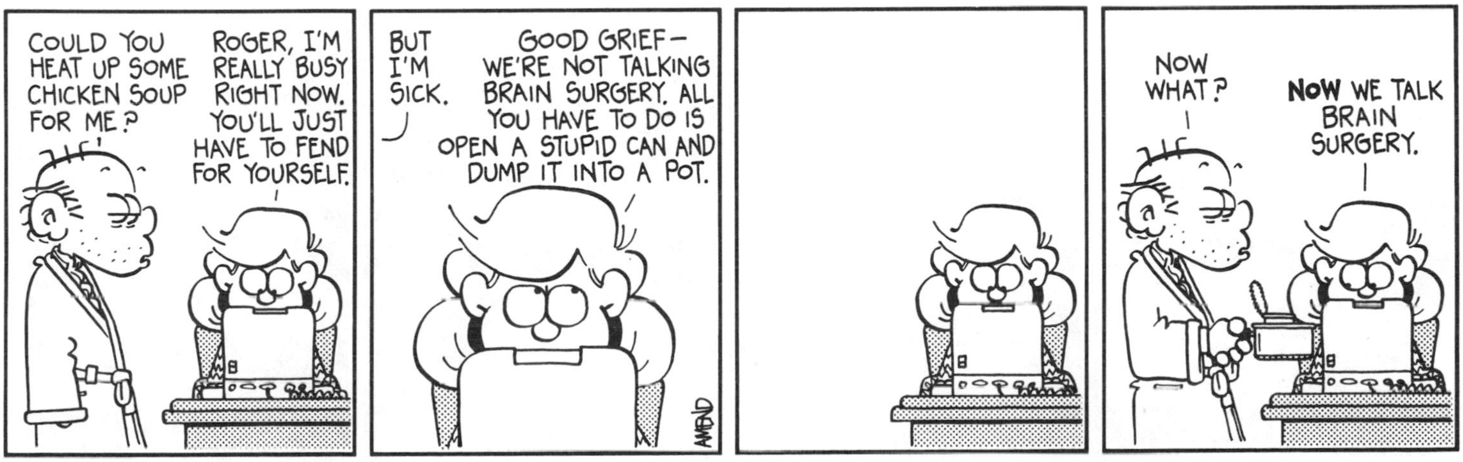
COULD YOU HEAT UP SOME CHICKEN SOUP FOR ME?
ROGER, I'M REALLY BUSY RIGHT NOW. YOU'LL JUST HAVE TO FEND FOR YOURSELF.
BUT I'M SICK.
GOOD GRIEF— WE'RE NOT TALKING BRAIN SURGERY. ALL YOU HAVE TO DO IS OPEN A STUPID CAN AND DUMP IT INTO A POT.
AMEND
NOW WHAT?
NOW WE TALK BRAIN SURGERY.

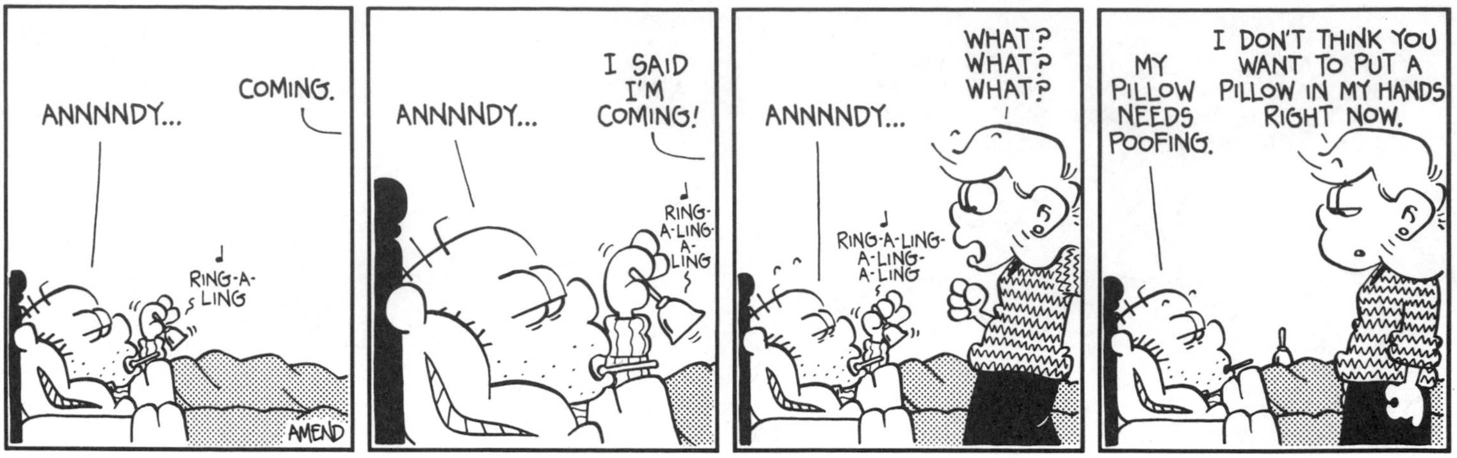
ANNNNDY...
COMING.
RING-A-LING
AMEND
ANNNNDY...
I SAID I'M COMING!
RING-A-LING-A-LING
ANNNNDY...
RING-A-LING-A-LING-A-LING
WHAT? WHAT? WHAT?
MY PILLOW NEEDS POOFING.
I DON'T THINK YOU WANT TO PUT A PILLOW IN MY HANDS RIGHT NOW.

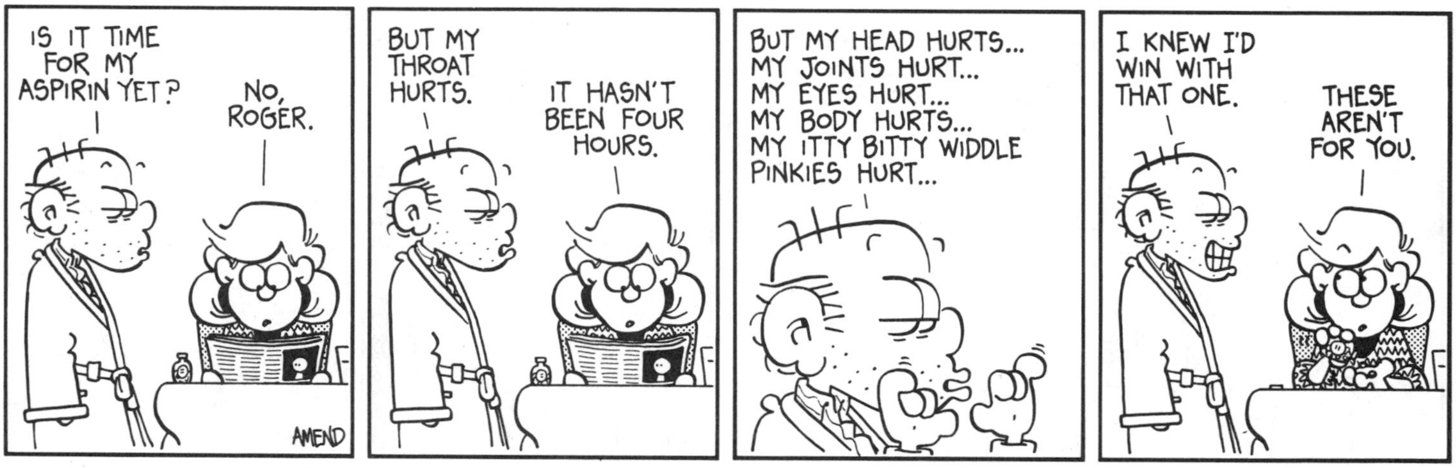
IS IT TIME FOR MY ASPIRIN YET?
NO, ROGER.
AMEND
BUT MY THROAT HURTS.
IT HASN'T BEEN FOUR HOURS.
BUT MY HEAD HURTS... MY JOINTS HURT... MY EYES HURT... MY BODY HURTS... MY ITTY BITTY WIDDLE PINKIES HURT...
I KNEW I'D WIN WITH THAT ONE.
THESE AREN'T FOR YOU.

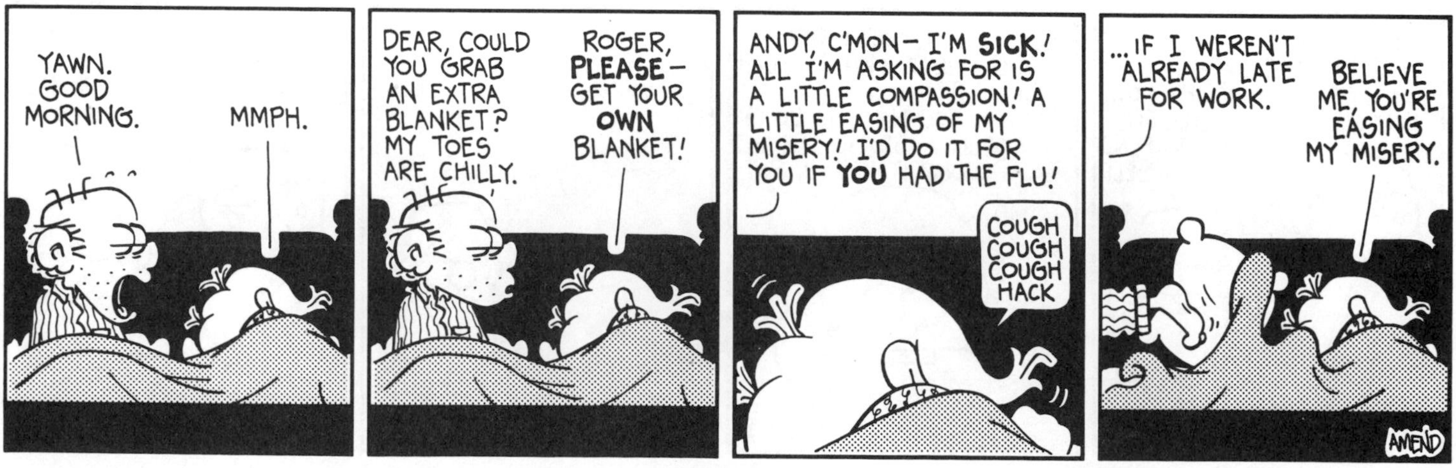
YAWN. GOOD MORNING.
MMPH.
DEAR, COULD YOU GRAB AN EXTRA BLANKET? MY TOES ARE CHILLY.
ROGER, **PLEASE** – GET YOUR **OWN** BLANKET!
ANDY, C'MON – I'M **SICK**! ALL I'M ASKING FOR IS A LITTLE COMPASSION! A LITTLE EASING OF MY MISERY! I'D DO IT FOR YOU IF **YOU** HAD THE FLU!
COUGH COUGH COUGH HACK
...IF I WEREN'T ALREADY LATE FOR WORK.
BELIEVE ME, YOU'RE EASING MY MISERY.
AMEND

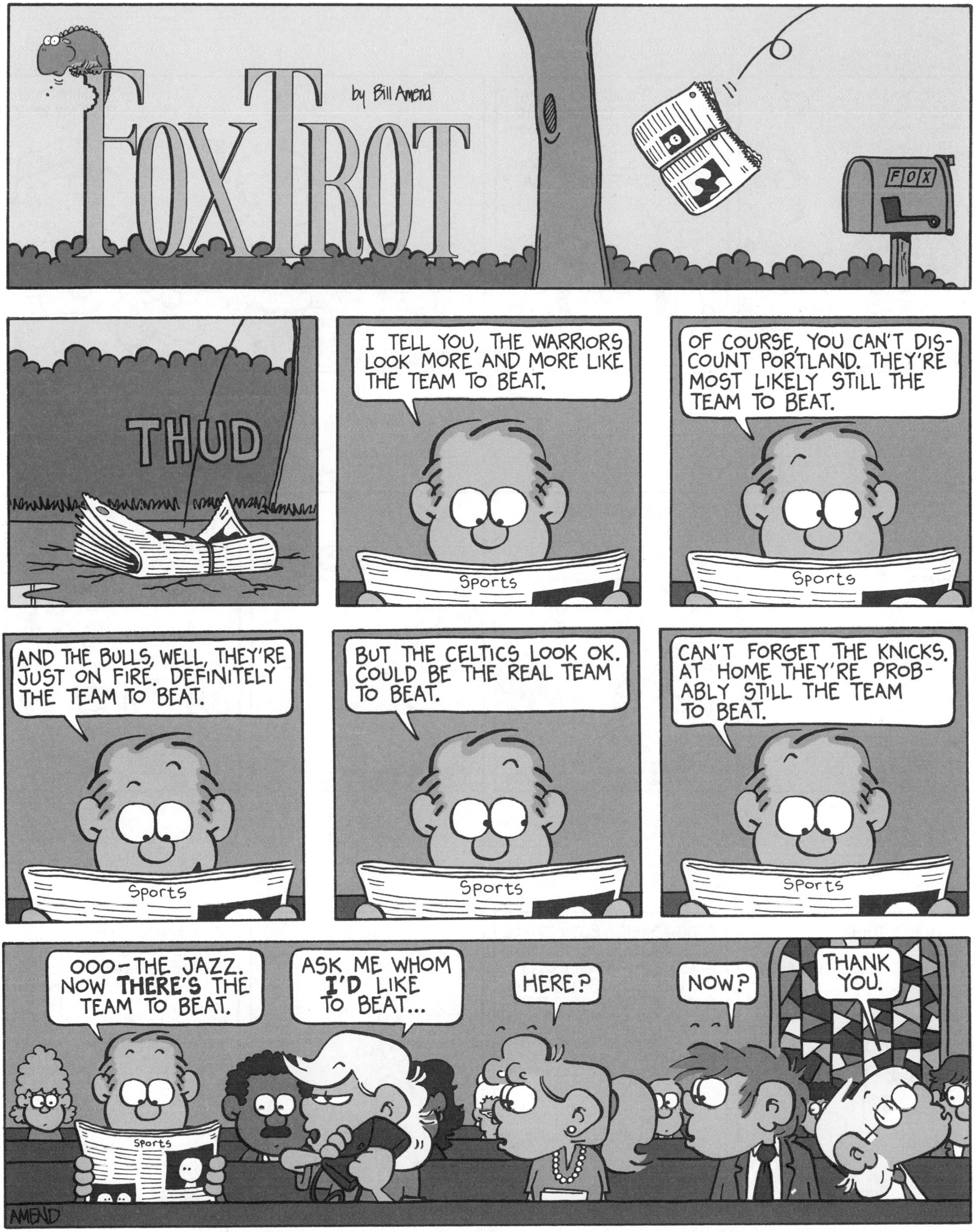
FoxTrot
by Bill Amend
FOX
THUD
Sports
I TELL YOU, THE WARRIORS LOOK MORE AND MORE LIKE THE TEAM TO BEAT.
OF COURSE, YOU CAN'T DIS-COUNT PORTLAND. THEY'RE MOST LIKELY STILL THE TEAM TO BEAT.
AND THE BULLS, WELL, THEY'RE JUST ON FIRE. DEFINITELY THE TEAM TO BEAT.
BUT THE CELTICS LOOK OK. COULD BE THE REAL TEAM TO BEAT.
CAN'T FORGET THE KNICKS. AT HOME THEY'RE PROB-ABLY STILL THE TEAM TO BEAT.
OOO-THE JAZZ. NOW THERE'S THE TEAM TO BEAT.
ASK ME WHOM I'D LIKE TO BEAT...
HERE?
NOW?
THANK YOU.
AMEND

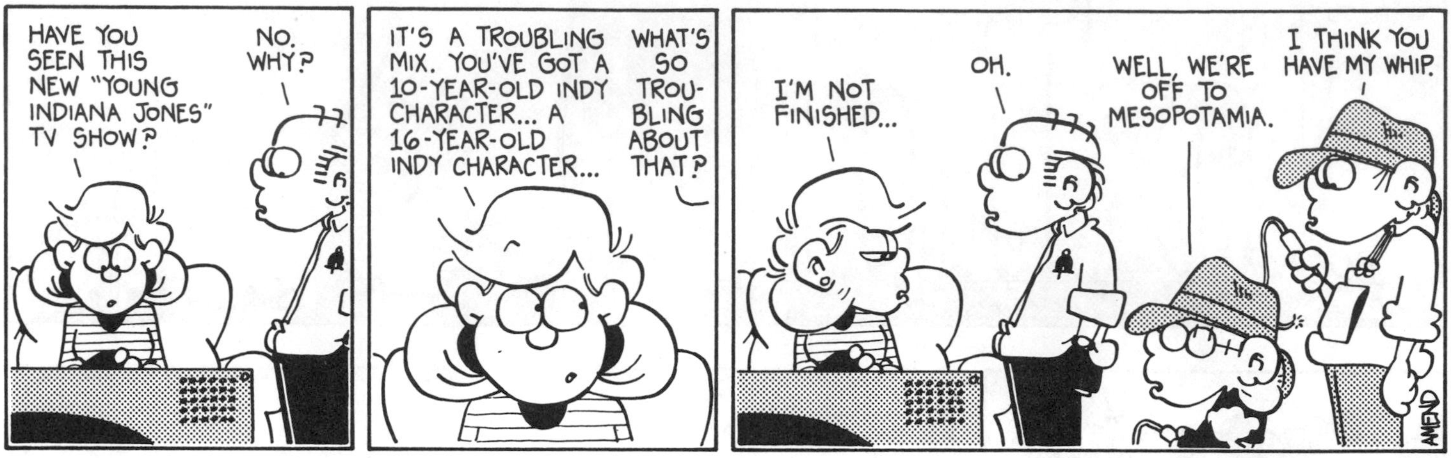
HAVE YOU SEEN THIS NEW "YOUNG INDIANA JONES" TV SHOW?
NO. WHY?
IT'S A TROUBLING MIX. YOU'VE GOT A 10-YEAR-OLD INDY CHARACTER... A 16-YEAR-OLD INDY CHARACTER...
WHAT'S SO TROUBLING ABOUT THAT?
I'M NOT FINISHED...
OH.
WELL, WE'RE OFF TO MESOPOTAMIA.
I THINK YOU HAVE MY WHIP.
AMEND

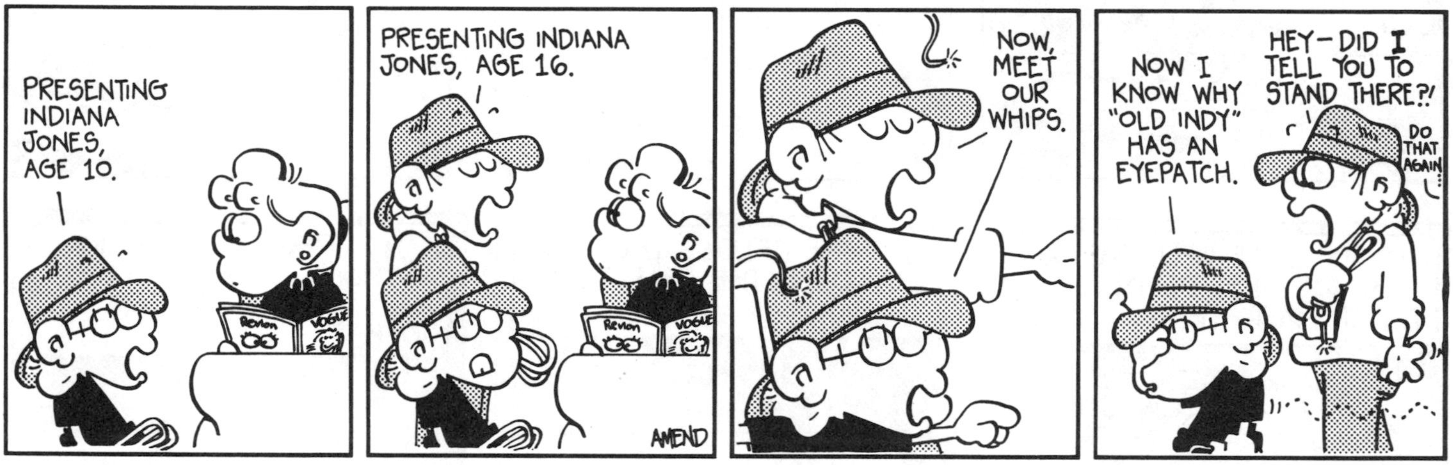
PRESENTING INDIANA JONES, AGE 10.
Revlon
VOGUE
PRESENTING INDIANA JONES, AGE 16.
AMEND
NOW, MEET OUR WHIPS.
NOW I KNOW WHY "OLD INDY" HAS AN EYEPATCH.
HEY—DID I TELL YOU TO STAND THERE?!
DO THAT AGAIN

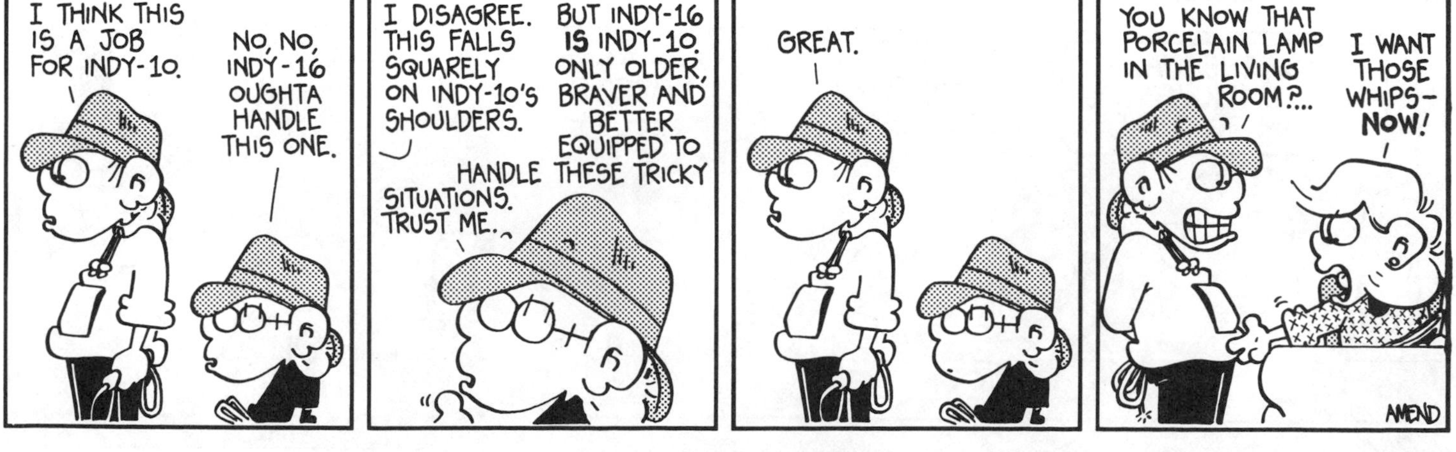
I THINK THIS IS A JOB FOR INDY-10.
NO, NO, INDY-16 OUGHTA HANDLE THIS ONE.
I DISAGREE. THIS FALLS SQUARELY ON INDY-10'S SHOULDERS.
BUT INDY-16 **IS** INDY-10. ONLY OLDER, BRAVER AND BETTER EQUIPPED TO HANDLE THESE TRICKY SITUATIONS. TRUST ME.
GREAT.
YOU KNOW THAT PORCELAIN LAMP IN THE LIVING ROOM?...
I WANT THOSE WHIPS—**NOW**!
AMEND

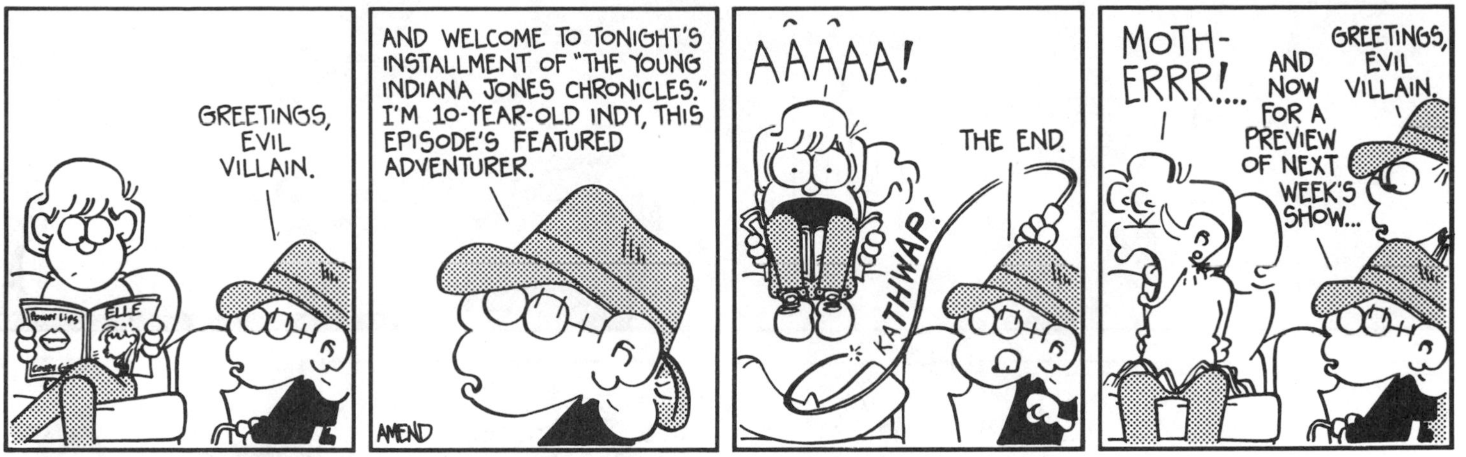
GREETINGS, EVIL VILLAIN.
ELLE
AND WELCOME TO TONIGHT'S INSTALLMENT OF "THE YOUNG INDIANA JONES CHRONICLES." I'M 10-YEAR-OLD INDY, THIS EPISODE'S FEATURED ADVENTURER.
AMEND
AÂÂÂA!
THE END.
KATHWAP!
MOTH-ERRR!...
AND NOW FOR A PREVIEW OF NEXT WEEK'S SHOW...
GREETINGS, EVIL VILLAIN.

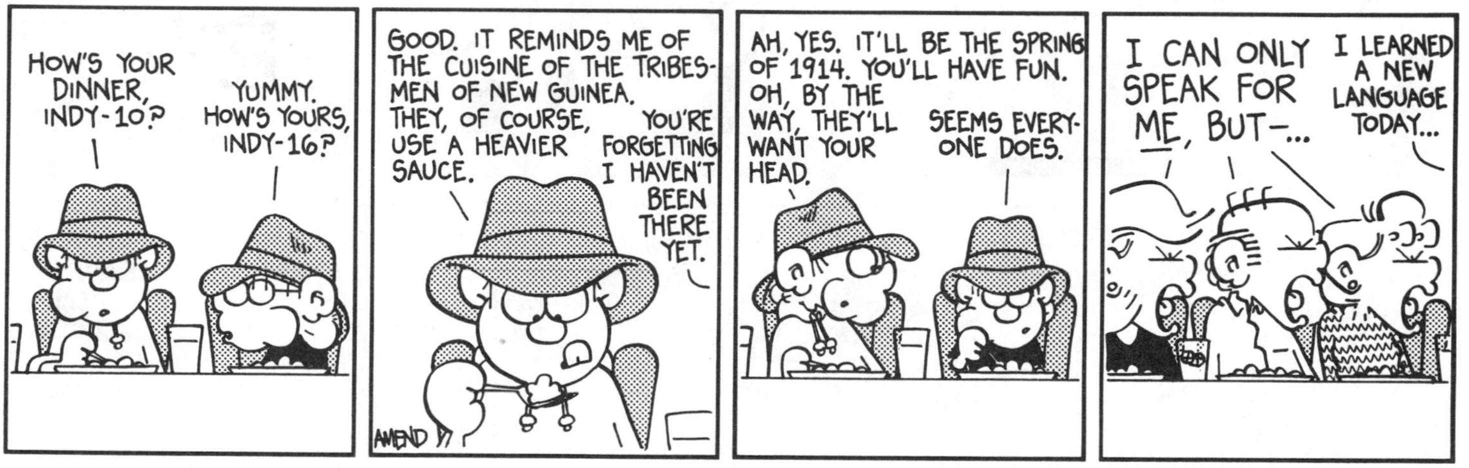
HOW'S YOUR DINNER, INDY-10?
YUMMY. HOW'S YOURS, INDY-16?
GOOD. IT REMINDS ME OF THE CUISINE OF THE TRIBESMEN OF NEW GUINEA. THEY, OF COURSE, USE A HEAVIER SAUCE.
YOU'RE FORGETTING I HAVEN'T BEEN THERE YET.
AMEND
AH, YES. IT'LL BE THE SPRING OF 1914. YOU'LL HAVE FUN. OH, BY THE WAY, THEY'LL WANT YOUR HEAD.
SEEMS EVERYONE DOES.
I CAN ONLY SPEAK FOR ME, BUT–...
I LEARNED A NEW LANGUAGE TODAY...

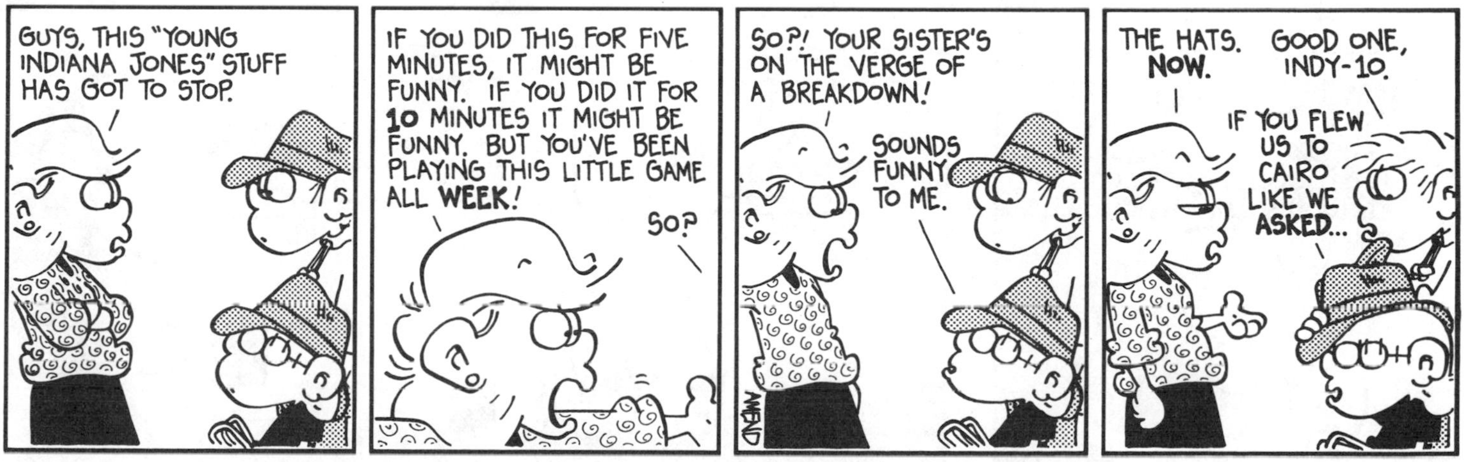
GUYS, THIS "YOUNG INDIANA JONES" STUFF HAS GOT TO STOP.
IF YOU DID THIS FOR FIVE MINUTES, IT MIGHT BE FUNNY. IF YOU DID IT FOR 10 MINUTES IT MIGHT BE FUNNY. BUT YOU'VE BEEN PLAYING THIS LITTLE GAME ALL WEEK!
SO?
SO?! YOUR SISTER'S ON THE VERGE OF A BREAKDOWN!
SOUNDS FUNNY TO ME.
AMEND
THE HATS. NOW.
GOOD ONE, INDY-10.
IF YOU FLEW US TO CAIRO LIKE WE ASKED...

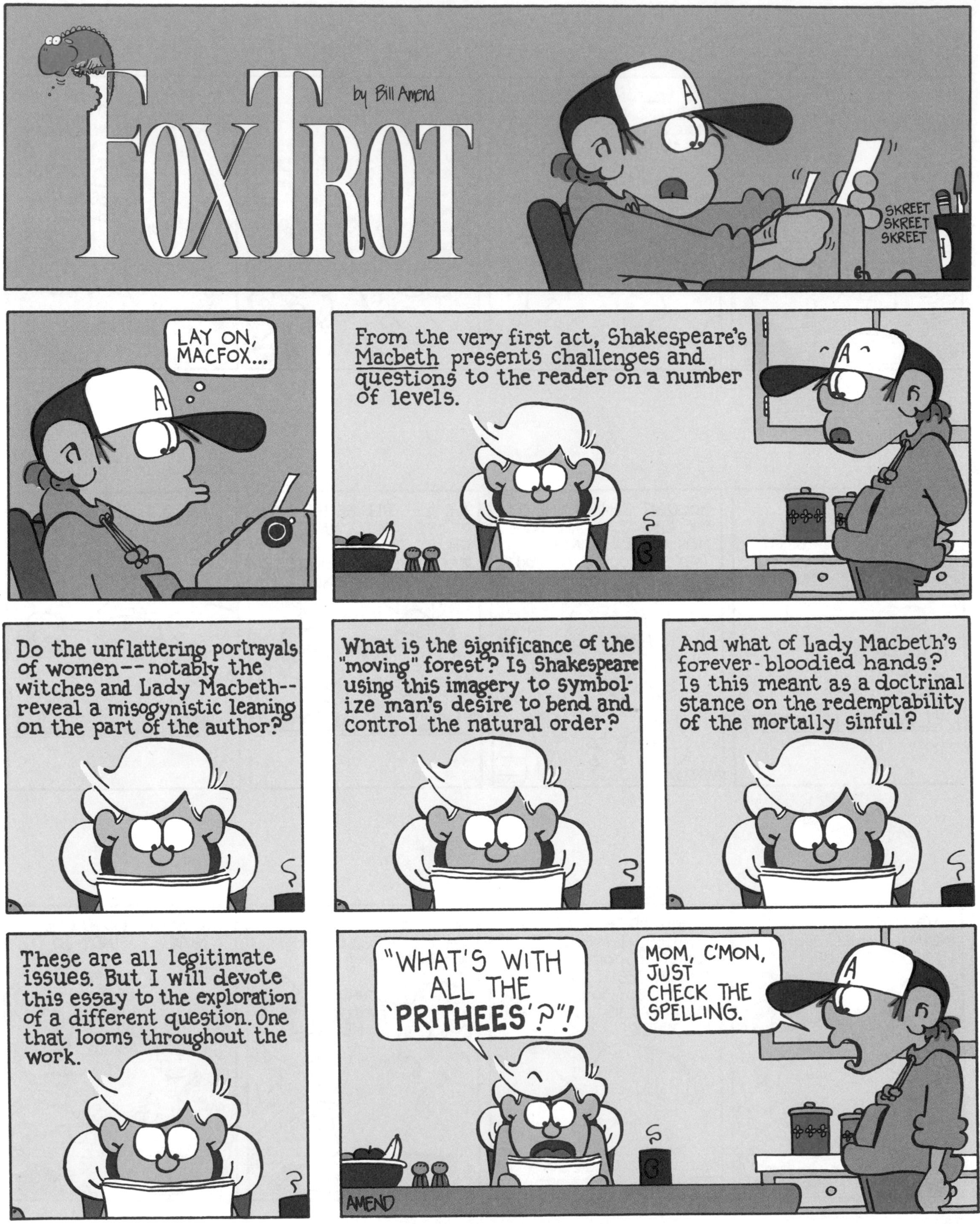
FoxTrot
by Bill Amend
SKREET SKREET SKREET
LAY ON, MACFOX...
From the very first act, Shakespeare's Macbeth presents challenges and questions to the reader on a number of levels.
Do the unflattering portrayals of women--notably the witches and Lady Macbeth--reveal a misogynistic leaning on the part of the author?
What is the significance of the "moving" forest? Is Shakespeare using this imagery to symbolize man's desire to bend and control the natural order?
And what of Lady Macbeth's forever-bloodied hands? Is this meant as a doctrinal stance on the redemptability of the mortally sinful?
These are all legitimate issues. But I will devote this essay to the exploration of a different question. One that looms throughout the work.
"WHAT'S WITH ALL THE 'PRITHEES'?"!
MOM, C'MON, JUST CHECK THE SPELLING.
AMEND

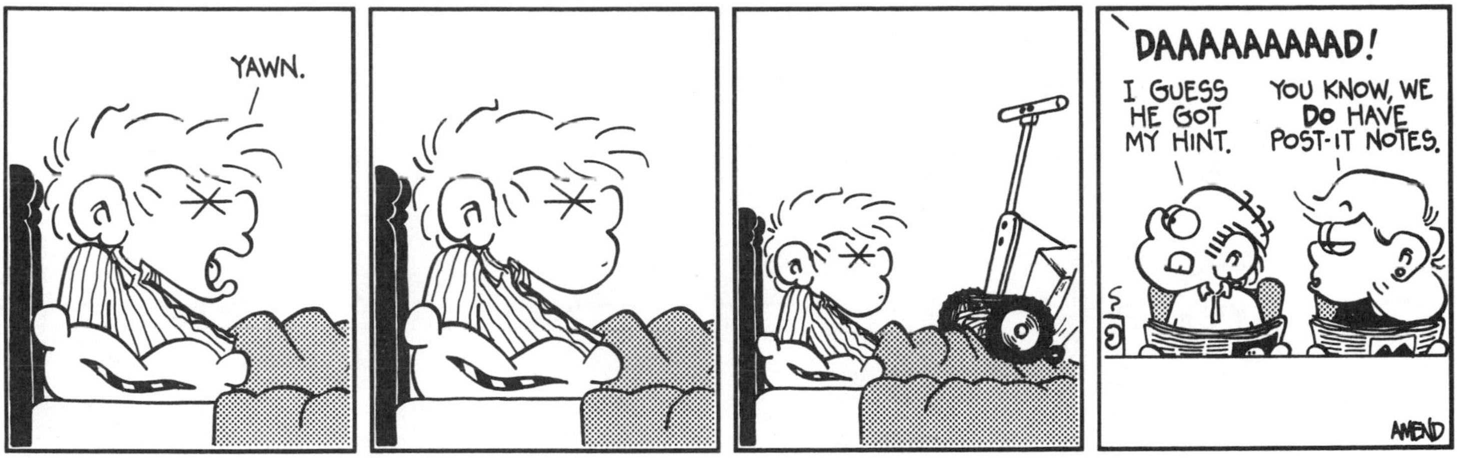
YAWN.
DAAAAAAAAAD!
I GUESS HE GOT MY HINT.
YOU KNOW, WE **DO** HAVE POST-IT NOTES.
AMEND

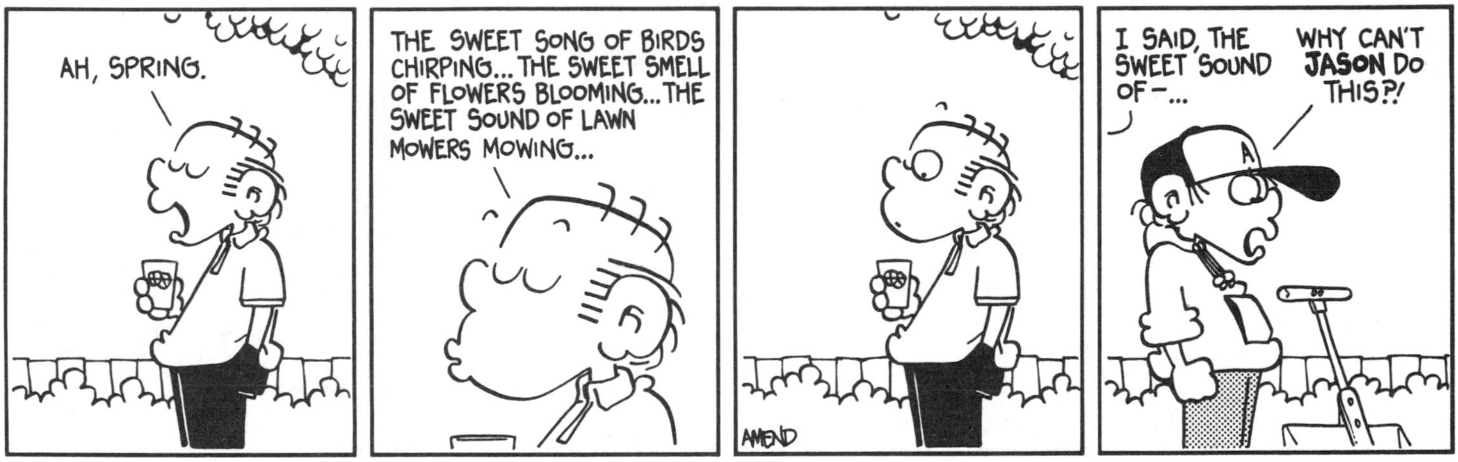
AH, SPRING.
THE SWEET SONG OF BIRDS CHIRPING... THE SWEET SMELL OF FLOWERS BLOOMING... THE SWEET SOUND OF LAWN MOWERS MOWING...
AMEND
I SAID, THE SWEET SOUND OF–...
WHY CAN'T **JASON** DO THIS?!

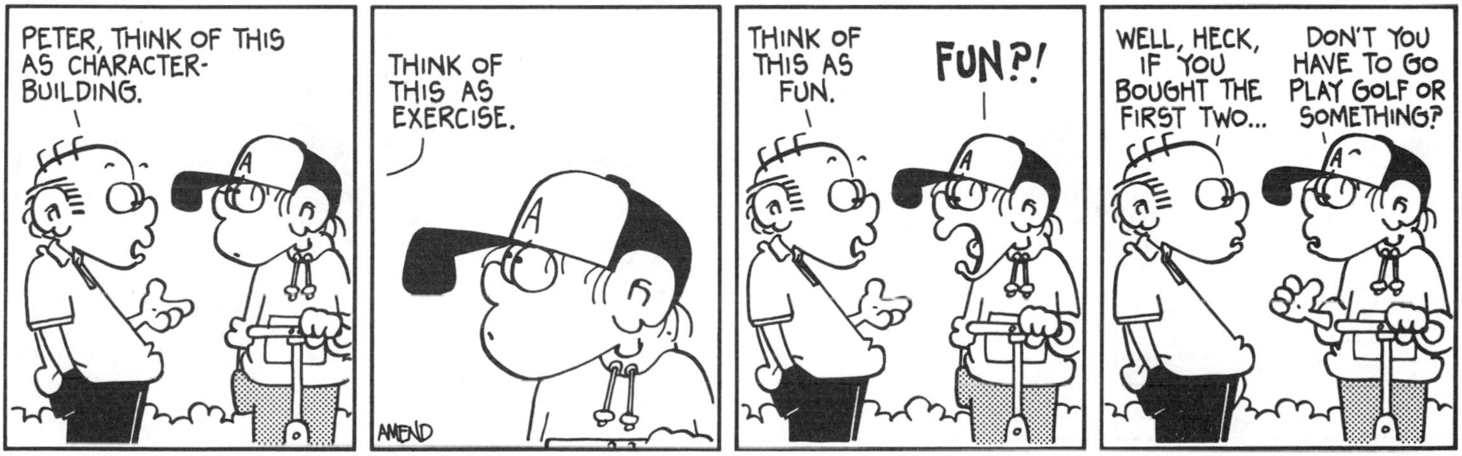
PETER, THINK OF THIS AS CHARACTER-BUILDING.
THINK OF THIS AS EXERCISE.
AMEND
THINK OF THIS AS FUN.
FUN?!
WELL, HECK, IF YOU BOUGHT THE FIRST TWO...
DON'T YOU HAVE TO GO PLAY GOLF OR SOMETHING?

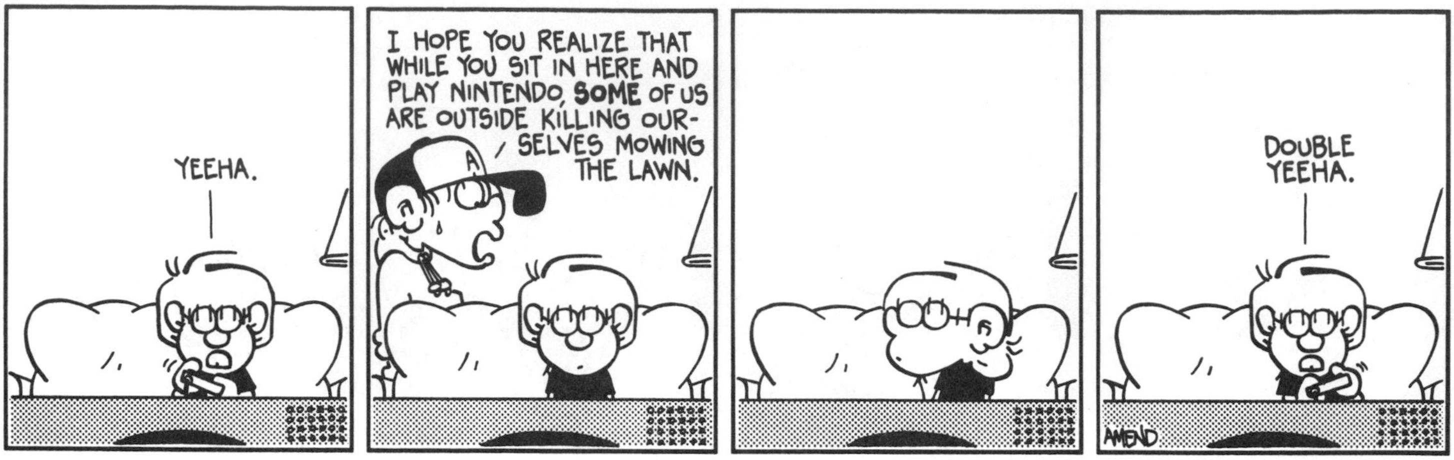
YEEHA.
I HOPE YOU REALIZE THAT WHILE YOU SIT IN HERE AND PLAY NINTENDO, SOME OF US ARE OUTSIDE KILLING OURSELVES MOWING THE LAWN.
DOUBLE YEEHA.
AMEND

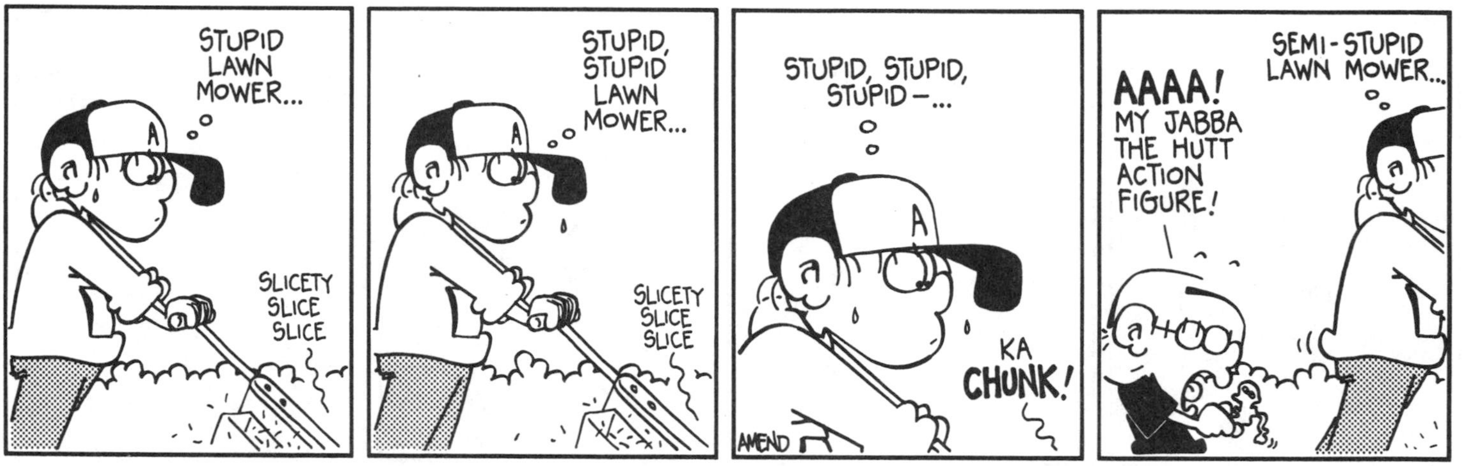
STUPID LAWN MOWER...
SLICETY SLICE SLICE
STUPID, STUPID LAWN MOWER...
SLICETY SLICE SLICE
STUPID, STUPID, STUPID—...
KA CHUNK!
AMEND
AAAA! MY JABBA THE HUTT ACTION FIGURE!
SEMI-STUPID LAWN MOWER...

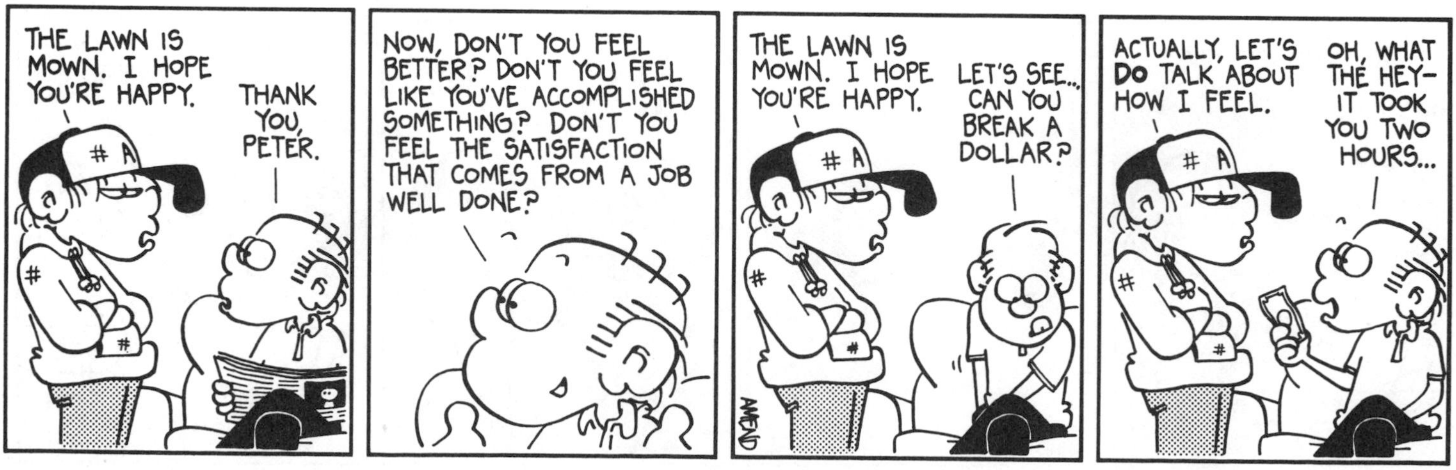
THE LAWN IS MOWN. I HOPE YOU'RE HAPPY.
THANK YOU, PETER.
NOW, DON'T YOU FEEL BETTER? DON'T YOU FEEL LIKE YOU'VE ACCOMPLISHED SOMETHING? DON'T YOU FEEL THE SATISFACTION THAT COMES FROM A JOB WELL DONE?
AMEND
THE LAWN IS MOWN. I HOPE YOU'RE HAPPY.
LET'S SEE... CAN YOU BREAK A DOLLAR?
ACTUALLY, LET'S DO TALK ABOUT HOW I FEEL.
OH, WHAT THE HEY—IT TOOK YOU TWO HOURS...

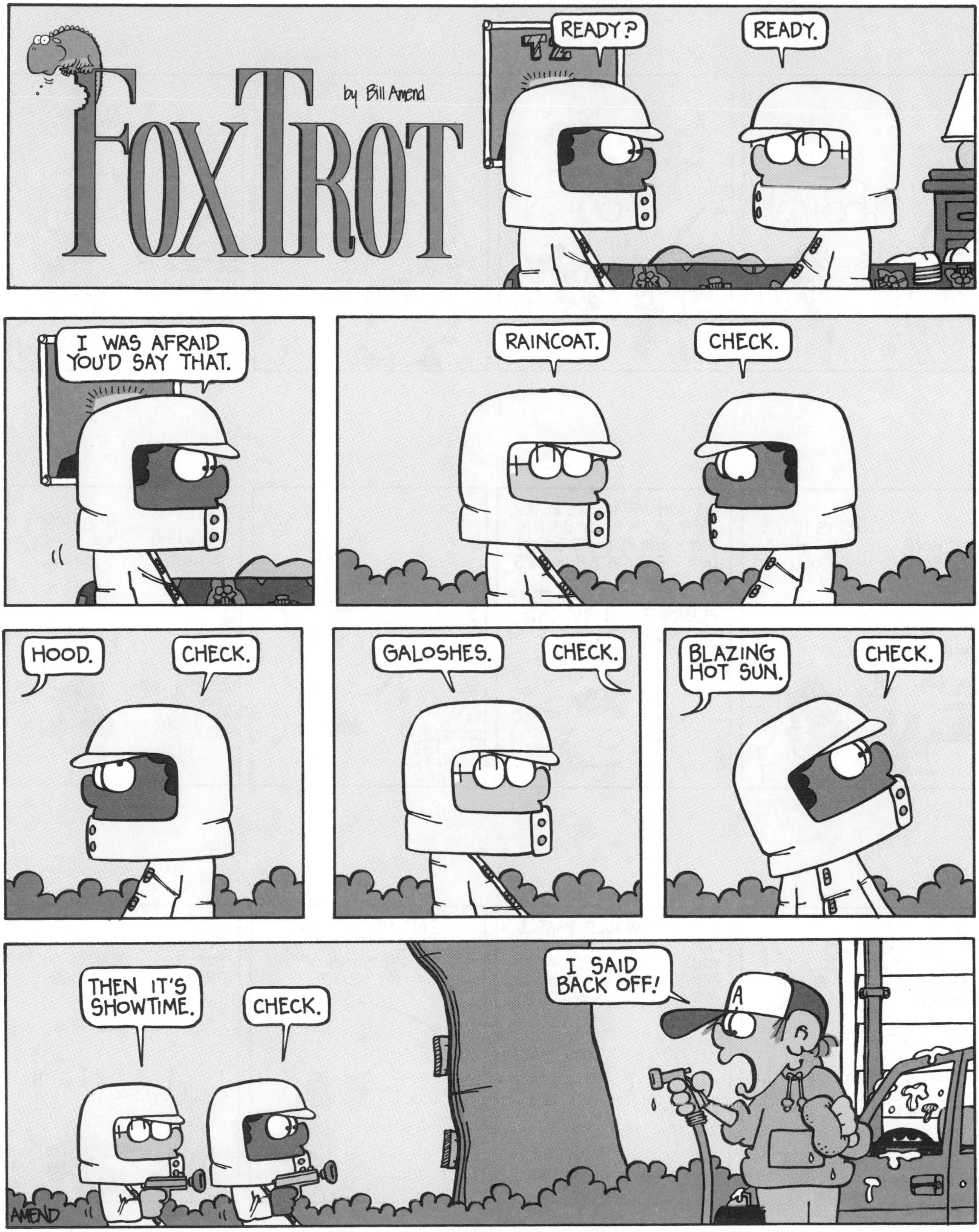
FoxTrot
by Bill Amend
READY?
READY.
I WAS AFRAID YOU'D SAY THAT.
RAINCOAT.
CHECK.
HOOD.
CHECK.
GALOSHES.
CHECK.
BLAZING HOT SUN.
CHECK.
THEN IT'S SHOWTIME.
CHECK.
I SAID BACK OFF!
AMEND

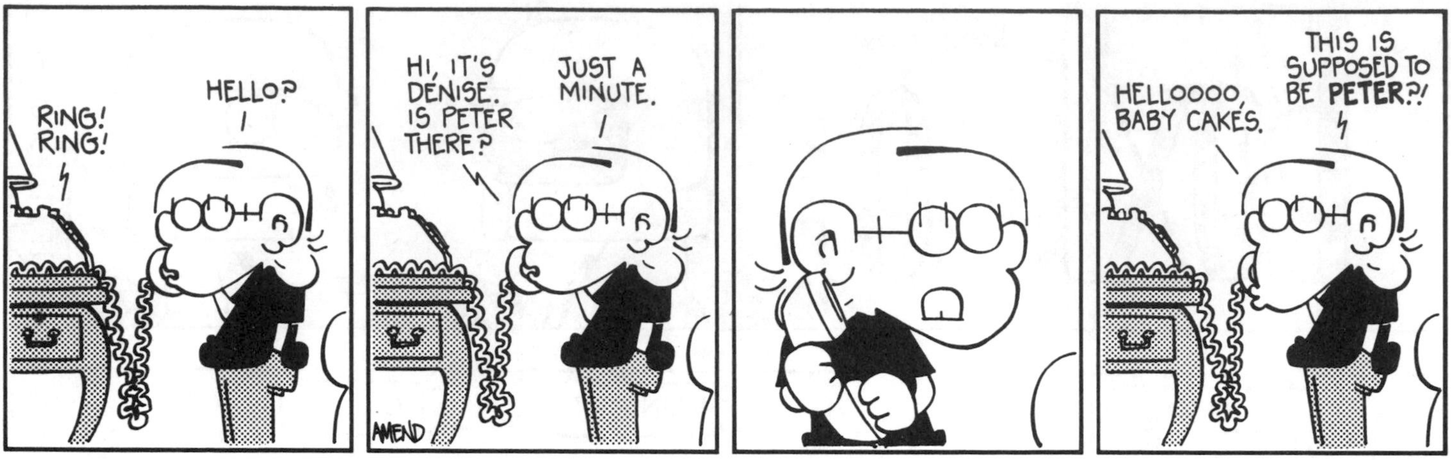
RING! RING!
HELLO?
HI, IT'S DENISE. IS PETER THERE?
JUST A MINUTE.
HELLOOOO, BABY CAKES.
THIS IS SUPPOSED TO BE **PETER**?!
AMEND

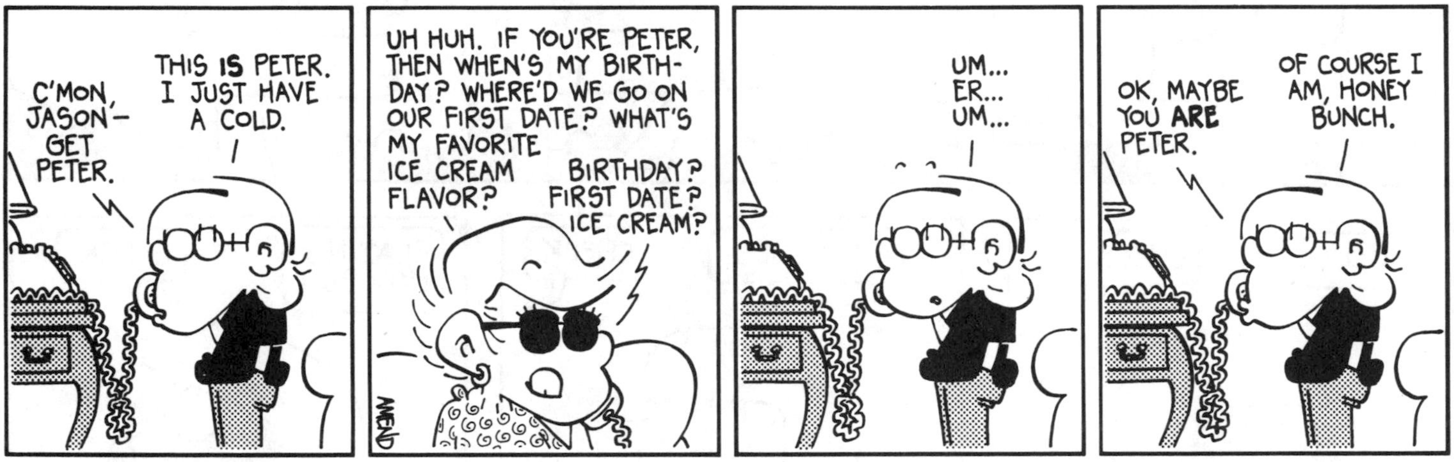
C'MON, JASON– GET PETER.
THIS **IS** PETER. I JUST HAVE A COLD.
UH HUH. IF YOU'RE PETER, THEN WHEN'S MY BIRTHDAY? WHERE'D WE GO ON OUR FIRST DATE? WHAT'S MY FAVORITE ICE CREAM FLAVOR?
BIRTHDAY? FIRST DATE? ICE CREAM?
UM... ER... UM...
OK, MAYBE YOU **ARE** PETER.
OF COURSE I AM, HONEY BUNCH.
AMEND

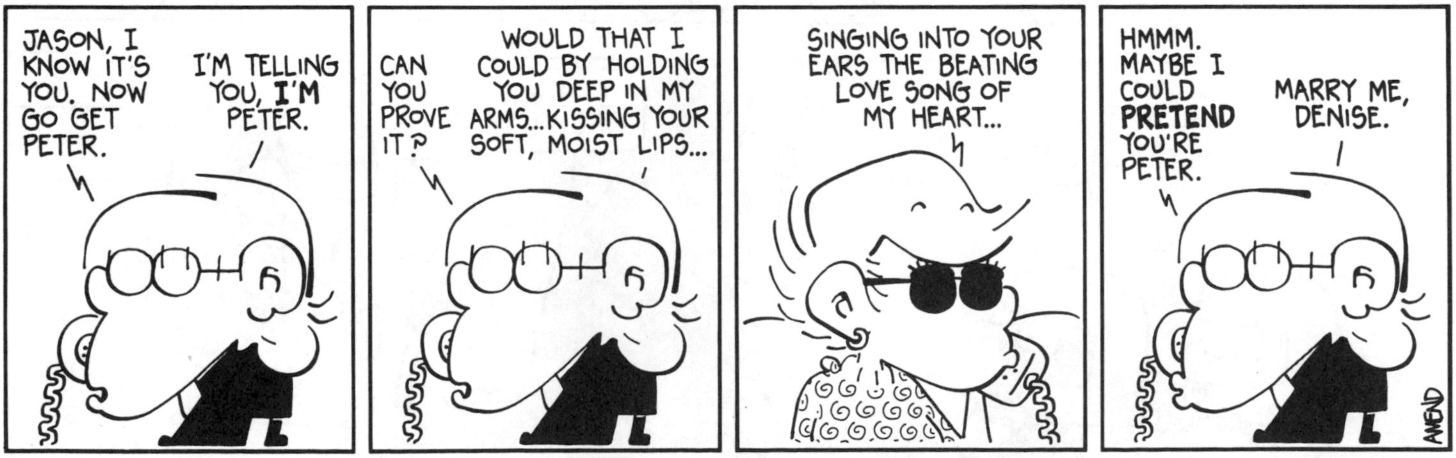
JASON, I KNOW IT'S YOU. NOW GO GET PETER.
I'M TELLING YOU, **I'M** PETER.
CAN YOU PROVE IT?
WOULD THAT I COULD BY HOLDING YOU DEEP IN MY ARMS...KISSING YOUR SOFT, MOIST LIPS...
SINGING INTO YOUR EARS THE BEATING LOVE SONG OF MY HEART...
HMMM. MAYBE I COULD **PRETEND** YOU'RE PETER.
MARRY ME, DENISE.
AMEND

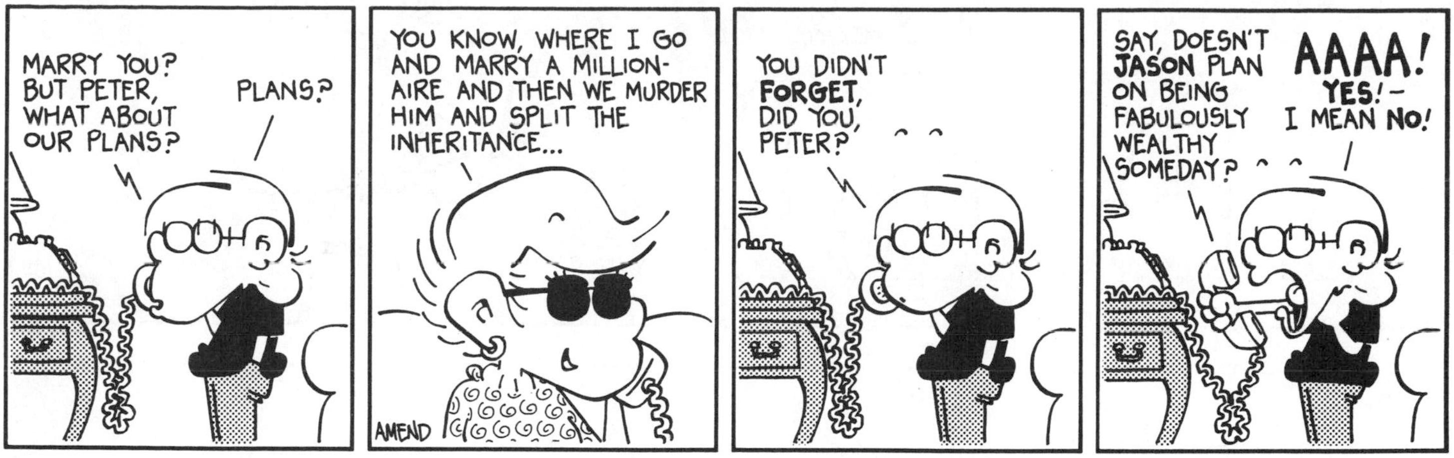
MARRY YOU? BUT PETER, WHAT ABOUT OUR PLANS?
PLANS?
YOU KNOW, WHERE I GO AND MARRY A MILLION-AIRE AND THEN WE MURDER HIM AND SPLIT THE INHERITANCE...
AMEND
YOU DIDN'T FORGET, DID YOU, PETER?
SAY, DOESN'T JASON PLAN ON BEING FABULOUSLY WEALTHY SOMEDAY?
AAAA! YES!– I MEAN NO!

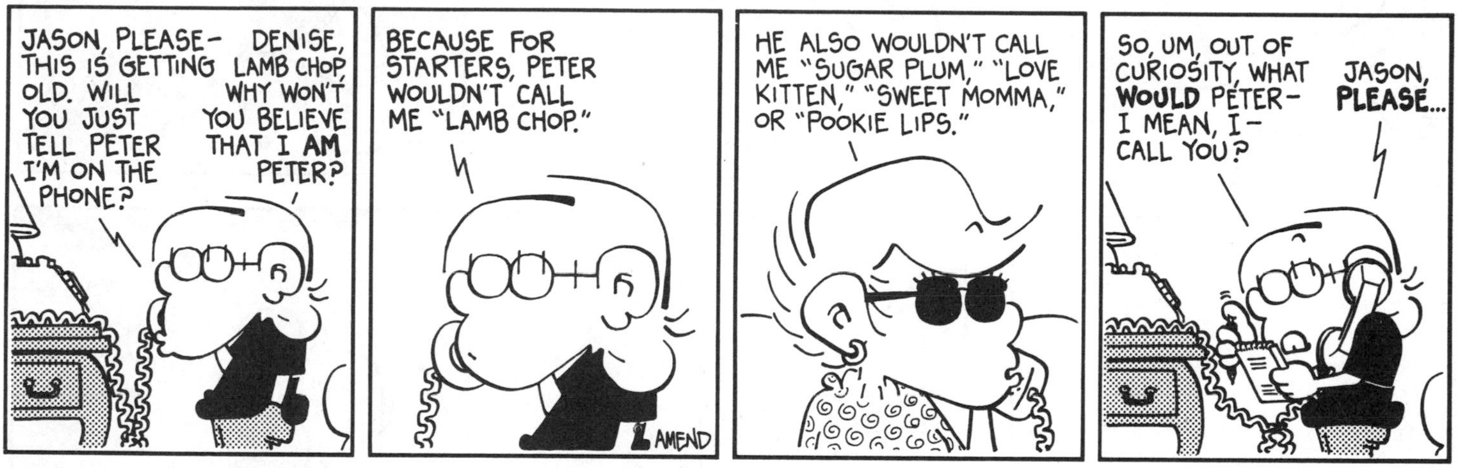
JASON, PLEASE– THIS IS GETTING OLD. WILL YOU JUST TELL PETER I'M ON THE PHONE?
DENISE, LAMB CHOP, WHY WON'T YOU BELIEVE THAT I AM PETER?
BECAUSE FOR STARTERS, PETER WOULDN'T CALL ME "LAMB CHOP."
AMEND
HE ALSO WOULDN'T CALL ME "SUGAR PLUM," "LOVE KITTEN," "SWEET MOMMA," OR "POOKIE LIPS."
SO, UM, OUT OF CURIOSITY, WHAT WOULD PETER– I MEAN, I– CALL YOU?
JASON, PLEASE...

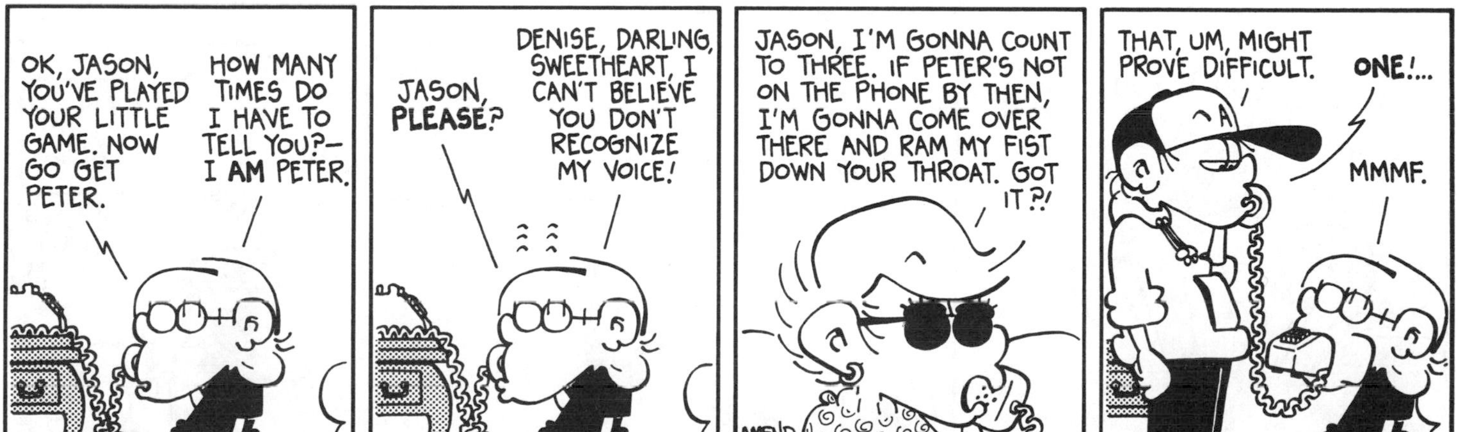
OK, JASON, YOU'VE PLAYED YOUR LITTLE GAME. NOW GO GET PETER.
HOW MANY TIMES DO I HAVE TO TELL YOU?– I AM PETER.
JASON, PLEASE?
DENISE, DARLING, SWEETHEART, I CAN'T BELIEVE YOU DON'T RECOGNIZE MY VOICE!
JASON, I'M GONNA COUNT TO THREE. IF PETER'S NOT ON THE PHONE BY THEN, I'M GONNA COME OVER THERE AND RAM MY FIST DOWN YOUR THROAT. GOT IT?!
AMEND
THAT, UM, MIGHT PROVE DIFFICULT.
ONE!...
MMMF.

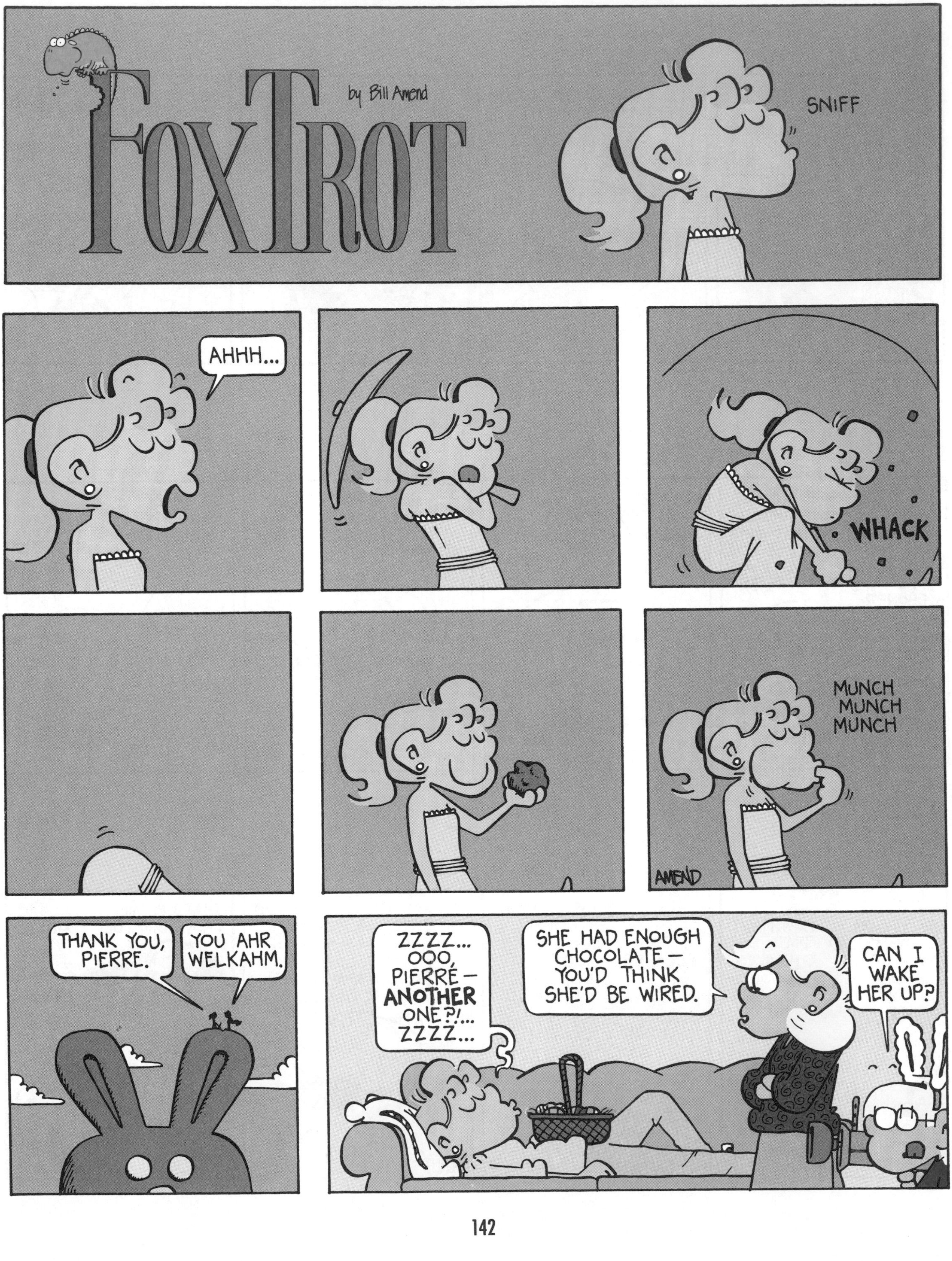
FoxTrot
by Bill Amend
SNIFF
AHHH...
WHACK
MUNCH MUNCH MUNCH
AMEND
THANK YOU, PIERRE.
YOU AHR WELKAHM.
ZZZZ... OOO, PIERRÉ— **ANOTHER** ONE?!... ZZZZ...
SHE HAD ENOUGH CHOCOLATE— YOU'D THINK SHE'D BE WIRED.
CAN I WAKE HER UP?

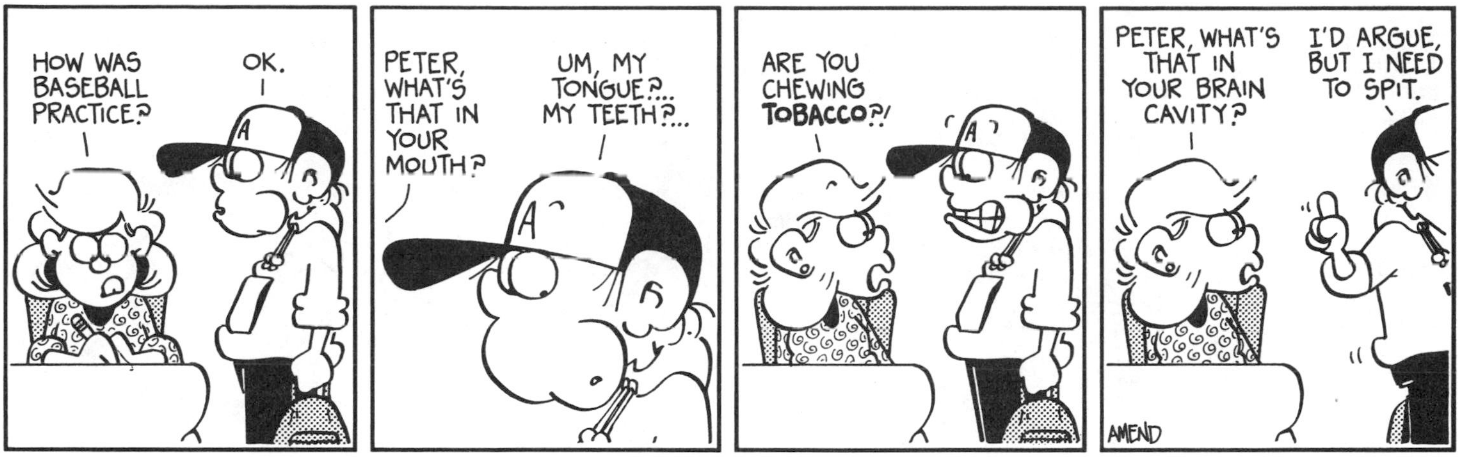

HOW WAS BASEBALL PRACTICE?
OK.
PETER, WHAT'S THAT IN YOUR MOUTH?
UM, MY TONGUE?... MY TEETH?...
ARE YOU CHEWING **TOBACCO**?!
PETER, WHAT'S THAT IN YOUR BRAIN CAVITY?
I'D ARGUE, BUT I NEED TO SPIT.
AMEND

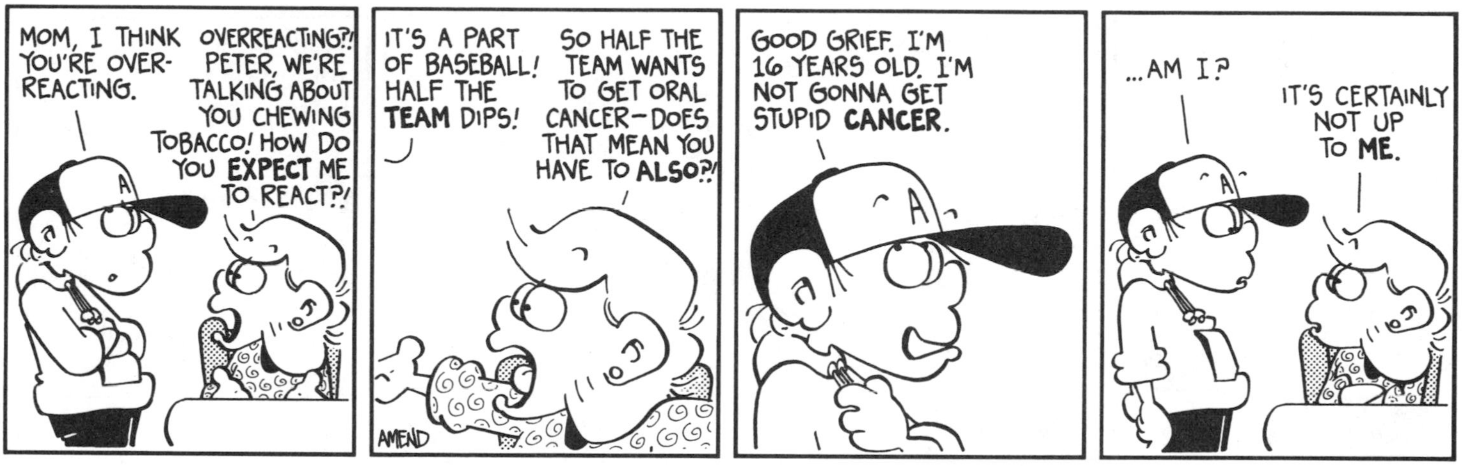

MOM, I THINK YOU'RE OVER-REACTING.
OVERREACTING?! PETER, WE'RE TALKING ABOUT YOU CHEWING TOBACCO! HOW DO YOU **EXPECT** ME TO REACT?!
IT'S A PART OF BASEBALL! HALF THE **TEAM** DIPS!
SO HALF THE TEAM WANTS TO GET ORAL CANCER—DOES THAT MEAN YOU HAVE TO **ALSO**?!
AMEND
GOOD GRIEF. I'M 16 YEARS OLD. I'M NOT GONNA GET STUPID **CANCER**.
...AM I?
IT'S CERTAINLY NOT UP TO **ME**.

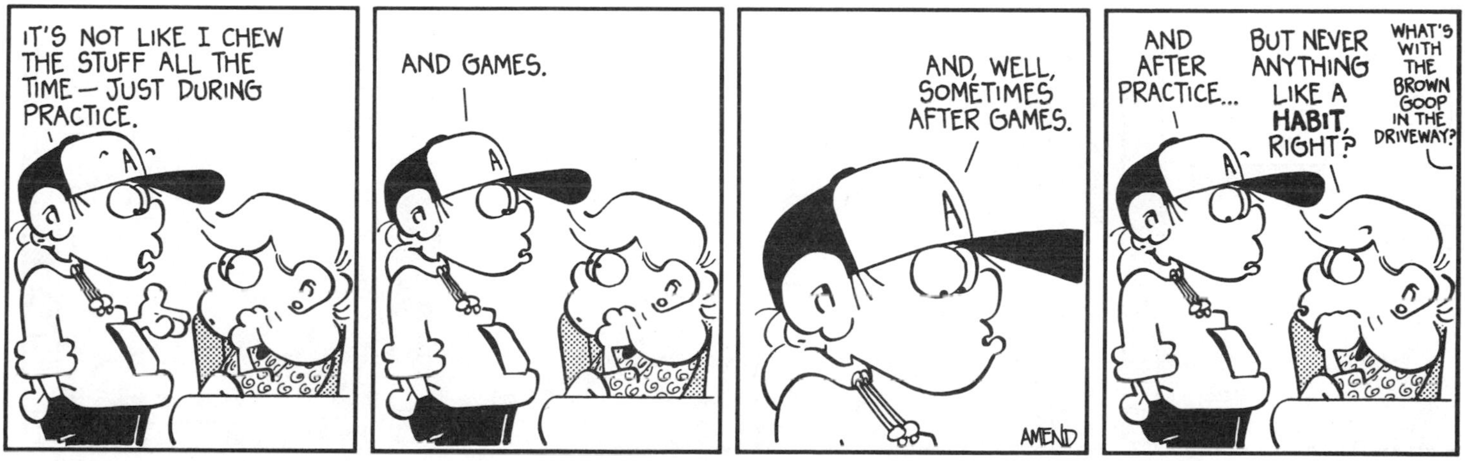

IT'S NOT LIKE I CHEW THE STUFF ALL THE TIME—JUST DURING PRACTICE.
AND GAMES.
AND, WELL, SOMETIMES AFTER GAMES.
AMEND
AND AFTER PRACTICE...
BUT NEVER ANYTHING LIKE A **HABIT**, RIGHT?
WHAT'S WITH THE BROWN GOOP IN THE DRIVEWAY?

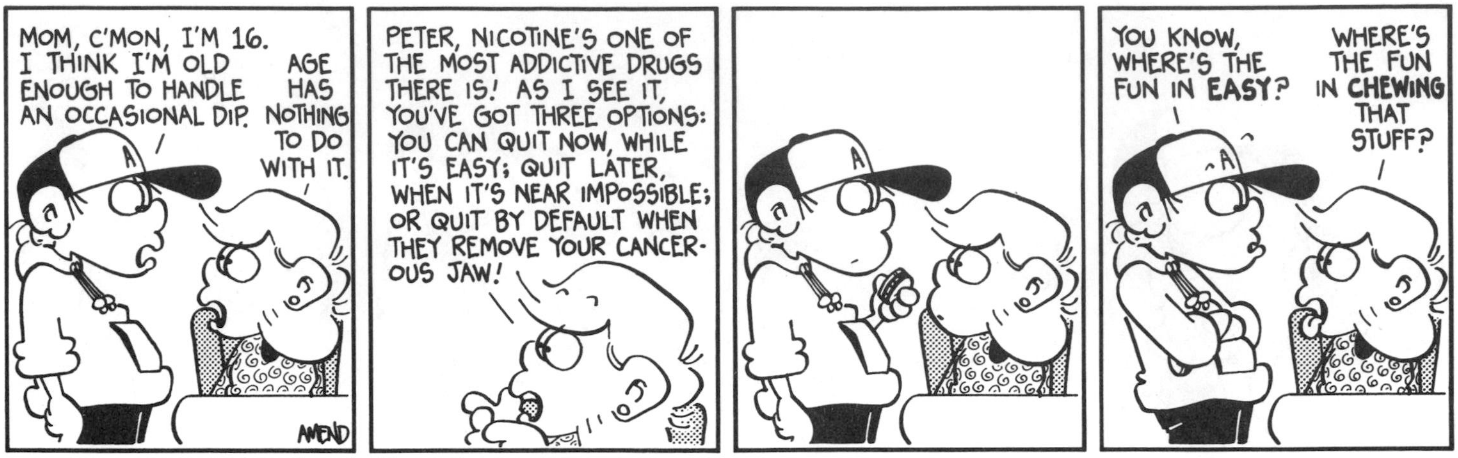
MOM, C'MON, I'M 16. I THINK I'M OLD ENOUGH TO HANDLE AN OCCASIONAL DIP.
AGE HAS NOTHING TO DO WITH IT.
AMEND
PETER, NICOTINE'S ONE OF THE MOST ADDICTIVE DRUGS THERE IS! AS I SEE IT, YOU'VE GOT THREE OPTIONS: YOU CAN QUIT NOW, WHILE IT'S EASY; QUIT LATER, WHEN IT'S NEAR IMPOSSIBLE; OR QUIT BY DEFAULT WHEN THEY REMOVE YOUR CANCEROUS JAW!
YOU KNOW, WHERE'S THE FUN IN EASY?
WHERE'S THE FUN IN CHEWING THAT STUFF?

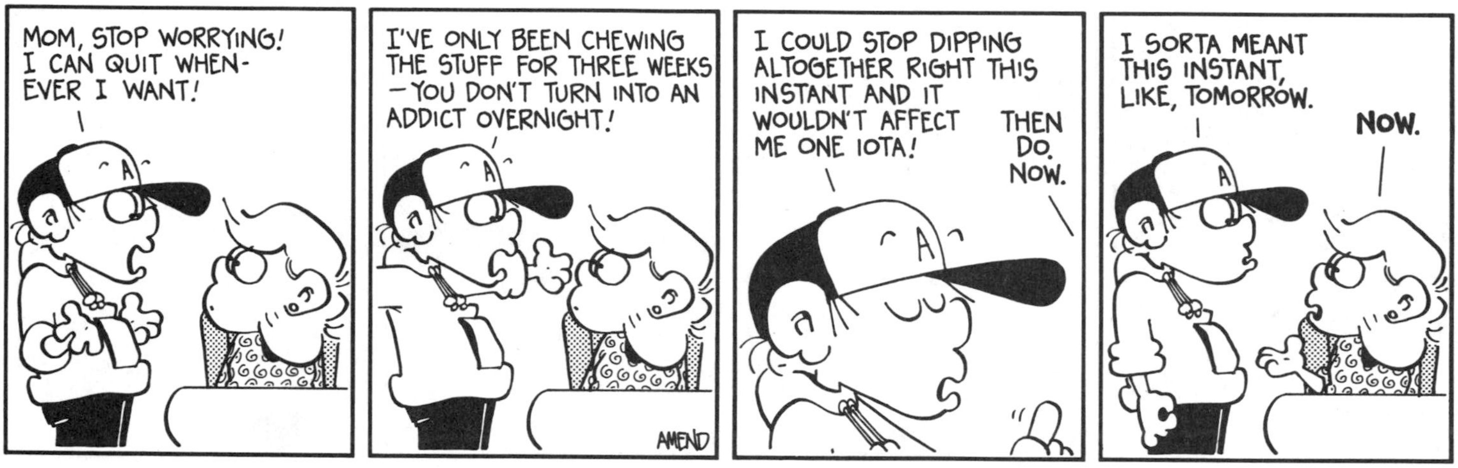
MOM, STOP WORRYING! I CAN QUIT WHENEVER I WANT!
I'VE ONLY BEEN CHEWING THE STUFF FOR THREE WEEKS —YOU DON'T TURN INTO AN ADDICT OVERNIGHT!
AMEND
I COULD STOP DIPPING ALTOGETHER RIGHT THIS INSTANT AND IT WOULDN'T AFFECT ME ONE IOTA!
THEN DO. NOW.
I SORTA MEANT THIS INSTANT, LIKE, TOMORROW.
NOW.

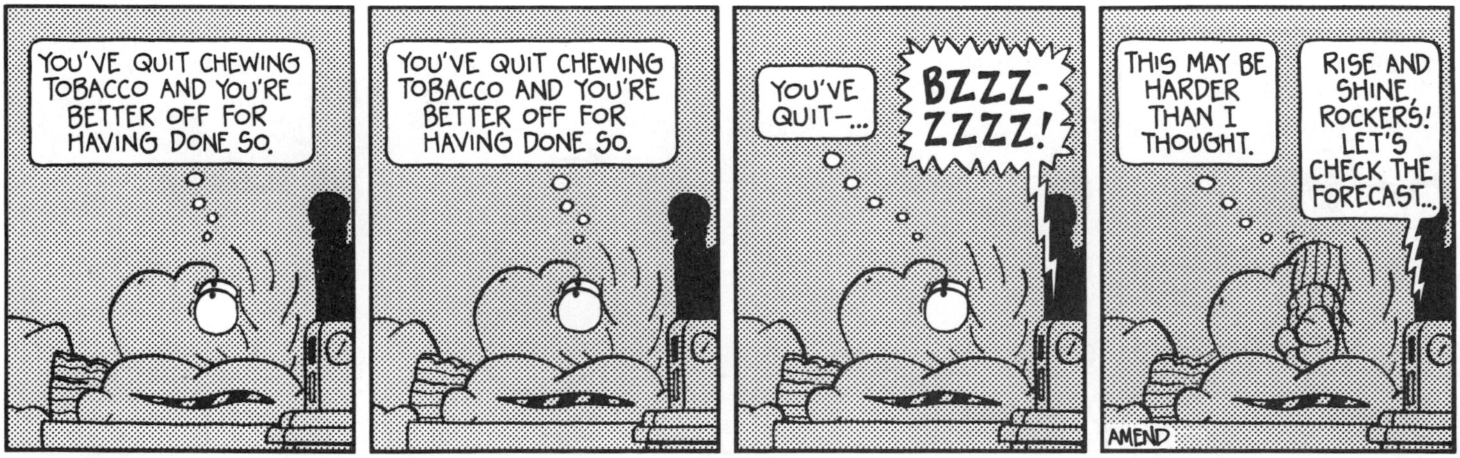
YOU'VE QUIT CHEWING TOBACCO AND YOU'RE BETTER OFF FOR HAVING DONE SO.
YOU'VE QUIT CHEWING TOBACCO AND YOU'RE BETTER OFF FOR HAVING DONE SO.
YOU'VE QUIT—...
BZZZ-ZZZZ!
THIS MAY BE HARDER THAN I THOUGHT.
RISE AND SHINE, ROCKERS! LET'S CHECK THE FORECAST...
AMEND

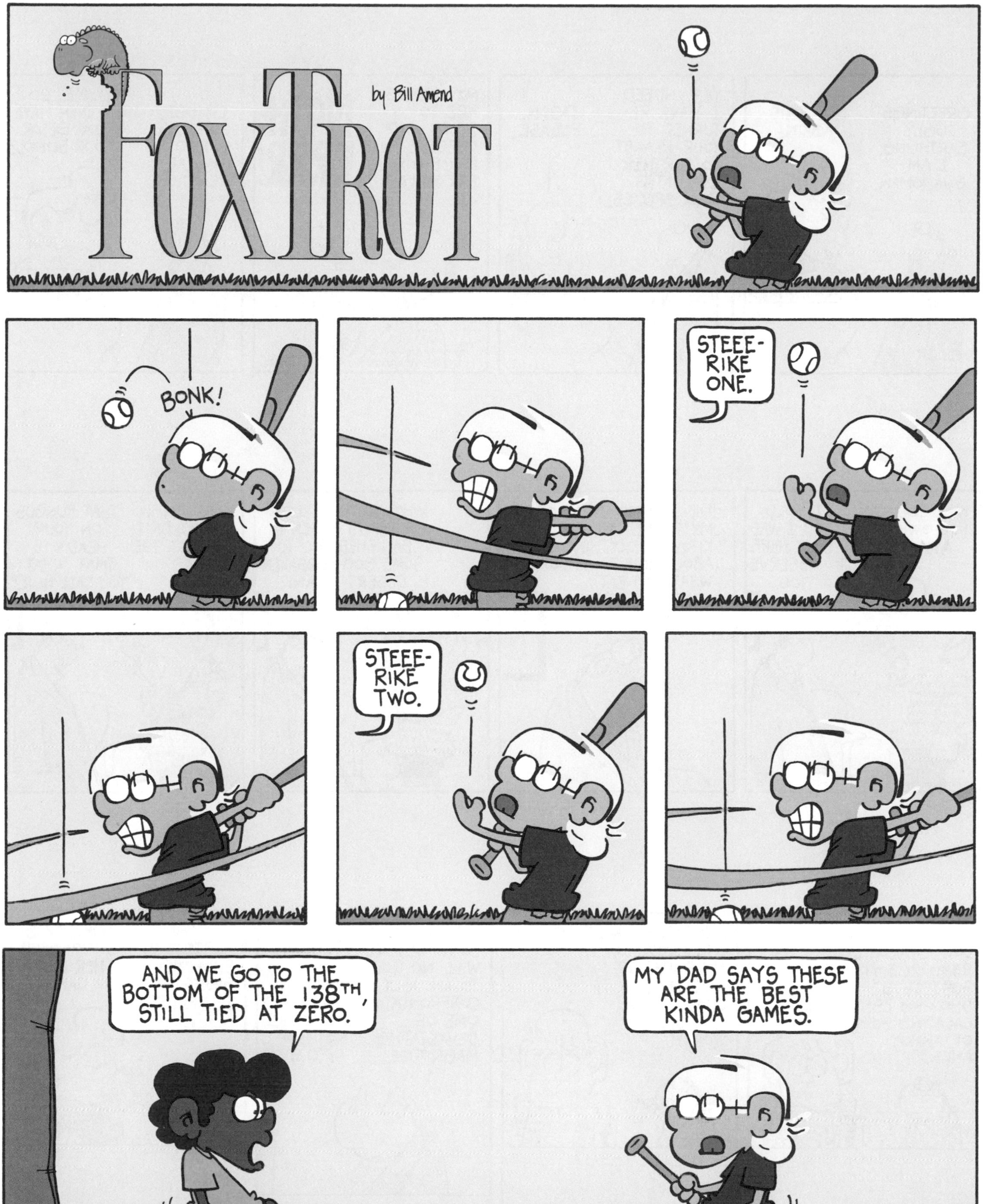
FoxTrot
by Bill Amend
BONK!
STEEE-RIKE ONE.
STEEE-RIKE TWO.
AND WE GO TO THE BOTTOM OF THE 138TH, STILL TIED AT ZERO.
MY DAD SAYS THESE ARE THE BEST KINDA GAMES.
AMEND

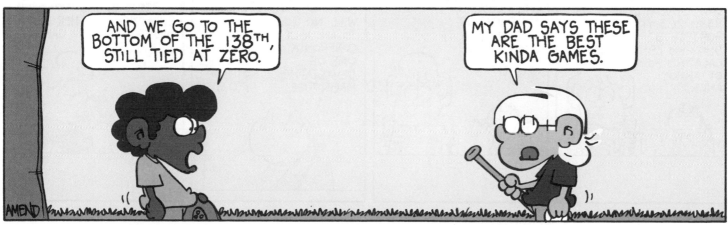

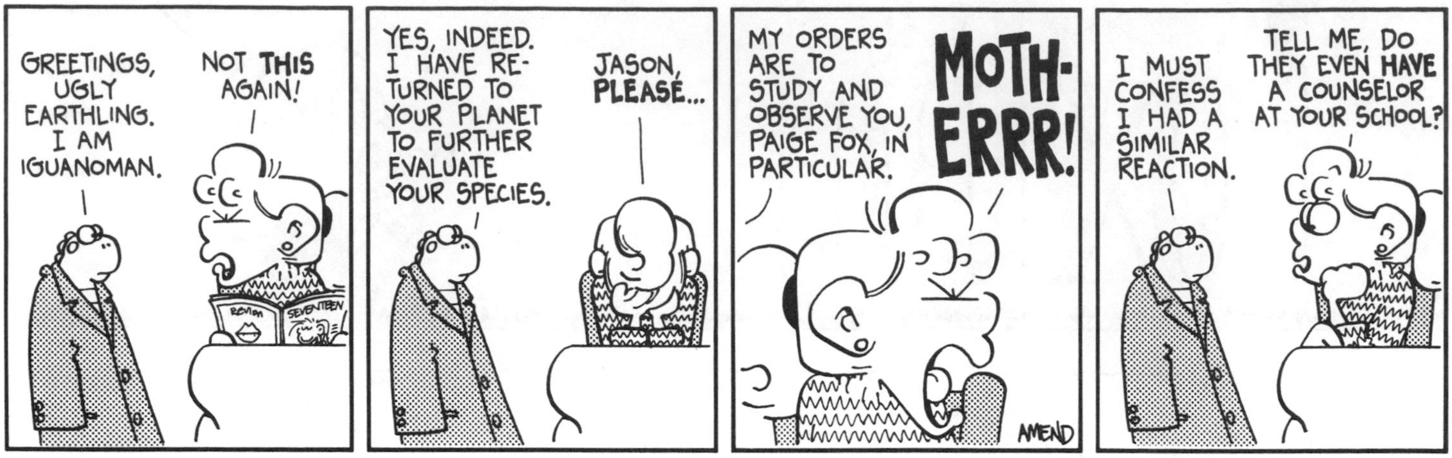
GREETINGS, UGLY EARTHLING. I AM IGUANOMAN.
NOT **THIS** AGAIN!
YES, INDEED. I HAVE RETURNED TO YOUR PLANET TO FURTHER EVALUATE YOUR SPECIES.
JASON, **PLEASE**...
MY ORDERS ARE TO STUDY AND OBSERVE YOU, PAIGE FOX, IN PARTICULAR.
MOTH-ERRR!
I MUST CONFESS I HAD A SIMILAR REACTION.
TELL ME, DO THEY EVEN **HAVE** A COUNSELOR AT YOUR SCHOOL?
AMEND

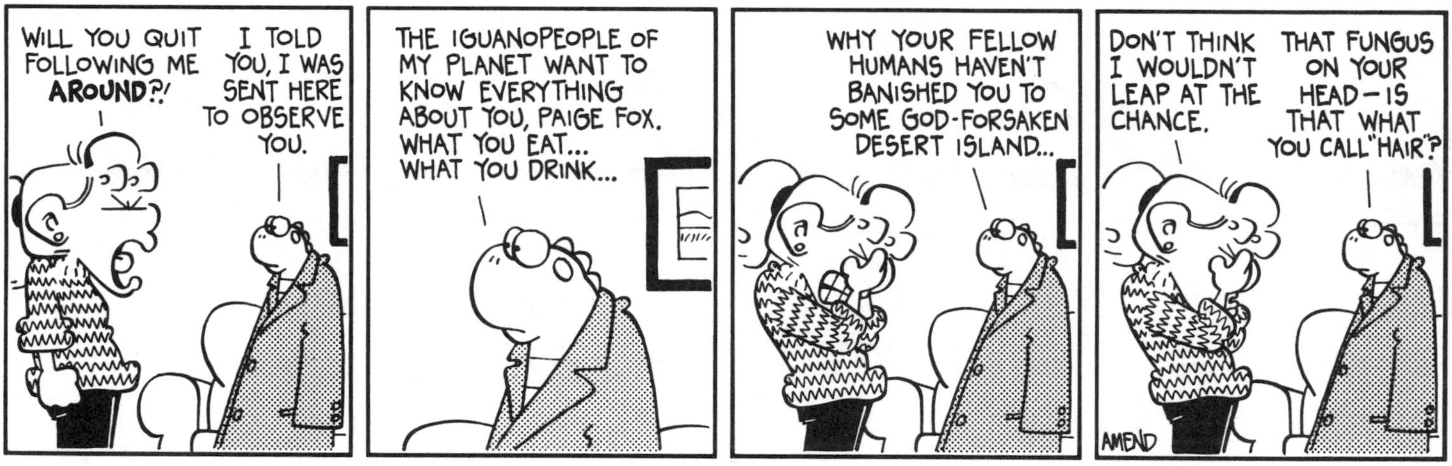
WILL YOU QUIT FOLLOWING ME **AROUND**?!
I TOLD YOU, I WAS SENT HERE TO OBSERVE YOU.
THE IGUANOPEOPLE OF MY PLANET WANT TO KNOW EVERYTHING ABOUT YOU, PAIGE FOX. WHAT YOU EAT... WHAT YOU DRINK...
WHY YOUR FELLOW HUMANS HAVEN'T BANISHED YOU TO SOME GOD-FORSAKEN DESERT ISLAND...
DON'T THINK I WOULDN'T LEAP AT THE CHANCE.
THAT FUNGUS ON YOUR HEAD—IS THAT WHAT YOU CALL "HAIR"?
AMEND

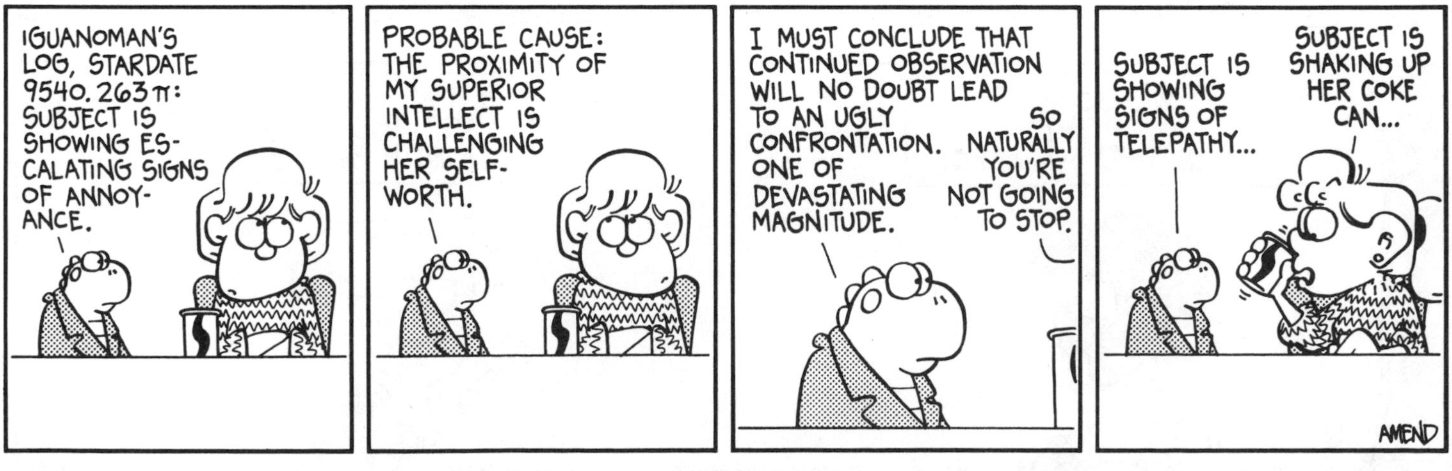
IGUANOMAN'S LOG, STARDATE 9540.263π: SUBJECT IS SHOWING ESCALATING SIGNS OF ANNOYANCE.
PROBABLE CAUSE: THE PROXIMITY OF MY SUPERIOR INTELLECT IS CHALLENGING HER SELF-WORTH.
I MUST CONCLUDE THAT CONTINUED OBSERVATION WILL NO DOUBT LEAD TO AN UGLY CONFRONTATION. ONE OF DEVASTATING MAGNITUDE.
SO NATURALLY YOU'RE NOT GOING TO STOP.
SUBJECT IS SHOWING SIGNS OF TELEPATHY...
SUBJECT IS SHAKING UP HER COKE CAN...
AMEND

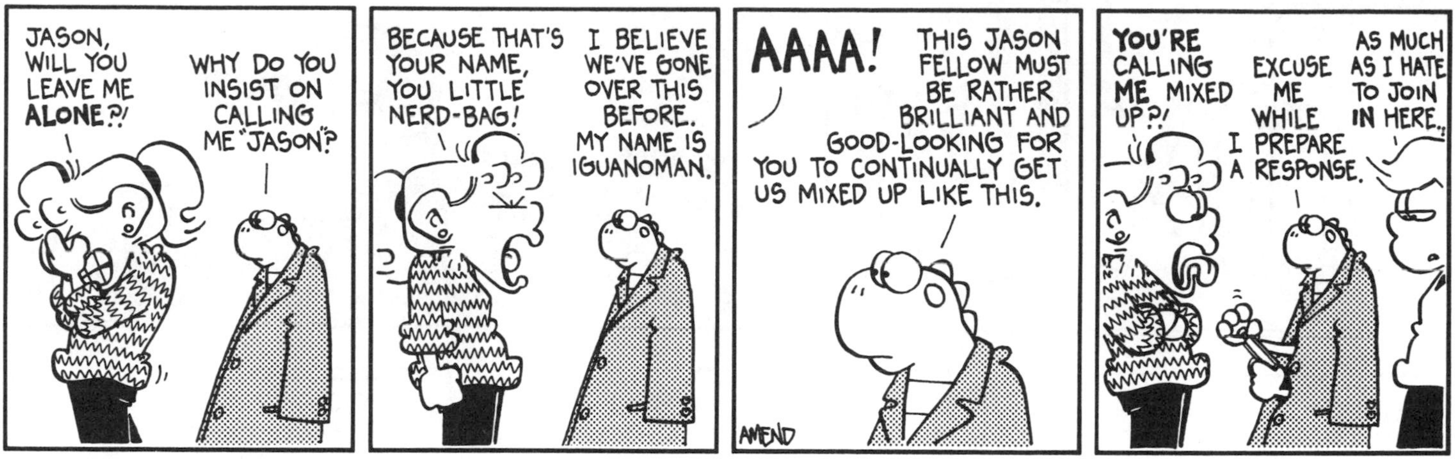
JASON, WILL YOU LEAVE ME **ALONE**?!
WHY DO YOU INSIST ON CALLING ME "JASON"?
BECAUSE THAT'S YOUR NAME, YOU LITTLE NERD-BAG!
I BELIEVE WE'VE GONE OVER THIS BEFORE. MY NAME IS IGUANOMAN.
AAAA!
THIS JASON FELLOW MUST BE RATHER BRILLIANT AND GOOD-LOOKING FOR YOU TO CONTINUALLY GET US MIXED UP LIKE THIS.
AMEND
YOU'RE CALLING **ME** MIXED UP?!
EXCUSE ME WHILE I PREPARE A RESPONSE.
AS MUCH AS I HATE TO JOIN **IN** HERE...

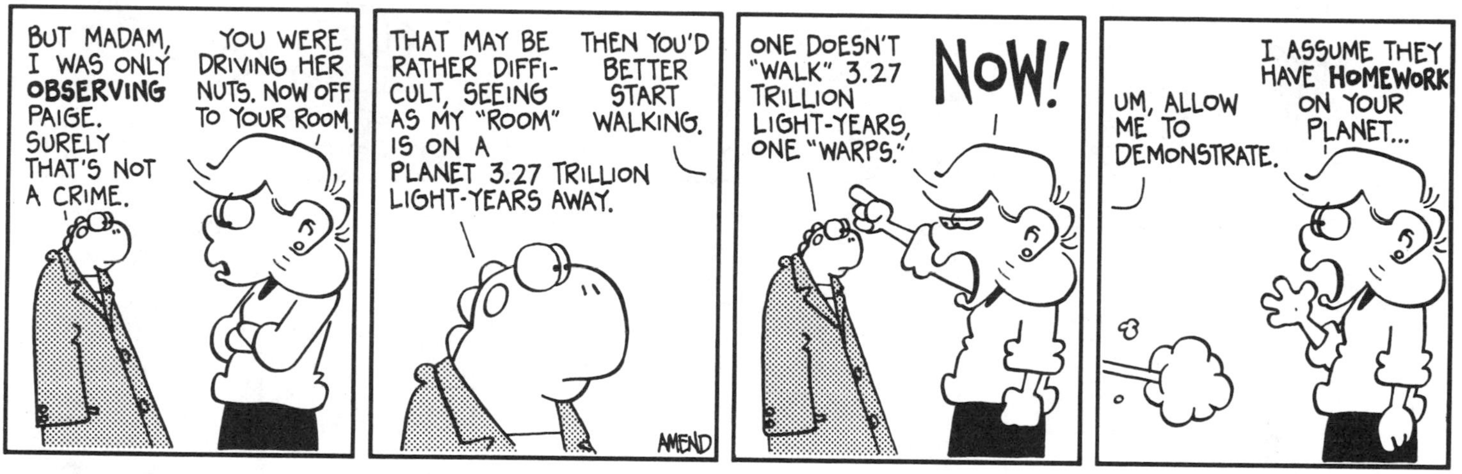
BUT MADAM, I WAS ONLY **OBSERVING** PAIGE. SURELY THAT'S NOT A CRIME.
YOU WERE DRIVING HER NUTS. NOW OFF TO YOUR ROOM.
THAT MAY BE RATHER DIFFICULT, SEEING AS MY "ROOM" IS ON A PLANET 3.27 TRILLION LIGHT-YEARS AWAY.
THEN YOU'D BETTER START WALKING.
AMEND
ONE DOESN'T "WALK" 3.27 TRILLION LIGHT-YEARS, ONE "WARPS."
NOW!
UM, ALLOW ME TO DEMONSTRATE.
I ASSUME THEY HAVE **HOMEWORK** ON YOUR PLANET...

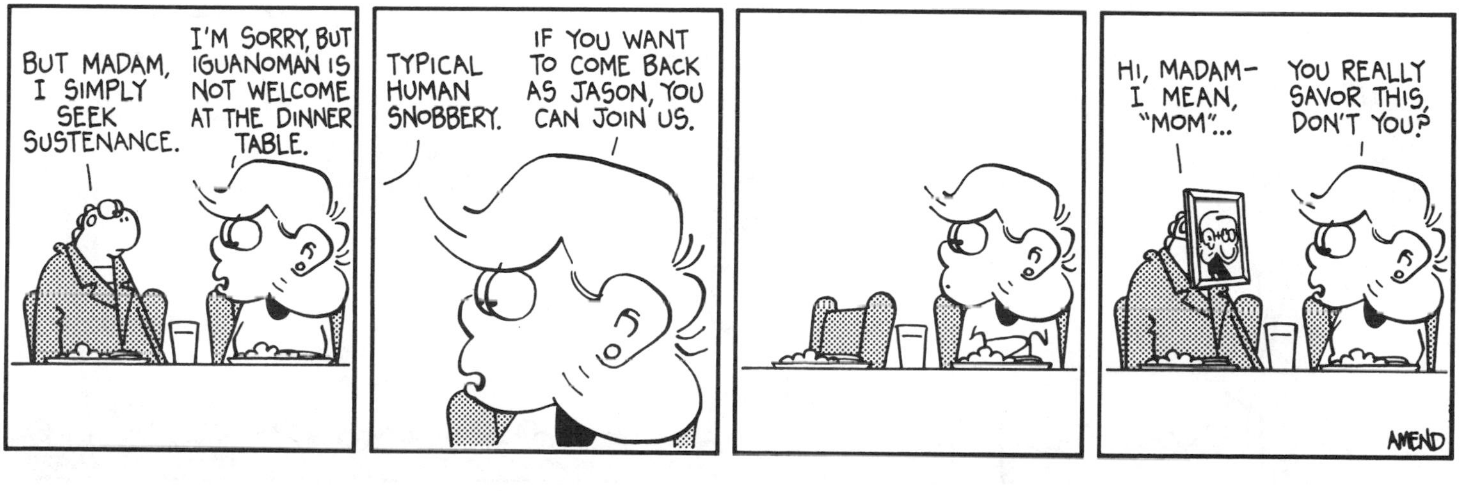
BUT MADAM, I SIMPLY SEEK SUSTENANCE.
I'M SORRY, BUT IGUANOMAN IS NOT WELCOME AT THE DINNER TABLE.
TYPICAL HUMAN SNOBBERY.
IF YOU WANT TO COME BACK AS JASON, YOU CAN JOIN US.
HI, MADAM— I MEAN, "MOM"...
YOU REALLY SAVOR THIS, DON'T YOU?
AMEND

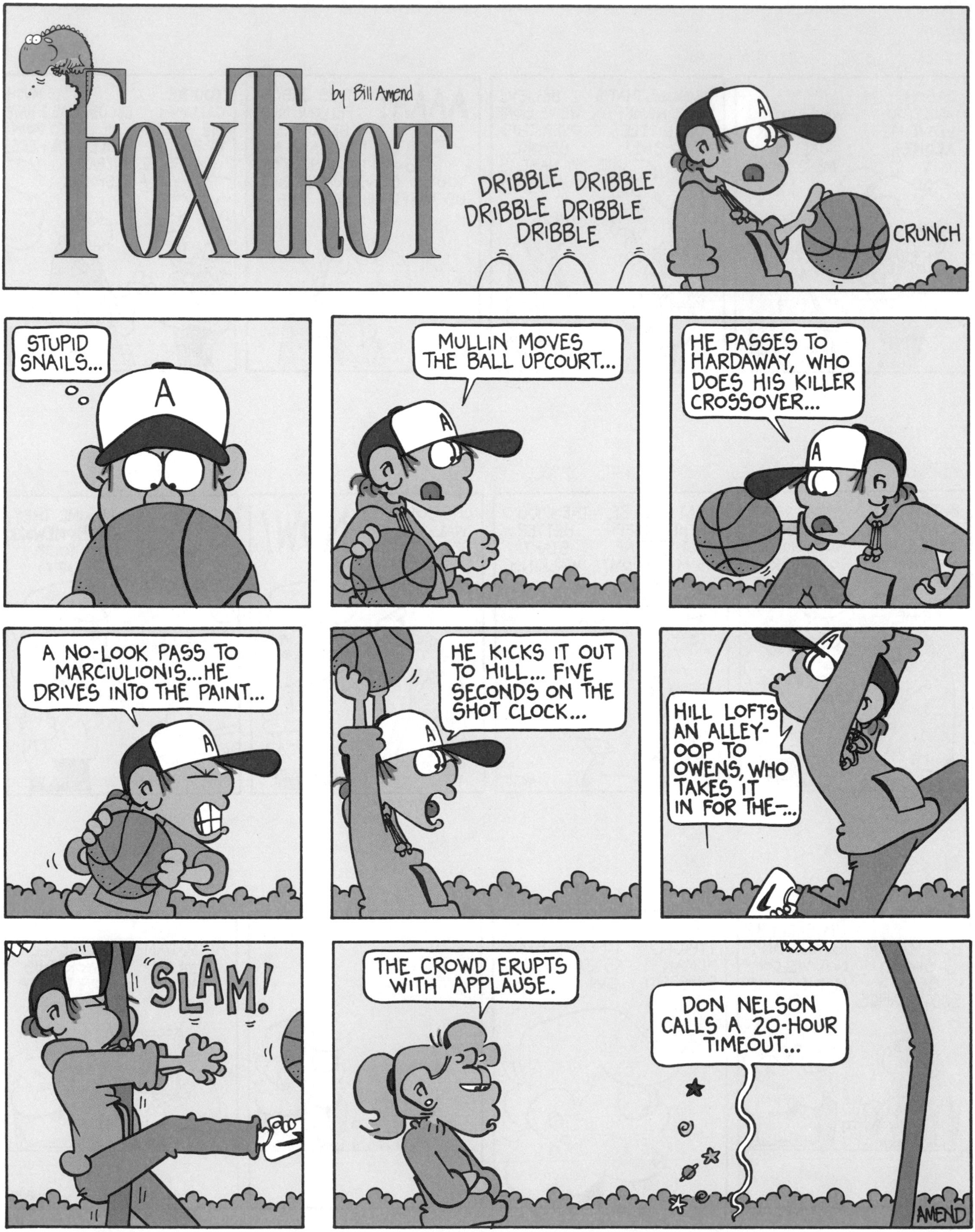
FoxTrot
by Bill Amend
DRIBBLE DRIBBLE DRIBBLE DRIBBLE DRIBBLE
CRUNCH
STUPID SNAILS...
MULLIN MOVES THE BALL UPCOURT...
HE PASSES TO HARDAWAY, WHO DOES HIS KILLER CROSSOVER...
A NO-LOOK PASS TO MARCIULIONIS...HE DRIVES INTO THE PAINT...
HE KICKS IT OUT TO HILL... FIVE SECONDS ON THE SHOT CLOCK...
HILL LOFTS AN ALLEY-OOP TO OWENS, WHO TAKES IT IN FOR THE—...
SLAM!
THE CROWD ERUPTS WITH APPLAUSE.
DON NELSON CALLS A 20-HOUR TIMEOUT...
AMEND

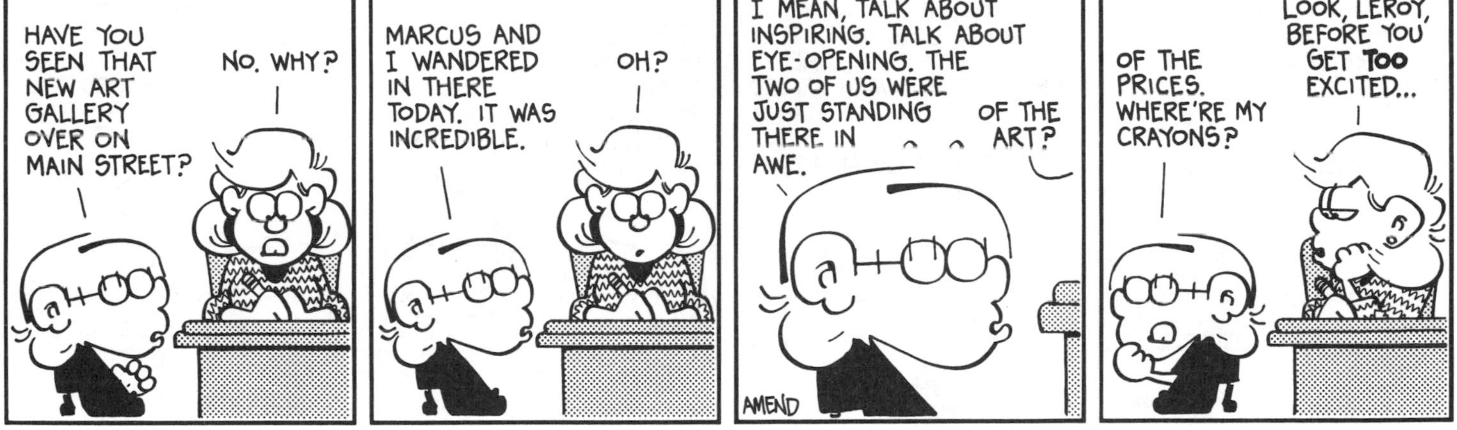
HAVE YOU SEEN THAT NEW ART GALLERY OVER ON MAIN STREET?
NO. WHY?
MARCUS AND I WANDERED IN THERE TODAY. IT WAS INCREDIBLE.
OH?
I MEAN, TALK ABOUT INSPIRING. TALK ABOUT EYE-OPENING. THE TWO OF US WERE JUST STANDING THERE IN AWE.
OF THE ART?
AMEND
LOOK, LEROY, BEFORE YOU GET **TOO** EXCITED...
OF THE PRICES. WHERE'RE MY CRAYONS?

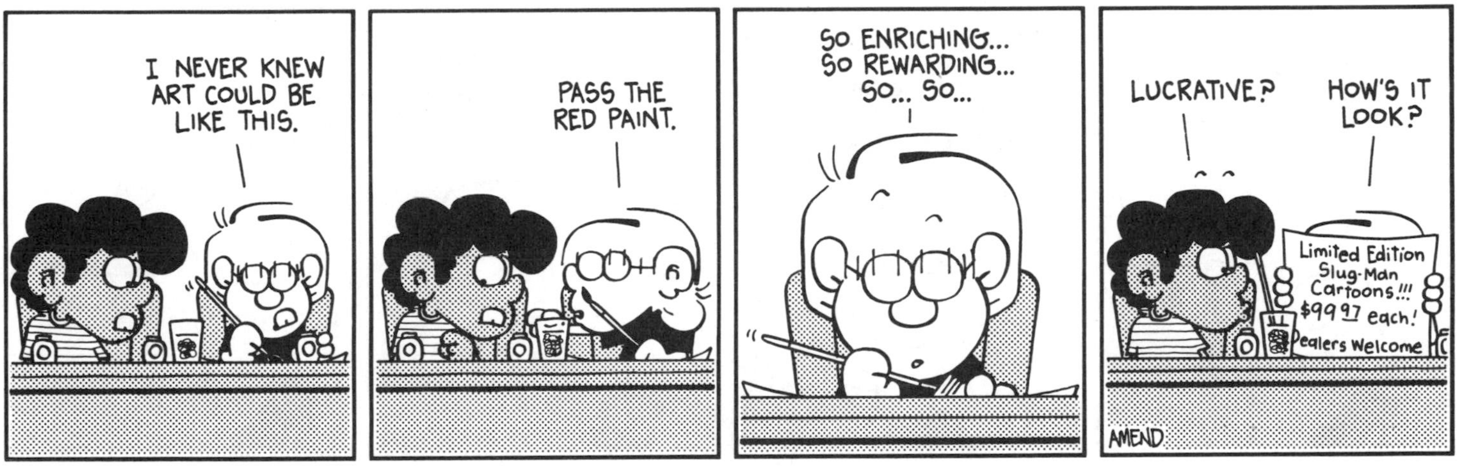
I NEVER KNEW ART COULD BE LIKE THIS.
PASS THE RED PAINT.
SO ENRICHING... SO REWARDING... SO... SO...
LUCRATIVE?
HOW'S IT LOOK?
Limited Edition Slug-Man Cartoons!!! $99.97 each! Dealers Welcome
AMEND

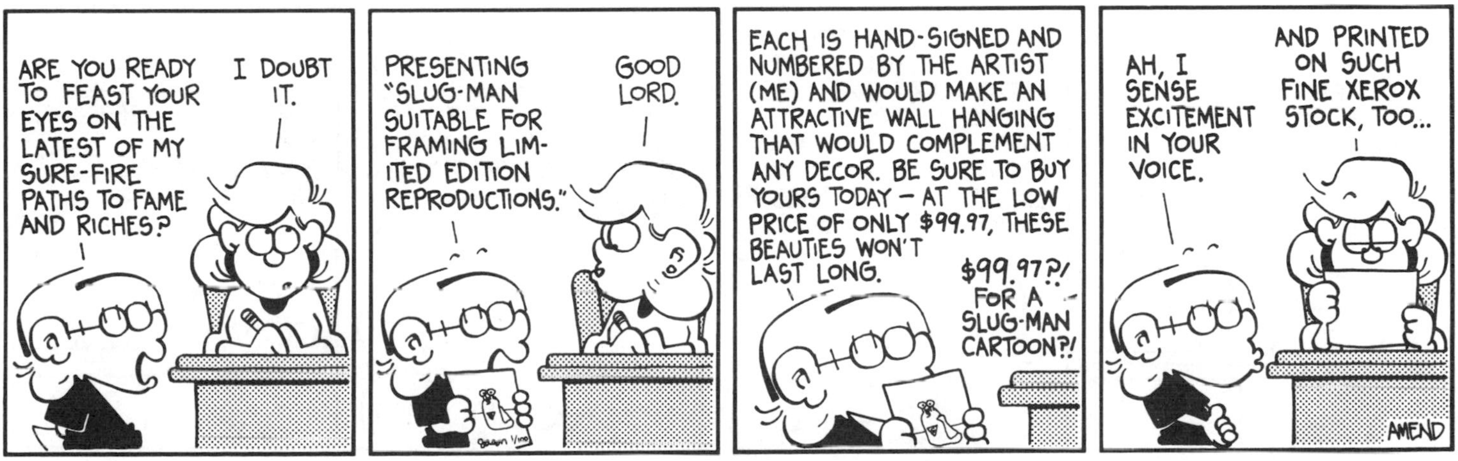
ARE YOU READY TO FEAST YOUR EYES ON THE LATEST OF MY SURE-FIRE PATHS TO FAME AND RICHES?
I DOUBT IT.
PRESENTING "SLUG-MAN SUITABLE FOR FRAMING LIMITED EDITION REPRODUCTIONS."
GOOD LORD.
EACH IS HAND-SIGNED AND NUMBERED BY THE ARTIST (ME) AND WOULD MAKE AN ATTRACTIVE WALL HANGING THAT WOULD COMPLEMENT ANY DECOR. BE SURE TO BUY YOURS TODAY – AT THE LOW PRICE OF ONLY $99.97, THESE BEAUTIES WON'T LAST LONG.
$99.97?! FOR A SLUG-MAN CARTOON?!
AH, I SENSE EXCITEMENT IN YOUR VOICE.
AND PRINTED ON SUCH FINE XEROX STOCK, TOO...
AMEND

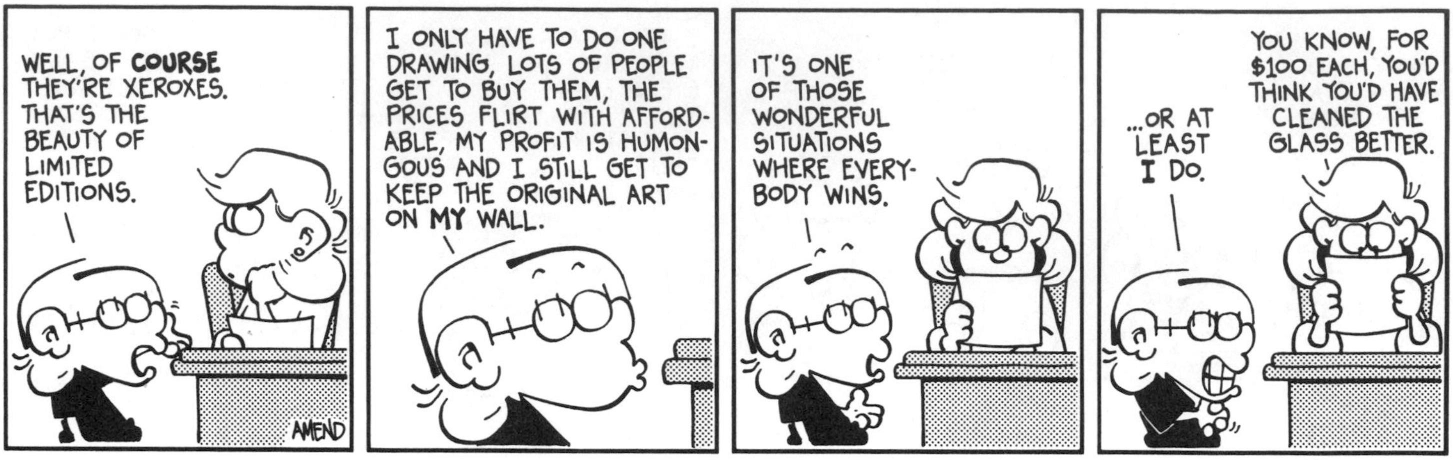

WELL, OF **COURSE** THEY'RE XEROXES. THAT'S THE BEAUTY OF LIMITED EDITIONS.
I ONLY HAVE TO DO ONE DRAWING, LOTS OF PEOPLE GET TO BUY THEM, THE PRICES FLIRT WITH AFFORDABLE, MY PROFIT IS HUMONGOUS AND I STILL GET TO KEEP THE ORIGINAL ART ON **MY** WALL.
IT'S ONE OF THOSE WONDERFUL SITUATIONS WHERE EVERYBODY WINS.
...OR AT LEAST **I** DO.
YOU KNOW, FOR $100 EACH, YOU'D THINK YOU'D HAVE CLEANED THE GLASS BETTER.
AMEND

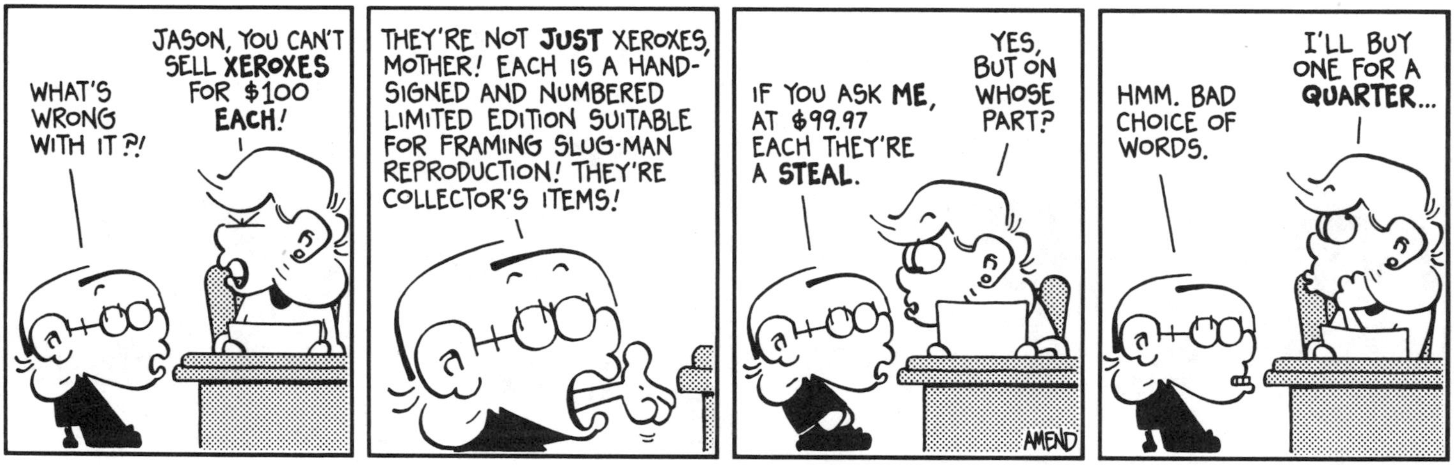

WHAT'S WRONG WITH IT?!
JASON, YOU CAN'T SELL **XEROXES** FOR $100 **EACH**!
THEY'RE NOT **JUST** XEROXES, MOTHER! EACH IS A HAND-SIGNED AND NUMBERED LIMITED EDITION SUITABLE FOR FRAMING SLUG-MAN REPRODUCTION! THEY'RE COLLECTOR'S ITEMS!
IF YOU ASK **ME**, AT $99.97 EACH THEY'RE A **STEAL**.
YES, BUT ON WHOSE PART?
HMM. BAD CHOICE OF WORDS.
I'LL BUY ONE FOR A **QUARTER**...
AMEND

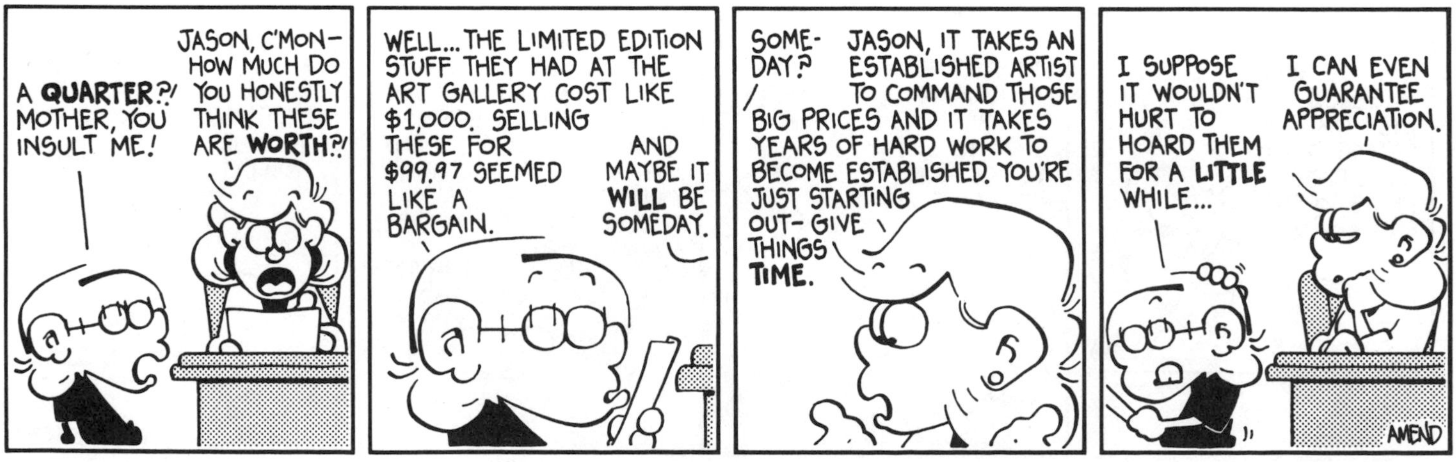

A **QUARTER**?! MOTHER, YOU INSULT ME!
JASON, C'MON— HOW MUCH DO YOU HONESTLY THINK THESE ARE **WORTH**?!
WELL... THE LIMITED EDITION STUFF THEY HAD AT THE ART GALLERY COST LIKE $1,000. SELLING THESE FOR $99.97 SEEMED LIKE A BARGAIN.
AND MAYBE IT **WILL** BE SOMEDAY.
SOMEDAY?
JASON, IT TAKES AN ESTABLISHED ARTIST TO COMMAND THOSE BIG PRICES AND IT TAKES YEARS OF HARD WORK TO BECOME ESTABLISHED. YOU'RE JUST STARTING OUT– GIVE THINGS **TIME**.
I SUPPOSE IT WOULDN'T HURT TO HOARD THEM FOR A **LITTLE** WHILE...
I CAN EVEN GUARANTEE APPRECIATION.
AMEND

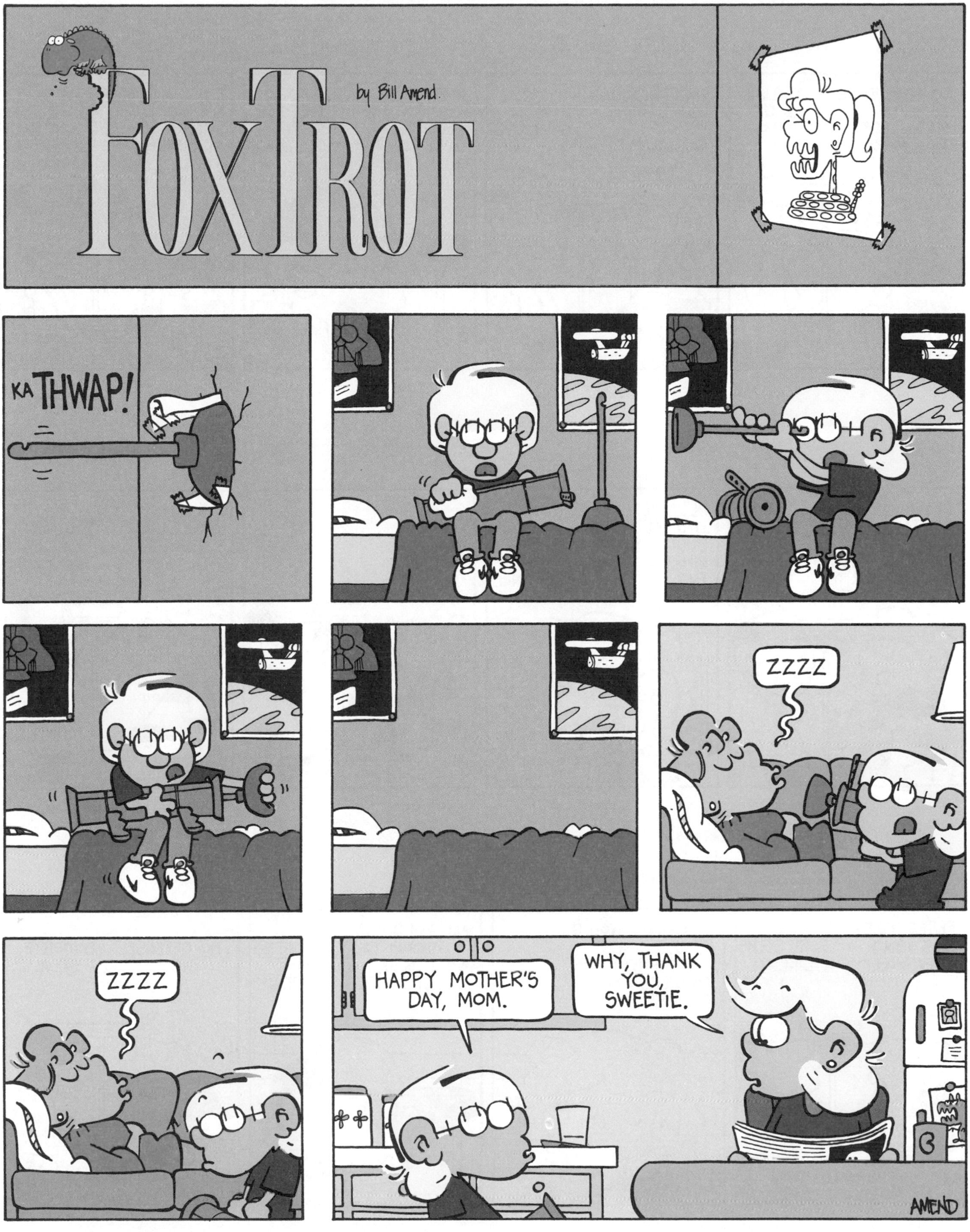
FoxTrot
by Bill Amend.
KA THWAP!
ZZZZ
ZZZZ
HAPPY MOTHER'S DAY, MOM.
WHY, THANK YOU, SWEETIE.
AMEND

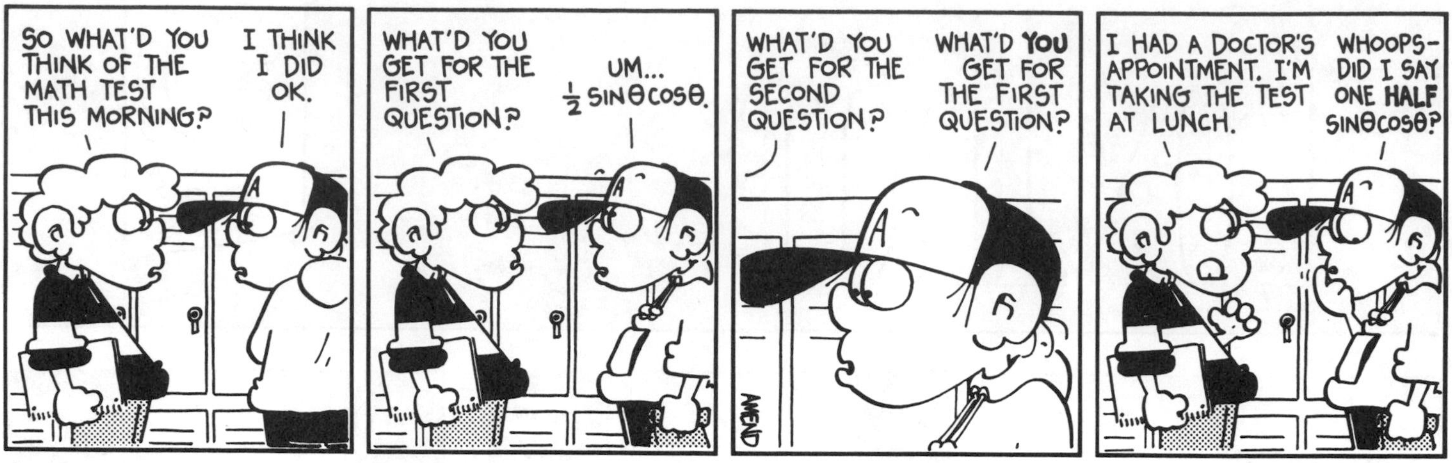
SO WHAT'D YOU THINK OF THE MATH TEST THIS MORNING?
I THINK I DID OK.
WHAT'D YOU GET FOR THE FIRST QUESTION?
UM... $\frac{1}{2}$ SINθCOSθ.
WHAT'D YOU GET FOR THE SECOND QUESTION?
WHAT'D **YOU** GET FOR THE FIRST QUESTION?
AMEND
I HAD A DOCTOR'S APPOINTMENT. I'M TAKING THE TEST AT LUNCH.
WHOOPS- DID I SAY ONE **HALF** SINθCOSθ?

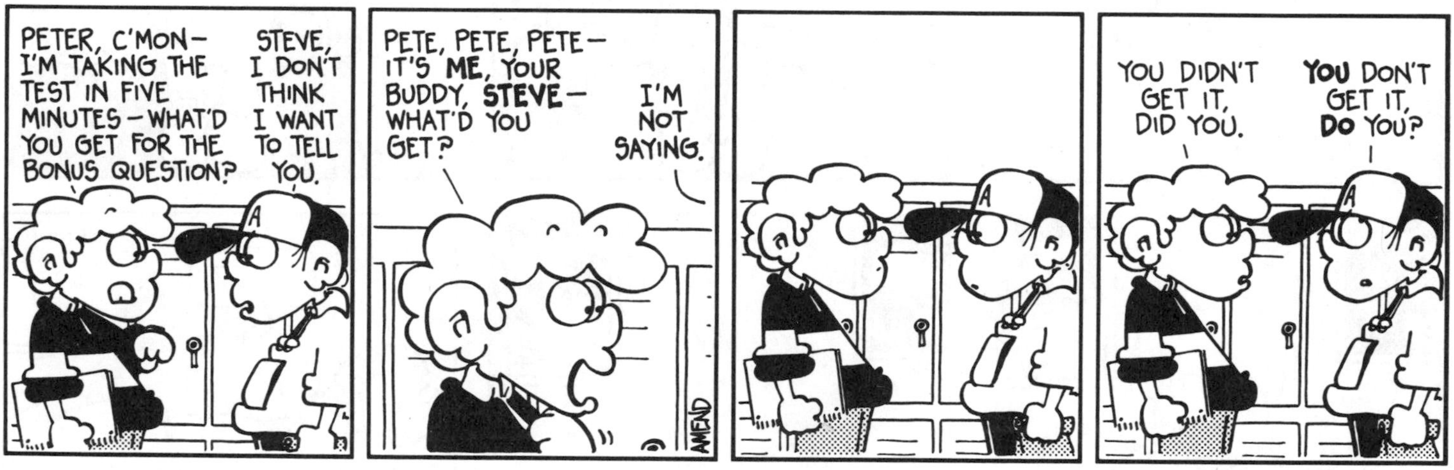
PETER, C'MON- I'M TAKING THE TEST IN FIVE MINUTES-WHAT'D YOU GET FOR THE BONUS QUESTION?
STEVE, I DON'T THINK I WANT TO TELL YOU.
PETE, PETE, PETE- IT'S **ME**, YOUR BUDDY, **STEVE**- WHAT'D YOU GET?
I'M NOT SAYING.
AMEND
YOU DIDN'T GET IT, DID YOU.
YOU DON'T GET IT, **DO** YOU?

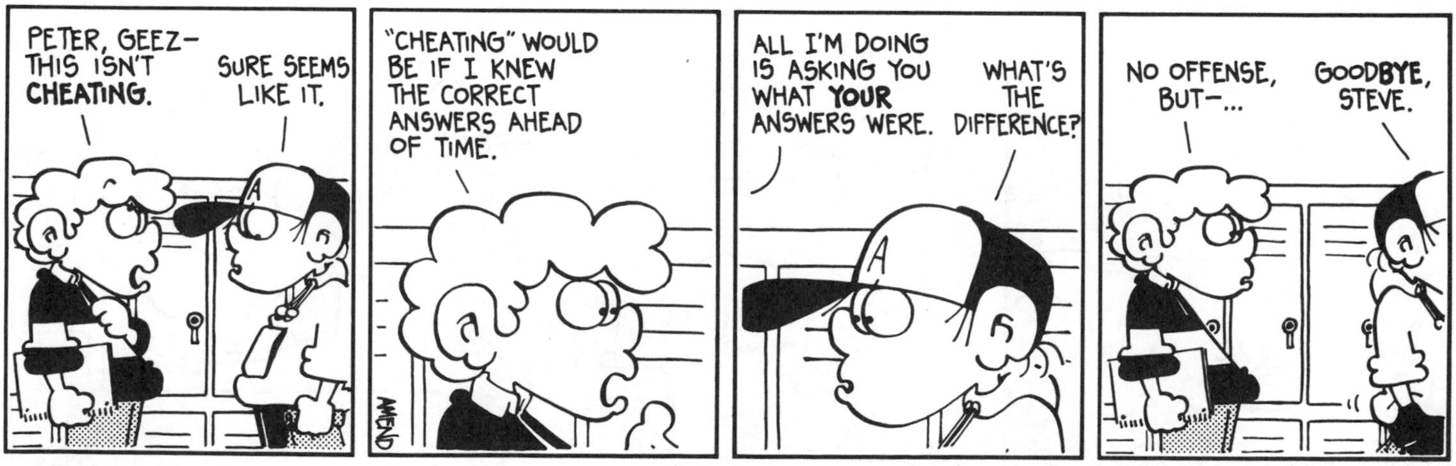
PETER, GEEZ- THIS ISN'T **CHEATING**.
SURE SEEMS LIKE IT.
"CHEATING" WOULD BE IF I KNEW THE CORRECT ANSWERS AHEAD OF TIME.
AMEND
ALL I'M DOING IS ASKING YOU WHAT **YOUR** ANSWERS WERE.
WHAT'S THE DIFFERENCE?
NO OFFENSE, BUT-...
GOOD**BYE**, STEVE.

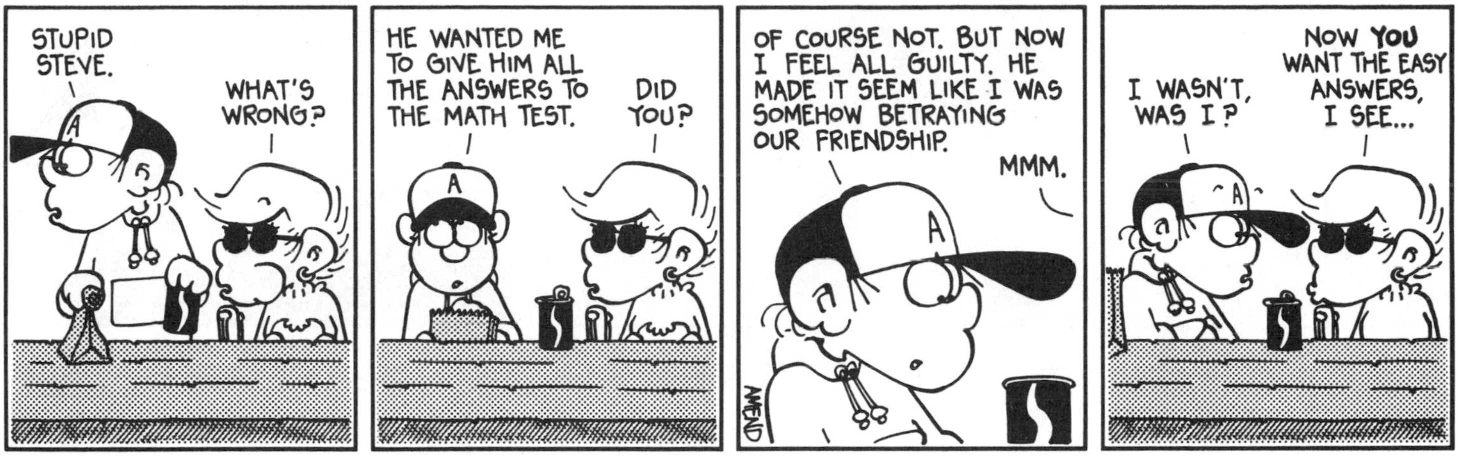
STUPID STEVE.
WHAT'S WRONG?
HE WANTED ME TO GIVE HIM ALL THE ANSWERS TO THE MATH TEST.
DID YOU?
OF COURSE NOT. BUT NOW I FEEL ALL GUILTY. HE MADE IT SEEM LIKE I WAS SOMEHOW BETRAYING OUR FRIENDSHIP.
MMM.
AMEND
I WASN'T, WAS I?
NOW **YOU** WANT THE EASY ANSWERS, I SEE...

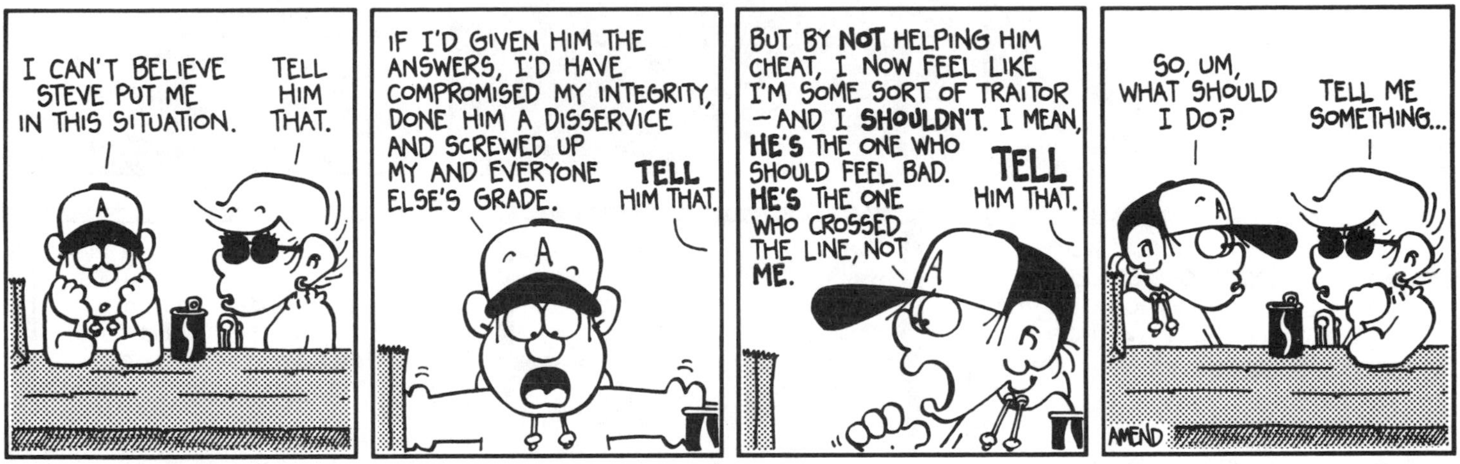
I CAN'T BELIEVE STEVE PUT ME IN THIS SITUATION.
TELL HIM THAT.
IF I'D GIVEN HIM THE ANSWERS, I'D HAVE COMPROMISED MY INTEGRITY, DONE HIM A DISSERVICE AND SCREWED UP MY AND EVERYONE ELSE'S GRADE.
TELL HIM THAT.
BUT BY **NOT** HELPING HIM CHEAT, I NOW FEEL LIKE I'M SOME SORT OF TRAITOR —AND I **SHOULDN'T**. I MEAN, **HE'S** THE ONE WHO SHOULD FEEL BAD. **HE'S** THE ONE WHO CROSSED THE LINE, NOT **ME**.
TELL HIM THAT.
SO, UM, WHAT SHOULD I DO?
TELL ME SOMETHING...
AMEND

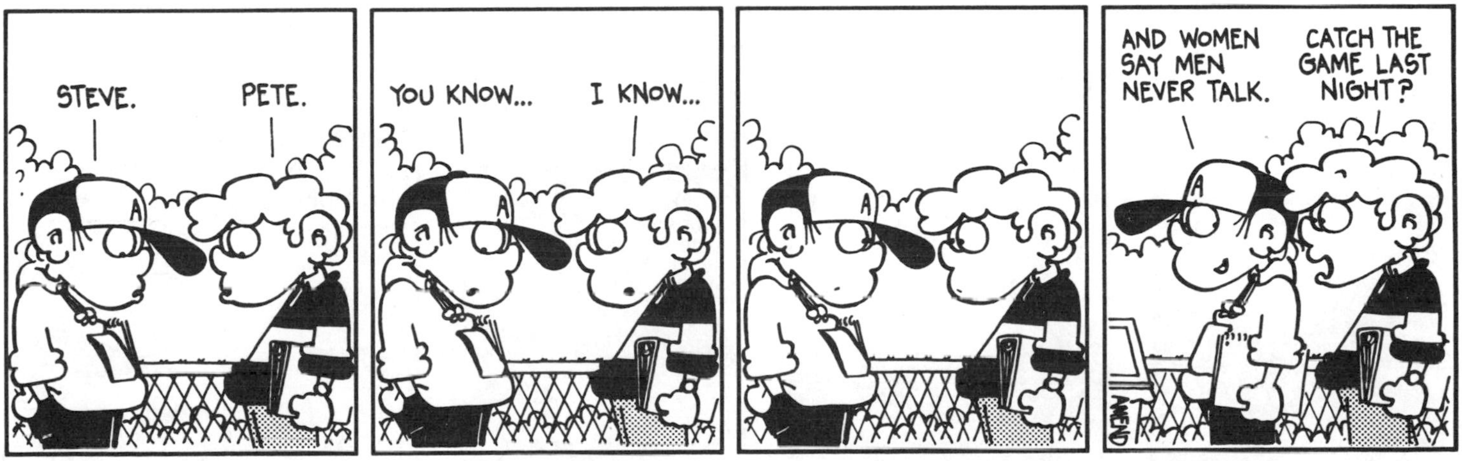
STEVE.
PETE.
YOU KNOW...
I KNOW...
AND WOMEN SAY MEN NEVER TALK.
CATCH THE GAME LAST NIGHT?
AMEND

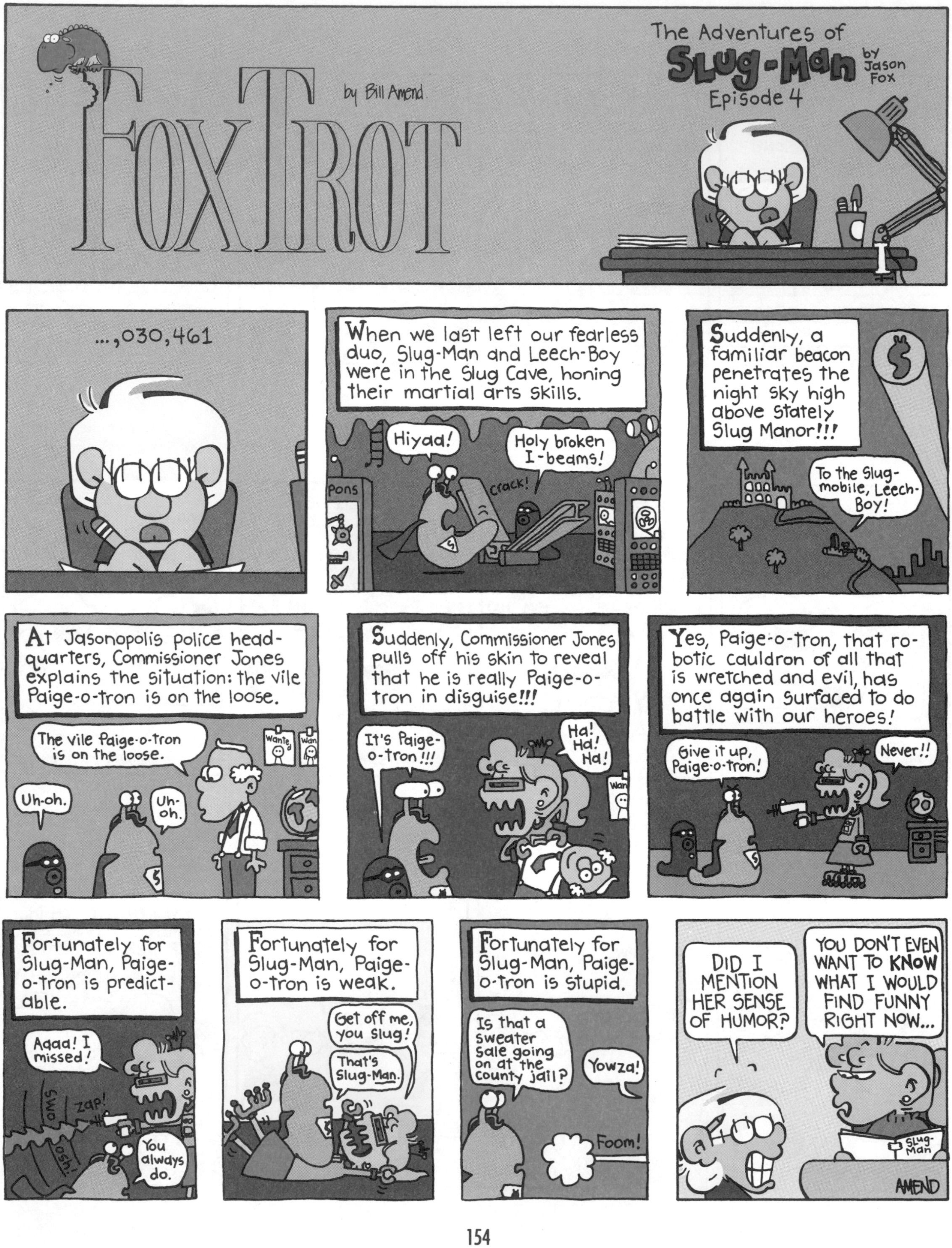
FoxTrot
by Bill Amend.
The Adventures of
Slug-Man
by Jason Fox
Episode 4
...,030,461
When we last left our fearless duo, Slug-Man and Leech-Boy were in the Slug Cave, honing their martial arts skills.
Hiyaa!
Holy broken I-beams!
Crack!
Suddenly, a familiar beacon penetrates the night sky high above stately Slug Manor!!!
To the Slug-mobile, Leech-Boy!
At Jasonopolis police head-quarters, Commissioner Jones explains the situation: the vile Paige-o-tron is on the loose.
The vile Paige-o-tron is on the loose.
Uh-oh.
Uh-oh.
Suddenly, Commissioner Jones pulls off his skin to reveal that he is really Paige-o-tron in disguise!!!
It's Paige-o-tron!!!
Ha! Ha! Ha!
Yes, Paige-o-tron, that robotic cauldron of all that is wretched and evil, has once again surfaced to do battle with our heroes!
Give it up, Paige-o-tron!
Never!!
Fortunately for Slug-Man, Paige-o-tron is predictable.
Aaaa! I missed!
Zap!
You always do.
Fortunately for Slug-Man, Paige-o-tron is weak.
Get off me, you slug!
That's Slug-Man.
Fortunately for Slug-Man, Paige-o-tron is stupid.
Is that a sweater sale going on at the county jail?
Yowza!
Foom!
DID I MENTION HER SENSE OF HUMOR?
YOU DON'T EVEN WANT TO KNOW WHAT I WOULD FIND FUNNY RIGHT NOW...
Slug-Man
AMEND

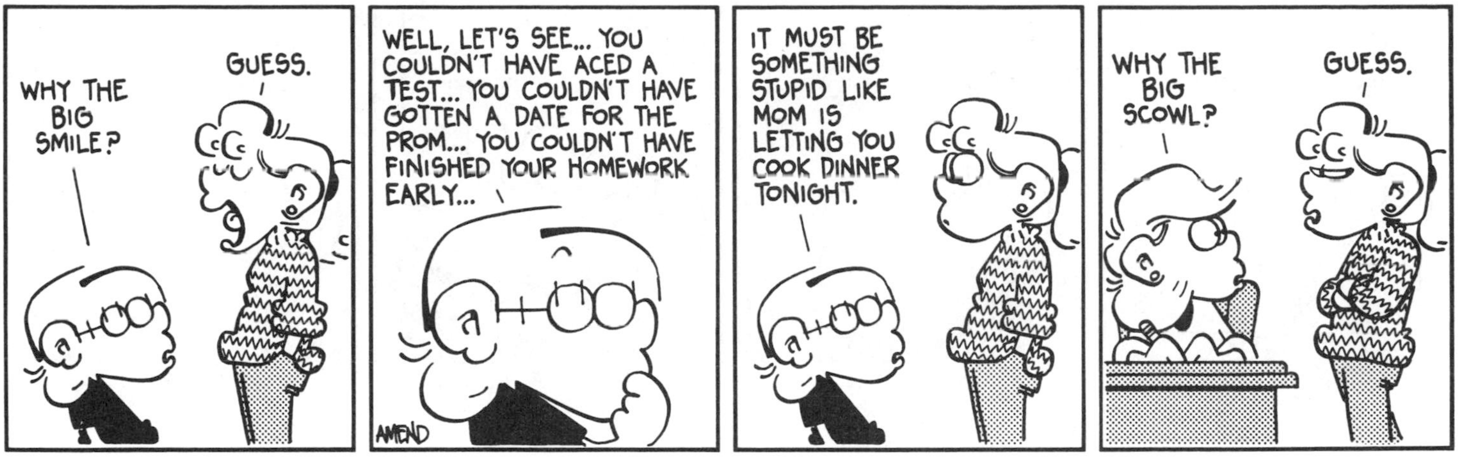
WHY THE BIG SMILE?
GUESS.
WELL, LET'S SEE... YOU COULDN'T HAVE ACED A TEST... YOU COULDN'T HAVE GOTTEN A DATE FOR THE PROM... YOU COULDN'T HAVE FINISHED YOUR HOMEWORK EARLY...
AMEND
IT MUST BE SOMETHING STUPID LIKE MOM IS LETTING YOU COOK DINNER TONIGHT.
WHY THE BIG SCOWL?
GUESS.

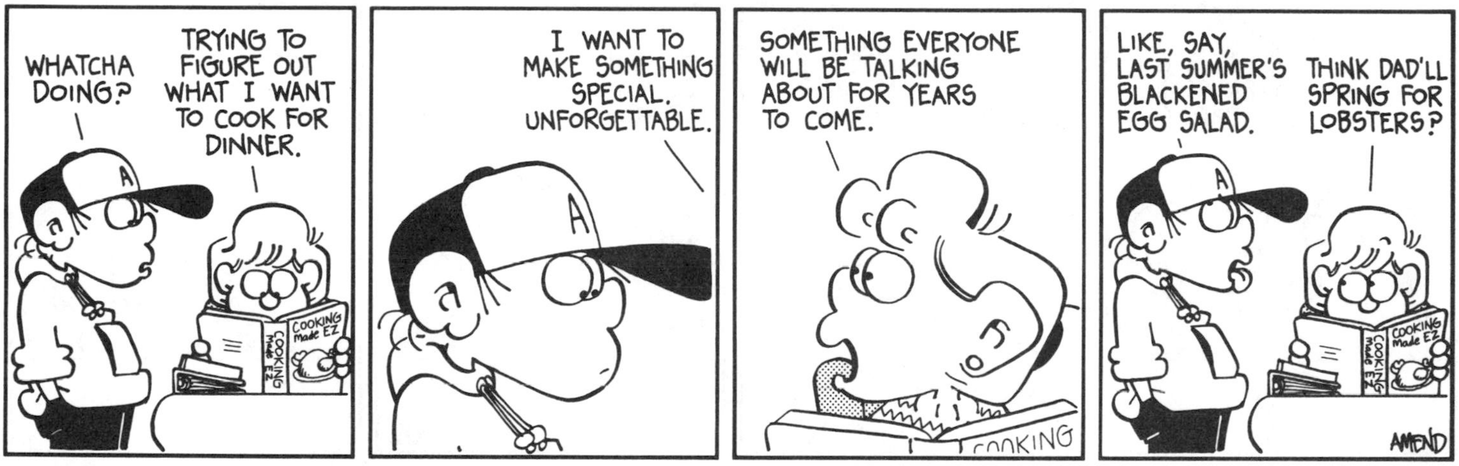
WHATCHA DOING?
TRYING TO FIGURE OUT WHAT I WANT TO COOK FOR DINNER.
COOKING Made EZ
I WANT TO MAKE SOMETHING SPECIAL. UNFORGETTABLE.
SOMETHING EVERYONE WILL BE TALKING ABOUT FOR YEARS TO COME.
COOKING
LIKE, SAY, LAST SUMMER'S BLACKENED EGG SALAD.
THINK DAD'LL SPRING FOR LOBSTERS?
COOKING Made EZ
AMEND

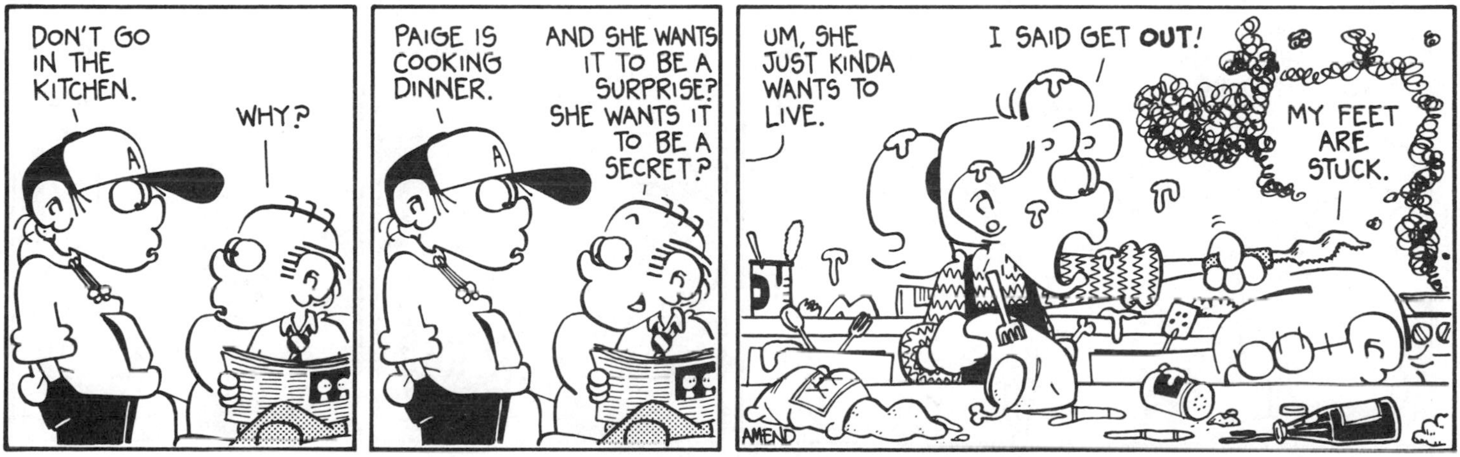
DON'T GO IN THE KITCHEN.
WHY?
PAIGE IS COOKING DINNER.
AND SHE WANTS IT TO BE A SURPRISE? SHE WANTS IT TO BE A SECRET?
UM, SHE JUST KINDA WANTS TO LIVE.
I SAID GET **OUT**!
MY FEET ARE STUCK.
AMEND

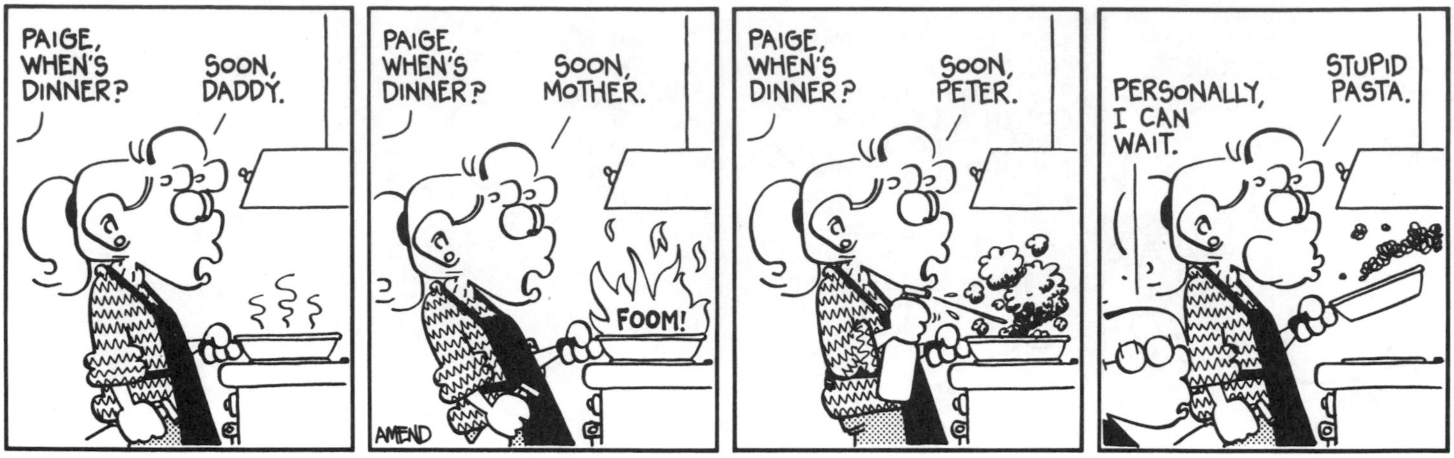
PAIGE, WHEN'S DINNER?
SOON, DADDY.
PAIGE, WHEN'S DINNER?
SOON, MOTHER.
FOOM!
AMEND
PAIGE, WHEN'S DINNER?
SOON, PETER.
PERSONALLY, I CAN WAIT.
STUPID PASTA.

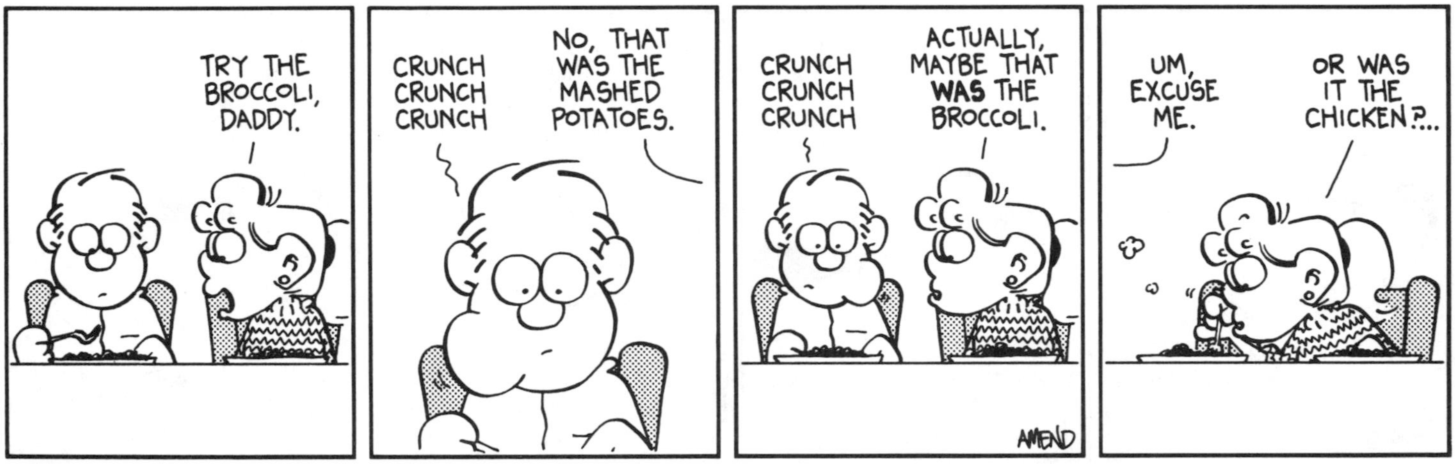
TRY THE BROCCOLI, DADDY.
CRUNCH CRUNCH CRUNCH
NO, THAT WAS THE MASHED POTATOES.
CRUNCH CRUNCH CRUNCH
ACTUALLY, MAYBE THAT **WAS** THE BROCCOLI.
AMEND
UM, EXCUSE ME.
OR WAS IT THE CHICKEN?...

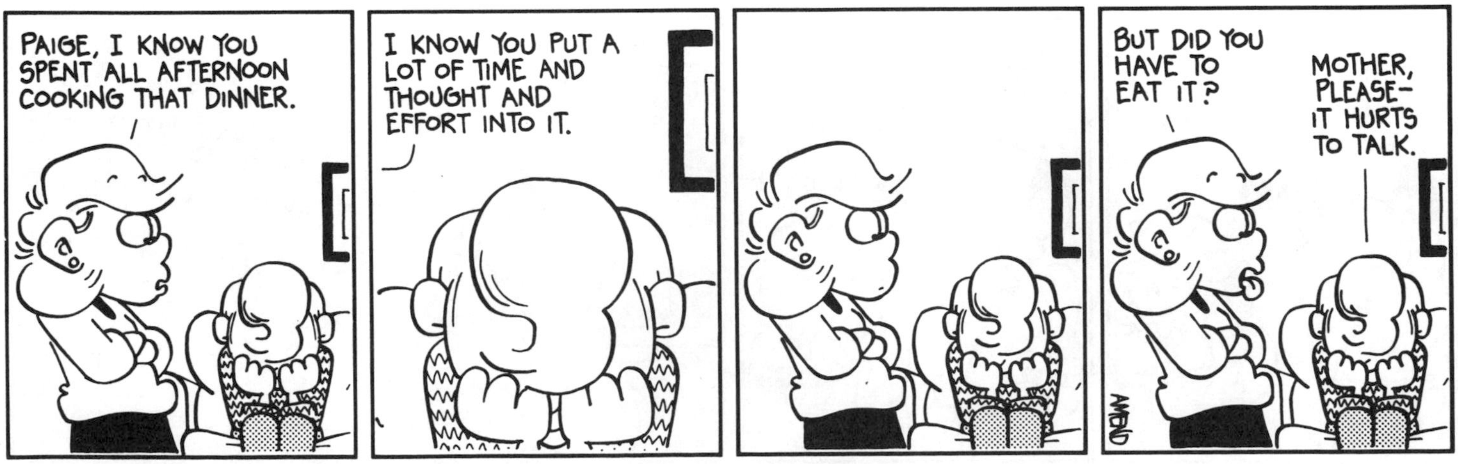
PAIGE, I KNOW YOU SPENT ALL AFTERNOON COOKING THAT DINNER.
I KNOW YOU PUT A LOT OF TIME AND THOUGHT AND EFFORT INTO IT.
AMEND
BUT DID YOU HAVE TO EAT IT?
MOTHER, PLEASE- IT HURTS TO TALK.

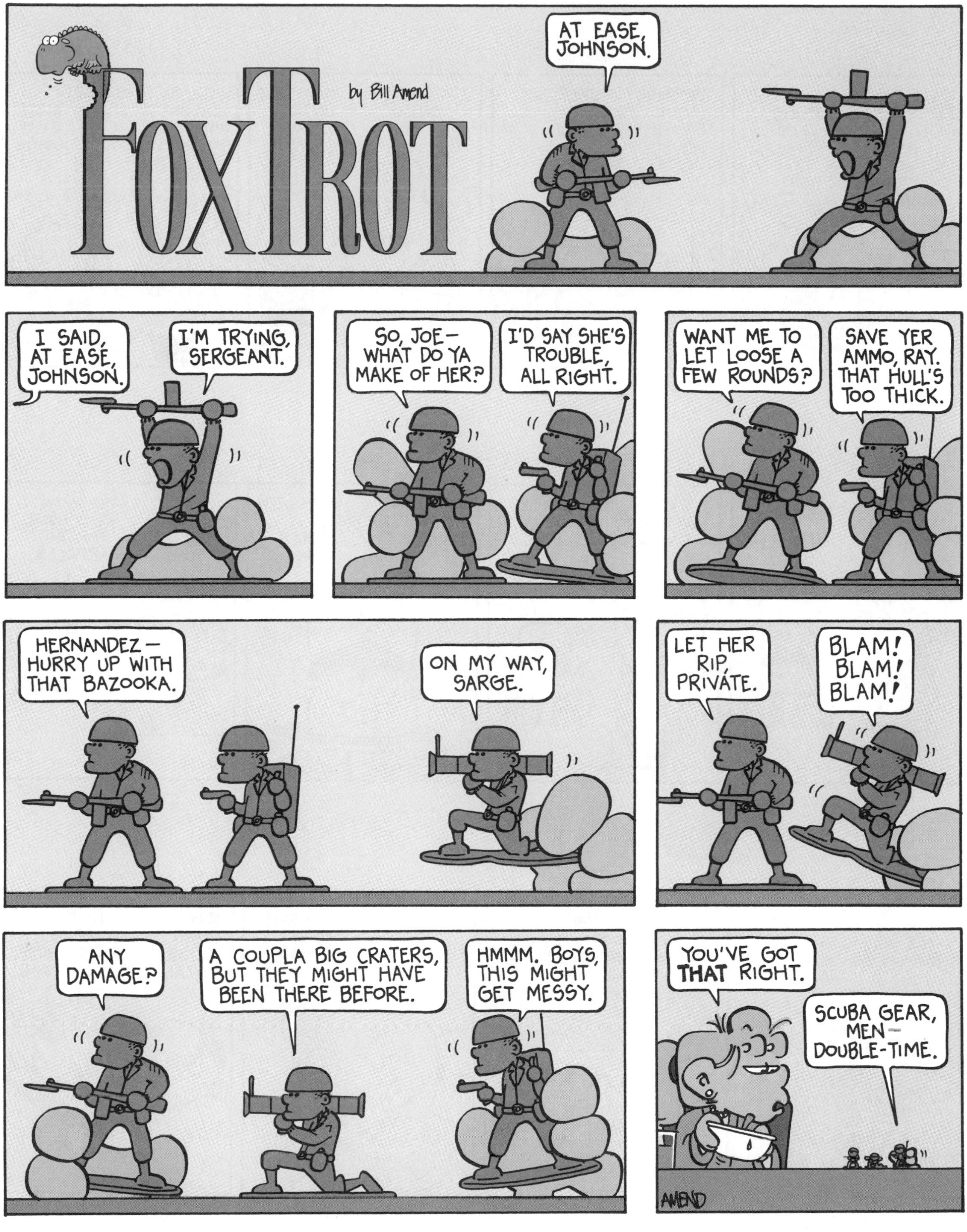
FoxTrot
by Bill Amend
AT EASE, JOHNSON.
I SAID, AT EASE, JOHNSON.
I'M TRYING, SERGEANT.
SO, JOE– WHAT DO YA MAKE OF HER?
I'D SAY SHE'S TROUBLE, ALL RIGHT.
WANT ME TO LET LOOSE A FEW ROUNDS?
SAVE YER AMMO, RAY. THAT HULL'S TOO THICK.
HERNANDEZ– HURRY UP WITH THAT BAZOOKA.
ON MY WAY, SARGE.
LET HER RIP, PRIVATE.
BLAM! BLAM! BLAM!
ANY DAMAGE?
A COUPLA BIG CRATERS, BUT THEY MIGHT HAVE BEEN THERE BEFORE.
HMMM. BOYS, THIS MIGHT GET MESSY.
YOU'VE GOT **THAT** RIGHT.
SCUBA GEAR, MEN– DOUBLE-TIME.
AMEND

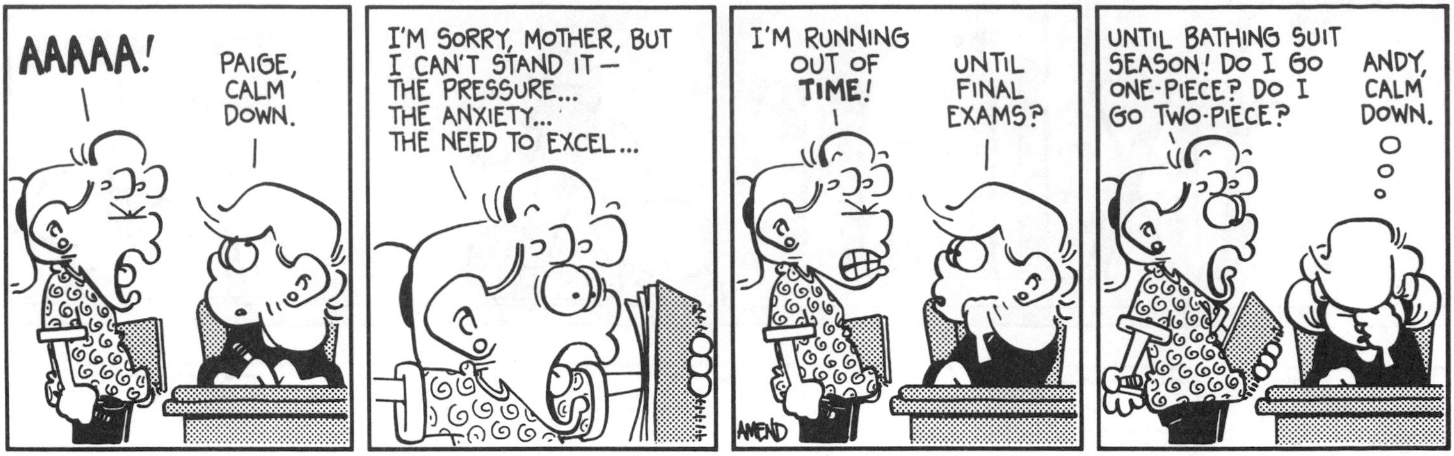
AAAAA!
PAIGE, CALM DOWN.
I'M SORRY, MOTHER, BUT I CAN'T STAND IT — THE PRESSURE... THE ANXIETY... THE NEED TO EXCEL...
I'M RUNNING OUT OF **TIME**!
UNTIL FINAL EXAMS?
UNTIL BATHING SUIT SEASON! DO I GO ONE-PIECE? DO I GO TWO-PIECE?
ANDY, CALM DOWN.
AMEND

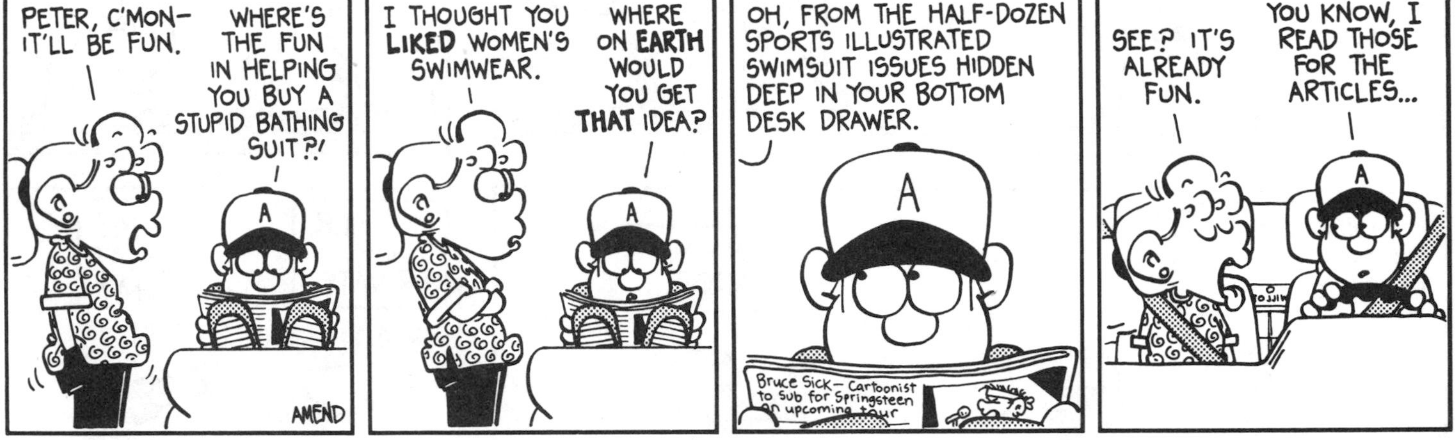
PETER, C'MON— IT'LL BE FUN.
WHERE'S THE FUN IN HELPING YOU BUY A STUPID BATHING SUIT?!
AMEND
I THOUGHT YOU **LIKED** WOMEN'S SWIMWEAR.
WHERE ON **EARTH** WOULD YOU GET **THAT** IDEA?
OH, FROM THE HALF-DOZEN SPORTS ILLUSTRATED SWIMSUIT ISSUES HIDDEN DEEP IN YOUR BOTTOM DESK DRAWER.
Bruce Sick— Cartoonist to Sub for Springsteen
SEE? IT'S ALREADY FUN.
YOU KNOW, I READ THOSE FOR THE ARTICLES...

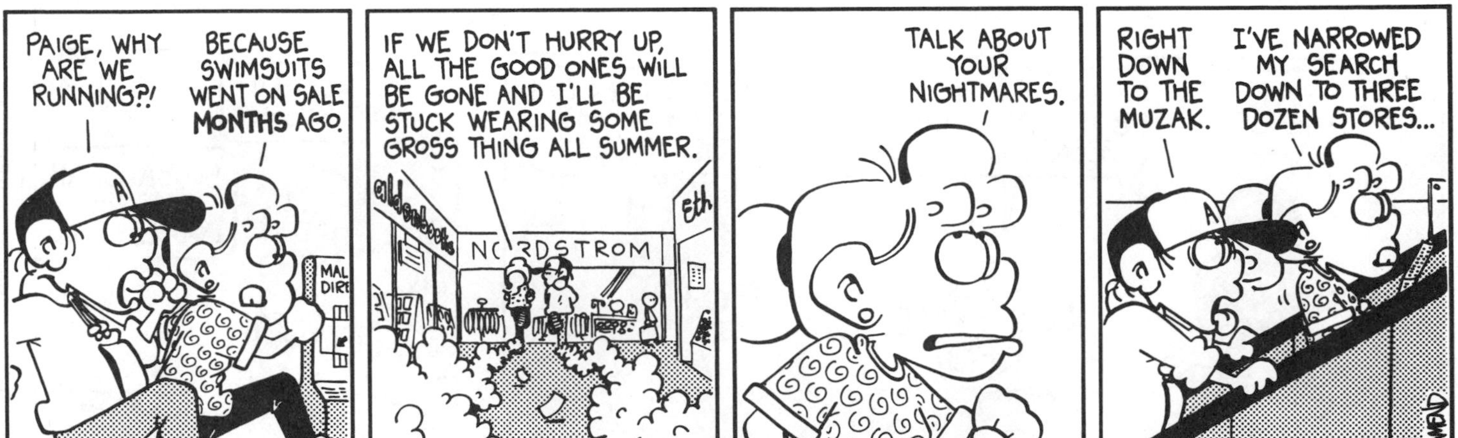
PAIGE, WHY ARE WE RUNNING?!
BECAUSE SWIMSUITS WENT ON SALE **MONTHS** AGO.
IF WE DON'T HURRY UP, ALL THE GOOD ONES WILL BE GONE AND I'LL BE STUCK WEARING SOME GROSS THING ALL SUMMER.
NORDSTROM
TALK ABOUT YOUR NIGHTMARES.
RIGHT DOWN TO THE MUZAK.
I'VE NARROWED MY SEARCH DOWN TO THREE DOZEN STORES...
AMEND

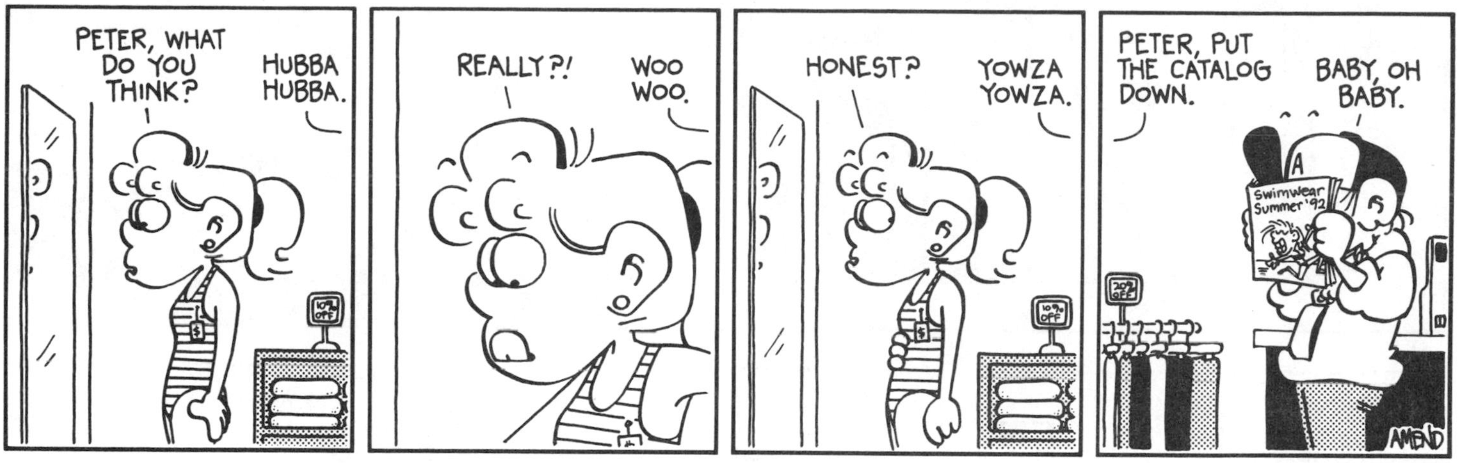
PETER, WHAT DO YOU THINK?
HUBBA HUBBA.
10% OFF
REALLY?!
WOO WOO.
HONEST?
YOWZA YOWZA.
10% OFF
PETER, PUT THE CATALOG DOWN.
BABY, OH BABY.
Swimwear Summer '92
20% OFF
AMEND

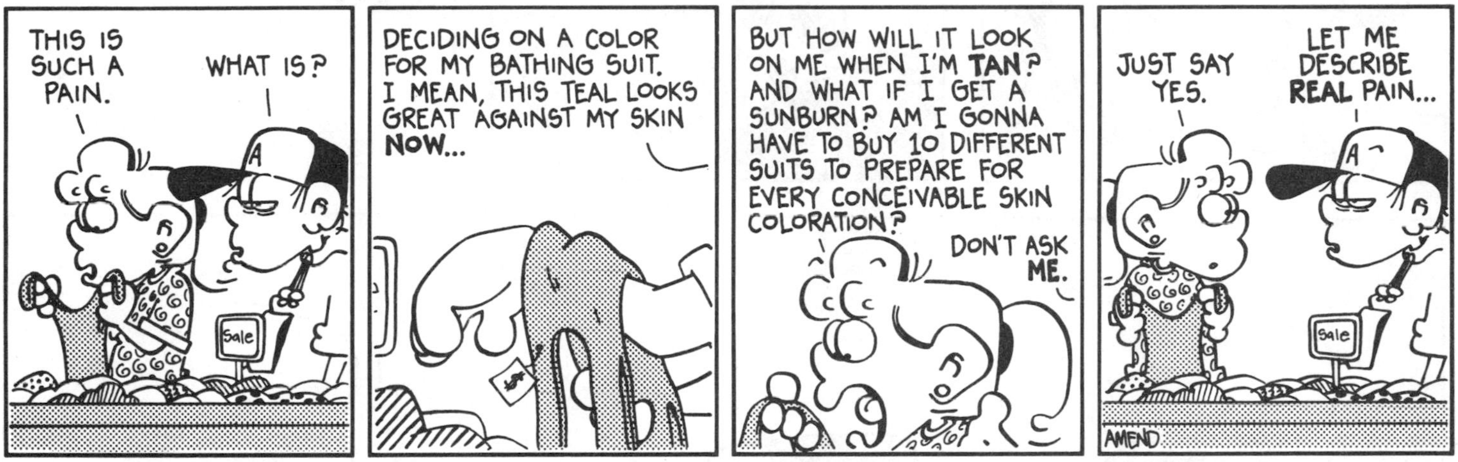
THIS IS SUCH A PAIN.
WHAT IS?
Sale
DECIDING ON A COLOR FOR MY BATHING SUIT. I MEAN, THIS TEAL LOOKS GREAT AGAINST MY SKIN **NOW**...
BUT HOW WILL IT LOOK ON ME WHEN I'M **TAN**? AND WHAT IF I GET A SUNBURN? AM I GONNA HAVE TO BUY 10 DIFFERENT SUITS TO PREPARE FOR EVERY CONCEIVABLE SKIN COLORATION?
DON'T ASK **ME**.
JUST SAY YES.
LET ME DESCRIBE **REAL** PAIN...
Sale
AMEND

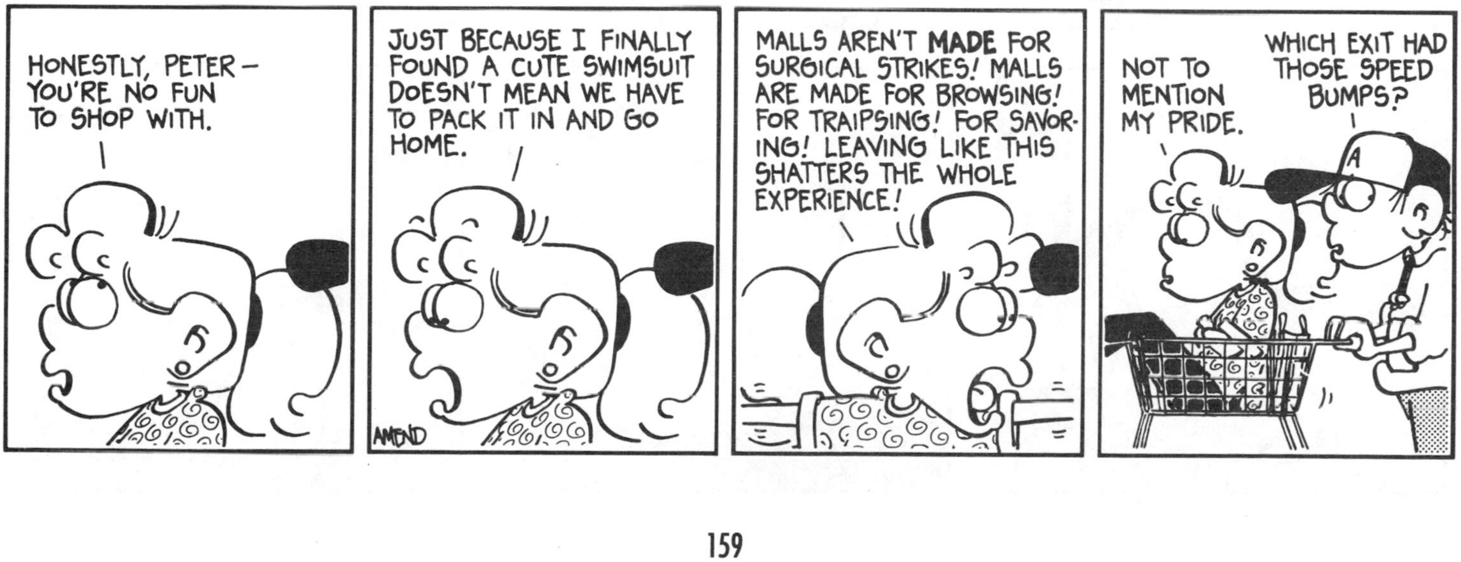
HONESTLY, PETER– YOU'RE NO FUN TO SHOP WITH.
JUST BECAUSE I FINALLY FOUND A CUTE SWIMSUIT DOESN'T MEAN WE HAVE TO PACK IT IN AND GO HOME.
AMEND
MALLS AREN'T **MADE** FOR SURGICAL STRIKES! MALLS ARE MADE FOR BROWSING! FOR TRAIPSING! FOR SAVORING! LEAVING LIKE THIS SHATTERS THE WHOLE EXPERIENCE!
NOT TO MENTION MY PRIDE.
WHICH EXIT HAD THOSE SPEED BUMPS?

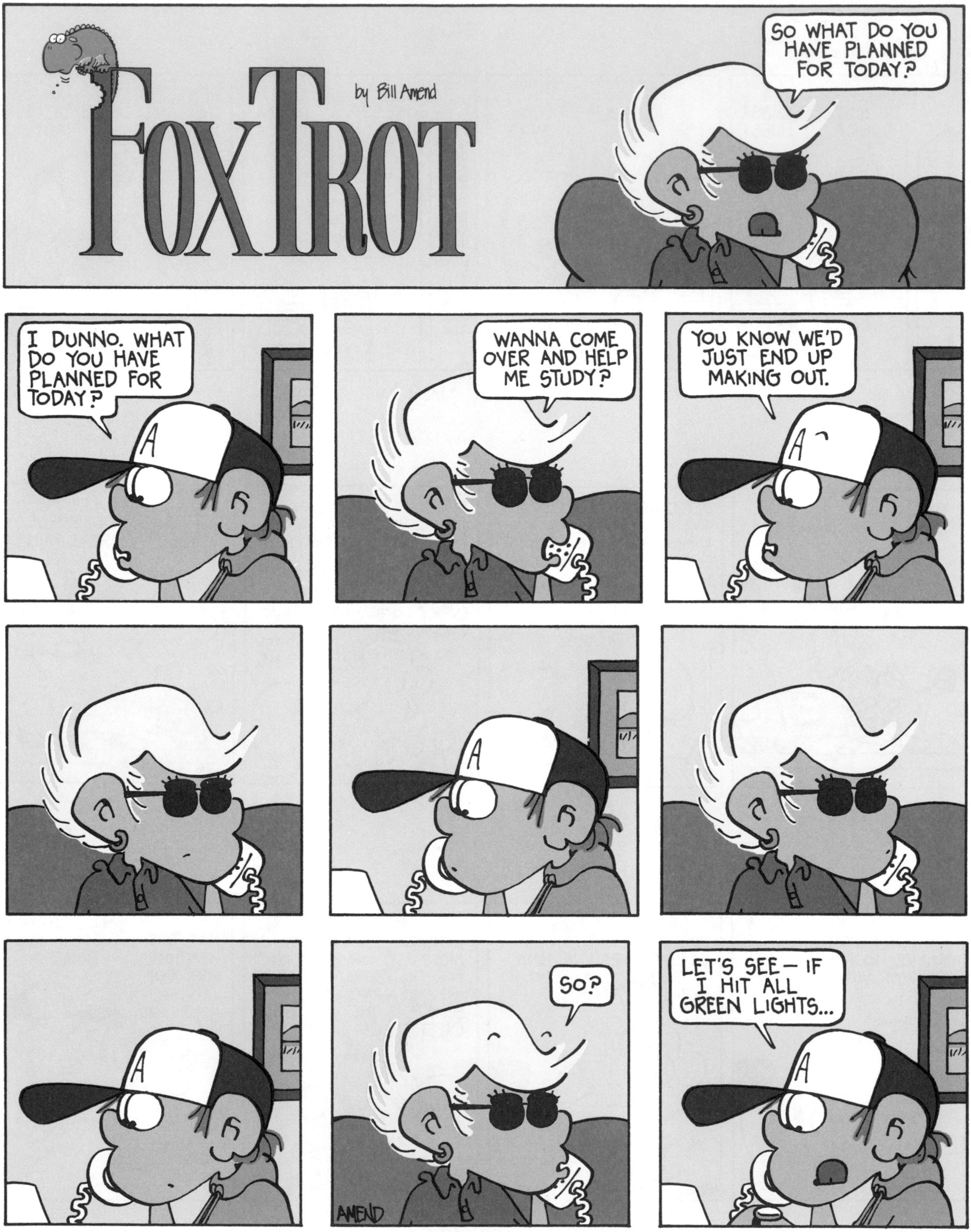

FoxTrot
by Bill Amend
SO WHAT DO YOU HAVE PLANNED FOR TODAY?
I DUNNO. WHAT DO YOU HAVE PLANNED FOR TODAY?
WANNA COME OVER AND HELP ME STUDY?
YOU KNOW WE'D JUST END UP MAKING OUT.
SO?
LET'S SEE– IF I HIT ALL GREEN LIGHTS...
AMEND

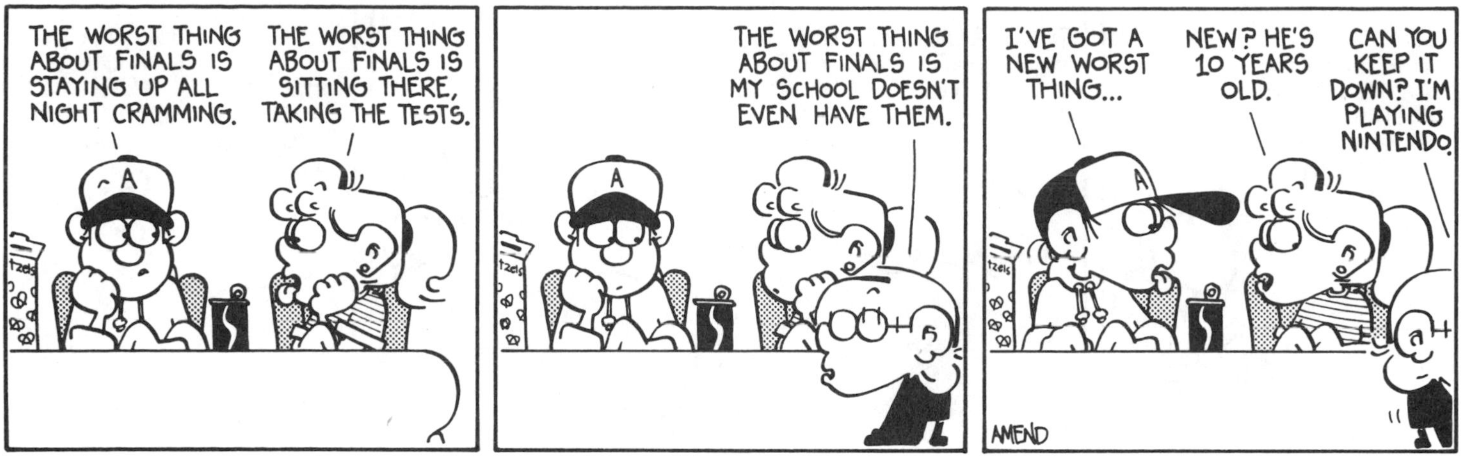
THE WORST THING ABOUT FINALS IS STAYING UP ALL NIGHT CRAMMING.
THE WORST THING ABOUT FINALS IS SITTING THERE, TAKING THE TESTS.
THE WORST THING ABOUT FINALS IS MY SCHOOL DOESN'T EVEN HAVE THEM.
I'VE GOT A NEW WORST THING...
NEW? HE'S 10 YEARS OLD.
CAN YOU KEEP IT DOWN? I'M PLAYING NINTENDO.

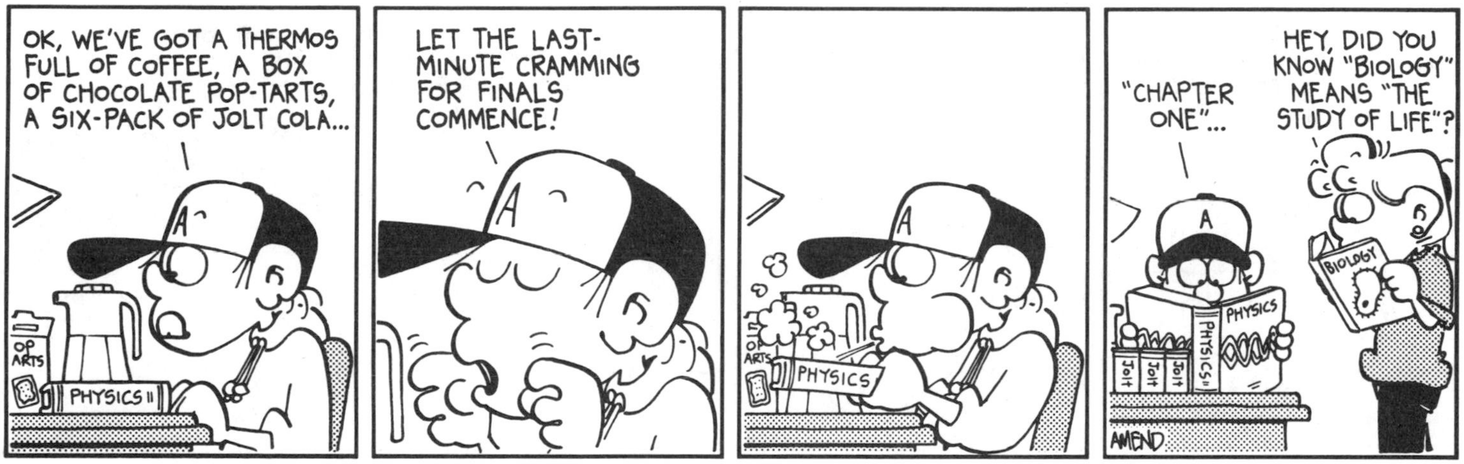
OK, WE'VE GOT A THERMOS FULL OF COFFEE, A BOX OF CHOCOLATE POP-TARTS, A SIX-PACK OF JOLT COLA...
LET THE LAST-MINUTE CRAMMING FOR FINALS COMMENCE!
"CHAPTER ONE"...
HEY, DID YOU KNOW "BIOLOGY" MEANS "THE STUDY OF LIFE"?

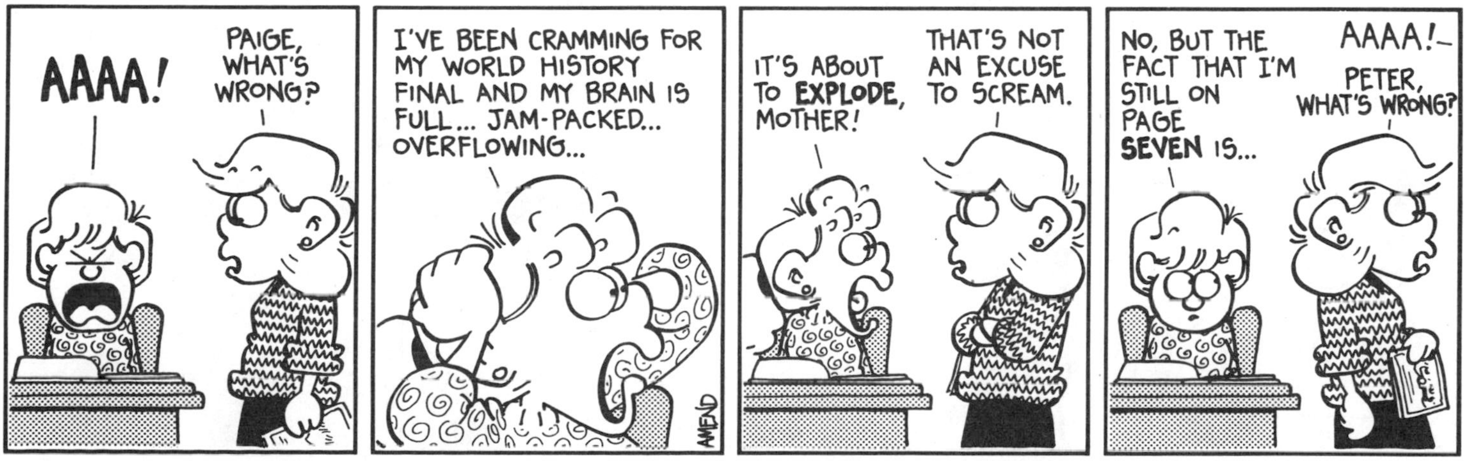
AAAA!
PAIGE, WHAT'S WRONG?
I'VE BEEN CRAMMING FOR MY WORLD HISTORY FINAL AND MY BRAIN IS FULL... JAM-PACKED... OVERFLOWING...
IT'S ABOUT TO EXPLODE, MOTHER!
THAT'S NOT AN EXCUSE TO SCREAM.
NO, BUT THE FACT THAT I'M STILL ON PAGE SEVEN IS...
AAAA!
PETER, WHAT'S WRONG?

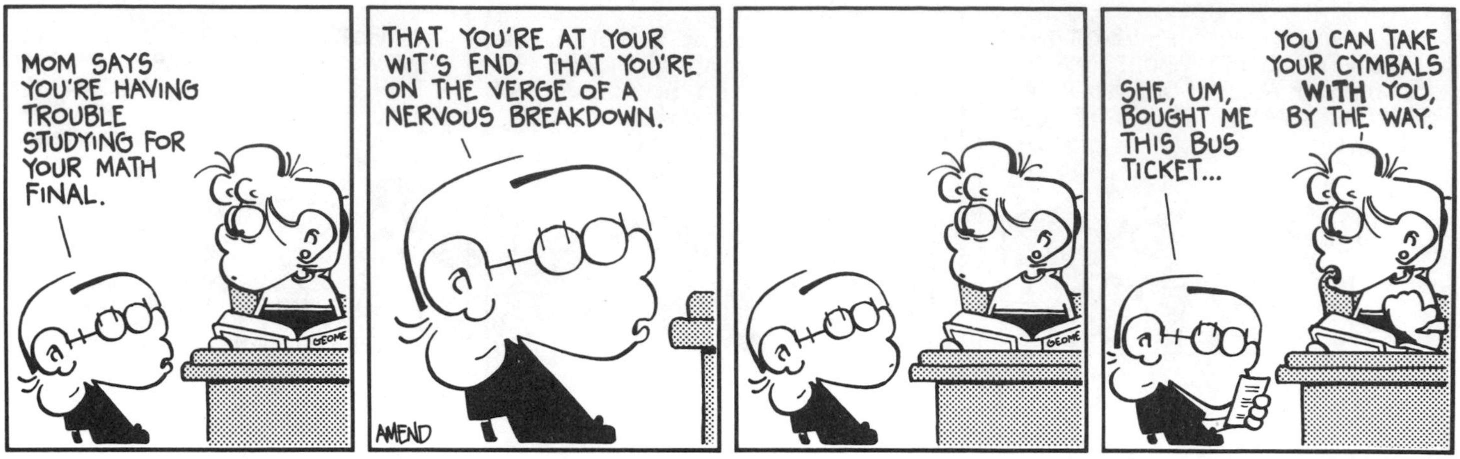
MOM SAYS YOU'RE HAVING TROUBLE STUDYING FOR YOUR MATH FINAL.
THAT YOU'RE AT YOUR WIT'S END. THAT YOU'RE ON THE VERGE OF A NERVOUS BREAKDOWN.
SHE, UM, BOUGHT ME THIS BUS TICKET...
YOU CAN TAKE YOUR CYMBALS WITH YOU, BY THE WAY.
AMEND

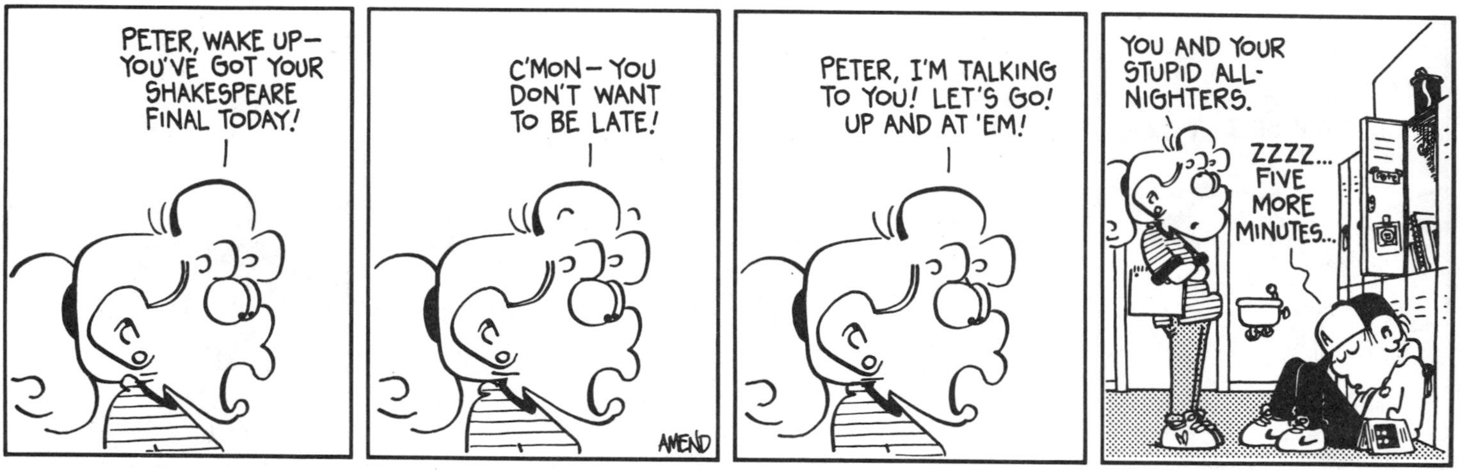
PETER, WAKE UP— YOU'VE GOT YOUR SHAKESPEARE FINAL TODAY!
C'MON— YOU DON'T WANT TO BE LATE!
PETER, I'M TALKING TO YOU! LET'S GO! UP AND AT 'EM!
YOU AND YOUR STUPID ALL-NIGHTERS.
ZZZZ... FIVE MORE MINUTES...
AMEND

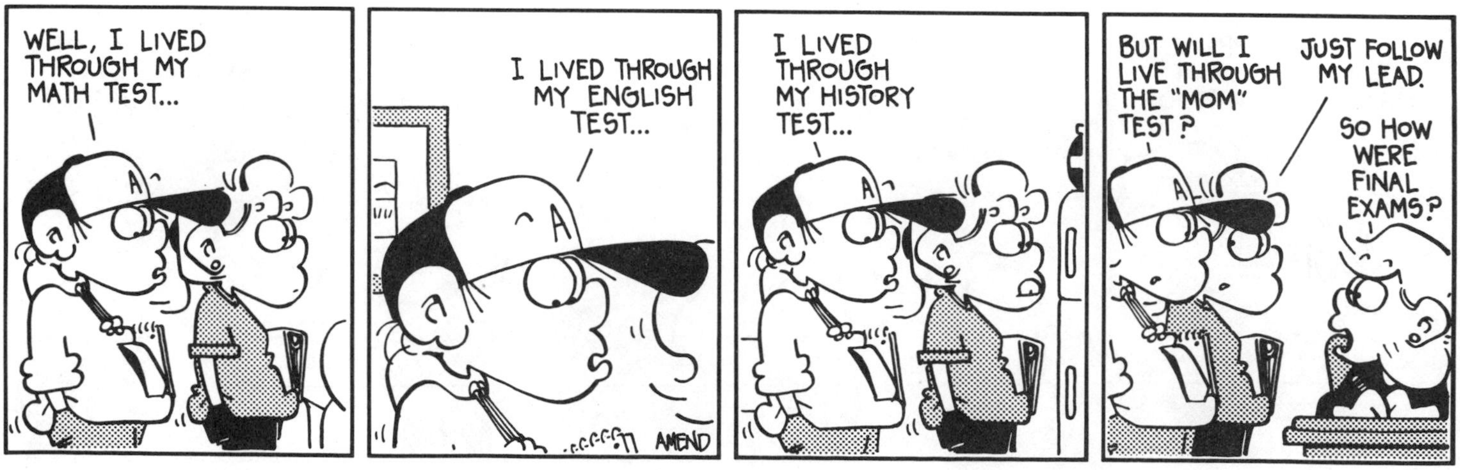
WELL, I LIVED THROUGH MY MATH TEST...
I LIVED THROUGH MY ENGLISH TEST...
I LIVED THROUGH MY HISTORY TEST...
BUT WILL I LIVE THROUGH THE "MOM" TEST?
JUST FOLLOW MY LEAD.
SO HOW WERE FINAL EXAMS?
AMEND

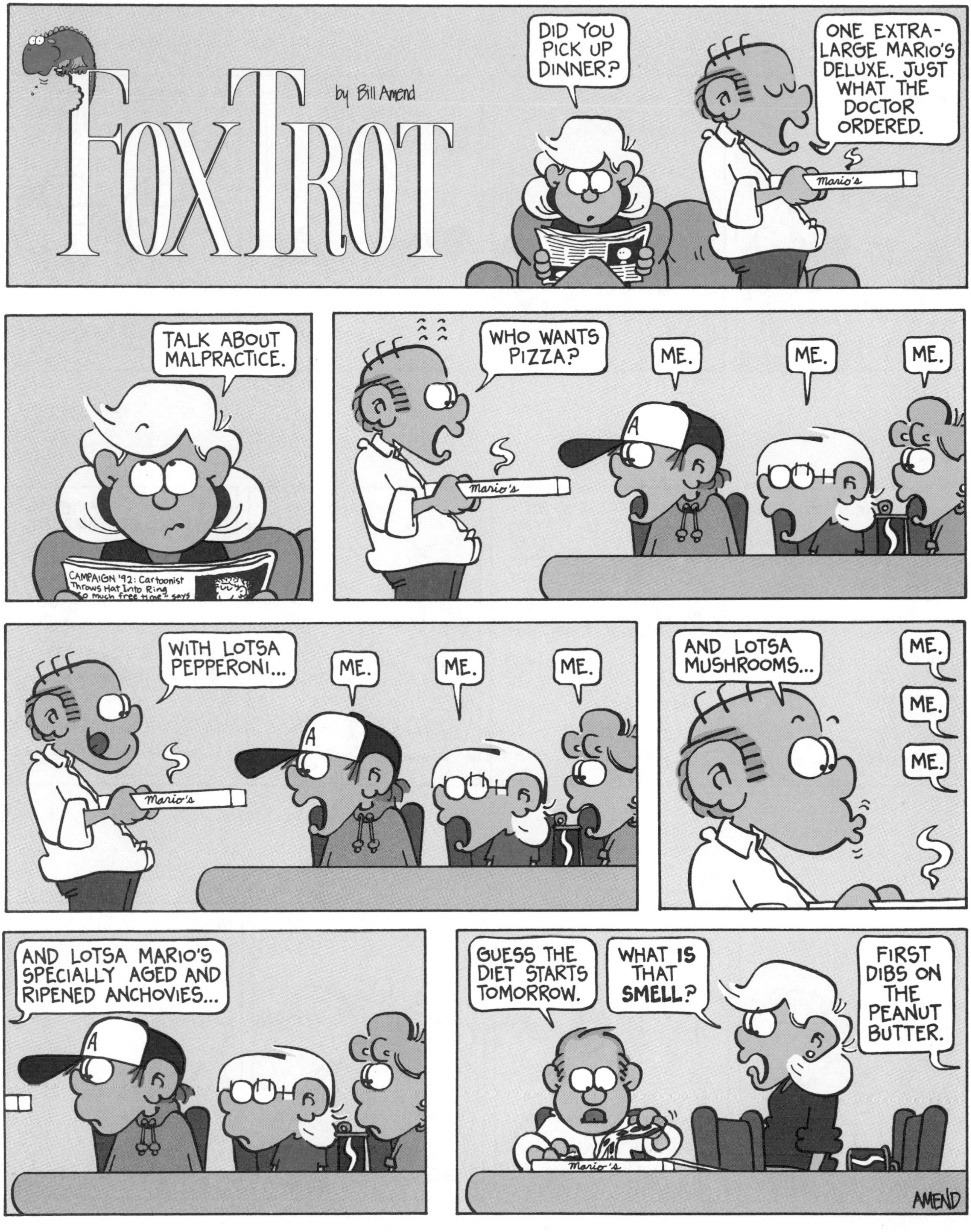
FoxTrot
by Bill Amend
DID YOU PICK UP DINNER?
ONE EXTRA-LARGE MARIO'S DELUXE. JUST WHAT THE DOCTOR ORDERED.
Mario's
TALK ABOUT MALPRACTICE.
CAMPAIGN '92: Cartoonist Throws Hat Into Ring
WHO WANTS PIZZA?
ME.
ME.
ME.
Mario's
WITH LOTSA PEPPERONI...
ME.
ME.
ME.
Mario's
AND LOTSA MUSHROOMS...
ME.
ME.
ME.
AND LOTSA MARIO'S SPECIALLY AGED AND RIPENED ANCHOVIES...
GUESS THE DIET STARTS TOMORROW.
WHAT IS THAT SMELL?
FIRST DIBS ON THE PEANUT BUTTER.
Mario's
AMEND

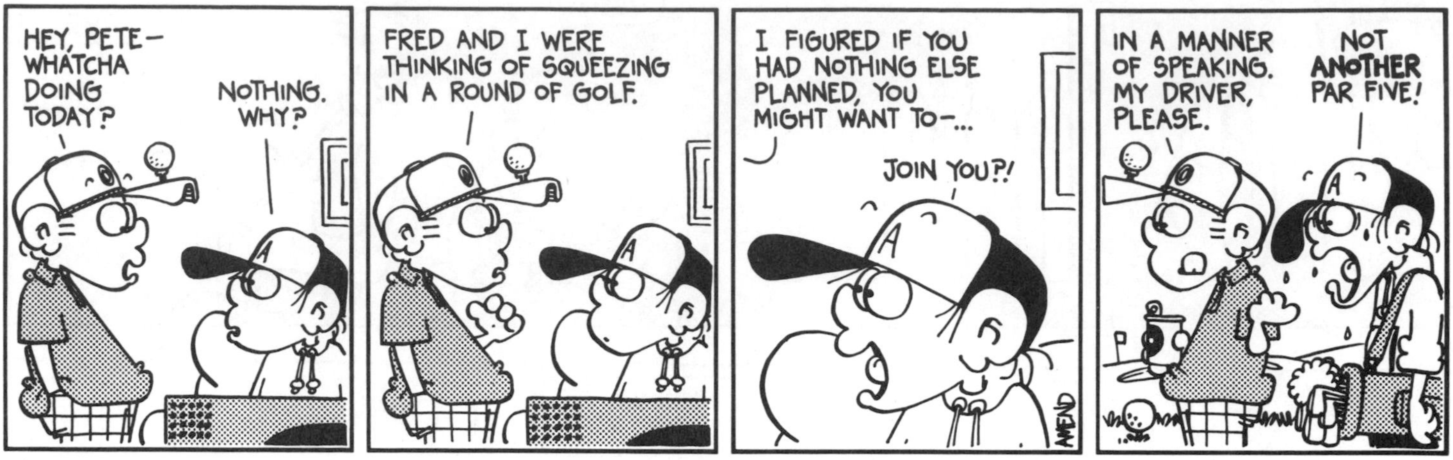
HEY, PETE— WHATCHA DOING TODAY?
NOTHING. WHY?
FRED AND I WERE THINKING OF SQUEEZING IN A ROUND OF GOLF.
I FIGURED IF YOU HAD NOTHING ELSE PLANNED, YOU MIGHT WANT TO—...
JOIN YOU?!
AMEND
IN A MANNER OF SPEAKING. MY DRIVER, PLEASE.
NOT **ANOTHER** PAR FIVE!

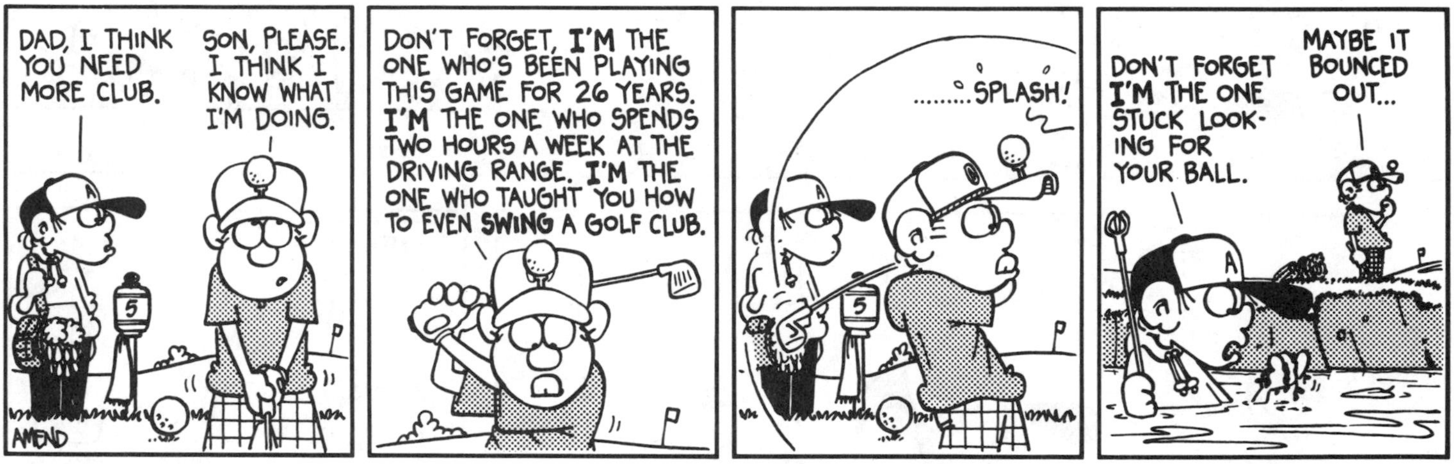
DAD, I THINK YOU NEED MORE CLUB.
SON, PLEASE. I THINK I KNOW WHAT I'M DOING.
5
AMEND
DON'T FORGET, **I'M** THE ONE WHO'S BEEN PLAYING THIS GAME FOR 26 YEARS. **I'M** THE ONE WHO SPENDS TWO HOURS A WEEK AT THE DRIVING RANGE. **I'M** THE ONE WHO TAUGHT YOU HOW TO EVEN **SWING** A GOLF CLUB.
.........SPLASH!
5
DON'T FORGET **I'M** THE ONE STUCK LOOKING FOR YOUR BALL.
MAYBE IT BOUNCED OUT...

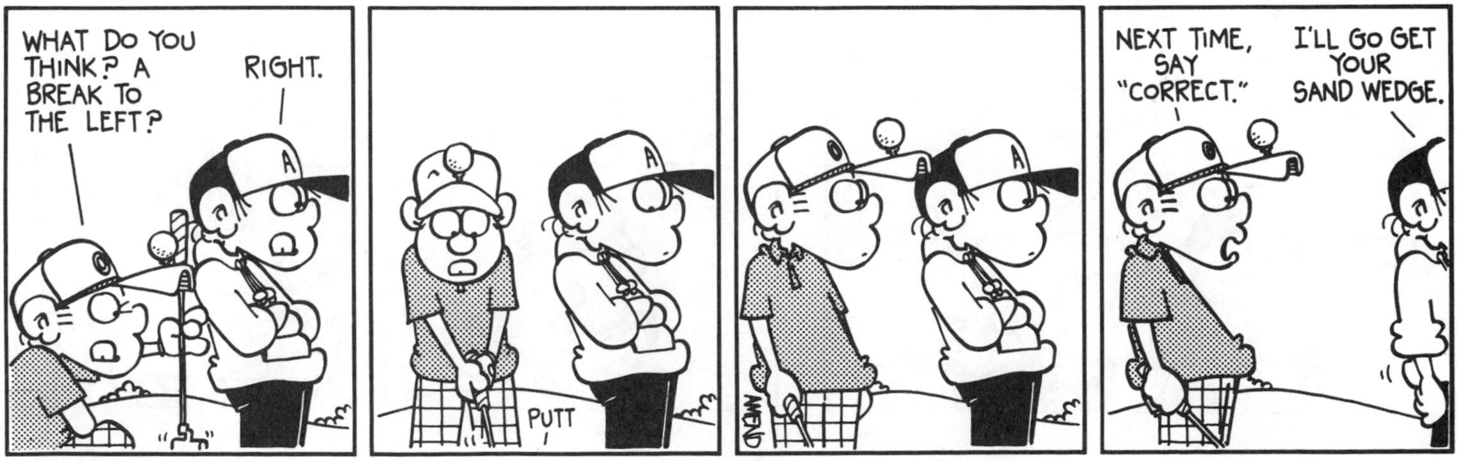
WHAT DO YOU THINK? A BREAK TO THE LEFT?
RIGHT.
PUTT
AMEND
NEXT TIME, SAY "CORRECT."
I'LL GO GET YOUR SAND WEDGE.

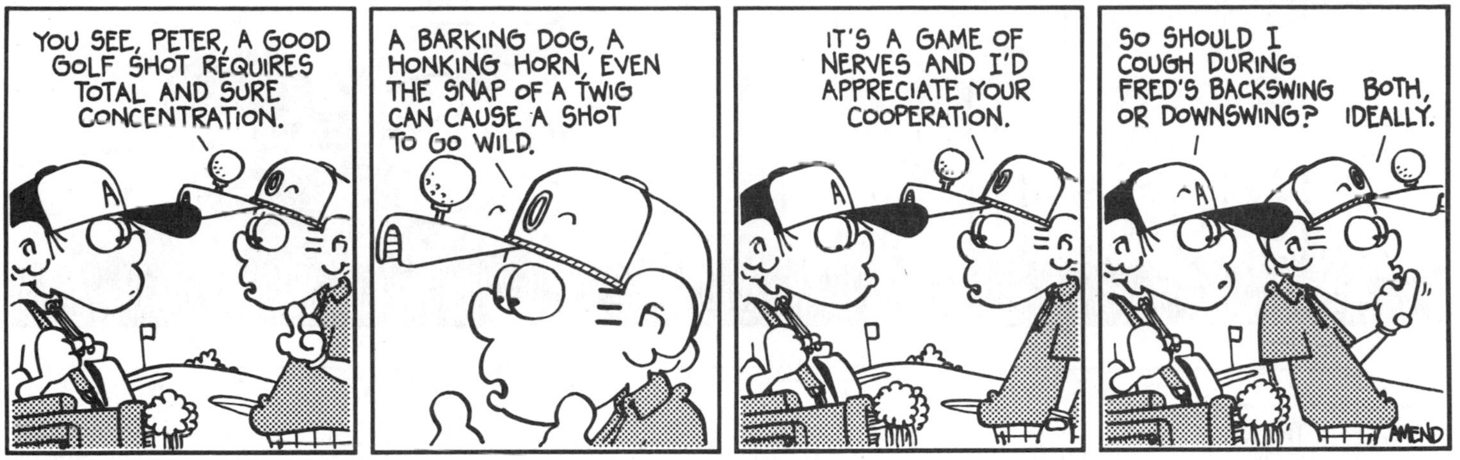
YOU SEE, PETER, A GOOD GOLF SHOT REQUIRES TOTAL AND SURE CONCENTRATION.
A BARKING DOG, A HONKING HORN, EVEN THE SNAP OF A TWIG CAN CAUSE A SHOT TO GO WILD.
IT'S A GAME OF NERVES AND I'D APPRECIATE YOUR COOPERATION.
SO SHOULD I COUGH DURING FRED'S BACKSWING OR DOWNSWING?
BOTH, IDEALLY.
AMEND

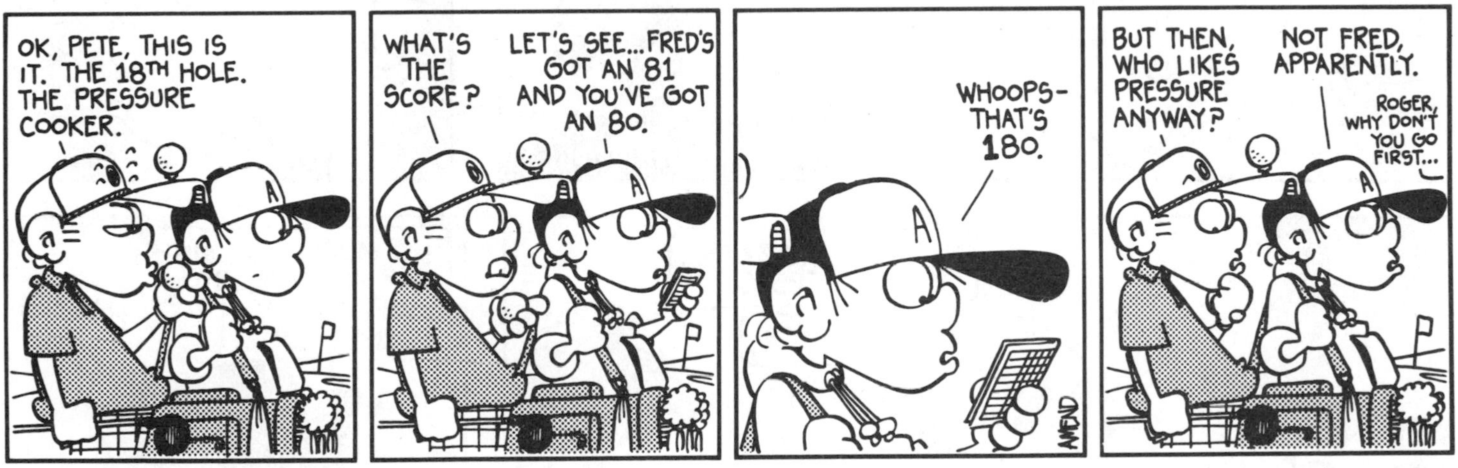
OK, PETE, THIS IS IT. THE 18TH HOLE. THE PRESSURE COOKER.
WHAT'S THE SCORE?
LET'S SEE... FRED'S GOT AN 81 AND YOU'VE GOT AN 80.
WHOOPS- THAT'S 180.
AMEND
BUT THEN, WHO LIKES PRESSURE ANYWAY?
NOT FRED, APPARENTLY.
ROGER, WHY DON'T YOU GO FIRST...

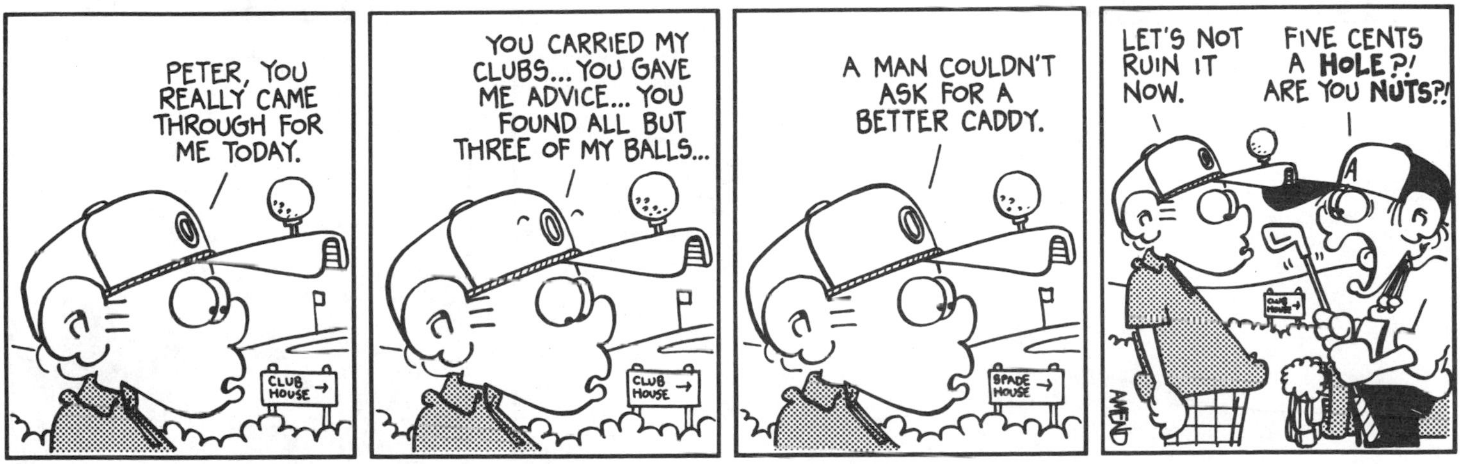
PETER, YOU REALLY CAME THROUGH FOR ME TODAY.
CLUB HOUSE
YOU CARRIED MY CLUBS... YOU GAVE ME ADVICE... YOU FOUND ALL BUT THREE OF MY BALLS...
CLUB HOUSE
A MAN COULDN'T ASK FOR A BETTER CADDY.
SPADE HOUSE
LET'S NOT RUIN IT NOW.
FIVE CENTS A HOLE?! ARE YOU NUTS?!
AMEND

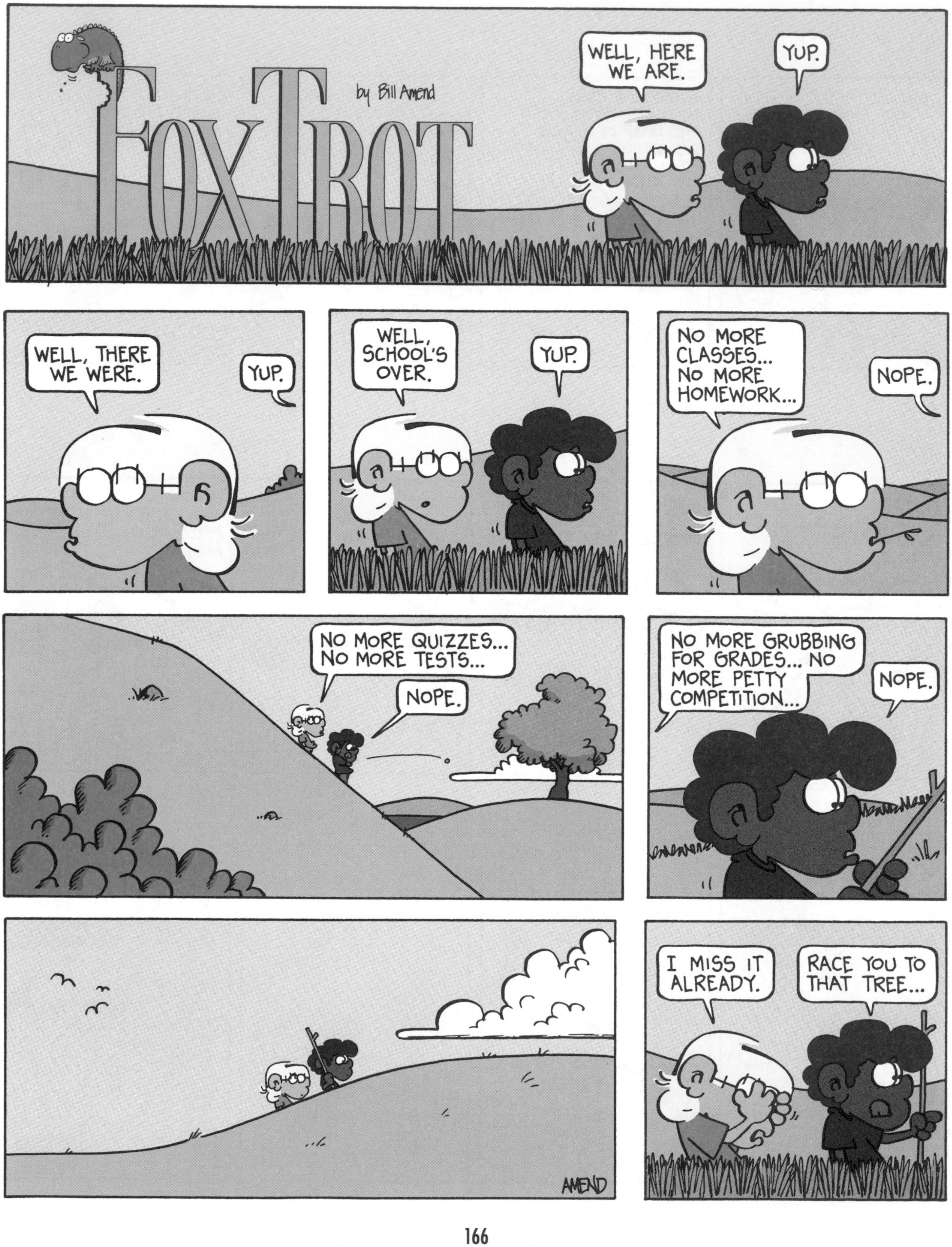
FoxTrot
by Bill Amend
WELL, HERE WE ARE.
YUP.
WELL, THERE WE WERE.
YUP.
WELL, SCHOOL'S OVER.
YUP.
NO MORE CLASSES... NO MORE HOMEWORK...
NOPE.
NO MORE QUIZZES... NO MORE TESTS...
NOPE.
NO MORE GRUBBING FOR GRADES... NO MORE PETTY COMPETITION...
NOPE.
AMEND
I MISS IT ALREADY.
RACE YOU TO THAT TREE...

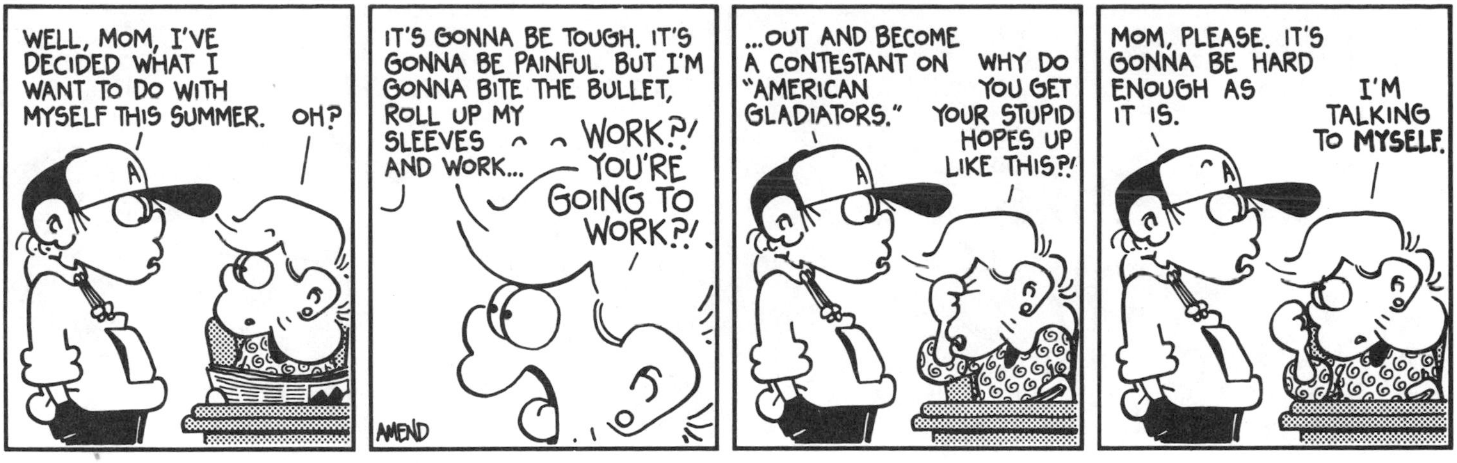
WELL, MOM, I'VE DECIDED WHAT I WANT TO DO WITH MYSELF THIS SUMMER.
OH?
IT'S GONNA BE TOUGH. IT'S GONNA BE PAINFUL. BUT I'M GONNA BITE THE BULLET, ROLL UP MY SLEEVES AND WORK...
WORK?! YOU'RE GOING TO WORK?!
AMEND
...OUT AND BECOME A CONTESTANT ON "AMERICAN GLADIATORS."
WHY DO YOU GET YOUR STUPID HOPES UP LIKE THIS?!
MOM, PLEASE. IT'S GONNA BE HARD ENOUGH AS IT IS.
I'M TALKING TO MYSELF.

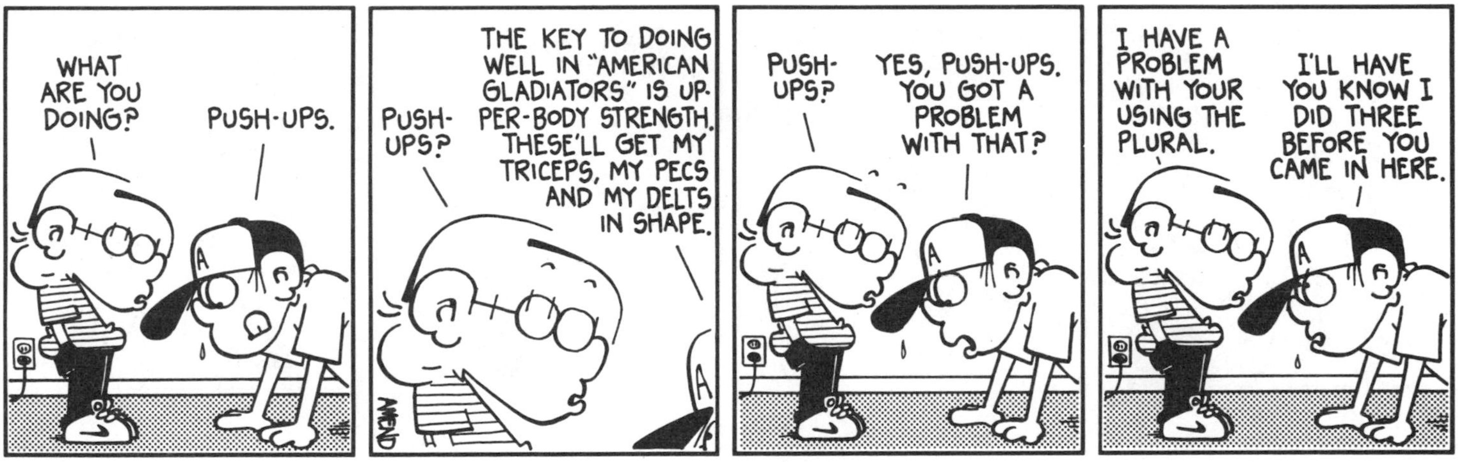
WHAT ARE YOU DOING?
PUSH-UPS.
PUSH-UPS?
THE KEY TO DOING WELL IN "AMERICAN GLADIATORS" IS UPPER-BODY STRENGTH. THESE'LL GET MY TRICEPS, MY PECS AND MY DELTS IN SHAPE.
AMEND
PUSH-UPS?
YES, PUSH-UPS. YOU GOT A PROBLEM WITH THAT?
I HAVE A PROBLEM WITH YOUR USING THE PLURAL.
I'LL HAVE YOU KNOW I DID THREE BEFORE YOU CAME IN HERE.

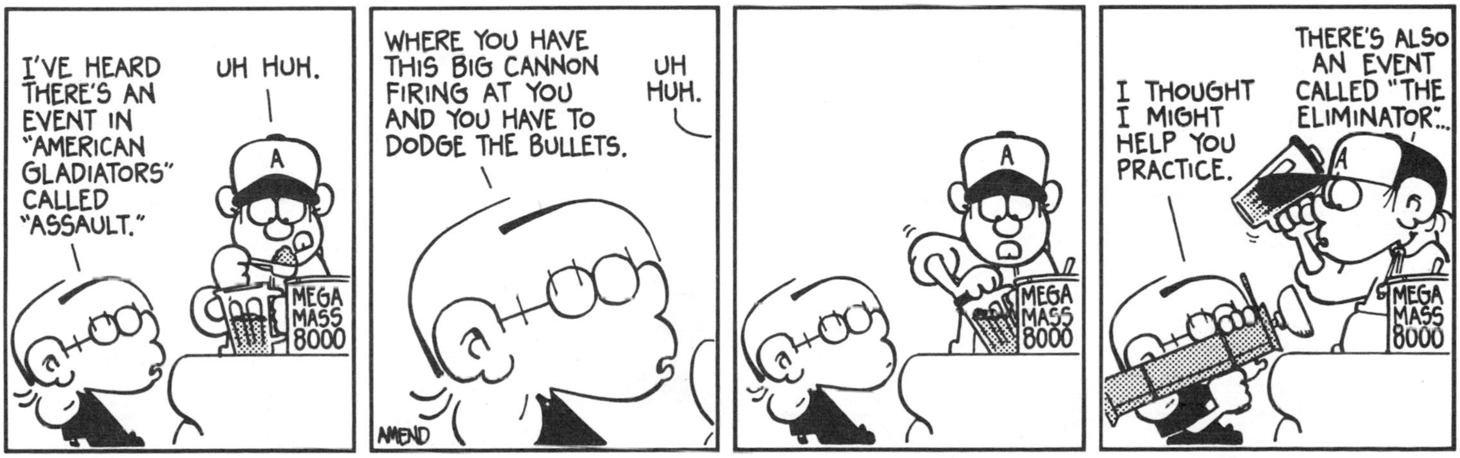
I'VE HEARD THERE'S AN EVENT IN "AMERICAN GLADIATORS" CALLED "ASSAULT."
UH HUH.
MEGA MASS 8000
WHERE YOU HAVE THIS BIG CANNON FIRING AT YOU AND YOU HAVE TO DODGE THE BULLETS.
UH HUH.
AMEND
MEGA MASS 8000
I THOUGHT I MIGHT HELP YOU PRACTICE.
THERE'S ALSO AN EVENT CALLED "THE ELIMINATOR"...
MEGA MASS 8000

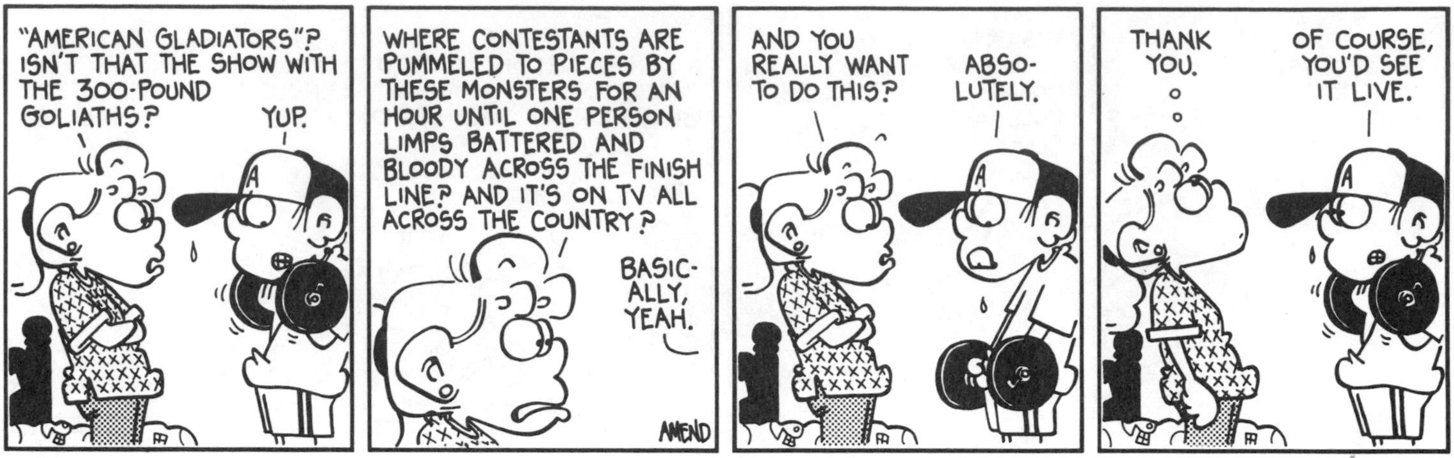
"AMERICAN GLADIATORS"? ISN'T THAT THE SHOW WITH THE 300-POUND GOLIATHS?
YUP.
WHERE CONTESTANTS ARE PUMMELED TO PIECES BY THESE MONSTERS FOR AN HOUR UNTIL ONE PERSON LIMPS BATTERED AND BLOODY ACROSS THE FINISH LINE? AND IT'S ON TV ALL ACROSS THE COUNTRY?
BASIC-ALLY, YEAH.
AMEND
AND YOU REALLY WANT TO DO THIS?
ABSO-LUTELY.
THANK YOU.
OF COURSE, YOU'D SEE IT LIVE.

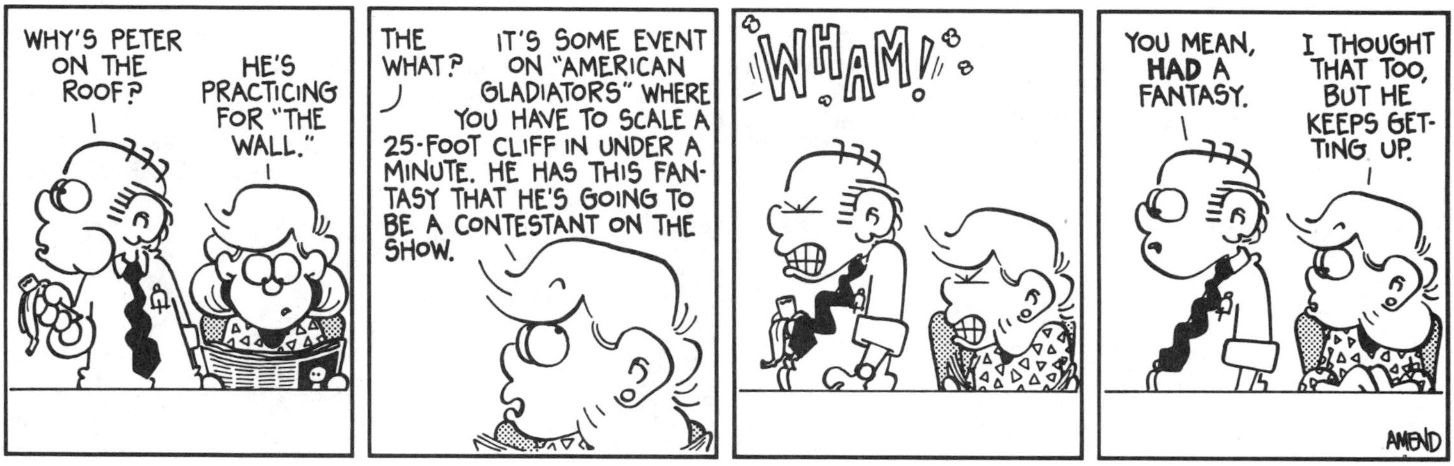
WHY'S PETER ON THE ROOF?
HE'S PRACTICING FOR "THE WALL."
THE WHAT?
IT'S SOME EVENT ON "AMERICAN GLADIATORS" WHERE YOU HAVE TO SCALE A 25-FOOT CLIFF IN UNDER A MINUTE. HE HAS THIS FANTASY THAT HE'S GOING TO BE A CONTESTANT ON THE SHOW.
WHAM!
YOU MEAN, **HAD** A FANTASY.
I THOUGHT THAT TOO, BUT HE KEEPS GETTING UP.
AMEND

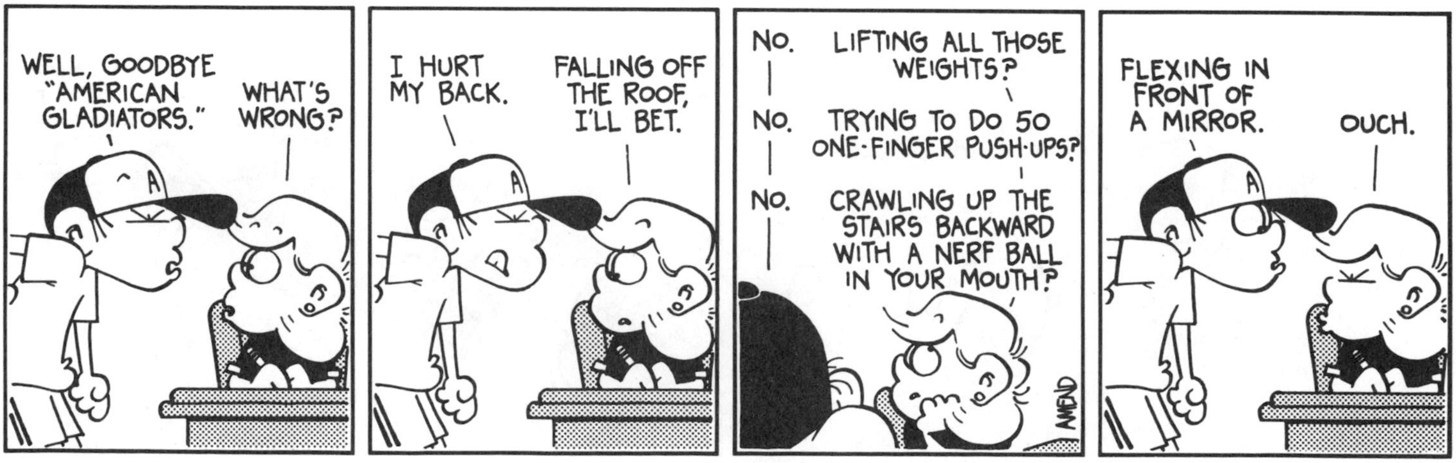
WELL, GOODBYE "AMERICAN GLADIATORS."
WHAT'S WRONG?
I HURT MY BACK.
FALLING OFF THE ROOF, I'LL BET.
NO.
LIFTING ALL THOSE WEIGHTS?
NO.
TRYING TO DO 50 ONE-FINGER PUSH-UPS?
NO.
CRAWLING UP THE STAIRS BACKWARD WITH A NERF BALL IN YOUR MOUTH?
AMEND
FLEXING IN FRONT OF A MIRROR.
OUCH.

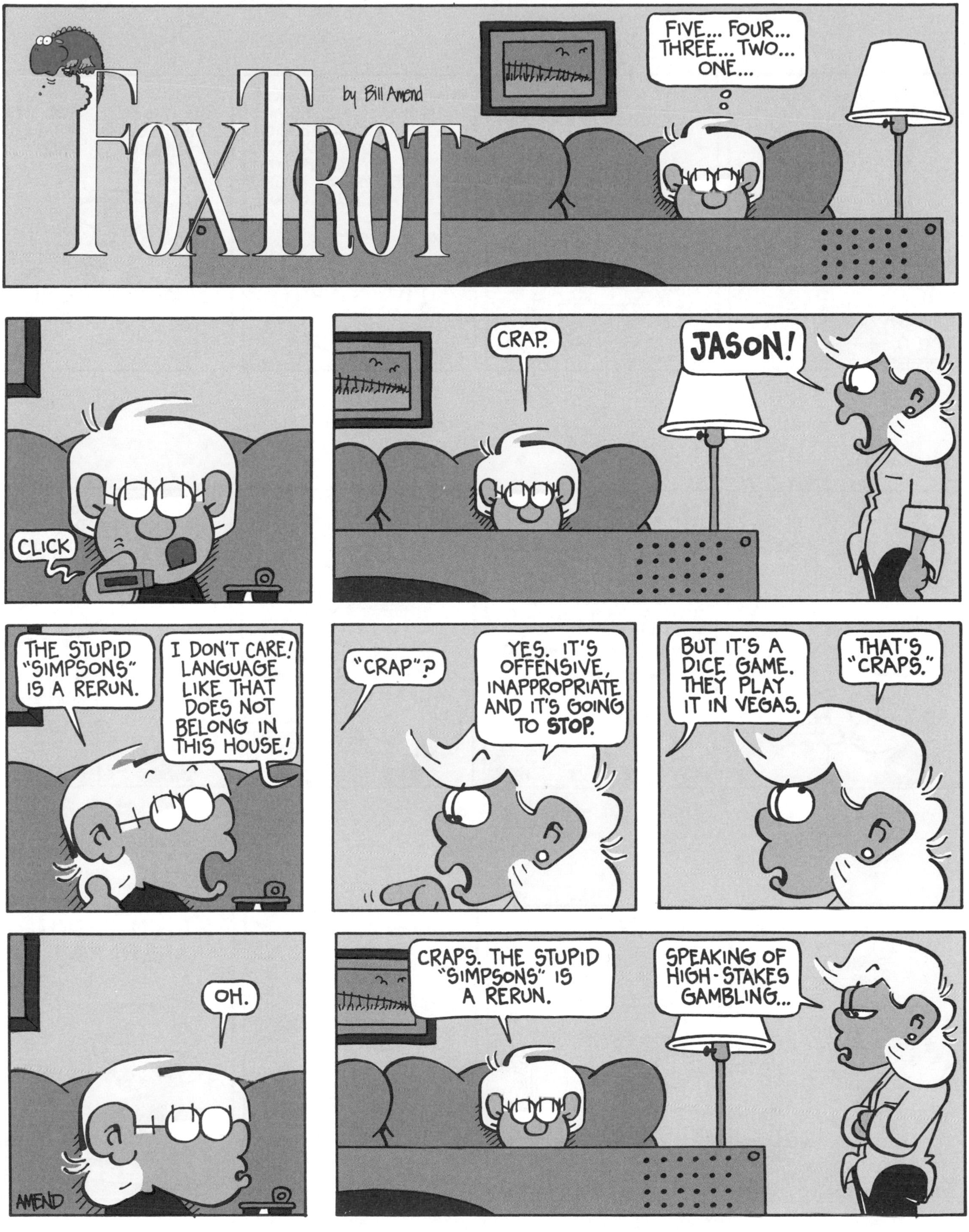
FoxTrot
by Bill Amend
FIVE... FOUR... THREE... TWO... ONE...
CLICK
CRAP.
JASON!
THE STUPID "SIMPSONS" IS A RERUN.
I DON'T CARE! LANGUAGE LIKE THAT DOES NOT BELONG IN THIS HOUSE!
"CRAP"?
YES. IT'S OFFENSIVE, INAPPROPRIATE AND IT'S GOING TO **STOP**.
BUT IT'S A DICE GAME. THEY PLAY IT IN VEGAS.
THAT'S "CRAPS."
OH.
AMEND
CRAPS. THE STUPID "SIMPSONS" IS A RERUN.
SPEAKING OF HIGH-STAKES GAMBLING...

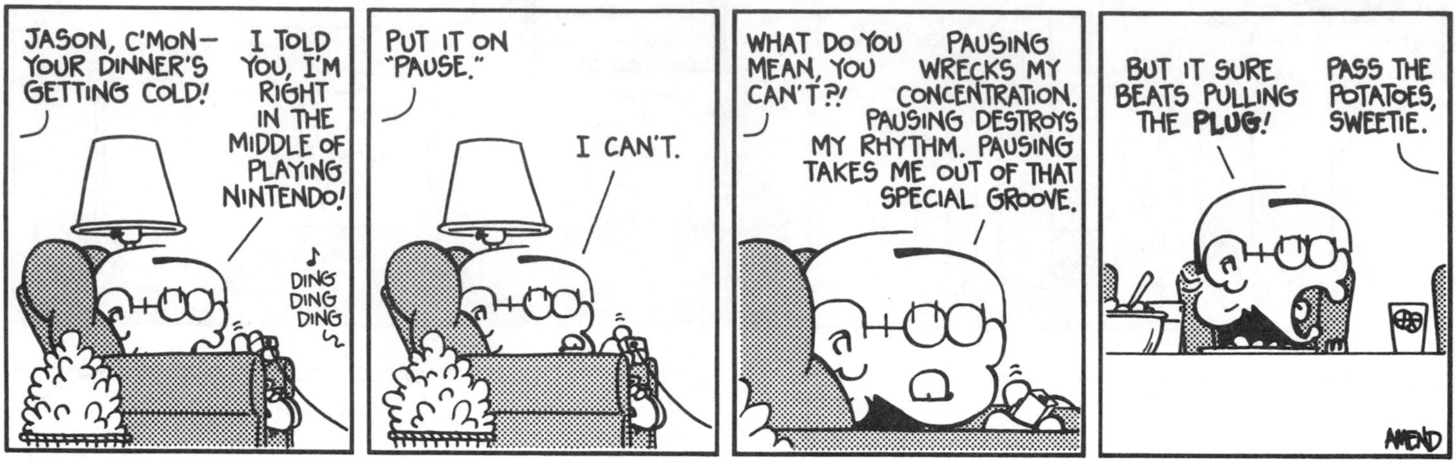
JASON, C'MON— YOUR DINNER'S GETTING COLD!
I TOLD YOU, I'M RIGHT IN THE MIDDLE OF PLAYING NINTENDO!
DING DING DING
PUT IT ON "PAUSE."
I CAN'T.
WHAT DO YOU MEAN, YOU CAN'T?!
PAUSING WRECKS MY CONCENTRATION. PAUSING DESTROYS MY RHYTHM. PAUSING TAKES ME OUT OF THAT SPECIAL GROOVE.
BUT IT SURE BEATS PULLING THE **PLUG**!
PASS THE POTATOES, SWEETIE.
AMEND

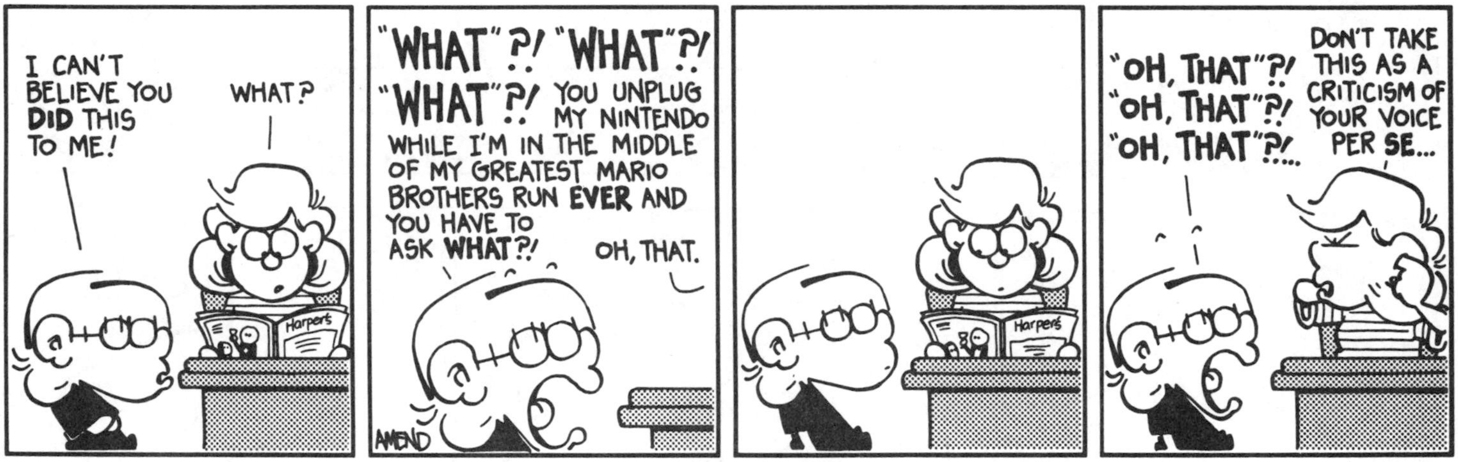
I CAN'T BELIEVE YOU **DID** THIS TO ME!
WHAT?
"WHAT"?! "WHAT"?! "WHAT"?! YOU UNPLUG MY NINTENDO WHILE I'M IN THE MIDDLE OF MY GREATEST MARIO BROTHERS RUN **EVER** AND YOU HAVE TO ASK **WHAT**?!
OH, THAT.
AMEND
"OH, THAT"?! "OH, THAT"?! "OH, THAT"?!...
DON'T TAKE THIS AS A CRITICISM OF YOUR VOICE PER **SE**...

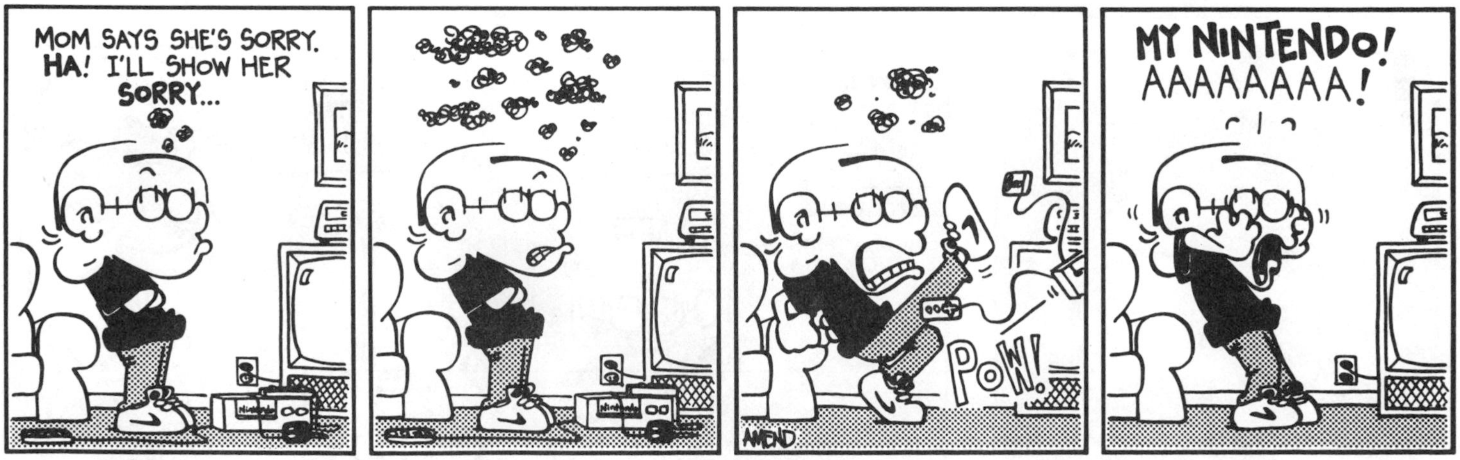
MOM SAYS SHE'S SORRY. **HA**! I'LL SHOW HER **SORRY**...
POW!
AMEND
MY NINTENDO!
AAAAAAAA!

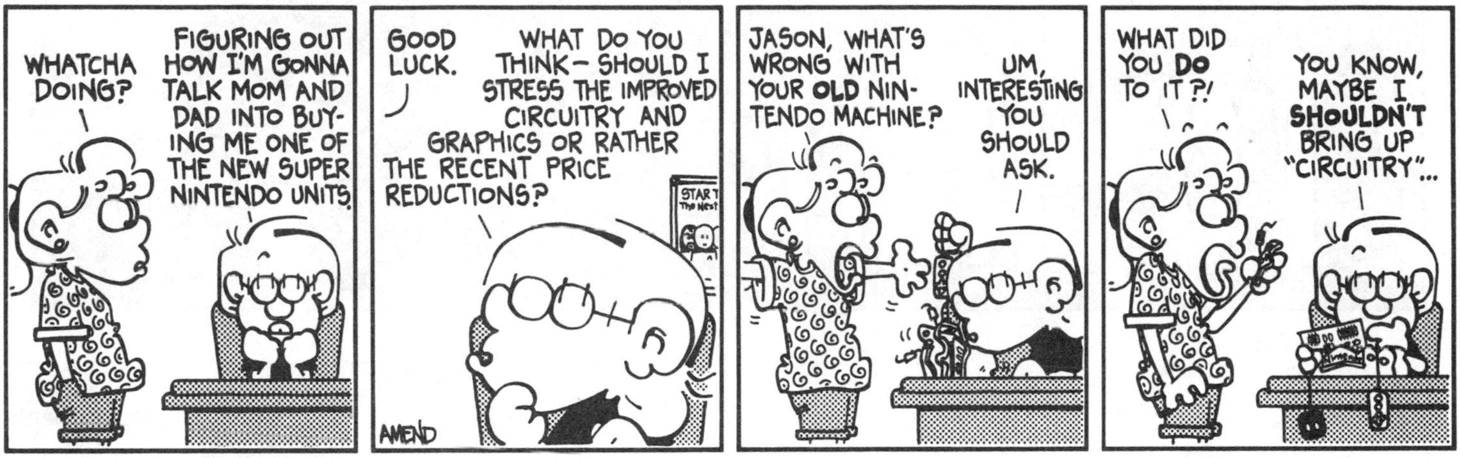
WHATCHA DOING?
FIGURING OUT HOW I'M GONNA TALK MOM AND DAD INTO BUYING ME ONE OF THE NEW SUPER NINTENDO UNITS.
GOOD LUCK.
WHAT DO YOU THINK—SHOULD I STRESS THE IMPROVED CIRCUITRY AND GRAPHICS OR RATHER THE RECENT PRICE REDUCTIONS?
AMEND
JASON, WHAT'S WRONG WITH YOUR **OLD** NINTENDO MACHINE?
UM, INTERESTING YOU SHOULD ASK.
WHAT DID YOU **DO** TO IT?!
YOU KNOW, MAYBE I **SHOULDN'T** BRING UP "CIRCUITRY"...

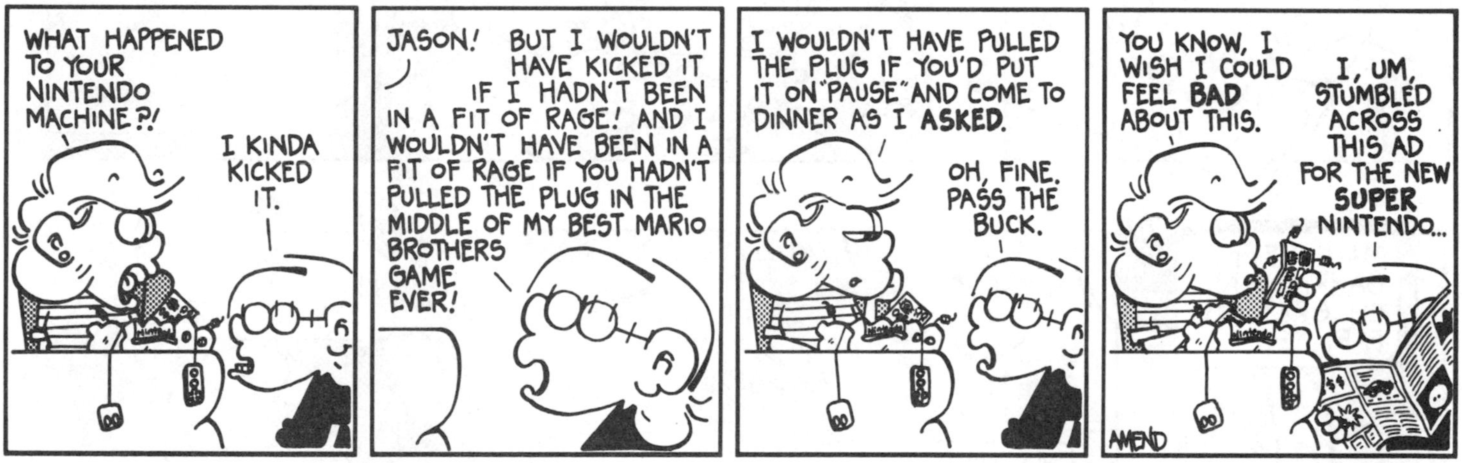
WHAT HAPPENED TO YOUR NINTENDO MACHINE?!
I KINDA KICKED IT.
JASON!
BUT I WOULDN'T HAVE KICKED IT IF I HADN'T BEEN IN A FIT OF RAGE! AND I WOULDN'T HAVE BEEN IN A FIT OF RAGE IF YOU HADN'T PULLED THE PLUG IN THE MIDDLE OF MY BEST MARIO BROTHERS GAME EVER!
I WOULDN'T HAVE PULLED THE PLUG IF YOU'D PUT IT ON "PAUSE" AND COME TO DINNER AS I **ASKED**.
OH, FINE. PASS THE BUCK.
YOU KNOW, I WISH I COULD FEEL **BAD** ABOUT THIS.
I, UM, STUMBLED ACROSS THIS AD FOR THE NEW **SUPER** NINTENDO...
AMEND

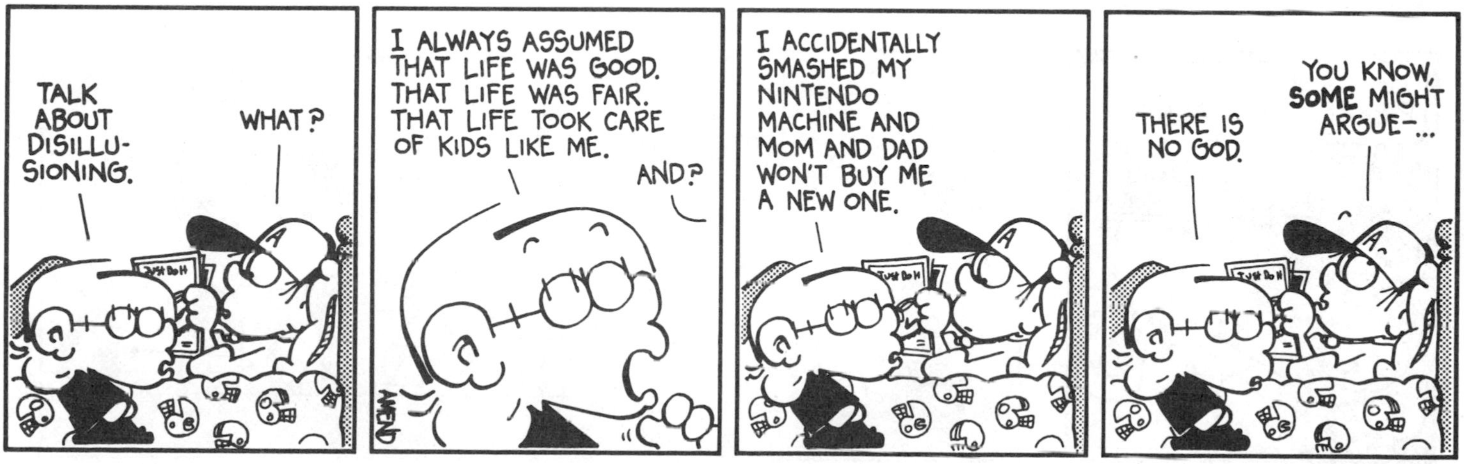
TALK ABOUT DISILLUSIONING.
WHAT?
I ALWAYS ASSUMED THAT LIFE WAS GOOD. THAT LIFE WAS FAIR. THAT LIFE TOOK CARE OF KIDS LIKE ME.
AND?
AMEND
I ACCIDENTALLY SMASHED MY NINTENDO MACHINE AND MOM AND DAD WON'T BUY ME A NEW ONE.
THERE IS NO GOD.
YOU KNOW, **SOME** MIGHT ARGUE—...

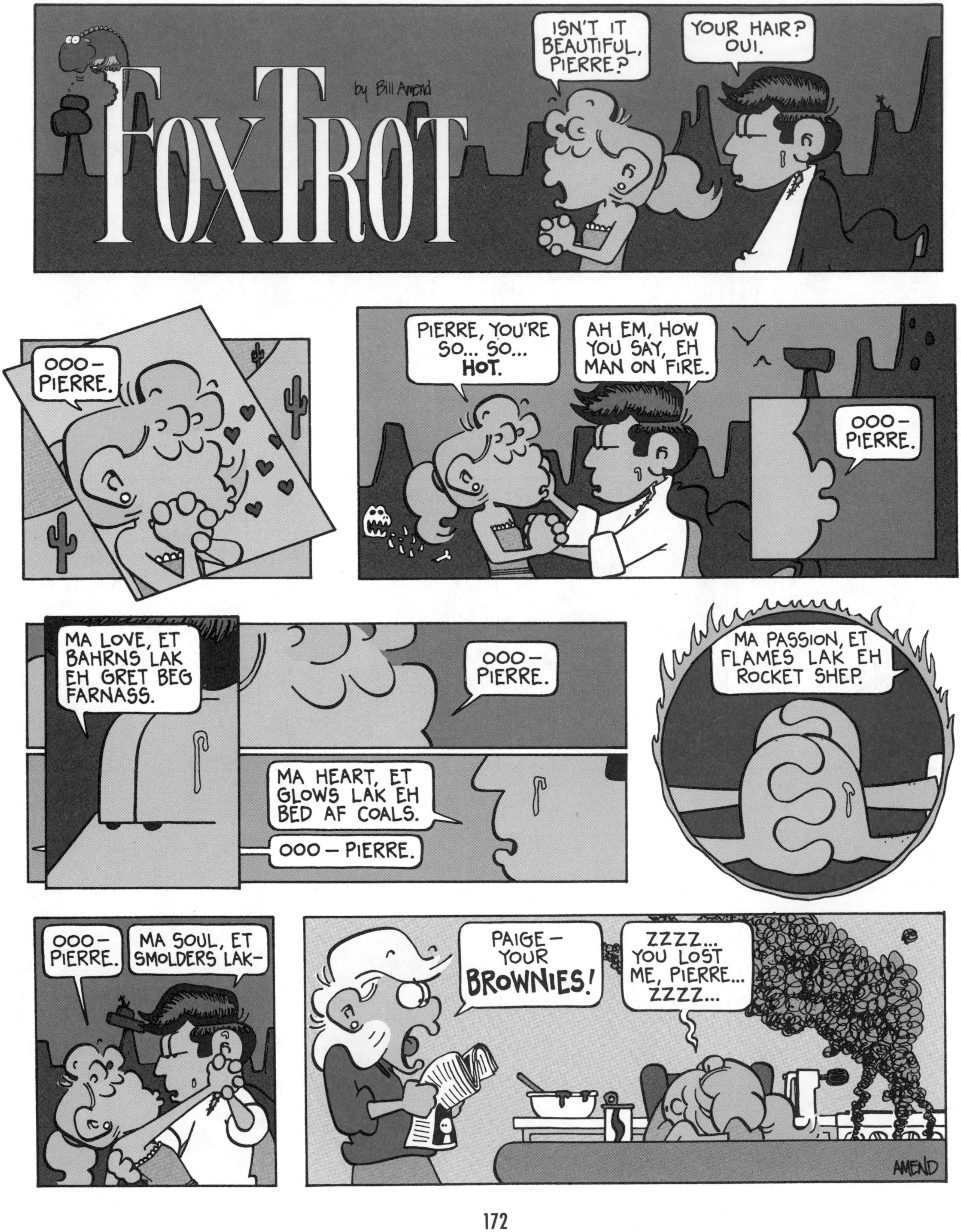
FoxTrot
by Bill Amend
ISN'T IT BEAUTIFUL, PIERRE?
YOUR HAIR? OUI.
OOO-PIERRE.
PIERRE, YOU'RE SO... SO... HOT.
AH EM, HOW YOU SAY, EH MAN ON FIRE.
OOO-PIERRE.
MA LOVE, ET BAHRNS LAK EH GRET BEG FARNASS.
OOO-PIERRE.
MA HEART, ET GLOWS LAK EH BED AF COALS.
OOO - PIERRE.
MA PASSION, ET FLAMES LAK EH ROCKET SHEP.
OOO-PIERRE.
MA SOUL, ET SMOLDERS LAK-
PAIGE - YOUR BROWNIES!
ZZZZ... YOU LOST ME, PIERRE... ZZZZ...
AMEND

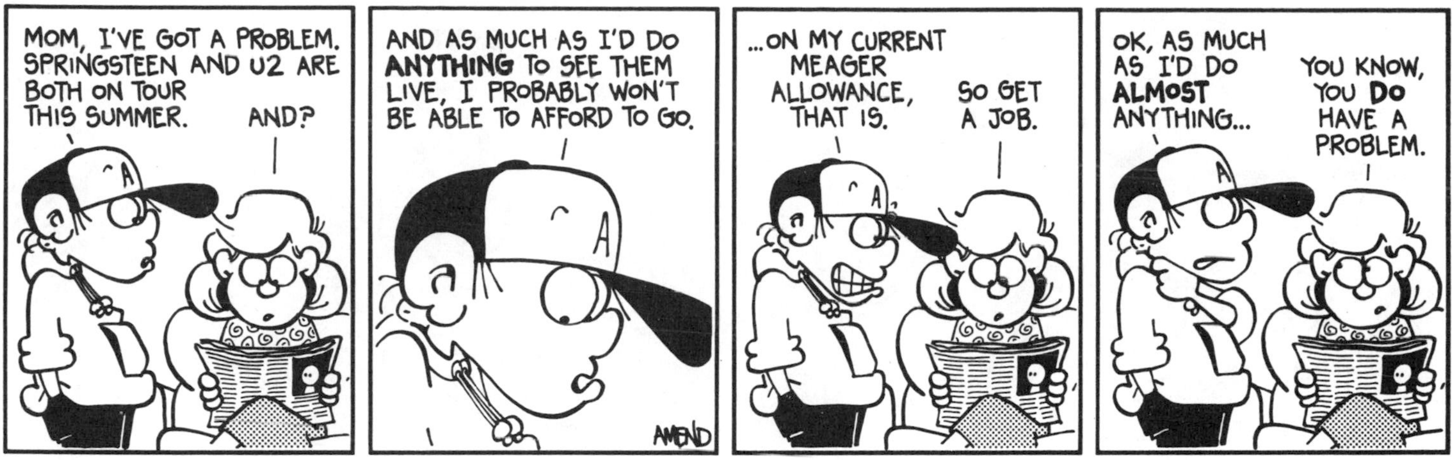
MOM, I'VE GOT A PROBLEM. SPRINGSTEEN AND U2 ARE BOTH ON TOUR THIS SUMMER.
AND?
AND AS MUCH AS I'D DO **ANYTHING** TO SEE THEM LIVE, I PROBABLY WON'T BE ABLE TO AFFORD TO GO.
AMEND
...ON MY CURRENT MEAGER ALLOWANCE, THAT IS.
SO GET A JOB.
OK, AS MUCH AS I'D DO **ALMOST** ANYTHING...
YOU KNOW, YOU **DO** HAVE A PROBLEM.

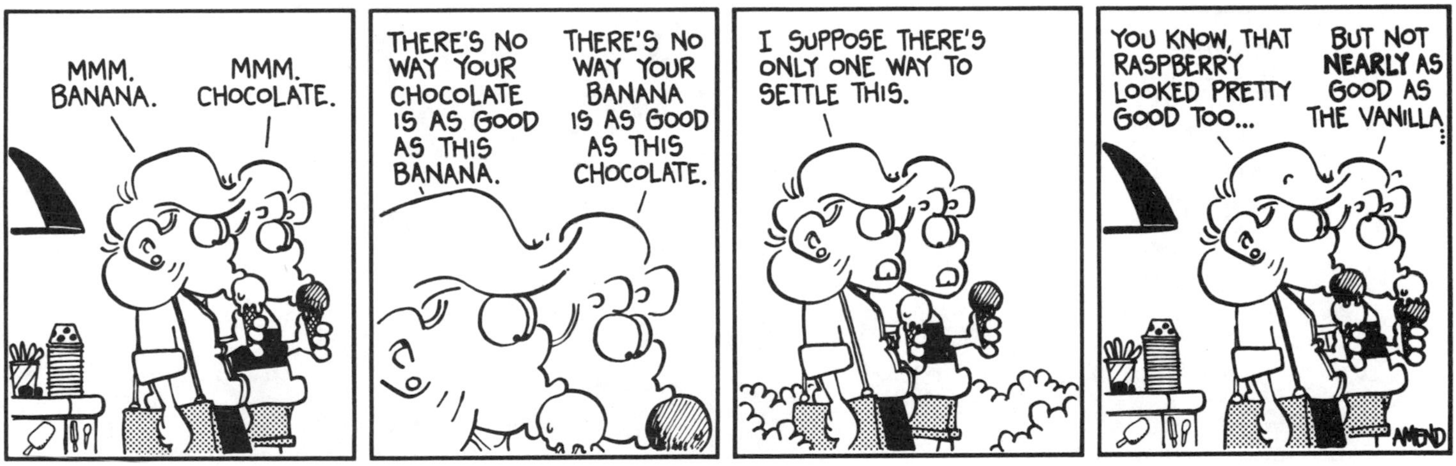
MMM. BANANA.
MMM. CHOCOLATE.
THERE'S NO WAY YOUR CHOCOLATE IS AS GOOD AS THIS BANANA.
THERE'S NO WAY YOUR BANANA IS AS GOOD AS THIS CHOCOLATE.
I SUPPOSE THERE'S ONLY ONE WAY TO SETTLE THIS.
YOU KNOW, THAT RASPBERRY LOOKED PRETTY GOOD TOO...
BUT NOT **NEARLY** AS GOOD AS THE VANILLA...
AMEND

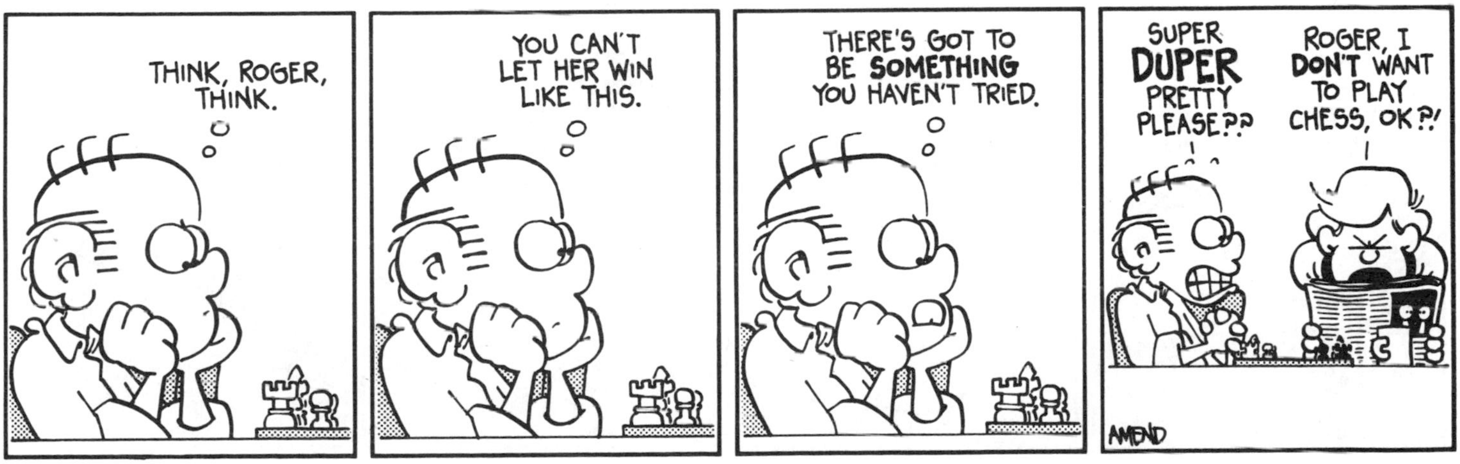
THINK, ROGER, THINK.
YOU CAN'T LET HER WIN LIKE THIS.
THERE'S GOT TO BE **SOMETHING** YOU HAVEN'T TRIED.
SUPER **DUPER** PRETTY PLEASE?!?
ROGER, I **DON'T** WANT TO PLAY CHESS, OK?!
AMEND

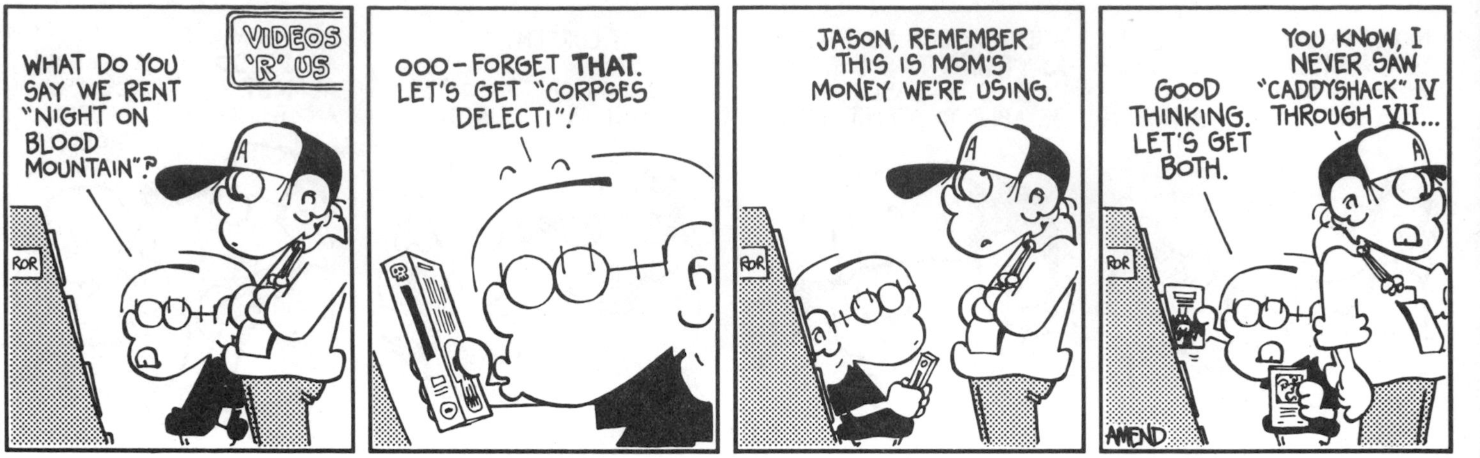
VIDEOS 'R' US
WHAT DO YOU SAY WE RENT "NIGHT ON BLOOD MOUNTAIN"?
RDR
OOO-FORGET **THAT**. LET'S GET "CORPSES DELECTI"!
JASON, REMEMBER THIS IS MOM'S MONEY WE'RE USING.
RDR
GOOD THINKING. LET'S GET BOTH.
YOU KNOW, I NEVER SAW "CADDYSHACK" IV THROUGH VII...
RDR
AMEND

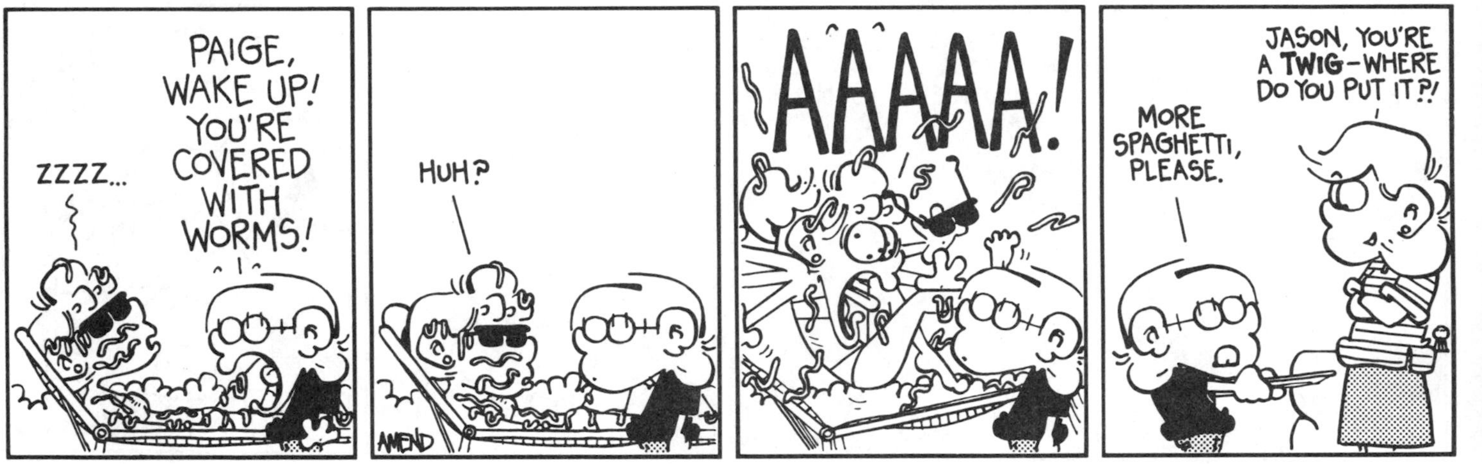
ZZZZ...
PAIGE, WAKE UP! YOU'RE COVERED WITH WORMS!
HUH?
AMEND
AAAAA!
MORE SPAGHETTI, PLEASE.
JASON, YOU'RE A **TWIG**-WHERE DO YOU PUT IT?!

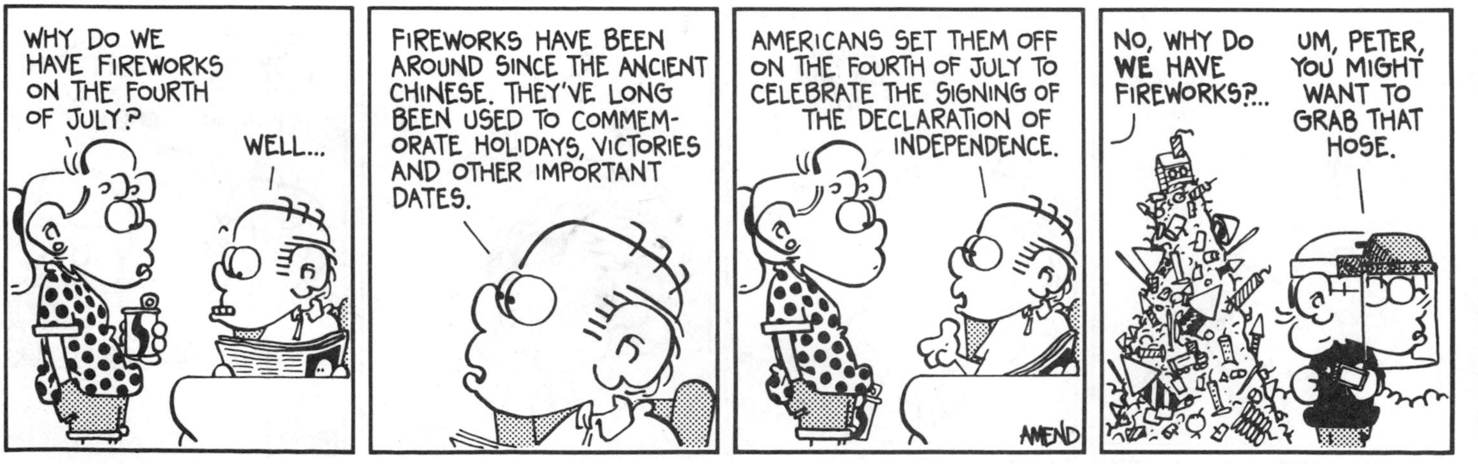
WHY DO WE HAVE FIREWORKS ON THE FOURTH OF JULY?
WELL...
FIREWORKS HAVE BEEN AROUND SINCE THE ANCIENT CHINESE. THEY'VE LONG BEEN USED TO COMMEMORATE HOLIDAYS, VICTORIES AND OTHER IMPORTANT DATES.
AMERICANS SET THEM OFF ON THE FOURTH OF JULY TO CELEBRATE THE SIGNING OF THE DECLARATION OF INDEPENDENCE.
AMEND
NO, WHY DO **WE** HAVE FIREWORKS?...
UM, PETER, YOU MIGHT WANT TO GRAB THAT HOSE.

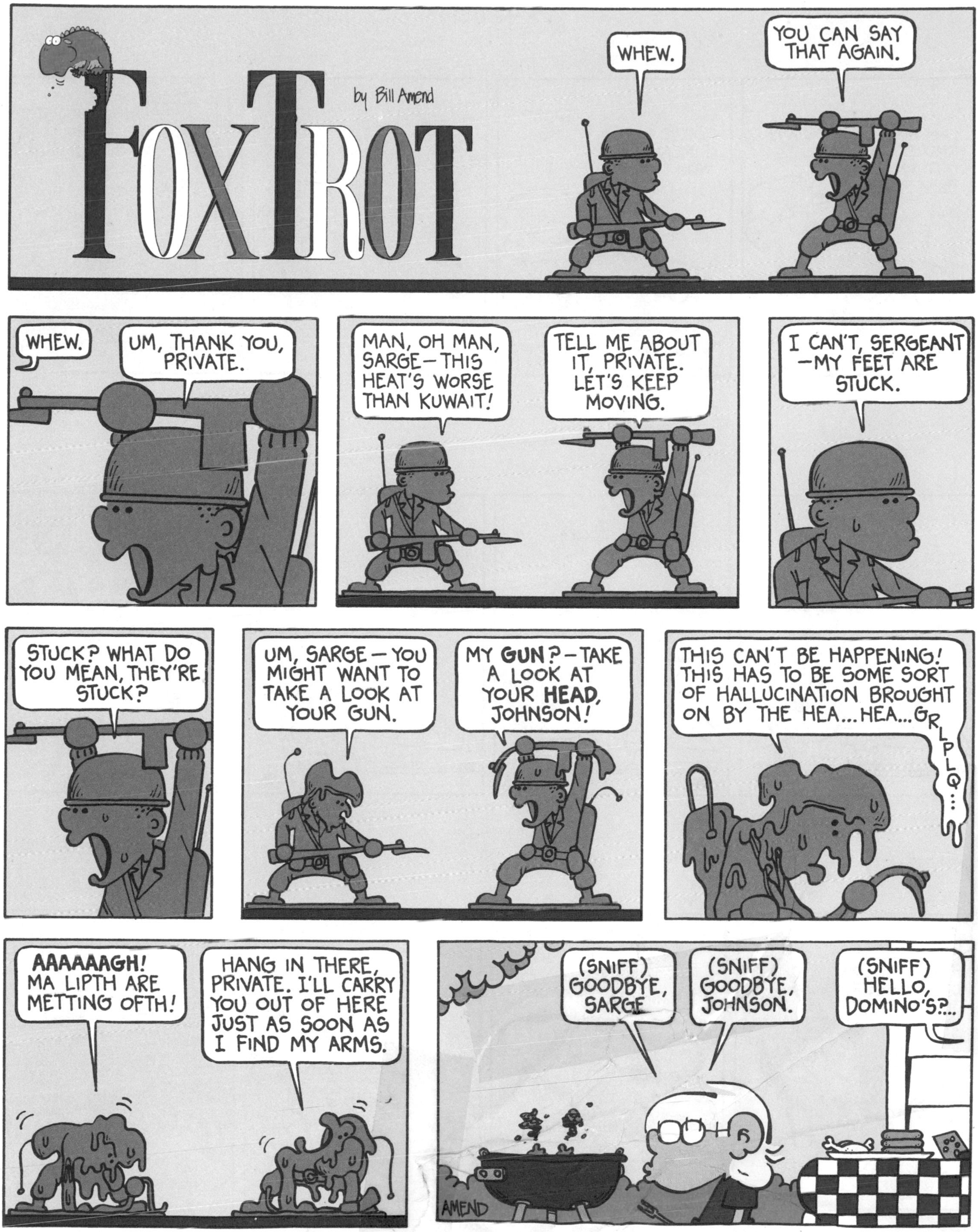
FoxTrot
by Bill Amend
WHEW.
YOU CAN SAY THAT AGAIN.
WHEW.
UM, THANK YOU, PRIVATE.
MAN, OH MAN, SARGE—THIS HEAT'S WORSE THAN KUWAIT!
TELL ME ABOUT IT, PRIVATE. LET'S KEEP MOVING.
I CAN'T, SERGEANT—MY FEET ARE STUCK.
STUCK? WHAT DO YOU MEAN, THEY'RE STUCK?
UM, SARGE—YOU MIGHT WANT TO TAKE A LOOK AT YOUR GUN.
MY **GUN**?—TAKE A LOOK AT YOUR **HEAD**, JOHNSON!
THIS CAN'T BE HAPPENING! THIS HAS TO BE SOME SORT OF HALLUCINATION BROUGHT ON BY THE HEA... HEA... GRLPLQ...
AAAAAAGH! MA LIPTH ARE METTING OFTH!
HANG IN THERE, PRIVATE. I'LL CARRY YOU OUT OF HERE JUST AS SOON AS I FIND MY ARMS.
(SNIFF) GOODBYE, SARGE.
(SNIFF) GOODBYE, JOHNSON.
(SNIFF) HELLO, DOMINO'S?...
AMEND

CAN MARCUS AND I GO OUT AND PLAY?
BY ALL MEANS.
YOU'RE SURE? I MEAN, YOU WON'T MIND?
TRUST ME.
AMEND
"SELECTIVE OMISSION" PAYS OFF ONCE AGAIN.
PAIGE SHOULD BE OUT BACK...

ZZZZ...
AMEND
ZZZZ...
AT LEAST WE KNOW THEY STICK.
PETER... BROTHER... FRIEND...
STRANG-LER...

PETER, MELLOW OUT— THEY'RE JUST RUBBER DARTS.
AMEND
OK, SO WE DIPPED THEM IN SOME PERMANENT LIQUID ADHESIVE...
I SWEAR, THE MINUTE I CAN **SEE** YOU TWO...

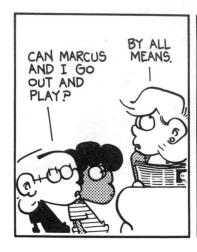

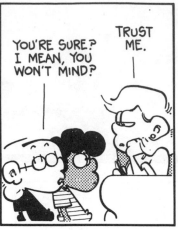

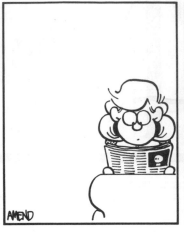

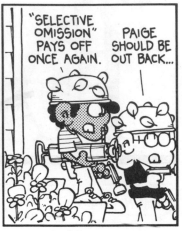

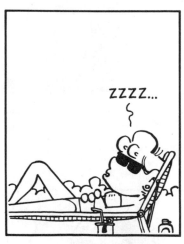

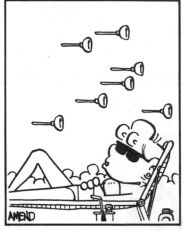

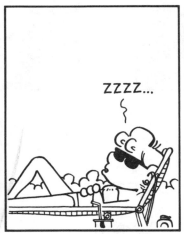

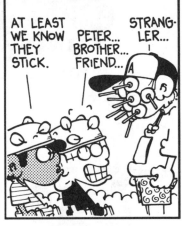

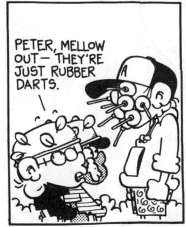

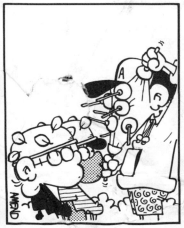

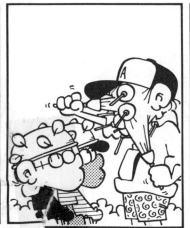

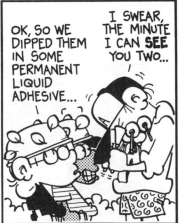

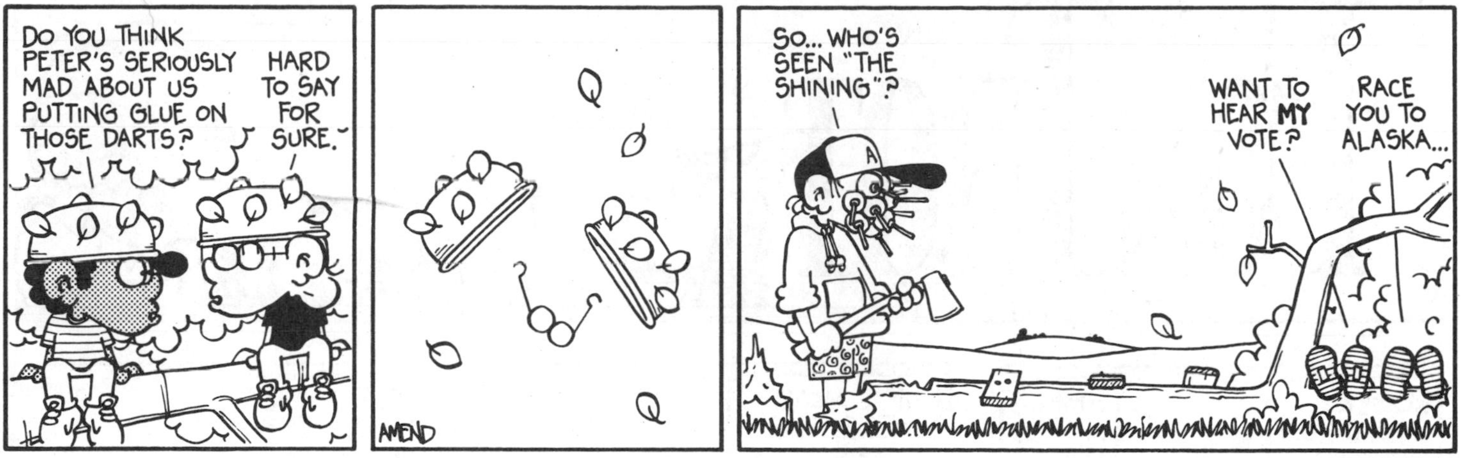
DO YOU THINK PETER'S SERIOUSLY MAD ABOUT US PUTTING GLUE ON THOSE DARTS?
HARD TO SAY FOR SURE.
AMEND
SO... WHO'S SEEN "THE SHINING"?
WANT TO HEAR **MY** VOTE?
RACE YOU TO ALASKA...

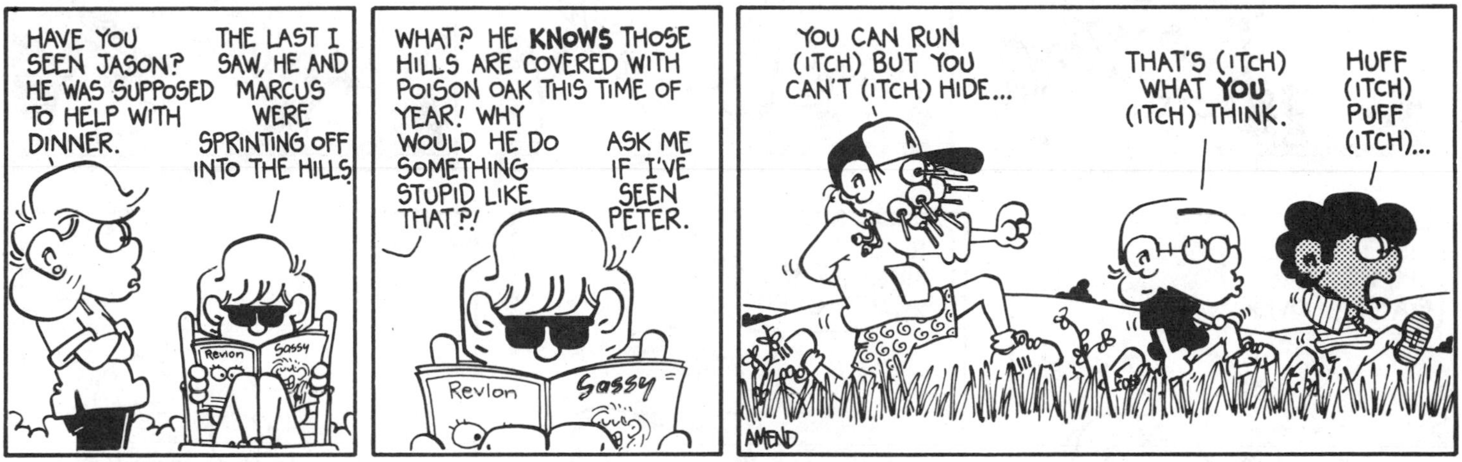
HAVE YOU SEEN JASON? HE WAS SUPPOSED TO HELP WITH DINNER.
THE LAST I SAW, HE AND MARCUS WERE SPRINTING OFF INTO THE HILLS.
Revlon
Sassy
WHAT? HE **KNOWS** THOSE HILLS ARE COVERED WITH POISON OAK THIS TIME OF YEAR! WHY WOULD HE DO SOMETHING STUPID LIKE THAT?!
ASK ME IF I'VE SEEN PETER.
YOU CAN RUN (ITCH) BUT YOU CAN'T (ITCH) HIDE...
THAT'S (ITCH) WHAT **YOU** (ITCH) THINK.
HUFF (ITCH) PUFF (ITCH)...
AMEND

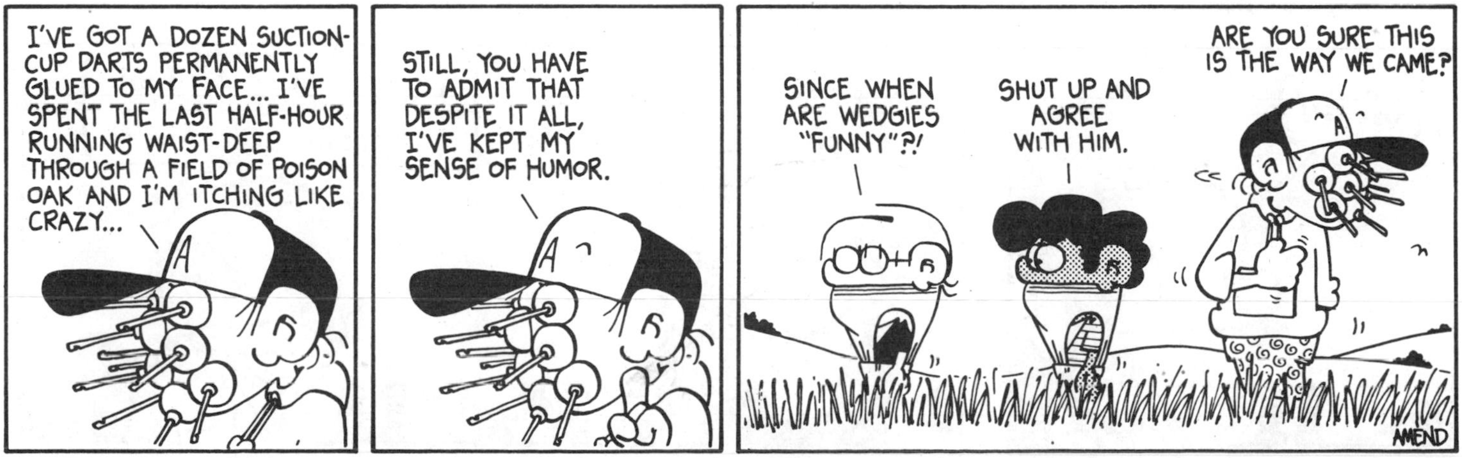
I'VE GOT A DOZEN SUCTION-CUP DARTS PERMANENTLY GLUED TO MY FACE... I'VE SPENT THE LAST HALF-HOUR RUNNING WAIST-DEEP THROUGH A FIELD OF POISON OAK AND I'M ITCHING LIKE CRAZY...
STILL, YOU HAVE TO ADMIT THAT DESPITE IT ALL, I'VE KEPT MY SENSE OF HUMOR.
SINCE WHEN ARE WEDGIES "FUNNY"?!
SHUT UP AND AGREE WITH HIM.
ARE YOU SURE THIS IS THE WAY WE CAME?
AMEND

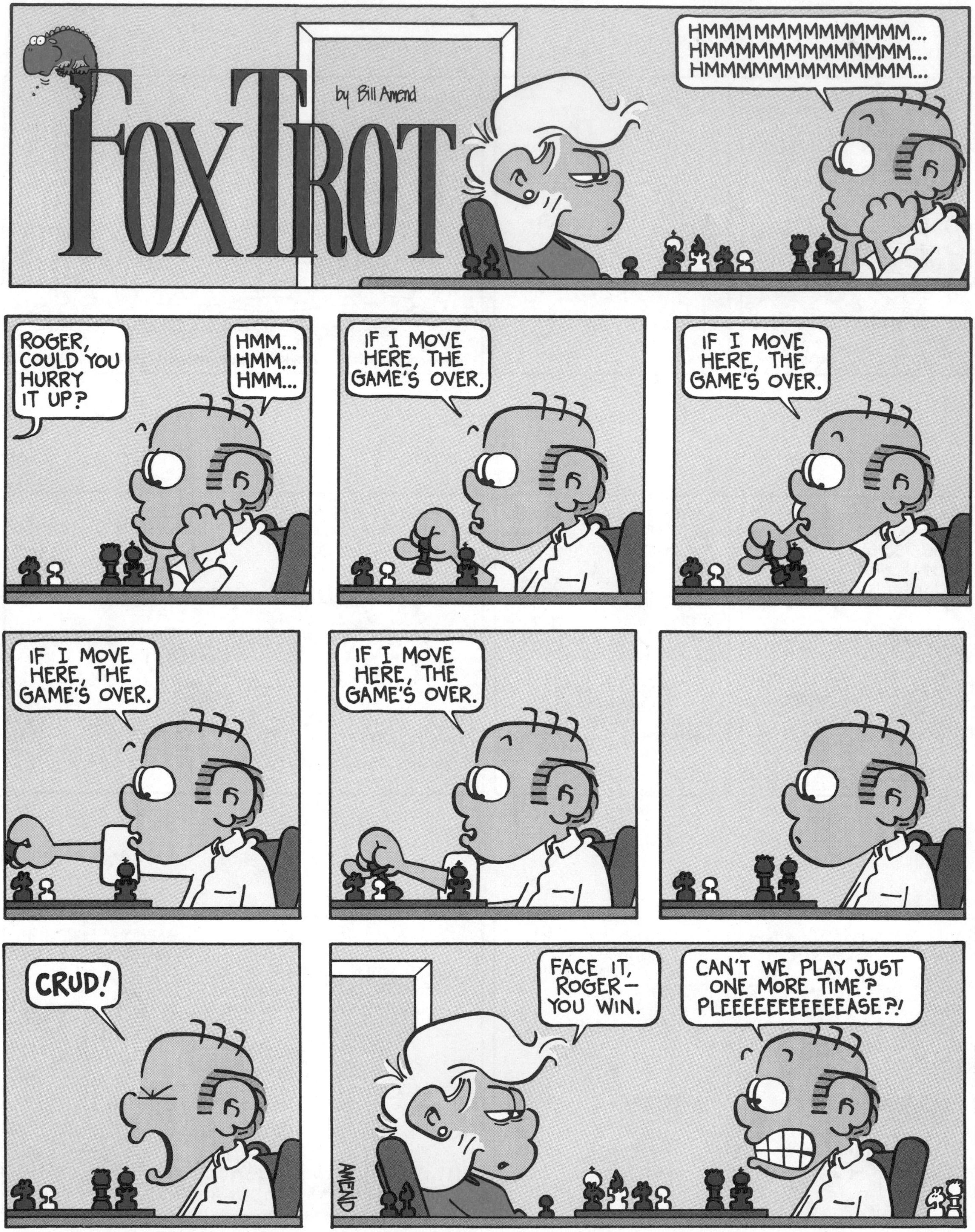
FoxTrot
by Bill Amend
HMMMMMMMMMMMMM... HMMMMMMMMMMMMM... HMMMMMMMMMMMMM...
ROGER, COULD YOU HURRY IT UP?
HMM... HMM... HMM...
IF I MOVE HERE, THE GAME'S OVER.
IF I MOVE HERE, THE GAME'S OVER.
IF I MOVE HERE, THE GAME'S OVER.
IF I MOVE HERE, THE GAME'S OVER.
CRUD!
FACE IT, ROGER — YOU WIN.
CAN'T WE PLAY JUST ONE MORE TIME? PLEEEEEEEEEEEASE?!
AMEND

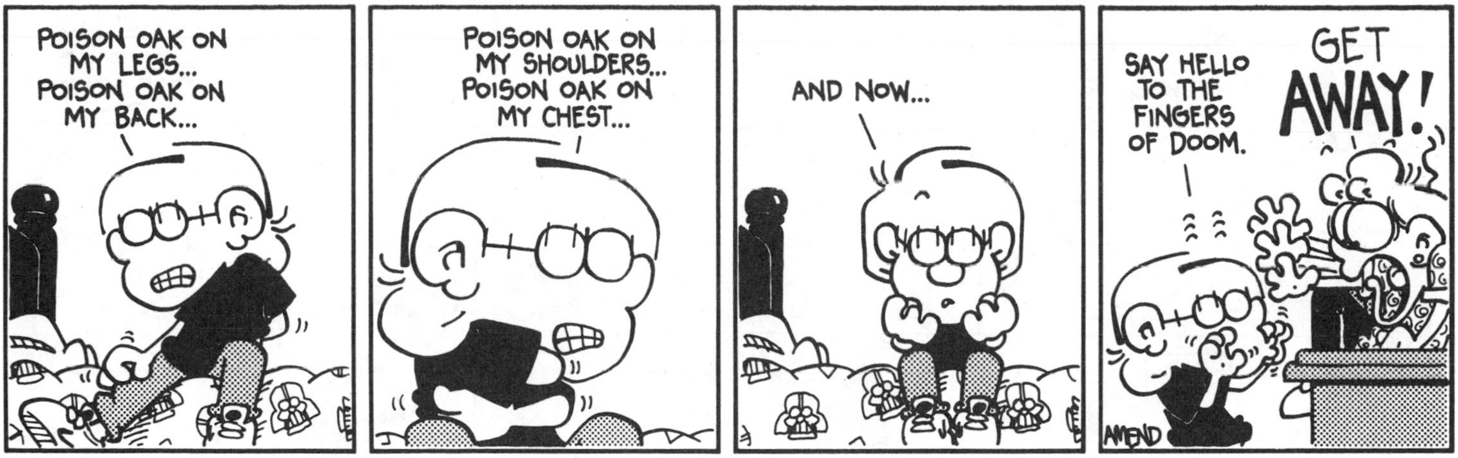
POISON OAK ON MY LEGS... POISON OAK ON MY BACK...
POISON OAK ON MY SHOULDERS... POISON OAK ON MY CHEST...
AND NOW...
SAY HELLO TO THE FINGERS OF DOOM.
GET AWAY!
AMEND

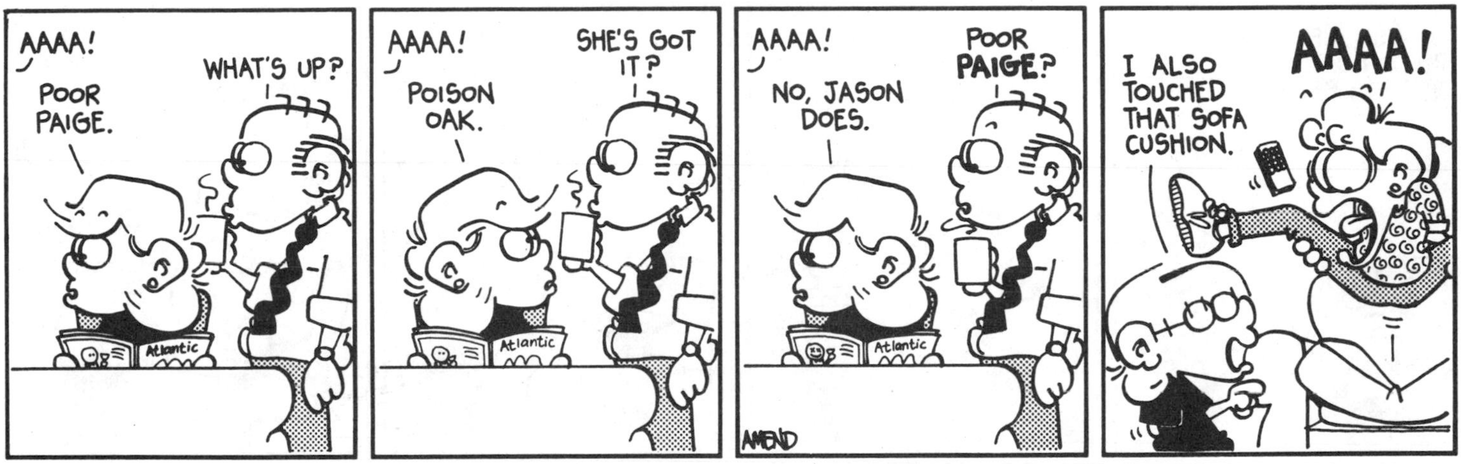
AAAA!
POOR PAIGE.
WHAT'S UP?
Atlantic
AAAA!
POISON OAK.
SHE'S GOT IT?
Atlantic
AAAA!
NO, JASON DOES.
POOR PAIGE?
Atlantic
AMEND
I ALSO TOUCHED THAT SOFA CUSHION.
AAAA!

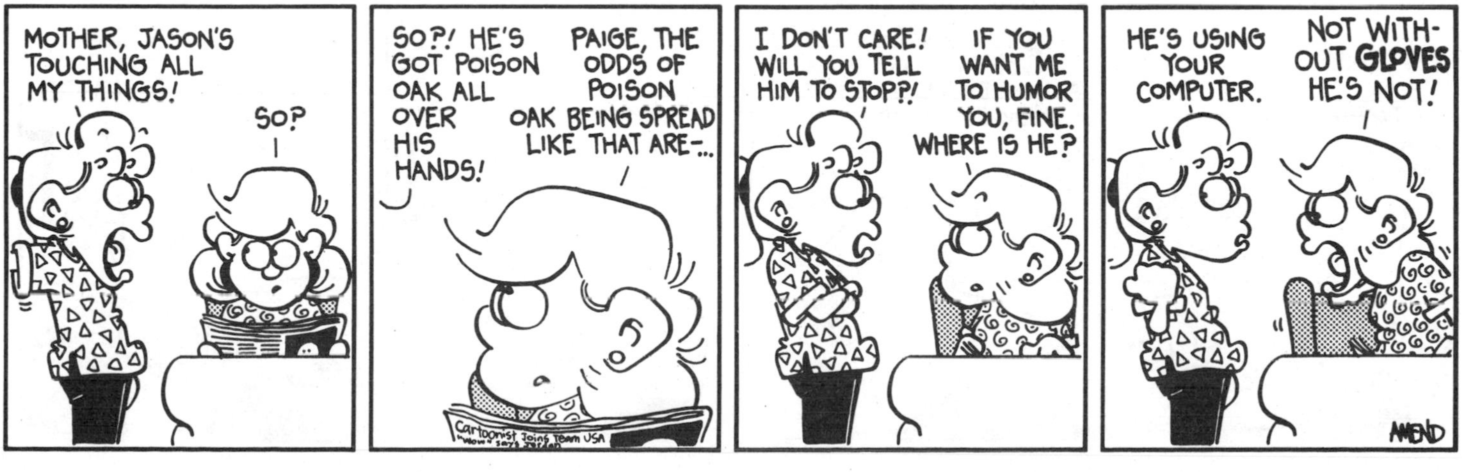
MOTHER, JASON'S TOUCHING ALL MY THINGS!
SO?
SO?! HE'S GOT POISON OAK ALL OVER HIS HANDS!
PAIGE, THE ODDS OF POISON OAK BEING SPREAD LIKE THAT ARE--...
Cartoonist Joins Team USA
I DON'T CARE! WILL YOU TELL HIM TO STOP?!
IF YOU WANT ME TO HUMOR YOU, FINE. WHERE IS HE?
HE'S USING YOUR COMPUTER.
NOT WITHOUT GLOVES HE'S NOT!
AMEND

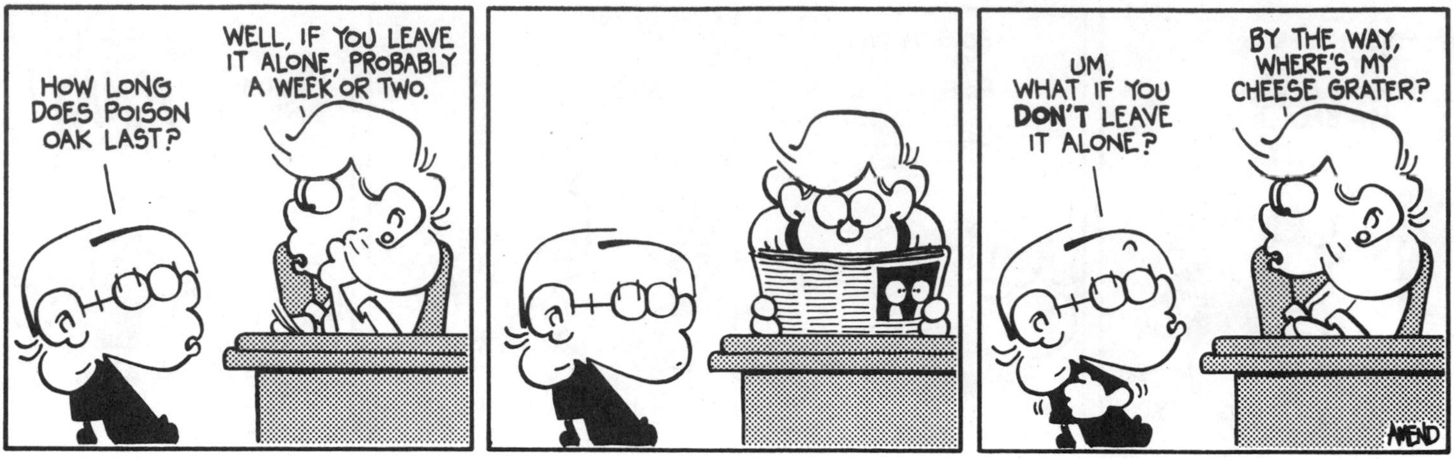
HOW LONG DOES POISON OAK LAST?
WELL, IF YOU LEAVE IT ALONE, PROBABLY A WEEK OR TWO.
UM, WHAT IF YOU **DON'T** LEAVE IT ALONE?
BY THE WAY, WHERE'S MY CHEESE GRATER?
AMEND

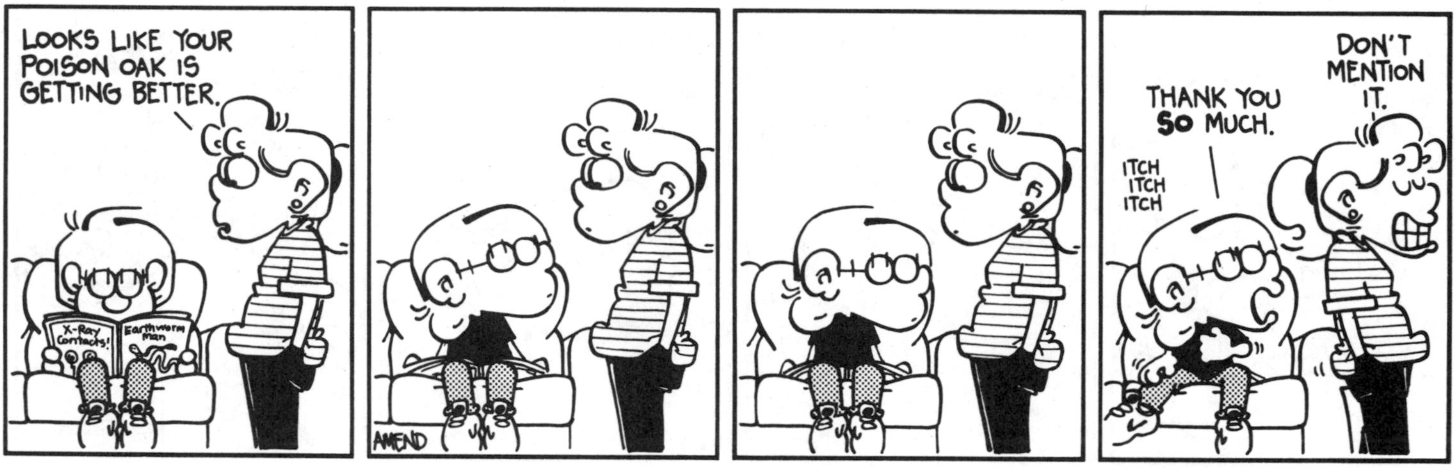
LOOKS LIKE YOUR POISON OAK IS GETTING BETTER.
X-Ray Contacts!
Earthworm Man
AMEND
ITCH ITCH ITCH
THANK YOU **SO** MUCH.
DON'T MENTION IT.

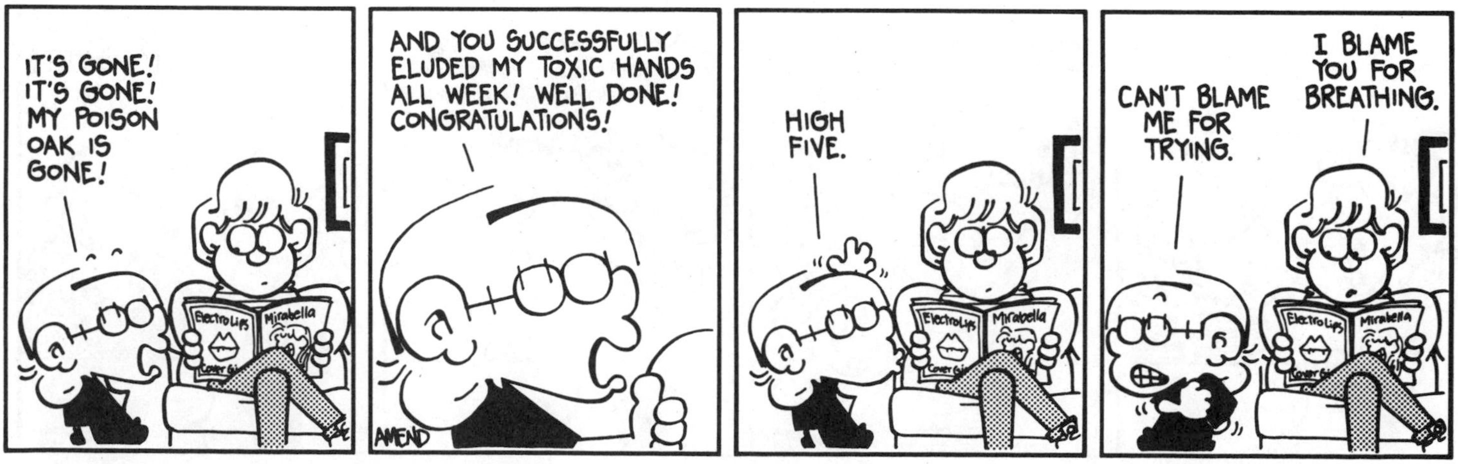
IT'S GONE! IT'S GONE! MY POISON OAK IS GONE!
ElectroLips
Mirabella
AND YOU SUCCESSFULLY ELUDED MY TOXIC HANDS ALL WEEK! WELL DONE! CONGRATULATIONS!
AMEND
HIGH FIVE.
CAN'T BLAME ME FOR TRYING.
I BLAME YOU FOR BREATHING.

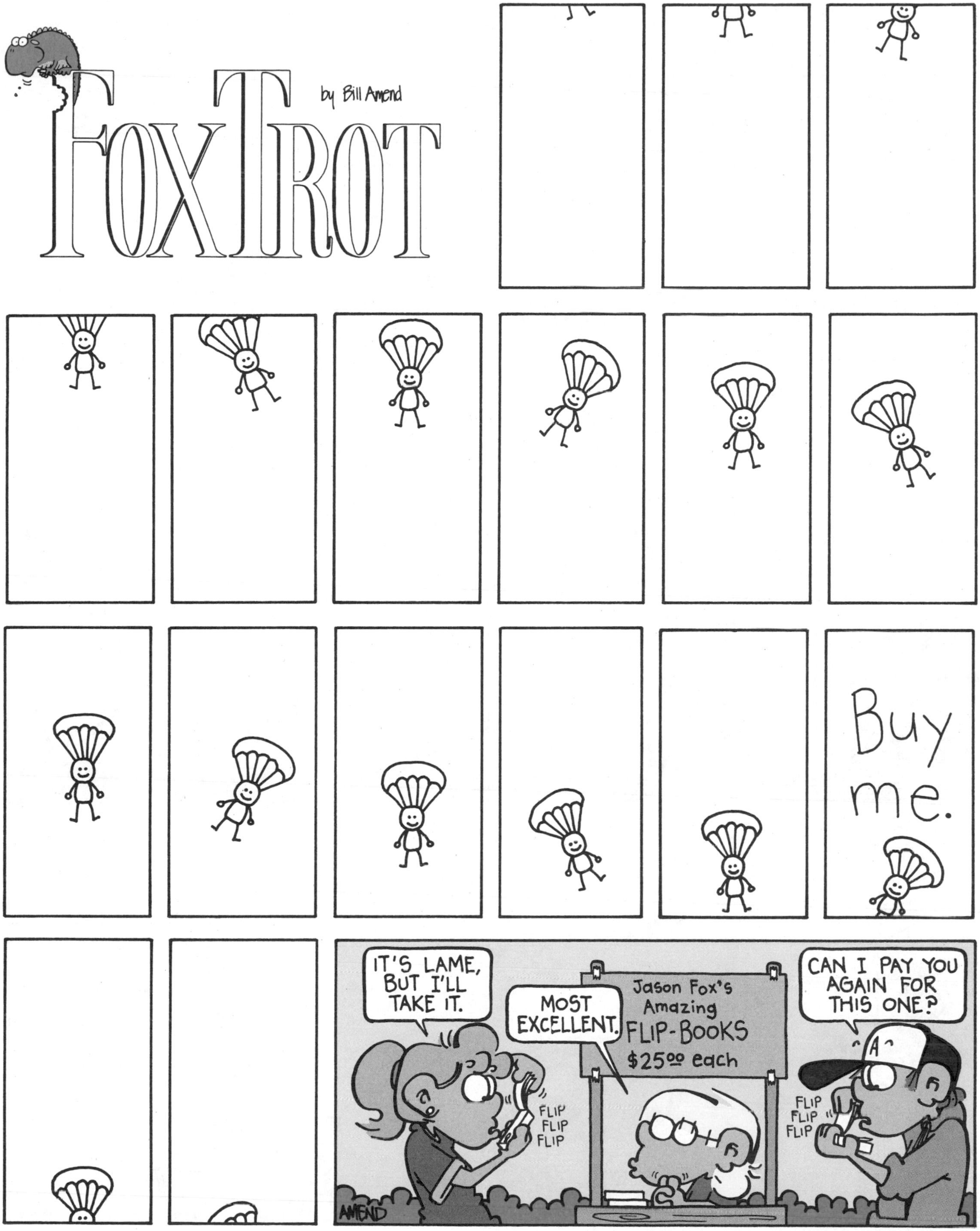
FoxTrot
by Bill Amend
Buy me.
IT'S LAME, BUT I'LL TAKE IT.
MOST EXCELLENT.
Jason Fox's Amazing FLIP-BOOKS $25⁰⁰ each
FLIP FLIP FLIP
FLIP FLIP FLIP
CAN I PAY YOU AGAIN FOR THIS ONE?
AMEND

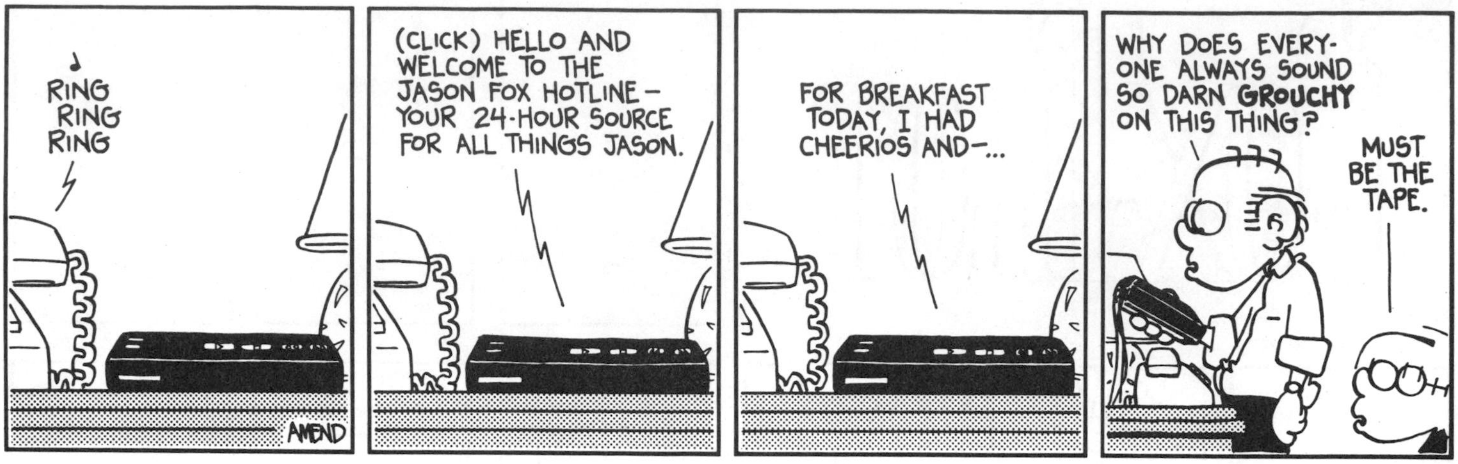
RING
RING
RING
AMEND
(CLICK) HELLO AND WELCOME TO THE JASON FOX HOTLINE— YOUR 24-HOUR SOURCE FOR ALL THINGS JASON.
FOR BREAKFAST TODAY, I HAD CHEERIOS AND—...
WHY DOES EVERY-ONE ALWAYS SOUND SO DARN **GROUCHY** ON THIS THING?
MUST BE THE TAPE.

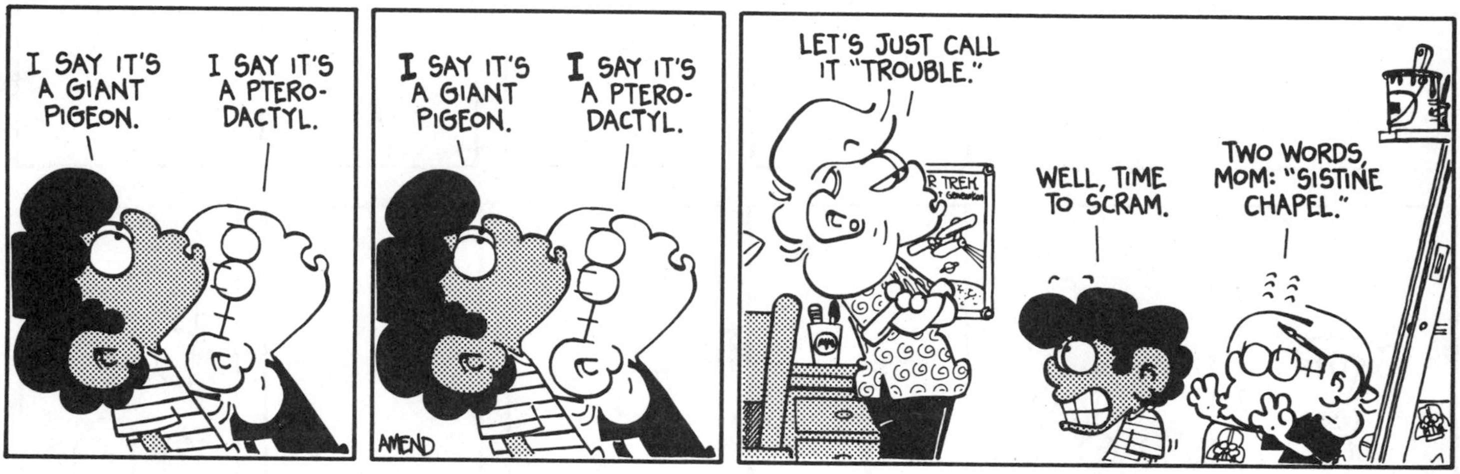
I SAY IT'S A GIANT PIGEON.
I SAY IT'S A PTERO-DACTYL.
I SAY IT'S A GIANT PIGEON.
I SAY IT'S A PTERO-DACTYL.
AMEND
LET'S JUST CALL IT "TROUBLE."
WELL, TIME TO SCRAM.
TWO WORDS, MOM: "SISTINE CHAPEL."

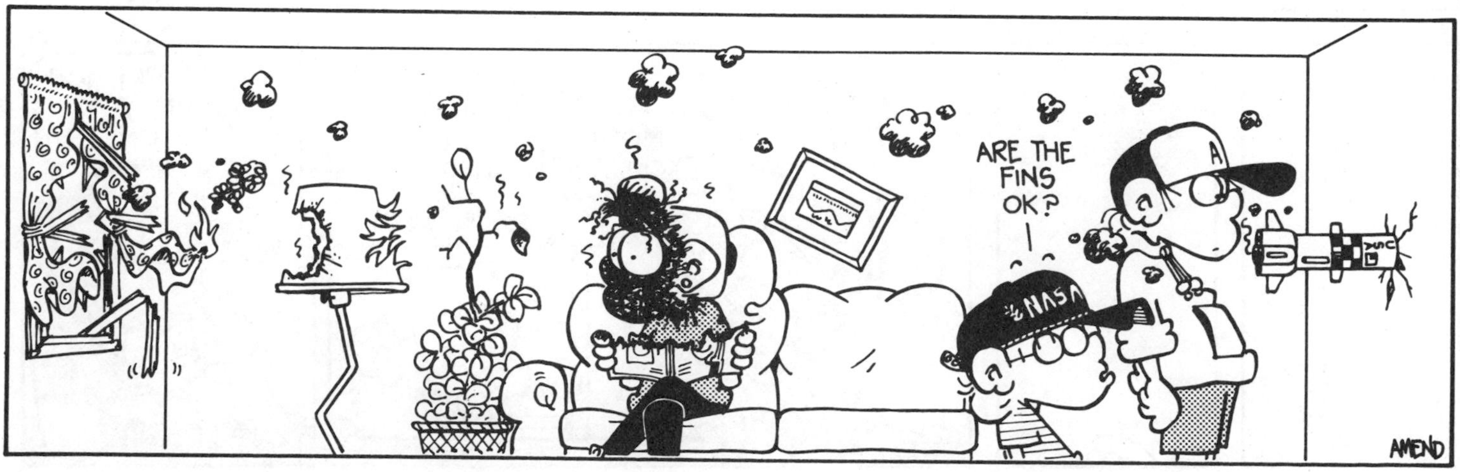
ARE THE FINS OK?
NASA
AMEND

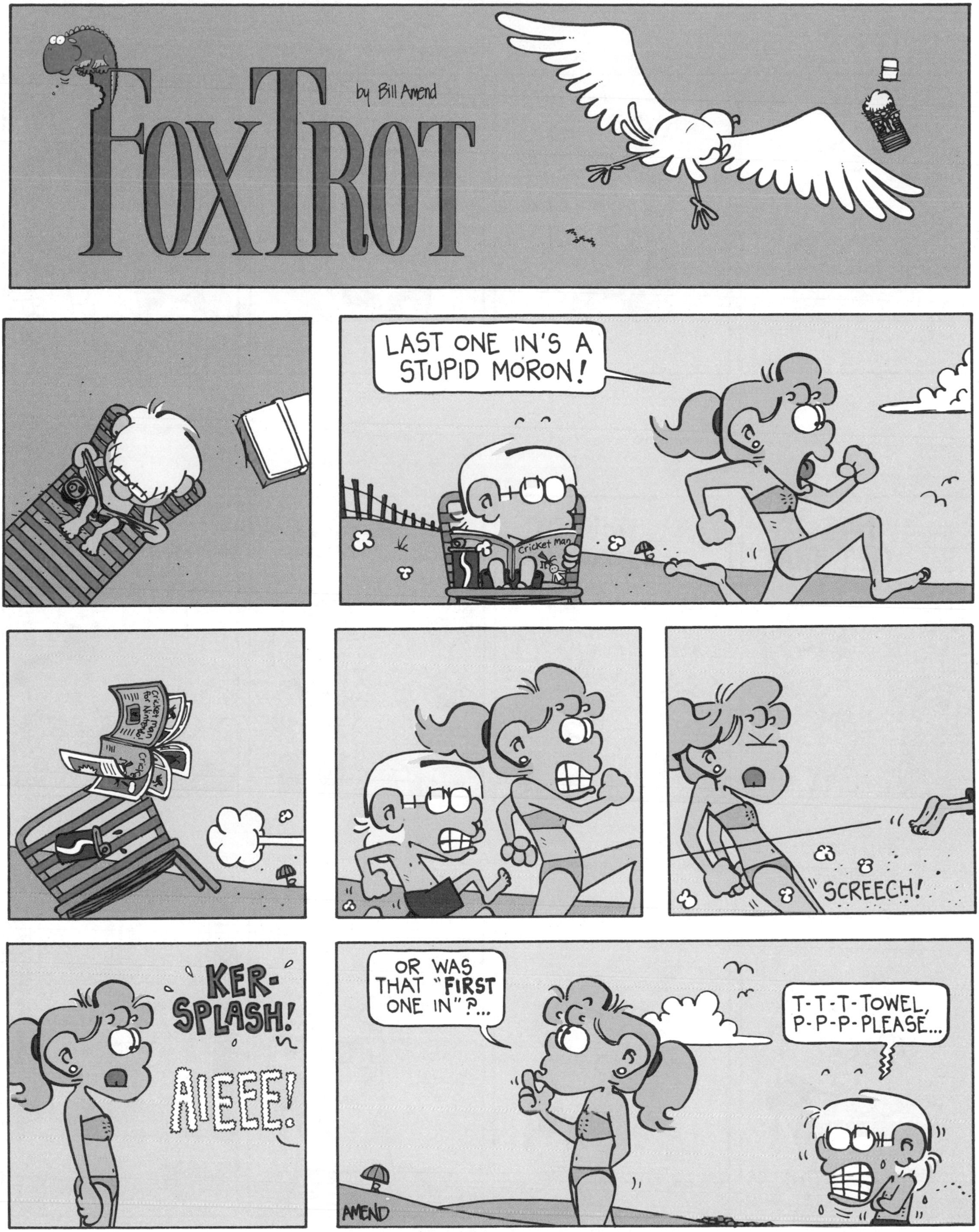
FoxTrot
by Bill Amend
LAST ONE IN'S A STUPID MORON!
Cricket Man
SCREECH!
KER-SPLASH!
AIEEE!
OR WAS THAT "FIRST ONE IN"?...
T-T-T-TOWEL, P-P-P-PLEASE...
AMEND

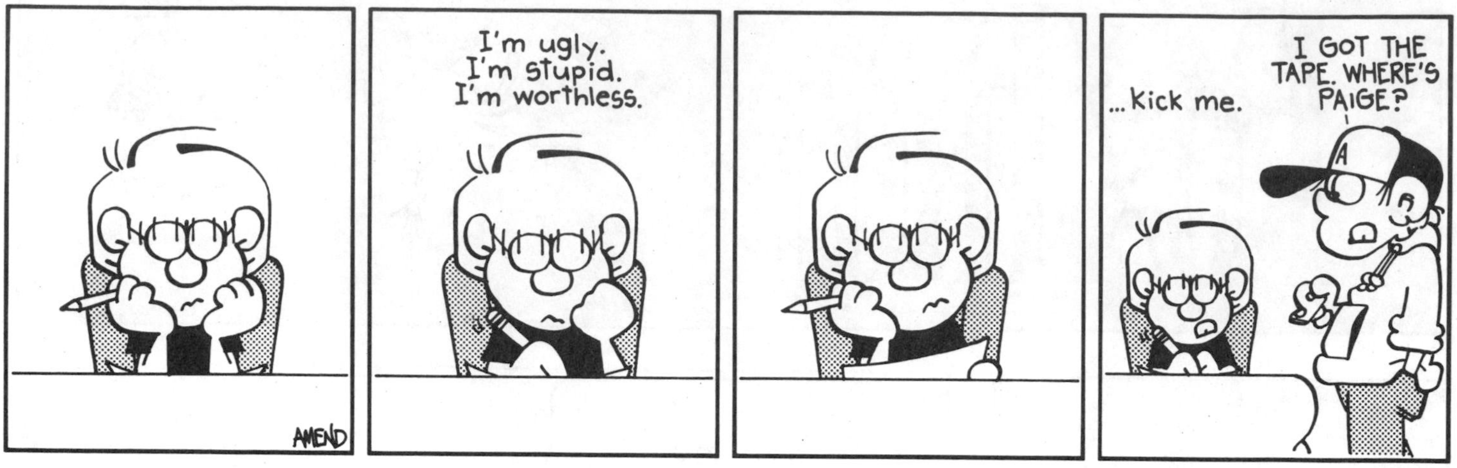
I'm ugly.
I'm stupid.
I'm worthless.
...kick me.
I GOT THE TAPE. WHERE'S PAIGE?
AMEND

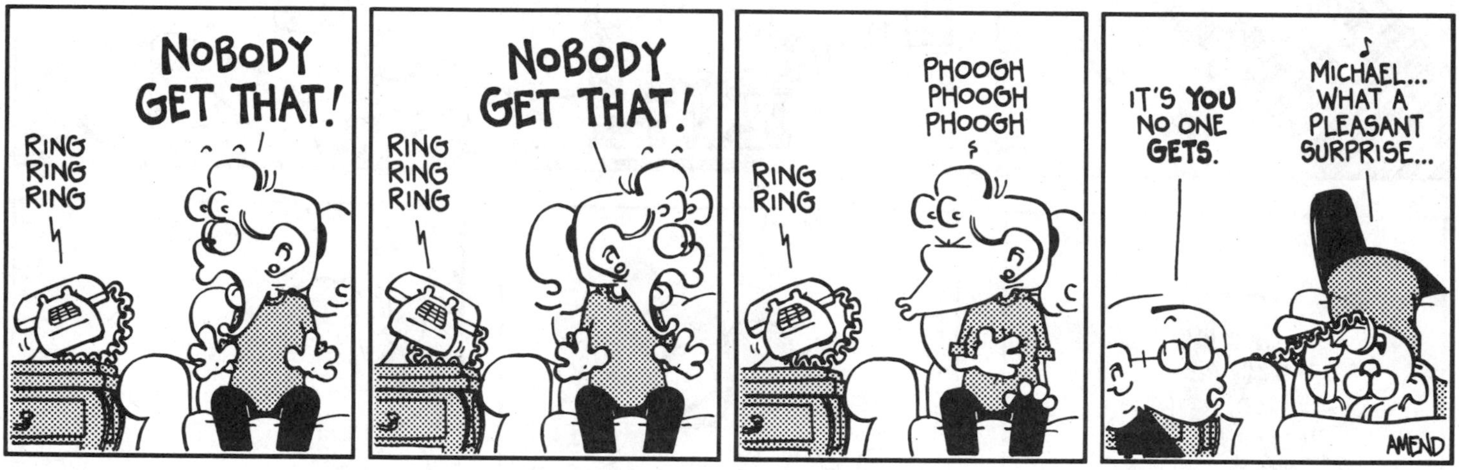
RING RING RING
NOBODY GET THAT!
RING RING RING
NOBODY GET THAT!
RING RING
PHOOGH PHOOGH PHOOGH
IT'S **YOU** NO ONE **GETS**.
MICHAEL... WHAT A PLEASANT SURPRISE...
AMEND

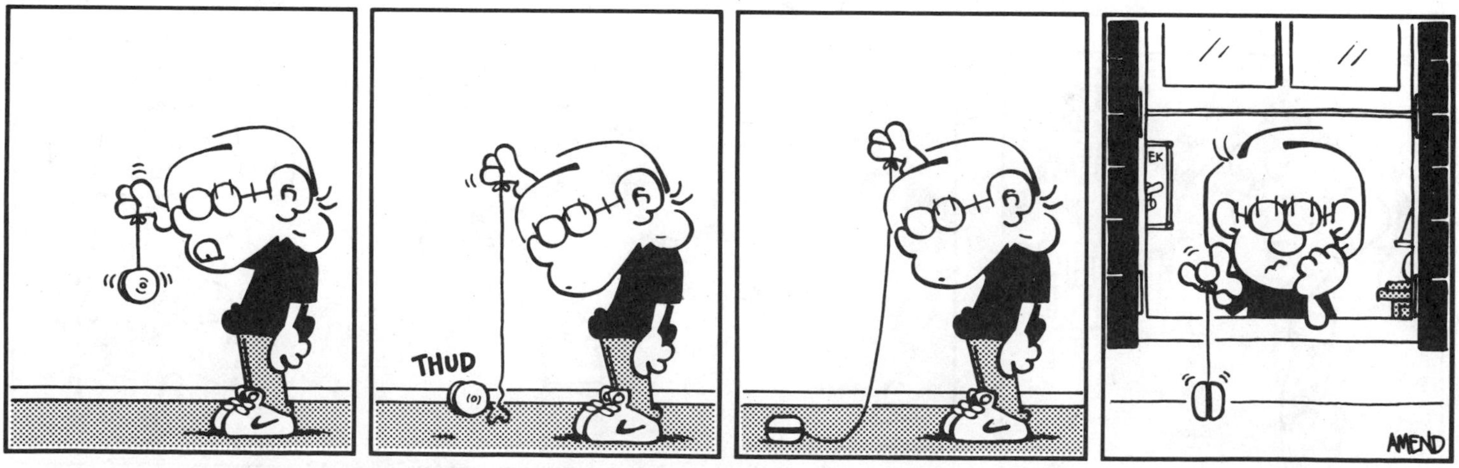
THUD
AMEND

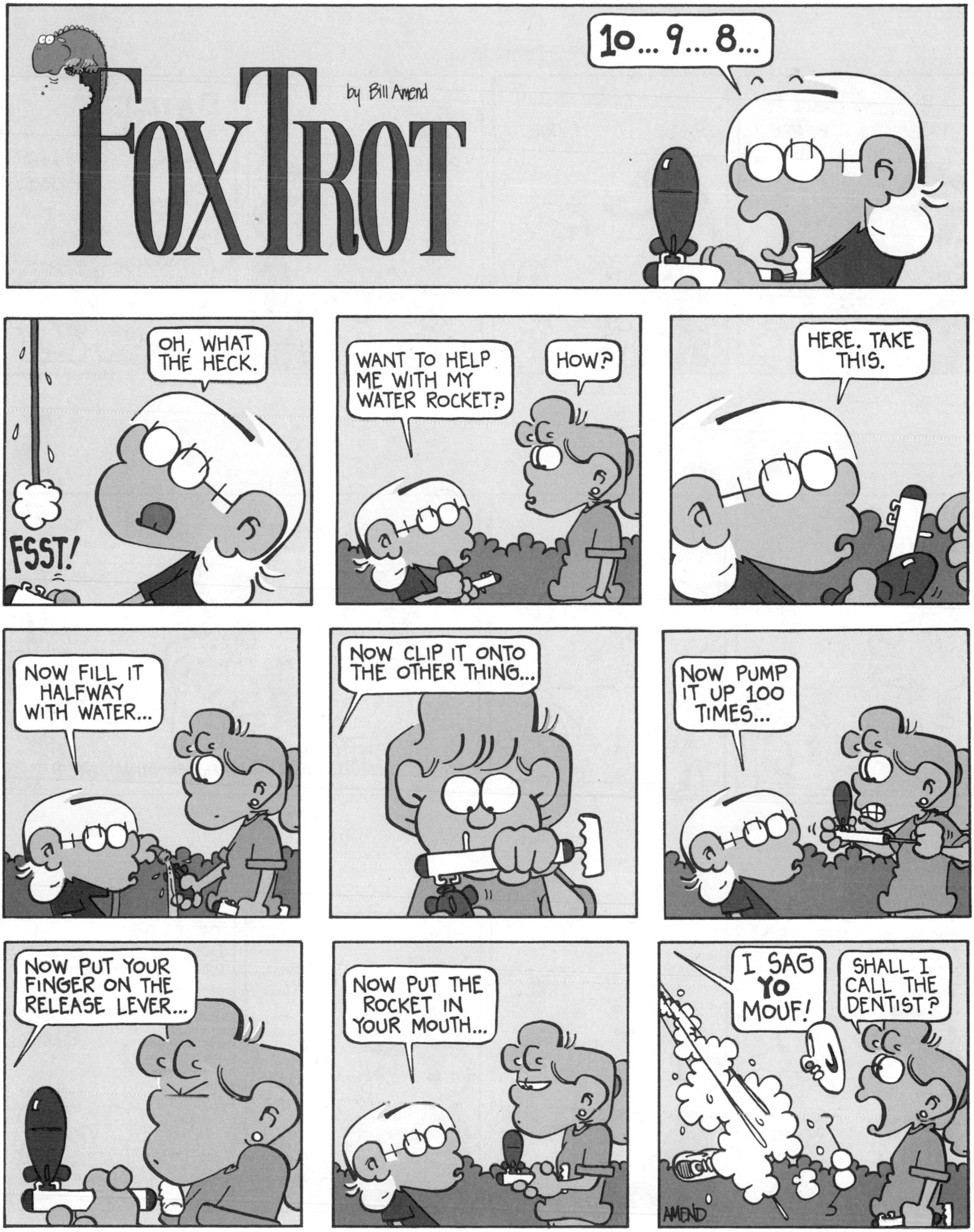
FoxTrot
by Bill Amend
10... 9... 8...
FSST!
OH, WHAT THE HECK.
WANT TO HELP ME WITH MY WATER ROCKET?
HOW?
HERE. TAKE THIS.
NOW FILL IT HALFWAY WITH WATER...
NOW CLIP IT ONTO THE OTHER THING...
NOW PUMP IT UP 100 TIMES...
NOW PUT YOUR FINGER ON THE RELEASE LEVER...
NOW PUT THE ROCKET IN YOUR MOUTH...
I SAG YO MOUF!
SHALL I CALL THE DENTIST?
AMEND

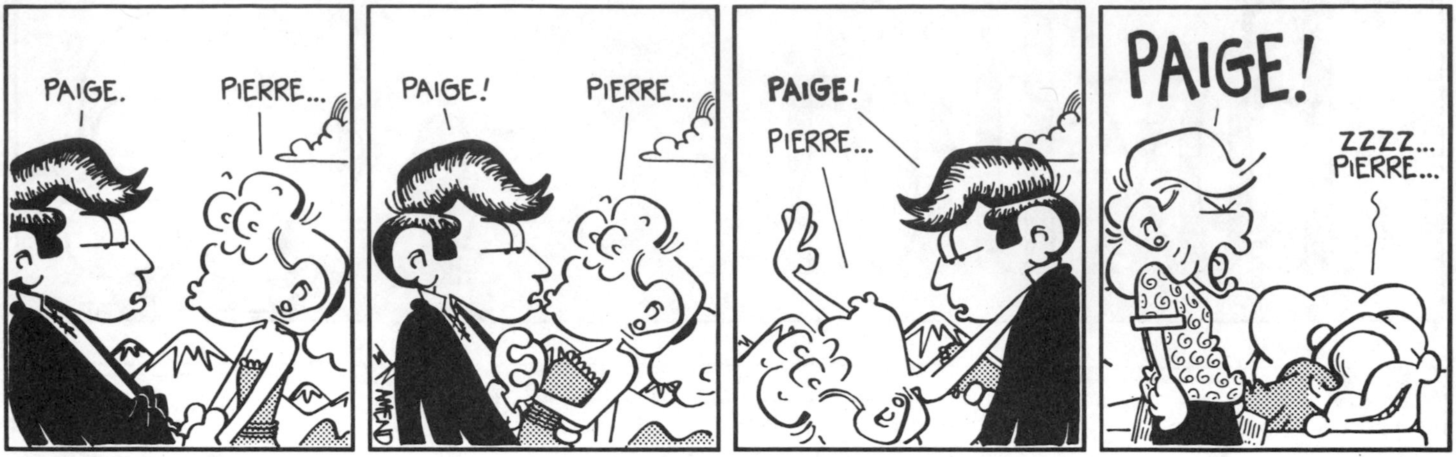
PAIGE.
PIERRE...
PAIGE!
PIERRE...
AMEND
PAIGE!
PIERRE...
PAIGE!
ZZZZ...
PIERRE...

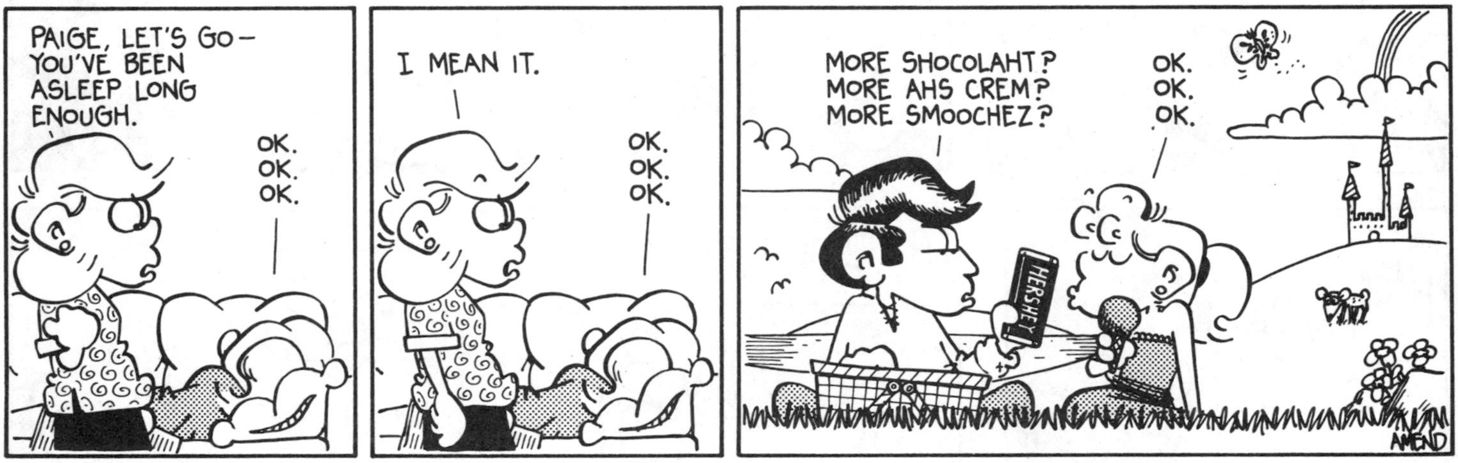
PAIGE, LET'S GO—
YOU'VE BEEN
ASLEEP LONG
ENOUGH.
OK.
OK.
OK.
I MEAN IT.
OK.
OK.
OK.
MORE SHOCOLAHT?
MORE AHS CREM?
MORE SMOOCHEZ?
OK.
OK.
OK.
HERSHEY
AMEND

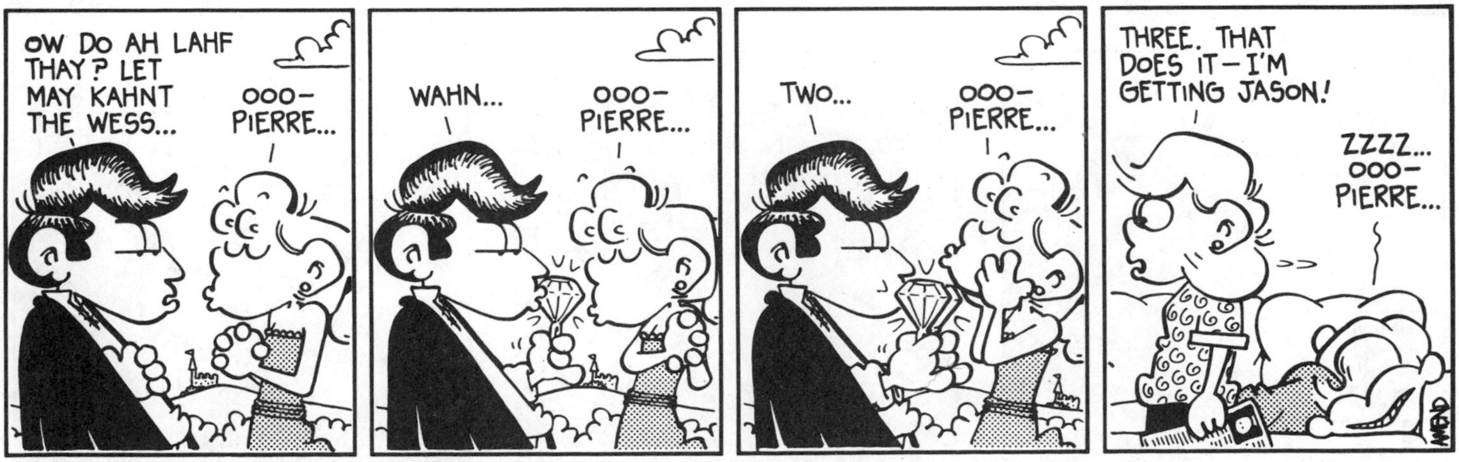
OW DO AH LAHF
THAY? LET
MAY KAHNT
THE WESS...
OOO-
PIERRE...
WAHN...
OOO-
PIERRE...
TWO...
OOO-
PIERRE...
THREE. THAT
DOES IT—I'M
GETTING JASON!
ZZZZ...
OOO-
PIERRE...
AMEND

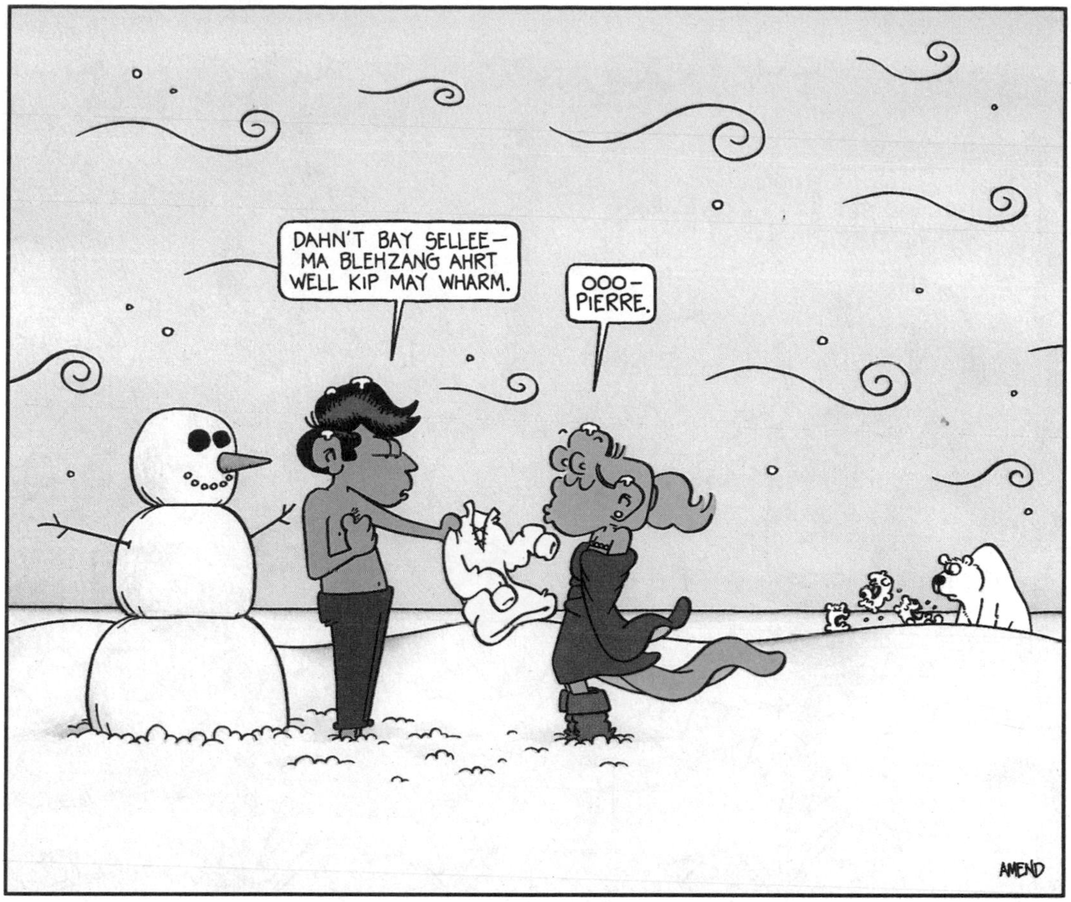
DAHN'T BAY SELLEE—
MA BLEHZANG AHRT
WELL KIP MAY WHARM.
OOO-
PIERRE.
AMEND

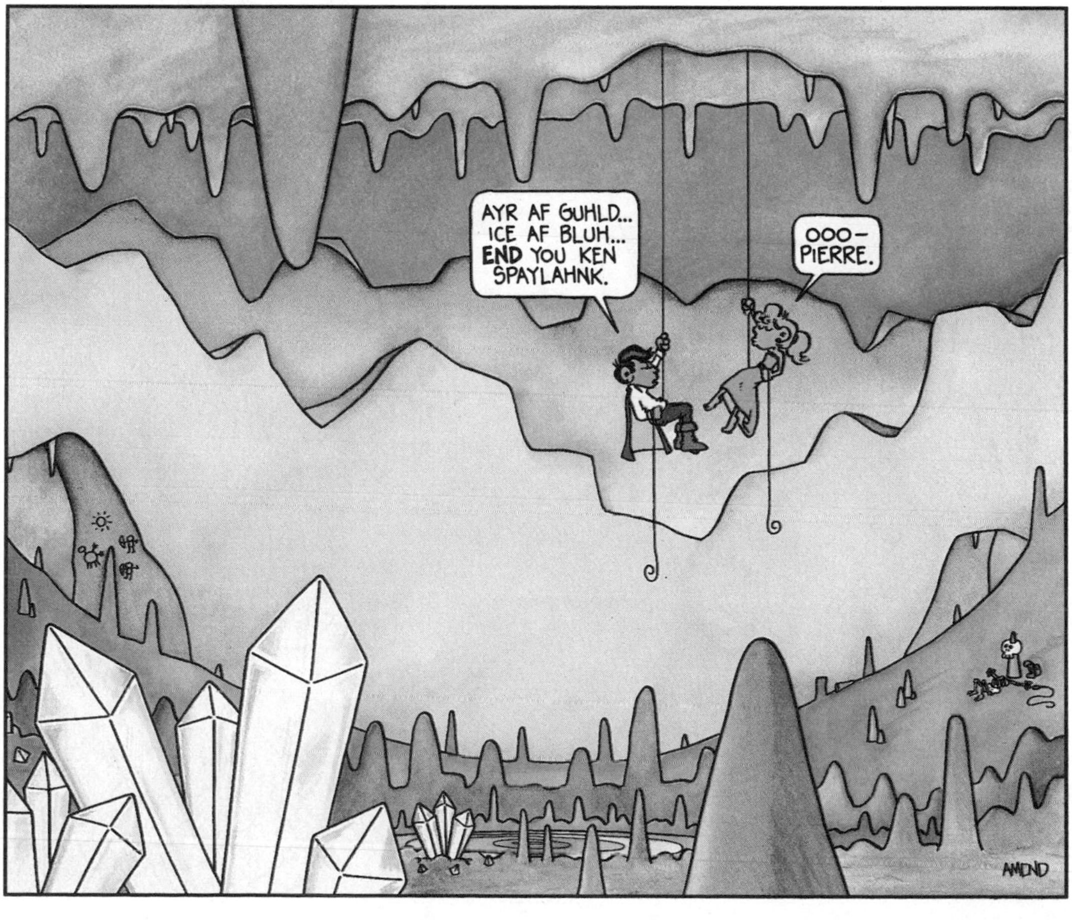
AYR AF GUHLD...
ICE AF BLUH...
END YOU KEN
SPAYLAHNK.
OOO-
PIERRE.
AMEND

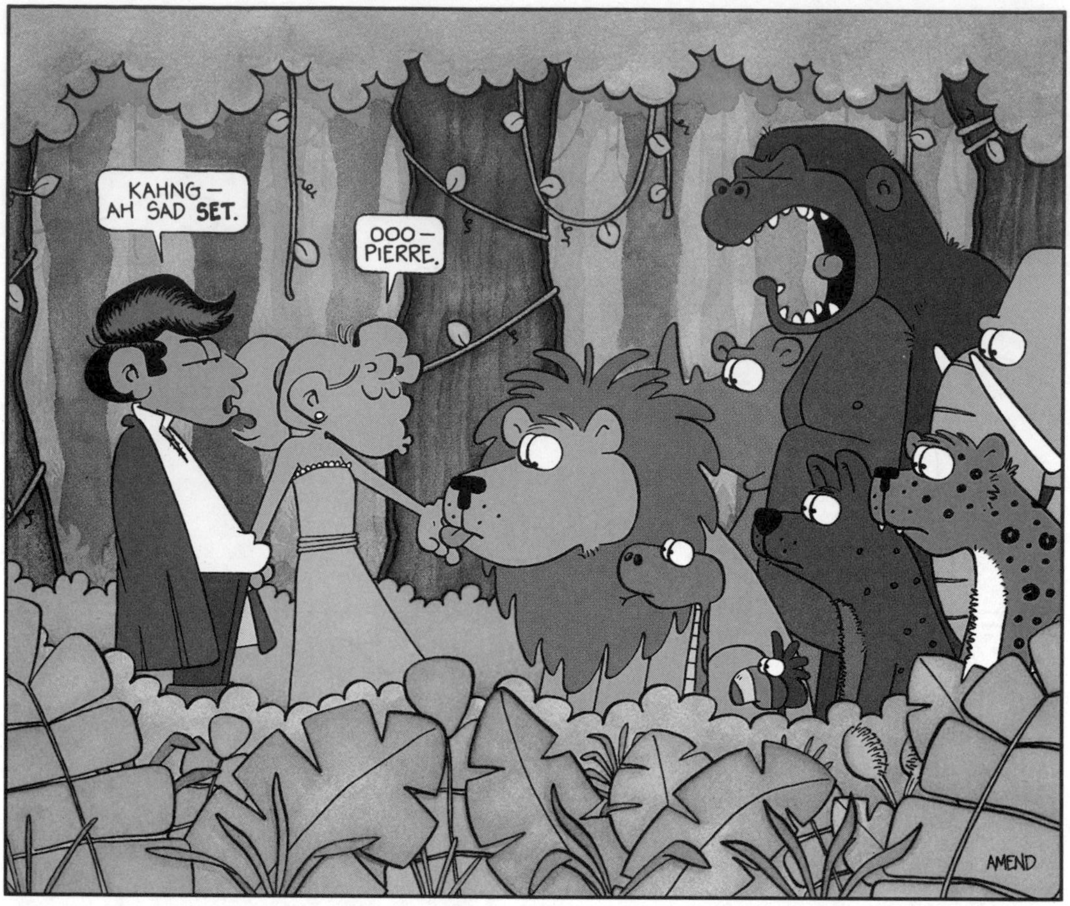
KAHNG— AH SAD **SET**.
OOO— PIERRE.
AMEND

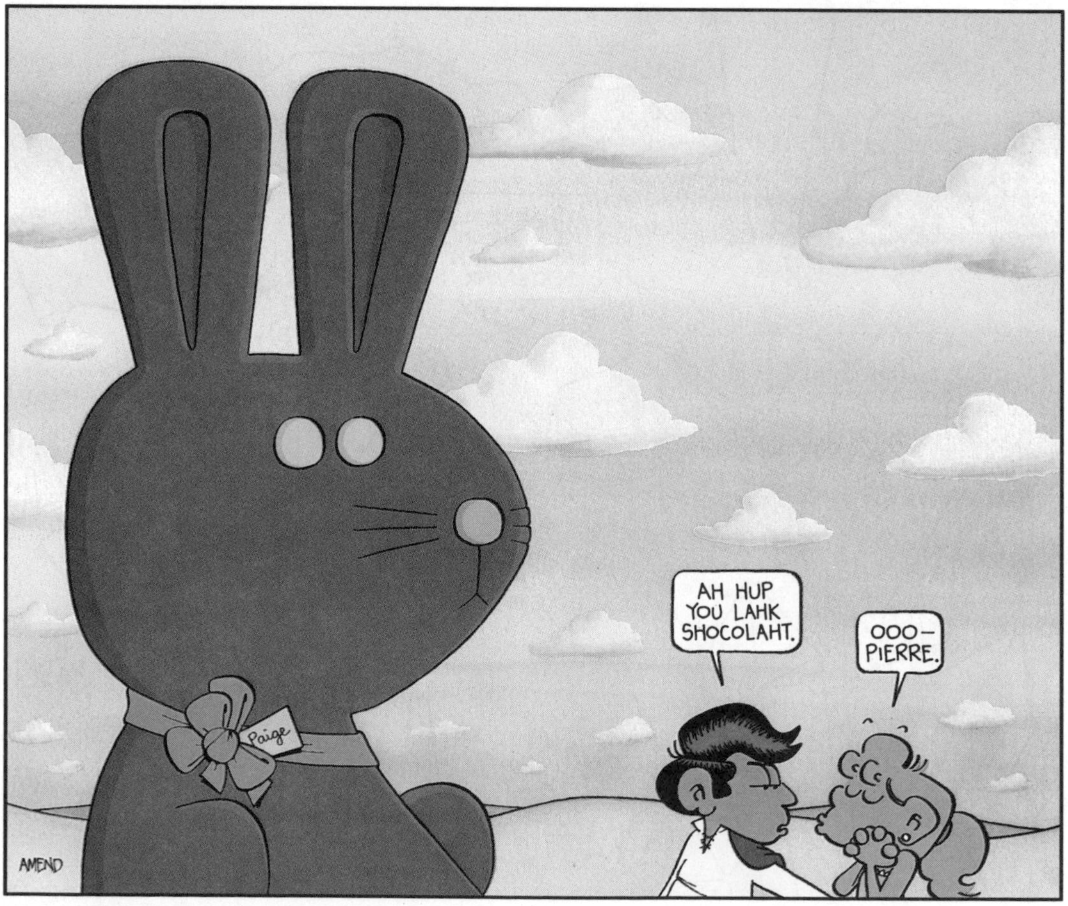
AH HUP YOU LAHK SHOCOLAHT.
OOO— PIERRE.
Paige
AMEND

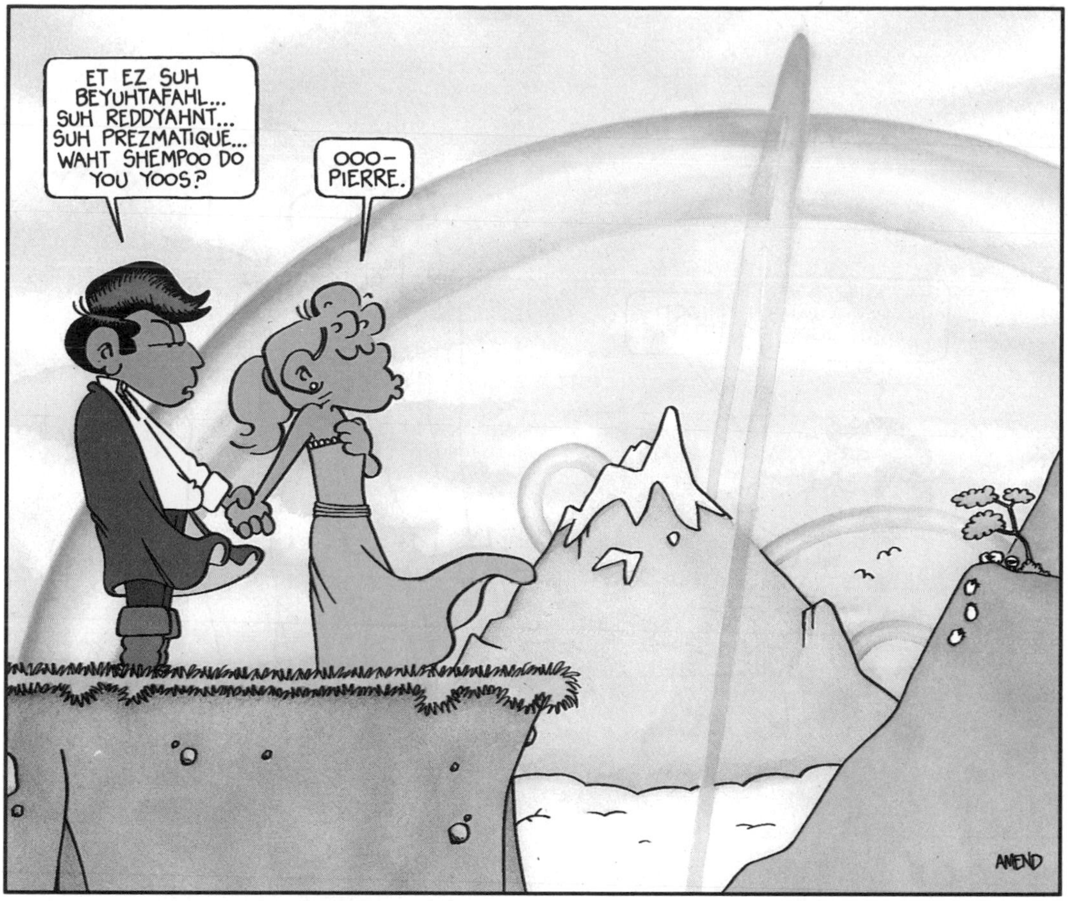
ET EZ SUH BEYUHTAFAHL... SUH REDDYAHNT... SUH PREZMATIQUE... WAHT SHEMPOO DO YOU YOOS?
OOO-PIERRE.
AMEND

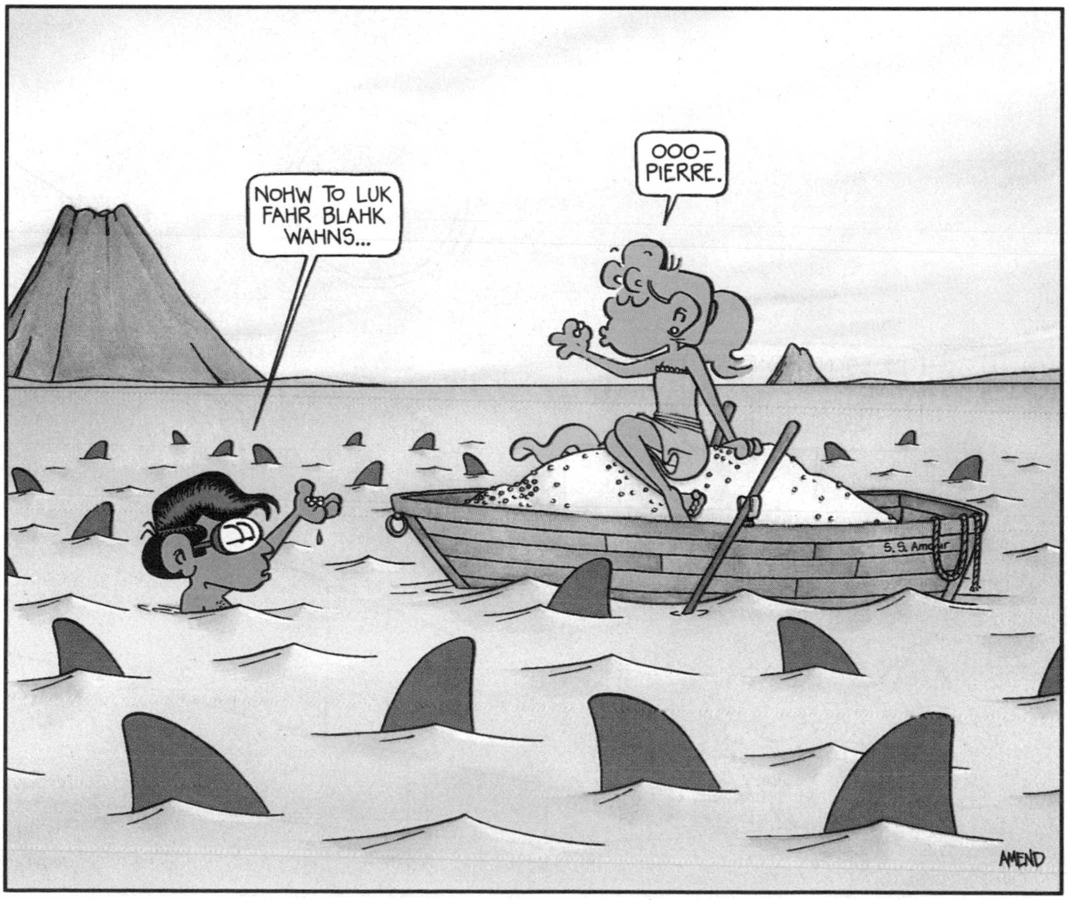
NOHW TO LUK FAHR BLAHK WAHNS...
OOO-PIERRE.
AMEND

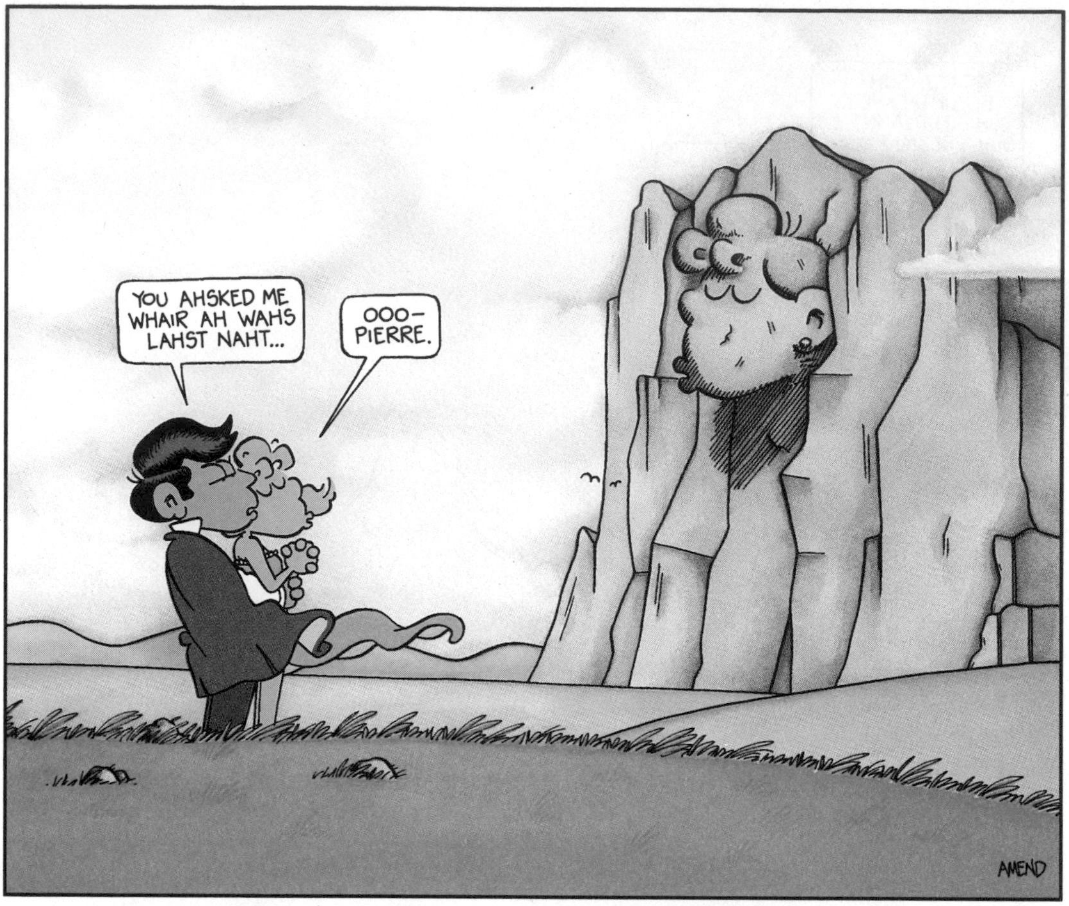
YOU AHSKED ME WHAIR AH WAHS LAHST NAHT...
OOO-PIERRE.
AMEND

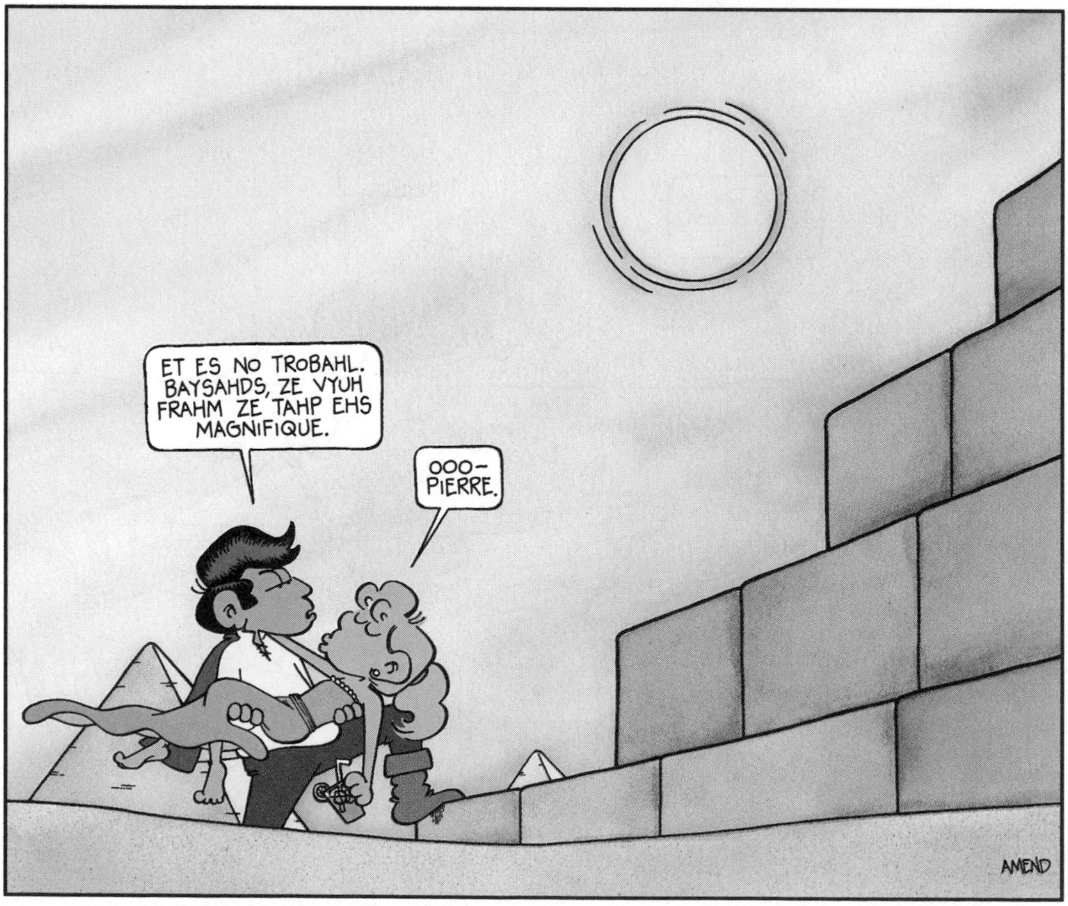
ET ES NO TROBAHL. BAYSAHDS, ZE VYUH FRAHM ZE TAHP EHS MAGNIFIQUE.
OOO-PIERRE.
AMEND

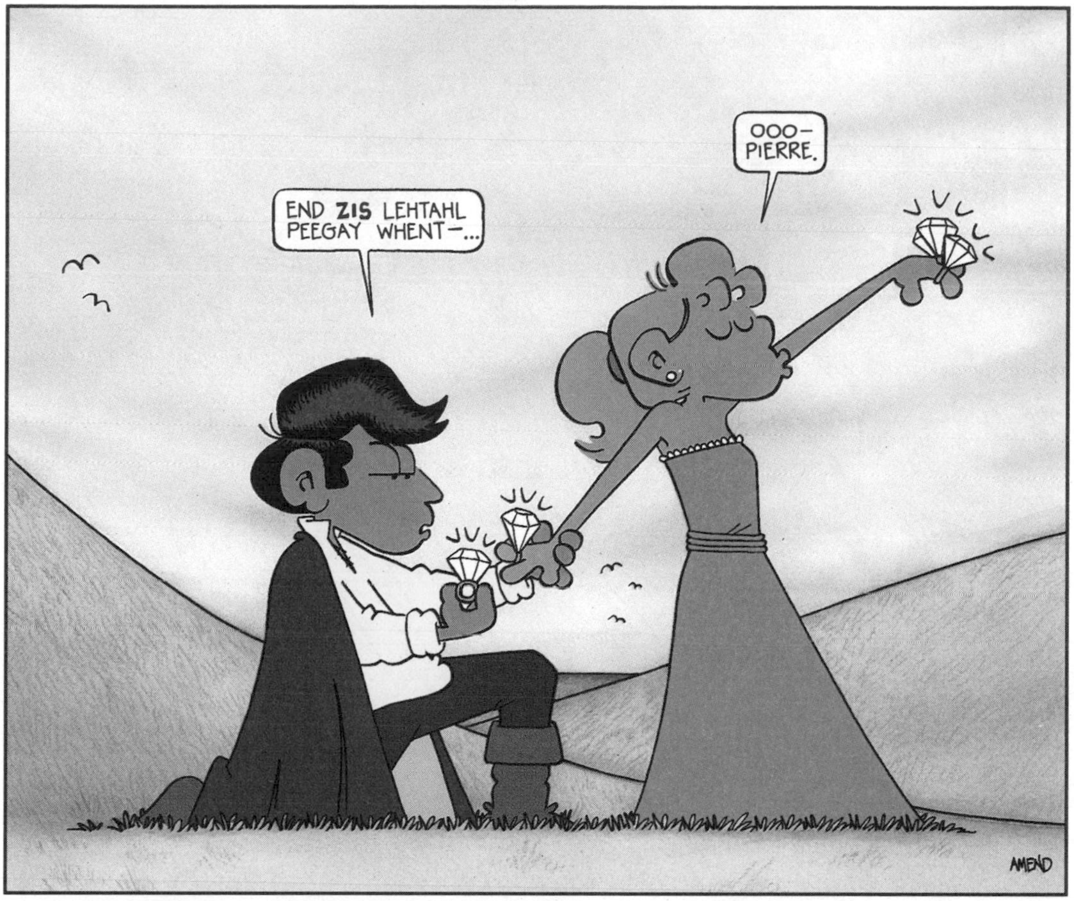
END ZIS LEHTAHL PEEGAY WHENT—...
OOO-PIERRE.
AMEND

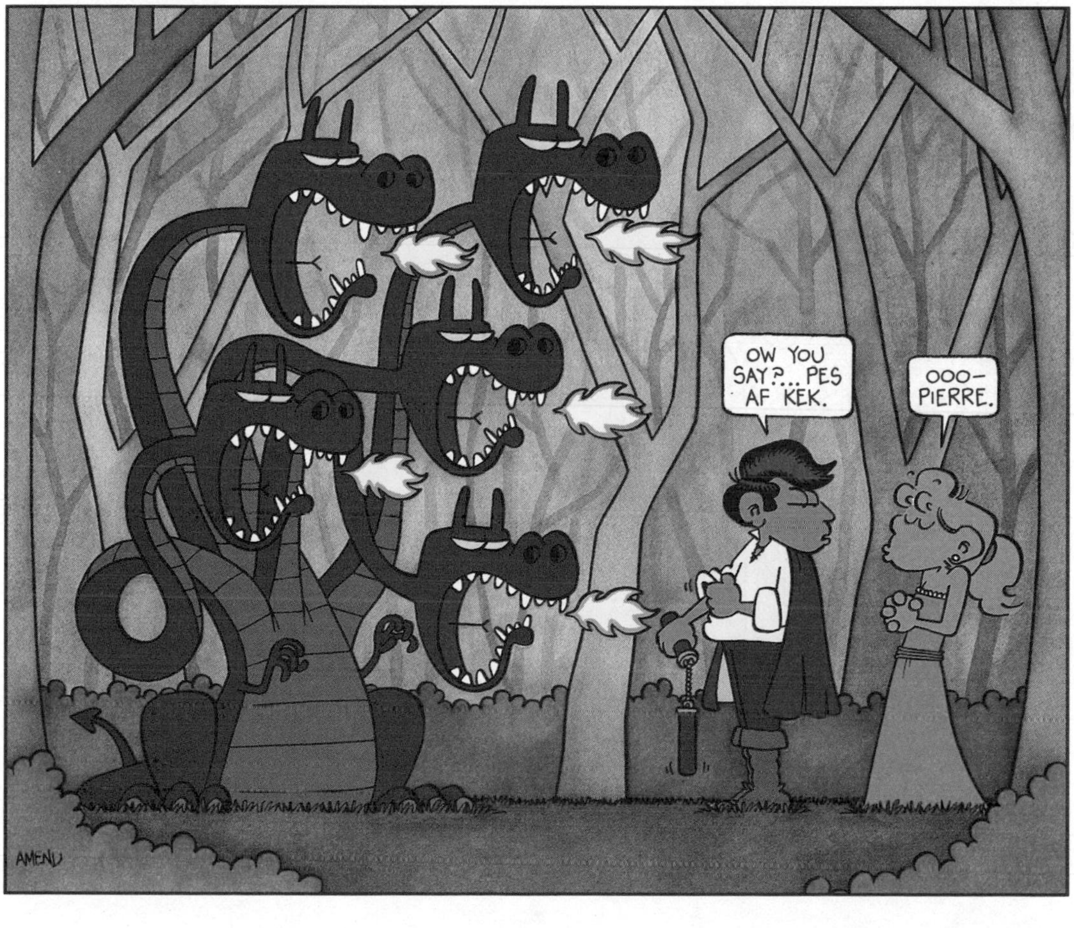
OW YOU SAY?... PES AF KEK.
OOO-PIERRE.
AMEND

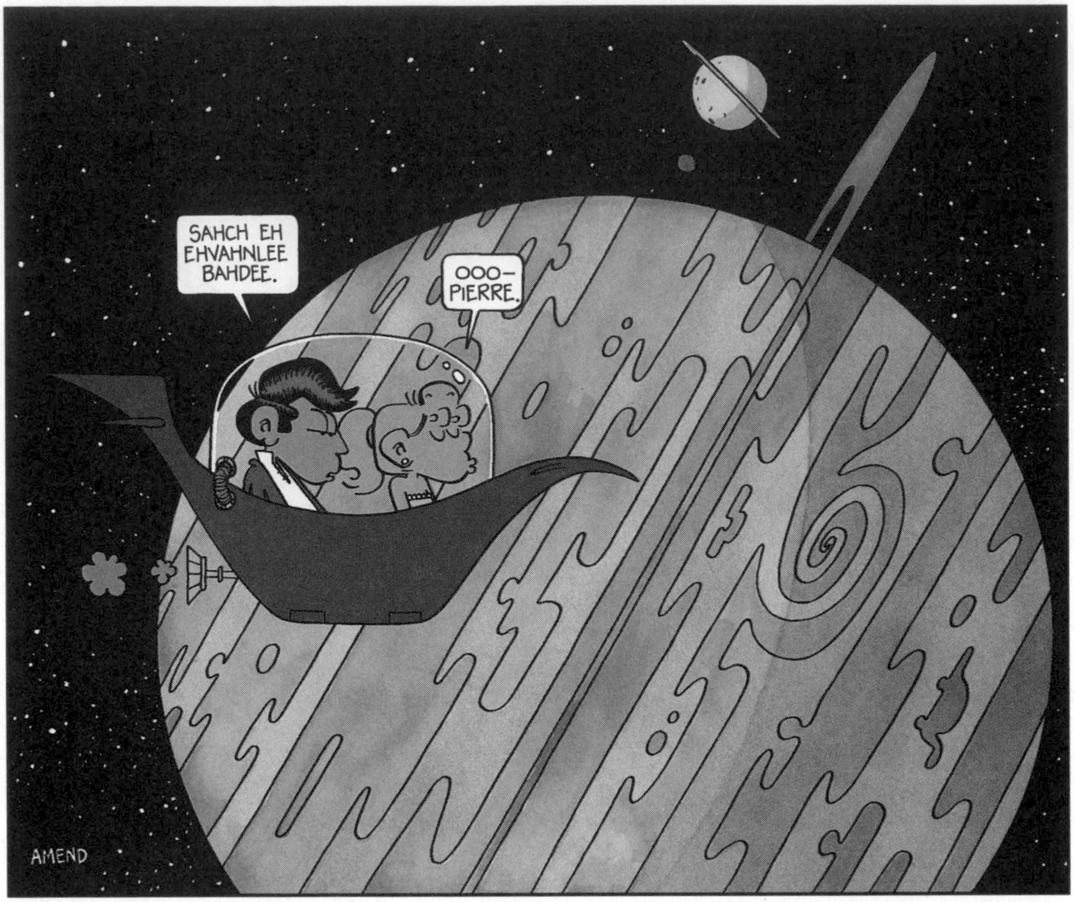
SAHCH EH EHVAHNLEE BAHDEE.
OOO- PIERRE.
AMEND

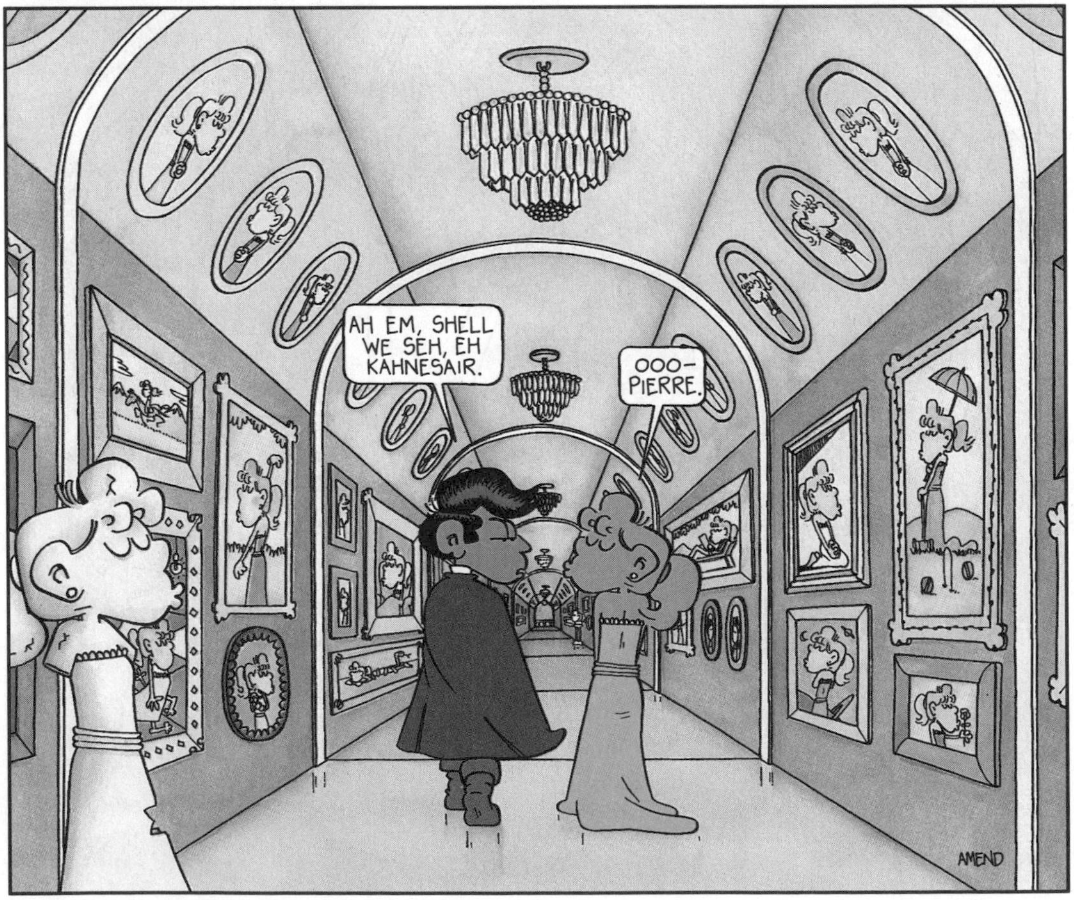
AH EM, SHELL WE SEH, EH KAHNESAIR.
OOO- PIERRE.
AMEND

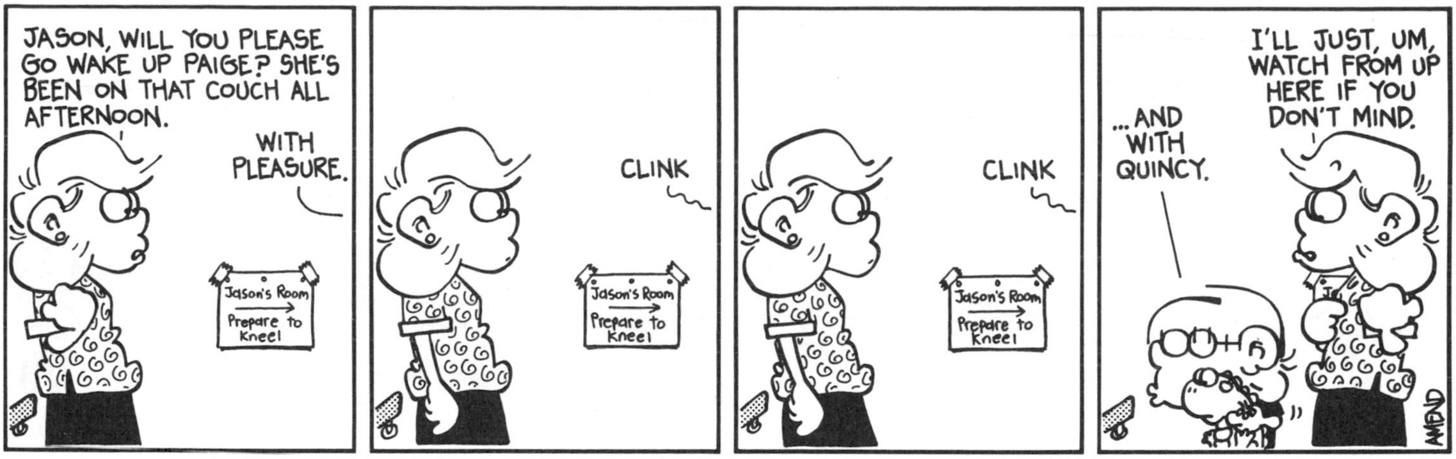
JASON, WILL YOU PLEASE GO WAKE UP PAIGE? SHE'S BEEN ON THAT COUCH ALL AFTERNOON.
WITH PLEASURE.
Jason's Room
Prepare to Kneel
CLINK
Jason's Room
Prepare to Kneel
CLINK
Jason's Room
Prepare to Kneel
...AND WITH QUINCY.
I'LL JUST, UM, WATCH FROM UP HERE IF YOU DON'T MIND.
AMEND

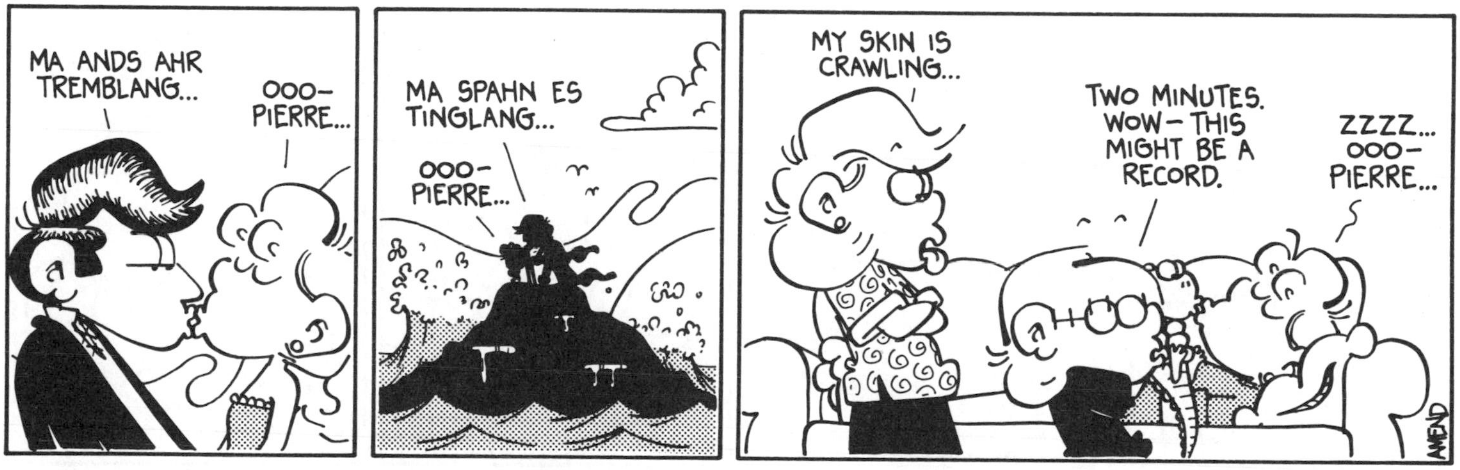
MA ANDS AHR TREMBLANG...
OOO-PIERRE...
MA SPAHN ES TINGLANG...
OOO-PIERRE...
MY SKIN IS CRAWLING...
TWO MINUTES. WOW–THIS MIGHT BE A RECORD.
ZZZZ... OOO-PIERRE...
AMEND

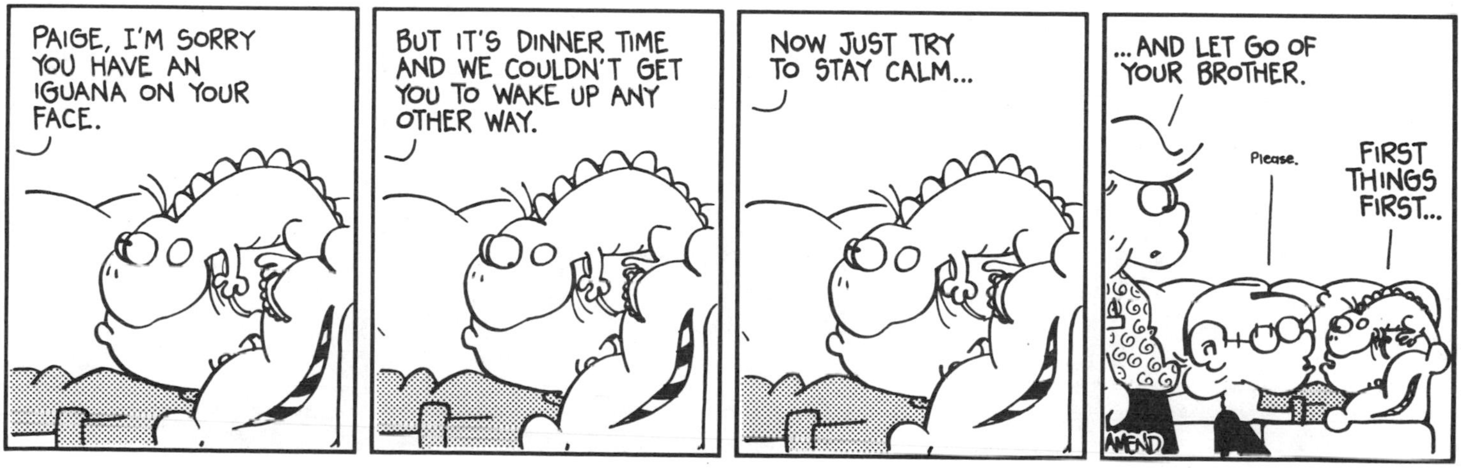
PAIGE, I'M SORRY YOU HAVE AN IGUANA ON YOUR FACE.
BUT IT'S DINNER TIME AND WE COULDN'T GET YOU TO WAKE UP ANY OTHER WAY.
NOW JUST TRY TO STAY CALM...
...AND LET GO OF YOUR BROTHER.
Please.
FIRST THINGS FIRST...
AMEND

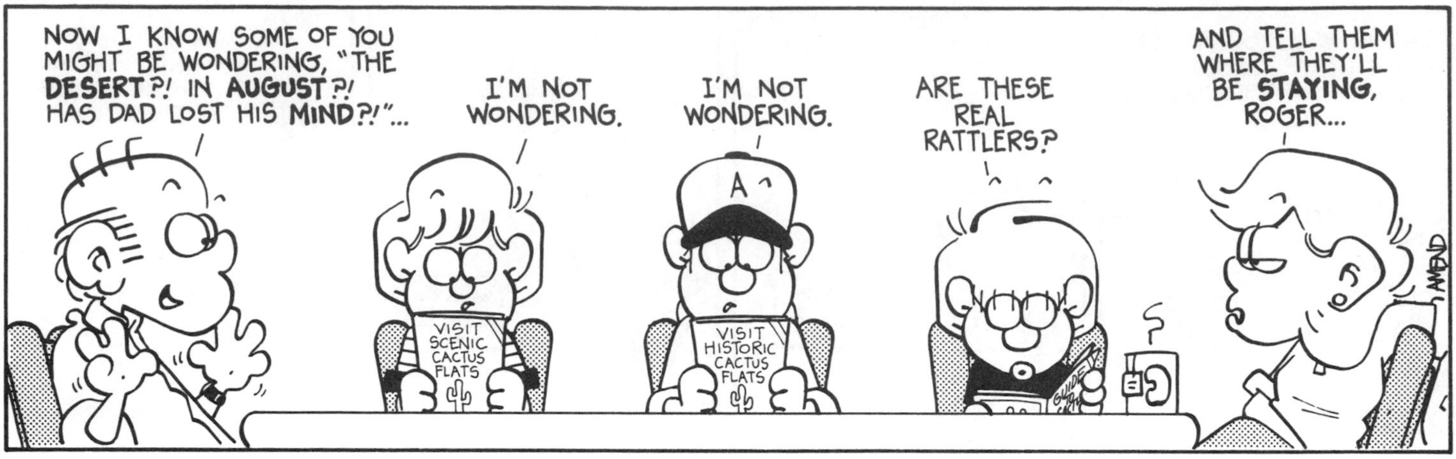
NOW I KNOW SOME OF YOU MIGHT BE WONDERING, "THE **DESERT**?! IN **AUGUST**?! HAS DAD LOST HIS **MIND**?!"...
I'M NOT WONDERING.
VISIT SCENIC CACTUS FLATS
I'M NOT WONDERING.
VISIT HISTORIC CACTUS FLATS
ARE THESE REAL RATTLERS?
AND TELL THEM WHERE THEY'LL BE **STAYING**, ROGER...
AMEND

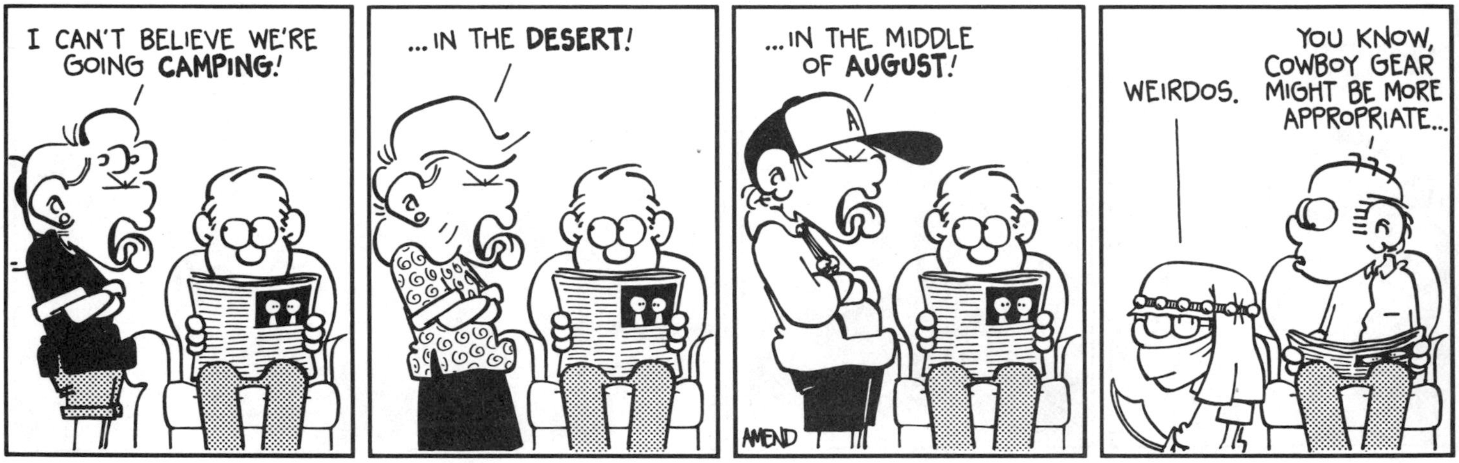
I CAN'T BELIEVE WE'RE GOING **CAMPING**!
...IN THE **DESERT**!
...IN THE MIDDLE OF **AUGUST**!
AMEND
WEIRDOS.
YOU KNOW, COWBOY GEAR MIGHT BE MORE APPROPRIATE...

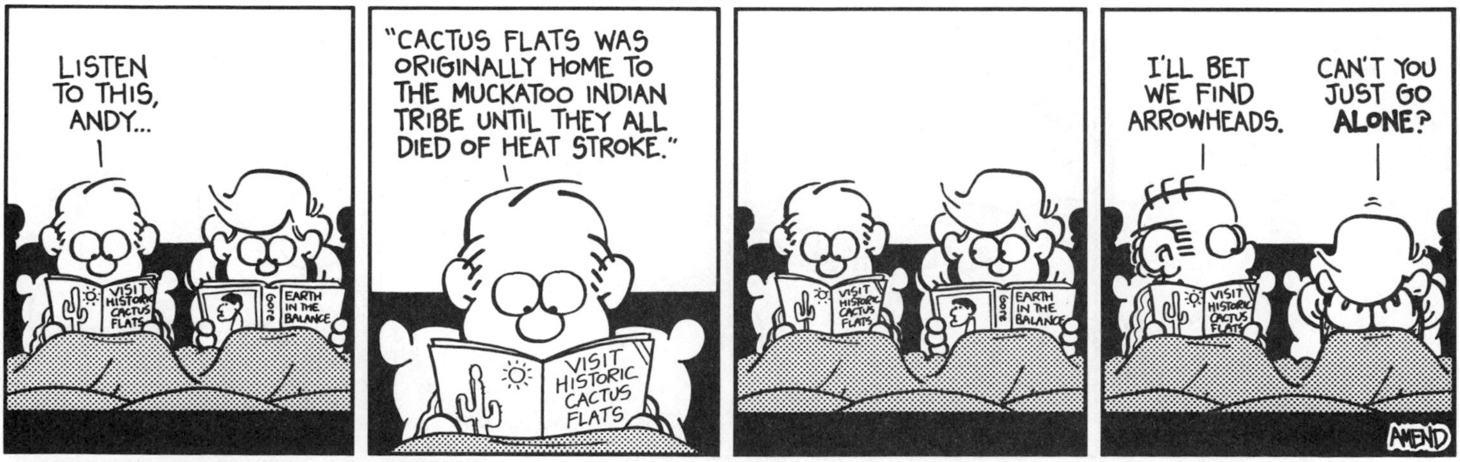
LISTEN TO THIS, ANDY...
EARTH IN THE BALANCE
GORE
"CACTUS FLATS WAS ORIGINALLY HOME TO THE MUCKATOO INDIAN TRIBE UNTIL THEY ALL DIED OF HEAT STROKE."
VISIT HISTORIC CACTUS FLATS
I'LL BET WE FIND ARROWHEADS.
CAN'T YOU JUST GO **ALONE**?
AMEND

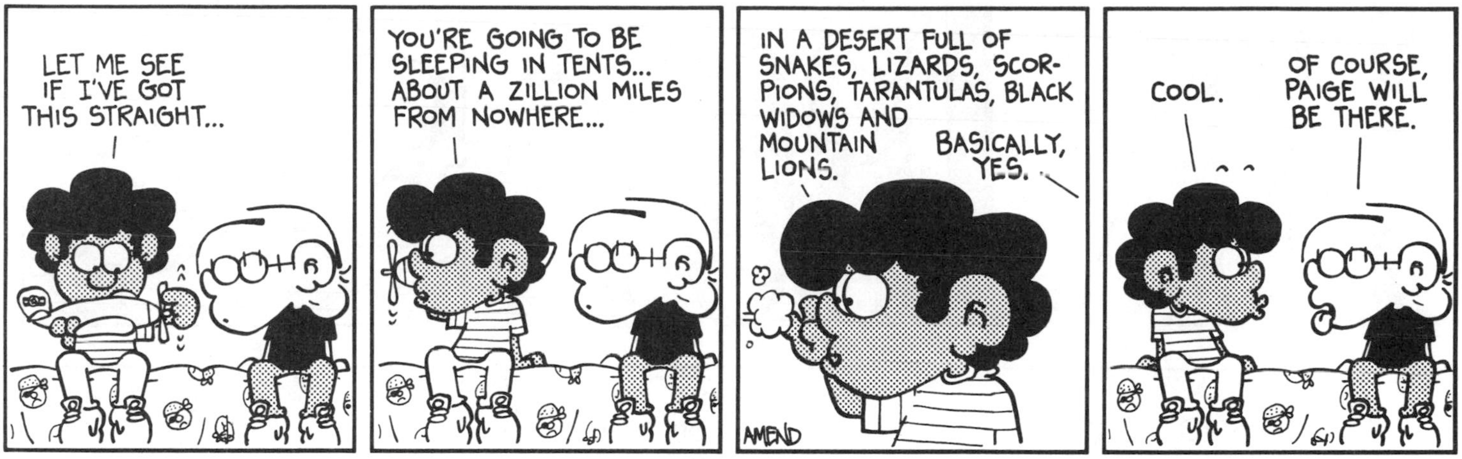
LET ME SEE IF I'VE GOT THIS STRAIGHT...
YOU'RE GOING TO BE SLEEPING IN TENTS... ABOUT A ZILLION MILES FROM NOWHERE...
IN A DESERT FULL OF SNAKES, LIZARDS, SCORPIONS, TARANTULAS, BLACK WIDOWS AND MOUNTAIN LIONS.
BASICALLY, YES.
AMEND
COOL.
OF COURSE, PAIGE WILL BE THERE.

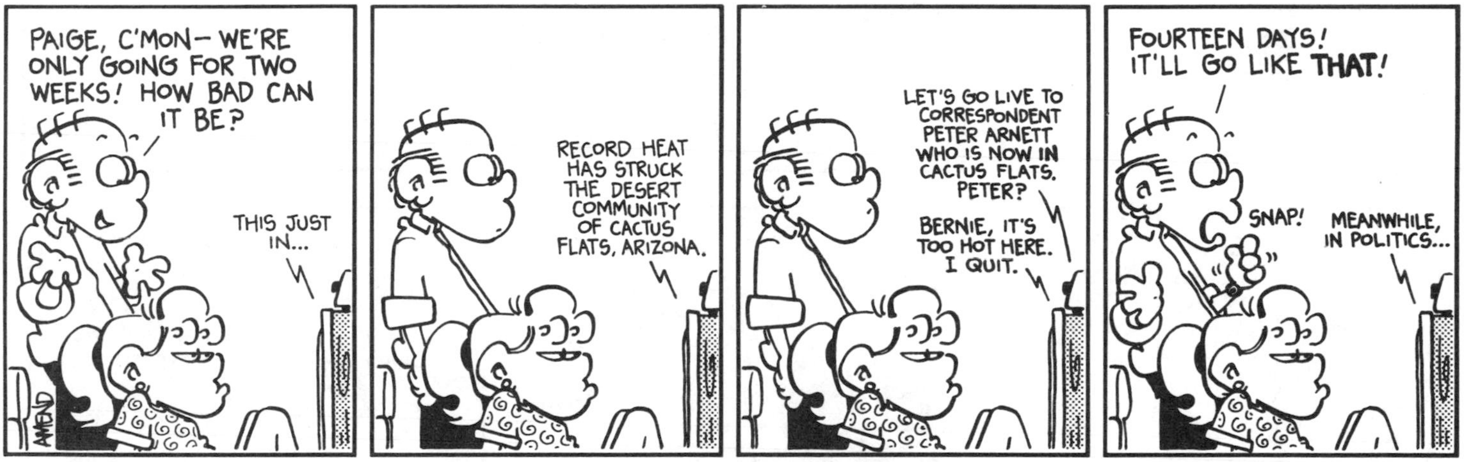
PAIGE, C'MON— WE'RE ONLY GOING FOR TWO WEEKS! HOW BAD CAN IT BE?
THIS JUST IN...
AMEND
RECORD HEAT HAS STRUCK THE DESERT COMMUNITY OF CACTUS FLATS, ARIZONA.
LET'S GO LIVE TO CORRESPONDENT PETER ARNETT WHO IS NOW IN CACTUS FLATS. PETER?
BERNIE, IT'S TOO HOT HERE. I QUIT.
FOURTEEN DAYS! IT'LL GO LIKE THAT!
SNAP!
MEANWHILE, IN POLITICS...

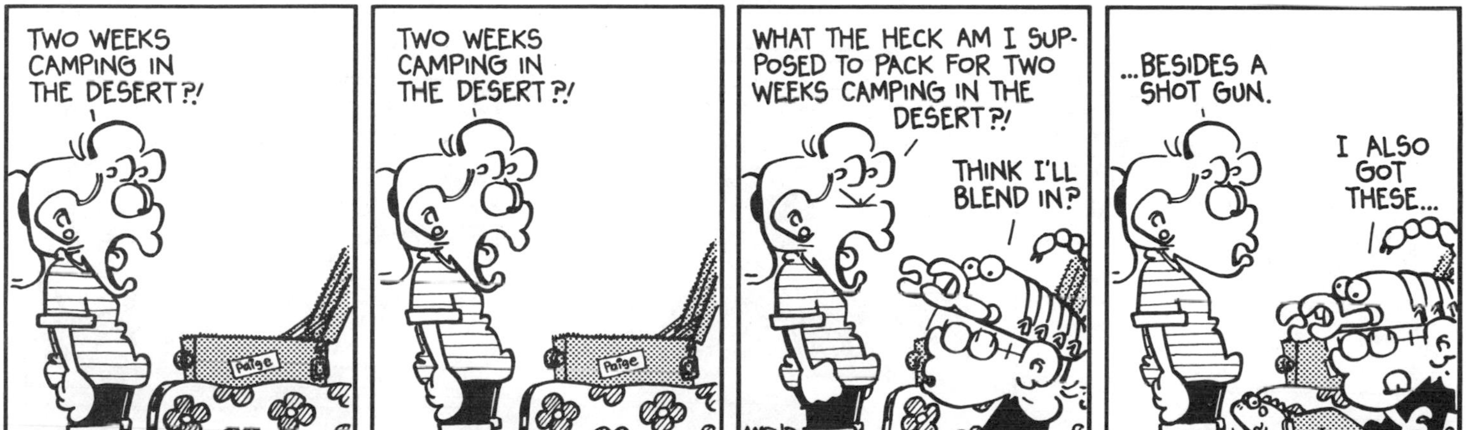
TWO WEEKS CAMPING IN THE DESERT?!
Paige
TWO WEEKS CAMPING IN THE DESERT?!
Paige
WHAT THE HECK AM I SUPPOSED TO PACK FOR TWO WEEKS CAMPING IN THE DESERT?!
THINK I'LL BLEND IN?
AMEND
...BESIDES A SHOT GUN.
I ALSO GOT THESE...

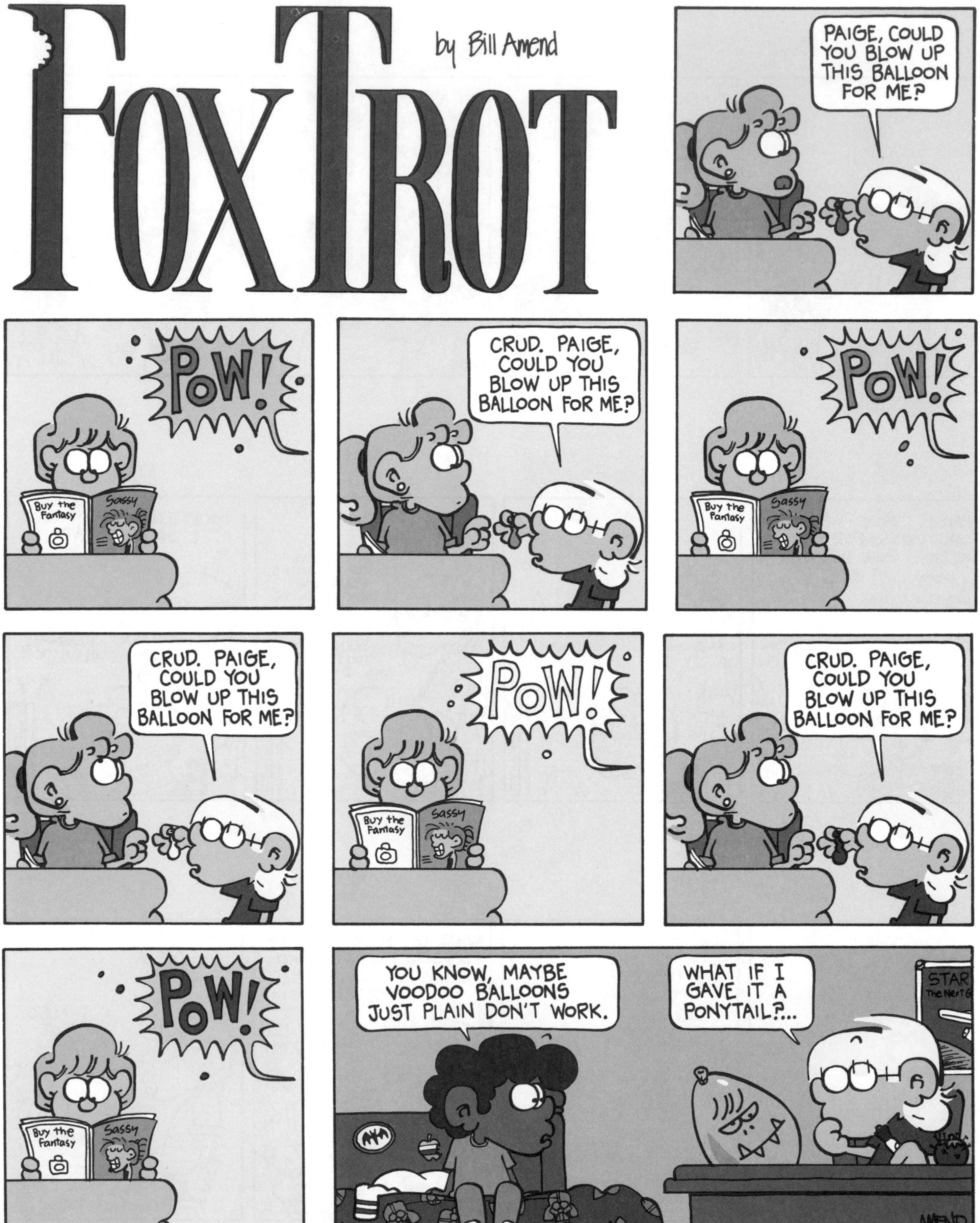
FoxTrot
by Bill Amend
PAIGE, COULD YOU BLOW UP THIS BALLOON FOR ME?
POW!
Buy the Fantasy
Sassy
CRUD. PAIGE, COULD YOU BLOW UP THIS BALLOON FOR ME?
POW!
CRUD. PAIGE, COULD YOU BLOW UP THIS BALLOON FOR ME?
POW!
CRUD. PAIGE, COULD YOU BLOW UP THIS BALLOON FOR ME?
POW!
YOU KNOW, MAYBE VOODOO BALLOONS JUST PLAIN DON'T WORK.
WHAT IF I GAVE IT A PONYTAIL?...
AMEND

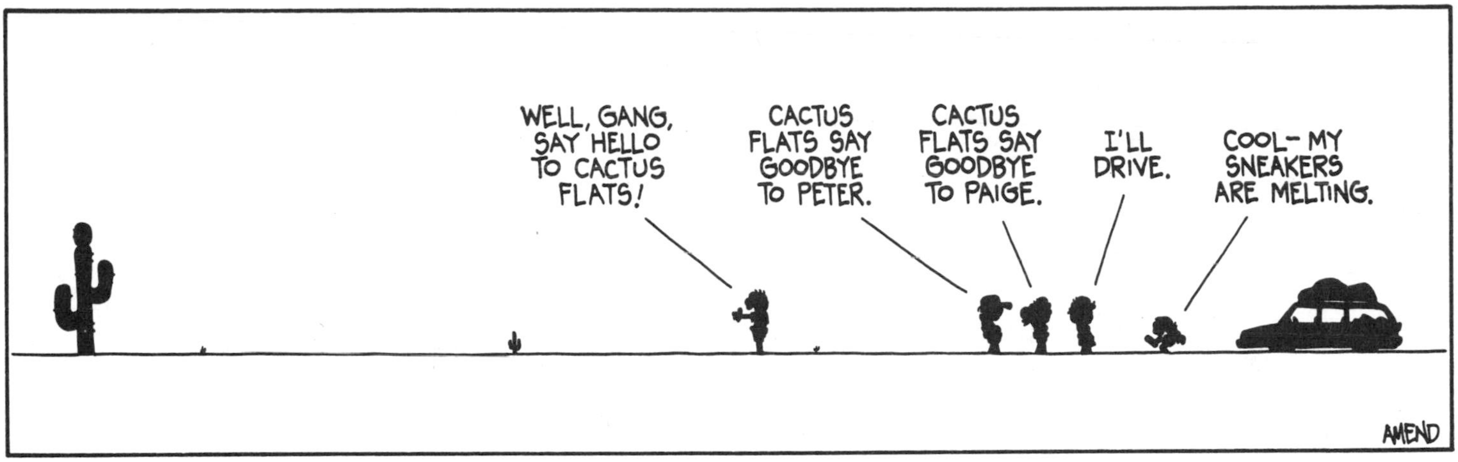
WELL, GANG, SAY HELLO TO CACTUS FLATS!
CACTUS FLATS SAY GOODBYE TO PETER.
CACTUS FLATS SAY GOODBYE TO PAIGE.
I'LL DRIVE.
COOL- MY SNEAKERS ARE MELTING.
AMEND

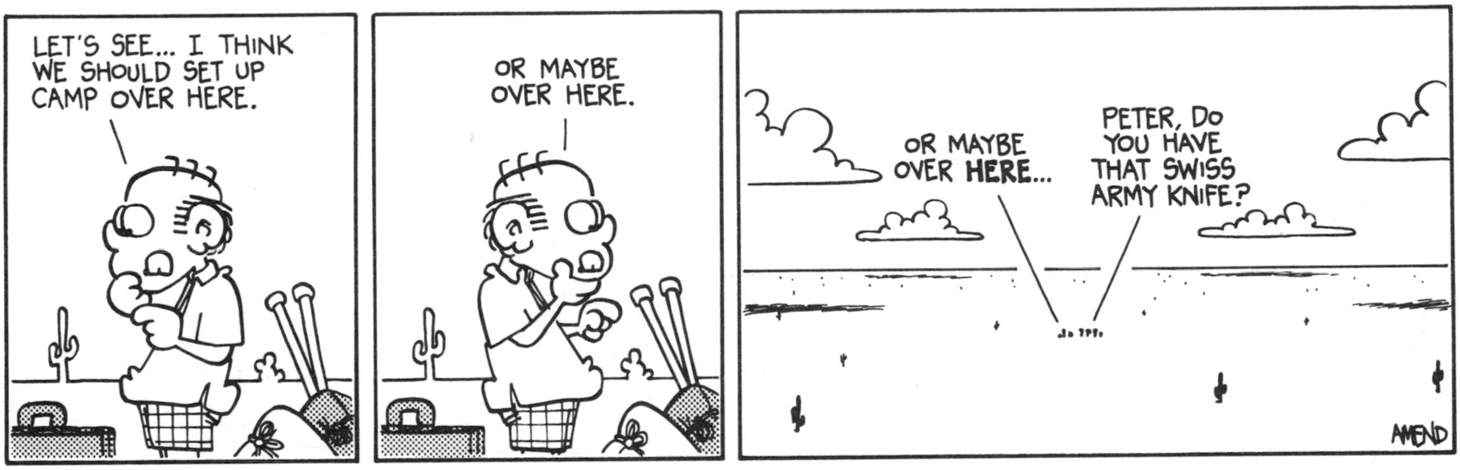
LET'S SEE... I THINK WE SHOULD SET UP CAMP OVER HERE.
OR MAYBE OVER HERE.
OR MAYBE OVER HERE...
PETER, DO YOU HAVE THAT SWISS ARMY KNIFE?
AMEND

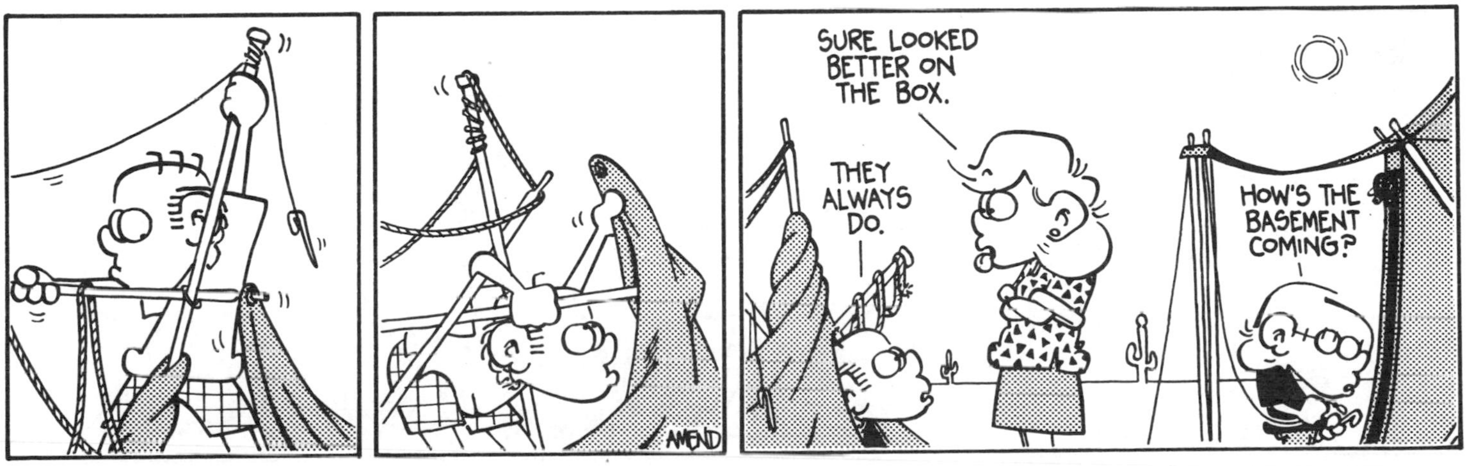
AMEND
SURE LOOKED BETTER ON THE BOX.
THEY ALWAYS DO.
HOW'S THE BASEMENT COMING?

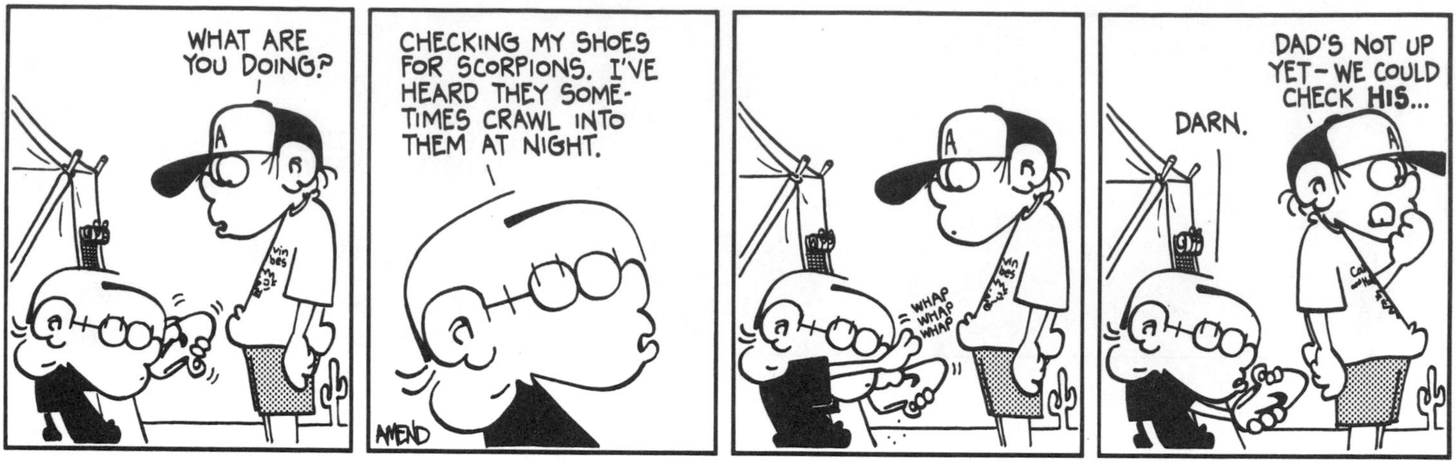
WHAT ARE YOU DOING?
CHECKING MY SHOES FOR SCORPIONS. I'VE HEARD THEY SOMETIMES CRAWL INTO THEM AT NIGHT.
AMEND
WHAP WHAP WHAP
DARN.
DAD'S NOT UP YET – WE COULD CHECK **HIS**...

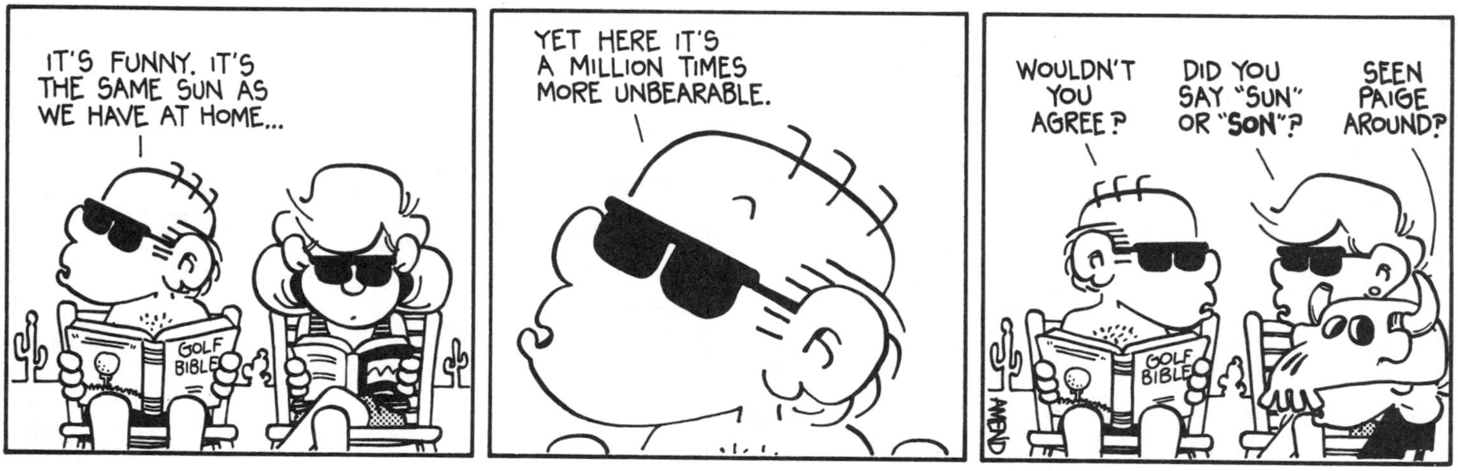
IT'S FUNNY. IT'S THE SAME SUN AS WE HAVE AT HOME...
GOLF BIBLE
YET HERE IT'S A MILLION TIMES MORE UNBEARABLE.
AMEND
WOULDN'T YOU AGREE?
DID YOU SAY "SUN" OR "**SON**"?
SEEN PAIGE AROUND?

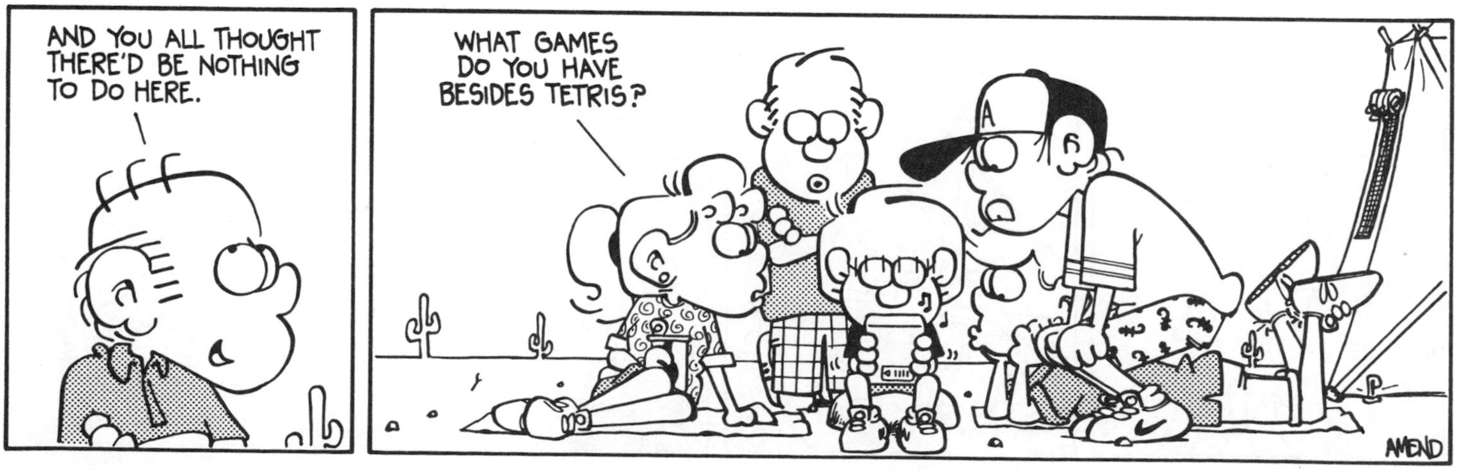
AND YOU ALL THOUGHT THERE'D BE NOTHING TO DO HERE.
WHAT GAMES DO YOU HAVE BESIDES TETRIS?
AMEND

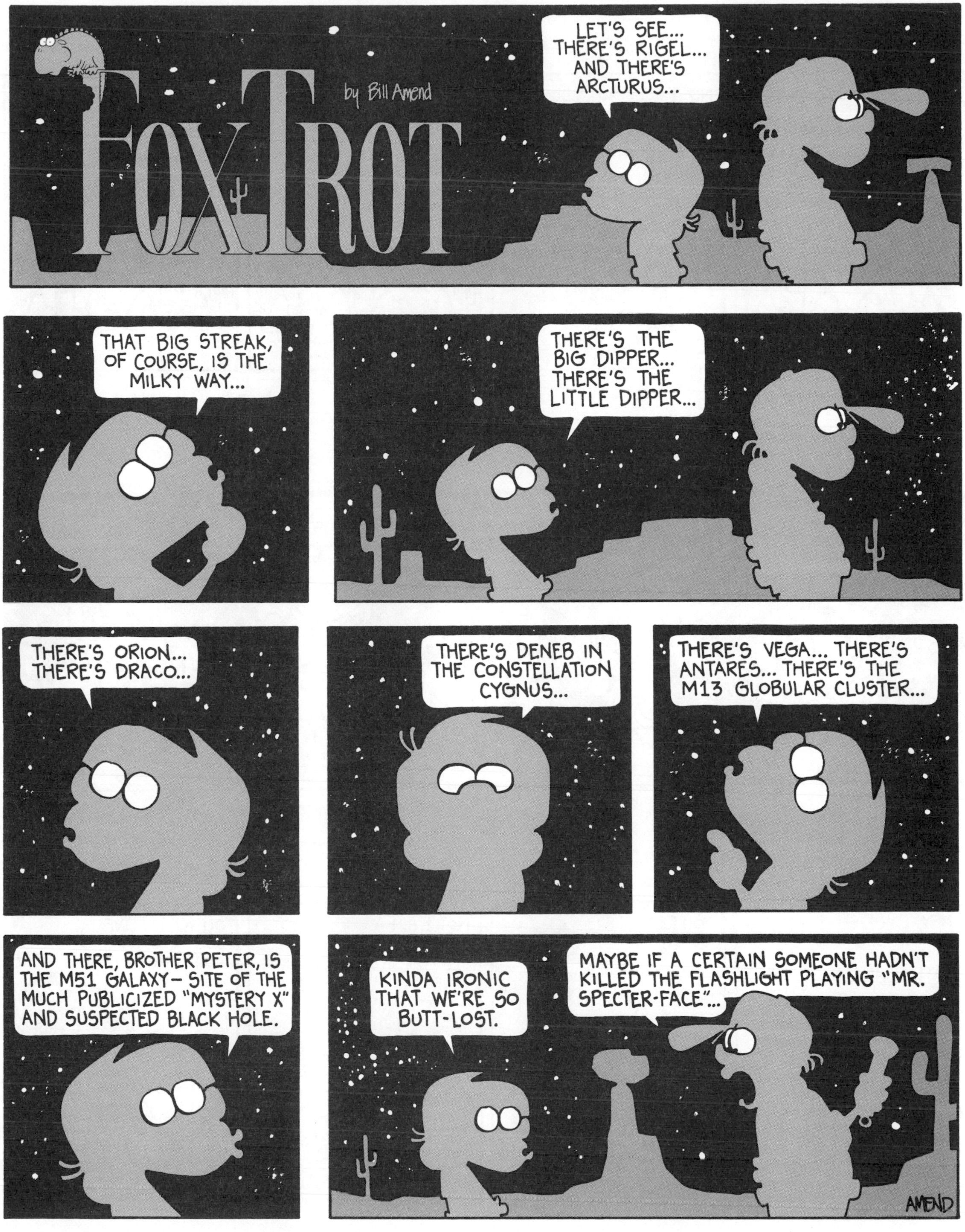
FoxTrot
by Bill Amend
LET'S SEE... THERE'S RIGEL... AND THERE'S ARCTURUS...
THAT BIG STREAK, OF COURSE, IS THE MILKY WAY...
THERE'S THE BIG DIPPER... THERE'S THE LITTLE DIPPER...
THERE'S ORION... THERE'S DRACO...
THERE'S DENEB IN THE CONSTELLATION CYGNUS...
THERE'S VEGA... THERE'S ANTARES... THERE'S THE M13 GLOBULAR CLUSTER...
AND THERE, BROTHER PETER, IS THE M51 GALAXY— SITE OF THE MUCH PUBLICIZED "MYSTERY X" AND SUSPECTED BLACK HOLE.
KINDA IRONIC THAT WE'RE SO BUTT-LOST.
MAYBE IF A CERTAIN SOMEONE HADN'T KILLED THE FLASHLIGHT PLAYING "MR. SPECTER-FACE"...
AMEND

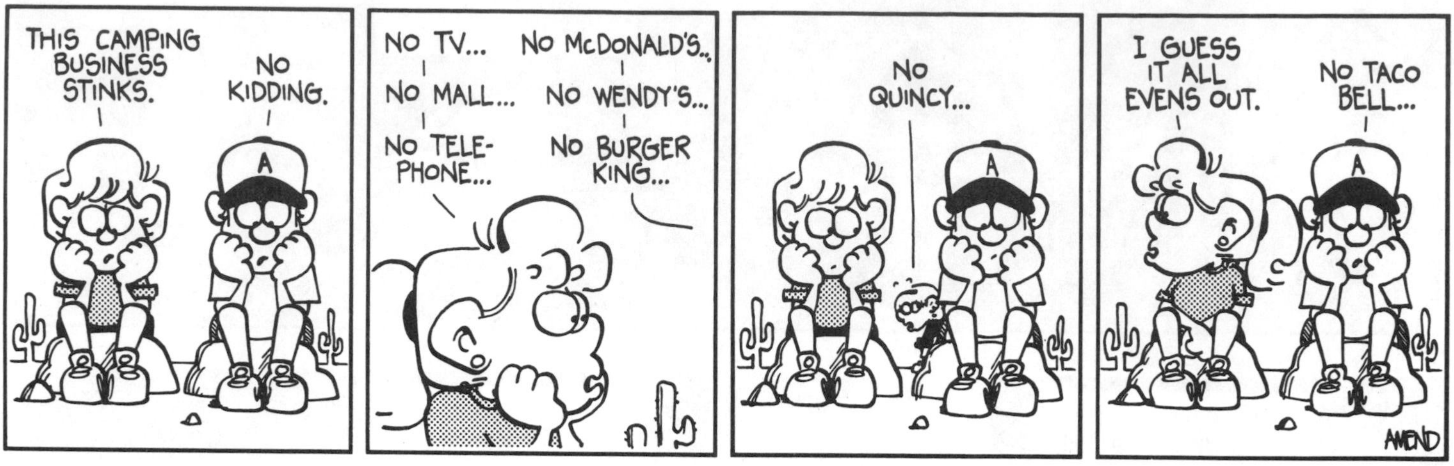
THIS CAMPING BUSINESS STINKS.
NO KIDDING.
NO TV...
NO MALL...
NO TELE-PHONE...
NO McDONALD'S..
NO WENDY'S...
NO BURGER KING...
NO QUINCY...
I GUESS IT ALL EVENS OUT.
NO TACO BELL...
AMEND

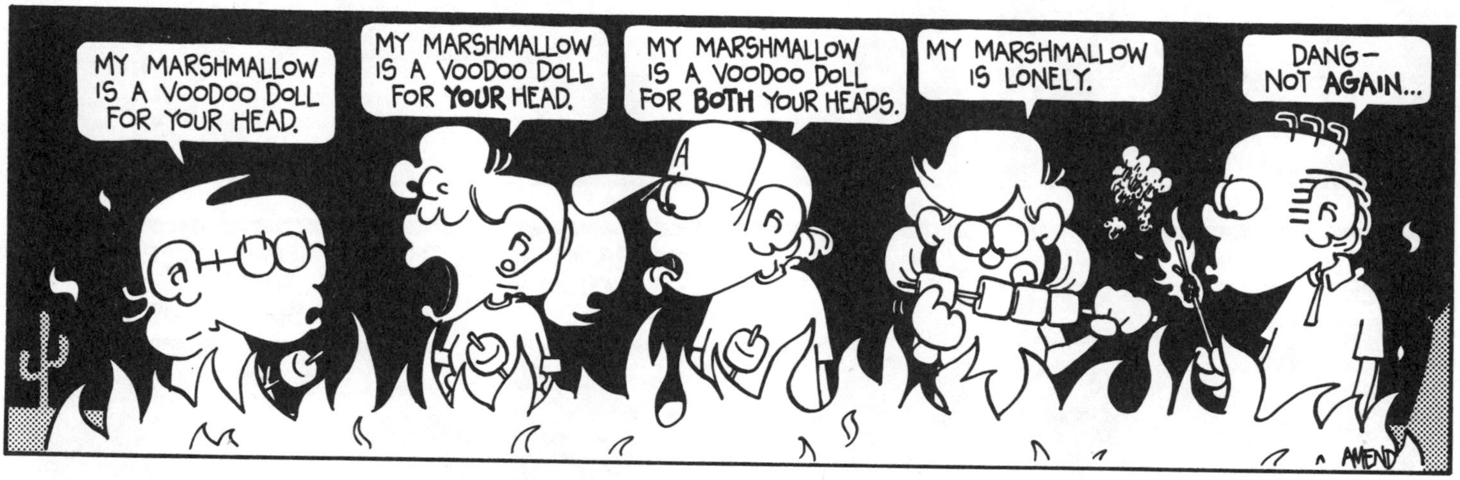
MY MARSHMALLOW IS A VOODOO DOLL FOR YOUR HEAD.
MY MARSHMALLOW IS A VOODOO DOLL FOR **YOUR** HEAD.
MY MARSHMALLOW IS A VOODOO DOLL FOR **BOTH** YOUR HEADS.
MY MARSHMALLOW IS LONELY.
DANG– NOT **AGAIN**...
AMEND

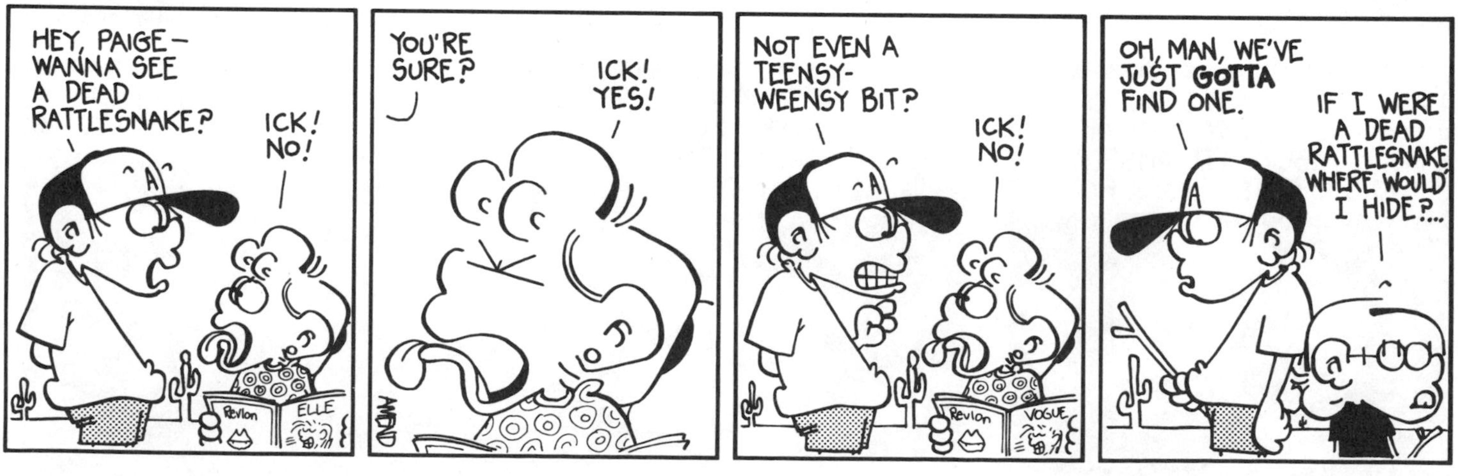
HEY, PAIGE– WANNA SEE A DEAD RATTLESNAKE?
ICK! NO!
Revlon
ELLE
YOU'RE SURE?
ICK! YES!
AMEND
NOT EVEN A TEENSY-WEENSY BIT?
ICK! NO!
Revlon
VOGUE
OH, MAN, WE'VE JUST **GOTTA** FIND ONE.
IF I WERE A DEAD RATTLESNAKE WHERE WOULD I HIDE?...

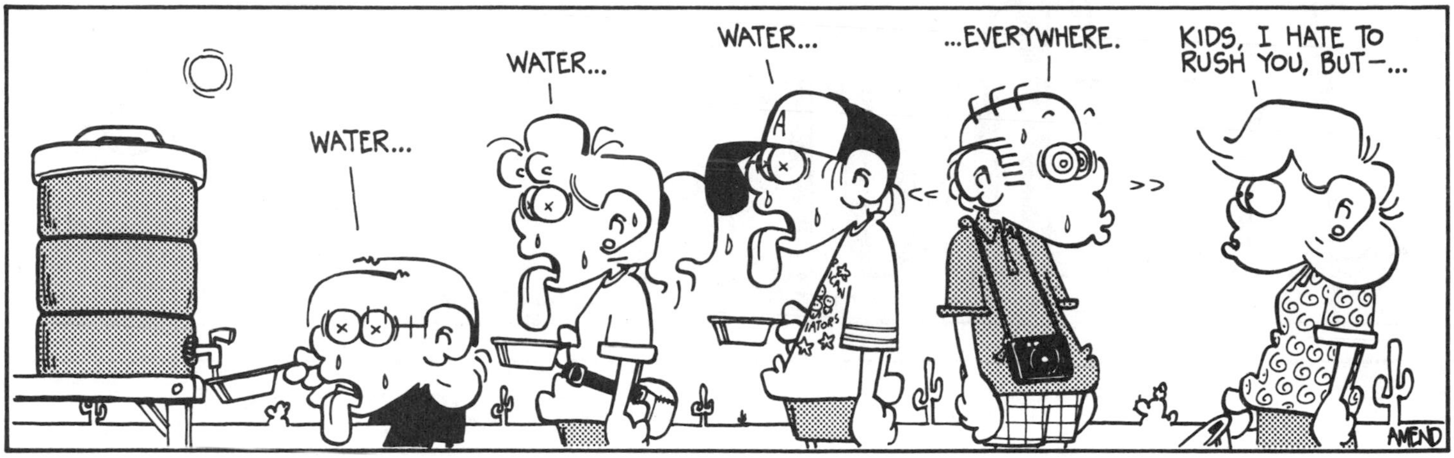
WATER...
WATER...
WATER...
...EVERYWHERE.
KIDS, I HATE TO RUSH YOU, BUT—...
AMEND

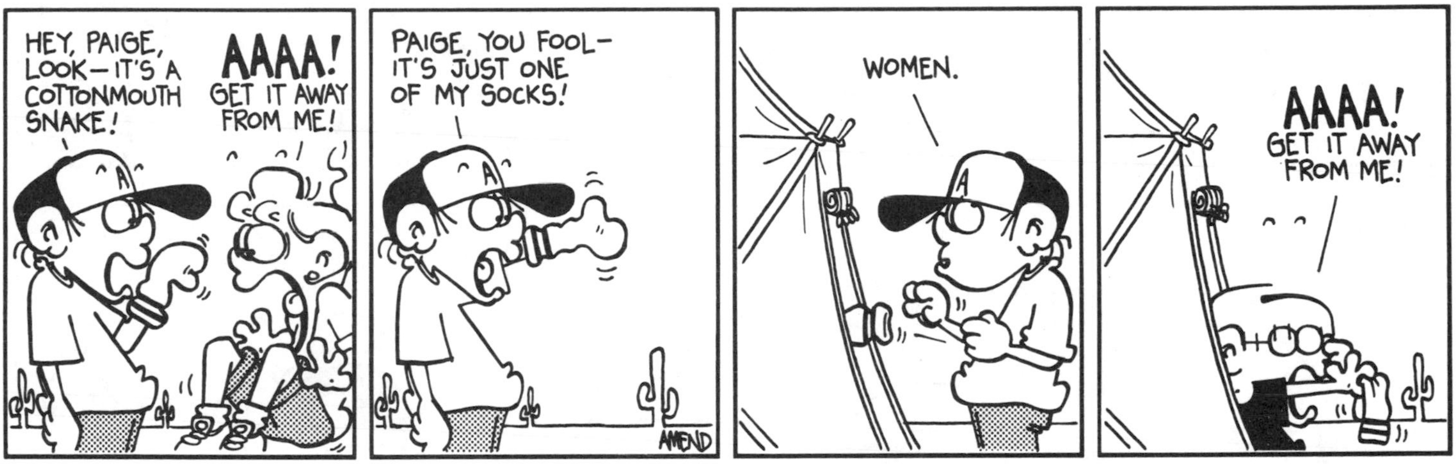
HEY, PAIGE, LOOK—IT'S A COTTONMOUTH SNAKE!
AAAA! GET IT AWAY FROM ME!
PAIGE, YOU FOOL—IT'S JUST ONE OF MY SOCKS!
AMEND
WOMEN.
AAAA! GET IT AWAY FROM ME!

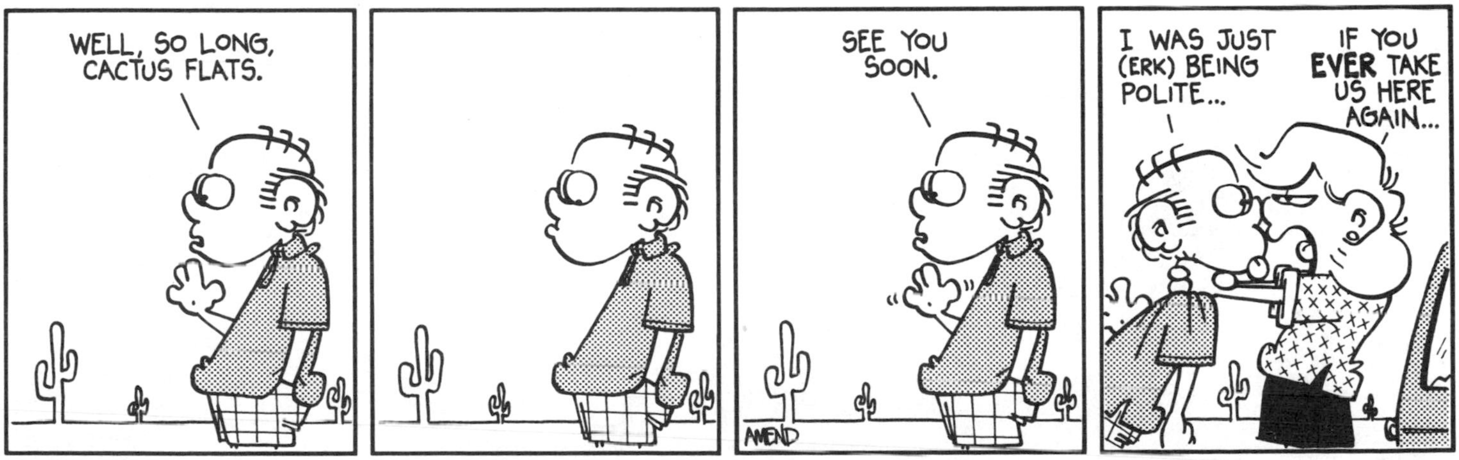
WELL, SO LONG, CACTUS FLATS.
SEE YOU SOON.
AMEND
I WAS JUST (ERK) BEING POLITE...
IF YOU EVER TAKE US HERE AGAIN...

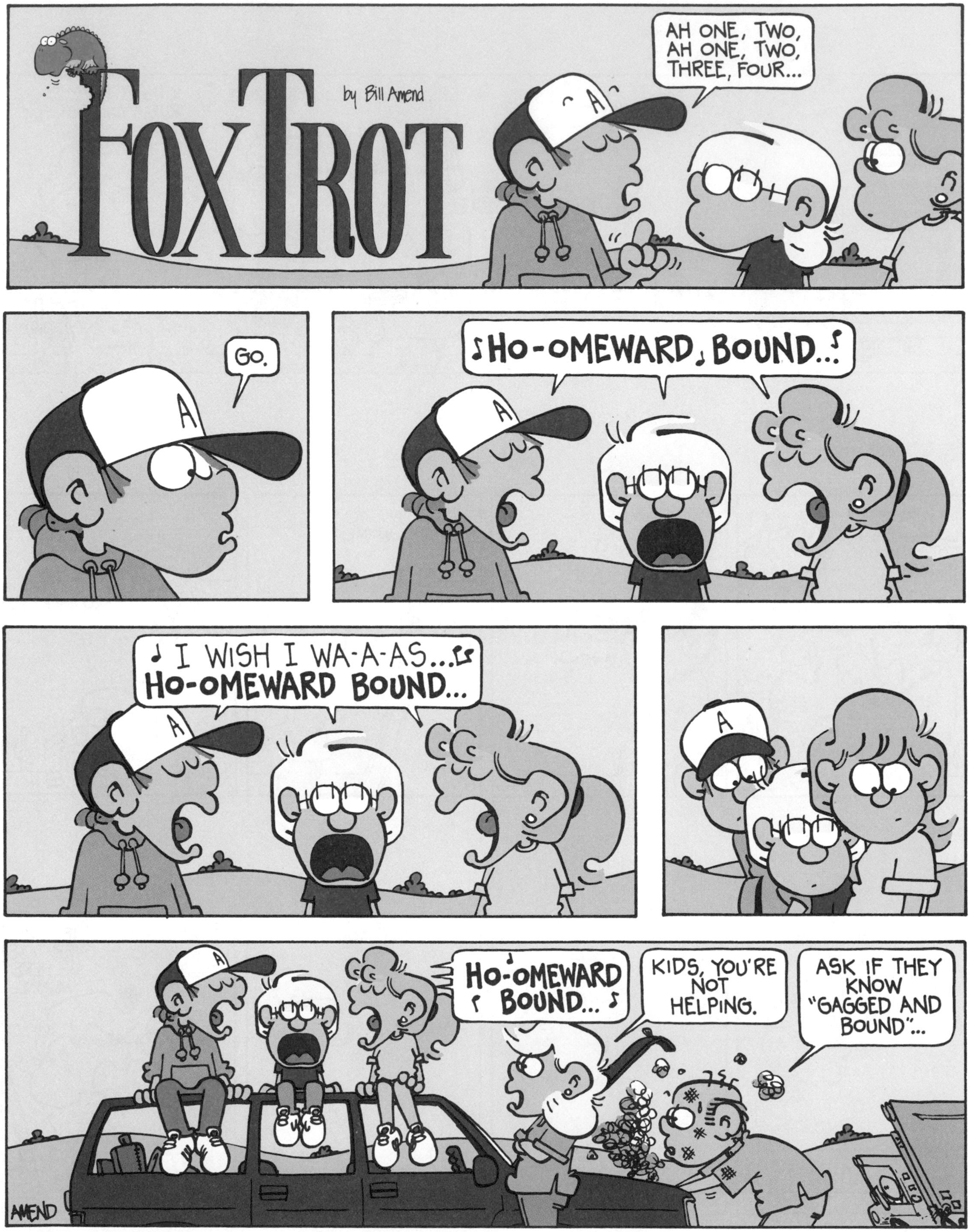
FoxTrot
by Bill Amend
AH ONE, TWO, AH ONE, TWO, THREE, FOUR...
GO.
HO-OMEWARD BOUND...
I WISH I WA-A-AS... HO-OMEWARD BOUND...
HO-OMEWARD BOUND...
KIDS, YOU'RE NOT HELPING.
ASK IF THEY KNOW "GAGGED AND BOUND"...
AMEND

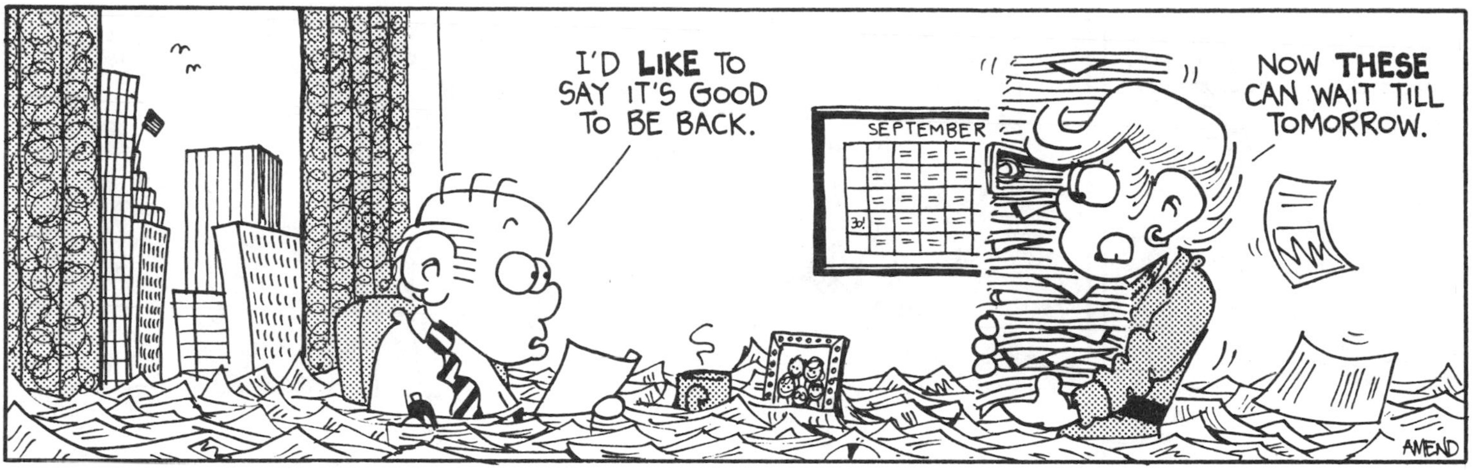
I'D **LIKE** TO SAY IT'S GOOD TO BE BACK.
SEPTEMBER
NOW **THESE** CAN WAIT TILL TOMORROW.

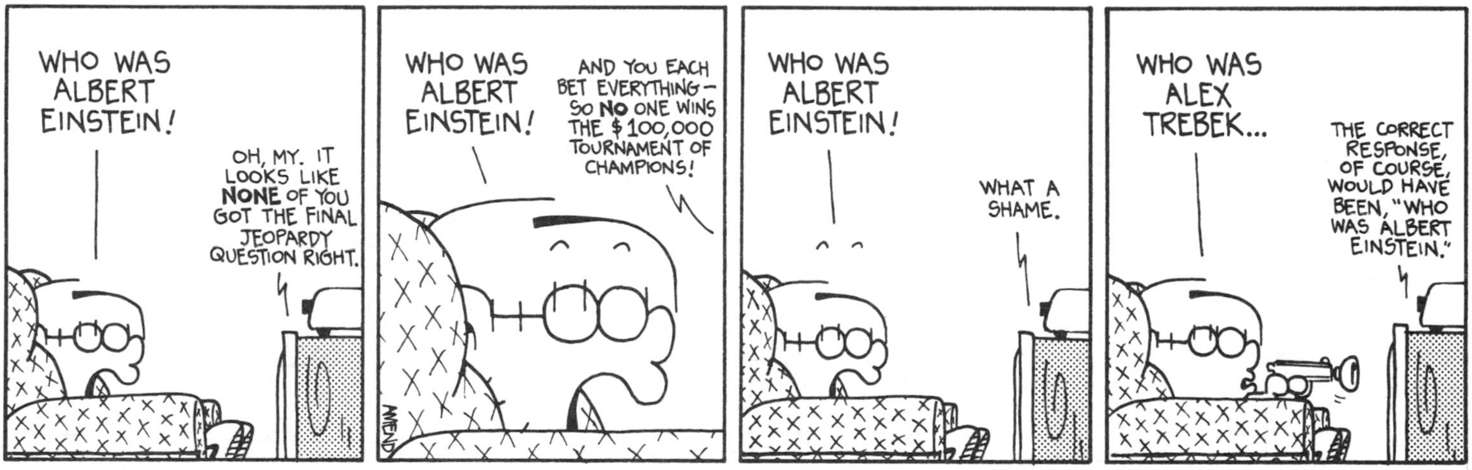
WHO WAS ALBERT EINSTEIN!
OH, MY. IT LOOKS LIKE **NONE** OF YOU GOT THE FINAL JEOPARDY QUESTION RIGHT.
WHO WAS ALBERT EINSTEIN!
AND YOU EACH BET EVERYTHING— SO **NO** ONE WINS THE $100,000 TOURNAMENT OF CHAMPIONS!
WHO WAS ALBERT EINSTEIN!
WHAT A SHAME.
WHO WAS ALEX TREBEK...
THE CORRECT RESPONSE, OF COURSE, WOULD HAVE BEEN, "WHO WAS ALBERT EINSTEIN."

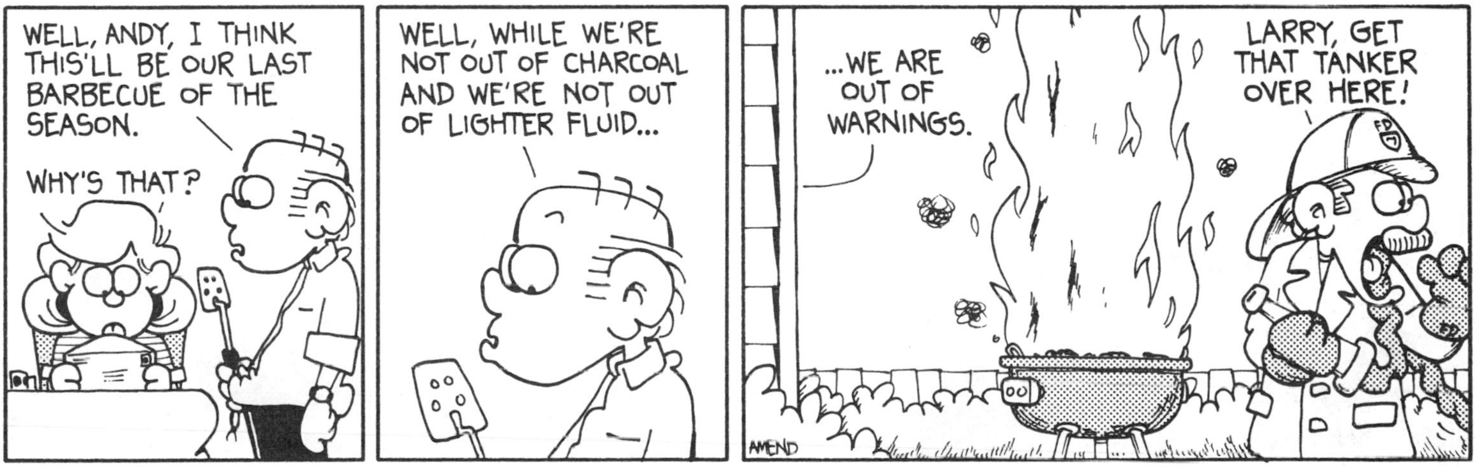
WELL, ANDY, I THINK THIS'LL BE OUR LAST BARBECUE OF THE SEASON.
WHY'S THAT?
WELL, WHILE WE'RE NOT OUT OF CHARCOAL AND WE'RE NOT OUT OF LIGHTER FLUID...
...WE ARE OUT OF WARNINGS.
LARRY, GET THAT TANKER OVER HERE!

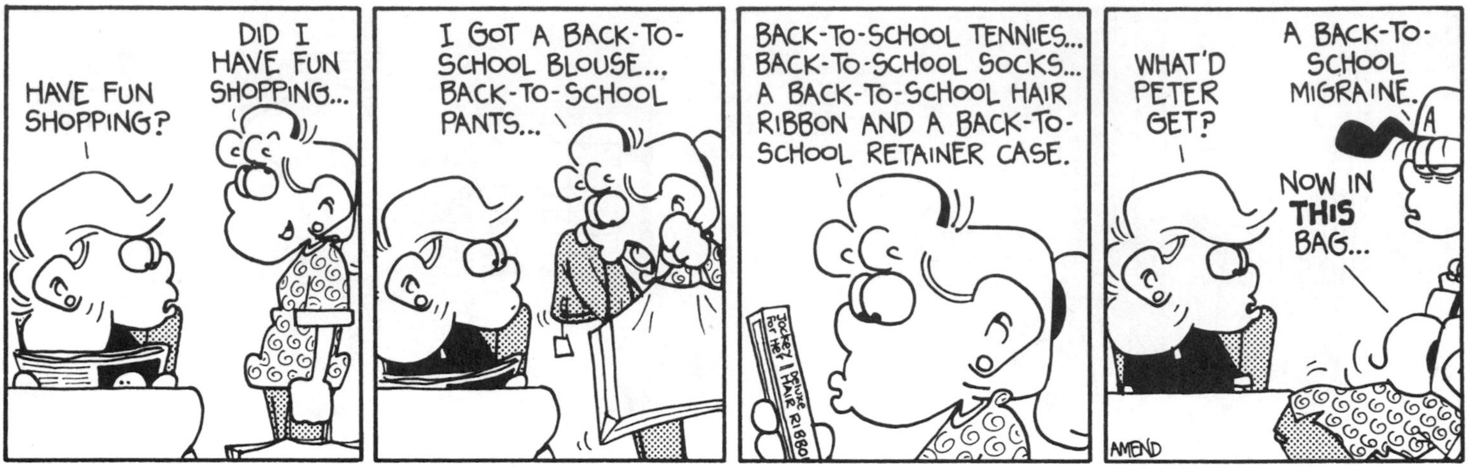
HAVE FUN SHOPPING?
DID I HAVE FUN SHOPPING...
I GOT A BACK-TO-SCHOOL BLOUSE... BACK-TO-SCHOOL PANTS...
BACK-TO-SCHOOL TENNIES... BACK-TO-SCHOOL SOCKS... A BACK-TO-SCHOOL HAIR RIBBON AND A BACK-TO-SCHOOL RETAINER CASE.
WHAT'D PETER GET?
A BACK-TO-SCHOOL MIGRAINE.
NOW IN **THIS** BAG...
AMEND

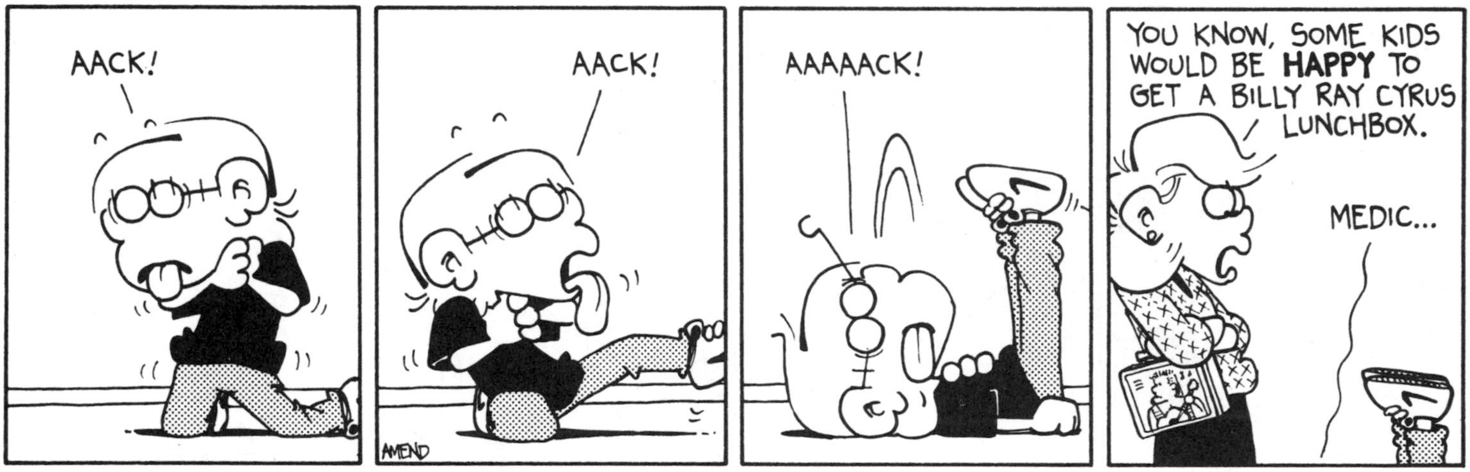
AACK!
AACK!
AMEND
AAAAACK!
YOU KNOW, SOME KIDS WOULD BE **HAPPY** TO GET A BILLY RAY CYRUS LUNCHBOX.
MEDIC...

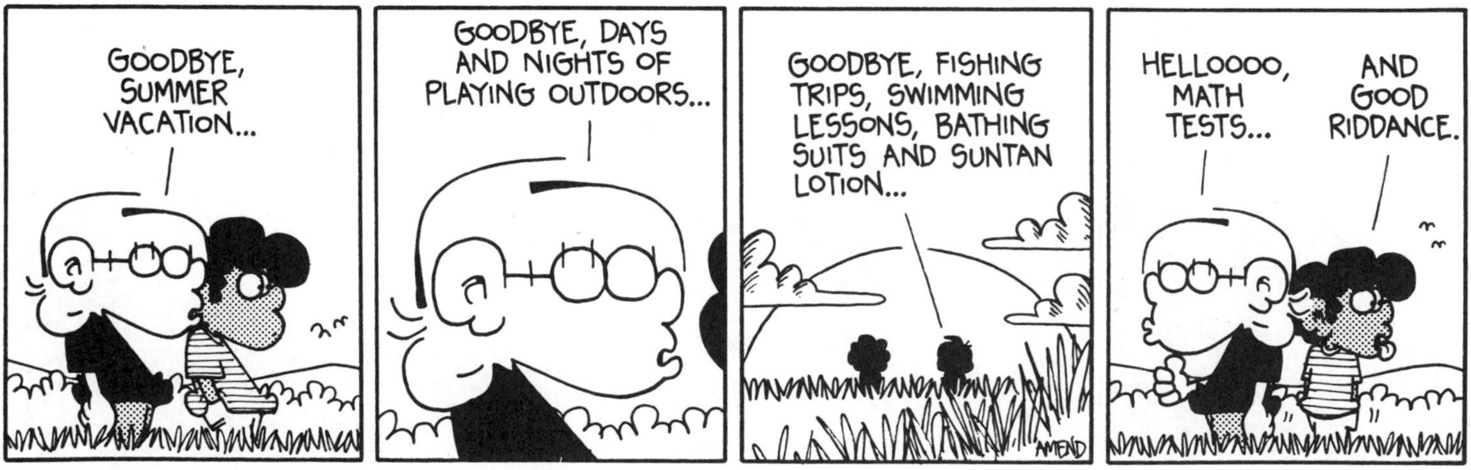
GOODBYE, SUMMER VACATION...
GOODBYE, DAYS AND NIGHTS OF PLAYING OUTDOORS...
GOODBYE, FISHING TRIPS, SWIMMING LESSONS, BATHING SUITS AND SUNTAN LOTION...
AMEND
HELLOOOO, MATH TESTS...
AND GOOD RIDDANCE.

FoxTrot
by Bill Amend
DRIBBLE
DRIBBLE
DRIBBLE
SLAM!
SLAM!
SLAM!
DAD, ARE YOU GONNA HELP ME WITH THIS OR NOT?!
WATCH THIS ONE, PETE...
Mr. Hoop's PRO Model
BASKETBALL
SET
AMEND

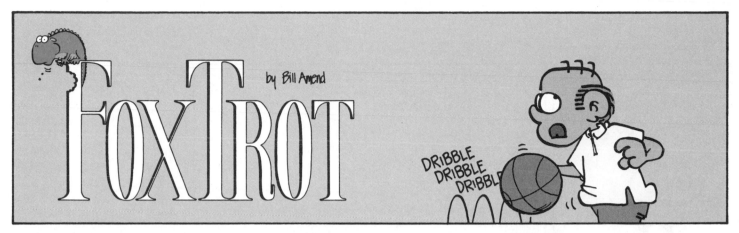

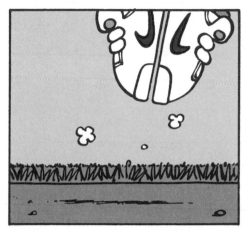

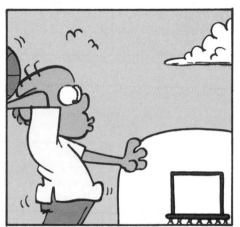

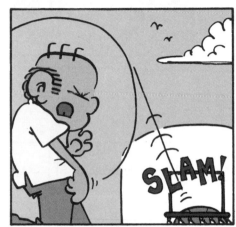

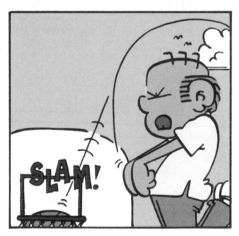

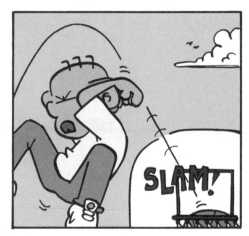

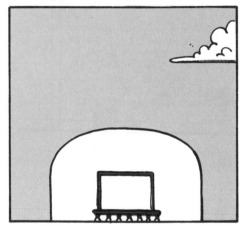

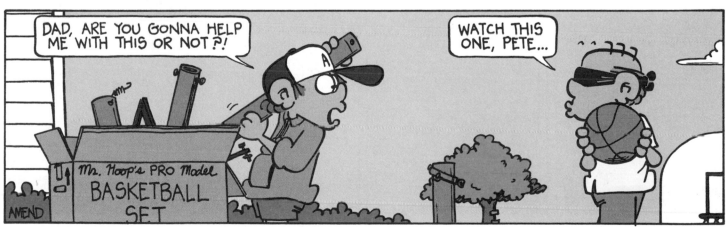

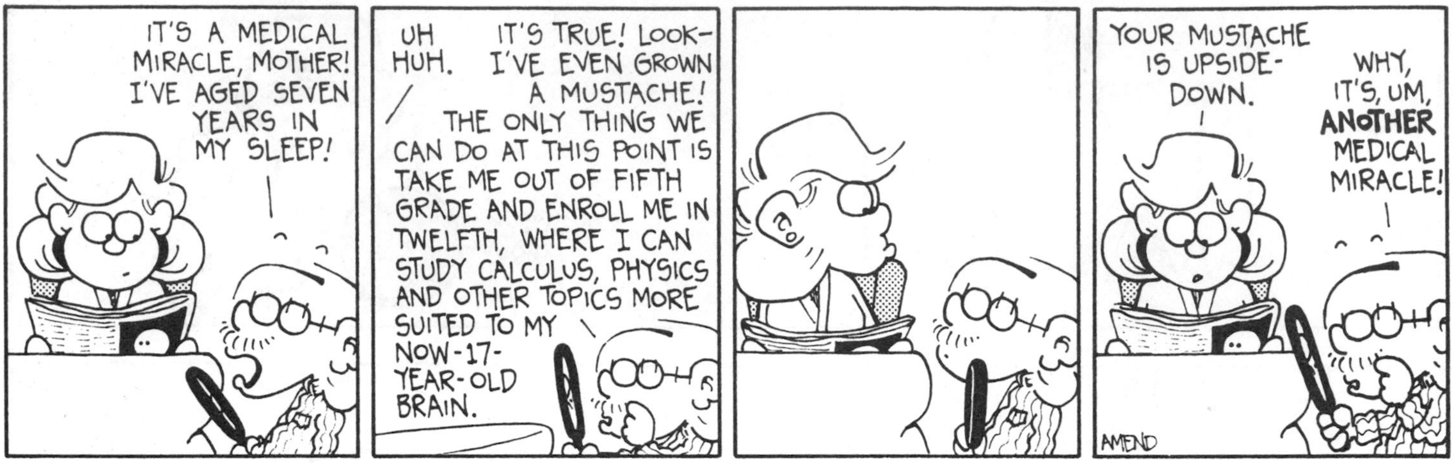
IT'S A MEDICAL MIRACLE, MOTHER! I'VE AGED SEVEN YEARS IN MY SLEEP!
UH HUH.
IT'S TRUE! LOOK– I'VE EVEN GROWN A MUSTACHE!
THE ONLY THING WE CAN DO AT THIS POINT IS TAKE ME OUT OF FIFTH GRADE AND ENROLL ME IN TWELFTH, WHERE I CAN STUDY CALCULUS, PHYSICS AND OTHER TOPICS MORE SUITED TO MY NOW-17-YEAR-OLD BRAIN.
YOUR MUSTACHE IS UPSIDE-DOWN.
WHY, IT'S, UM, **ANOTHER** MEDICAL MIRACLE!
AMEND

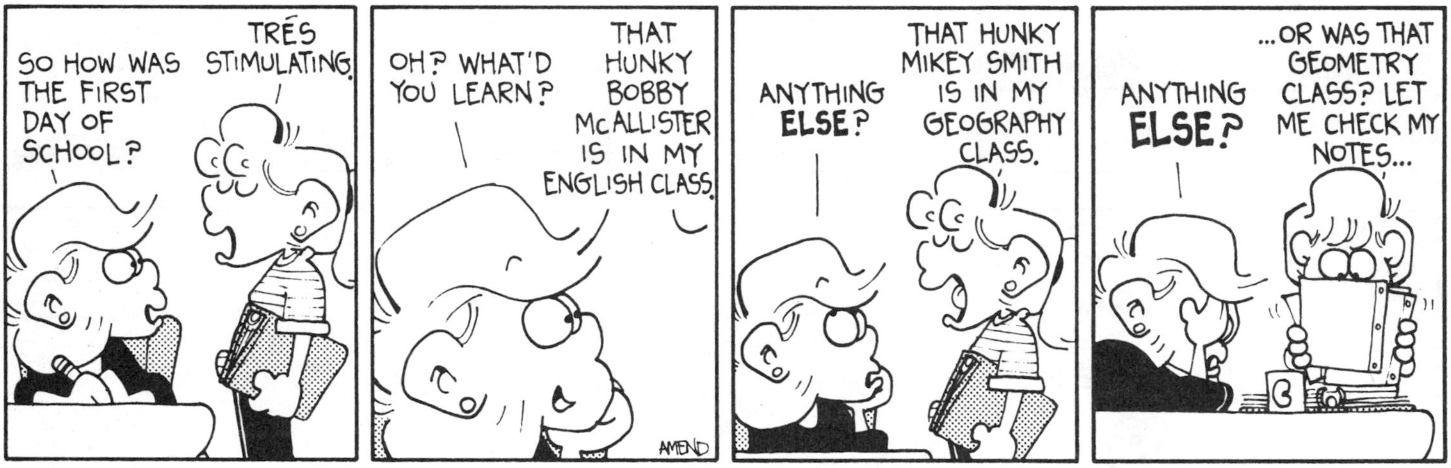
SO HOW WAS THE FIRST DAY OF SCHOOL?
TRÉS STIMULATING.
OH? WHAT'D YOU LEARN?
THAT HUNKY BOBBY McALLISTER IS IN MY ENGLISH CLASS.
AMEND
ANYTHING **ELSE**?
THAT HUNKY MIKEY SMITH IS IN MY GEOGRAPHY CLASS.
ANYTHING **ELSE?**
...OR WAS THAT GEOMETRY CLASS? LET ME CHECK MY NOTES...

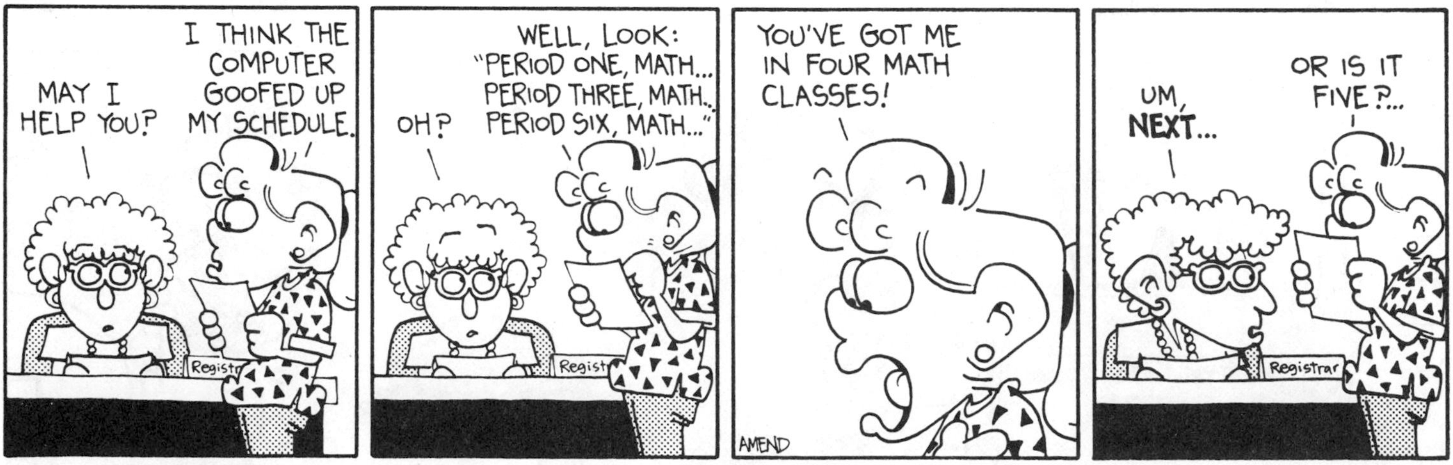
MAY I HELP YOU?
I THINK THE COMPUTER GOOFED UP MY SCHEDULE.
Registr
OH?
WELL, LOOK: "PERIOD ONE, MATH... PERIOD THREE, MATH... PERIOD SIX, MATH..."
Regist
YOU'VE GOT ME IN FOUR MATH CLASSES!
AMEND
UM, **NEXT**...
OR IS IT FIVE?...
Registrar

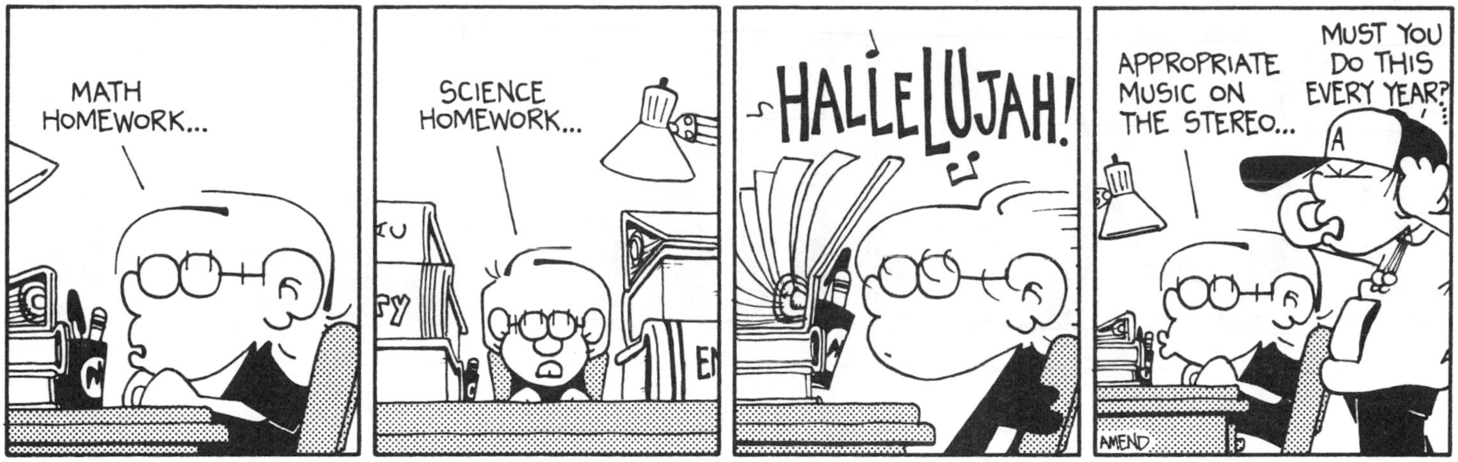
MATH HOMEWORK...
SCIENCE HOMEWORK...
HALLELUJAH!
APPROPRIATE MUSIC ON THE STEREO...
MUST YOU DO THIS EVERY YEAR?
AMEND

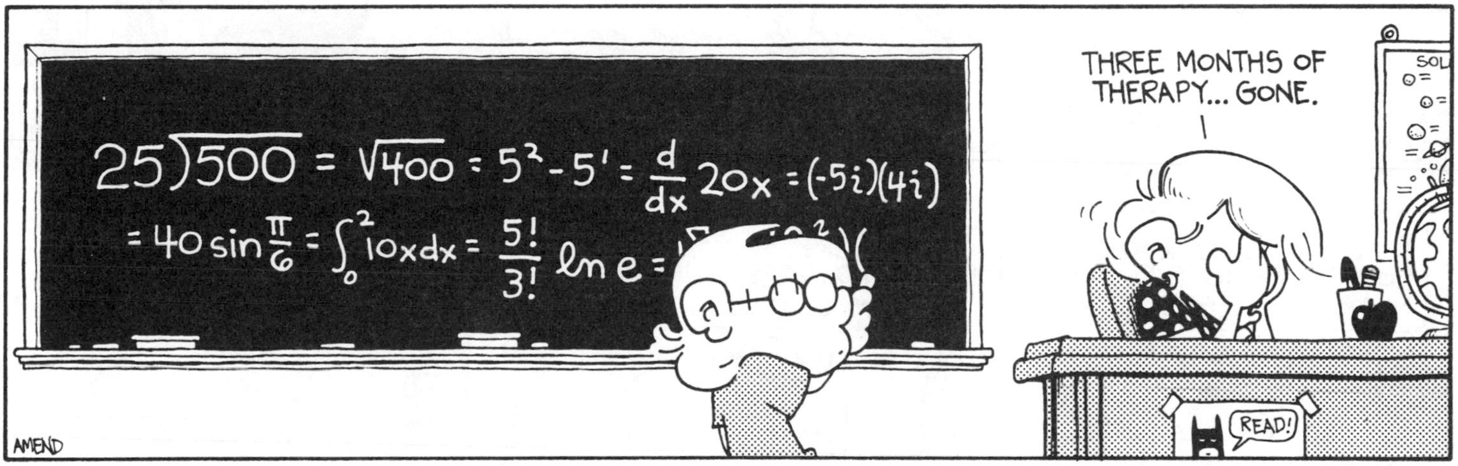
$25\overline{)500} = \sqrt{400} = 5^2 - 5' = \frac{d}{dx} 20x = (-5i)(4i)$
$= 40 \sin\frac{\pi}{6} = \int_0^2 10x\,dx = \frac{5!}{3!} \ln e =$
THREE MONTHS OF THERAPY... GONE.
READ!
AMEND

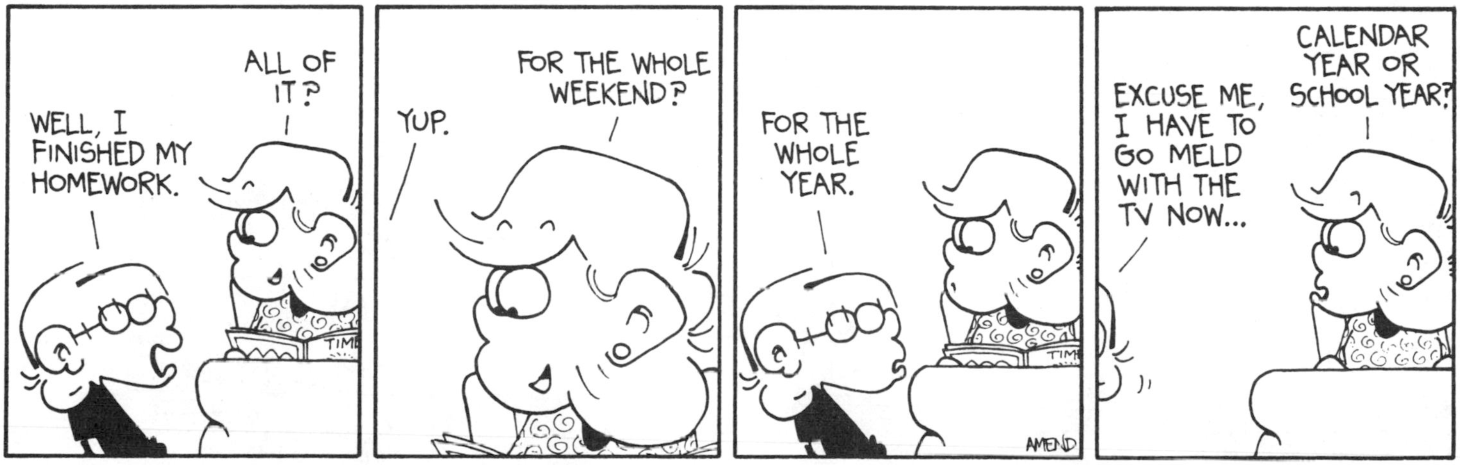
WELL, I FINISHED MY HOMEWORK.
ALL OF IT?
YUP.
FOR THE WHOLE WEEKEND?
FOR THE WHOLE YEAR.
EXCUSE ME, I HAVE TO GO MELD WITH THE TV NOW...
CALENDAR YEAR OR SCHOOL YEAR?
AMEND

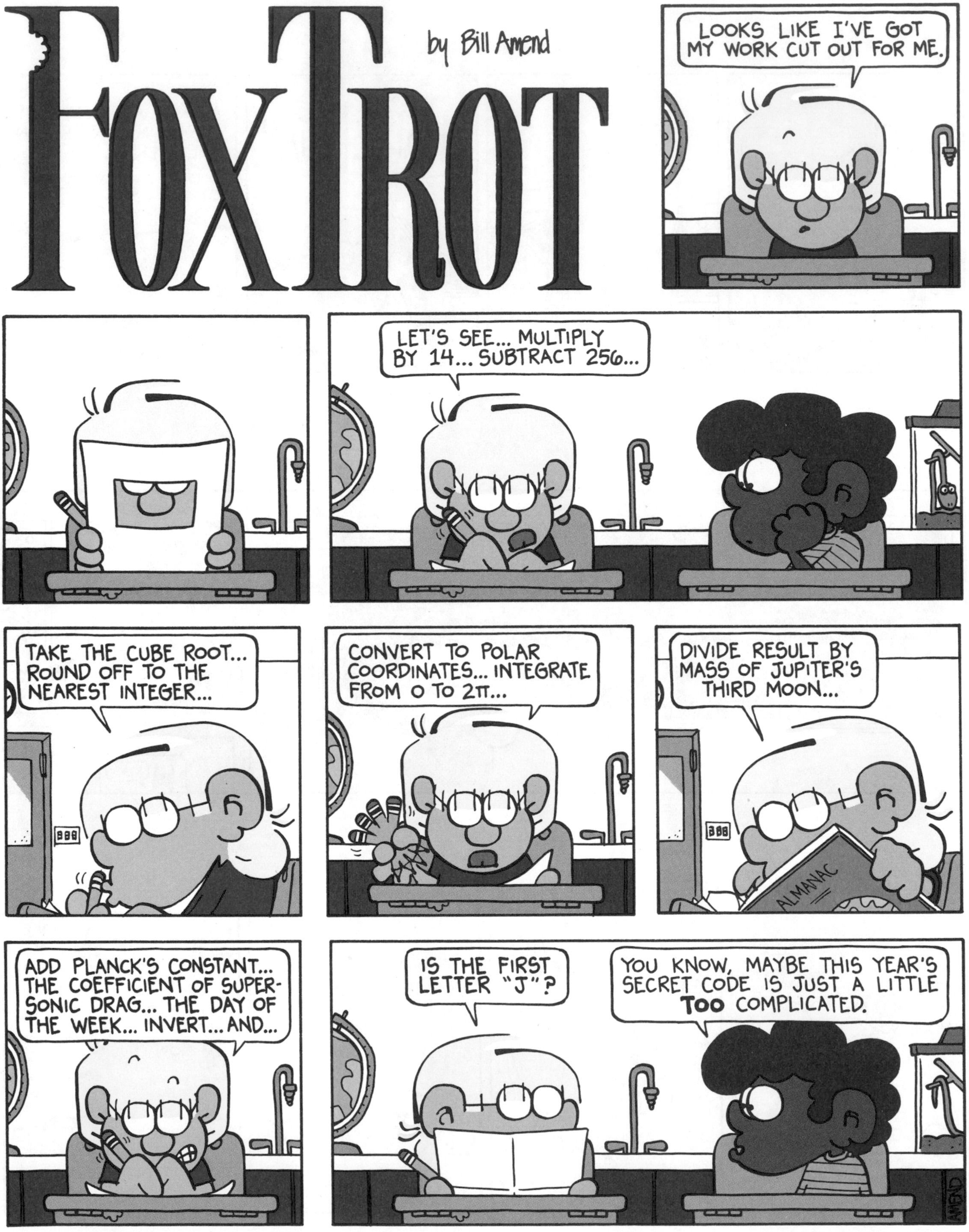
FoxTrot
by Bill Amend
LOOKS LIKE I'VE GOT MY WORK CUT OUT FOR ME.
LET'S SEE... MULTIPLY BY 14... SUBTRACT 256...
TAKE THE CUBE ROOT... ROUND OFF TO THE NEAREST INTEGER...
CONVERT TO POLAR COORDINATES... INTEGRATE FROM 0 TO 2π...
DIVIDE RESULT BY MASS OF JUPITER'S THIRD MOON...
ALMANAC
ADD PLANCK'S CONSTANT... THE COEFFICIENT OF SUPER-SONIC DRAG... THE DAY OF THE WEEK... INVERT... AND...
IS THE FIRST LETTER "J"?
YOU KNOW, MAYBE THIS YEAR'S SECRET CODE IS JUST A LITTLE **TOO** COMPLICATED.
AMEND

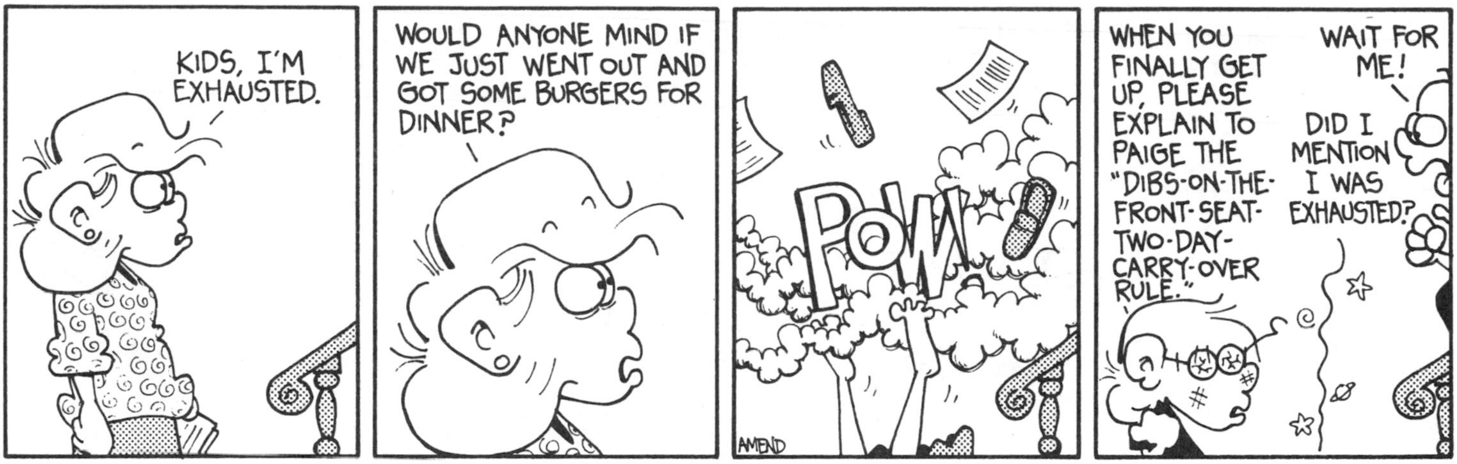
KIDS, I'M EXHAUSTED.
WOULD ANYONE MIND IF WE JUST WENT OUT AND GOT SOME BURGERS FOR DINNER?
POW!
AMEND
WHEN YOU FINALLY GET UP, PLEASE EXPLAIN TO PAIGE THE "DIBS-ON-THE-FRONT-SEAT-TWO-DAY-CARRY-OVER RULE."
WAIT FOR ME!
DID I MENTION I WAS EXHAUSTED?

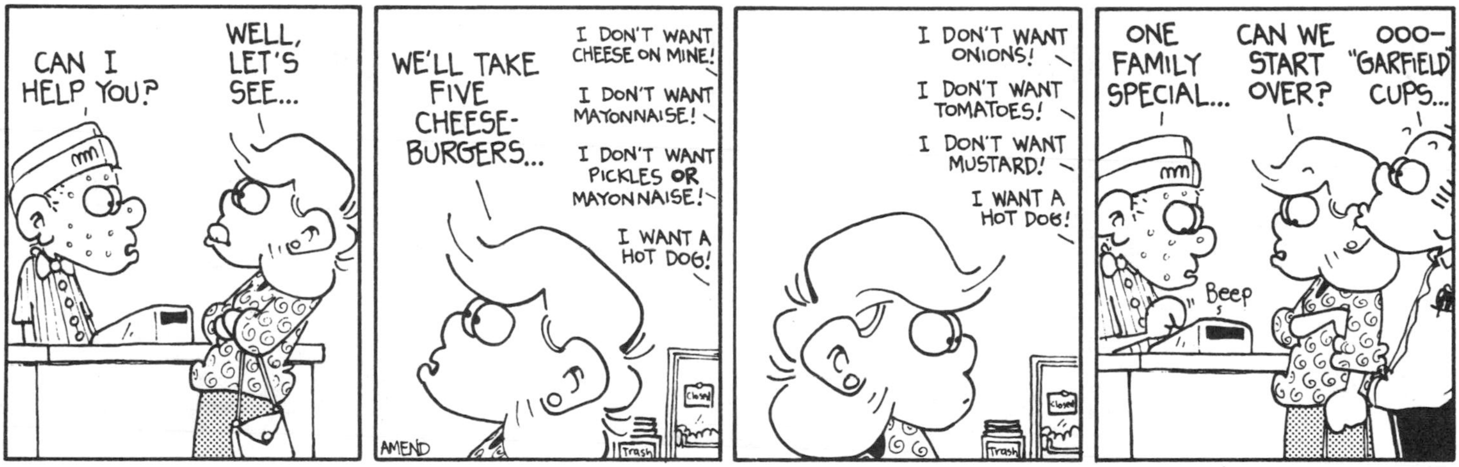
CAN I HELP YOU?
WELL, LET'S SEE...
WE'LL TAKE FIVE CHEESE-BURGERS...
I DON'T WANT CHEESE ON MINE!
I DON'T WANT MAYONNAISE!
I DON'T WANT PICKLES OR MAYONNAISE!
I WANT A HOT DOG!
AMEND
I DON'T WANT ONIONS!
I DON'T WANT TOMATOES!
I DON'T WANT MUSTARD!
I WANT A HOT DOG!
ONE FAMILY SPECIAL...
CAN WE START OVER?
OOO— "GARFIELD" CUPS...
Beep

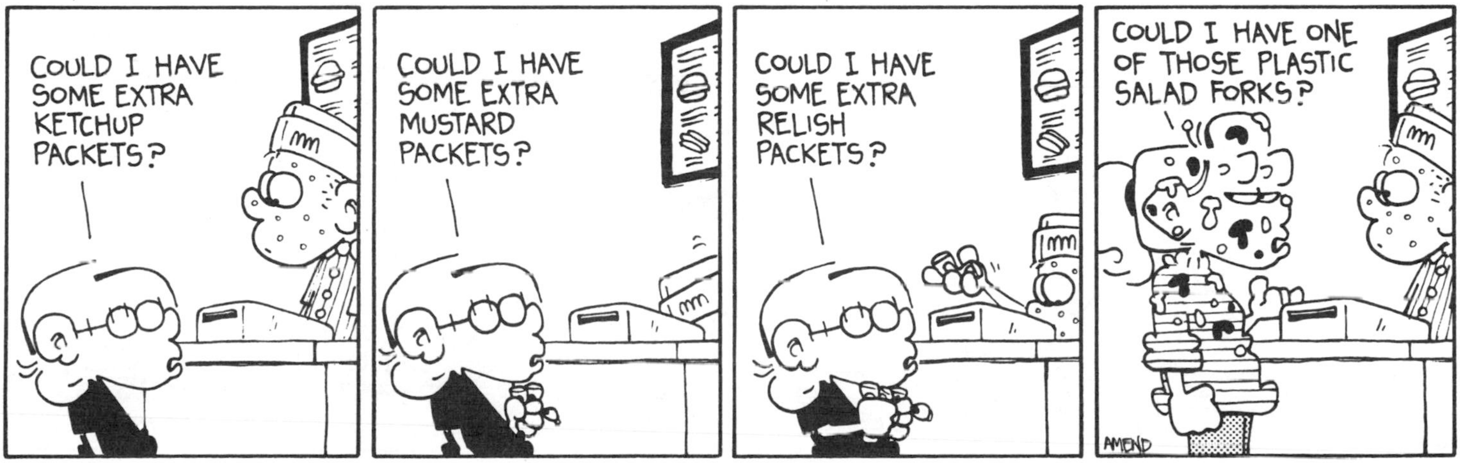
COULD I HAVE SOME EXTRA KETCHUP PACKETS?
COULD I HAVE SOME EXTRA MUSTARD PACKETS?
COULD I HAVE SOME EXTRA RELISH PACKETS?
COULD I HAVE ONE OF THOSE PLASTIC SALAD FORKS?
AMEND

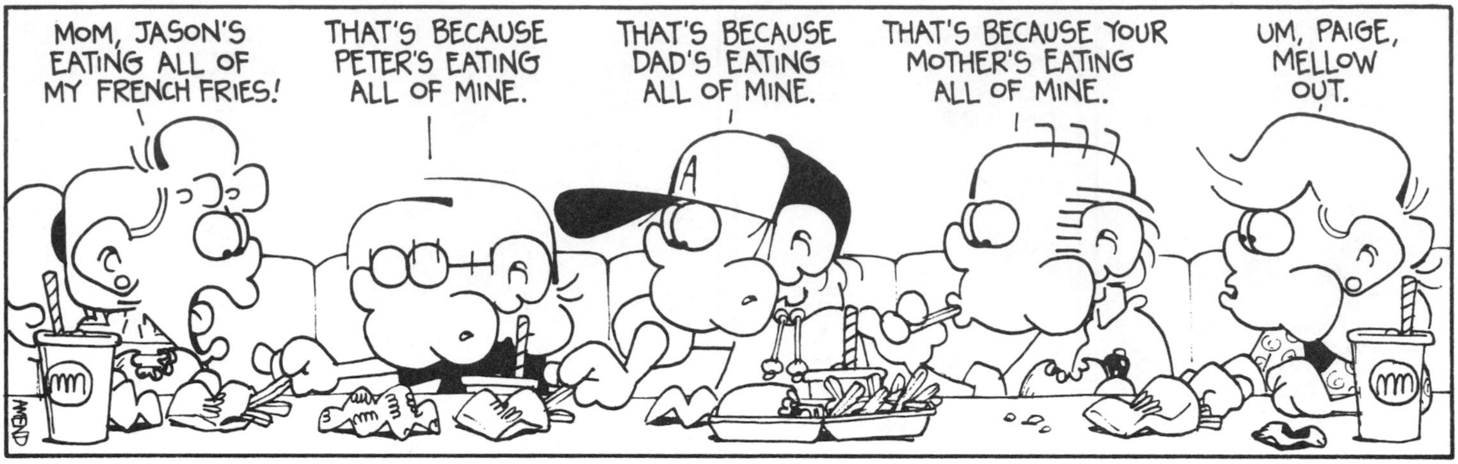
MOM, JASON'S EATING ALL OF MY FRENCH FRIES!
THAT'S BECAUSE PETER'S EATING ALL OF MINE.
THAT'S BECAUSE DAD'S EATING ALL OF MINE.
THAT'S BECAUSE YOUR MOTHER'S EATING ALL OF MINE.
UM, PAIGE, MELLOW OUT.
AMEND

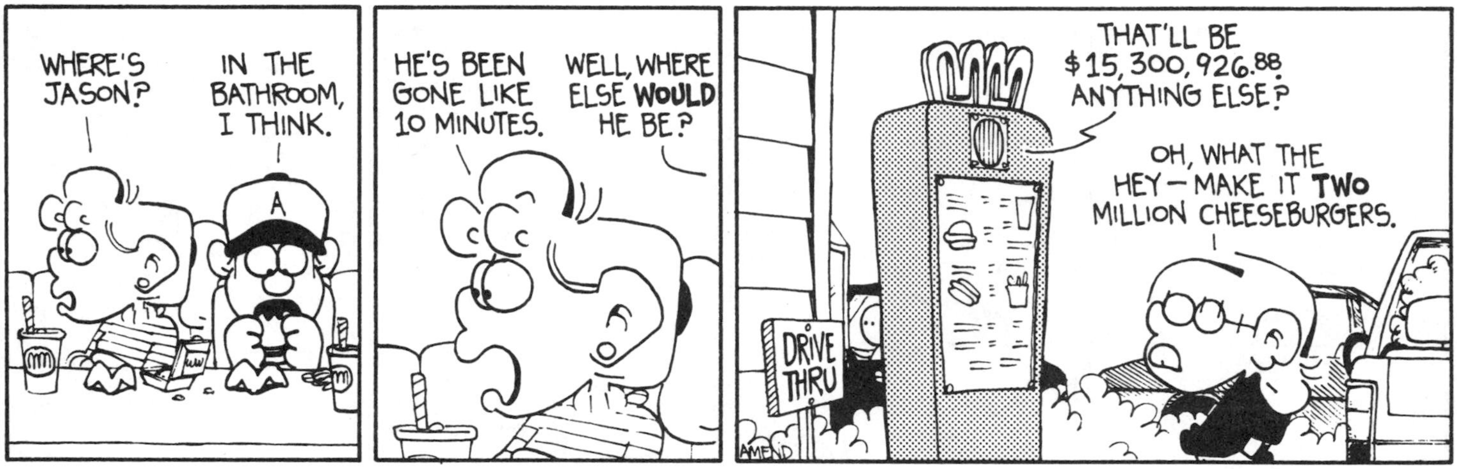
WHERE'S JASON?
IN THE BATHROOM, I THINK.
HE'S BEEN GONE LIKE 10 MINUTES.
WELL, WHERE ELSE **WOULD** HE BE?
THAT'LL BE $15,300,926.88 ANYTHING ELSE?
OH, WHAT THE HEY—MAKE IT **TWO** MILLION CHEESEBURGERS.
DRIVE THRU
AMEND

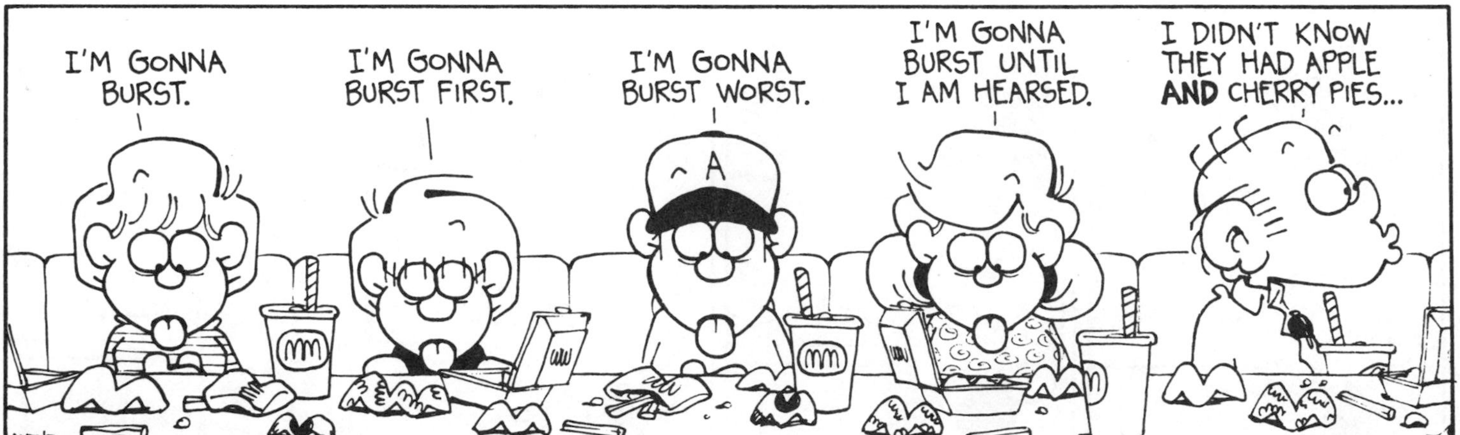
I'M GONNA BURST.
I'M GONNA BURST FIRST.
I'M GONNA BURST WORST.
I'M GONNA BURST UNTIL I AM HEARSED.
I DIDN'T KNOW THEY HAD APPLE **AND** CHERRY PIES...
AMEND

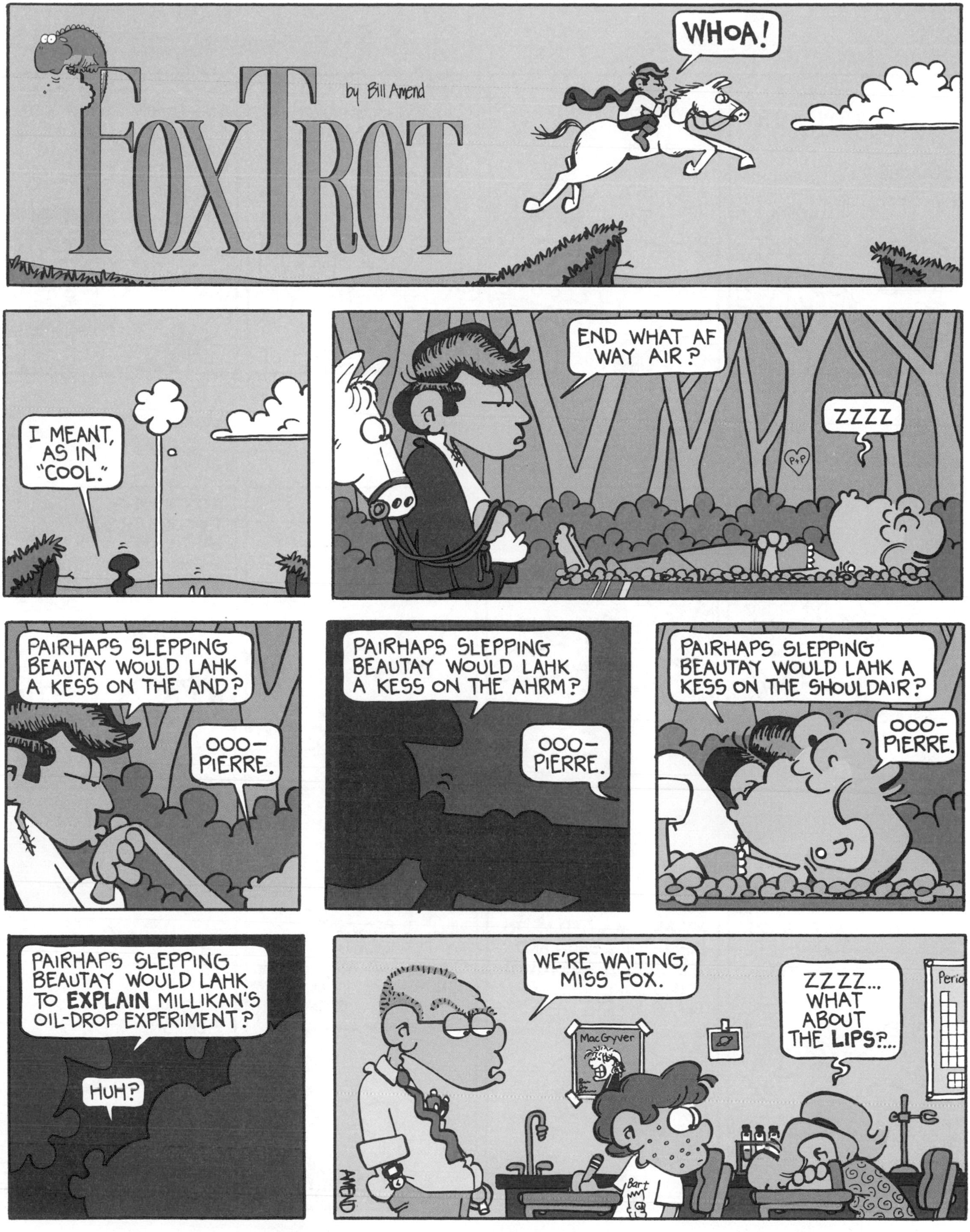
FoxTrot
by Bill Amend
WHOA!
I MEANT, AS IN "COOL."
END WHAT AF WAY AIR?
ZZZZ
P+P
PAIRHAPS SLEPPING BEAUTAY WOULD LAHK A KESS ON THE AND?
OOO-PIERRE.
PAIRHAPS SLEPPING BEAUTAY WOULD LAHK A KESS ON THE AHRM?
OOO-PIERRE.
PAIRHAPS SLEPPING BEAUTAY WOULD LAHK A KESS ON THE SHOULDAIR?
OOO-PIERRE.
PAIRHAPS SLEPPING BEAUTAY WOULD LAHK TO EXPLAIN MILLIKAN'S OIL-DROP EXPERIMENT?
HUH?
WE'RE WAITING, MISS FOX.
ZZZZ... WHAT ABOUT THE LIPS?...
MacGyver
Bart
AMEND

HEE HEE HEE...

WHAT'S SO FUNNY?

TOMORROW'S MY DAY TO BRING SOMETHING FOR SHOW AND TELL.

YEAH, SO?

I'M BRINGING QUINCY. THE GIRLS ARE ALL GONNA HAVE HEART ATTACKS.

YOU DON'T KNOW ANY-THING ABOUT LIABILITY LAW, DO YOU?

YOU KNOW, MOST KIDS JUST BRING STAMP COLLECTIONS...

WHAT'S IN THE BOX?

I'M BRINGING QUINCY TO SCHOOL FOR SHOW AND TELL.

Live Animal

MISS O'MALLEY **SAID** YOU COULD?

Live Animal

I MEAN, YOU DID **ASK**, RIGHT?

DIDN'T WE GO THROUGH THIS LAST YEAR WITH YOUR TICK FARM?

WAS IT **MY** FAULT THEY GOT LOOSE?!

MISS O'MALLEY?

WHY, JASON, **YOU'RE** HERE EARLY.

Live Animal

Read!

MY MOM WANTED ME TO DISCUSS MY SHOW AND TELL PRESENTATION WITH YOU BEFORE CLASS STARTS.

WHY'S THAT?

WELL, I BROUGHT MY PET IGUANA, QUINCY, AND HE TENDS TO BE SOMETHING OF A HAND-FUL.

AND SO SHE WANTED MY PERMISSION?

INDEMNI-FICATION.

A REGULAR CARL LEWIS, I SEE.

Live Animal

Read!

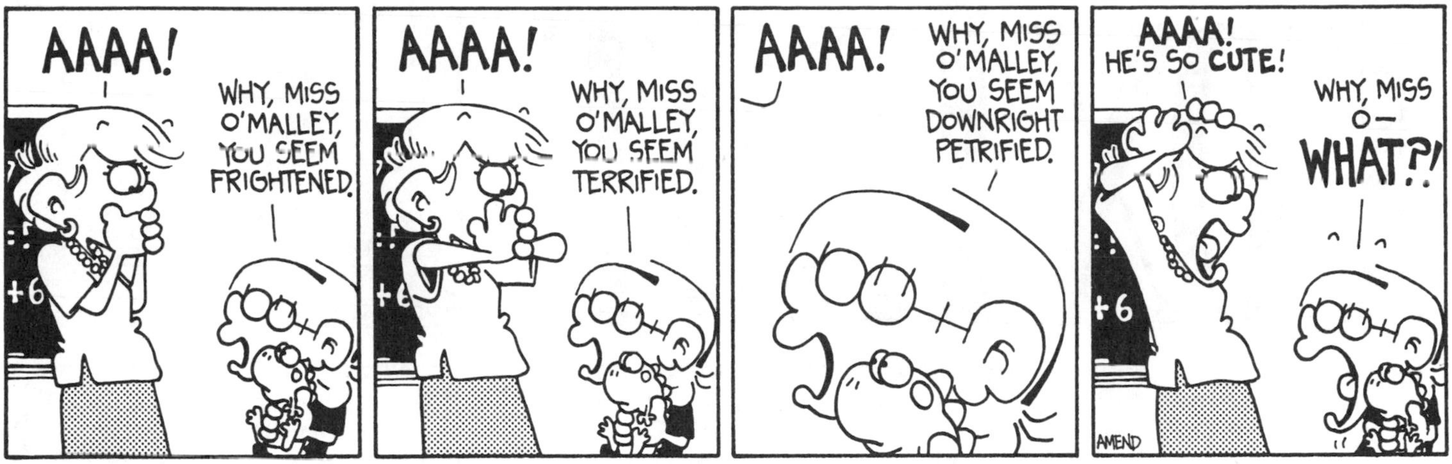
AAAA!
WHY, MISS O'MALLEY, YOU SEEM FRIGHTENED.
AAAA!
WHY, MISS O'MALLEY, YOU SEEM TERRIFIED.
AAAA!
WHY, MISS O'MALLEY, YOU SEEM DOWNRIGHT PETRIFIED.
AAAA! HE'S SO CUTE!
WHY, MISS O—
WHAT?!
AMEND

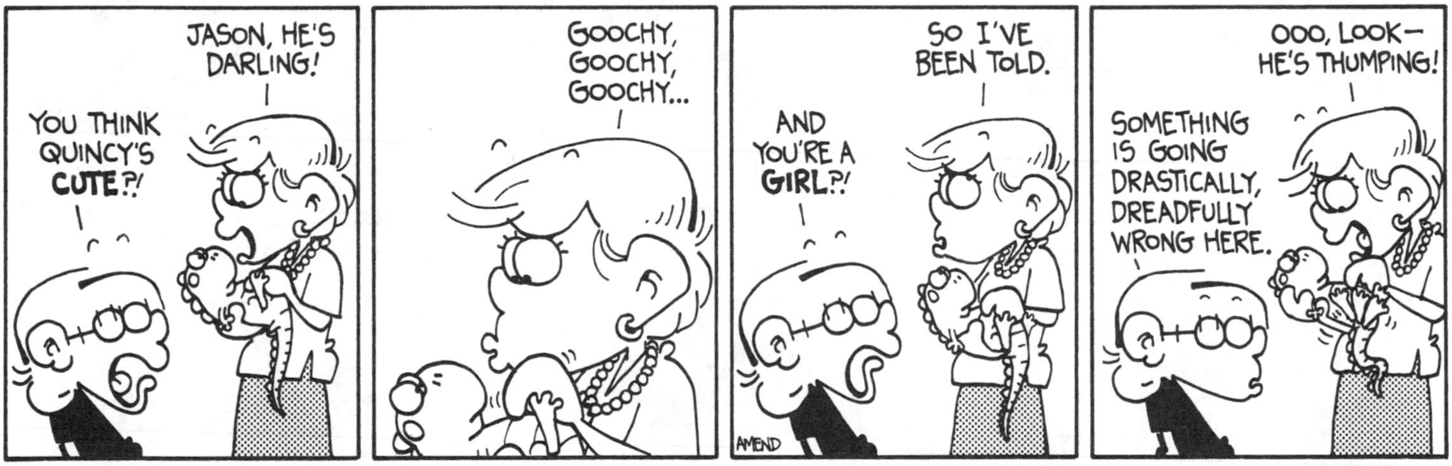
JASON, HE'S DARLING!
YOU THINK QUINCY'S CUTE?!
GOOCHY, GOOCHY, GOOCHY...
SO I'VE BEEN TOLD.
AND YOU'RE A GIRL?!
AMEND
OOO, LOOK— HE'S THUMPING!
SOMETHING IS GOING DRASTICALLY, DREADFULLY WRONG HERE.

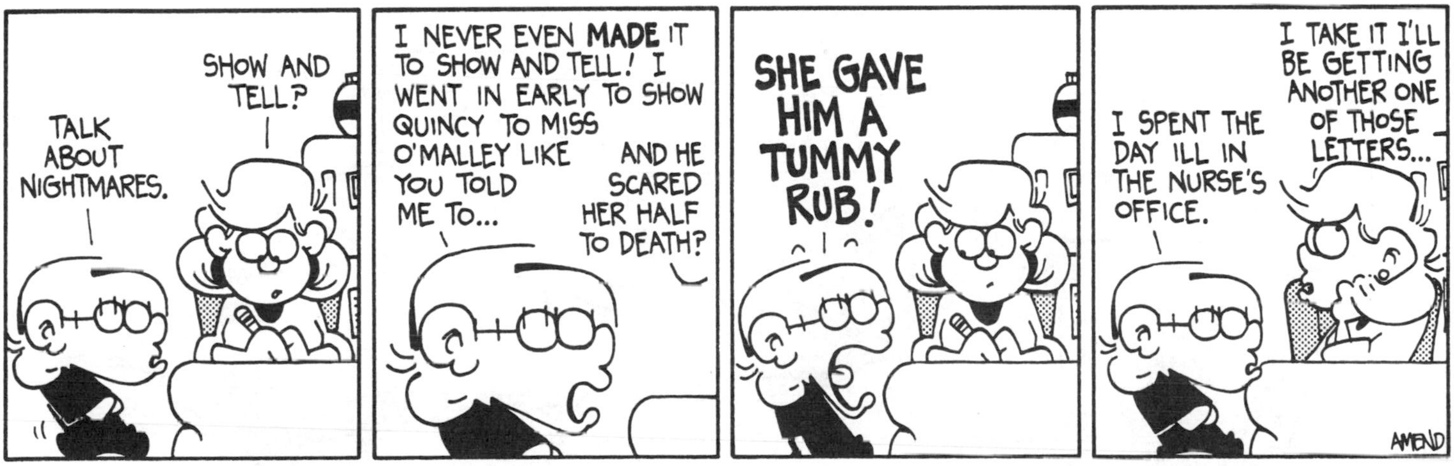
SHOW AND TELL?
TALK ABOUT NIGHTMARES.
I NEVER EVEN MADE IT TO SHOW AND TELL! I WENT IN EARLY TO SHOW QUINCY TO MISS O'MALLEY LIKE YOU TOLD ME TO...
AND HE SCARED HER HALF TO DEATH?
SHE GAVE HIM A TUMMY RUB!
I TAKE IT I'LL BE GETTING ANOTHER ONE OF THOSE LETTERS...
I SPENT THE DAY ILL IN THE NURSE'S OFFICE.
AMEND

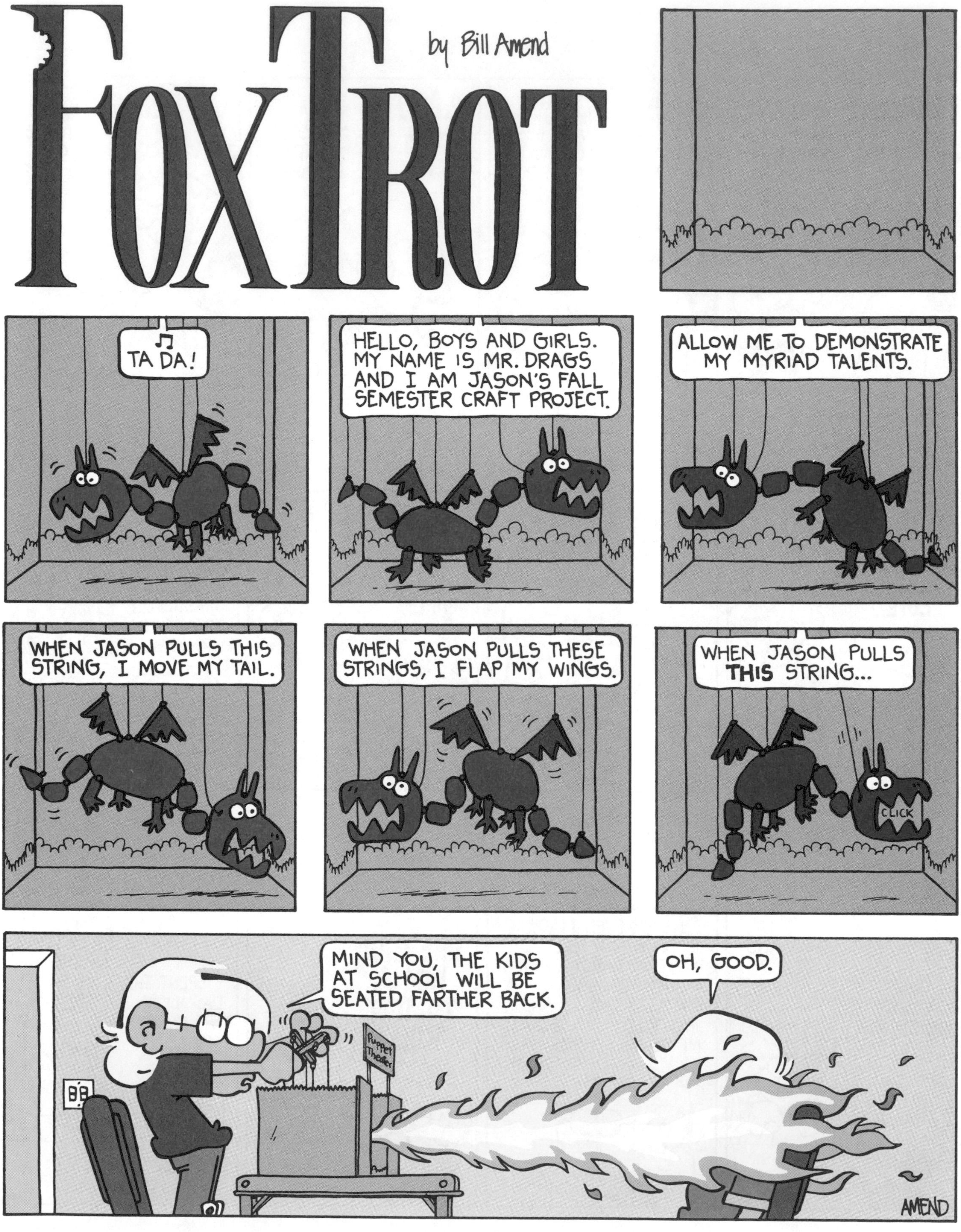
FoxTrot
by Bill Amend
♫ TA DA!
HELLO, BOYS AND GIRLS. MY NAME IS MR. DRAGS AND I AM JASON'S FALL SEMESTER CRAFT PROJECT.
ALLOW ME TO DEMONSTRATE MY MYRIAD TALENTS.
WHEN JASON PULLS THIS STRING, I MOVE MY TAIL.
WHEN JASON PULLS THESE STRINGS, I FLAP MY WINGS.
WHEN JASON PULLS **THIS** STRING...
CLICK
MIND YOU, THE KIDS AT SCHOOL WILL BE SEATED FARTHER BACK.
OH, GOOD.
Puppet Theater
AMEND

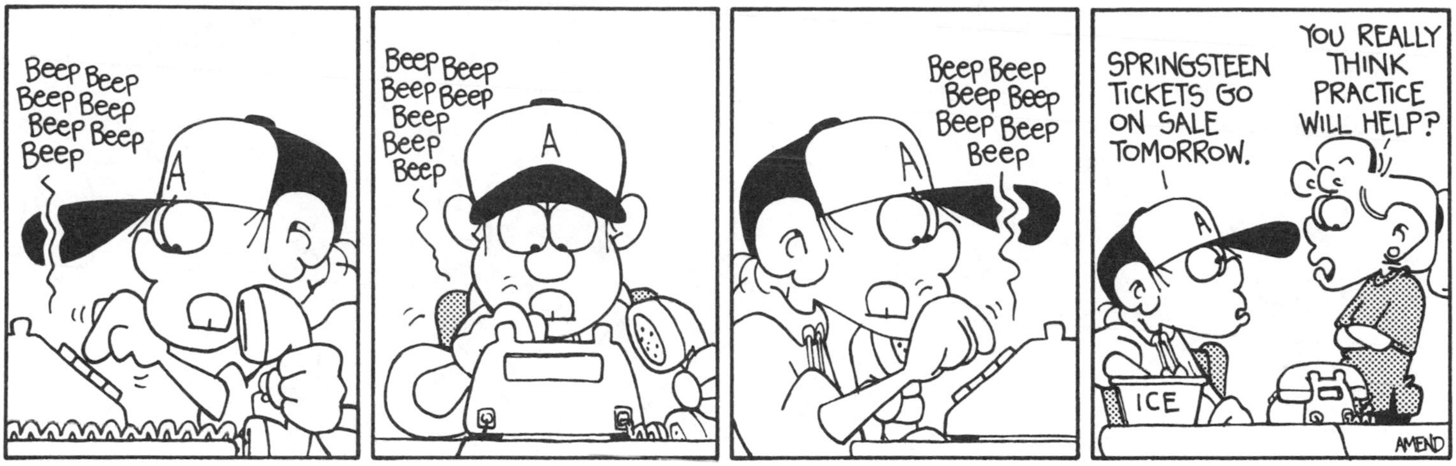
Beep Beep Beep Beep Beep Beep Beep
Beep Beep Beep Beep Beep
Beep Beep Beep Beep Beep Beep Beep
SPRINGSTEEN TICKETS GO ON SALE TOMORROW.
YOU REALLY THINK PRACTICE WILL HELP?
ICE
AMEND

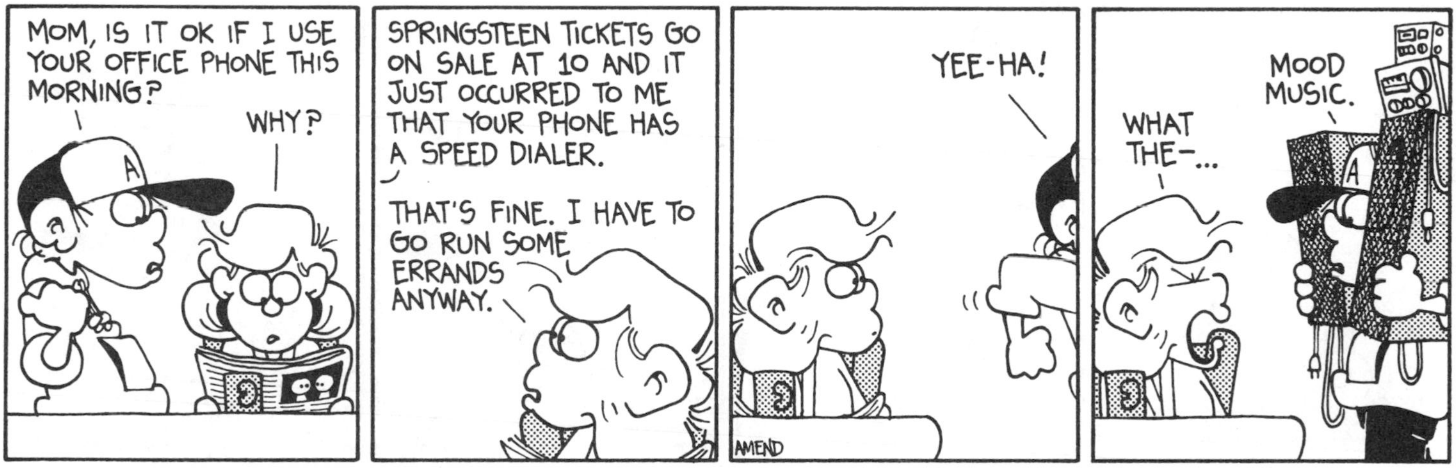
MOM, IS IT OK IF I USE YOUR OFFICE PHONE THIS MORNING?
WHY?
SPRINGSTEEN TICKETS GO ON SALE AT 10 AND IT JUST OCCURRED TO ME THAT YOUR PHONE HAS A SPEED DIALER.
THAT'S FINE. I HAVE TO GO RUN SOME ERRANDS ANYWAY.
YEE-HA!
AMEND
WHAT THE-...
MOOD MUSIC.

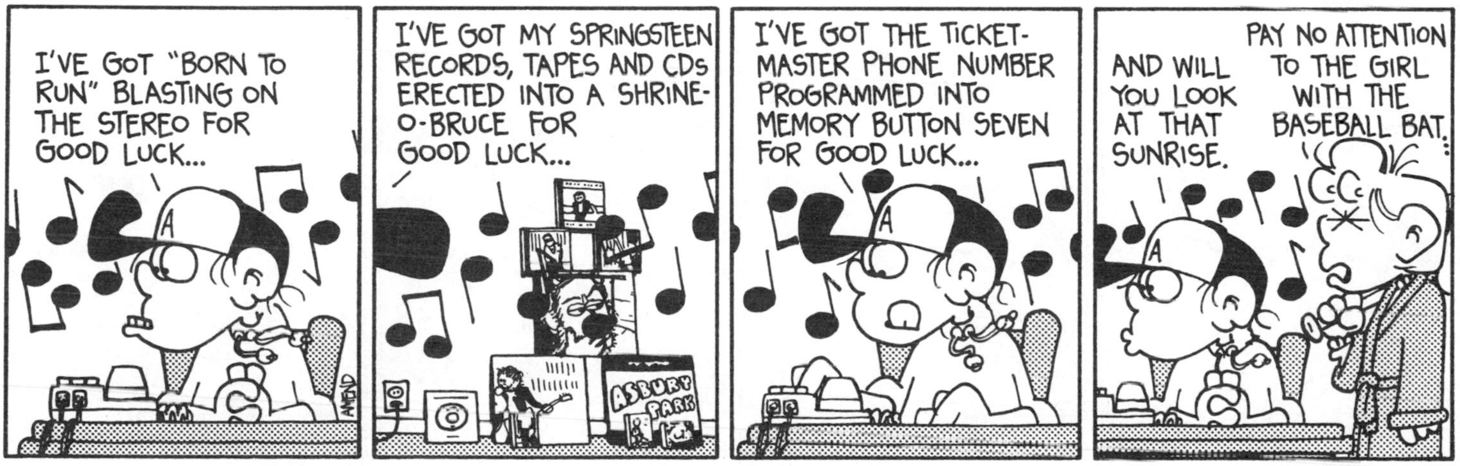
I'VE GOT "BORN TO RUN" BLASTING ON THE STEREO FOR GOOD LUCK...
AMEND
I'VE GOT MY SPRINGSTEEN RECORDS, TAPES AND CDs ERECTED INTO A SHRINE-O-BRUCE FOR GOOD LUCK...
ASBURY PARK
I'VE GOT THE TICKET-MASTER PHONE NUMBER PROGRAMMED INTO MEMORY BUTTON SEVEN FOR GOOD LUCK...
AND WILL YOU LOOK AT THAT SUNRISE.
PAY NO ATTENTION TO THE GIRL WITH THE BASEBALL BAT.

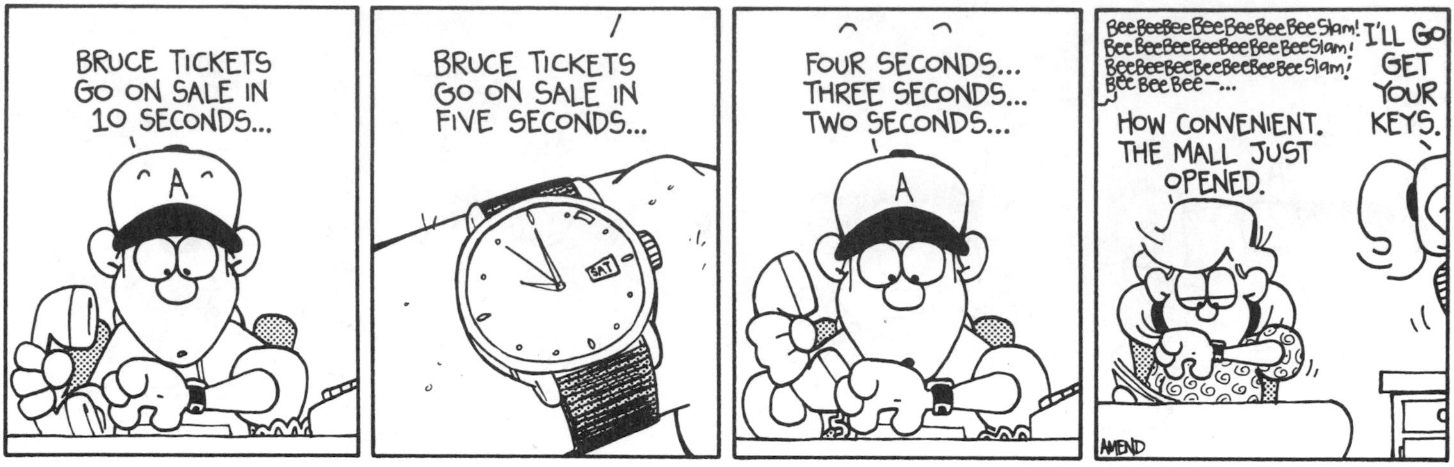
BRUCE TICKETS GO ON SALE IN 10 SECONDS...
BRUCE TICKETS GO ON SALE IN FIVE SECONDS...
SAT
FOUR SECONDS... THREE SECONDS... TWO SECONDS...
BeeBeeBeeBeeBeeBeeBeeSlam! BeeBeeBeeBeeBeeBeeBeeSlam! BeeBeeBeeBeeBeeBeeBeeSlam! BeeBeeBee—...
I'LL GO GET YOUR KEYS.
HOW CONVENIENT. THE MALL JUST OPENED.
AMEND

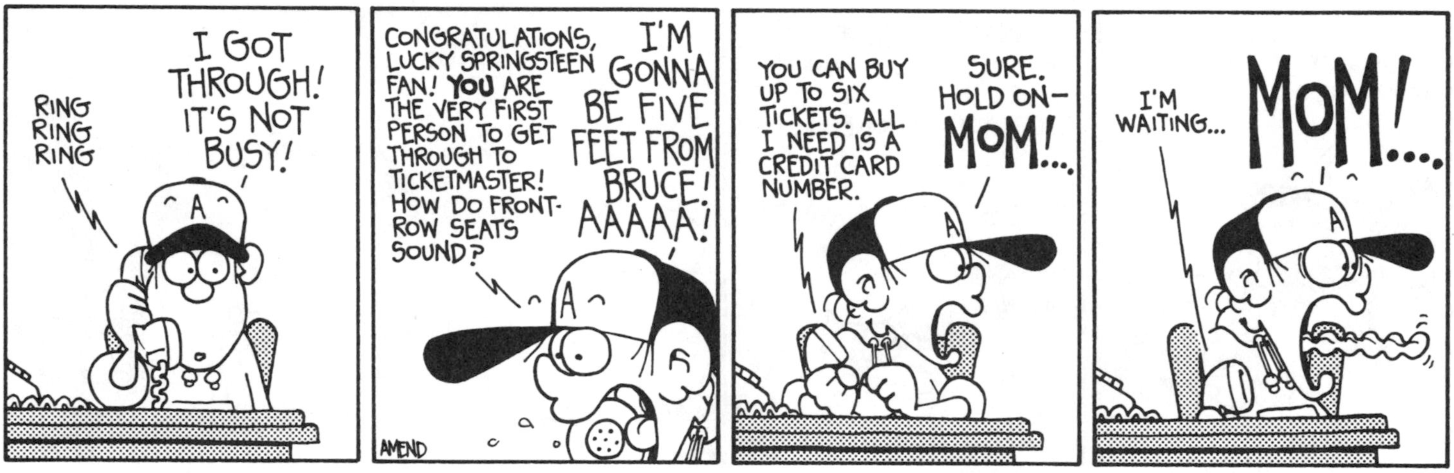
RING RING RING
I GOT THROUGH! IT'S NOT BUSY!
CONGRATULATIONS, LUCKY SPRINGSTEEN FAN! YOU ARE THE VERY FIRST PERSON TO GET THROUGH TO TICKETMASTER! HOW DO FRONT-ROW SEATS SOUND?
I'M GONNA BE FIVE FEET FROM BRUCE! AAAAA!
AMEND
YOU CAN BUY UP TO SIX TICKETS. ALL I NEED IS A CREDIT CARD NUMBER.
SURE. HOLD ON— MOM!...
I'M WAITING...
MOM!....

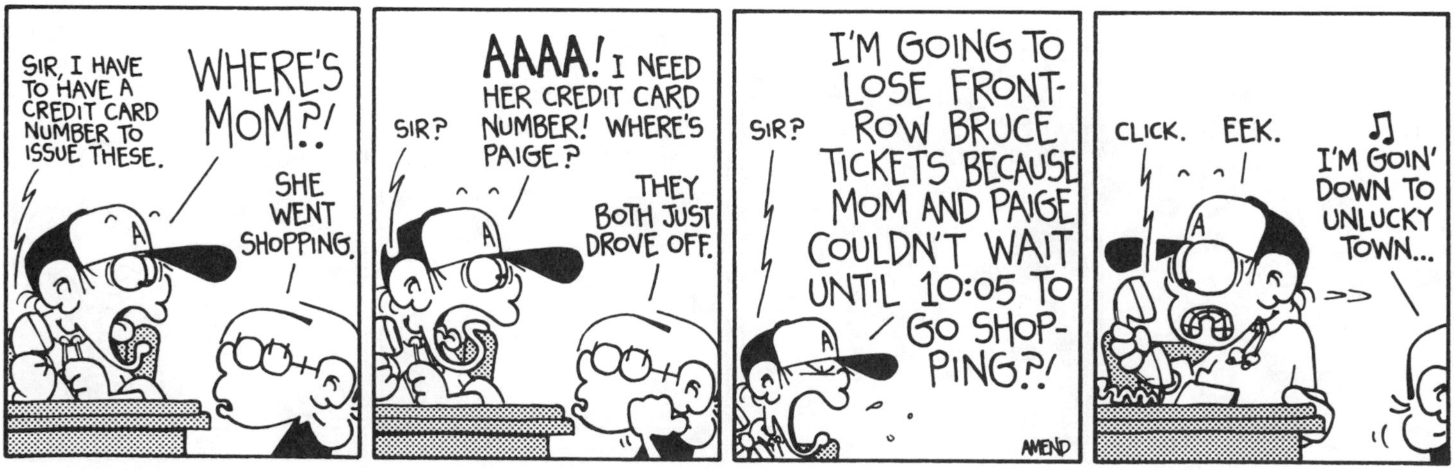
SIR, I HAVE TO HAVE A CREDIT CARD NUMBER TO ISSUE THESE.
WHERE'S MOM?!
SHE WENT SHOPPING.
SIR?
AAAA! I NEED HER CREDIT CARD NUMBER! WHERE'S PAIGE?
THEY BOTH JUST DROVE OFF.
SIR?
I'M GOING TO LOSE FRONT-ROW BRUCE TICKETS BECAUSE MOM AND PAIGE COULDN'T WAIT UNTIL 10:05 TO GO SHOPPING?!
AMEND
CLICK.
EEK.
♫ I'M GOIN' DOWN TO UNLUCKY TOWN...

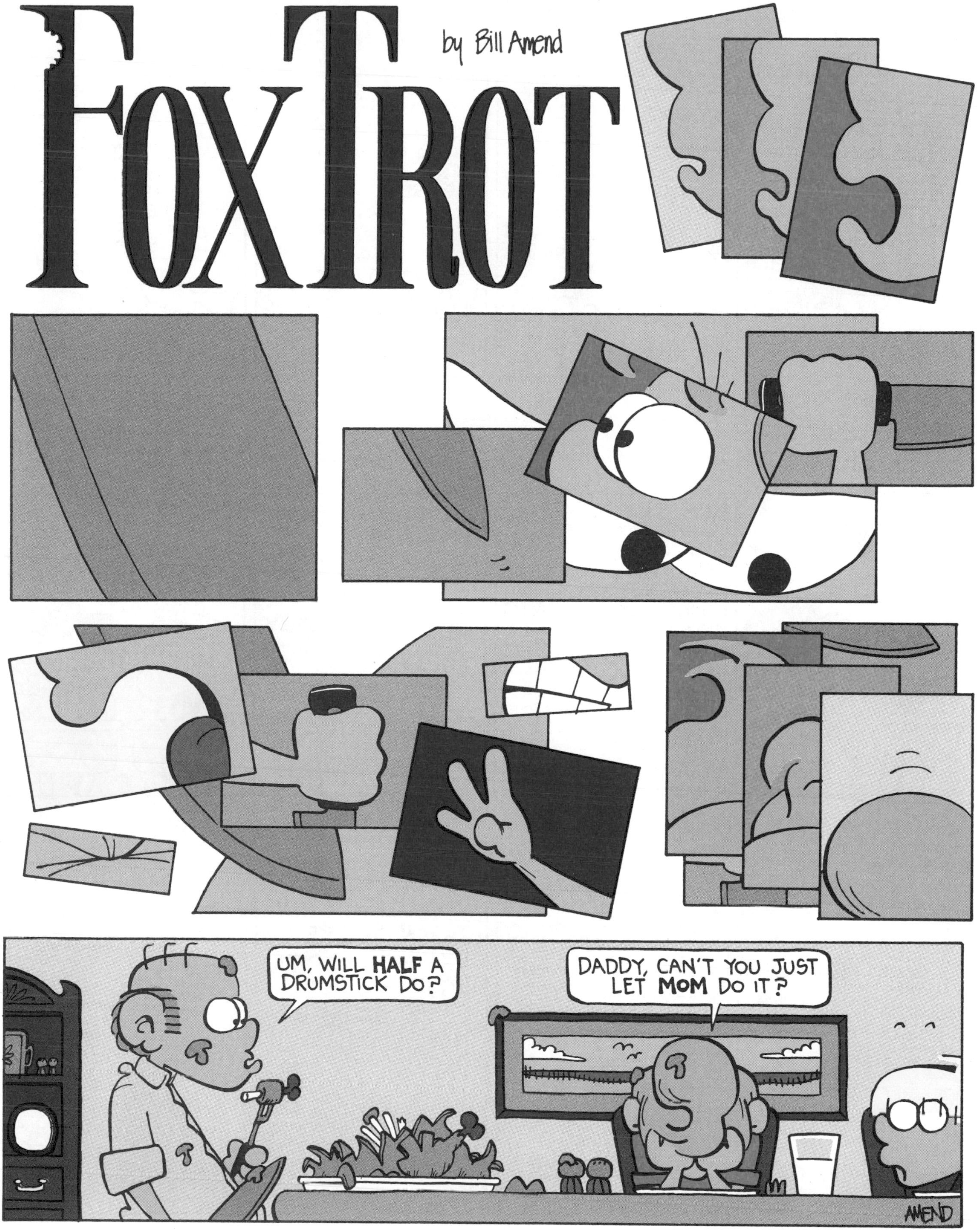
FoxTrot
by Bill Amend
UM, WILL HALF A DRUMSTICK DO?
DADDY, CAN'T YOU JUST LET MOM DO IT?
AMEND

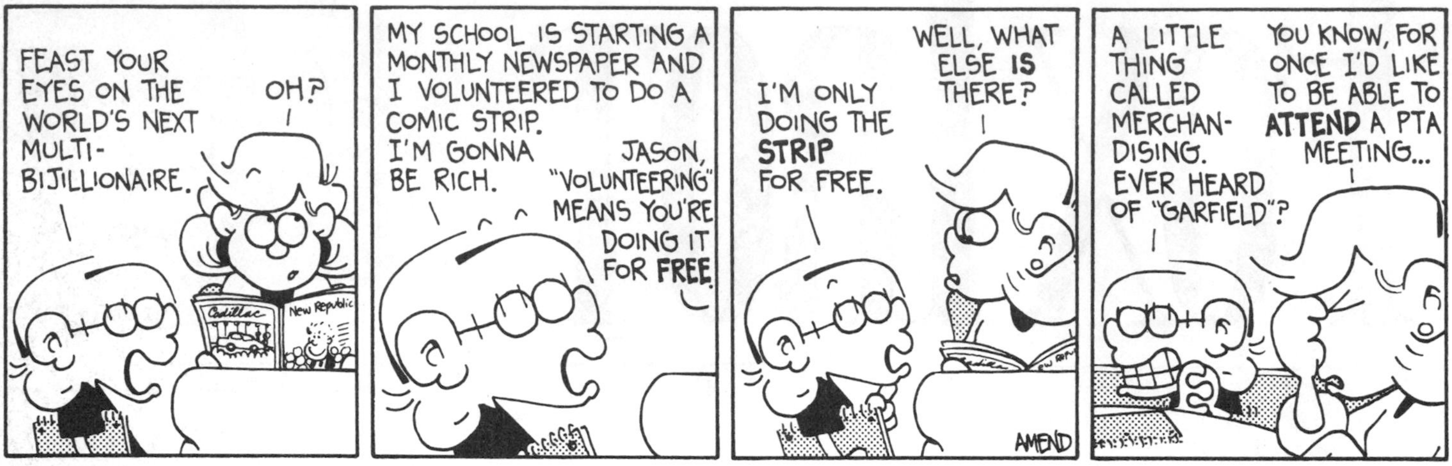
FEAST YOUR EYES ON THE WORLD'S NEXT MULTI-BIJILLIONAIRE.
OH?
New Republic
MY SCHOOL IS STARTING A MONTHLY NEWSPAPER AND I VOLUNTEERED TO DO A COMIC STRIP. I'M GONNA BE RICH.
JASON, "VOLUNTEERING" MEANS YOU'RE DOING IT FOR **FREE**.
I'M ONLY DOING THE **STRIP** FOR FREE.
WELL, WHAT ELSE **IS** THERE?
AMEND
A LITTLE THING CALLED MERCHAN-DISING. EVER HEARD OF "GARFIELD"?
YOU KNOW, FOR ONCE I'D LIKE TO BE ABLE TO **ATTEND** A PTA MEETING...

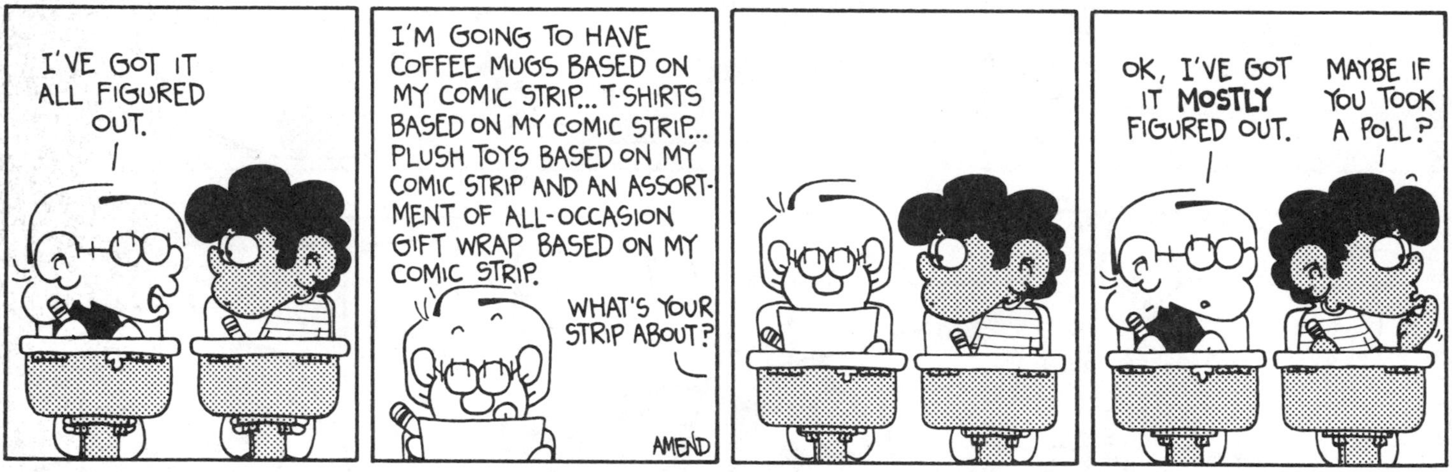
I'VE GOT IT ALL FIGURED OUT.
I'M GOING TO HAVE COFFEE MUGS BASED ON MY COMIC STRIP... T-SHIRTS BASED ON MY COMIC STRIP... PLUSH TOYS BASED ON MY COMIC STRIP AND AN ASSORT-MENT OF ALL-OCCASION GIFT WRAP BASED ON MY COMIC STRIP.
WHAT'S YOUR STRIP ABOUT?
AMEND
OK, I'VE GOT IT **MOSTLY** FIGURED OUT.
MAYBE IF YOU TOOK A POLL?

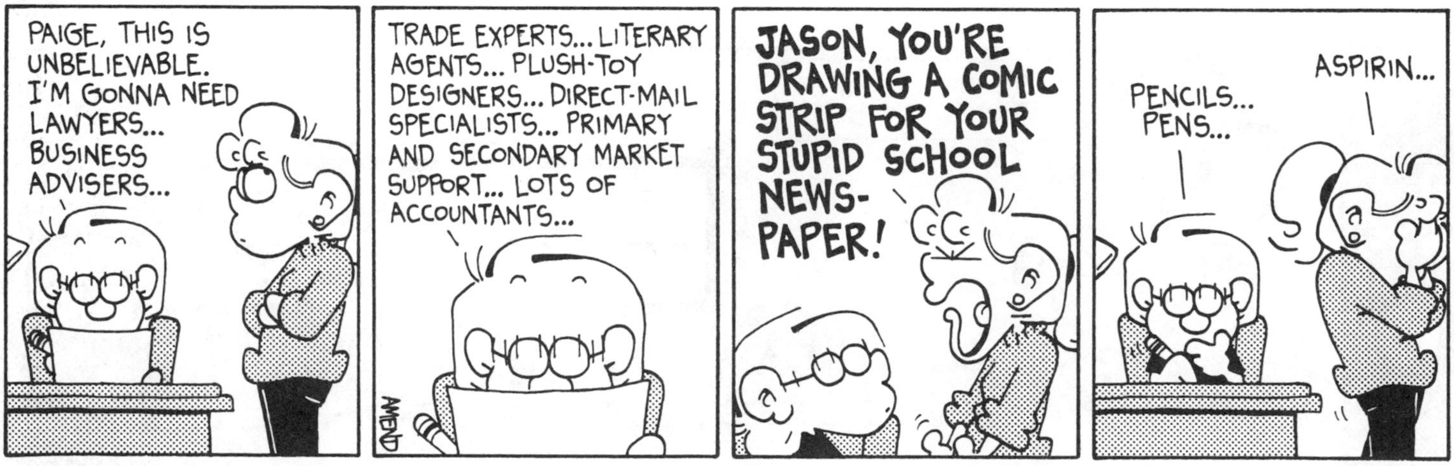
PAIGE, THIS IS UNBELIEVABLE. I'M GONNA NEED LAWYERS... BUSINESS ADVISERS...
TRADE EXPERTS... LITERARY AGENTS... PLUSH-TOY DESIGNERS... DIRECT-MAIL SPECIALISTS... PRIMARY AND SECONDARY MARKET SUPPORT... LOTS OF ACCOUNTANTS...
AMEND
JASON, YOU'RE DRAWING A COMIC STRIP FOR YOUR STUPID SCHOOL NEWS-PAPER!
PENCILS... PENS...
ASPIRIN...

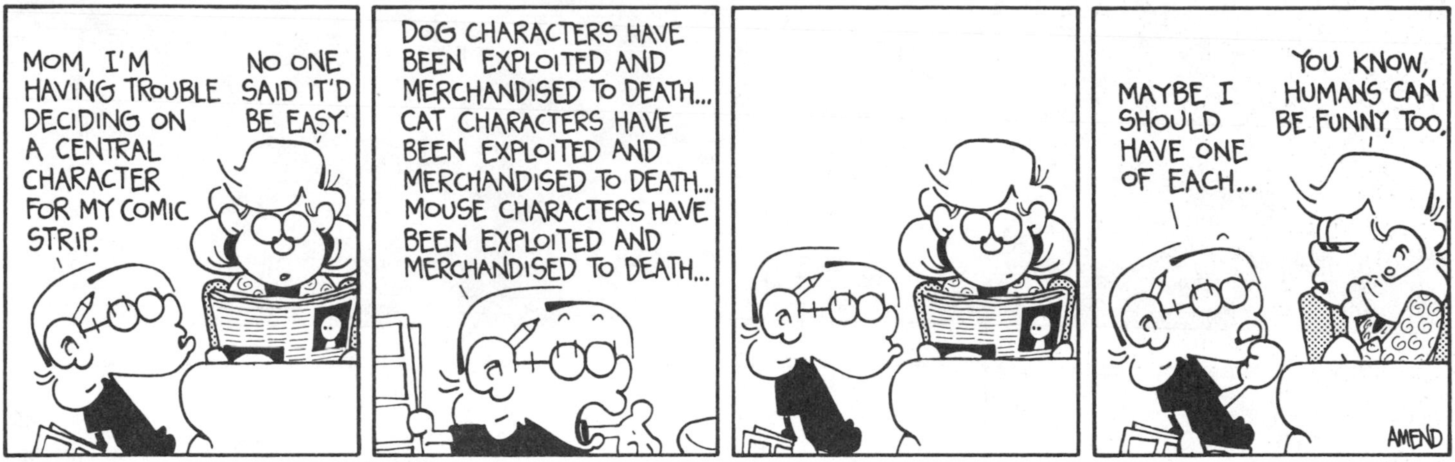
MOM, I'M HAVING TROUBLE DECIDING ON A CENTRAL CHARACTER FOR MY COMIC STRIP.
NO ONE SAID IT'D BE EASY.
DOG CHARACTERS HAVE BEEN EXPLOITED AND MERCHANDISED TO DEATH... CAT CHARACTERS HAVE BEEN EXPLOITED AND MERCHANDISED TO DEATH... MOUSE CHARACTERS HAVE BEEN EXPLOITED AND MERCHANDISED TO DEATH...
MAYBE I SHOULD HAVE ONE OF EACH...
YOU KNOW, HUMANS CAN BE FUNNY, TOO.
AMEND

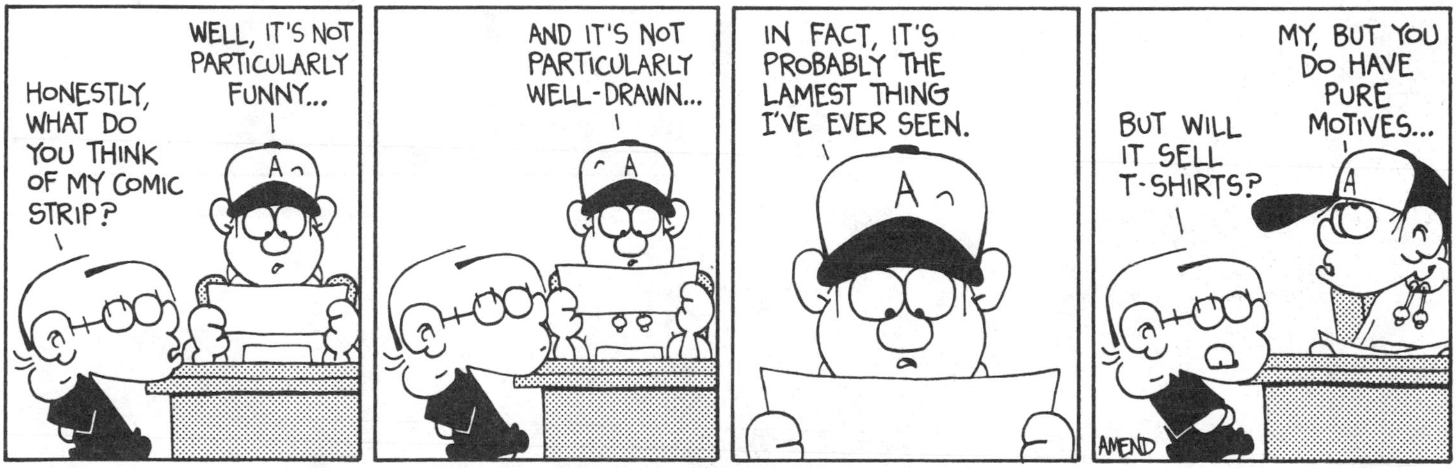
HONESTLY, WHAT DO YOU THINK OF MY COMIC STRIP?
WELL, IT'S NOT PARTICULARLY FUNNY...
AND IT'S NOT PARTICULARLY WELL-DRAWN...
IN FACT, IT'S PROBABLY THE LAMEST THING I'VE EVER SEEN.
BUT WILL IT SELL T-SHIRTS?
MY, BUT YOU DO HAVE PURE MOTIVES...
AMEND

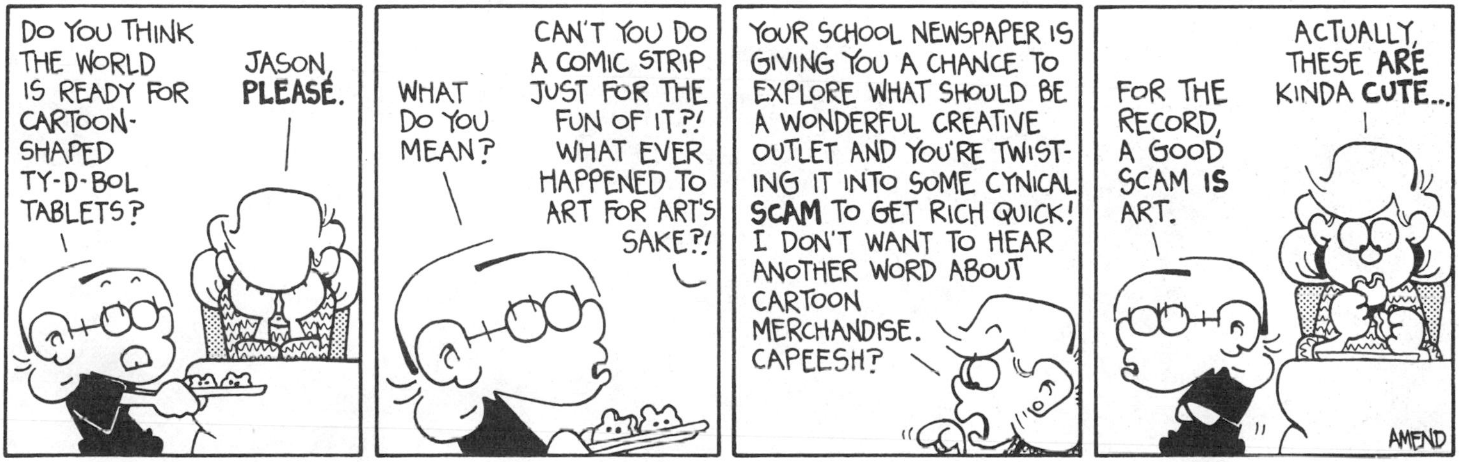
DO YOU THINK THE WORLD IS READY FOR CARTOON-SHAPED TY-D-BOL TABLETS?
JASON, **PLEASE**.
WHAT DO YOU MEAN?
CAN'T YOU DO A COMIC STRIP JUST FOR THE FUN OF IT?! WHAT EVER HAPPENED TO ART FOR ART'S SAKE?!
YOUR SCHOOL NEWSPAPER IS GIVING YOU A CHANCE TO EXPLORE WHAT SHOULD BE A WONDERFUL CREATIVE OUTLET AND YOU'RE TWISTING IT INTO SOME CYNICAL **SCAM** TO GET RICH QUICK! I DON'T WANT TO HEAR ANOTHER WORD ABOUT CARTOON MERCHANDISE. CAPEESH?
FOR THE RECORD, A GOOD SCAM **IS** ART.
ACTUALLY, THESE **ARE** KINDA **CUTE**...
AMEND

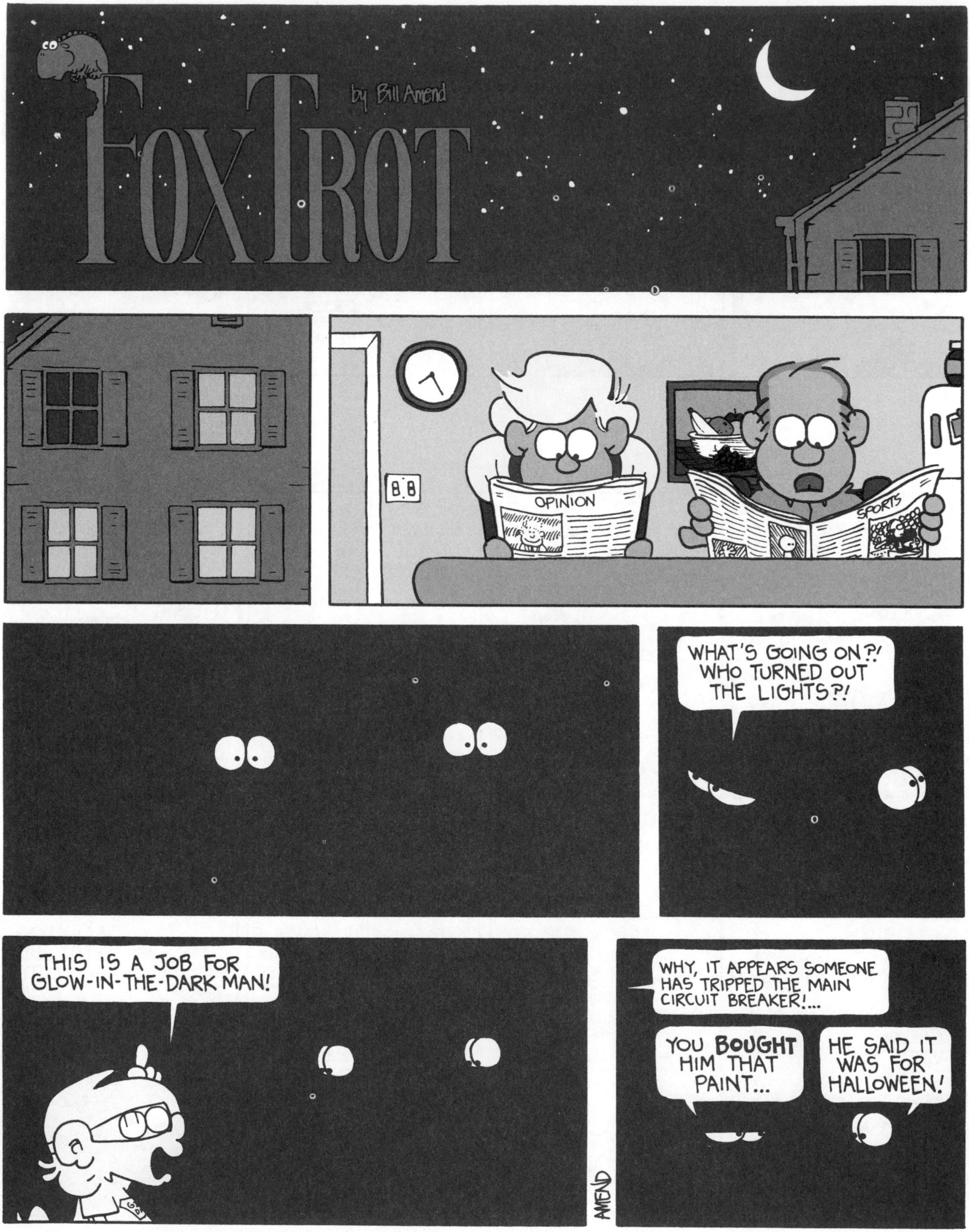
FoxTrot
by Bill Amend
OPINION
SPORTS
WHAT'S GOING ON?! WHO TURNED OUT THE LIGHTS?!
THIS IS A JOB FOR GLOW-IN-THE-DARK MAN!
WHY, IT APPEARS SOMEONE HAS TRIPPED THE MAIN CIRCUIT BREAKER!...
YOU BOUGHT HIM THAT PAINT...
HE SAID IT WAS FOR HALLOWEEN!
AMEND

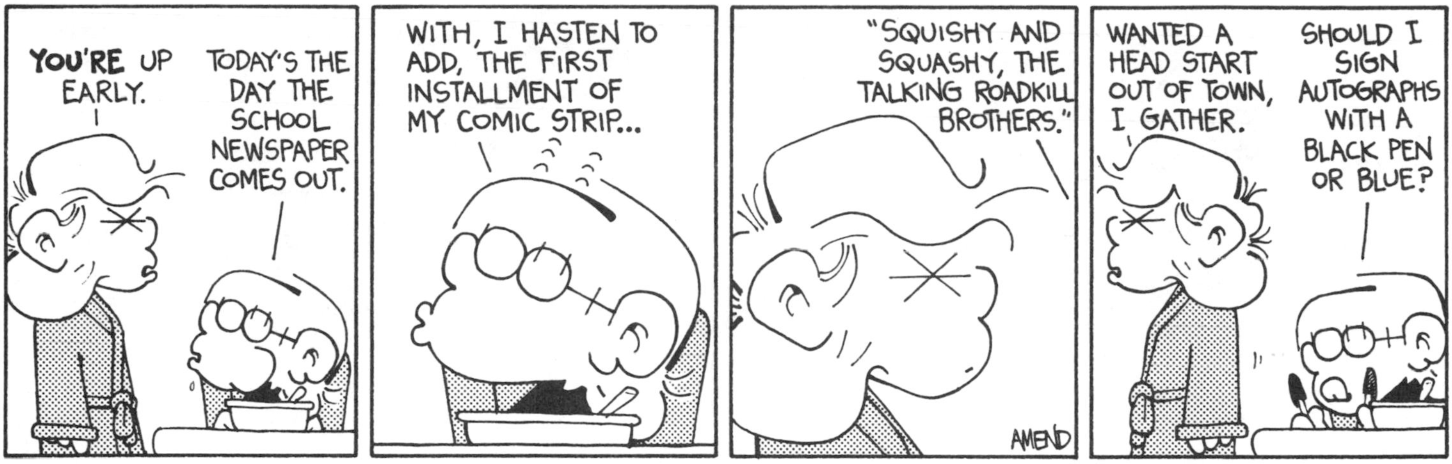
YOU'RE UP EARLY.
TODAY'S THE DAY THE SCHOOL NEWSPAPER COMES OUT.
WITH, I HASTEN TO ADD, THE FIRST INSTALLMENT OF MY COMIC STRIP...
"SQUISHY AND SQUASHY, THE TALKING ROADKILL BROTHERS."
AMEND
WANTED A HEAD START OUT OF TOWN, I GATHER.
SHOULD I SIGN AUTOGRAPHS WITH A BLACK PEN OR BLUE?

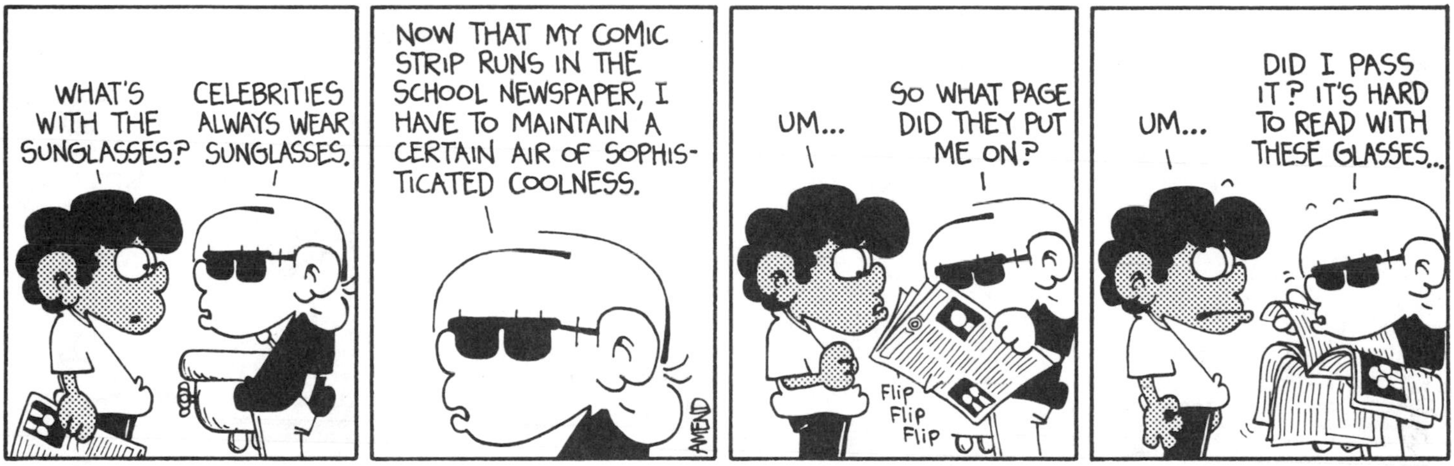
WHAT'S WITH THE SUNGLASSES?
CELEBRITIES ALWAYS WEAR SUNGLASSES.
NOW THAT MY COMIC STRIP RUNS IN THE SCHOOL NEWSPAPER, I HAVE TO MAINTAIN A CERTAIN AIR OF SOPHISTICATED COOLNESS.
AMEND
UM...
SO WHAT PAGE DID THEY PUT ME ON?
FLIP FLIP FLIP
UM...
DID I PASS IT? IT'S HARD TO READ WITH THESE GLASSES...

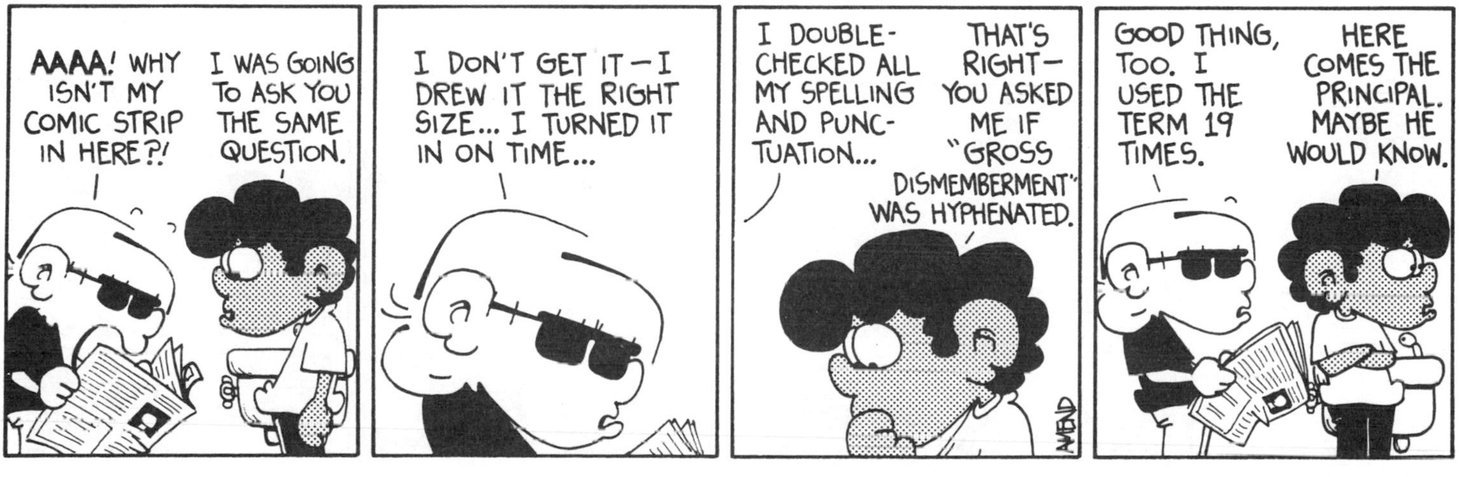
AAAA! WHY ISN'T MY COMIC STRIP IN HERE?!
I WAS GOING TO ASK YOU THE SAME QUESTION.
I DON'T GET IT—I DREW IT THE RIGHT SIZE... I TURNED IT IN ON TIME...
I DOUBLE-CHECKED ALL MY SPELLING AND PUNCTUATION...
THAT'S RIGHT—YOU ASKED ME IF "GROSS DISMEMBERMENT" WAS HYPHENATED.
AMEND
GOOD THING, TOO. I USED THE TERM 19 TIMES.
HERE COMES THE PRINCIPAL. MAYBE HE WOULD KNOW.

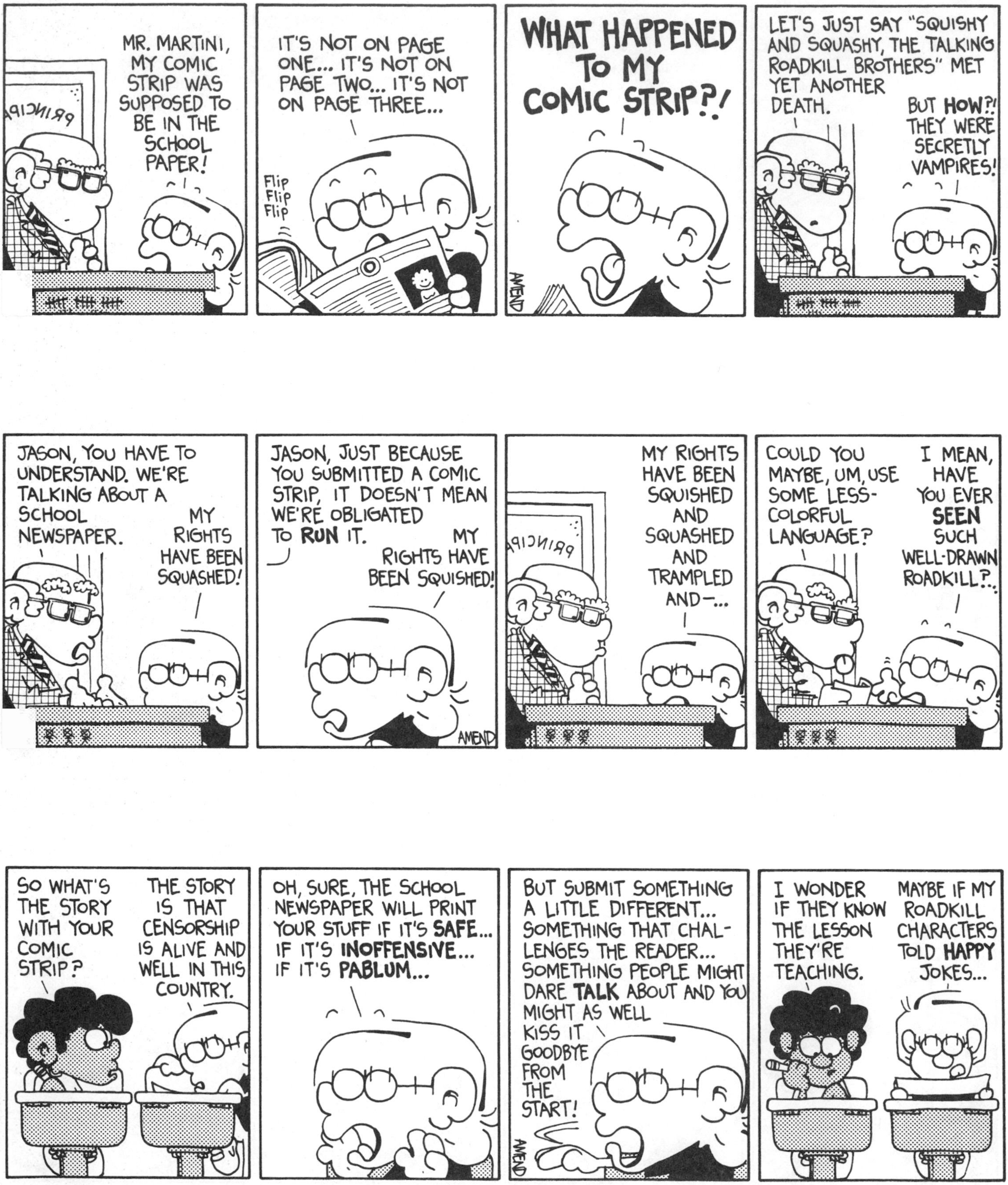
MR. MARTINI, MY COMIC STRIP WAS SUPPOSED TO BE IN THE SCHOOL PAPER!
IT'S NOT ON PAGE ONE... IT'S NOT ON PAGE TWO... IT'S NOT ON PAGE THREE...
Flip Flip Flip
WHAT HAPPENED TO MY COMIC STRIP?!
AMEND
LET'S JUST SAY "SQUISHY AND SQUASHY, THE TALKING ROADKILL BROTHERS" MET YET ANOTHER DEATH.
BUT HOW?! THEY WERE SECRETLY VAMPIRES!
JASON, YOU HAVE TO UNDERSTAND. WE'RE TALKING ABOUT A SCHOOL NEWSPAPER.
MY RIGHTS HAVE BEEN SQUASHED!
JASON, JUST BECAUSE YOU SUBMITTED A COMIC STRIP, IT DOESN'T MEAN WE'RE OBLIGATED TO RUN IT.
MY RIGHTS HAVE BEEN SQUISHED!
AMEND
MY RIGHTS HAVE BEEN SQUISHED AND SQUASHED AND TRAMPLED AND—...
COULD YOU MAYBE, UM, USE SOME LESS-COLORFUL LANGUAGE?
I MEAN, HAVE YOU EVER SEEN SUCH WELL-DRAWN ROADKILL?..
SO WHAT'S THE STORY WITH YOUR COMIC STRIP?
THE STORY IS THAT CENSORSHIP IS ALIVE AND WELL IN THIS COUNTRY.
OH, SURE, THE SCHOOL NEWSPAPER WILL PRINT YOUR STUFF IF IT'S SAFE... IF IT'S INOFFENSIVE... IF IT'S PABLUM...
BUT SUBMIT SOMETHING A LITTLE DIFFERENT... SOMETHING THAT CHALLENGES THE READER... SOMETHING PEOPLE MIGHT DARE TALK ABOUT AND YOU MIGHT AS WELL KISS IT GOODBYE FROM THE START!
AMEND
I WONDER IF THEY KNOW THE LESSON THEY'RE TEACHING.
MAYBE IF MY ROADKILL CHARACTERS TOLD HAPPY JOKES...

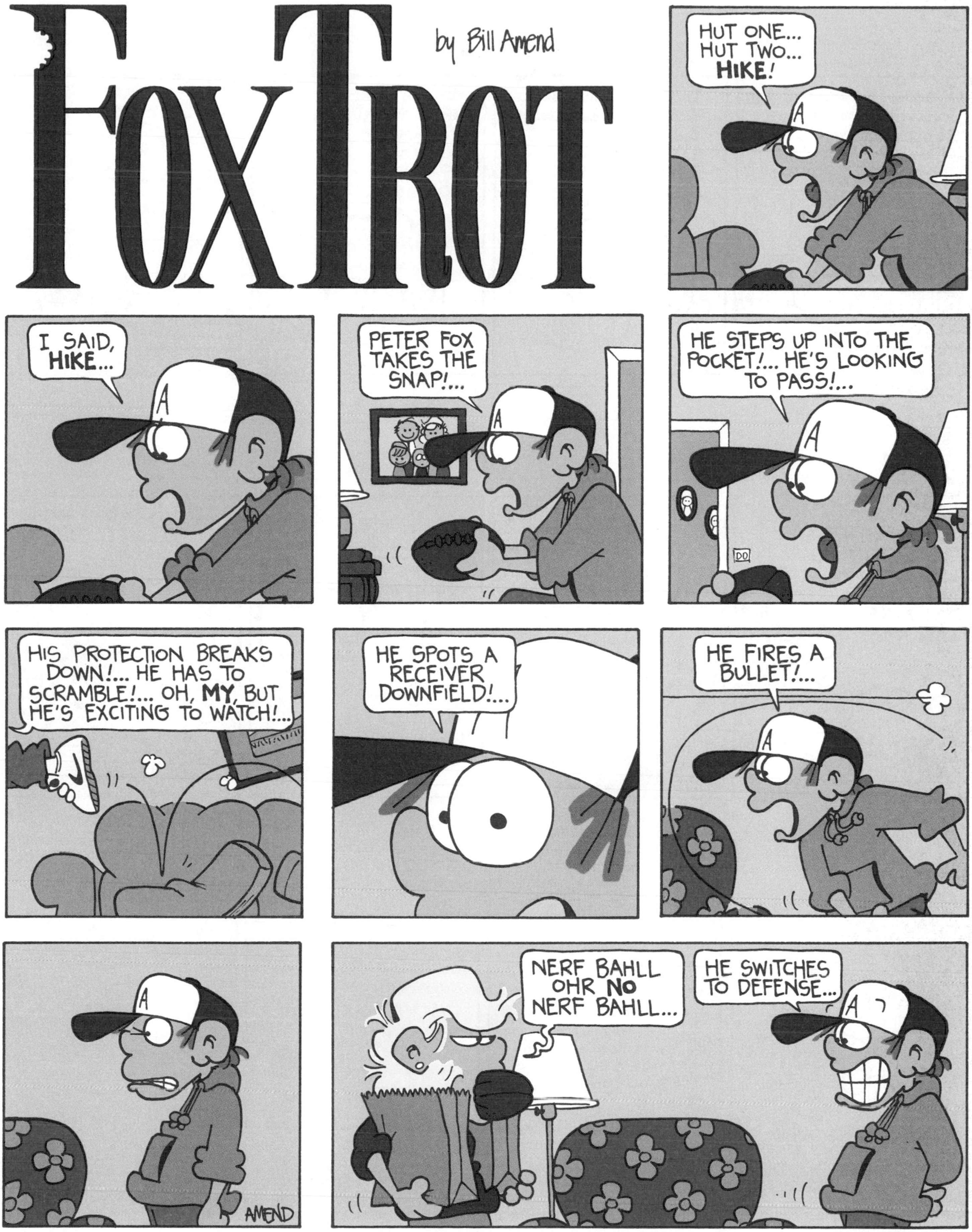
FoxTrot
by Bill Amend
HUT ONE... HUT TWO... **HIKE**!
I SAID, **HIKE**...
PETER FOX TAKES THE SNAP!...
HE STEPS UP INTO THE POCKET!... HE'S LOOKING TO PASS!...
HIS PROTECTION BREAKS DOWN!... HE HAS TO SCRAMBLE!... OH, **MY**, BUT HE'S EXCITING TO WATCH!...
HE SPOTS A RECEIVER DOWNFIELD!...
HE FIRES A BULLET!...
NERF BAHLL OHR **NO** NERF BAHLL...
HE SWITCHES TO DEFENSE...
AMEND

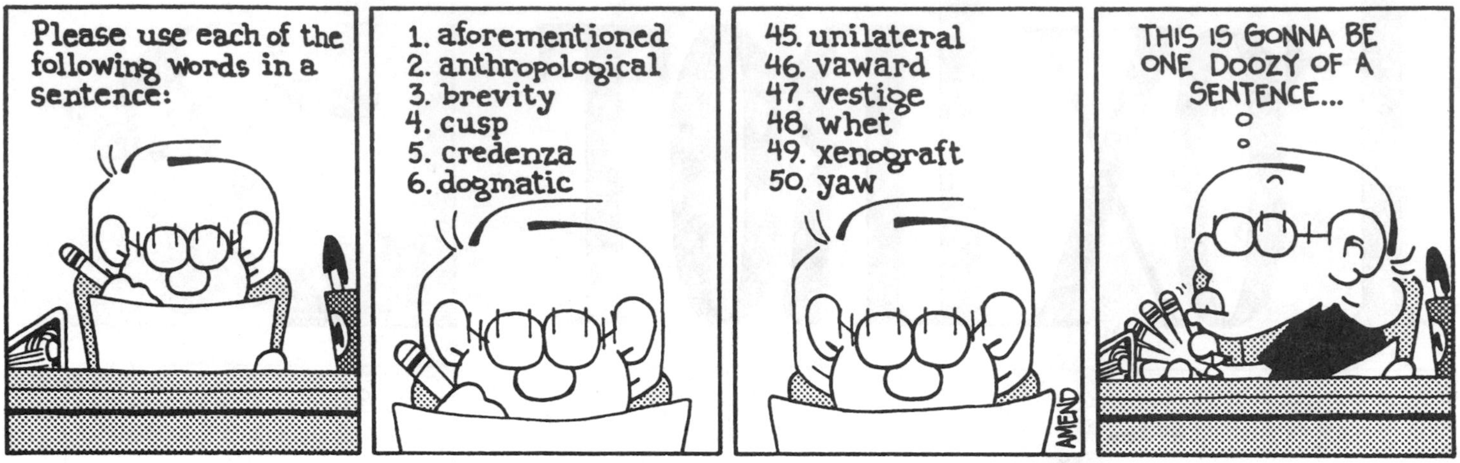
Please use each of the following words in a sentence:
1. aforementioned
2. anthropological
3. brevity
4. cusp
5. credenza
6. dogmatic
45. unilateral
46. vaward
47. vestige
48. whet
49. xenograft
50. yaw
AMEND
THIS IS GONNA BE ONE DOOZY OF A SENTENCE...

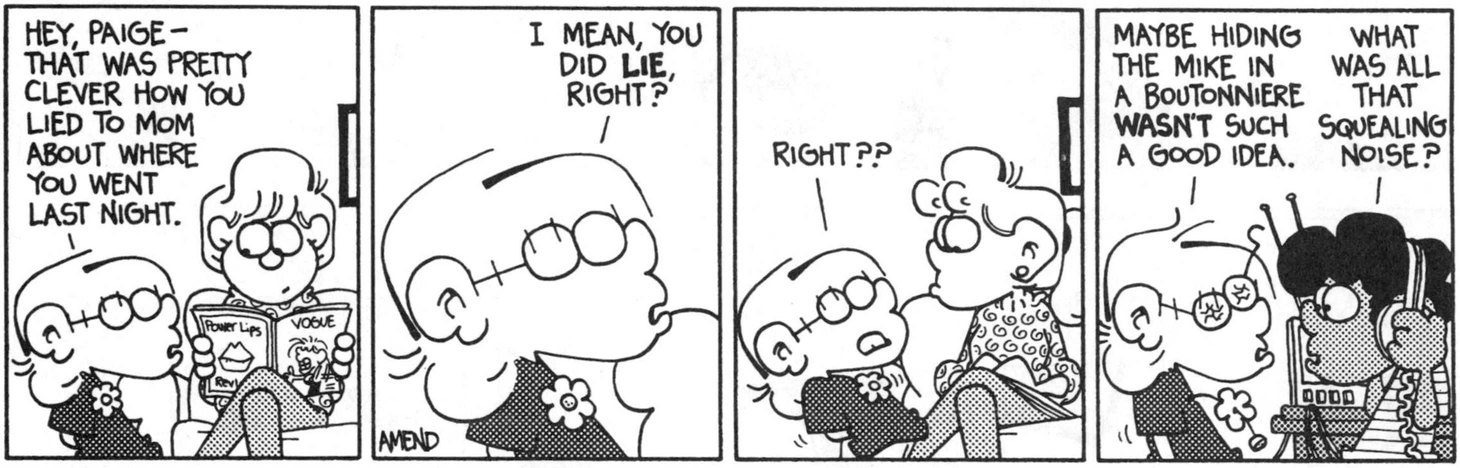
HEY, PAIGE— THAT WAS PRETTY CLEVER HOW YOU LIED TO MOM ABOUT WHERE YOU WENT LAST NIGHT.
Power Lips
VOGUE
I MEAN, YOU DID **LIE**, RIGHT?
AMEND
RIGHT??
MAYBE HIDING THE MIKE IN A BOUTONNIERE **WASN'T** SUCH A GOOD IDEA.
WHAT WAS ALL THAT SQUEALING NOISE?

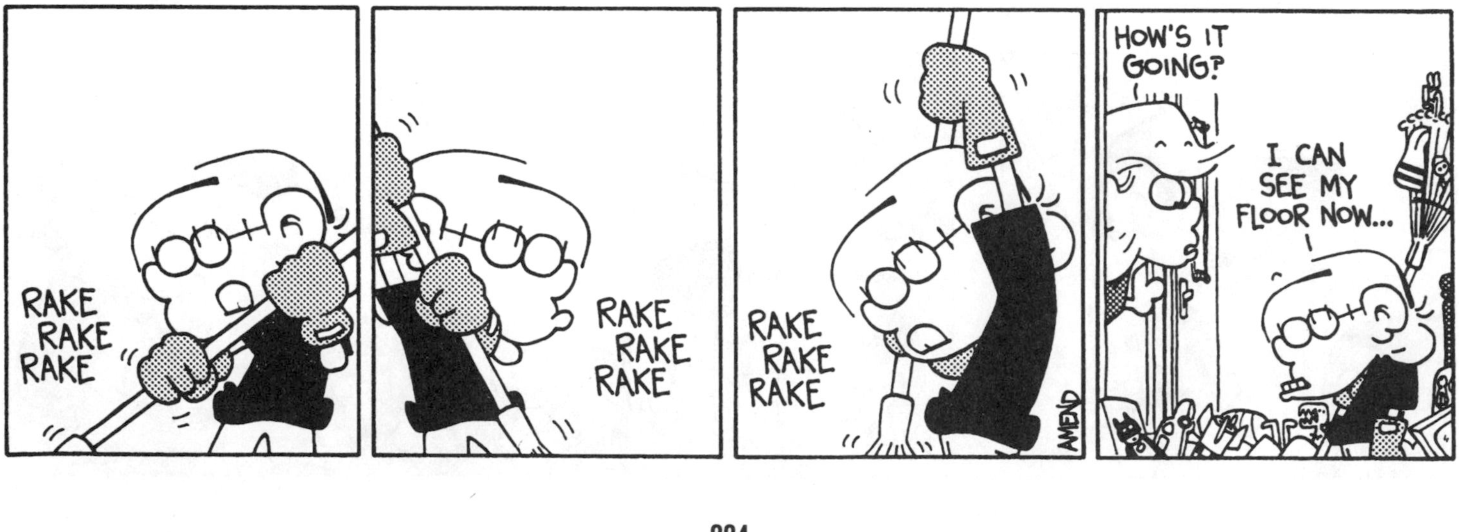
RAKE RAKE RAKE
RAKE RAKE RAKE
RAKE RAKE RAKE
AMEND
HOW'S IT GOING?
I CAN SEE MY FLOOR NOW...

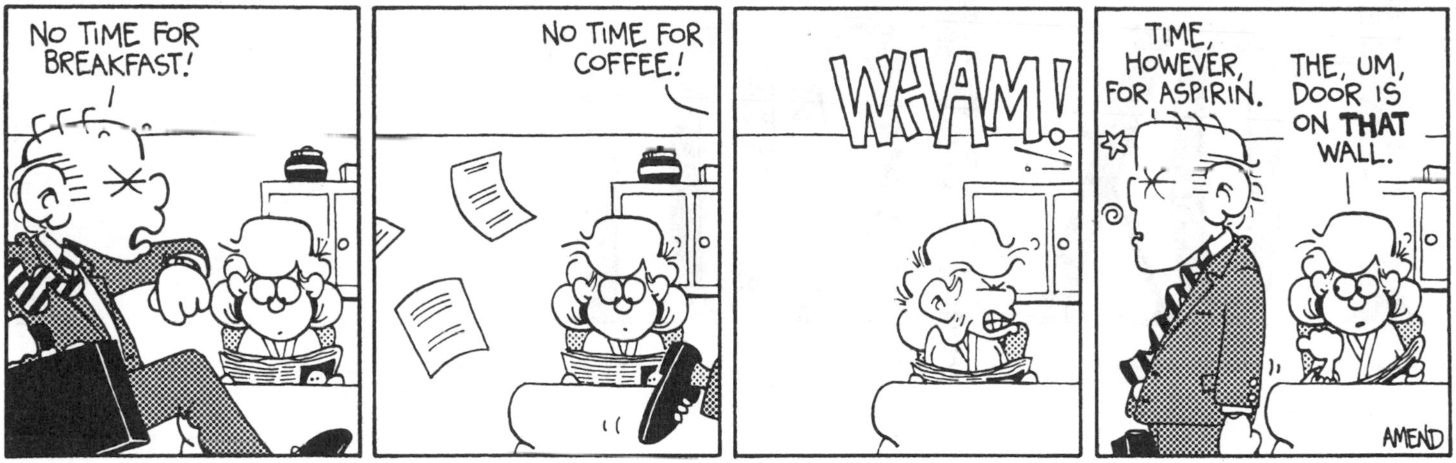
NO TIME FOR BREAKFAST!
NO TIME FOR COFFEE!
WHAM!
TIME, HOWEVER, FOR ASPIRIN.
THE, UM, DOOR IS ON THAT WALL.
AMEND

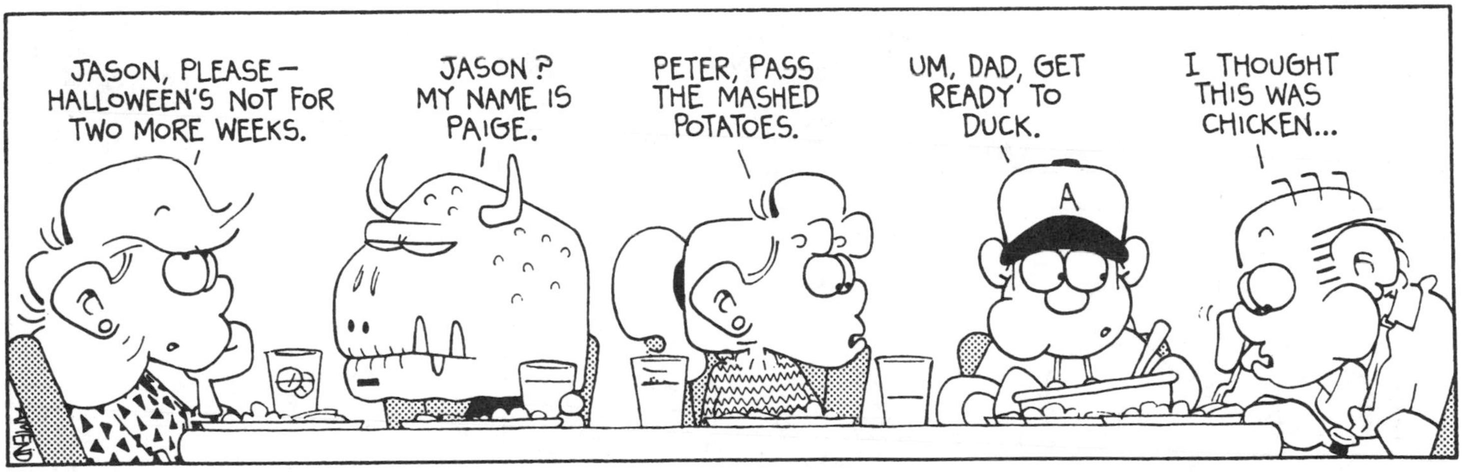
JASON, PLEASE— HALLOWEEN'S NOT FOR TWO MORE WEEKS.
JASON? MY NAME IS PAIGE.
PETER, PASS THE MASHED POTATOES.
UM, DAD, GET READY TO DUCK.
I THOUGHT THIS WAS CHICKEN...
A

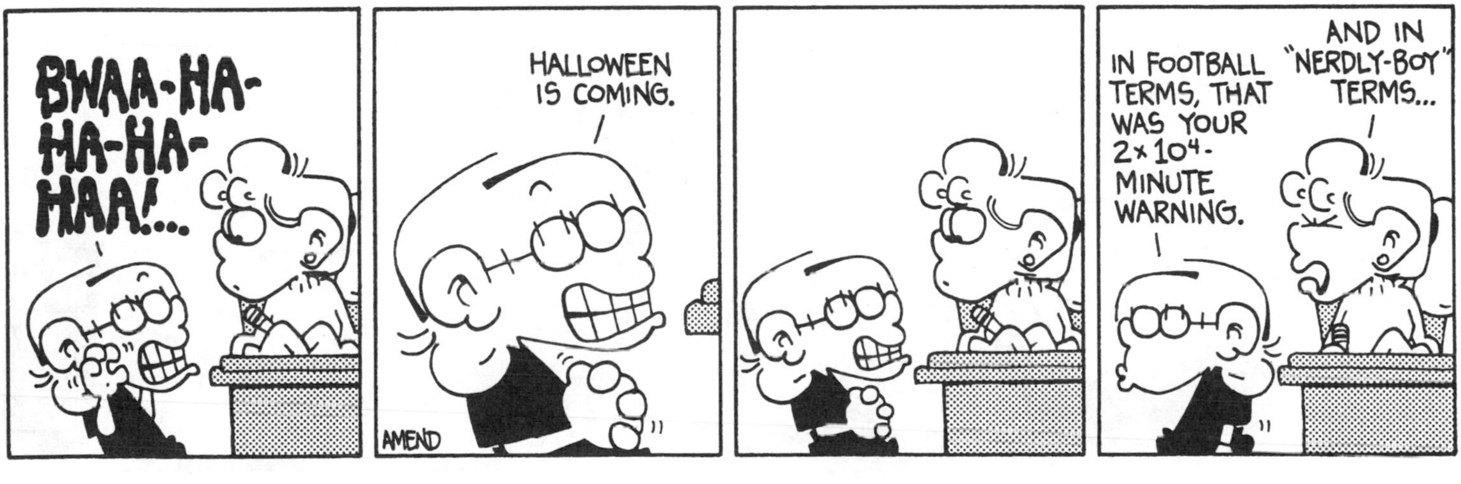
BWAA-HA-HA-HA-HAA!...
HALLOWEEN IS COMING.
AMEND
IN FOOTBALL TERMS, THAT WAS YOUR 2×10⁴-MINUTE WARNING.
AND IN "NERDLY-BOY" TERMS...

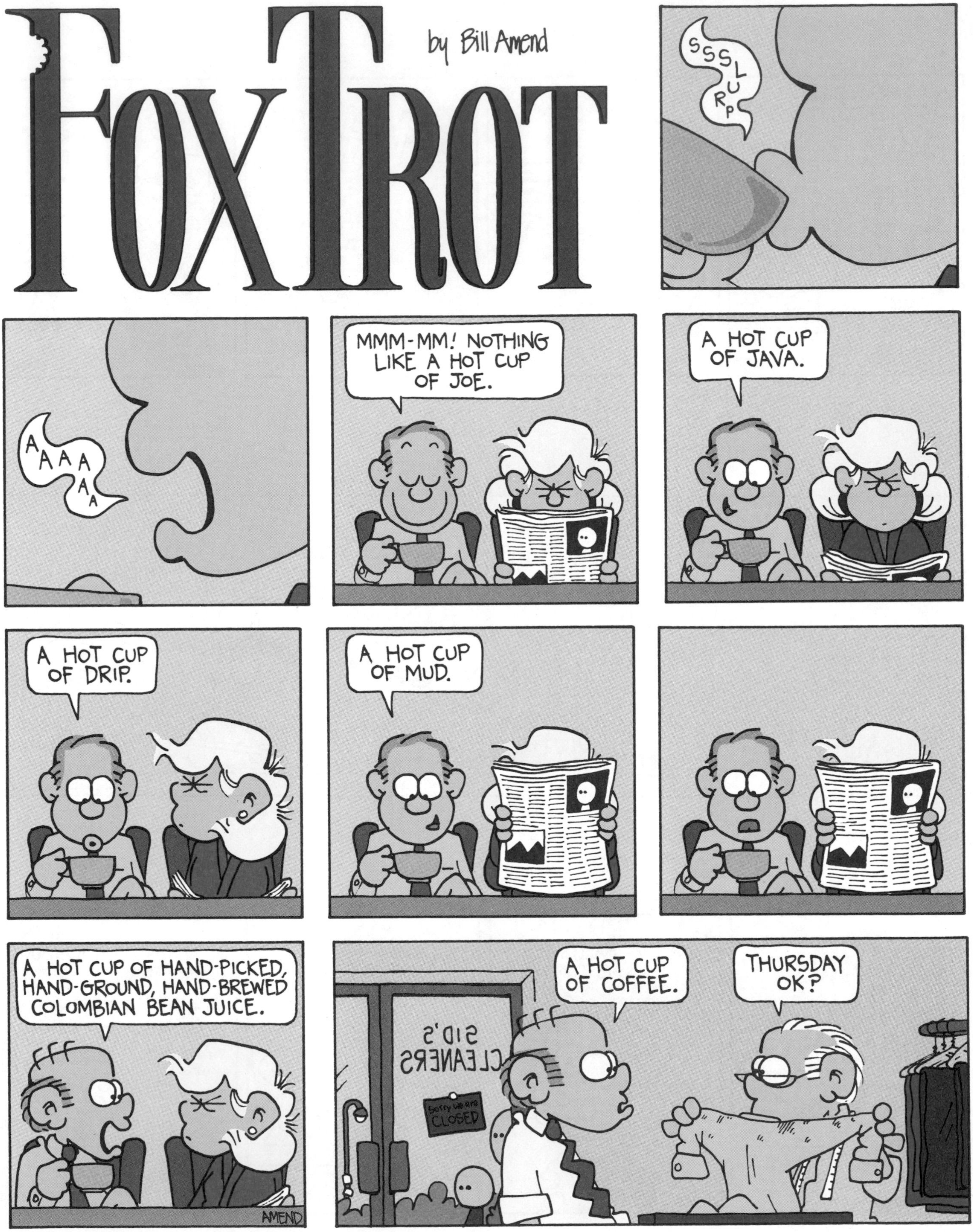
FoxTrot
by Bill Amend
SSSLURP
AAAAAAA
MMM-MM! NOTHING LIKE A HOT CUP OF JOE.
A HOT CUP OF JAVA.
A HOT CUP OF DRIP.
A HOT CUP OF MUD.
A HOT CUP OF HAND-PICKED, HAND-GROUND, HAND-BREWED COLOMBIAN BEAN JUICE.
AMEND
SID'S CLEANERS
Sorry we are CLOSED
A HOT CUP OF COFFEE.
THURSDAY OK?

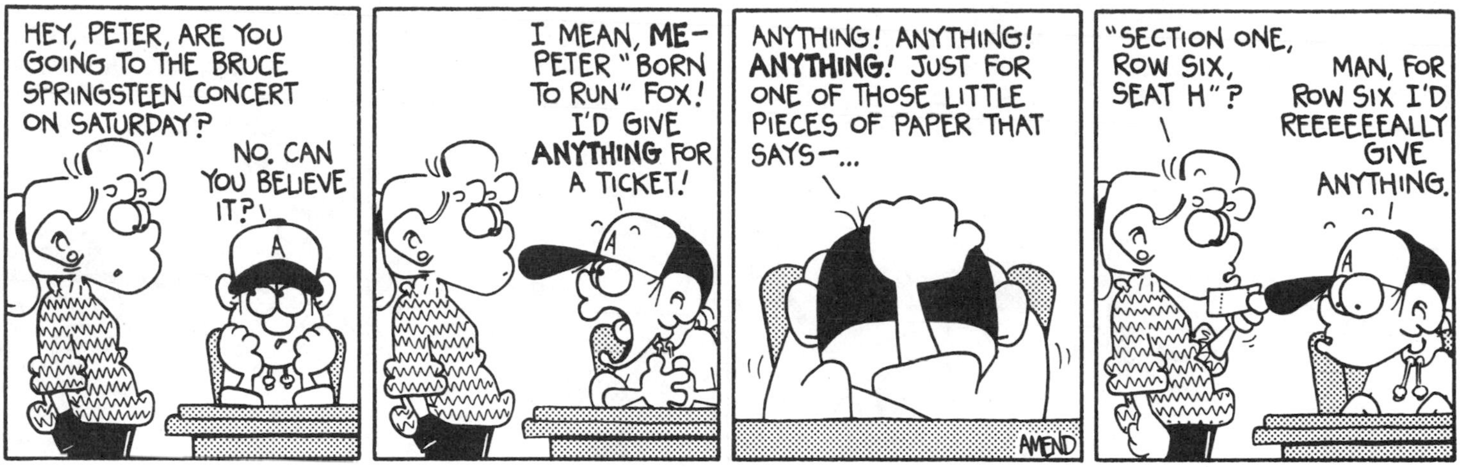
HEY, PETER, ARE YOU GOING TO THE BRUCE SPRINGSTEEN CONCERT ON SATURDAY?
NO. CAN YOU BELIEVE IT?
I MEAN, ME–PETER "BORN TO RUN" FOX! I'D GIVE ANYTHING FOR A TICKET!
ANYTHING! ANYTHING! ANYTHING! JUST FOR ONE OF THOSE LITTLE PIECES OF PAPER THAT SAYS–...
AMEND
"SECTION ONE, ROW SIX, SEAT H"?
MAN, FOR ROW SIX I'D REEEEEEALLY GIVE ANYTHING.

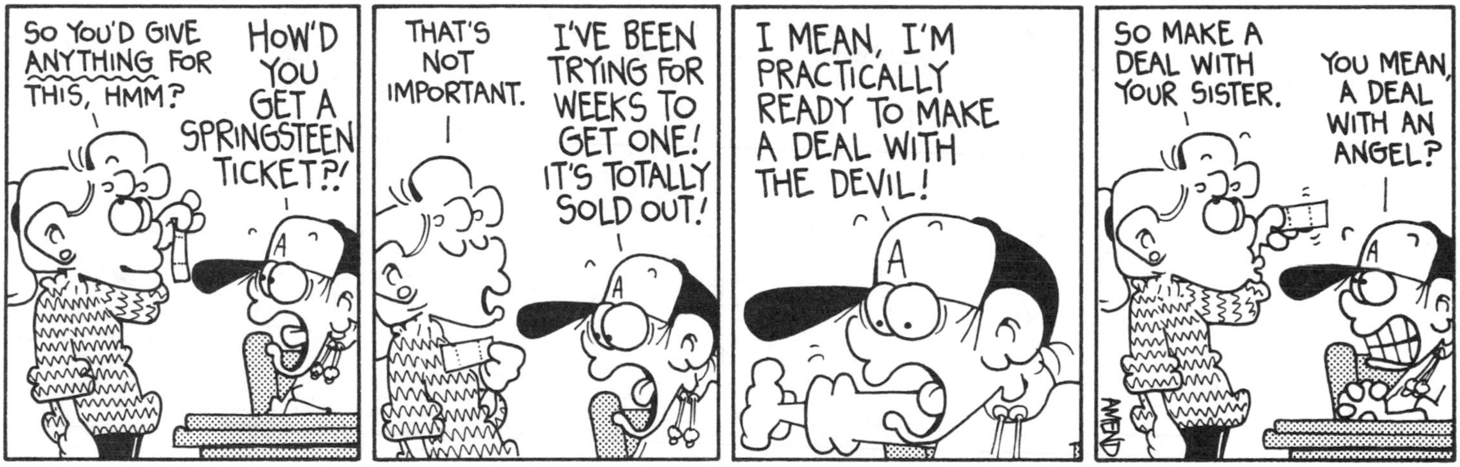
SO YOU'D GIVE ANYTHING FOR THIS, HMM?
HOW'D YOU GET A SPRINGSTEEN TICKET?!
THAT'S NOT IMPORTANT.
I'VE BEEN TRYING FOR WEEKS TO GET ONE! IT'S TOTALLY SOLD OUT!
I MEAN, I'M PRACTICALLY READY TO MAKE A DEAL WITH THE DEVIL!
SO MAKE A DEAL WITH YOUR SISTER.
YOU MEAN, A DEAL WITH AN ANGEL?
AMEND

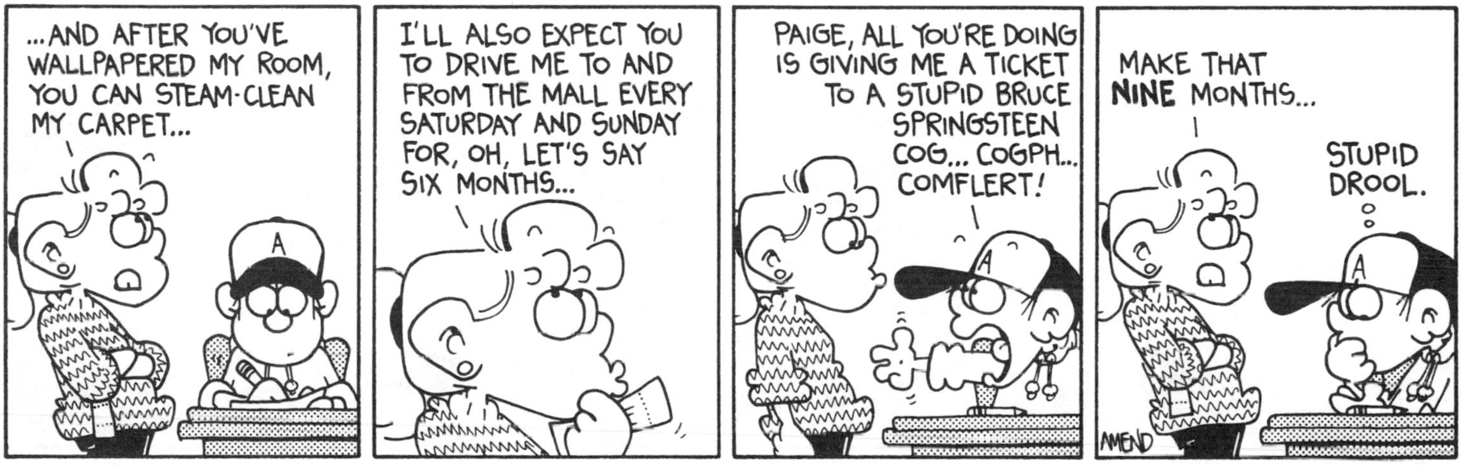
...AND AFTER YOU'VE WALLPAPERED MY ROOM, YOU CAN STEAM-CLEAN MY CARPET...
I'LL ALSO EXPECT YOU TO DRIVE ME TO AND FROM THE MALL EVERY SATURDAY AND SUNDAY FOR, OH, LET'S SAY SIX MONTHS...
PAIGE, ALL YOU'RE DOING IS GIVING ME A TICKET TO A STUPID BRUCE SPRINGSTEEN COG... COGPH... COMFLERT!
MAKE THAT NINE MONTHS...
STUPID DROOL.
AMEND

Panel 1: PETER, DO YOU WANT THIS SPRINGSTEEN TICKET OR NOT? / PAIGE, YOU'RE ASKING TOO MUCH!

Panel 2: LOOK, I'LL DO YOUR HOMEWORK... I'LL CLEAN YOUR ROOM... I'LL DRIVE YOU TO AND FROM THE MALL... I'LL BUTTER YOUR TOAST ON SUNDAYS...

Panel 3: BUT I WILL **NOT** ORDER VANITY LICENSE PLATES THAT SAY "ILUV210"!

Panel 4: YOU KNOW, I'LL BET IN ROW SIX YOU CAN COUNT BRUCE'S EARRINGS. / I'LL GET A BUMPER STICKER! PAIGE, **PLEASE!**

Panel 5: WELL, PETER, I THINK WE'VE WORKED OUT A PRETTY GOOD DEAL. / I AGREE.

Panel 6: YOU GET A SIXTH ROW BRUCE SPRINGSTEEN TICKET... I GET NINE MONTHS OF MISCELLANEOUS CHORES AND FAVORS OUT OF YOU... I'D SAY WE'RE **BOTH** WINNERS. / I AGREE.

Panel 7: HERE'S YOUR TICKET. / COME TO PAPPA, BABY, OH, BABY!...

Panel 8: NOT THAT SOME OF US AREN'T ALSO **LOSERS**. / IS IT ME, OR IS THIS THING GLOWING?

Panel 9: YOU ARE LOOKING AT THE HAPPIEST KID ON EARTH RIGHT NOW.

Panel 10: NOTHING COULD BUM ME OUT. NOTHING COULD RUIN MY MOOD. / DID PAIGE GIVE YOU THE BRUCE SPRINGSTEEN TICKET I GOT FOR YOU?

Panel 11: (no dialogue)

Panel 12: EXCUSE ME A MINUTE. / WHY DO YOU HAVE YOUR SISTER'S LAUNDRY?

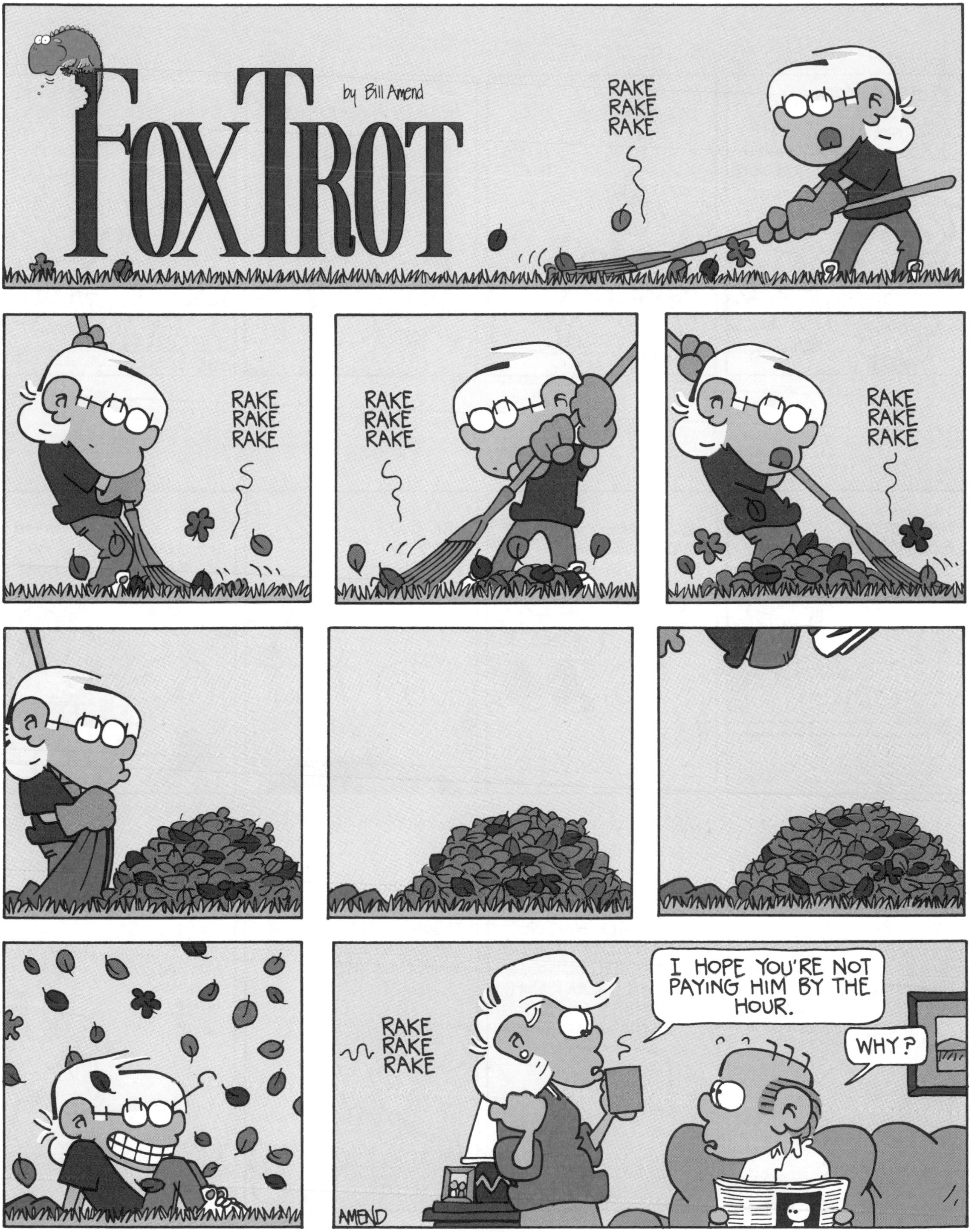
FoxTrot
by Bill Amend
RAKE
RAKE
RAKE
RAKE
RAKE
RAKE
RAKE
RAKE
RAKE
RAKE
RAKE
RAKE
RAKE
RAKE
RAKE
I HOPE YOU'RE NOT PAYING HIM BY THE HOUR.
WHY?
AMEND

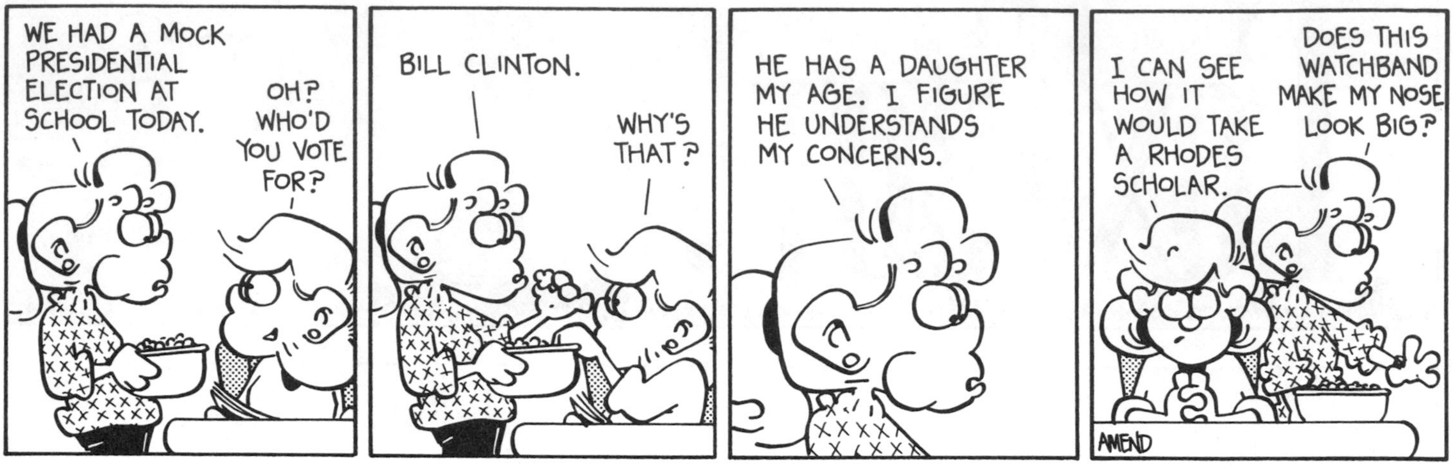
WE HAD A MOCK PRESIDENTIAL ELECTION AT SCHOOL TODAY.
OH? WHO'D YOU VOTE FOR?
BILL CLINTON.
WHY'S THAT?
HE HAS A DAUGHTER MY AGE. I FIGURE HE UNDERSTANDS MY CONCERNS.
I CAN SEE HOW IT WOULD TAKE A RHODES SCHOLAR.
DOES THIS WATCHBAND MAKE MY NOSE LOOK BIG?
AMEND

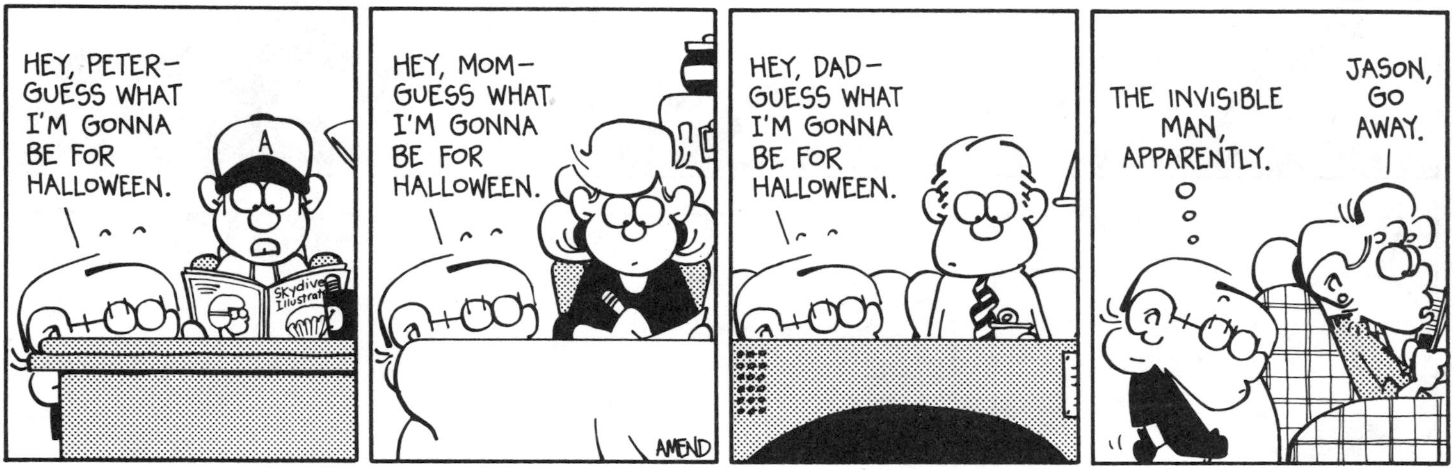
HEY, PETER- GUESS WHAT I'M GONNA BE FOR HALLOWEEN.
HEY, MOM- GUESS WHAT I'M GONNA BE FOR HALLOWEEN.
AMEND
HEY, DAD- GUESS WHAT I'M GONNA BE FOR HALLOWEEN.
THE INVISIBLE MAN, APPARENTLY.
JASON, GO AWAY.

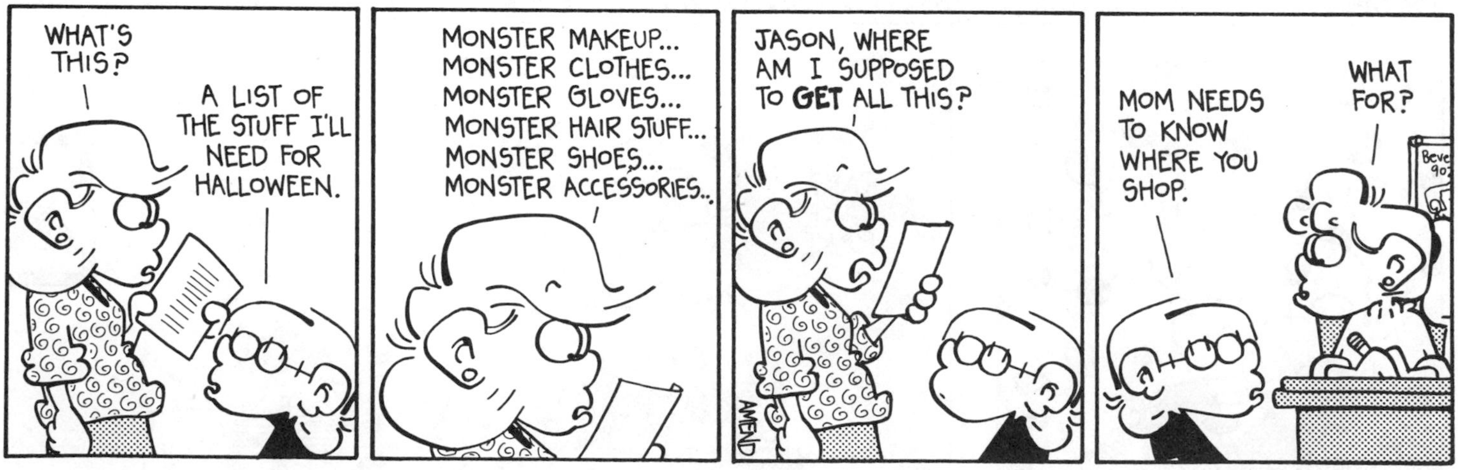
WHAT'S THIS?
A LIST OF THE STUFF I'LL NEED FOR HALLOWEEN.
MONSTER MAKEUP... MONSTER CLOTHES... MONSTER GLOVES... MONSTER HAIR STUFF... MONSTER SHOES... MONSTER ACCESSORIES...
JASON, WHERE AM I SUPPOSED TO **GET** ALL THIS?
AMEND
MOM NEEDS TO KNOW WHERE YOU SHOP.
WHAT FOR?

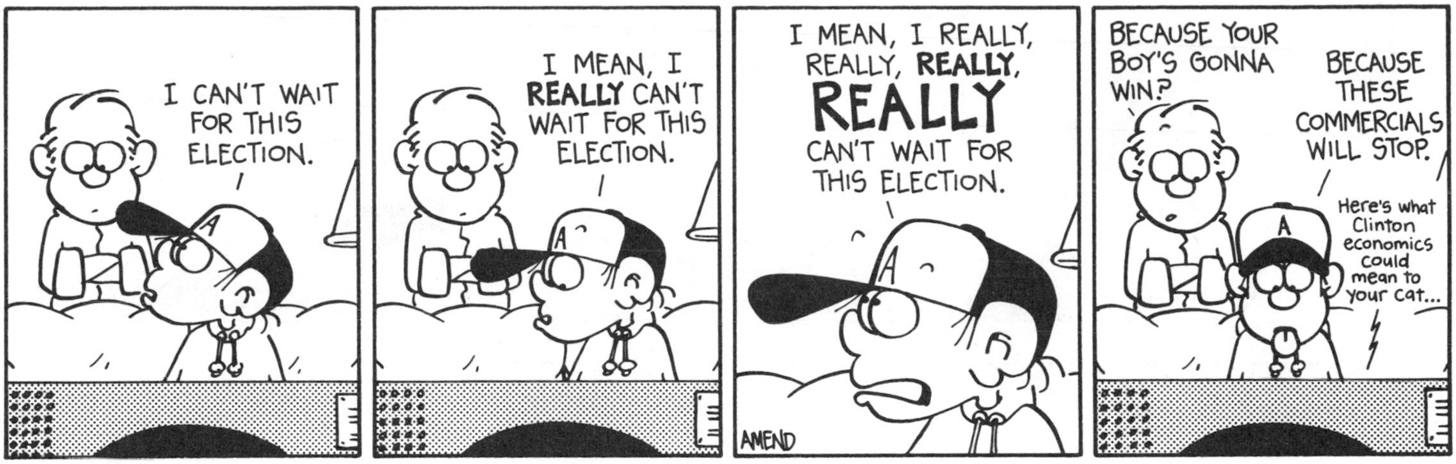
I CAN'T WAIT FOR THIS ELECTION.
I MEAN, I **REALLY** CAN'T WAIT FOR THIS ELECTION.
I MEAN, I REALLY, REALLY, **REALLY**, **REALLY** CAN'T WAIT FOR THIS ELECTION.
AMEND
BECAUSE YOUR BOY'S GONNA WIN?
BECAUSE THESE COMMERCIALS WILL STOP.
Here's what Clinton economics could mean to your cat...

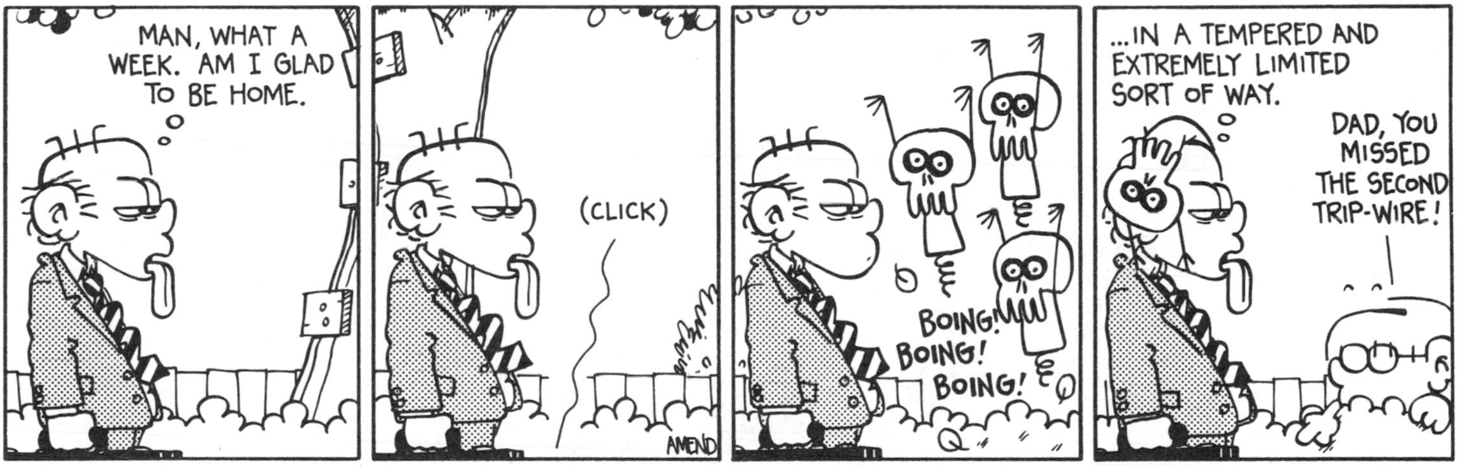
MAN, WHAT A WEEK. AM I GLAD TO BE HOME.
(CLICK)
AMEND
BOING! BOING! BOING!
...IN A TEMPERED AND EXTREMELY LIMITED SORT OF WAY.
DAD, YOU MISSED THE SECOND TRIP-WIRE!

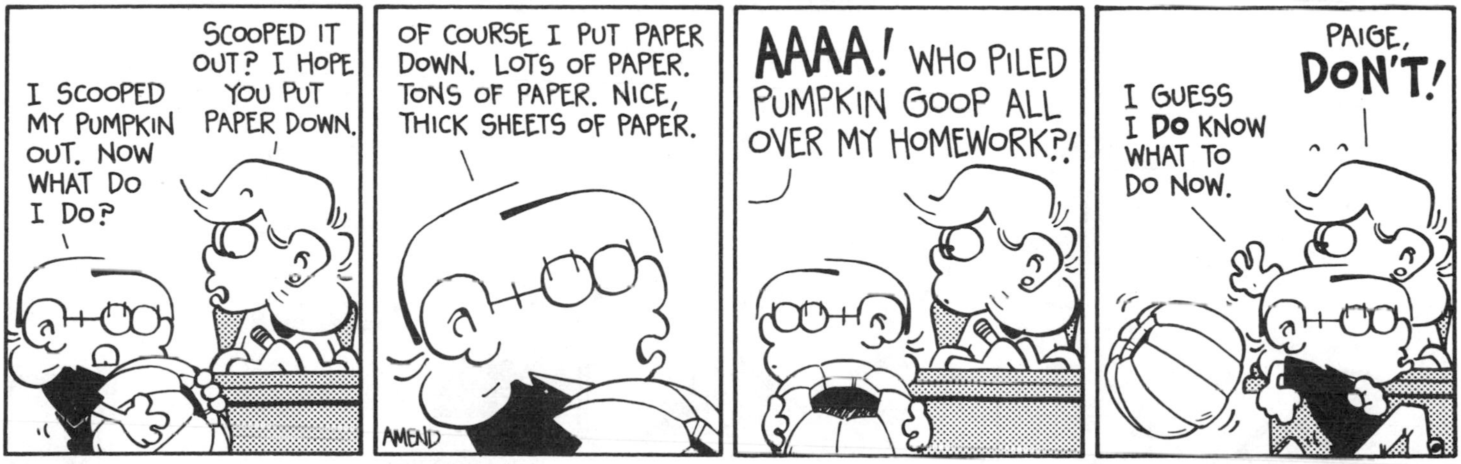
I SCOOPED MY PUMPKIN OUT. NOW WHAT DO I DO?
SCOOPED IT OUT? I HOPE YOU PUT PAPER DOWN.
OF COURSE I PUT PAPER DOWN. LOTS OF PAPER. TONS OF PAPER. NICE, THICK SHEETS OF PAPER.
AMEND
AAAA! WHO PILED PUMPKIN GOOP ALL OVER MY HOMEWORK?!
I GUESS I **DO** KNOW WHAT TO DO NOW.
PAIGE, **DON'T!**

FoxTrot
by Bill Amend
DID NOT!
DID TOO!
DID TOO!
DID NOT!
DID NOT!
DID TOO!
DID TOO!
DID NOT!
DID NOT!
DID TOO!
DID TOO!
DID NOT!
DID NOT!
DID TOO!
DID TOO!
DID NOT!
TWO MORE DAYS...
AND NOW, FOR A POST-DEBATE ANALYSIS, HERE'S JOHN CHANCELLOR...
AMEND

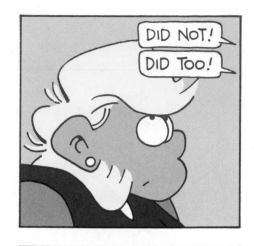

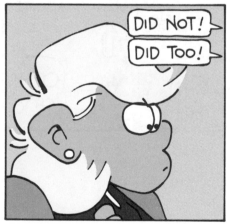

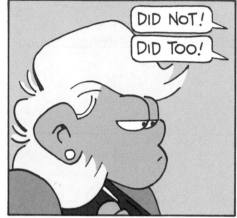

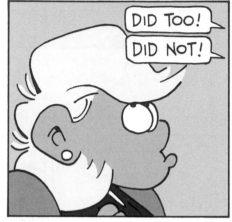

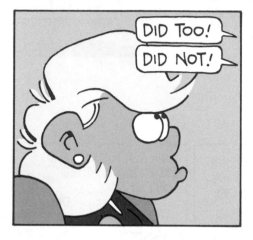

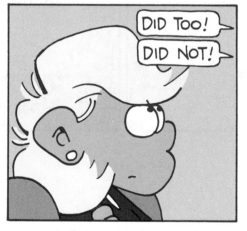

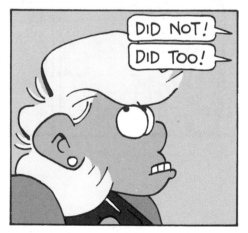

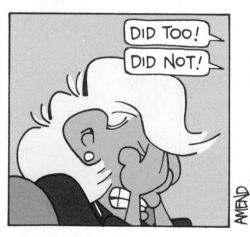

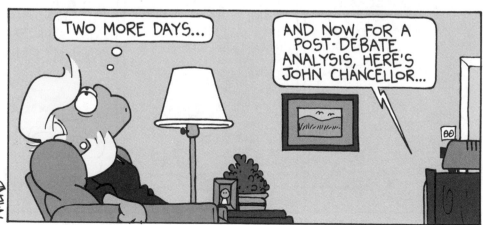

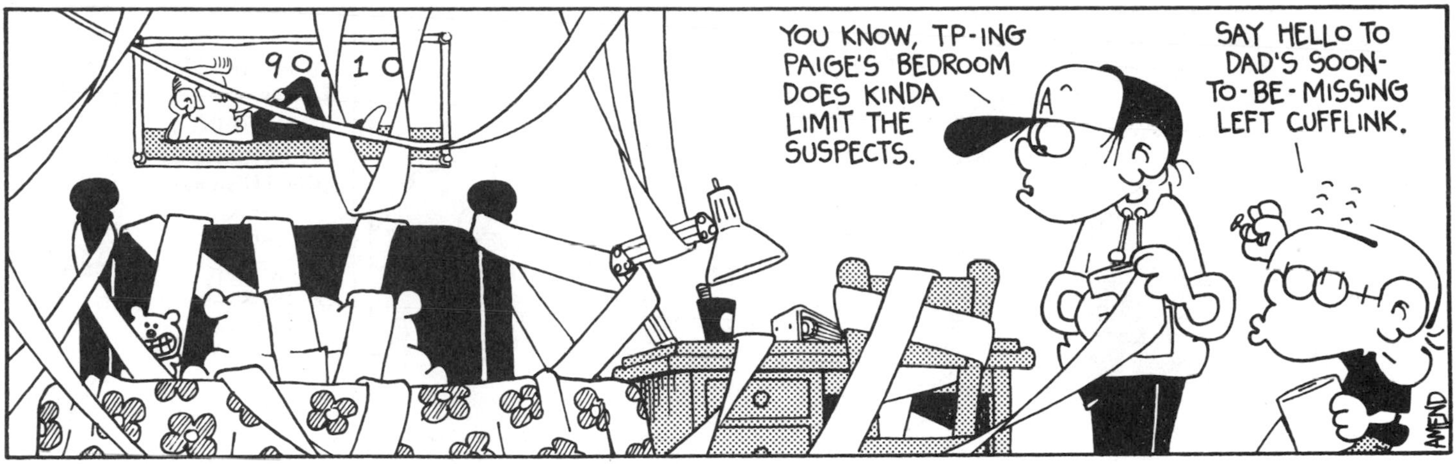
YOU KNOW, TP-ING PAIGE'S BEDROOM DOES KINDA LIMIT THE SUSPECTS.
SAY HELLO TO DAD'S SOON-TO-BE-MISSING LEFT CUFFLINK.

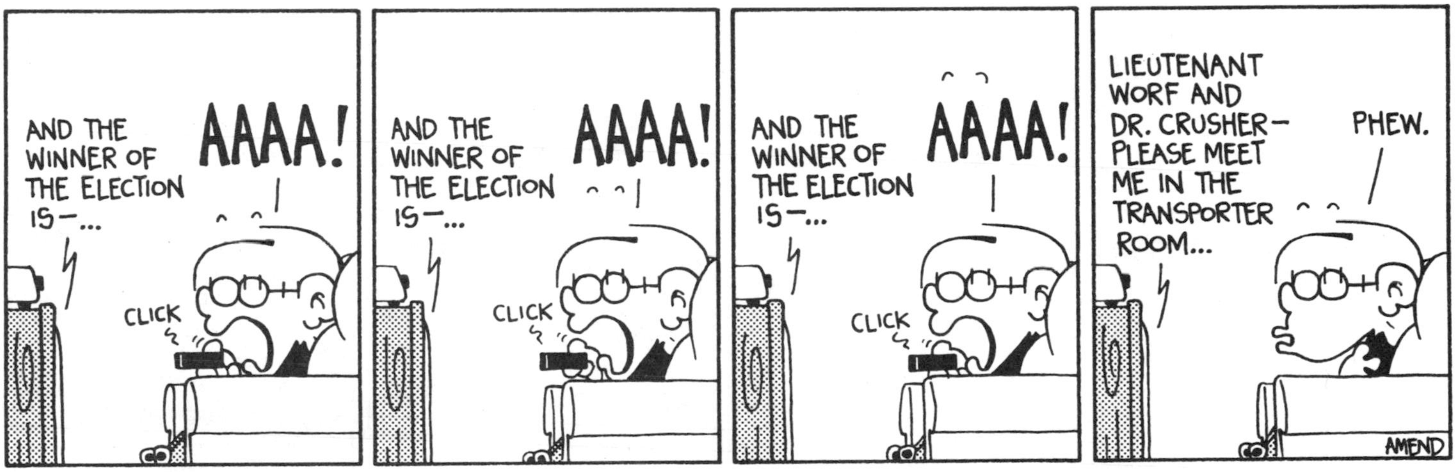
AND THE WINNER OF THE ELECTION IS—...
AAAA!
CLICK
AND THE WINNER OF THE ELECTION IS—...
AAAA!
CLICK
AND THE WINNER OF THE ELECTION IS—...
AAAA!
CLICK
LIEUTENANT WORF AND DR. CRUSHER—PLEASE MEET ME IN THE TRANSPORTER ROOM...
PHEW.

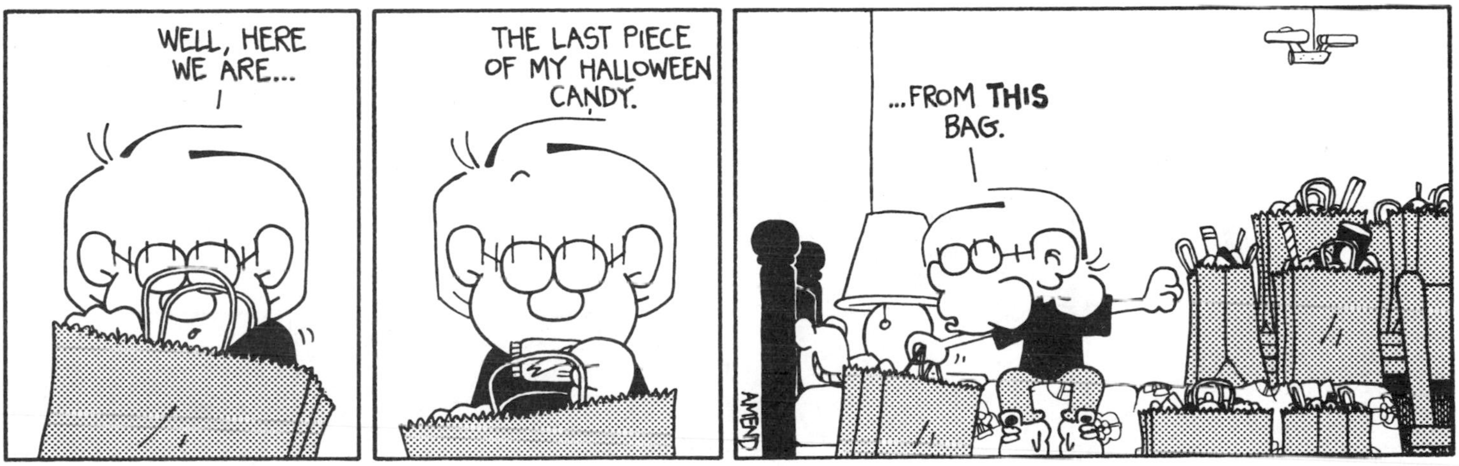
WELL, HERE WE ARE...
THE LAST PIECE OF MY HALLOWEEN CANDY.
...FROM THIS BAG.

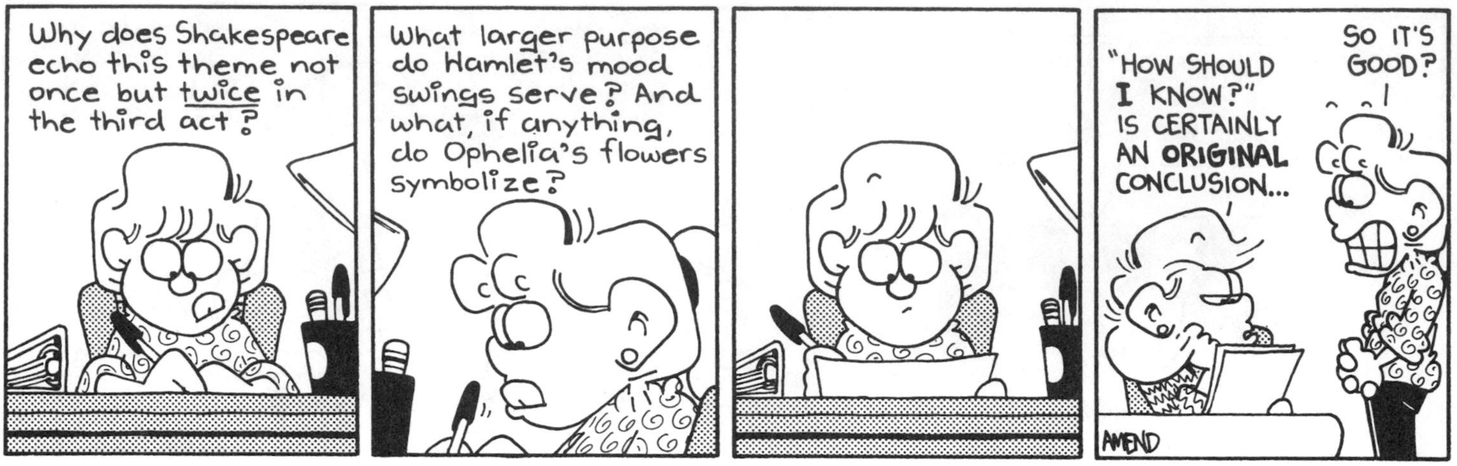
Why does Shakespeare echo this theme not once but twice in the third act?
What larger purpose do Hamlet's mood swings serve? And what, if anything, do Ophelia's flowers symbolize?
"HOW SHOULD I KNOW?" IS CERTAINLY AN ORIGINAL CONCLUSION...
SO IT'S GOOD?
AMEND

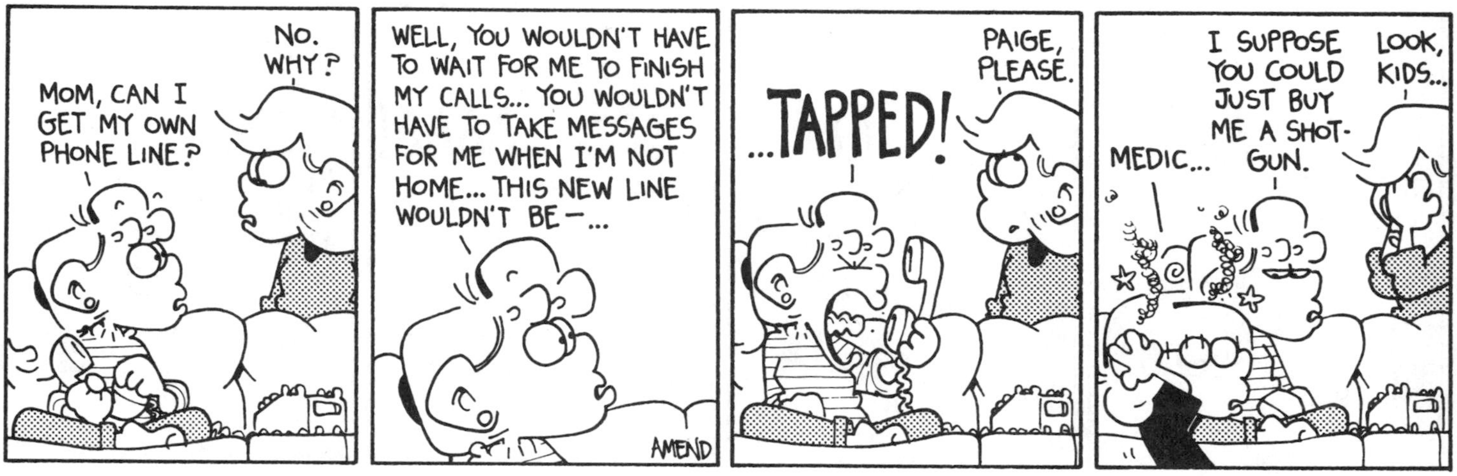
MOM, CAN I GET MY OWN PHONE LINE?
NO. WHY?
WELL, YOU WOULDN'T HAVE TO WAIT FOR ME TO FINISH MY CALLS... YOU WOULDN'T HAVE TO TAKE MESSAGES FOR ME WHEN I'M NOT HOME... THIS NEW LINE WOULDN'T BE—...
AMEND
...TAPPED!
PAIGE, PLEASE.
MEDIC...
I SUPPOSE YOU COULD JUST BUY ME A SHOT-GUN.
LOOK, KIDS...

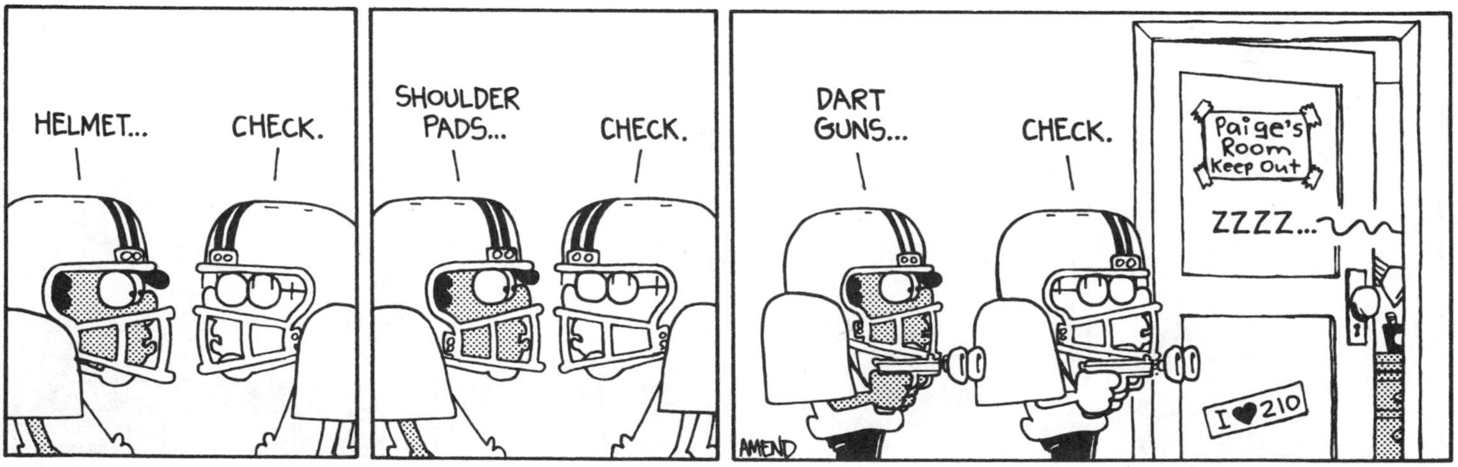
HELMET...
CHECK.
SHOULDER PADS...
CHECK.
DART GUNS...
CHECK.
Paige's Room Keep Out
ZZZZ...
I ♥ 210
AMEND

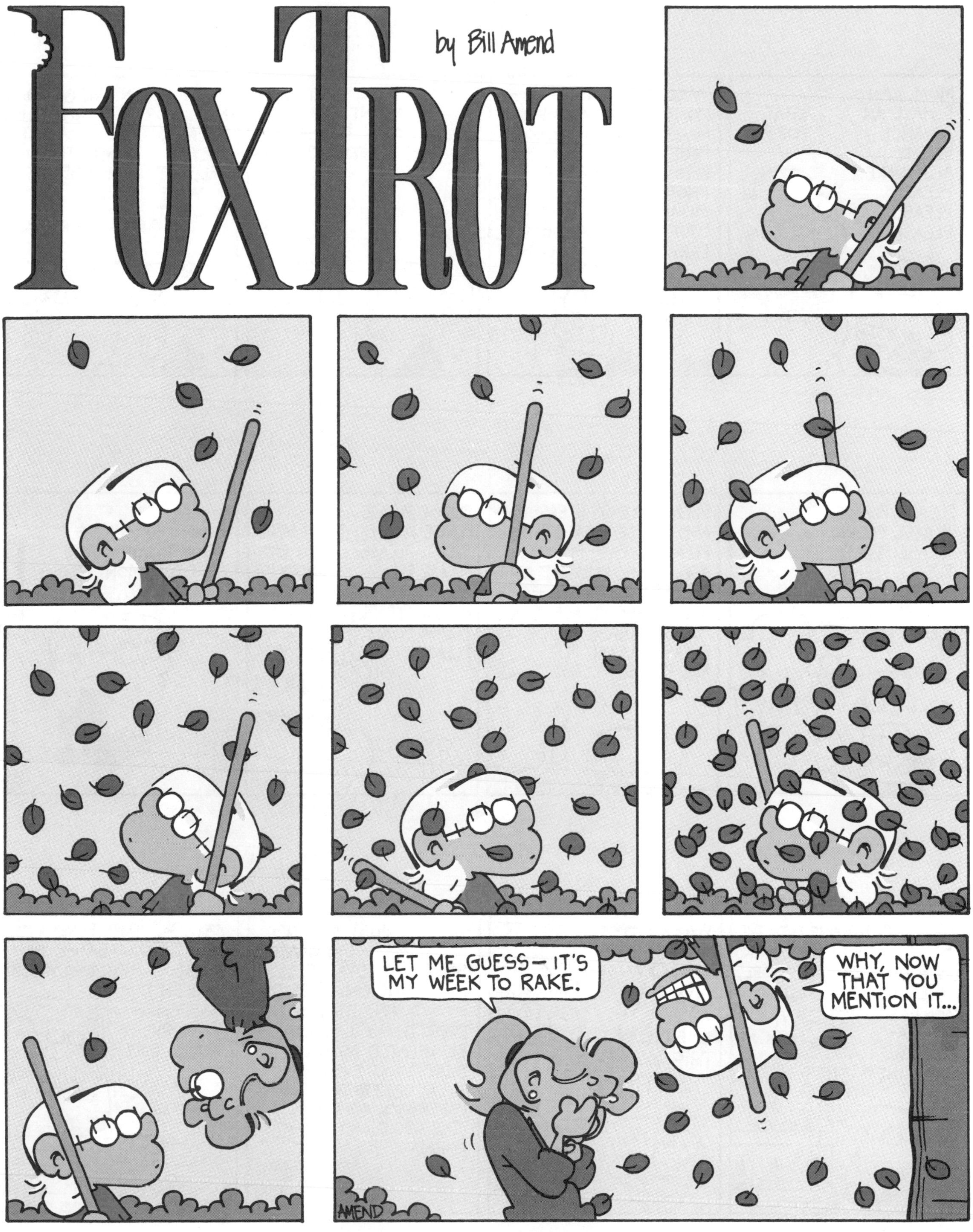
FoxTrot
by Bill Amend
LET ME GUESS — IT'S MY WEEK TO RAKE.
WHY, NOW THAT YOU MENTION IT...
AMEND

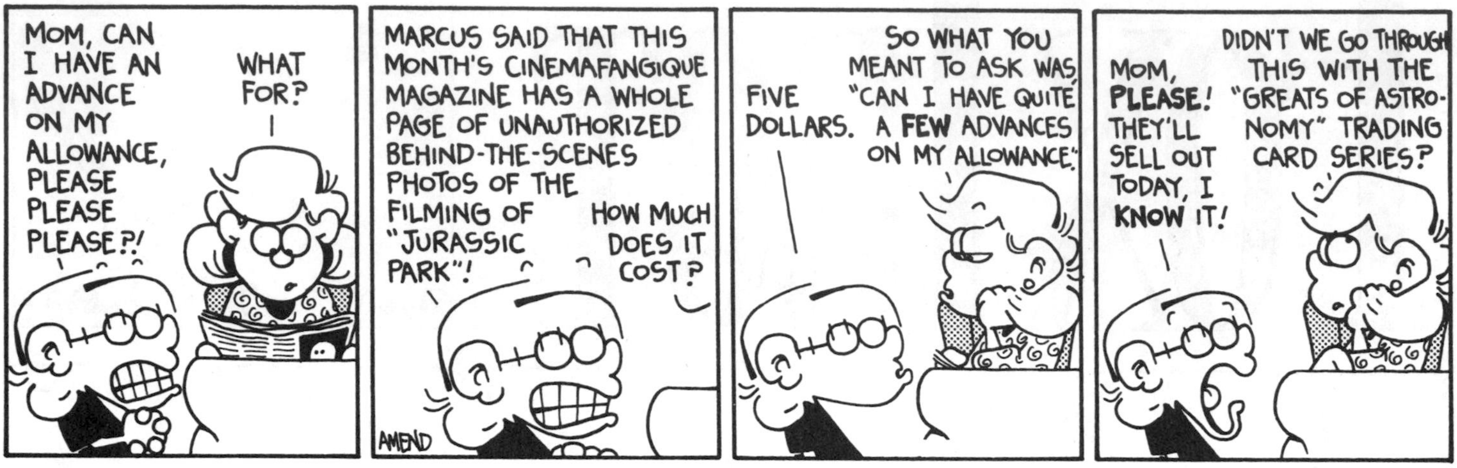
MOM, CAN I HAVE AN ADVANCE ON MY ALLOWANCE, PLEASE PLEASE PLEASE?!
WHAT FOR?
MARCUS SAID THAT THIS MONTH'S CINEMAFANGIQUE MAGAZINE HAS A WHOLE PAGE OF UNAUTHORIZED BEHIND-THE-SCENES PHOTOS OF THE FILMING OF "JURASSIC PARK"!
HOW MUCH DOES IT COST?
AMEND
FIVE DOLLARS.
SO WHAT YOU MEANT TO ASK WAS, "CAN I HAVE QUITE A **FEW** ADVANCES ON MY ALLOWANCE."
MOM, **PLEASE**! THEY'LL SELL OUT TODAY, I **KNOW** IT!
DIDN'T WE GO THROUGH THIS WITH THE "GREATS OF ASTRONOMY" TRADING CARD SERIES?

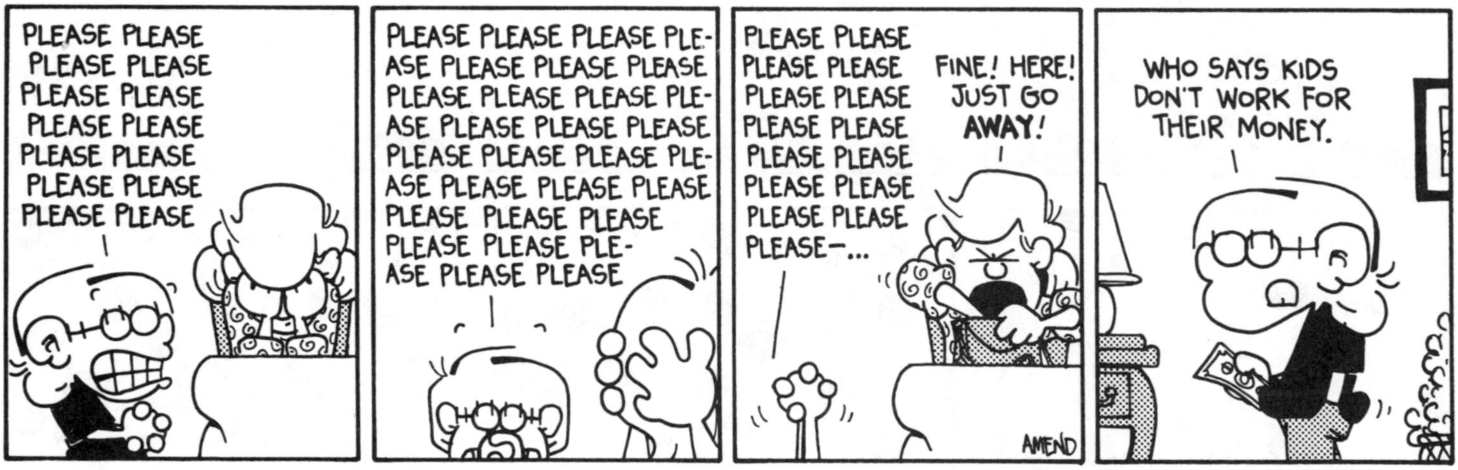
PLEASE PLEASE PLEASE PLEASE PLEASE PLEASE PLEASE PLEASE PLEASE PLEASE PLEASE PLEASE PLEASE PLEASE
PLEASE PLEASE PLEASE PLE-ASE PLEASE PLEASE PLEASE PLEASE PLEASE PLEASE PLE-ASE PLEASE PLEASE PLEASE PLEASE PLEASE PLEASE PLE-ASE PLEASE PLEASE PLEASE PLEASE PLEASE PLEASE PLEASE PLEASE PLE-ASE PLEASE PLEASE
PLEASE PLEASE PLEASE PLEASE PLEASE PLEASE PLEASE PLEASE PLEASE PLEASE PLEASE PLEASE PLEASE PLEASE PLEASE–...
FINE! HERE! JUST GO **AWAY**!
AMEND
WHO SAYS KIDS DON'T WORK FOR THEIR MONEY.

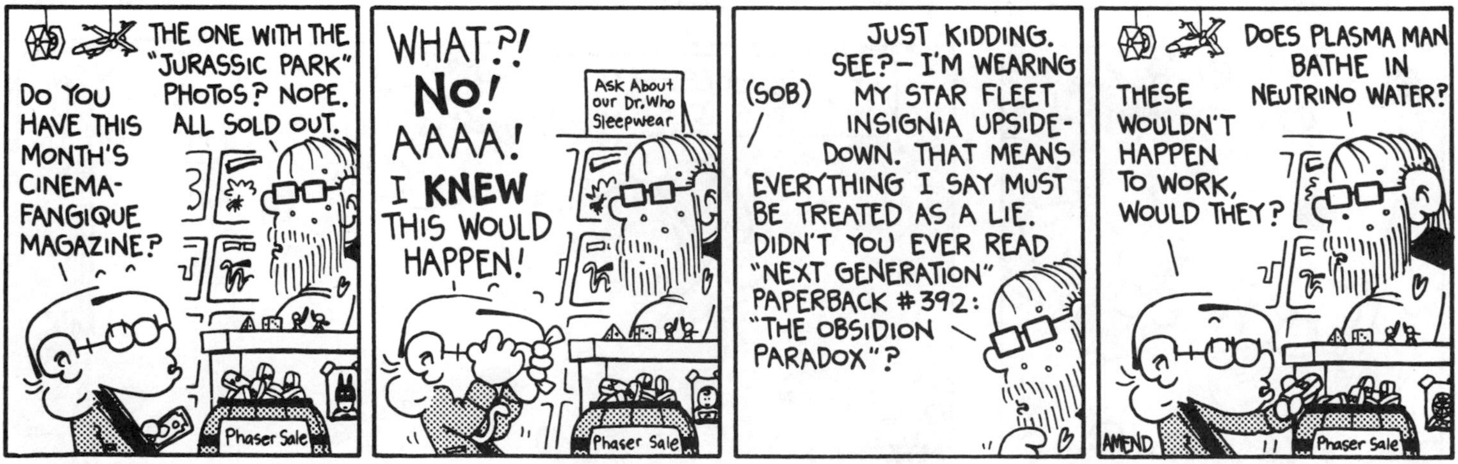
DO YOU HAVE THIS MONTH'S CINEMA-FANGIQUE MAGAZINE?
THE ONE WITH THE "JURASSIC PARK" PHOTOS? NOPE. ALL SOLD OUT.
Phaser Sale
WHAT?! **NO**! AAAA! I **KNEW** THIS WOULD HAPPEN!
Ask About our Dr. Who Sleepwear
Phaser Sale
(SOB)
JUST KIDDING. SEE?– I'M WEARING MY STAR FLEET INSIGNIA UPSIDE-DOWN. THAT MEANS EVERYTHING I SAY MUST BE TREATED AS A LIE. DIDN'T YOU EVER READ "NEXT GENERATION" PAPERBACK #392: "THE OBSIDION PARADOX"?
THESE WOULDN'T HAPPEN TO WORK, WOULD THEY?
DOES PLASMA MAN BATHE IN NEUTRINO WATER?
AMEND
Phaser Sale

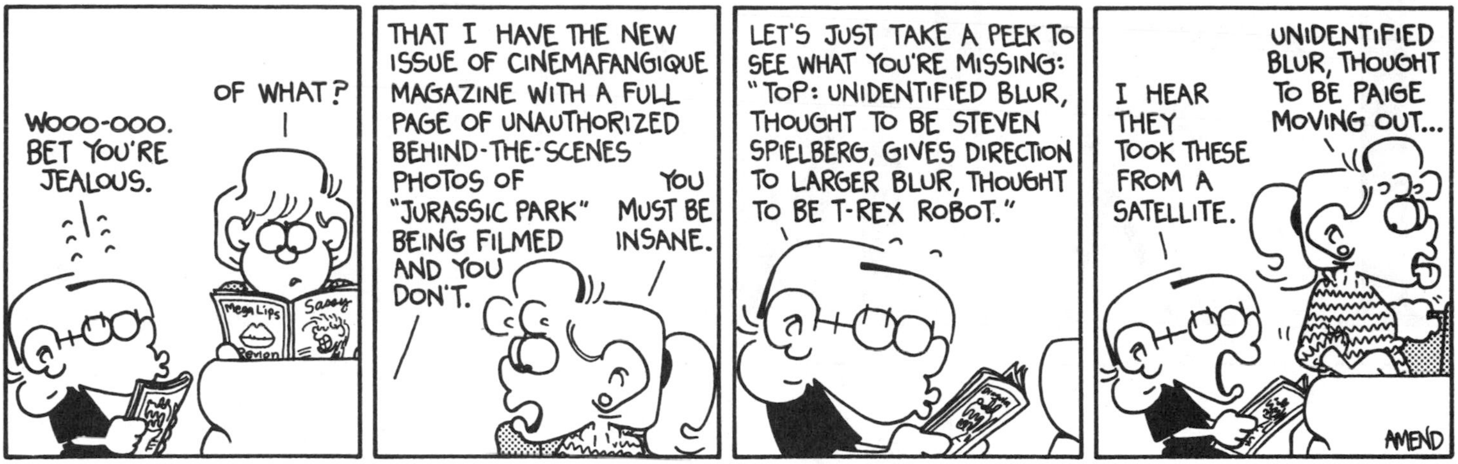
WOOO-OOO. BET YOU'RE JEALOUS.
OF WHAT?
Mega Lips
Revlon
Sassy
THAT I HAVE THE NEW ISSUE OF CINEMAFANGIQUE MAGAZINE WITH A FULL PAGE OF UNAUTHORIZED BEHIND-THE-SCENES PHOTOS OF "JURASSIC PARK" BEING FILMED AND YOU DON'T.
YOU MUST BE INSANE.
LET'S JUST TAKE A PEEK TO SEE WHAT YOU'RE MISSING: "TOP: UNIDENTIFIED BLUR, THOUGHT TO BE STEVEN SPIELBERG, GIVES DIRECTION TO LARGER BLUR, THOUGHT TO BE T-REX ROBOT."
I HEAR THEY TOOK THESE FROM A SATELLITE.
UNIDENTIFIED BLUR, THOUGHT TO BE PAIGE MOVING OUT...
AMEND

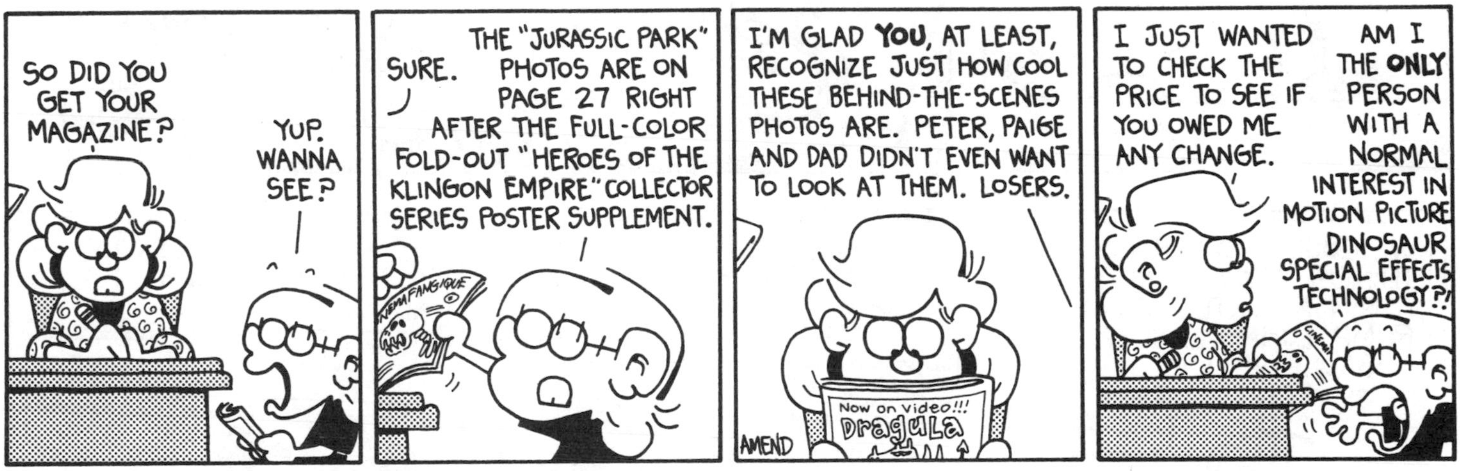
SO DID YOU GET YOUR MAGAZINE?
YUP. WANNA SEE?
SURE.
THE "JURASSIC PARK" PHOTOS ARE ON PAGE 27 RIGHT AFTER THE FULL-COLOR FOLD-OUT "HEROES OF THE KLINGON EMPIRE" COLLECTOR SERIES POSTER SUPPLEMENT.
CINEMAFANGIQUE
I'M GLAD YOU, AT LEAST, RECOGNIZE JUST HOW COOL THESE BEHIND-THE-SCENES PHOTOS ARE. PETER, PAIGE AND DAD DIDN'T EVEN WANT TO LOOK AT THEM. LOSERS.
Now on video!!!
Dragula
AMEND
I JUST WANTED TO CHECK THE PRICE TO SEE IF YOU OWED ME ANY CHANGE.
AM I THE ONLY PERSON WITH A NORMAL INTEREST IN MOTION PICTURE DINOSAUR SPECIAL EFFECTS TECHNOLOGY?!

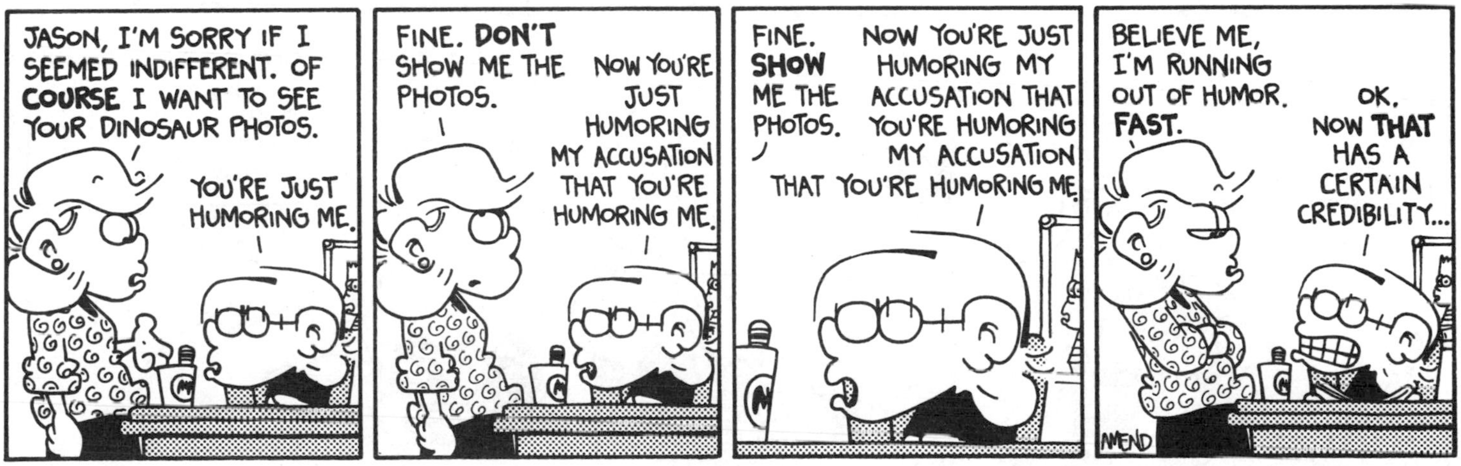
JASON, I'M SORRY IF I SEEMED INDIFFERENT. OF COURSE I WANT TO SEE YOUR DINOSAUR PHOTOS.
YOU'RE JUST HUMORING ME.
FINE. DON'T SHOW ME THE PHOTOS.
NOW YOU'RE JUST HUMORING MY ACCUSATION THAT YOU'RE HUMORING ME.
FINE. SHOW ME THE PHOTOS.
NOW YOU'RE JUST HUMORING MY ACCUSATION THAT YOU'RE HUMORING MY ACCUSATION THAT YOU'RE HUMORING ME.
BELIEVE ME, I'M RUNNING OUT OF HUMOR. FAST.
OK. NOW THAT HAS A CERTAIN CREDIBILITY...
AMEND

FoxTrot
by Bill Amend

SO, RAPHAEL, WHAT DO YOU WANT TO DO TODAY?

I DON'T KNOW, DONATELLO. WHAT DO YOU WANT TO DO TODAY?

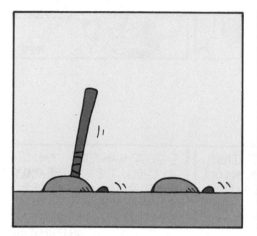

WE COULD DO LOTS OF THINGS IF ONLY WE HAD A NINJA TURTLE ACTION PUMP LUNAR LANDER ASSAULT VEHICLE.

SO TRUE.

OR A BATTERY-OPERATED, REMOTE-CONTROLLED NINJA TURTLE DUST COPTER AND COMMAND CENTER.

TELL ME ABOUT IT.

OR A DELUXE NINJA TURTLE AQUA SUB ACTIVITY PACK.

LIKE MARCUS HAS.

OR, DARE I MENTION IT?...

THE NEW NINJA TURTLE SEWER FORTRESS SCALE MODEL CONSTRUCTION SET WITH REALGLO™ LASER ARSENAL?

WHY DON'T I TELL YOU WHAT TO DO.

YOU KNOW, THE DUST COPTER WILL GET ME OUT OF THE HOUSE...

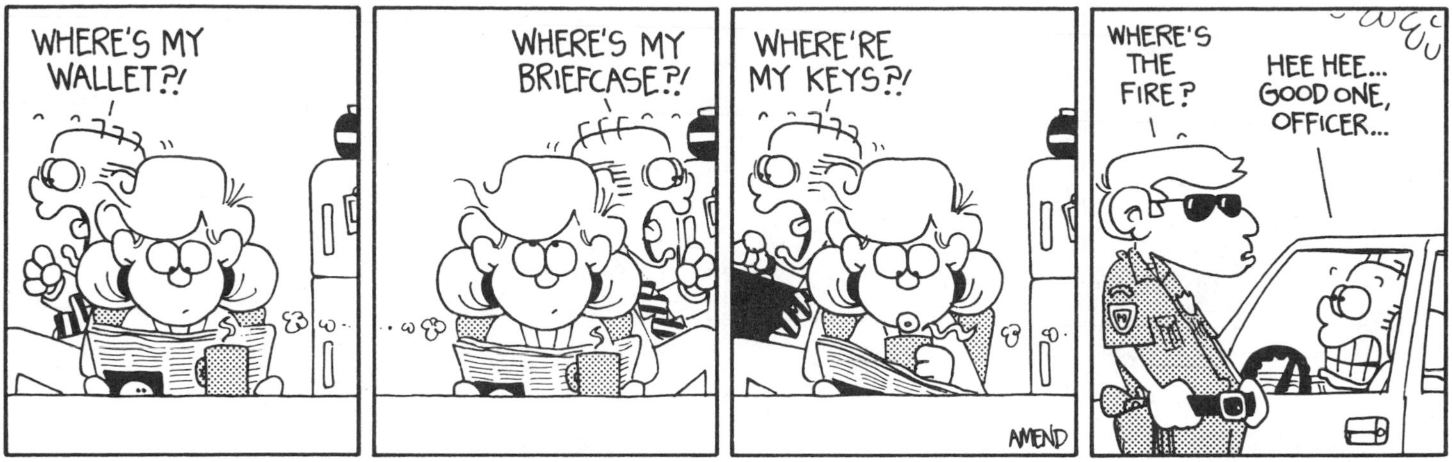
WHERE'S MY WALLET?!
WHERE'S MY BRIEFCASE?!
WHERE'RE MY KEYS?!
AMEND
WHERE'S THE FIRE?
HEE HEE... GOOD ONE, OFFICER...

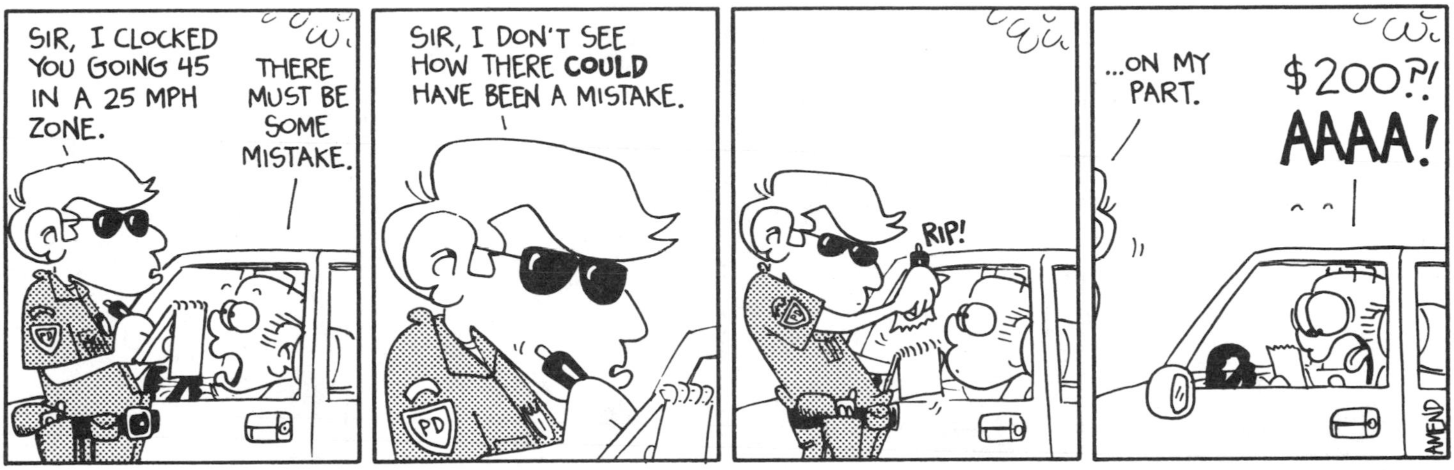
SIR, I CLOCKED YOU GOING 45 IN A 25 MPH ZONE.
THERE MUST BE SOME MISTAKE.
SIR, I DON'T SEE HOW THERE **COULD** HAVE BEEN A MISTAKE.
RIP!
...ON MY PART.
$200?!
AAAA!
AMEND

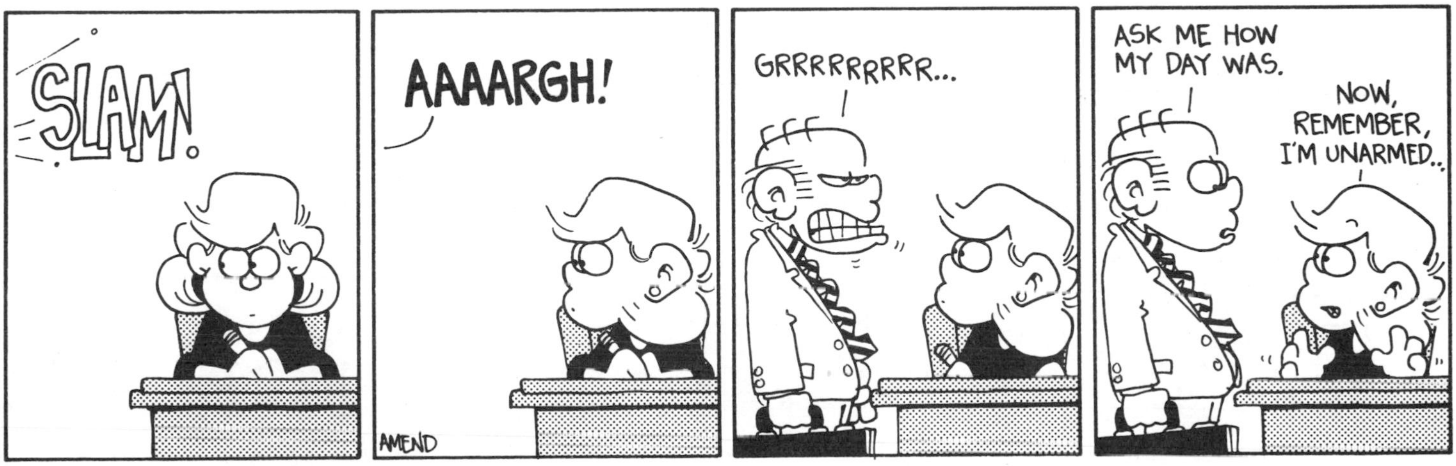
SLAM!
AAAARGH!
AMEND
GRRRRRRRRR...
ASK ME HOW MY DAY WAS.
NOW, REMEMBER, I'M UNARMED...

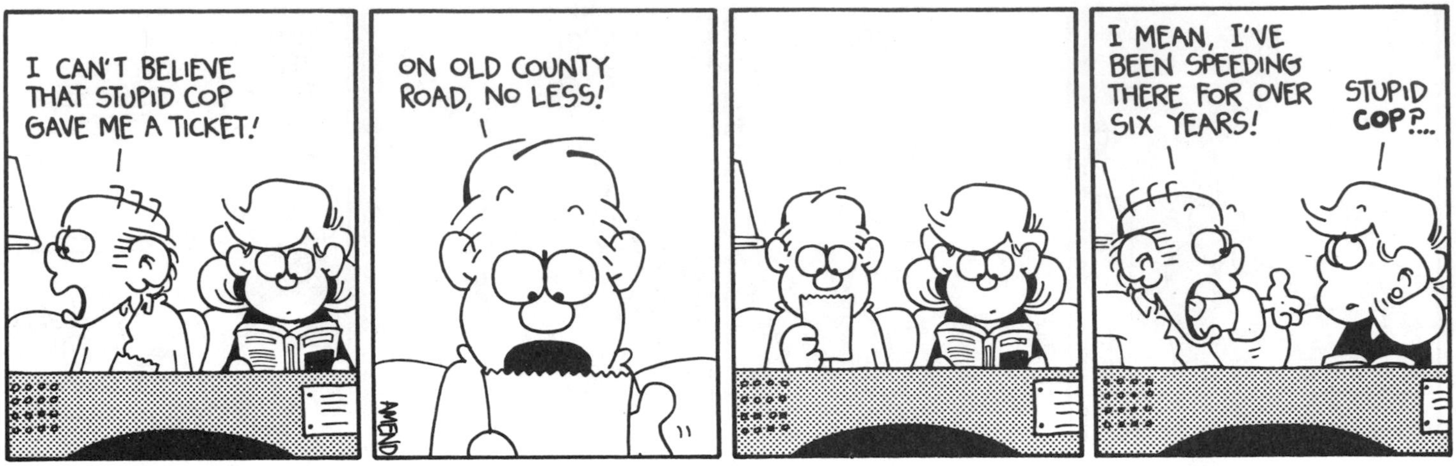
I CAN'T BELIEVE THAT STUPID COP GAVE ME A TICKET!
ON OLD COUNTY ROAD, NO LESS!
AMEND
I MEAN, I'VE BEEN SPEEDING THERE FOR OVER SIX YEARS!
STUPID **COP**?...

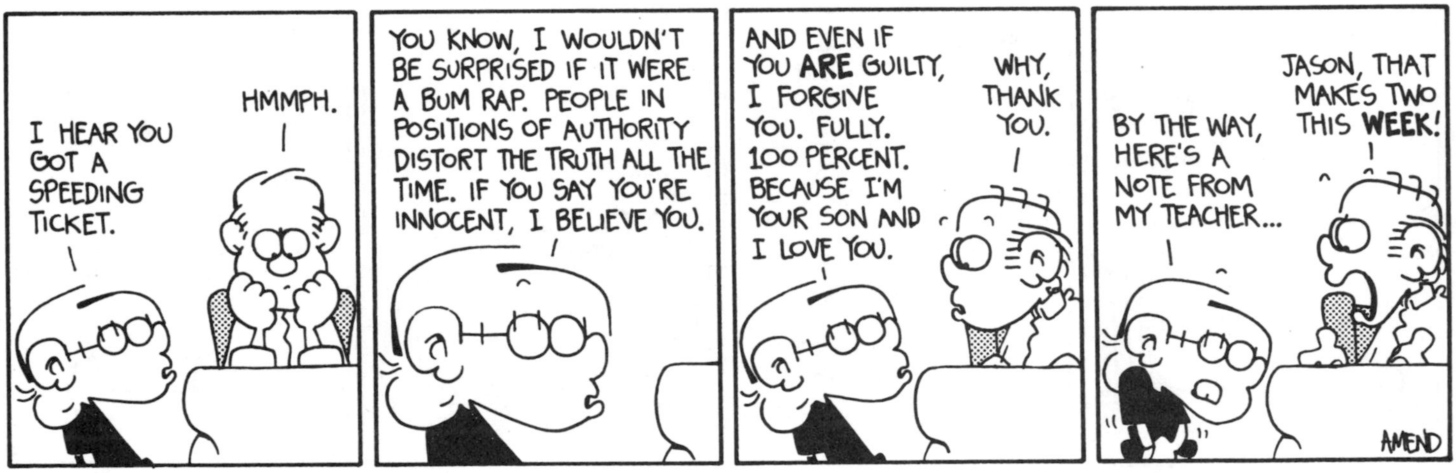
I HEAR YOU GOT A SPEEDING TICKET.
HMMPH.
YOU KNOW, I WOULDN'T BE SURPRISED IF IT WERE A BUM RAP. PEOPLE IN POSITIONS OF AUTHORITY DISTORT THE TRUTH ALL THE TIME. IF YOU SAY YOU'RE INNOCENT, I BELIEVE YOU.
AND EVEN IF YOU **ARE** GUILTY, I FORGIVE YOU. FULLY. 100 PERCENT. BECAUSE I'M YOUR SON AND I LOVE YOU.
WHY, THANK YOU.
BY THE WAY, HERE'S A NOTE FROM MY TEACHER...
JASON, THAT MAKES TWO THIS **WEEK**!
AMEND

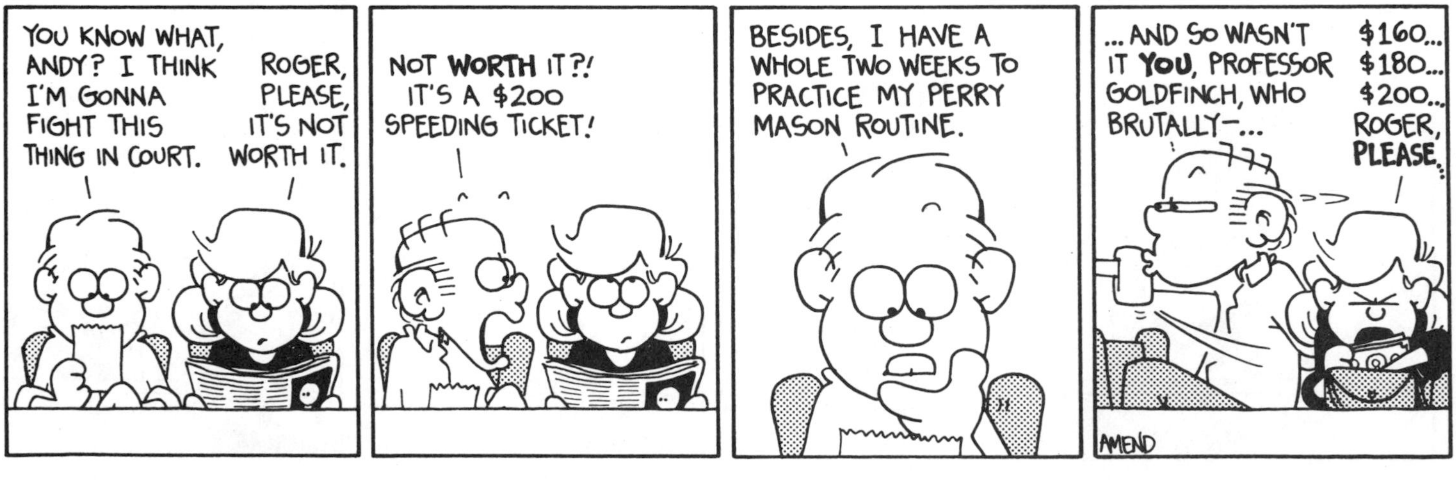
YOU KNOW WHAT, ANDY? I THINK I'M GONNA FIGHT THIS THING IN COURT.
ROGER, PLEASE, IT'S NOT WORTH IT.
NOT **WORTH** IT?! IT'S A $200 SPEEDING TICKET!
BESIDES, I HAVE A WHOLE TWO WEEKS TO PRACTICE MY PERRY MASON ROUTINE.
...AND SO WASN'T IT **YOU**, PROFESSOR GOLDFINCH, WHO BRUTALLY–...
$160... $180... $200... ROGER, **PLEASE**...
AMEND

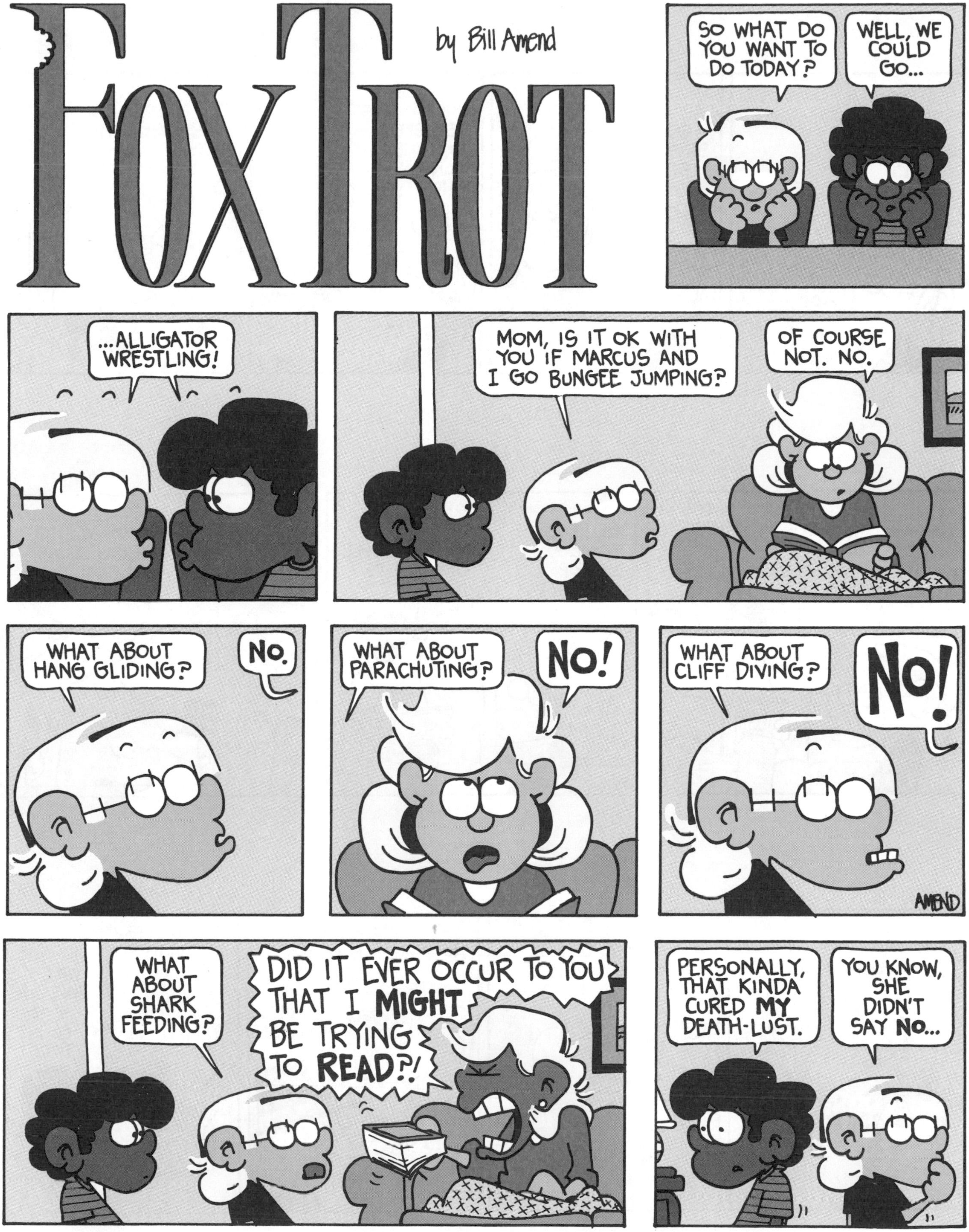
FoxTrot
by Bill Amend
SO WHAT DO YOU WANT TO DO TODAY?
WELL, WE COULD GO...
...ALLIGATOR WRESTLING!
MOM, IS IT OK WITH YOU IF MARCUS AND I GO BUNGEE JUMPING?
OF COURSE NOT. NO.
WHAT ABOUT HANG GLIDING?
NO.
WHAT ABOUT PARACHUTING?
NO!
WHAT ABOUT CLIFF DIVING?
NO!
AMEND
WHAT ABOUT SHARK FEEDING?
DID IT EVER OCCUR TO YOU THAT I **MIGHT** BE TRYING TO **READ**?!
PERSONALLY, THAT KINDA CURED **MY** DEATH-LUST.
YOU KNOW, SHE DIDN'T SAY **NO**...

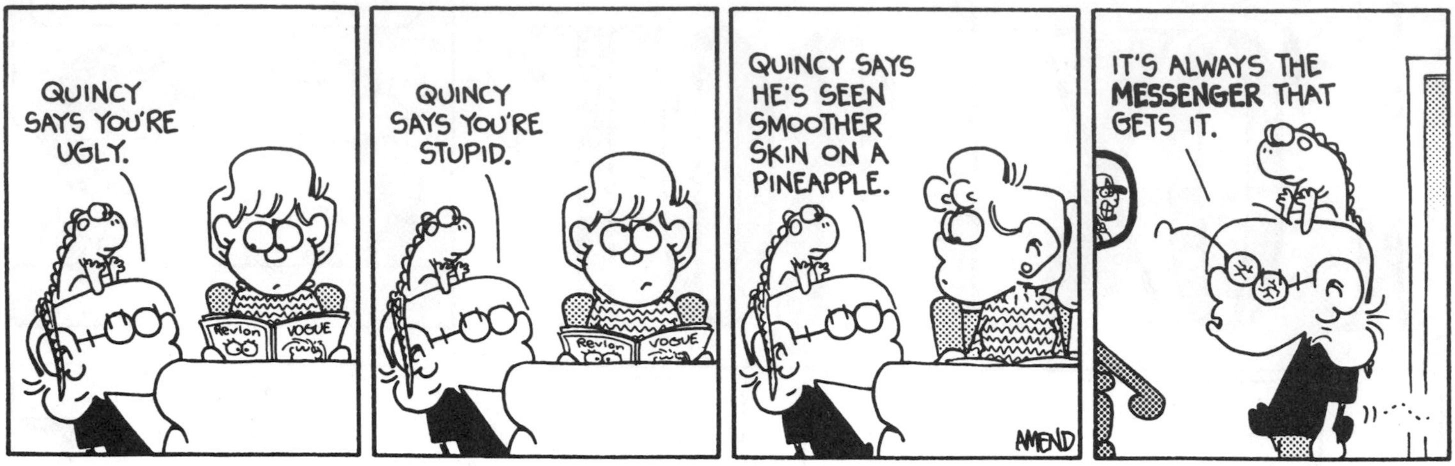
QUINCY SAYS YOU'RE UGLY.
Revlon
VOGUE
QUINCY SAYS YOU'RE STUPID.
Revlon
VOGUE
QUINCY SAYS HE'S SEEN SMOOTHER SKIN ON A PINEAPPLE.
AMEND
IT'S ALWAYS THE **MESSENGER** THAT GETS IT.

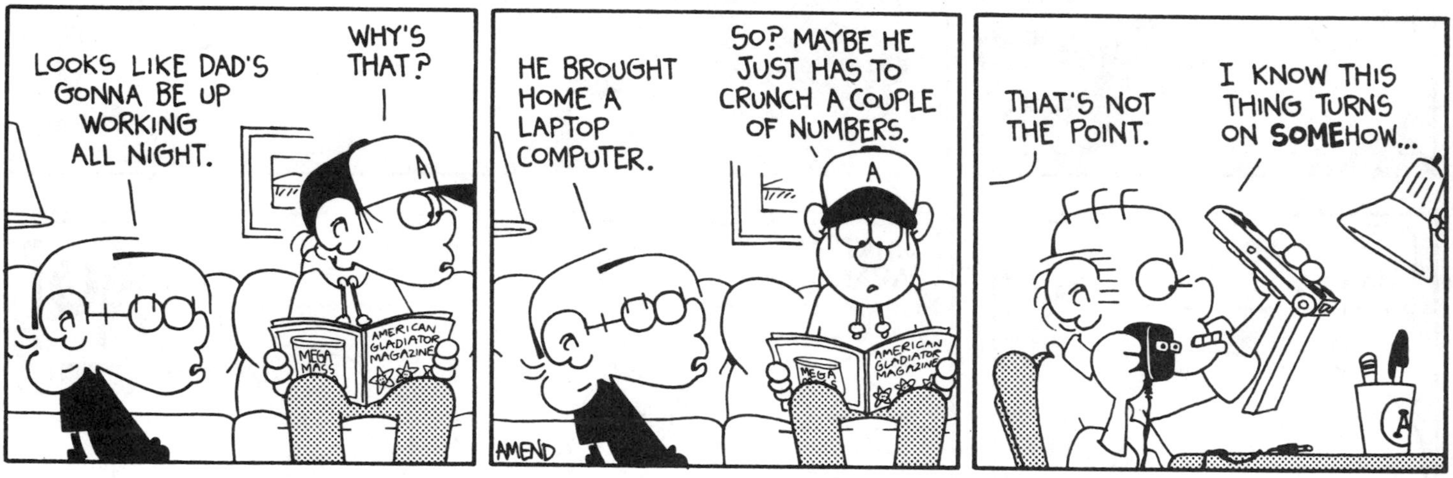
LOOKS LIKE DAD'S GONNA BE UP WORKING ALL NIGHT.
WHY'S THAT?
MEGA MASS
AMERICAN GLADIATOR MAGAZINE
HE BROUGHT HOME A LAPTOP COMPUTER.
SO? MAYBE HE JUST HAS TO CRUNCH A COUPLE OF NUMBERS.
AMEND
THAT'S NOT THE POINT.
I KNOW THIS THING TURNS ON **SOME**HOW...

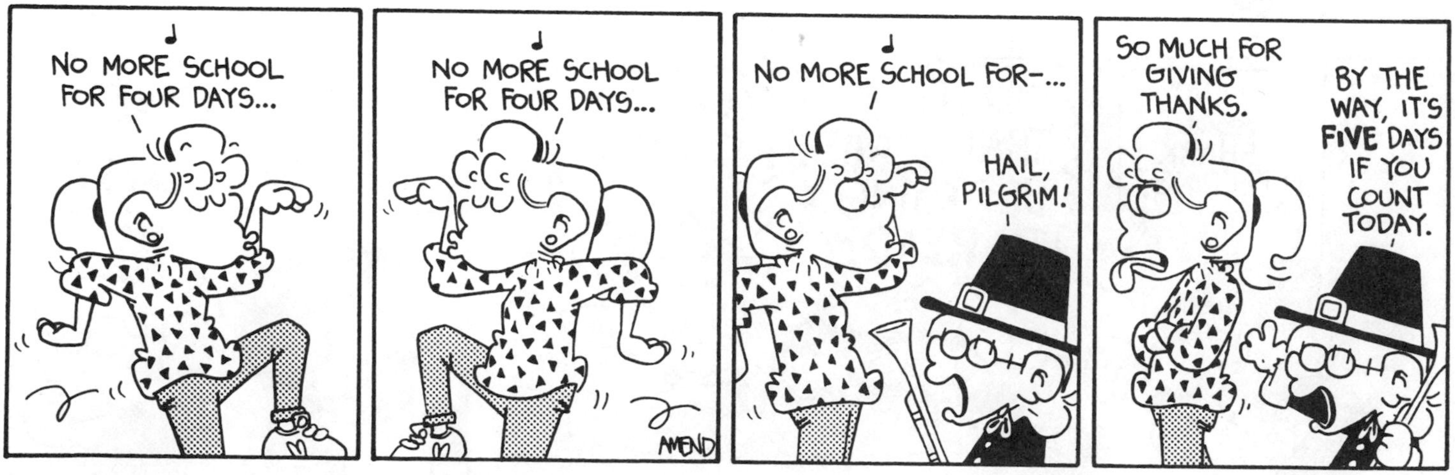
NO MORE SCHOOL FOR FOUR DAYS...
NO MORE SCHOOL FOR FOUR DAYS...
AMEND
NO MORE SCHOOL FOR-...
HAIL, PILGRIM!
SO MUCH FOR GIVING THANKS.
BY THE WAY, IT'S **FIVE** DAYS IF YOU COUNT TODAY.

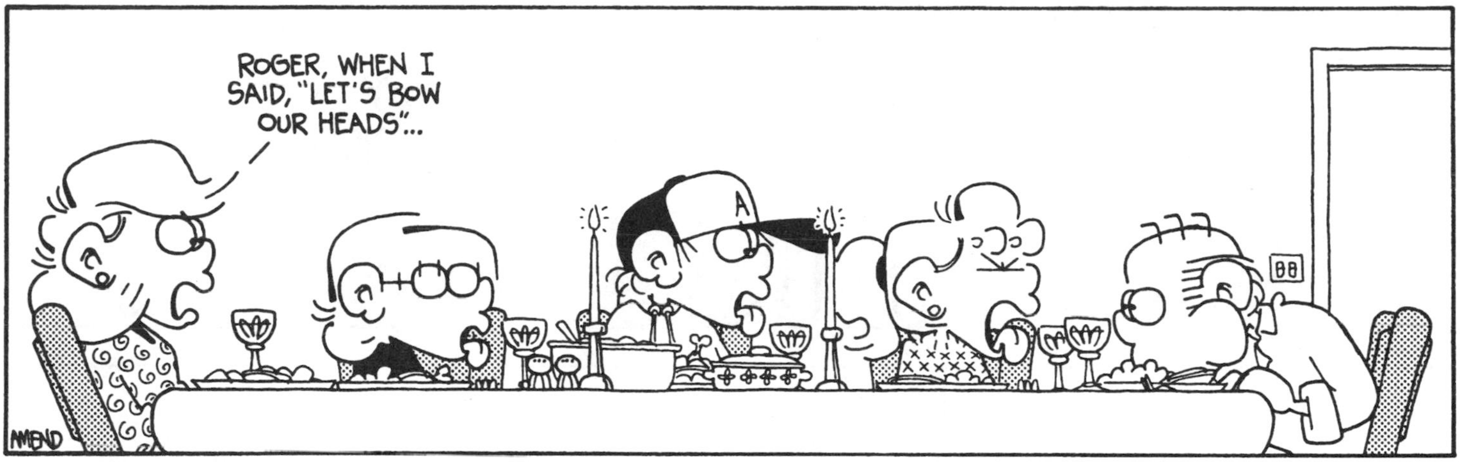
ROGER, WHEN I SAID, "LET'S BOW OUR HEADS"...
AMEND

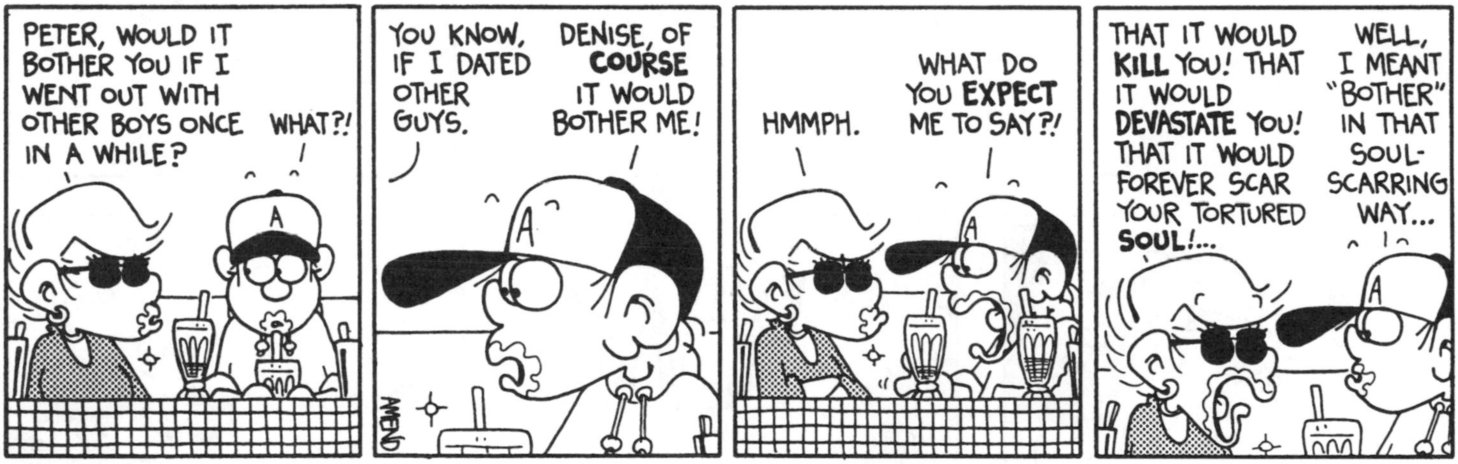
PETER, WOULD IT BOTHER YOU IF I WENT OUT WITH OTHER BOYS ONCE IN A WHILE?
WHAT?!
YOU KNOW, IF I DATED OTHER GUYS.
DENISE, OF **COURSE** IT WOULD BOTHER ME!
AMEND
HMMPH.
WHAT DO YOU **EXPECT** ME TO SAY?!
THAT IT WOULD **KILL** YOU! THAT IT WOULD **DEVASTATE** YOU! THAT IT WOULD FOREVER SCAR YOUR TORTURED **SOUL**!...
WELL, I MEANT "BOTHER" IN THAT SOUL-SCARRING WAY...

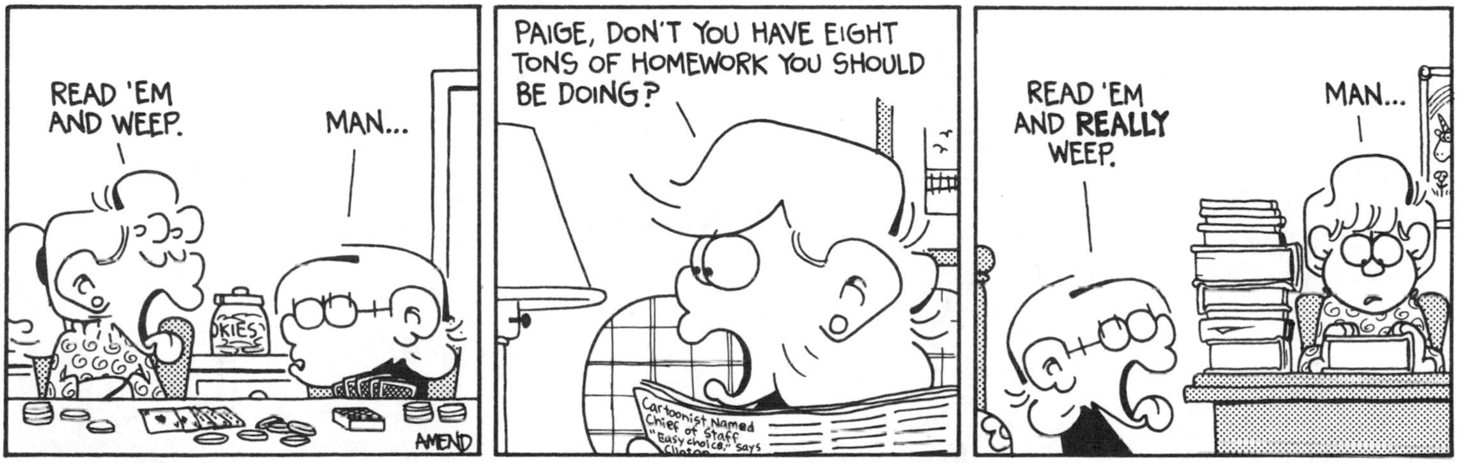
READ 'EM AND WEEP.
MAN...
AMEND
PAIGE, DON'T YOU HAVE EIGHT TONS OF HOMEWORK YOU SHOULD BE DOING?
Cartoonist Named Chief of Staff
"Easy choice," says
READ 'EM AND **REALLY** WEEP.
MAN...

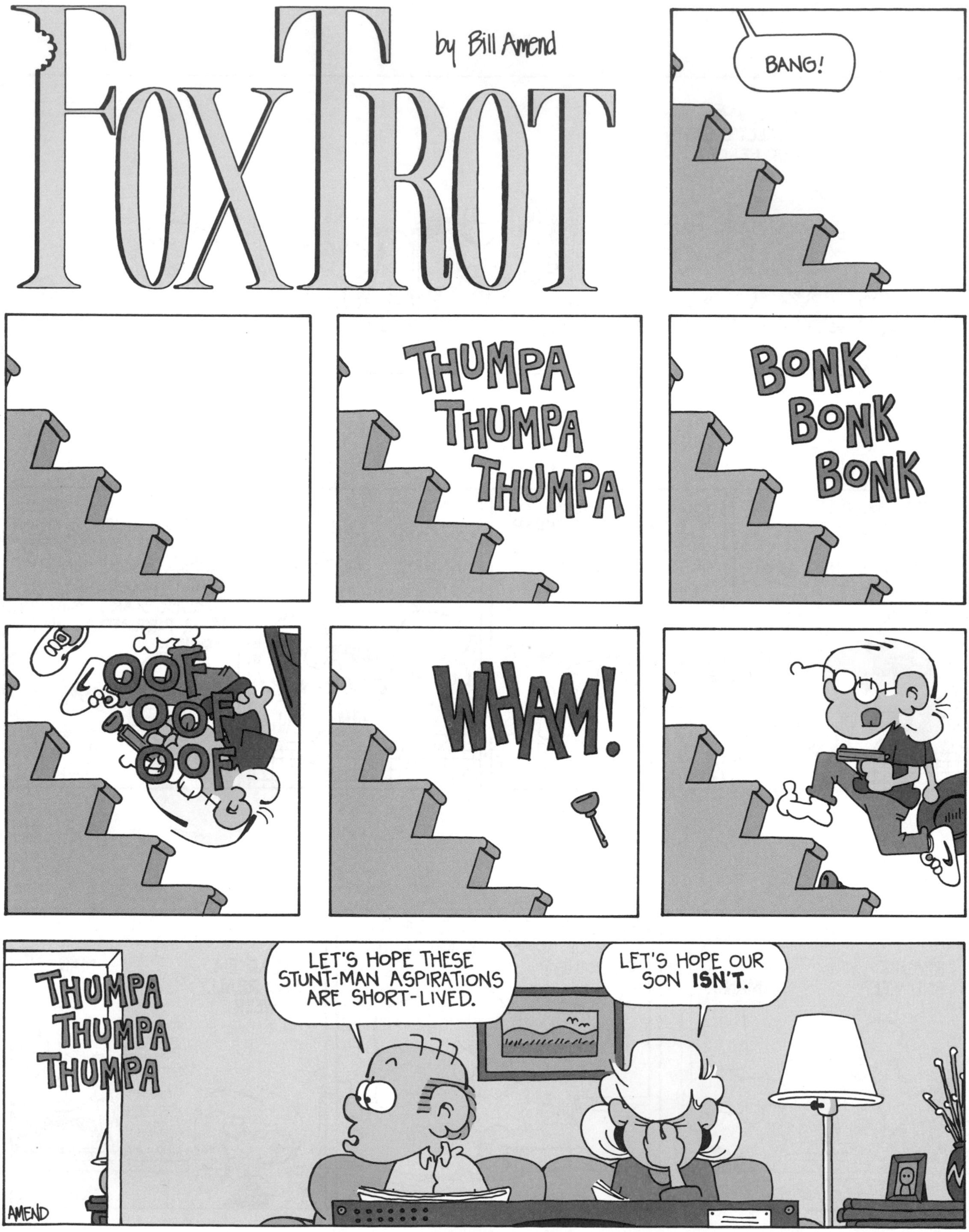
FOXTROT
by Bill Amend
BANG!
THUMPA THUMPA THUMPA
BONK BONK BONK
OOF OOF OOF
WHAM!
THUMPA THUMPA THUMPA
LET'S HOPE THESE STUNT-MAN ASPIRATIONS ARE SHORT-LIVED.
LET'S HOPE OUR SON **ISN'T**.
AMEND

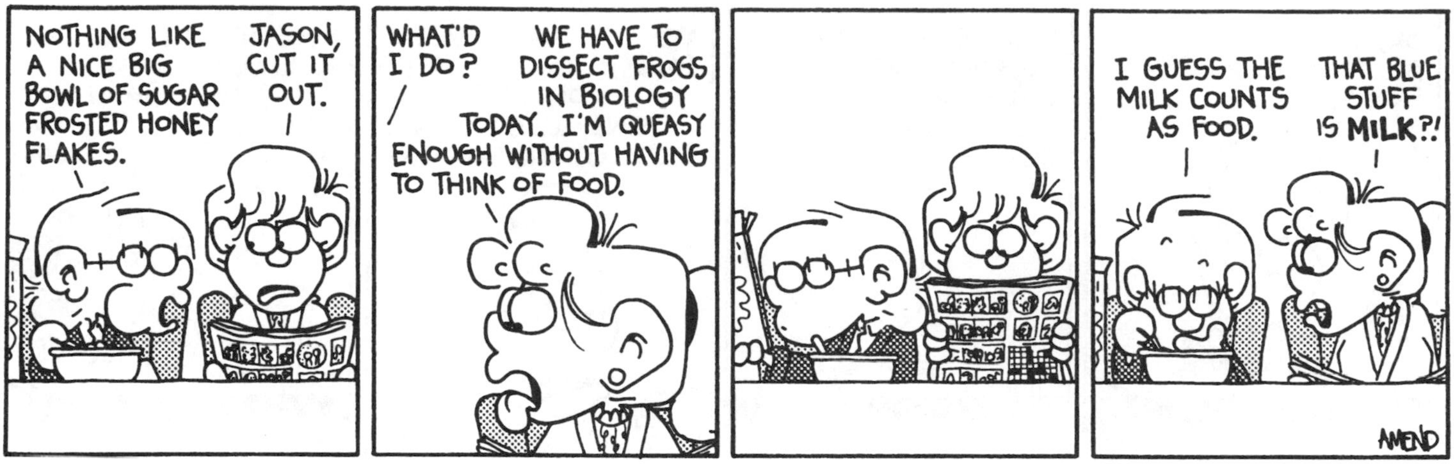
NOTHING LIKE A NICE BIG BOWL OF SUGAR FROSTED HONEY FLAKES.
JASON, CUT IT OUT.
WHAT'D I DO?
WE HAVE TO DISSECT FROGS IN BIOLOGY TODAY. I'M QUEASY ENOUGH WITHOUT HAVING TO THINK OF FOOD.
I GUESS THE MILK COUNTS AS FOOD.
THAT BLUE STUFF IS **MILK**?!
AMEND

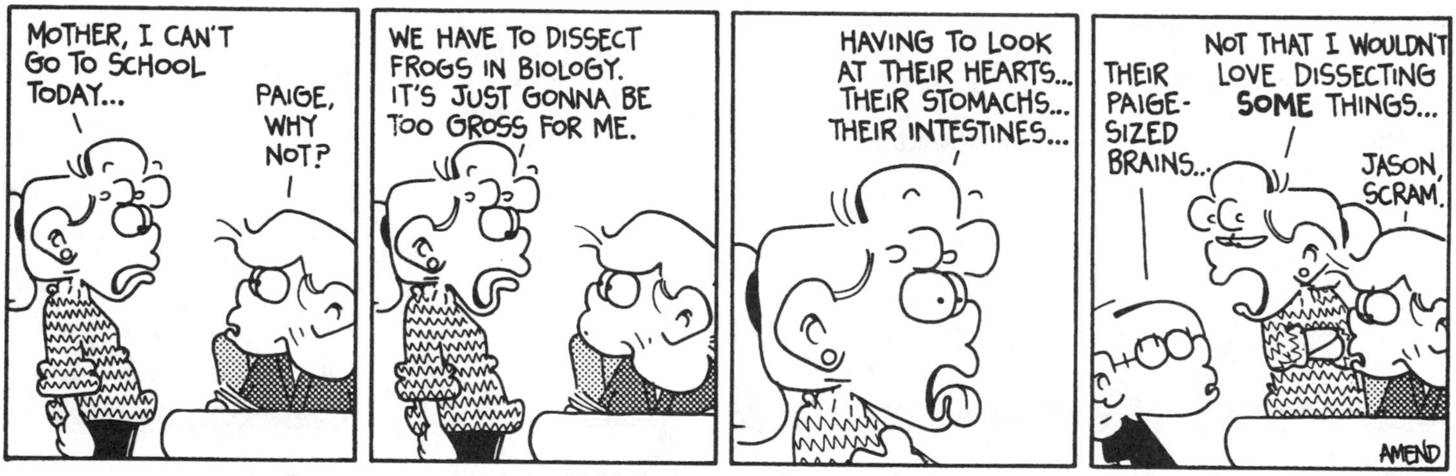
MOTHER, I CAN'T GO TO SCHOOL TODAY...
PAIGE, WHY NOT?
WE HAVE TO DISSECT FROGS IN BIOLOGY. IT'S JUST GONNA BE TOO GROSS FOR ME.
HAVING TO LOOK AT THEIR HEARTS... THEIR STOMACHS... THEIR INTESTINES...
THEIR PAIGE-SIZED BRAINS...
NOT THAT I WOULDN'T LOVE DISSECTING **SOME** THINGS...
JASON, SCRAM.
AMEND

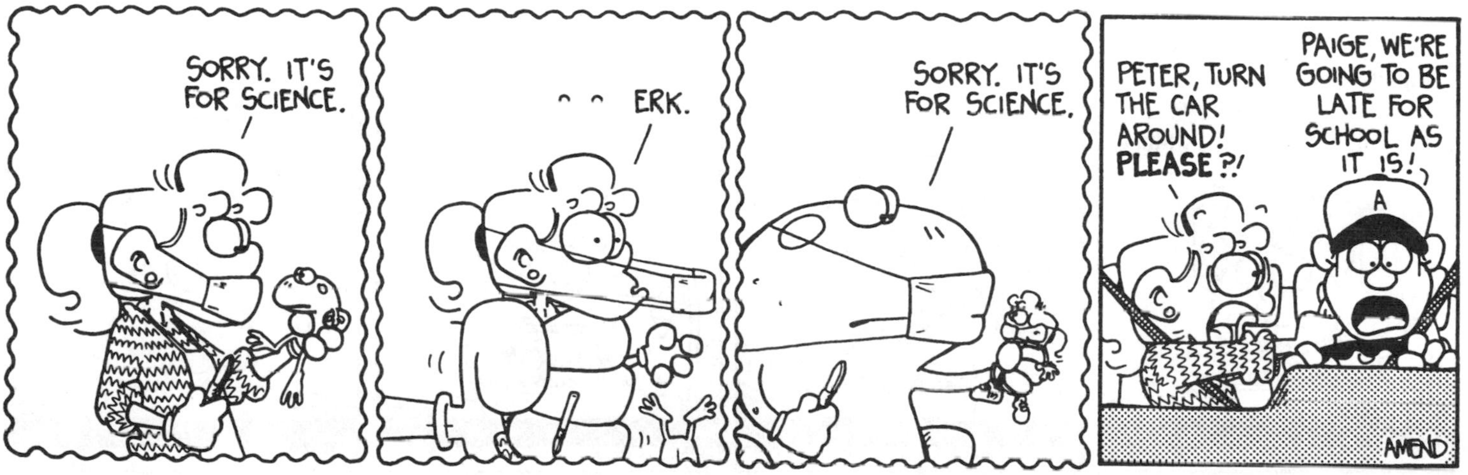
SORRY. IT'S FOR SCIENCE.
ERK.
SORRY. IT'S FOR SCIENCE.
PETER, TURN THE CAR AROUND! **PLEASE**?!
PAIGE, WE'RE GOING TO BE LATE FOR SCHOOL AS IT IS!
AMEND

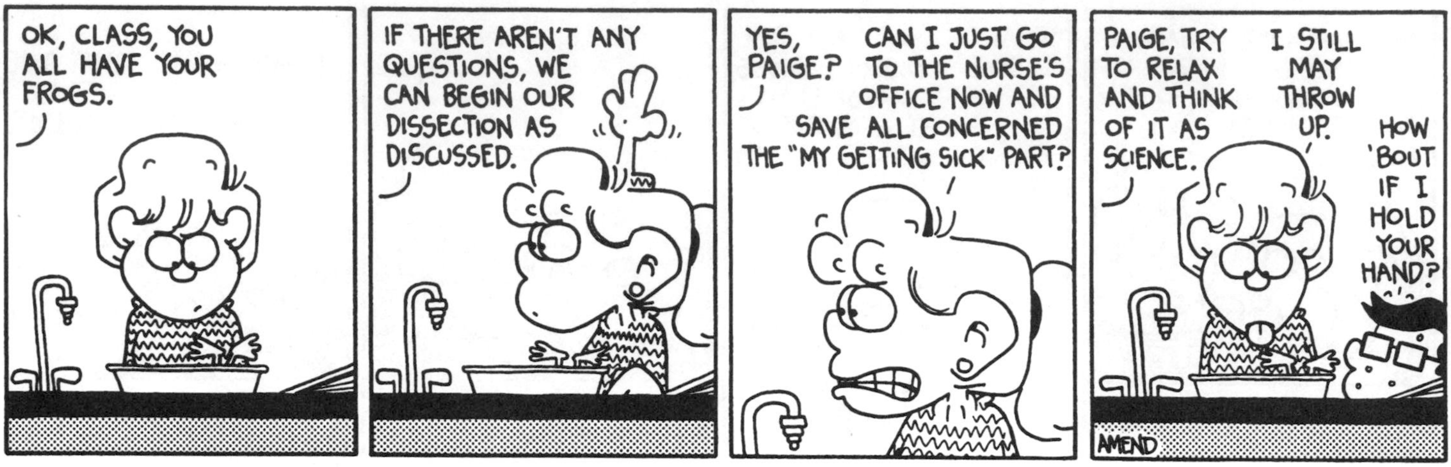
OK, CLASS, YOU ALL HAVE YOUR FROGS.
IF THERE AREN'T ANY QUESTIONS, WE CAN BEGIN OUR DISSECTION AS DISCUSSED.
YES, PAIGE?
CAN I JUST GO TO THE NURSE'S OFFICE NOW AND SAVE ALL CONCERNED THE "MY GETTING SICK" PART?
PAIGE, TRY TO RELAX AND THINK OF IT AS SCIENCE.
I STILL MAY THROW UP.
HOW 'BOUT IF I HOLD YOUR HAND?
AMEND

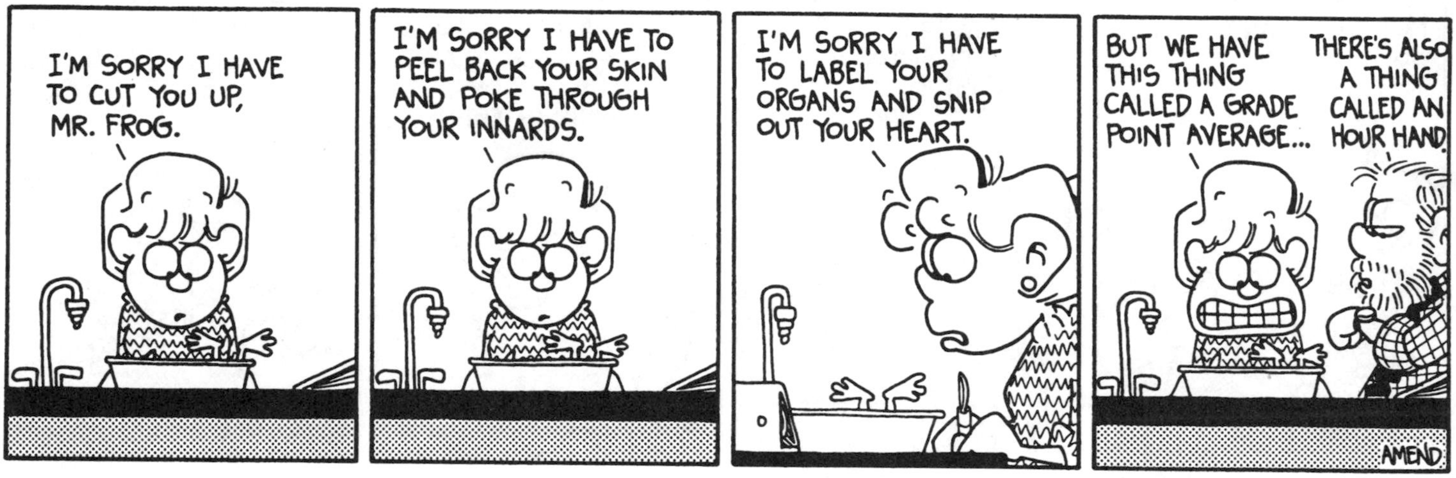
I'M SORRY I HAVE TO CUT YOU UP, MR. FROG.
I'M SORRY I HAVE TO PEEL BACK YOUR SKIN AND POKE THROUGH YOUR INNARDS.
I'M SORRY I HAVE TO LABEL YOUR ORGANS AND SNIP OUT YOUR HEART.
BUT WE HAVE THIS THING CALLED A GRADE POINT AVERAGE...
THERE'S ALSO A THING CALLED AN HOUR HAND.
AMEND

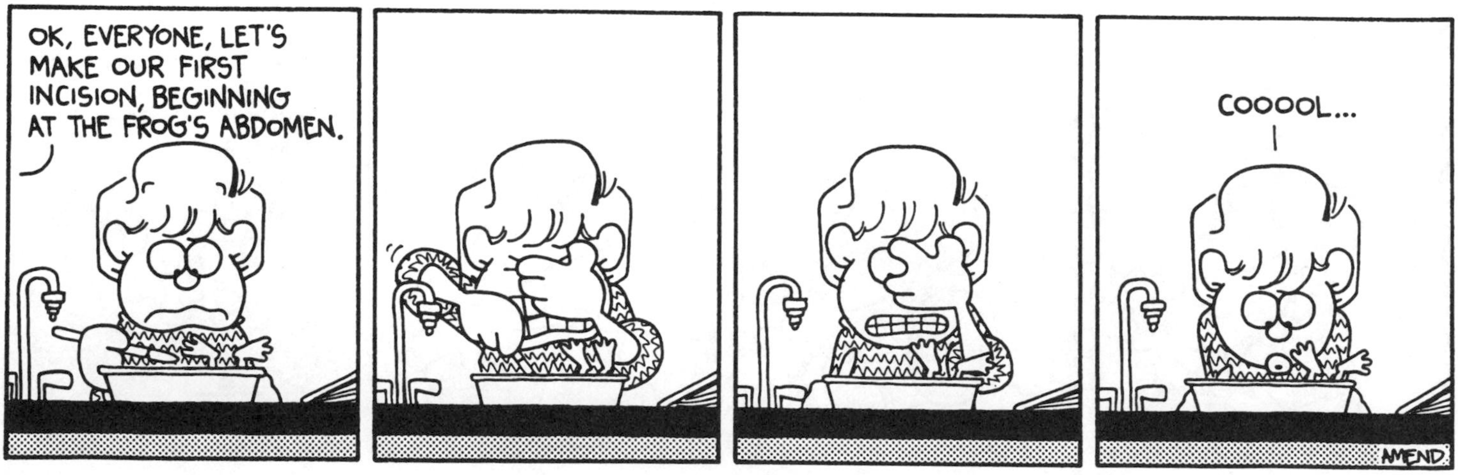
OK, EVERYONE, LET'S MAKE OUR FIRST INCISION, BEGINNING AT THE FROG'S ABDOMEN.
COOOOL...
AMEND

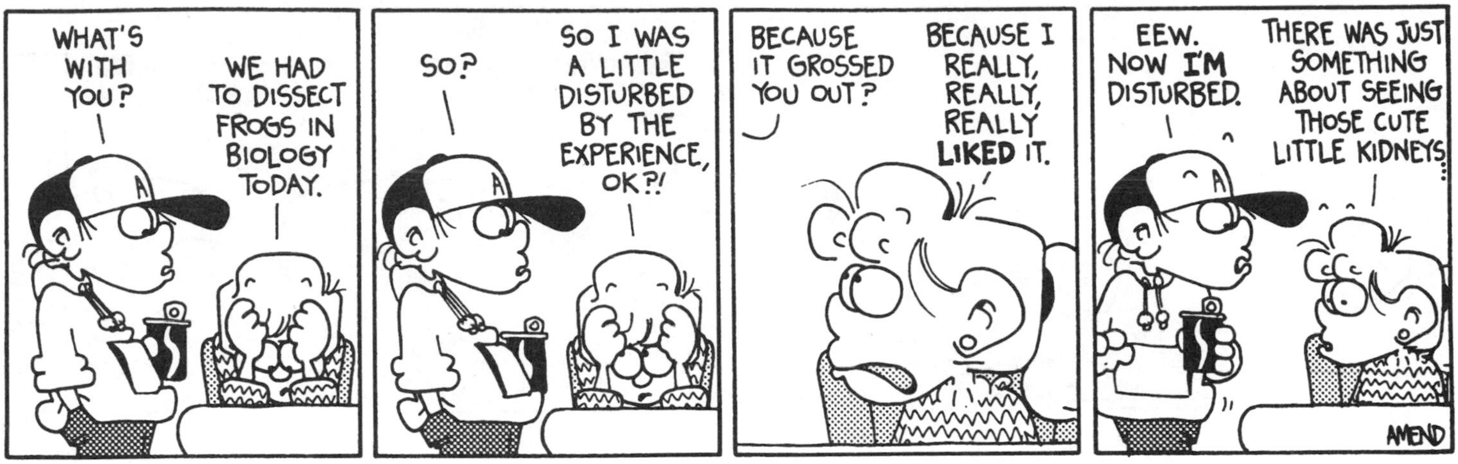
WHAT'S WITH YOU?
WE HAD TO DISSECT FROGS IN BIOLOGY TODAY.
SO?
SO I WAS A LITTLE DISTURBED BY THE EXPERIENCE, OK?!
BECAUSE IT GROSSED YOU OUT?
BECAUSE I REALLY, REALLY, REALLY **LIKED** IT.
EEW. NOW **I'M** DISTURBED.
THERE WAS JUST SOMETHING ABOUT SEEING THOSE CUTE LITTLE KIDNEYS...
AMEND

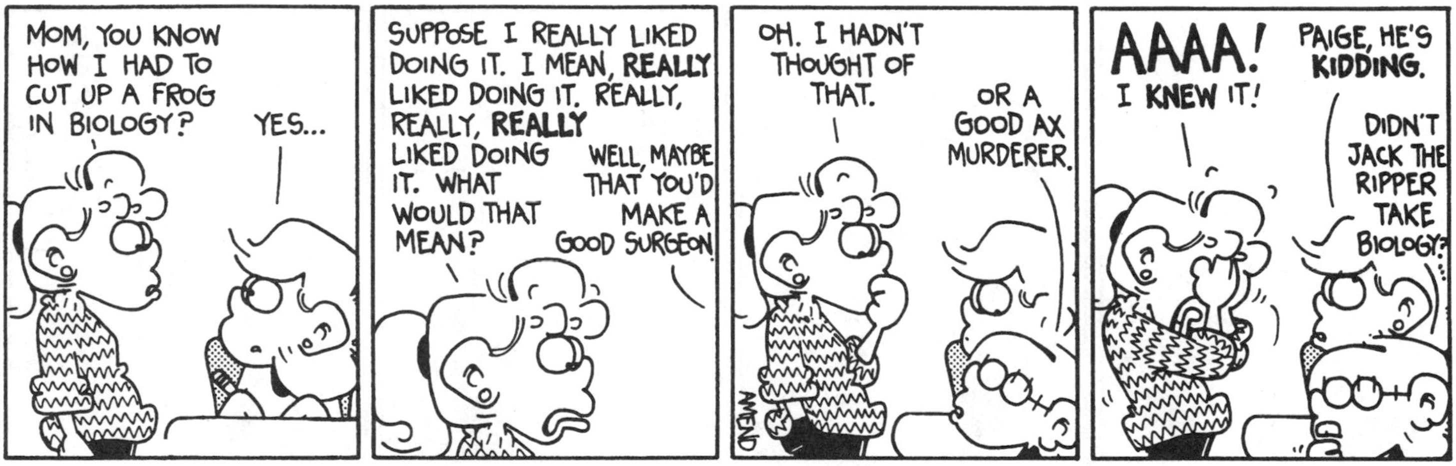
MOM, YOU KNOW HOW I HAD TO CUT UP A FROG IN BIOLOGY?
YES...
SUPPOSE I REALLY LIKED DOING IT. I MEAN, **REALLY** LIKED DOING IT. REALLY, REALLY, **REALLY** LIKED DOING IT. WHAT WOULD THAT MEAN?
WELL, MAYBE THAT YOU'D MAKE A GOOD SURGEON.
OH. I HADN'T THOUGHT OF THAT.
OR A GOOD AX MURDERER.
AMEND
AAAA! I **KNEW** IT!
PAIGE, HE'S **KIDDING**.
DIDN'T JACK THE RIPPER TAKE BIOLOGY?

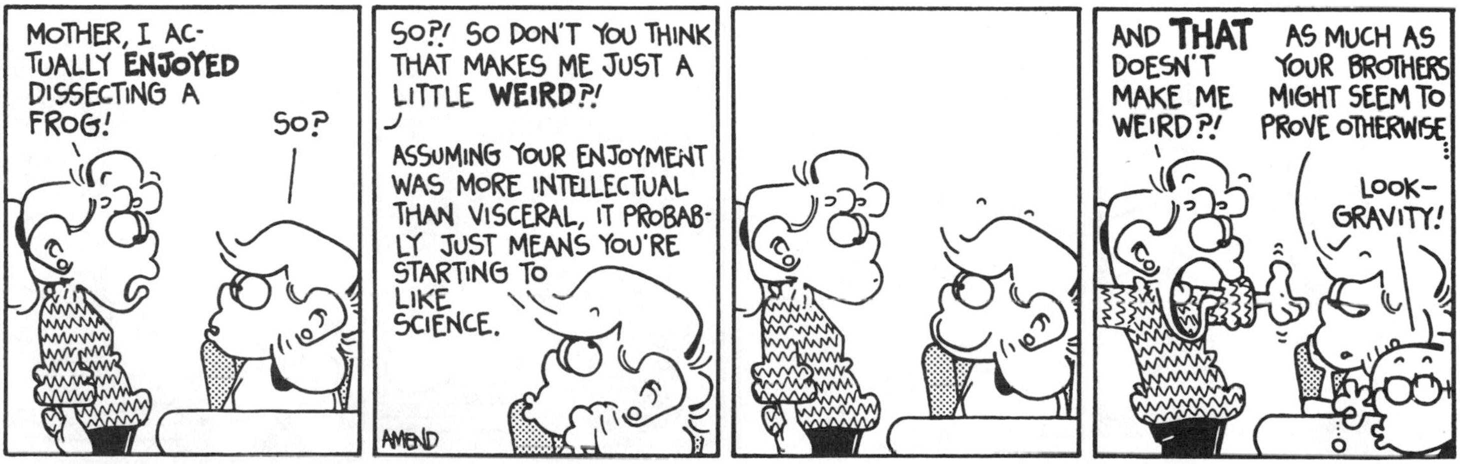
MOTHER, I ACTUALLY **ENJOYED** DISSECTING A FROG!
SO?
SO?! SO DON'T YOU THINK THAT MAKES ME JUST A LITTLE **WEIRD**?!
ASSUMING YOUR ENJOYMENT WAS MORE INTELLECTUAL THAN VISCERAL, IT PROBABLY JUST MEANS YOU'RE STARTING TO LIKE SCIENCE.
AMEND
AND **THAT** DOESN'T MAKE ME WEIRD?!
AS MUCH AS YOUR BROTHERS MIGHT SEEM TO PROVE OTHERWISE...
LOOK– GRAVITY!

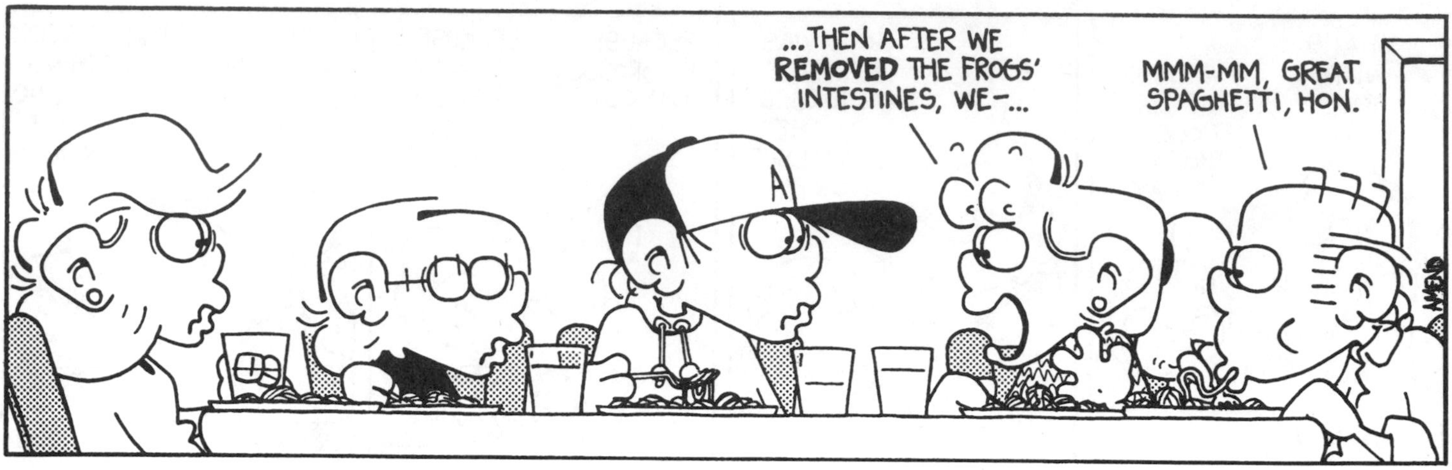
...THEN AFTER WE **REMOVED** THE FROGS' INTESTINES, WE-...
MMM-MM, GREAT SPAGHETTI, HON.
AMEND

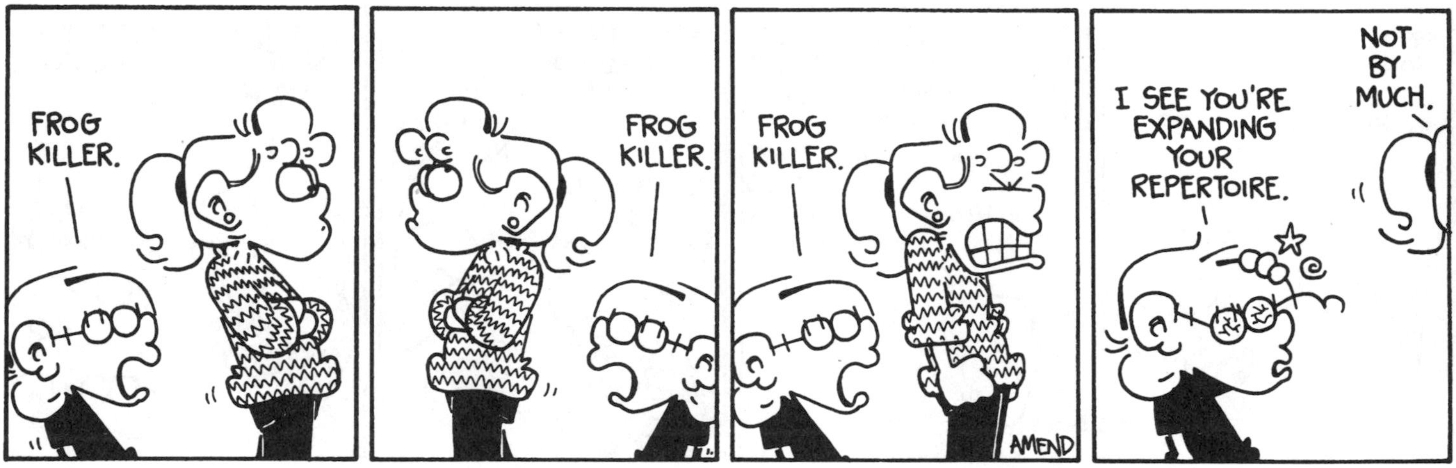
FROG KILLER.
FROG KILLER.
FROG KILLER.
AMEND
I SEE YOU'RE EXPANDING YOUR REPERTOIRE.
NOT BY MUCH.

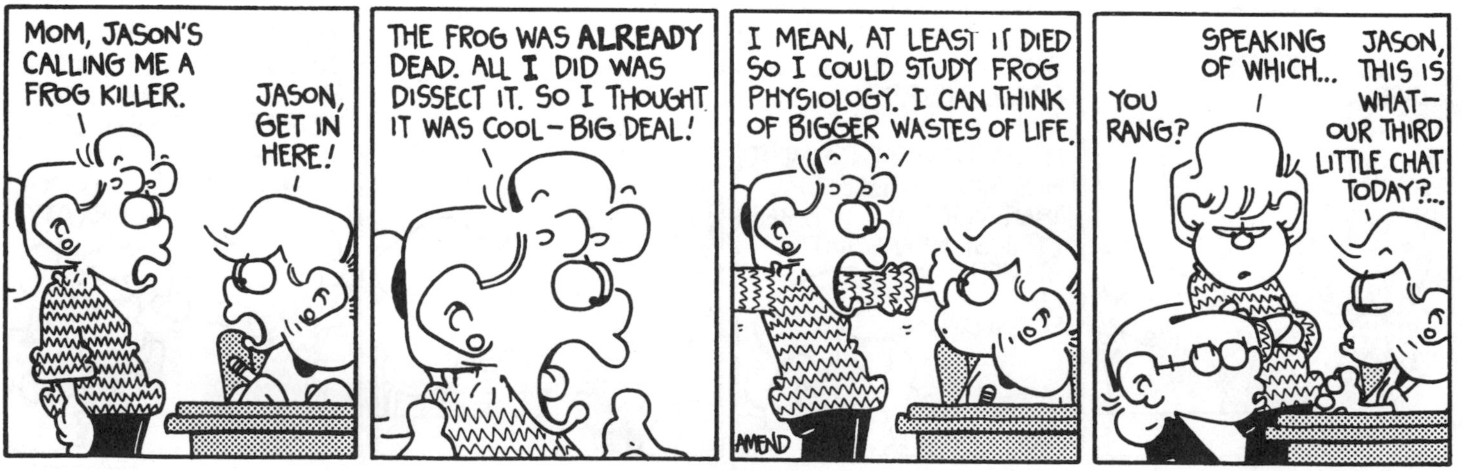
MOM, JASON'S CALLING ME A FROG KILLER.
JASON, GET IN HERE!
THE FROG WAS **ALREADY** DEAD. ALL **I** DID WAS DISSECT IT. SO I THOUGHT IT WAS COOL – BIG DEAL!
I MEAN, AT LEAST IT DIED SO I COULD STUDY FROG PHYSIOLOGY. I CAN THINK OF BIGGER WASTES OF LIFE.
AMEND
YOU RANG?
SPEAKING OF WHICH...
JASON, THIS IS WHAT– OUR THIRD LITTLE CHAT TODAY?...

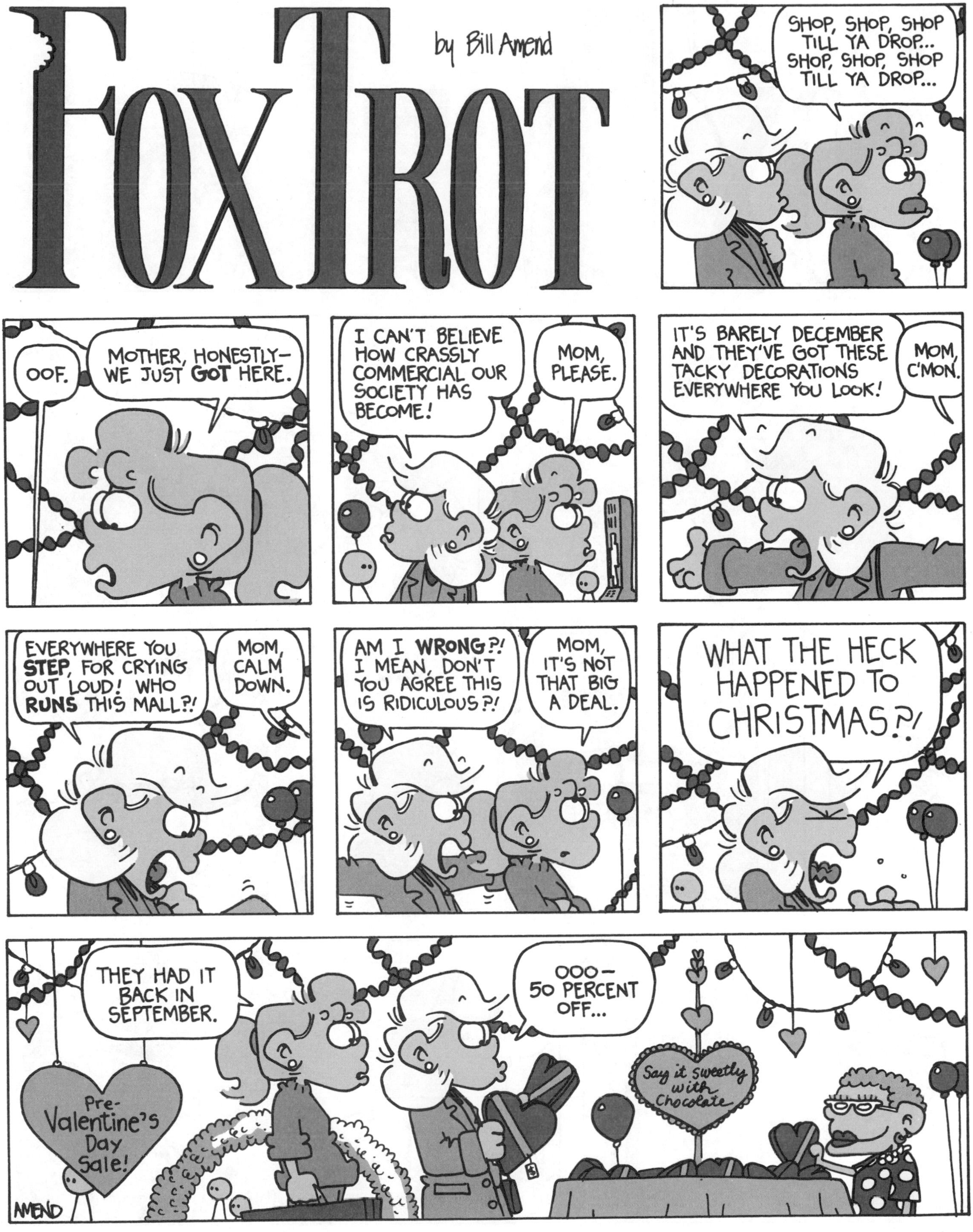
FoxTrot
by Bill Amend
SHOP, SHOP, SHOP TILL YA DROP... SHOP, SHOP, SHOP TILL YA DROP...
OOF.
MOTHER, HONESTLY— WE JUST **GOT** HERE.
I CAN'T BELIEVE HOW CRASSLY COMMERCIAL OUR SOCIETY HAS BECOME!
MOM, PLEASE.
IT'S BARELY DECEMBER AND THEY'VE GOT THESE TACKY DECORATIONS EVERYWHERE YOU LOOK!
MOM, C'MON.
EVERYWHERE YOU **STEP**, FOR CRYING OUT LOUD! WHO **RUNS** THIS MALL?!
MOM, CALM DOWN.
AM I **WRONG**?! I MEAN, DON'T YOU AGREE THIS IS RIDICULOUS?!
MOM, IT'S NOT THAT BIG A DEAL.
WHAT THE HECK HAPPENED TO CHRISTMAS?!
THEY HAD IT BACK IN SEPTEMBER.
OOO— 50 PERCENT OFF...
Pre-Valentine's Day Sale!
Say it sweetly with Chocolate
AMEND

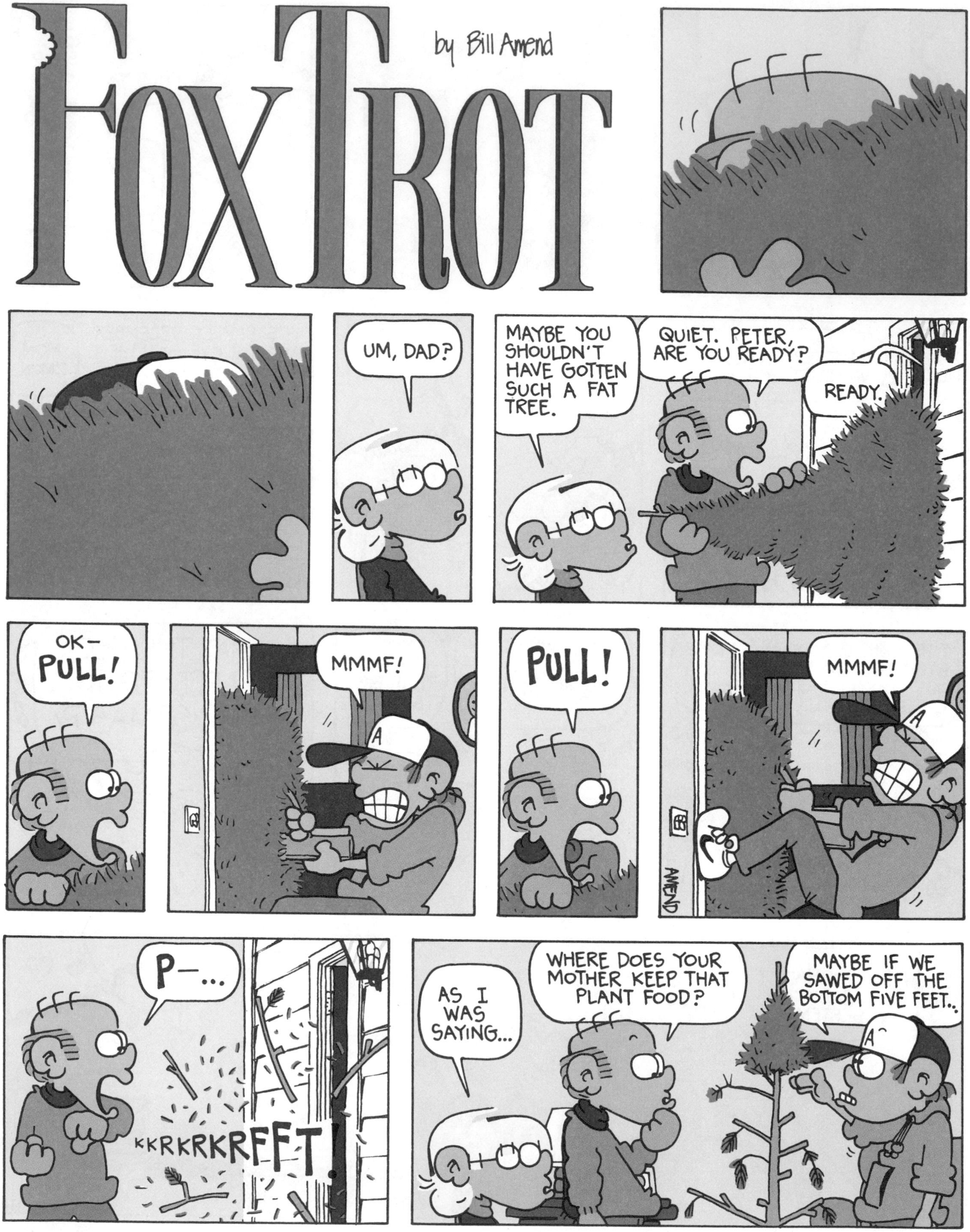
FoxTrot
by Bill Amend
UM, DAD?
MAYBE YOU SHOULDN'T HAVE GOTTEN SUCH A FAT TREE.
QUIET. PETER, ARE YOU READY?
READY.
OK– PULL!
MMMF!
PULL!
MMMF!
AMEND
P–...
KKRKRKRFFT!
AS I WAS SAYING...
WHERE DOES YOUR MOTHER KEEP THAT PLANT FOOD?
MAYBE IF WE SAWED OFF THE BOTTOM FIVE FEET..

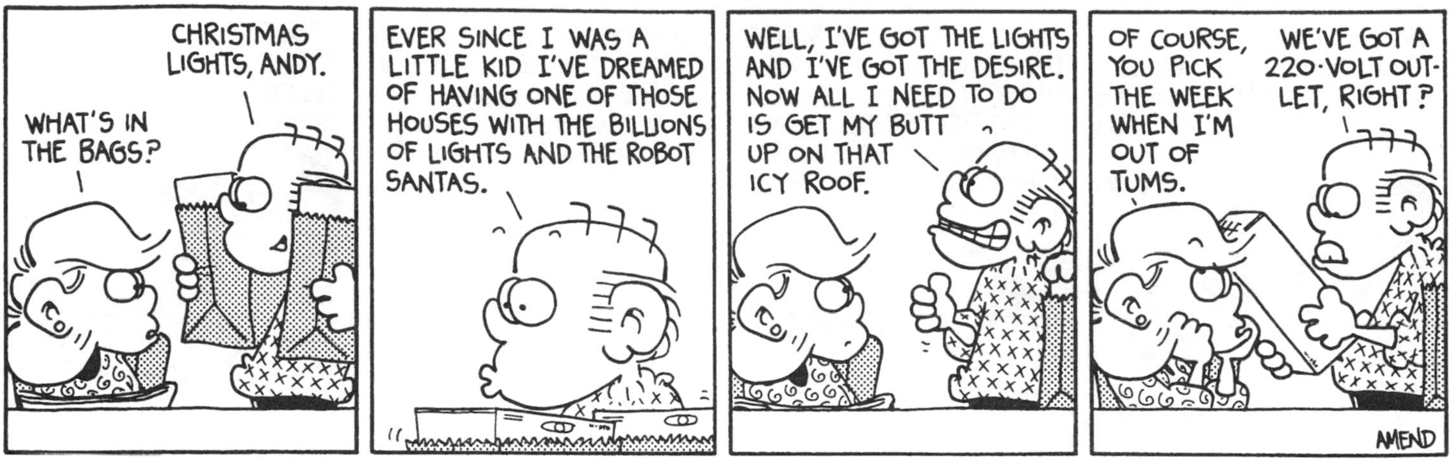
WHAT'S IN THE BAGS?
CHRISTMAS LIGHTS, ANDY.
EVER SINCE I WAS A LITTLE KID I'VE DREAMED OF HAVING ONE OF THOSE HOUSES WITH THE BILLIONS OF LIGHTS AND THE ROBOT SANTAS.
WELL, I'VE GOT THE LIGHTS AND I'VE GOT THE DESIRE. NOW ALL I NEED TO DO IS GET MY BUTT UP ON THAT ICY ROOF.
OF COURSE, YOU PICK THE WEEK WHEN I'M OUT OF TUMS.
WE'VE GOT A 220-VOLT OUTLET, RIGHT?
AMEND

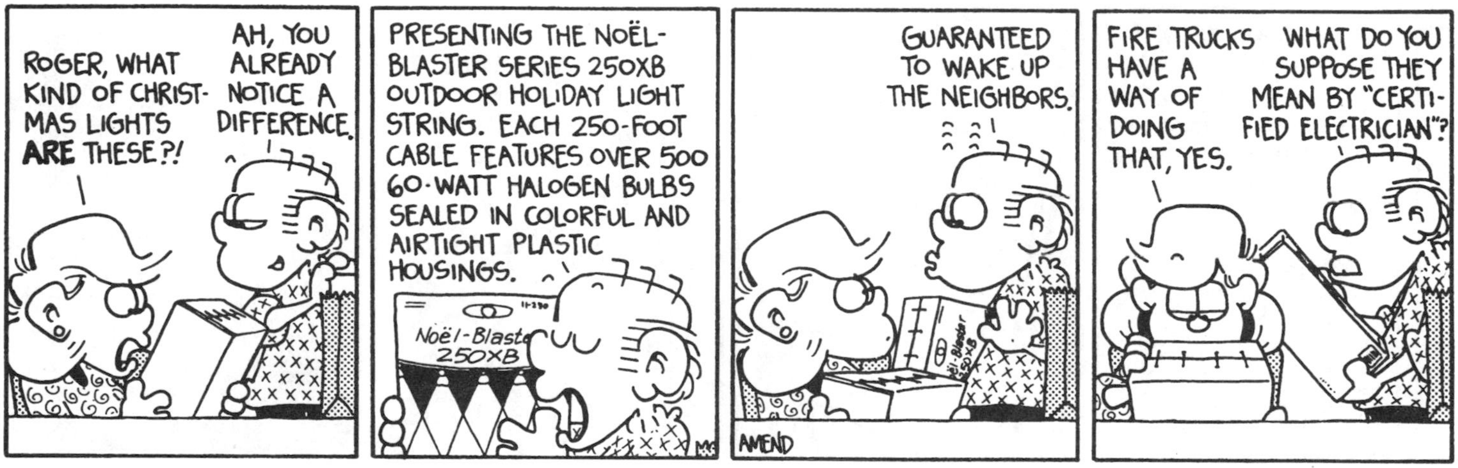
ROGER, WHAT KIND OF CHRISTMAS LIGHTS **ARE** THESE?!
AH, YOU ALREADY NOTICE A DIFFERENCE.
PRESENTING THE NOËL-BLASTER SERIES 250XB OUTDOOR HOLIDAY LIGHT STRING. EACH 250-FOOT CABLE FEATURES OVER 500 60-WATT HALOGEN BULBS SEALED IN COLORFUL AND AIRTIGHT PLASTIC HOUSINGS.
Noël-Blaster 250XB
GUARANTEED TO WAKE UP THE NEIGHBORS.
AMEND
FIRE TRUCKS HAVE A WAY OF DOING THAT, YES.
WHAT DO YOU SUPPOSE THEY MEAN BY "CERTIFIED ELECTRICIAN"?

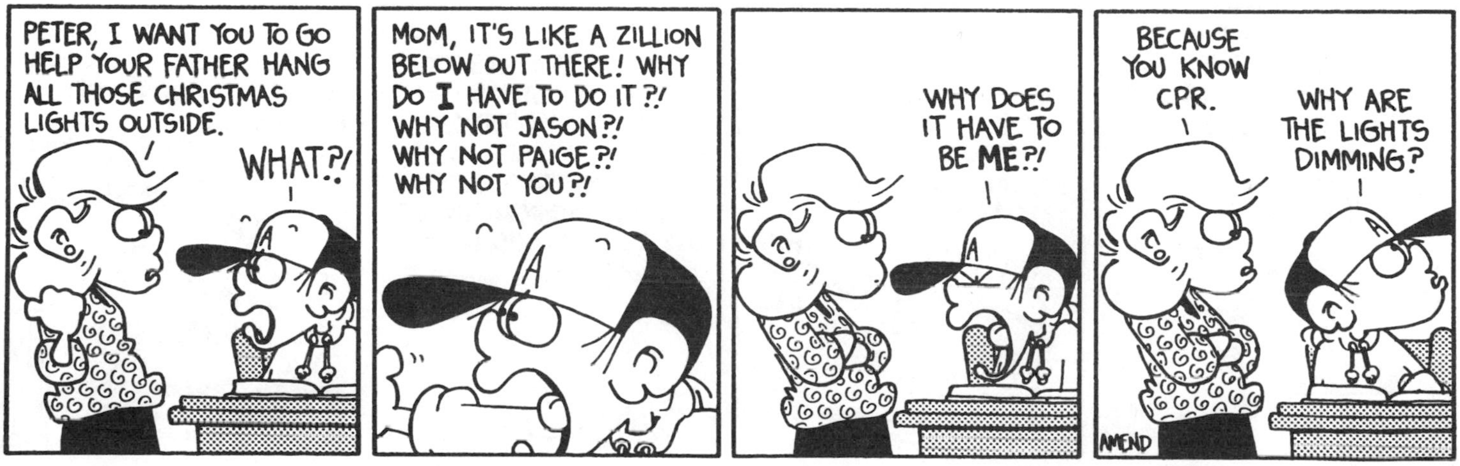
PETER, I WANT YOU TO GO HELP YOUR FATHER HANG ALL THOSE CHRISTMAS LIGHTS OUTSIDE.
WHAT?!
MOM, IT'S LIKE A ZILLION BELOW OUT THERE! WHY DO **I** HAVE TO DO IT?! WHY NOT JASON?! WHY NOT PAIGE?! WHY NOT YOU?!
WHY DOES IT HAVE TO BE **ME**?!
BECAUSE YOU KNOW CPR.
WHY ARE THE LIGHTS DIMMING?
AMEND

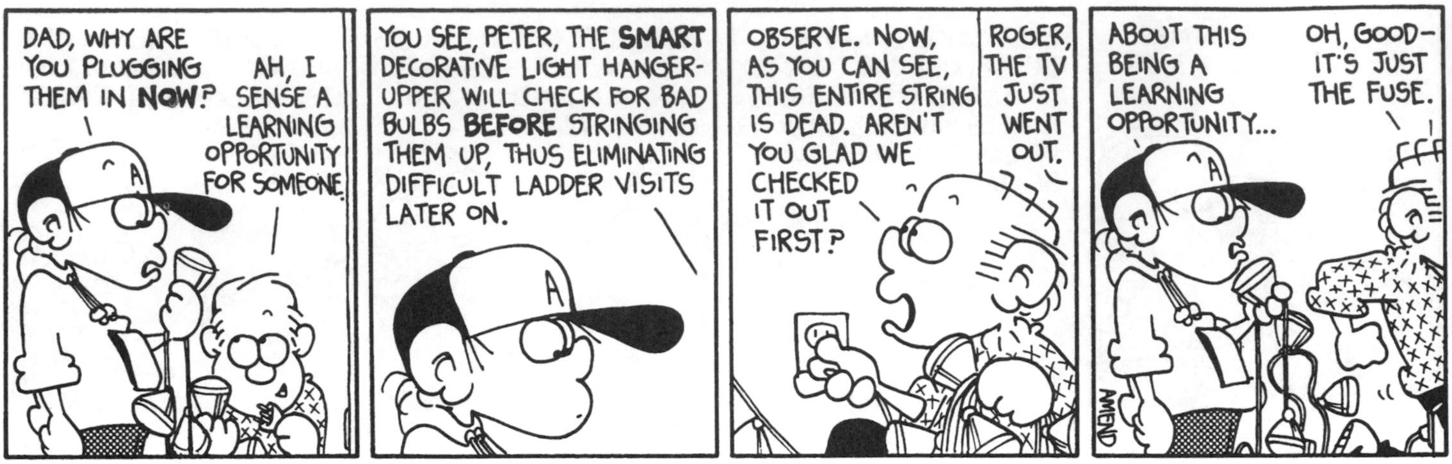
DAD, WHY ARE YOU PLUGGING THEM IN NOW?
AH, I SENSE A LEARNING OPPORTUNITY FOR SOMEONE.
YOU SEE, PETER, THE SMART DECORATIVE LIGHT HANGER-UPPER WILL CHECK FOR BAD BULBS BEFORE STRINGING THEM UP, THUS ELIMINATING DIFFICULT LADDER VISITS LATER ON.
OBSERVE. NOW, AS YOU CAN SEE, THIS ENTIRE STRING IS DEAD. AREN'T YOU GLAD WE CHECKED IT OUT FIRST?
ROGER, THE TV JUST WENT OUT.
ABOUT THIS BEING A LEARNING OPPORTUNITY...
OH, GOOD– IT'S JUST THE FUSE.
AMEND

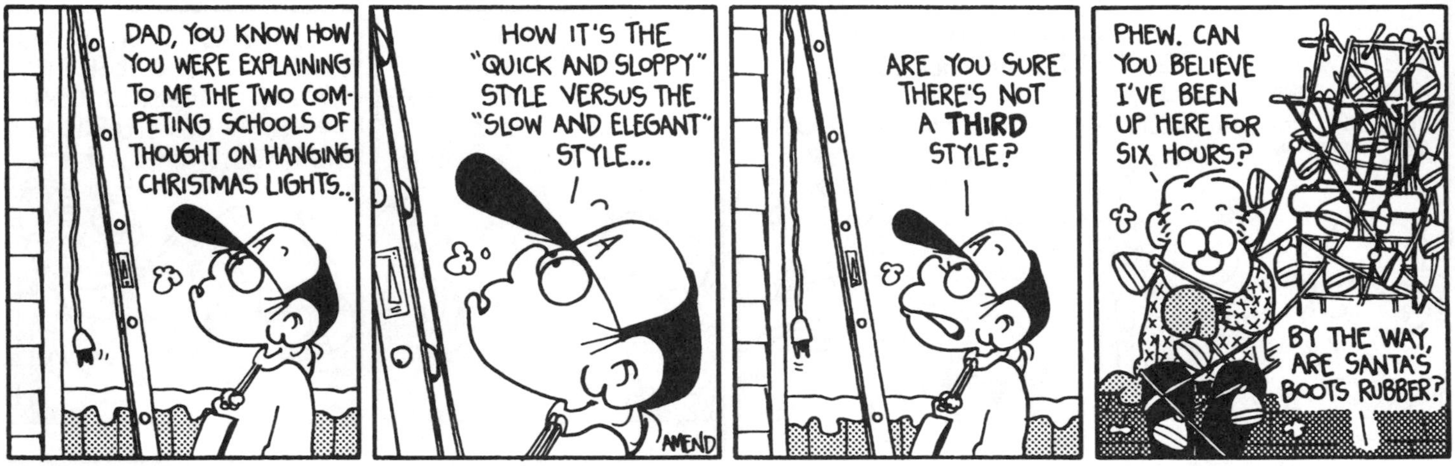
DAD, YOU KNOW HOW YOU WERE EXPLAINING TO ME THE TWO COMPETING SCHOOLS OF THOUGHT ON HANGING CHRISTMAS LIGHTS...
HOW IT'S THE "QUICK AND SLOPPY" STYLE VERSUS THE "SLOW AND ELEGANT" STYLE...
AMEND
ARE YOU SURE THERE'S NOT A THIRD STYLE?
PHEW. CAN YOU BELIEVE I'VE BEEN UP HERE FOR SIX HOURS?
BY THE WAY, ARE SANTA'S BOOTS RUBBER?

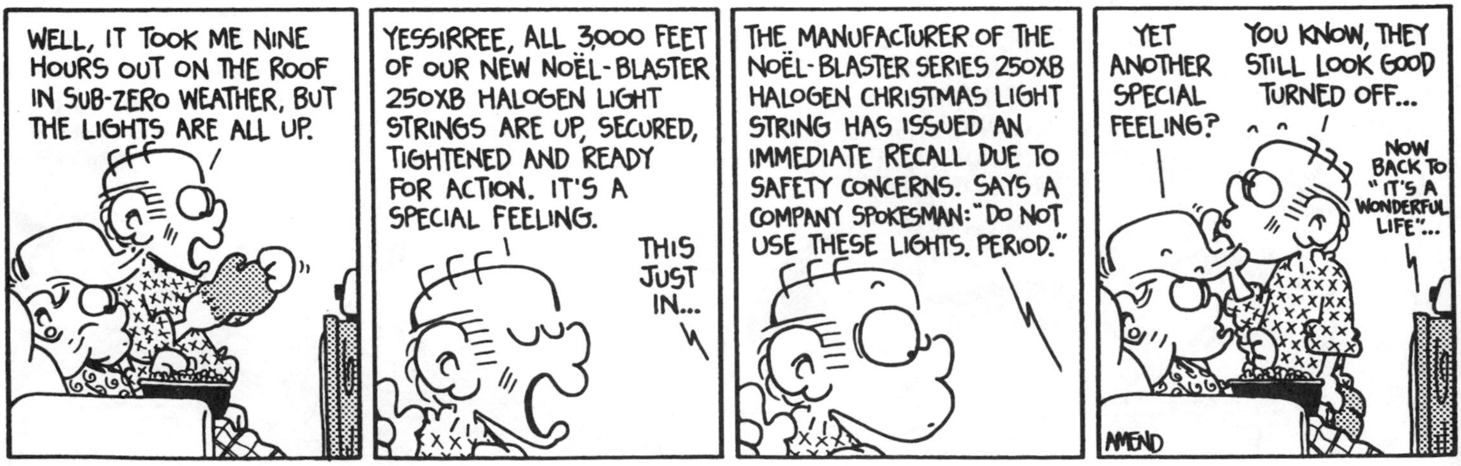
WELL, IT TOOK ME NINE HOURS OUT ON THE ROOF IN SUB-ZERO WEATHER, BUT THE LIGHTS ARE ALL UP.
YESSIRREE, ALL 3,000 FEET OF OUR NEW NOËL-BLASTER 250XB HALOGEN LIGHT STRINGS ARE UP, SECURED, TIGHTENED AND READY FOR ACTION. IT'S A SPECIAL FEELING.
THIS JUST IN...
THE MANUFACTURER OF THE NOËL-BLASTER SERIES 250XB HALOGEN CHRISTMAS LIGHT STRING HAS ISSUED AN IMMEDIATE RECALL DUE TO SAFETY CONCERNS. SAYS A COMPANY SPOKESMAN: "DO NOT USE THESE LIGHTS. PERIOD."
YET ANOTHER SPECIAL FEELING?
YOU KNOW, THEY STILL LOOK GOOD TURNED OFF...
NOW BACK TO "IT'S A WONDERFUL LIFE"...
AMEND

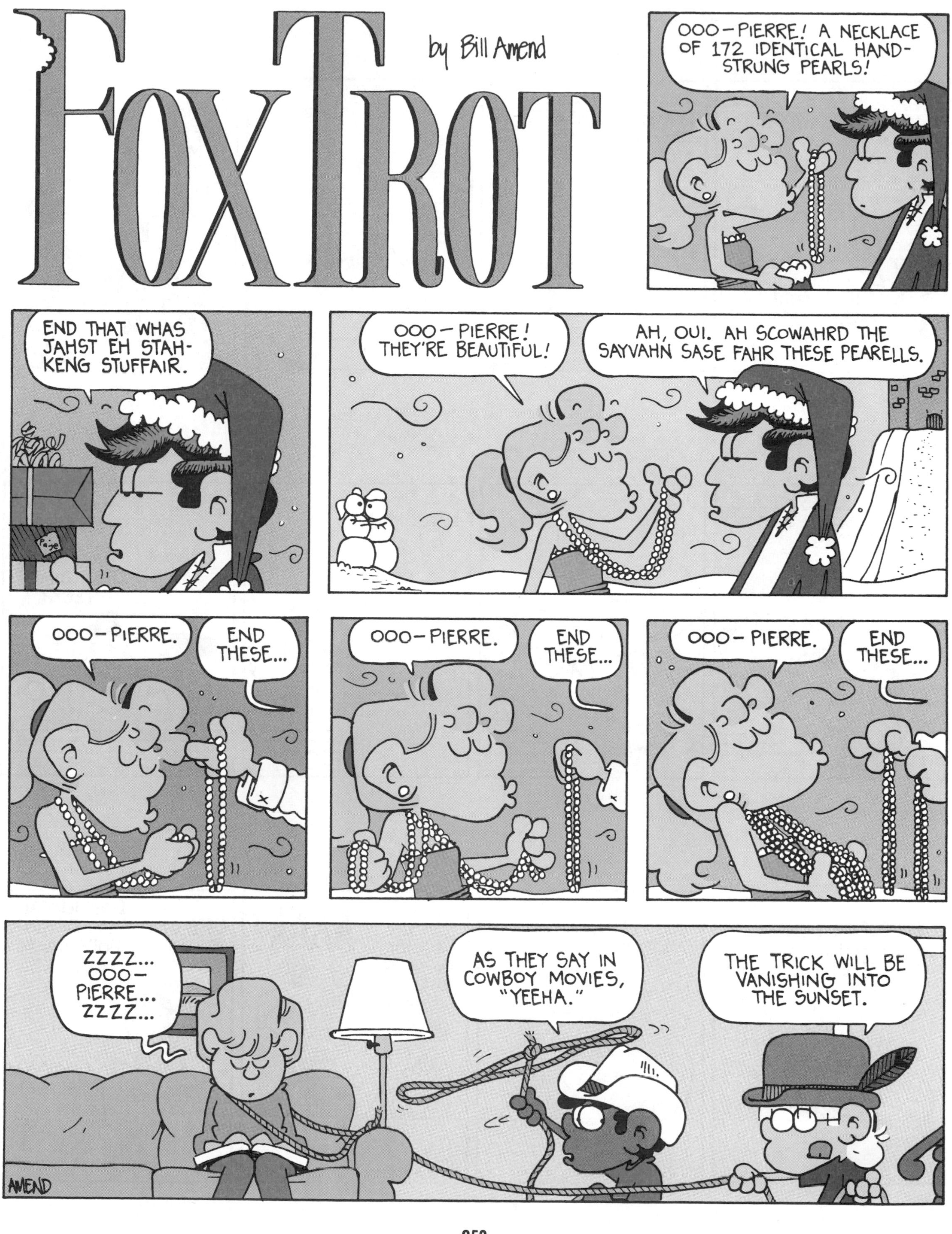
FoxTrot
by Bill Amend
OOO-PIERRE! A NECKLACE OF 172 IDENTICAL HAND-STRUNG PEARLS!
END THAT WHAS JAHST EH STAH-KENG STUFFAIR.
OOO-PIERRE! THEY'RE BEAUTIFUL!
AH, OUI. AH SCOWAHRD THE SAYVAHN SASE FAHR THESE PEARELLS.
OOO-PIERRE.
END THESE...
OOO-PIERRE.
END THESE...
OOO-PIERRE.
END THESE...
ZZZZ... OOO-PIERRE... ZZZZ...
AS THEY SAY IN COWBOY MOVIES, "YEEHA."
THE TRICK WILL BE VANISHING INTO THE SUNSET.
AMEND

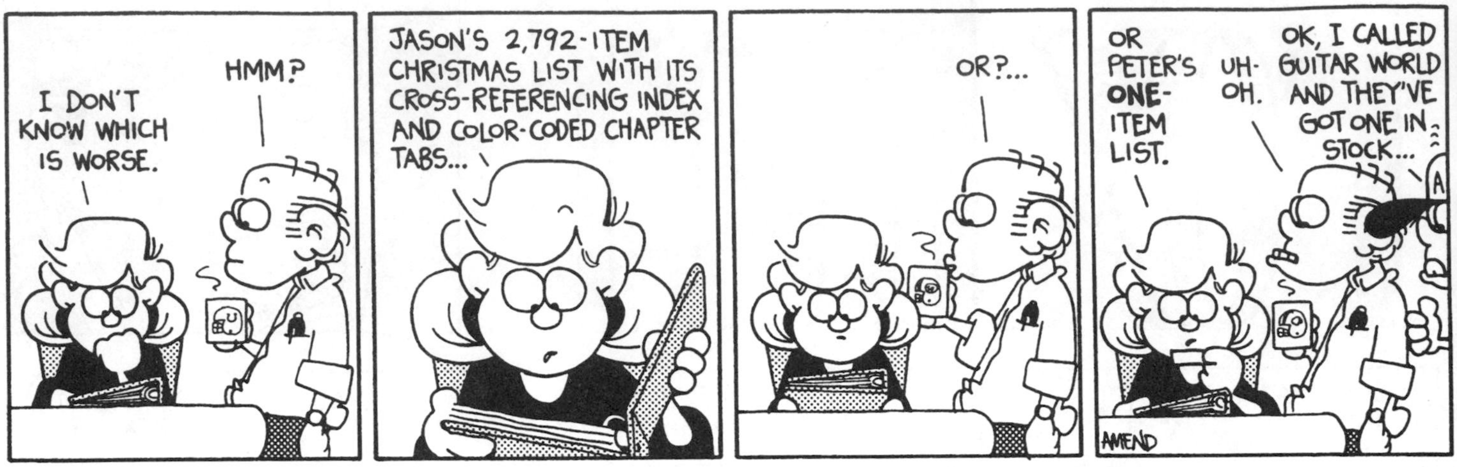
I DON'T KNOW WHICH IS WORSE.
HMM?
JASON'S 2,792-ITEM CHRISTMAS LIST WITH ITS CROSS-REFERENCING INDEX AND COLOR-CODED CHAPTER TABS...
OR?...
OR PETER'S **ONE**-ITEM LIST.
UH-OH.
OK, I CALLED GUITAR WORLD AND THEY'VE GOT ONE IN STOCK...
AMEND

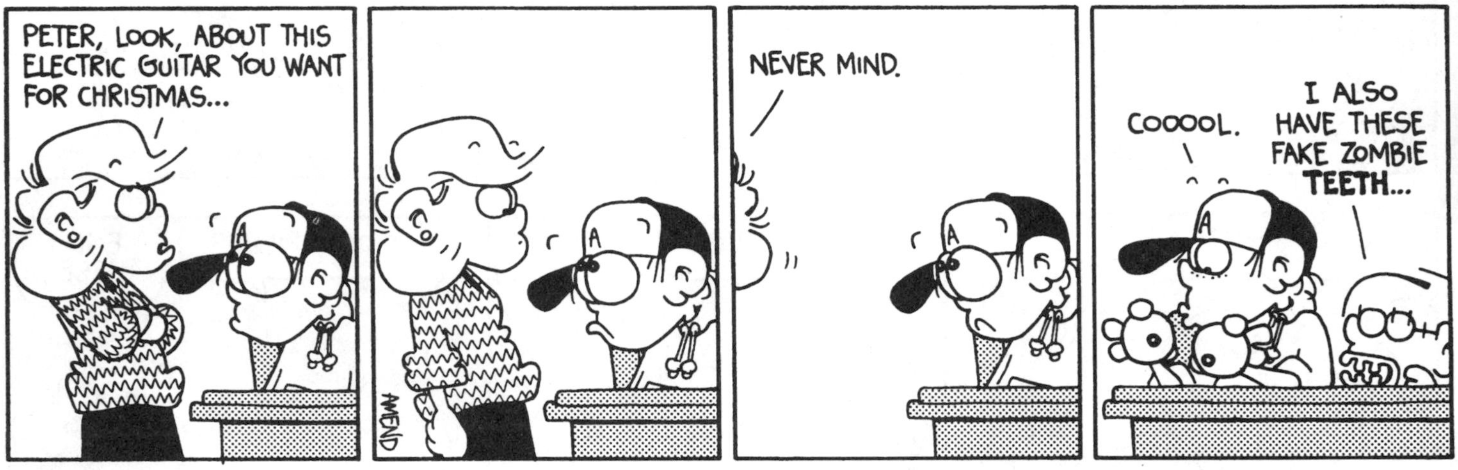
PETER, LOOK, ABOUT THIS ELECTRIC GUITAR YOU WANT FOR CHRISTMAS...
AMEND
NEVER MIND.
COOOOL.
I ALSO HAVE THESE FAKE ZOMBIE **TEETH**...

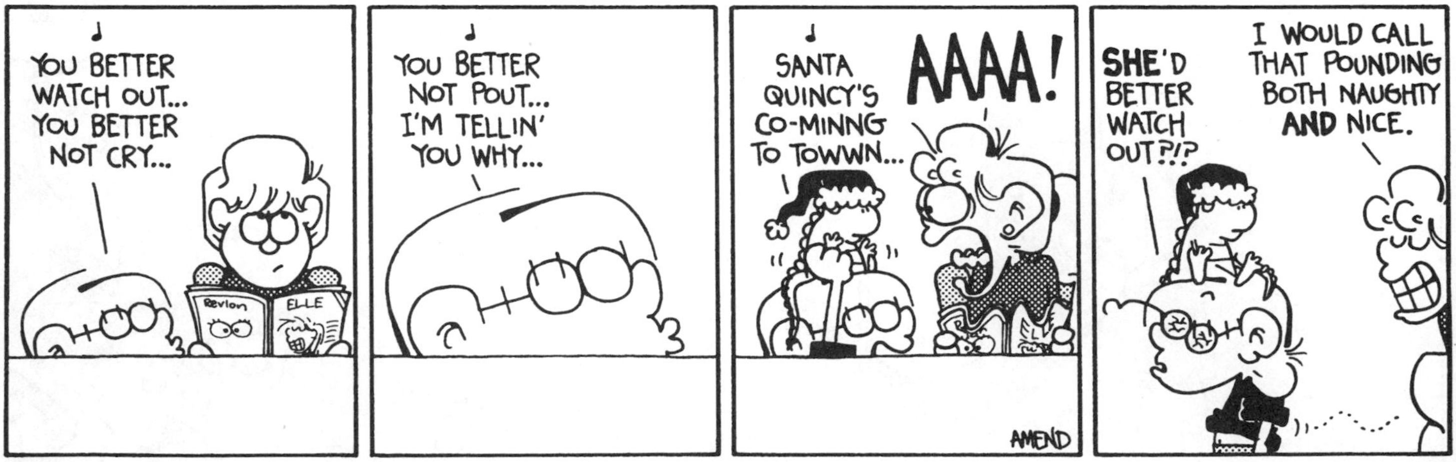
YOU BETTER WATCH OUT... YOU BETTER NOT CRY...
Revlon
ELLE
YOU BETTER NOT POUT... I'M TELLIN' YOU WHY...
SANTA QUINCY'S CO-MINNG TO TOWWN...
AAAA!
AMEND
SHE'D BETTER WATCH OUT?!?
I WOULD CALL THAT POUNDING BOTH NAUGHTY **AND** NICE.

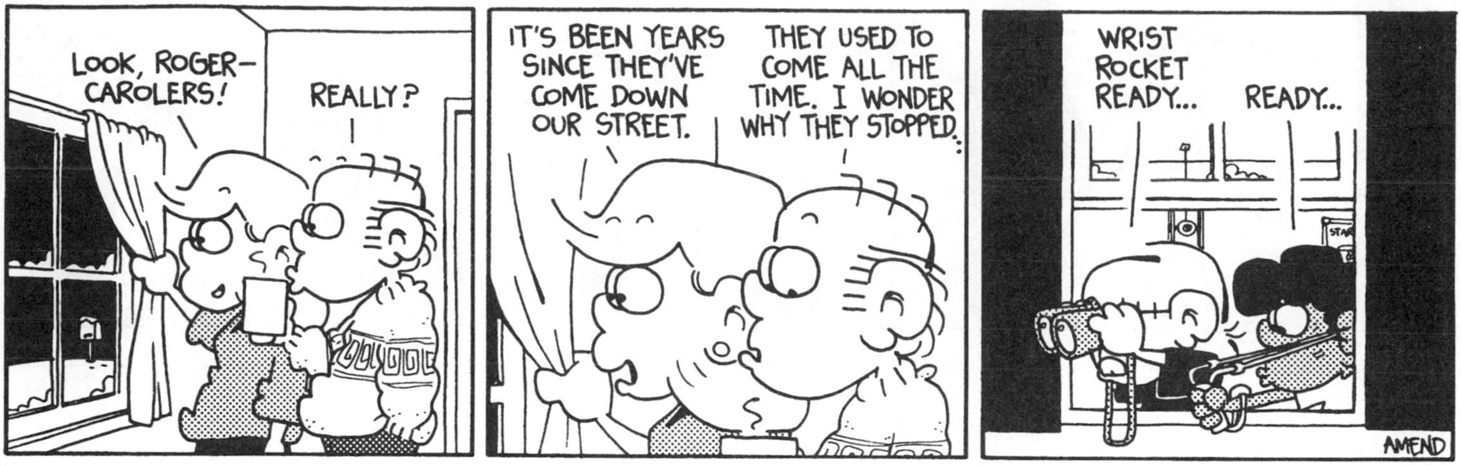
LOOK, ROGER—CAROLERS!
REALLY?
IT'S BEEN YEARS SINCE THEY'VE COME DOWN OUR STREET.
THEY USED TO COME ALL THE TIME. I WONDER WHY THEY STOPPED.
WRIST ROCKET READY...
READY...
AMEND

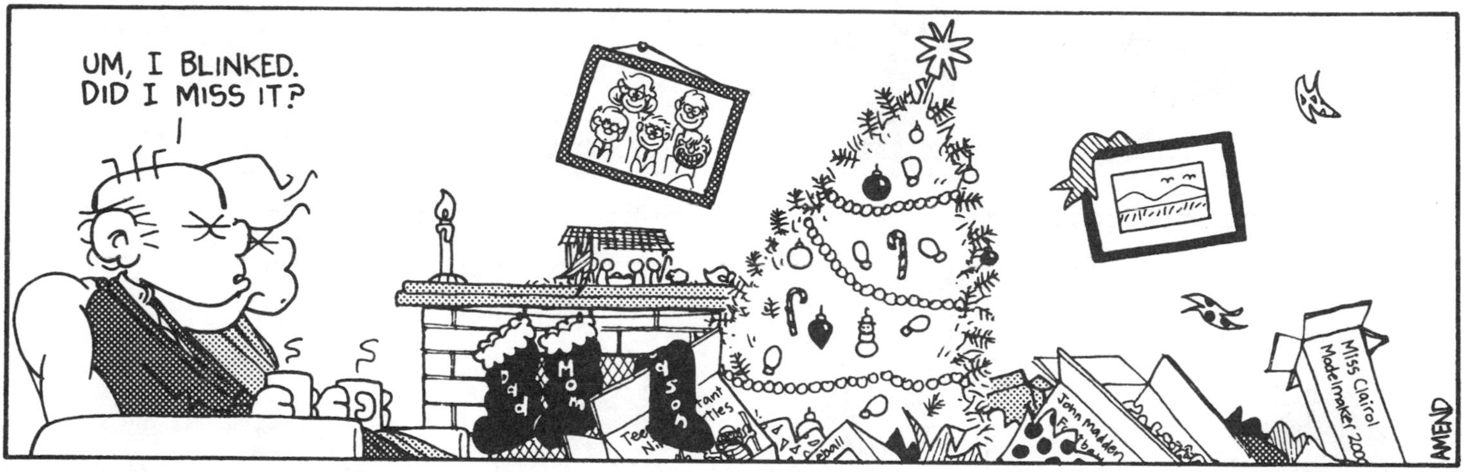
UM, I BLINKED. DID I MISS IT?
Dad
Mom
Jason
Miss Clairol Modelmaker 2000
AMEND

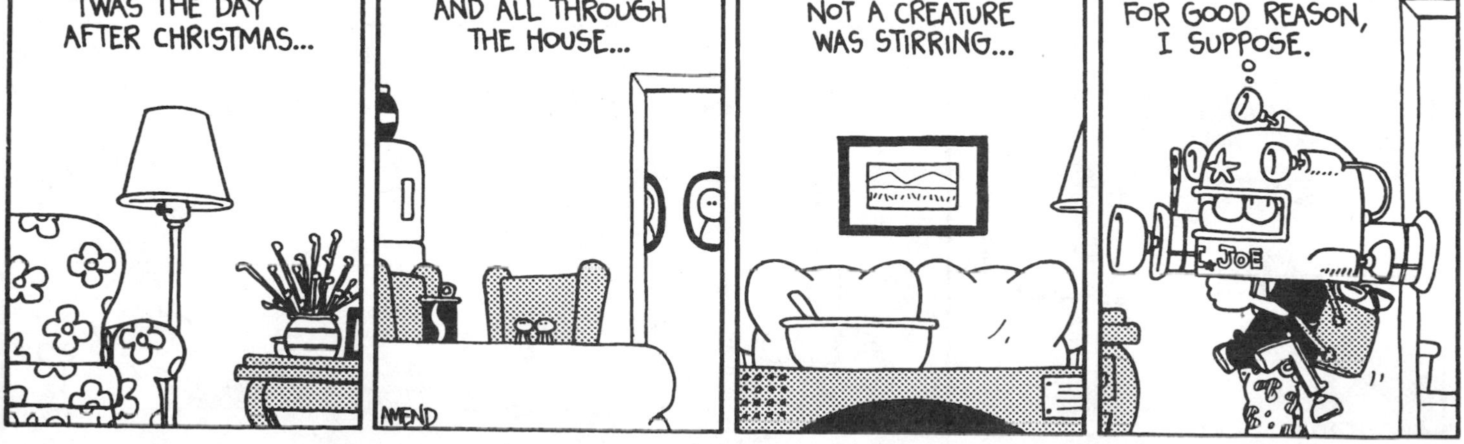
TWAS THE DAY AFTER CHRISTMAS...
AND ALL THROUGH THE HOUSE...
AMEND
NOT A CREATURE WAS STIRRING...
FOR GOOD REASON, I SUPPOSE.
JOE

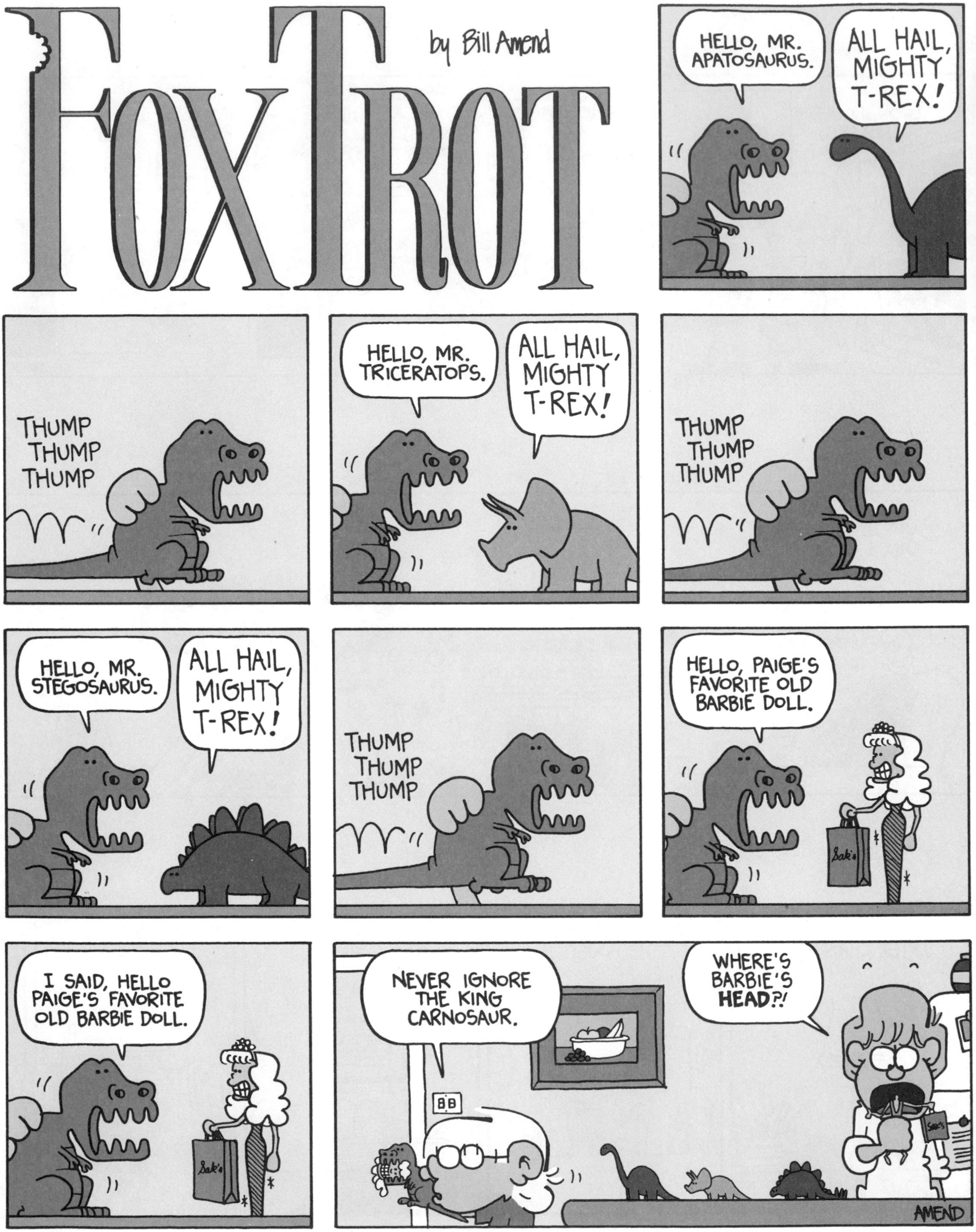
FoxTrot
by Bill Amend
HELLO, MR. APATOSAURUS.
ALL HAIL, MIGHTY T-REX!
THUMP THUMP THUMP
HELLO, MR. TRICERATOPS.
ALL HAIL, MIGHTY T-REX!
THUMP THUMP THUMP
HELLO, MR. STEGOSAURUS.
ALL HAIL, MIGHTY T-REX!
THUMP THUMP THUMP
HELLO, PAIGE'S FAVORITE OLD BARBIE DOLL.
I SAID, HELLO PAIGE'S FAVORITE OLD BARBIE DOLL.
NEVER IGNORE THE KING CARNOSAUR.
WHERE'S BARBIE'S **HEAD**?!
AMEND